Prussia

Art and Architecture

NEC SOLI CEDIT
SUUM CUIQUE

Prussia

Art and Architecture

Edited by Gert Streidt and Peter Feierabend

Photos by Klaus Frahm and Hagen Immel

With contributions from Klaus Arlt, Ernst Badstübner, Gerd Bartoschek,

Annette Dorgerloh, Hans-Joachim Giersberg, Burkhardt Göres, Sepp-Gustav Gröschel,

Saskia Hüneke, Claudia Meckel, Bernd Nicolai, Wasilissa Pachomova-Göres, Karola Paepke,

Corina Pertschi, Heinz Schönemann, Michael Seiler, Irmtraud Thierse,

Christoph Martin Vogtherr

Note:
Unless otherwise stated, dimensions given represent height x breadth x depth. Where the present location of the object shown is not stated, it is in private ownership or an unidentified collection.
Frontispiece: domed hall of the Bode Museum in Berlin, with equestrian statue of the Great Elector by Andreas Schlüter (copy). Photo © Klaus Frahm

The layout of these two pages makes use of an aquarelle drawing by Karl Friedrich Schinkel (see page 312: design for an Unter den Linden store, Berlin 1827, original size: 18.7 x 55.4 cm. Preussischer Kulturbesitz, Staatliche Museen, Berlin.

Concept: Gert Streidt
Design: Peter Feierabend, Anne-Claire Martin, Philine Rath
Project Coordination: Birgit Dunker
Picture Research: Katharina Bahr
Production Manager: Detlev Schaper
Production: Marc Voges
Reproduction: Typografik, Cologne

Original title: Preußen, Kunst und Architektur

Translation from German: Paul Aston, Helen Atkins, Peter Barton, Anthea Bell and Christine Shuttleworth in association with Goodfellow & Egan, Cambridge
Editor of the English-language edition: Chris Murray in association with Goodfellow & Egan, Cambridge
Typesetting: Goodfellow & Egan, Cambridge
Overall Project Management: Jackie Dobbyne in association with Goodfellow & Egan, Cambridge
Project Coordination: Bettina Kaufmann and Nadja Bremse
Production Manager: Detlev Schaper

Printing and Binding: Neue Stalling, Oldenburg

Printed in Germany

ISBN 3-8290-2590-4

10 9 8 7 6 5 4 3 2 1

CONTENTS

INTRODUCTION 6
Gert Streidt

The March of Brandenburg: German Colonization and the Heartland of Prussia: 928–1640

CHRONOLOGY 14

ARCHITECTURE, SCULPTURE, AND PAINTING 18
Ernst Badstübner

Prussia Becomes a Kingdom: 1640–1740

CHRONOLOGY 72

ARCHITECTURE, URBAN PLANNING AND GARDEN DESIGN 76
Irmtraud Thierse

SCULPTURE 118
Sepp-Gustav Gröschel

PAINTING 132
Gerd Bartoschek

THE APPLIED ARTS 144
Burkhardt Göres

Prussia Under Frederick the Great: 1740–1786

CHRONOLOGY 154

Architecture, Urban Planning and Garden Design 158
Hans-Joachim Giersberg

Sculpture 224
Saskia Hüneke

Painting 238
Gerd Bartoschek

The Applied Arts 246
Wasilissa Pachomova-Göres

Carriage Building at the Prussian Court in the 18th Century 258
Claudia Meckel

Textile Furnishing in the Palaces of Potsdam and Berlin 262
Karola Paepke

The Age of Revolutions 1786–1871

Chronology 268

Architecture and Urban Planning 272
Heinz Schönemann

Landscape Gardening in the Potsdam Parks 336
Michael Seiler

Sculpture 348
Saskia Hüneke

Painting 362
Christoph Martin Vogtherr

The Applied Arts 402
Burkhardt Göres

Prussia and the German Empire 1871–1918

Chronology 412

Architecture and Urban Development 416
Bernd Nicolai

Sculpture and Painting 456
Annette Dorgerloh

Urban Planning and Berlin's "Green Lungs" 490
Bernd Nicolai

Cemeteries and Tombs in Brandenburg and Berlin 494
Klaus Arlt

Glossary 506

Artist Biographies 508
Corina Pertschi

Index of Place Names 515
Index of Personal Names 517
Further Reading 519
Picture Credits 520
Acknowledgments 520

INTRODUCTION

Gert Streidt

Stendal, Ünglinger Gate (around 1450/1460)
Detail of the façade

Frankfurt an der Oder Marienkirche (1522)
Vault of sacristy

Although Prussia is now very much a part of the past, it can still arouse strong – and conflicting – emotions. Some see Prussia as an all-powerful authoritarian state that, dominated by the military, pursued a ruthless program of territorial aggrandizement that entailed the systematic subjugation of its neighbors. Others see in Prussia an enlightened, rationalist state that always tolerated foreign influences, and even understood how to utilize them to its advantage, thereby ensuring its citizens a good standard of living. During the Cold War, such assessments of Prussia's role in history were sharpened by ideological differences.

But now that the Iron Curtain itself has become a part of history, and the countries of Europe have resumed normal relations, perhaps Prussia can be discussed dispassionately, free of facile prejudices. The unending stream of literature on the subject certainly suggests that there is an urgent need to come to terms with the past in order fully to understand the present.

And to do this we must accept Prussia in all its complexity, resisting the temptation to single out one feature as a peg on which to hang facile generalizations. It is only by admitting, for example, that Prussian tolerance was as much an aspect of Prussia's development as its militarism and regimentation that we will be able to understand the rise of Prussia as a great European power, as well as its recent disappearance into history.

So what is left of the state that was formally dissolved by an Allied Control Council law dated February 25, 1947? From Prussia's heyday we still have, above all, its artistic legacy, the subject of this book – its remarkable architecture, gardens, painting, and sculpture. These are the expression of Prussia's own view of itself, and of its aristocracy's desire for elegant display. The destruction of World War II wreaked immeasurable damage to this legacy. Among the major losses were the city palaces of Berlin and Potsdam: both of these buildings ranked among the glories of Prussian, and European, architecture. Badly damaged by bombs during the war, they were later demolished by the German socialist state, which was keen to be rid of what it considered symbols of an unwanted legacy of Prussian history. The open, desolate spaces where they once stood give a clear impression of how prominently the palaces featured in the cityscapes of Berlin and Potsdam. However, despite the many, the surviving evidence of Prussia's artistic achievements is ample evidence of the former importance of this state, both as a German state and a European power.

For five centuries, from the year 1415 until 1918, Brandenburg and Prussia were ruled by the Hohenzollern dynasty. They exercised their artistic patronage for almost as long, firmly imposing their dynastic needs and artistic tastes on the development of the arts in Prussia. In each age they were successful in attracting fine artists, for a basic feature of the Hohenzollerns' policy was to measure themselves against European standards and to entrust important commissions to leading representatives of the latest trends. Works by such figures served as models for Prussian artists and prompted imitation throughout the country. Berlin and Potsdam were the main artistic centers of Prussia; that was where the ruling house, and therefore the principal patrons, lived. Developments in the provinces – for example in Silesia, which was annexed to Prussia in the 18th century, or in the Rhineland provinces which were acquired after 1815 – followed their own course based on quite different historical circumstances. Yet the Hohenzollerns were quite ready to summon artists from the provinces to Berlin, relying on the city to act as an artistic beacon throughout the country. One important example was Carl Gotthard Langhans, whom Frederick William II brought from Silesia to Berlin, where he developed into one of the leading architects of Prussia. Another was Peter Joseph Lenné, called to Potsdam in 1816; it was not until he started work in Berlin and Postdam that conditions allowed his true abilities to flower.

It took centuries for Prussia to forge its sundry territories, sometimes geographically far flung, into a single, unified state. "Prussia" is still generally identified with the region lying between the Elbe and Oder rivers, and centered on Berlin. In fact, this territory was the March of Brandenburg, which only became part of the state of Prussia in 1701, after a long history of its own.

The "first Prussia" was the area settled by a Lithuanian clan who were known as the Prus, on either side of the Lower Vistula, thus forming East

Potsdam, palace stables (1746)
Detail of façade
Georg Wenzeslaus von Knobelsdorff

*Along Germany's troubled eastern borders, several towns and cities are now known by their Russian or Polish names. As this is a book about German cultural history, the German forms have been retained throughout, though the present names are indicated in this introduction (where the historical sweep of the text makes them particularly relevant), on the maps, and in the index of places.

and West Prussia. In the 13th century, these pagan Baltic peoples were subjugated by the Teutonic Knights, who used indescribable brutality to defeat them. As the Knights did not consider themselves conquerors but the bringers of the true faith and of civilization, they set about founding a state of their own, which by the following century was flourishing. The Grand Master of the Order lived in fortified Marienburg (now Malbork), which formed a high point of medieval architecture. The economy boomed, enabling all classes to make a living. The far-flung trade connections that subsequently developed led to the rapid growth of the cities of Königsberg (Kaliningrad) and Danzig (Gdansk).*

In the 15th century, wars against Poland and Lithuania gradually sapped the energies of this Teutonic state, and finally it collapsed. West Prussia fell entirely into Polish hands, while East Prussia became a fiefdom of the Polish crown. It was only in 1618 that East Prussia passed by line of succession to the Elector of Brandenburg, and thereafter remained linked with Brandenburg through its ruler.

In the other core territory of the later Prussia, the March of Brandenburg, century succeeded century as the area slowly forged itself into a state, constantly threatened from outside and rendered unstable within by frequent change of ruler. Up to the 13th century, the March was populated by Slav tribes, though German colonizers had first entered the area in the 10th century. After a lengthy struggle, they finally overcame Slav resistance and established themselves as rulers. To consolidate their power, they brought in more German settlers and monks. The monks' ostensible task was to Christianize the remaining Slav population, but thanks to their knowledge of building technology, crafts, and agriculture, they also acted as an important force in social and economic development. The new rulers – which up to 1411 included the Ascania, Wittelsbach, and Luxemburg dynasties, and the Margraves of Moravia – set about erecting castles and fortified houses as power bases. The monks of the Cistercian and Premonstratensian orders built monasteries, which soon developed into economic and cultural centers. Whereas only a few ruins are left of the castles, the surviving monasteries in Zinna, Lehnin, and Chorin bear impressive witness to the advanced building capabilities of the period. Massive cathedrals, most notably those in the settlements of Brandenburg and Havelberg, were intended to impress the new Christian converts with the power of the Church. Yet it is not just cathedrals that form outstanding examples of medieval church architecture in the March of Brandenburg. In the settlements that developed in the shadow of castles and episcopal seats – often sites originally settled by Slavs – the townsfolk also wanted churches. Initially, these tended to be small, but in time they came to occupy a central position in the townscape, as in Prenzlau or

Jüterbog. As the towns increasingly emancipated themselves from their rulers in the second half of the 13th century, town halls, expressions of the growing self-confidence of the burghers, began to spring up alongside churches. In many cases (for example in Perleberg) the town halls are almost the equal of the churches, with which they had now formed an architectural unit.

The Wittelsbachs, Luxemburgs, and especially the Margraves of Moravia, who were in power in the 14th century, did very little to fashion the March of Brandenburg into a state. Mostly they handed the administration to governors from outside, whose activities were limited to collecting taxes. Robber barons grew strong and arrogant, prompting the towns to form defensive leagues. When Frederick IV, the burgrave of Nuremberg, assumed power in Brandenburg in 1415 as the first Hohenzollern ruler, a strong central hand was sorely lacking that could stop the state from falling apart piecemeal. Over the next two centuries the electors of Brandenburg devoted themselves to the task of preserving unity, though with varying degrees of success; Frederick II and Joachim II were among the most able rulers of this period. In 1443 Frederick II made a decision of historic importance for the later Prussian capital by starting work on a castle in Cölln, across the Spree from the later Berlin. A little less than a century later, in 1538, the architect Caspar Theiss rebuilt the castle as a stately Renaissance palace, whose influence can be traced on the buildings that were erected by the Marcher aristocracy.

The Thirty Years' War (1618-1648) devastated the region. It is no exaggeration to say that it put back social and economic development in Brandenburg by 100 years. This applied also to artistic activity, which after all depended on economic prosperity as a precondition. The gap between Brandenburg and European development as a whole widened. In other countries, it was a time of incomparable artistic creativity. Since the stylistic watershed of around 1600 in Rome and Bologna, which saw the emergence of the Baroque, Italy had experienced an artistic upturn that produced an immeasurable wealth of achievements in architecture, sculpture and painting. In Holland, the 17th century saw the onset of an unparalleled golden age in painting; under Louis XIV, a classicizing national style developed in France, and in Spain it was the century of Velázquez and Ribera.

Against this background, it is indeed difficult to over-estimate the achievement of the Great Elector Frederick William in reconstructing the country. When he assumed power in 1640, the country was bleeding to death. Brandenburg had been a principal theater of the War, and the country lost half its population overall, though in some areas 90 percent had been wiped out. Numerous villages had been laid waste, and castles and churches lay in ruins. Although under the Treaty of Westphalia (1648) Brandenburg acquired 30,000 square kilometers (11,580 square miles) of additional territory, thus increasing its size by over a third, the need for strong central control in this enlarged state was so much the more pressing. The Great Elector succeeded in extricating the March of Brandenburg from the power games of the European powers, and building up an orderly state administration and a strong army. The foundations were laid on which successor Hohenzollern rulers could build. He continued Brandenburg's immigration policy, which became a basic feature of Brandenburger and Prussian state doctrine: those persecuted in other countries would find refuge in Brandenburg. The immigrants brought know-how and skills with them that were highly welcome in Brandenburg. About 20,000 Huguenots came from France after 1685, for example, and in the process

Potsdam, Sanssouci Palace (1745–1747)
Section of wall in the library
Georg Wenzeslaus von Knobelsdorff

Potsdam, town house in Schlossstrasse (1751)
Georg Wenzeslaus von Knobelsdorff

created completely new occupational classes. The Great Elector's strategy, quite simply, was to encourage progress, and for this he sought inspiration mainly in the advanced economies of Holland and Flanders. He had studied in Leiden, married a princess from the House of Orange, and imported Dutch architects, artists, engineers, and craftsmen.

The Great Elector's successors kept firmly to the same policy, which became paramount in artistic matters as well. They kept up with general European developments, and demonstrated great skill in the choice of artists they commissioned. Prussian history books say little about Elector Frederick III, the Great Elector's immediate successor; he is mostly depicted as a characterless spendthrift who, dominated by favorites, took the state to the brink of ruin. This judgment is unfair, for he took a step that was decisive for the later rise of Prussia to the rank of great power: in 1701, Elector Frederick III reconstituted his realm as the kingdom of Prussia, restyled himself King Frederick I of Prussia, and set a lavish theatrical tone for his new kingdom that involved an impressive promotion of the arts. He had already established an Academy of the Arts in Berlin in 1696, followed by an Academy of Science in 1700. The leading artistic force to emerge in this period was Andreas Schlüter from Danzig, whose was important as both an architect and as a sculptor.

The party could not last, and Frederick I's successor Frederick William I clamped down on it altogether, limiting expenditure to what the country could afford. He turned his administration into the most modern state machine in Europe, and devoted himself above all to building up his army. It was not until 1740, when his son Frederick the Great took over, that the muses returned to Brandenburg-Prussia. Frederick launched a jamboree of the arts on a hitherto unknown scale, taking modern French art, classical antiquity, and the architecture of Palladio as his pantheon. He sent his favorite architect Georg Wenzeslaus von Knobelsdorff on study tours to France and Italy, entrusted major commissions in sculpture and painting to French artists, and set out to establish the Rococo style, which was so strongly marked by his own ideas that art historians actually describe the Prussian version of the style as Frederician Rococo. And once he had established an artistic principle, however, he stuck with it until he died in 1786. Consequently, the succession of his nephew Frederick William III inevitably marked the beginning of a new era in the arts, giving Prussia the chance it needed to catch up with European developments. The artistic talents that created Prussian classicism and gave Berlin its classical face were all trained around 1800. The first decades of the 19th century were among the most productive periods ever in the arts of Prussia.

Promoting the glory of the state was no longer the sole criterion of content. The social changes brought about as a result of the crisis in the Prussia of old, and its collapse under Napoleon's onslaught, also sought expression in art, with artists supporting the struggle against Napoleonic rule by adopting fervently patriotic themes. And artists now addressed their work to completely new sections of the population. The middle classes began to acquire great quantities of art to furnish their houses and apartments, a trend that boosted artistic output and led to

Opposite
Berlin, Brandenburg Gate
Portal
Carl Gotthard Langhans (1789–1791) and Johann Heinrich Strack (1867–1868)

Far left
Potsdam, Palm Hall, Orangery in the New Garden (1791)
Section of wall
Carl Gotthard Langhans

Left
Berlin, New Pavilion, park of Charlottenburg Palace (1824–1825)
Corner of Garden Room
Karl Friedrich Schinkel

This page, far left
Potsdam, Babelsberg Palace (1834–1849)
Vault of the ballroom
Karl Friedrich Schinkel, Ludwig Persius, Johann Heinrich Strack

Left
Berlin, City Courts, Littenstrasse (1896–1904)
Detail of façade
Paul Thoemer, Rudolf Mönnich, Otto Schmalz

Opposite
Berlin, Rotunda, Old Museum (Altes Museum) (1825–1830)
Karl Friedrich Schinkel

Berlin, Assembly shop of AEG's turbine factory in Huttenstrasse (1909)
Detail of façade
Peter Behrens

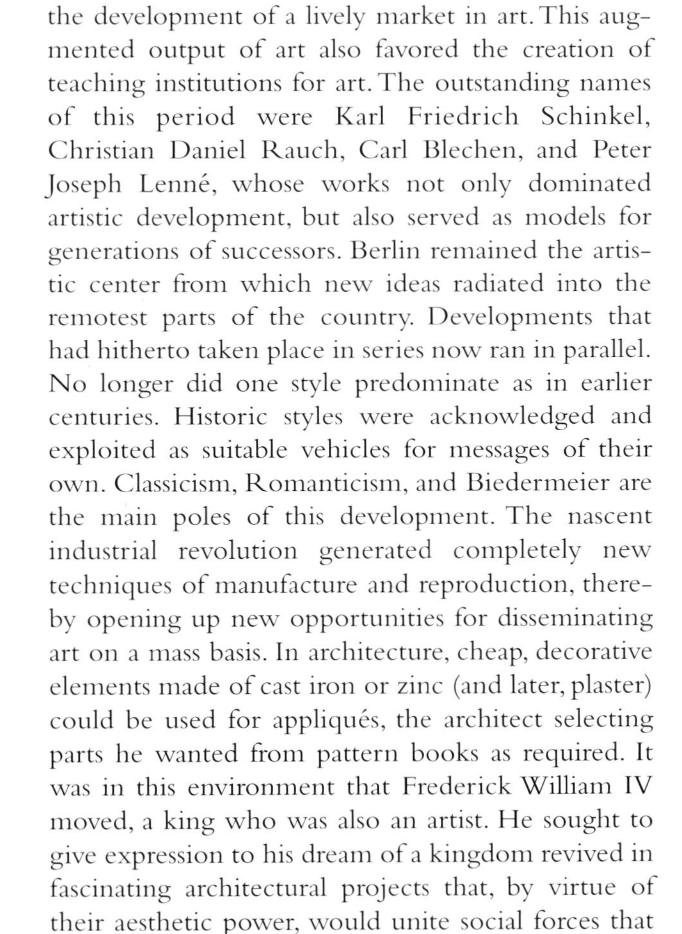

the development of a lively market in art. This augmented output of art also favored the creation of teaching institutions for art. The outstanding names of this period were Karl Friedrich Schinkel, Christian Daniel Rauch, Carl Blechen, and Peter Joseph Lenné, whose works not only dominated artistic development, but also served as models for generations of successors. Berlin remained the artistic center from which new ideas radiated into the remotest parts of the country. Developments that had hitherto taken place in series now ran in parallel. No longer did one style predominate as in earlier centuries. Historic styles were acknowledged and exploited as suitable vehicles for messages of their own. Classicism, Romanticism, and Biedermeier are the main poles of this development. The nascent industrial revolution generated completely new techniques of manufacture and reproduction, thereby opening up new opportunities for disseminating art on a mass basis. In architecture, cheap, decorative elements made of cast iron or zinc (and later, plaster) could be used for appliqués, the architect selecting parts he wanted from pattern books as required. It was in this environment that Frederick William IV moved, a king who was also an artist. He sought to give expression to his dream of a kingdom revived in fascinating architectural projects that, by virtue of their aesthetic power, would unite social forces that were drifting asunder. He initiated – particularly in Potsdam – an overall ensemble of architecture and gardens that has now been included in UNESCO's World Heritage List as a unique cultural landscape.

When Germany was united in 1871, Prussia became absorbed in the German Reich. In a sense, this was the point at which Prussia began to pass into history. The new role of world power for the kingdom that had become the leading power in Germany ill suited it. The arts were allotted mainly the role of producing showpieces for the self-glorification of a Kaiser-dominated realm. Huge monumental projects such as the Niederwald monument by the Rhine in Rüdesheim or the Kaiser Wilhelm national monument in Berlin were intended to make manifest the historic legitimization of the German Reich. The empty pathos of many of these monuments – which were not, incidentally, just a German phenomenon – did not go unnoticed by contemporaries, as the flourishing of caricature during the Kaiser period indicates. The melting pot of all these developments was Berlin, which, in the years after 1871, developed into a metropolis at lightning speed. Imperial Berlin also provided a focus for new artistic movements arising from the rejection of official state art, chief of which were the Secession and Expressionism – movements that brought Prussia to the forefront of world art. The Modern style, which would be international in character, was about to emerge.

The March of Brandenburg: German Colonization and the Heartland of Prussia

928–1640

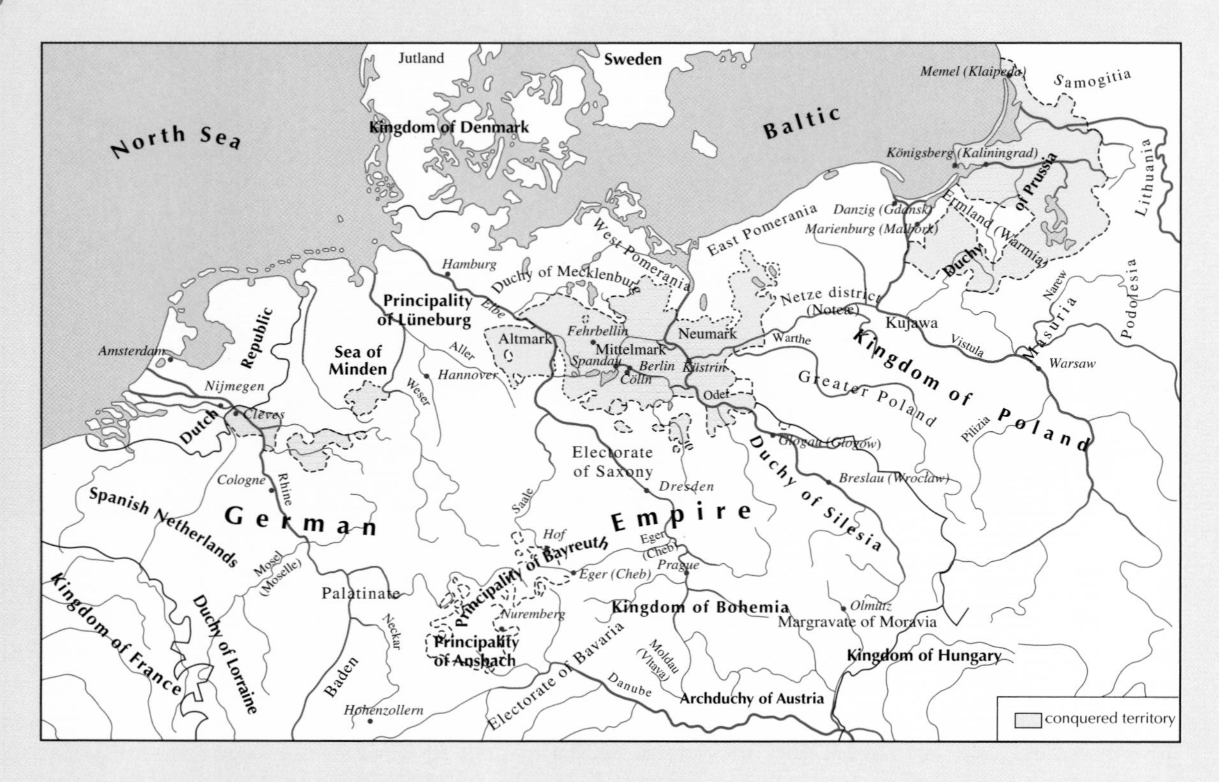

928–983 The Saxon emperors secure their eastern frontiers in conflicts with the Slavs. Marcher territories are organized, the construction of castles and foundation of bishoprics being used to bolster territorial claims.

928/929 To counter a simultaneous threat from the Slavs and Magyars, King Henry I undertakes a campaign against the Slav Havellers (Slav tribe in Havelland) and conquers their main fort of "Brennaburg" (Brandenburg).

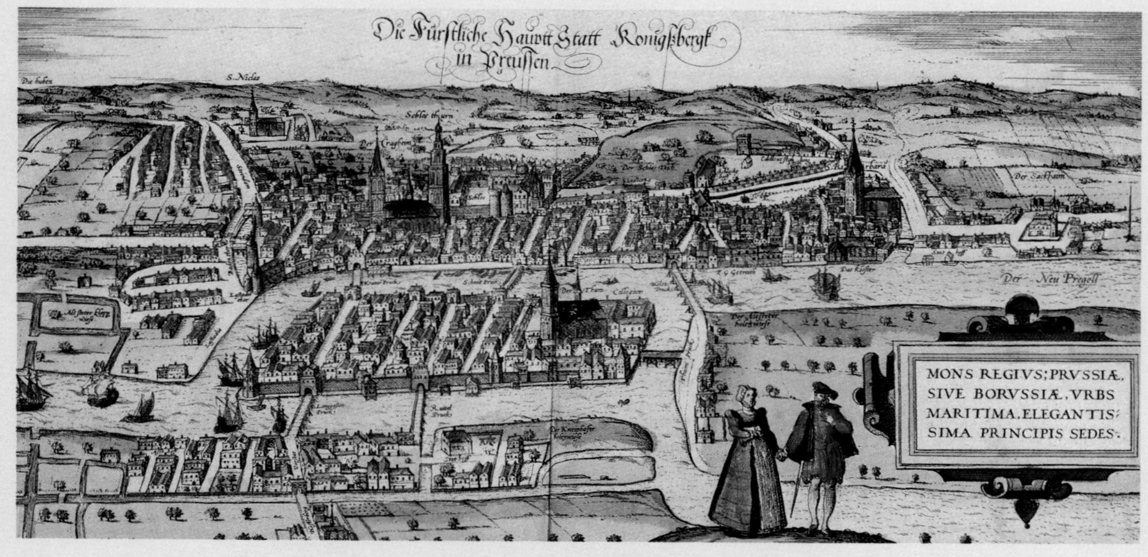

Prospect of Königsberg, colored copperplate engraving by Braun and Hogenberg (c. 1590)

936 By the death of Henry I, all tribes between the Middle Elbe and Middle Oder owe tribute to the German king.

948 At the Magdeburg Assembly of Princes, the bishoprics of Brandenburg and Havelberg are established.

968 Emperor Otto the Great founds the bishoprics of Oldenburg in Holstein, Meissen, Merseburg, and Zeitz. Magdeburg, elevated to archdiocese, controls not only these new sees, but also Brandenburg and Havelberg.

983 Major Slav uprising. Supported by numerous Slav tribes, the Redars (from the Usedom area) attack the settlement of Havelberg and kill the German garrison. Area east of the Elbe remains under Slav control until the mid-12th century.

993 King Otto III issues document in Merseburg granting the localities of Poztupimi (Potsdam) and Geliti (Geltow) on the island of Chotiemuizles to the abbey of Quedlinburg. The gift remains ineffective as the places are still in pagan hands.

1028 King Mieszko II of Poland lays eastern Saxony waste, and inflicts heavy damage on the tribal area of the Slavic Lusatians (who occupied area between Elbe and Oder) and ravages Haveller area even more gravely.

1128 On his second mission to Pomerania, Bishop Otto of Bamberg travels by boat down the Elbe and reaches Havelberg, where the pagan population is celebrating a festival in honor of their god Gerovit.

Elector Albrecht Achilles, copper engraving

1130–1320 The "great movement eastwards": with support from the margraves, Emperor Lothar III institutes a political and ecclesiastical policy of moving eastwards to occupy lands held by non-Christians.

1134–1320 The Ascanians come to prominence. Albert the Bear and his successors extend their possessions and improve their economy. German peasants and burghers are summoned into the new territory. Existing Slav settlements, now placed under "German law," are taken over by German settlers.

1134 Albert the Bear is enfeoffed by Emperor Lothar – presumably at the Imperial Assembly in Halberstadt – with the Nordmark (the territory of today's Altmark), formerly Haveller territory.

1140 Bishop Wigger of Brandenburg founds an abbey for Premonstratensian canons in Leitzkau, located in the Nordmark.

1147 The founder of the Cistercian order, Bernard of Clairvaux, and Pope Eugene III call for a crusade against the Wends (west Slav tribes). Princes and knights from northeast Germany join in, as do the Danes and the Poles.

1150 The Slav prince of Brandenburg, Pribislav-Henry, dies. His widow Petrissa enables Albert the Bear to take over Brandenburg fort by agreement and provide it with a joint German-Slav garrison. Albert the Bear styles himself Margrave of Brandenburg.

1160 Beginning of systematic settlement of Elbe-Havel-Spree basin by nobility, burghers, and peasants from the Schwabengau area (Harz), the Netherlands, the Rhineland, and Westphalia.

1165 Foundation stone for a cathedral church laid on the cathedral island of Brandenburg.

1170 Havelberg Cathedral is consecrated in the presence of Albert the Bear and his sons.

1171 Archbishop Wichmann of Magdeburg founds the Cistercian monastery of Zinna near Jüterbog.

1180 Margrave Otto I founds the Cistercian abbey of Lehnin as the family monastery of the Ascanian dynasty. The first abbot, Sibold, is killed by pagans.

1183 Margrave Otto I founds a Benedictine nunnery in Arendsee, in his territory west of the Elbe.

c. 1200 The Teutonic Order settles in Teltow district, near Potsdam. It establishes a fortified base (Tempelhof) and settlements at Mariendorf, Marienfelde, and Richardsdorf (now Rixdorf-Neukölln).

1220 Margrave Albrecht II dies and is buried in Ascanian family monastery of Lehnin. His successors are his similarly aged sons John I and Otto III, who have a close personal relationship, and act jointly to become the most important Ascanian regents in Brandenburg.

1226–1525 The Teutonic Knights govern Prussia (the territory of modern East Prussia) as an independent state.

1226 The Golden Bull of Rimini empowers the Teutonic Knights to rule the territory of the Lithuanian Prus (later called East Prussia).

1232 Margraves John I and Otto III endow the Marienkirche in the Cistercian nunnery of Neuendorf in the Altmark. In the following decades, the brothers founded several monasteries: Franciscan in Görlitz, Bautzen, and Berlin; Dominican in Strausberg and Seehausen; Cistercian in Mariensee on the Pehlitzwerder (later moved to Chorin); and Benedictine (nuns) in Spandau.

1258 Margraves John I and Otto III end their joint rule and divide the March of Brandenburg between them.

Elector Joachim I, painting by Lucas Cranach the Elder, 1529

1265/1266 During the winter, Margrave III takes part in a crusade against the Lithuanian Prus. While there, he builds a settlement called "Brandenburg" (later town was known as Brunsberg, and is now Braniewo) on the Frisches Haff (a freshwater lagoon on the Baltic coast, now called Vislinski Zaliv) southwest of Königsberg (Kaliningrad). Except for a small wooden tower, it is quickly destroyed by the Ermlanders.

Elector Joachim II, painting by Lucas Cranach the Younger (c. 1550)

In the summer 1266, Otto III undertakes a further campaign in Prussia to rebuild his "Brandenburg." The name is the first evidence of a connection between Brandenburg and Prussia.

1285 The arts, philosophy, and theology can be studied in Neuruppin, a settlement 80 kilometers (50 miles) northwest of Berlin.

From 1288 Entries in Hamburg's book of debtors confirms particularly lively trade links between the March of Brandenburg and Hamburg up to 1320. The names of merchants from Berlin-Cölln are entered more than 20 times. They deliver "Berlin rye" and marchland oak to the Hamburgers, goods transported by boats along the Spree, Havel, and Elbe rivers.

1299 The oldest recorded school teaching Latin in the March is a reference to a certain "Marienschule" (St. Mary's School) in Spandau.

Margrave Albrecht III founds a family monastery and burial site at Zisterze Himmelpfort near Lychen, a daughter house of Lehnin.

1320 The Ascania dynasty fails to produce an heir, and the March of Brandenburg returns to the control of the German Emperor as a "vacant imperial fief."

1323–1373 The Wittelsbach dynasty. King Louis the Bavarian grants his son Ludwig the fief of the March of

Elector John George, painting by Andreas Riehl the Younger (c. 1596)

Brandenburg. Financial dependency on the estates and political complications lead to the sale of the March to the Emperor Charles IV in 1373.

1334 The twin town of Berlin-Cölln issues a legal code. Among other regulations, it limits certain behavior in taverns, the serving of beer, and the amount that can be bet in bowls and dicing. Ceiling also set on expenditure at weddings and for wedding presents, as well as the expenditure on clothes and jewelry.

1336 Inquisition proceedings against 14 inhabitants on the town of Angermünde accused of Satanism ends in the death penalty at the stake.

1349–1350 The plague, the Black Death, rife in many European territories including Germany for years, spreads into the March of Brandenburg. Persecution of the Jews starts throughout the country: they are accused of causing the plague by poisoning wells.

1356 The Golden Bull of the Emperor Charles IV numbers the Margrave of Brandenburg, in his capacity as Imperial Chamberlain, as one of the four secular electors. From now on they, together with the three spiritual electors, will elect the German King. The electorate is indivisible; no elector may hold two electoral votes.

1373–1415 The Luxemburg Emperor Charles IV takes over the administration of the March of Brandenburg on behalf of his sons. He has a "province book" drawn up with a precise record of all taxes. Under his successors, the March drifts into anarchy. Robber baron plunders the region and towns have to set up defensive leagues.

1383 The priest of the village of Wilsnack discovers three eucharistic hosts on the altar of his fire-stricken church. They are undamaged, but each bears a drop of blood. During a Mass conducted by the Bishop of Havelberg, the hosts begin to bleed profusely. As a result of the excitement caused, the "Wilsnack Walk" begins and Wilsnack develops into a major pilgrimage center.

1388–1411 The March of Brandenburg is mortgaged to the Margraves of Moravia. The new margraves are seen even more rarely in their Brandenburg possessions than the Wittelsbach regents, and hand over the administration to outside nominees and provincial governors, whose principal task is to collect taxes.

1410 Teutonic Knights are heavily defeated by the Poles in the battle of Tannenberg.

1411 Margrave Joseph of Moravia dies without heir. The March of Brandenburg returns to the Empire.

Sigismund appoints his closest adviser, the Burgrave Frederick VI of Nuremberg, of the Swabian house of Hohenzollern, as administrator and lord of the March of Brandenburg. This marks the beginning of Hohenzollern rule in the March of Brandenburg.

1411–1918 Hohenzollern rule in Brandenburg.

1415 At the Council of Constance, Emperor Sigismund confers the rank of margrave, elector, and chamberlain of the Holy Roman Empire of the German Nation on Burgrave Frederick VI (1371–1440). As Margrave of Brandenburg, he retitles himself Frederick I.

1427 Civil unrest in the March following the approval

Elector Joachim Frederick, copper engraving by Peter Rollos (c. 1630)

of the Hussite tax in the imperial war-tax law. The towns are in constant opposition to taxes that are not directly used in the March of Brandenburg, and so this imperial measure is likewise generally rejected.

1432 Bohemian Hussites attack the March of Brandenburg, plundering and sacking settlements around Berlin, Fürstenwalde, Strausberg, and Bernau, where the Hussites finally withdraw after fruitless attacks on the strongly walled city.

1440–1470 Elector Frederick II (1413–1471) is able to consolidate his position in the interior, restricts the influence of the Church, recaptures fragments of lost territory, and attempts to push his frontiers toward the Baltic by attacking Pomerania.

1443 A foundation stone is laid for a castle on a site that is ceded to the Elector at Cölln on the Spree. The citizens of the double town subsequently hamper its construction, because they see the castle as a "stronghold", which is threatening to "curb their ancient freedoms." Building workers are prevented from entering the town. Additionally, the stone is taken away, and a barrier is erected. In the end, however, these measures fail to prevent completion of the castle.

1451 Elector Frederick moves into the castle at Cölln, where henceforth he holds his courts during his visits to the towns along the Spree, carries out administrative duties, and issues documents.

1454 The Teutonic Knights decided to mortgage Neumark to the Elector Frederick II for the sum of 40,000 Rhenish florins.

1466 In the second Treaty of Thorn, the King of Poland gains overlordship of the Teutonic Knights' territory in Prussia.

1470–1486 Reign of Elector Albrecht Achilles (1414–1486).

1473 Albrecht Achilles issues a dynastic decree, the *Dispositio Achillea,* ensuring the succession of the Hohenzollern dynasty. According to this, the territory of Brandenburg must not be split up, sold, or mortgaged; it is always to be handed on to the firstborn of the dynasty as a whole, undivided.

1474 The chancellor of the March, Bishop Friedrich Sesselmann, reports a rapidly spreading epidemic with thousands of victims in towns large and small. There is a sudden increase in the number of pilgrims on the Wilsnack Walk (see 1383).

1477 The *studium generale* for the Dominican province of Saxony, hitherto based in Erfurt and Magdeburg, is moved to the Dominican monastery in Cölln. This theological institution, which is reserved for members of the Order, is the first college in Brandenburg.

1486–1499 Reign of Elector John Cicero (1455–1499).

1488 The Provincial Assembly approves the beer levy, an indirect tax on consumption, amounting to 12 pfennig on every tun of beer.

1499–1535 Reign of the Elector Joachim I (1484–1535).

1503 The estates complain of breaches of the peace and robberies throughout the March of Brandenburg and ask the Elector for strict measures against robbers and their henchmen.

In order to get rid all of their debts, the estates demand that the Elector expel the Jews from Brandenburg at Michaelmas.

1506 A university is founded at Frankfurt (Oder). During its existence, it acts as an intermediary of culture and science between eastern and western Europe.

1514 A register of books at the Cistercian monastery of Lehnin lists titles of 986 manuscripts bound in 557 volumes. For the most part they are theological works, but there are legal, philosophical, and medical works among them. Scarcely any are classical writings, but the prophecies of the nun Hildegard of Bingen (1098–1179) are represented.

1517 The Augustinian monk Martin Luther publishes in Wittenberg, which belongs to the diocese of Brandenburg, his 95 theses about church malpractices, especially the selling of indulgences.

1518 A provincial assembly (Landtag) agrees on the introduction of standard wages for farm laborers and maids. Rates differ according to the type of landscape.

1524 The court astrologer of Brandenburg Johannes Carion prophesies a great flood. The electoral family and courtiers take refuge on Tempelhof Hill (modern Kreuzberg in Berlin). However, the catastrophe fails to appear, but lightning strikes four horses and a wagoner on the return journey.

1525 The Teutonic Knights' state in later East Prussia is reconstituted as the Duchy of Prussia, under the suzerainty of Poland.

1535–1571 Reign of Elector Joachim II (1506–1571). He introduces the Reformation in the March of Brandenburg, and revives the economy by modernizing the administration, by promoting trade and crafts, and by setting in hand new building works.

Elector John Sigismund, painting, German school (c. 1610)

Elector George William, copper engraving by Peter Rollos (c. 1630)

1535 A notice issued for the official residence of the Elector of Brandenburg regulates the order of the day in the castle at Cölln an der Spree. In the words of a description: "Daily life begins and ends early. The gates are opened at four in summer and five in winter … The council meets at six in summer and seven in winter. Early every morning the court goes to church, even in Protestant times …"

1544 Founding of a university at Königsberg.

1564 A census carried out this year shows that around 100,000 inhabitants live in about 16,500 houses in the towns of Brandenburg, while 165,000 inhabitants occupy 33,000 houses in the country. Thus, excluding "young children," 300,000 people live in Brandenburg. The largest town in Brandenburg at the time is already the up-and-coming royal residence of Berlin (1,316 houses without hearths), followed by Stendal (1,210), and Brandenburg-Havel (1,174).

1569 Joachim II is jointly enfeoffed with the Duchy of Prussia by the King of Poland. It is because of his close family connections with the Catholic royal house of Poland that he is able to undertake this momentous action for the history of Brandenburg.

1571–1598 Reign of Elector John George (1525–1598).

1572 The guaranteed sales of urban goods, particularly the forced purchases of beer by village tapsters in the country, are once again arranged to the advantage of the towns. Trade and crafts are, with few exceptions, forbidden in the country, thus ensuring the economic prosperity of the towns.

1574 Following the Saxon precedent, the buildings of Berlin's Franciscan monastery, unused since the Reformation, are taken over for a new general school of learning for sons of Brandenburg burghers.

1598–1608 Reign of Elector Joachim Frederick (1546–1608).

1601 Joachim Frederick has the first glass factory in the March of Brandenburg built in Grimnitz (near the later Joachimstal) and imports Bohemian glassmakers to run it.

1604 The Privy Council is founded as the central organ of government.

1608–1619 Reign of Elector John Sigismund (1572–1619).

1609 After the death of the last duke of Jülich-Kleve-Berg (between Cologne and Aachen) the Hohenzollerns of Brandenberg successfully assert their claims of succession in the territory of Jülich-Berg. However, it takes them until 1614 to secure their rule in Cleves, in the County of Mark, and Ravensberg. Brandenburg policy now concerned with expansion in the west as well as in the east.

1613 Elector John Sigismund officially goes over to Calvinism. This change of confession by the ruling house of Brandenburg, based on both conviction and dynastic ambition, fails to win the support among the estates and population of town and country alike. Until the immigration of the Huguenots, Calvinism remains an elitist minority religion in Brandenburg.

1615 In Berlin, quarrels between orthodox Lutherans and Calvinists lead to street fights and civil disorder.

1618 With the death of the last Franconian Hohenzollern as Duke of Prussia, the Brandenburg electors acquire nominal control in Prussia, which henceforth is linked to the Brandenburg heartland through its ruler.

1618–1648 Thirty Years' War rages.

1619–1640 Reign of Elector George William (1595–1640). Militarily unequipped, Brandenburg becomes the battlefield for foreign armies. The consequences of this are devastating destruction and partial depopulation of the country.

1626 A tax introduced in this year for the first time, the *Kontribution*, is intended to fund the creation of a standing army in Brandenburg. The tax remains in force throughout the period of absolutist rule.

1631 The Elector of Brandenburg is forced into an alliance with Sweden by the Swedish king Gustav Adolf, who threatens to occupy Berlin-Cölln.

1636 One of the biggest battles of the entire Thirty Years' War takes place at Scharffenberg near Wittstock in the Prignitz region. Some 23,000 Swedish soldiers defeat the imperial army of 30,000 and thus secure the long-term superiority of Sweden in the north German area.

ARCHITECTURE, SCULPTURE, AND PAINTING

Ernst Badstübner

From the Beginnings to the 13th century

Can the names of the March (or Electorate) of Brandenburg and the Kingdom of Prussia be linked with a distinct region – with a precise historical and geographical entity? The history of Brandenburg, the area that stretches from the Harz river to the Lower Vistula, or more narrowly between the Elbe and Oder, will allow this only to a limited extent. The geographical name Brandenburg first appears in the 12th century, when Albert the Bear, Count of Ballenstedt-Aschersleben, titled himself Margrave of Brandenburg after capturing the Slav castle of Brennaburg on the river Havel in 1157. Albert, of the Ascanian dynasty, had previously held the fief of the Altmark (west of the Elbe) from the Emperor Lothar I von Supplinburg since 1134.

The territory we are now describing was called "Prussia" only because it became the heart of the state when its rulers – who from the 14th century were the Electors of Brandenburg – from 1701 had themselves crowned king in Königsberg in the former Duchy of Prussia, even though they maintained their official residences in Berlin and Potsdam. So in the early period – from the Middle Ages to the early 17th century Renaissance – our subject, at least in name, will be Brandenburg rather than Prussia. But the historical roots go back beyond the 12th century to the 10th century, when the Ottonians (the German kings) and Holy Roman Emperors from the House of Saxony gained a foothold in the territory west of the Elbe, which had been settled by West Slavs since the 6th century, and endeavored to establish a border march. (The Semnonii, mentioned by Roman writers as living in this area at the beginning of the era in question, and memorably evoked in the painting *The Camp of the Semnonii*, 1837, by Carl Blechen, was in fact a Germanic tribe that later migrated westwards; see page 376.)

As early as 789, Charlemagne attempted to exact tribute from the Elbe Slavs. Over a hundred years later the Duke of the Saxons, after being elected German king as Henry I in 919, went on the offensive against these Slav tribes more single-mindedly. In this he enjoyed the support of the aristocratic clans: like the ruling house, they too had their seats in the region north of the Harz. Over the winter of 928–929, Henry I captured Brandenburg (the castle of Brennaburg on the Havel), and on September 5, 929, he defeated the Vilz (Wieleci) tribe at Lenzen, just over the Elbe. Henry's son, King Otto I, then installed the Counts Hermann Billung and Gero as rulers of the annexed areas. Having founded the nunnery of Gernrode beside his castle in the Harz, Gero then seized control of the territory as far as the Oder in the east and the March of Lausitz in the south.

In 937, Otto established a Benedictine monastery in Magdeburg dedicated to St. Maurice, and he was able to endow this immediately with possessions beyond the Elbe. In 948 came the creation of two bishoprics for the Slav-populated Lower Elbe-Oder region: these episcopal seats were established in Brandenburg and Havelberg, in other words in pagan locations that were becoming increasingly important both in political and religious terms. Finally, in 968, Otto was able to create a new archbishopric in Magdeburg to which the dioceses east of the Elbe were subject, thus enabling old ties to the Archbishop of Mainz to be severed. This ecclesiastical organization of the country was accompanied by a military one: "burgraves" (counts based on a single castle) ruled the area and exercised justice from "burg-wards" (forts). It seemed that conditions had been established for lasting rule over the Elbe Slavs. But in 983, in an uprising directly after the death of the Emperor Otto II in Italy, the Slavs regained their independence, which they defended successfully until the 12th century.

So the royal and episcopal fortified seats in Brandenburg and Havelberg, where the first churches were presumably built of wood, were wiped out in 983. Church and Empire had to withdraw their frontiers to the Elbe again. Attempts at reconquest led to constant conflict but remained unsuccessful. Interestingly, margraves and bishops with titles from beyond the Elbe kept their offices and rank, and thus ensured a continuous succession of claimants for the lost territories. After the rule of the Salians from Franconia gave way to Saxon control in the person of Duke Lothar von Supplinburg – who became German king in 1125 and Holy Roman Emperor in 1133 – the granting of fiefs relating to land east of

Leitzkau, ruin of the former Premonstratensian church of Sancta Maria in Monte
View down the nave towards the west end of the basilica (begun c. 1140, consecrated 1155)

Characteristic features of this architecture are the alternation of circular and rectangular piers to carry the round-arched arcades and the high nave wall pierced with arched clerestory windows. At the west end, the nave opens into a very wide tower arch and tower porch, above which are the openings of the prince's gallery.

the Elbe was resumed, with the Saxon nobility as beneficiaries: the act of enfeoffment was always intended to encourage reconquest. Once again clans from the Harz area were at the forefront of eastwards expansion, notably the Ascania dynasty in Havelland and the Prignitz, and the Wettin dynasty in Lausitz and Spreeland. The Archbishop of Magdeburg directed his territorial claims at the "corner" between the Elbe and Havel rivers, the Jüterbog district, and the Fläming Hills. At the beginning of the 13th century, these three main claimants came into conflict over access to the Oder, the eventual victors being the Ascanians.

The Ascanian to be granted the fief of the Nordmark (the territory of today's Altmark) in 1134 was Albert the Bear, who was Count of Ballenstedt-Aschersleben. Even before that, in 1130, the Zauche area in the southwest had fallen into his lap as a baptismal gift for his son Otto, and the ruler of the Haveller Slavs, Pribislav, who had been christened Henry on his conversion to Christianity, had nominated him as his successor.

Albert came into this legacy in 1150 when Pribislav died, and he spent much of his reign occupying more and more of Brandenburg. The Ascanians deliberately built up their fief, the March of Brandenburg, as a territorial overlordship. Around 1170 in Brandenburg they founded their first town, the new town of Brandenburg on the southern bank of the Havel.

On the island in the Havel, a royal burgrave now asserted the rights of the Empire once again and eventually the bishop moved into his seat. In 1180, Margrave Otto I laid the foundations for the first Cistercian monastery in the March of Brandenburg.

The effort of the Ascanian dynasty was also focused on extending its territory eastwards and northwards. They are presumed to have occupied the western Teltow district also in the 1170s, as far as the later settlements of the Templars in Tempelhof, Mariendorf, and Marienfelde, which today (since 1920, in fact) have formed part of the urban area of Greater Berlin.

Along with the Havelland, the old Slav fort of Spandau, situated at the confluence of the Havel and Spree, had also passed into Ascanian hands and had been furnished with a new castle. Settlement is also thought to have taken place in the Spree Valley between Teltow and the Barnim district, where Berlin developed.

Under Margrave Otto II, efforts were made to expand in a northeasterly direction around 1200, beyond a temporary frontier formed by the Nuthe and Havel rivers. Traveling upriver on the Havel, the Ascanians circled round the Barnim Plateau and reached the lower Oder near Oderberg and Schwedt. Campaigns against the Danes, who in 1168 had begun the conquest of the southern Baltic coastal area by capturing the island of Rügen, took the margraves of Brandenburg to the coast. This is apparently how, passing through the Stargard area, the first occupations and settlements came into being around Löwenberg, Gransee, Zehdenick, and the upper Barnim.

On his accession in 1205, Albert II continued this movement. In 1214 he built the castles of Eberswalde and Oderberg "against the Slavs," a term which in the margravial chronicle (at the end of the 13th century) refers in fact to the Pomeranians and the Danes. These outposts in the vicinity of the Oder assumed bases along the Havel, which can in fact be seen in the frontier forts where towns later developed, such as Spandau, Bötzow (renamed Oranienburg in the 17th century), Liebenwalde, and Biesenthal.

Jerichow, former Premonstratensian church (mid-12th–13th centuries)
Above: View from west
Opposite: Nave, looking towards east end (second half of the 12th century)

As can be seen, this cruciform basilica possesses two imposing towers on the west front, flanking a lower central tower house. This used to be a typical feature of the first daughter houses of the Abbey of Our Lady in Magdeburg, whose tower house provided the model. The building also exhibits an accomplished mastery of brick, a building material that is surprising at this date in an area east of the Elbe.

In the first decades of the 13th century, the lower Barnim and eastern Teltow were in the hands of the Wettin dynasty. At the end of the 12th century, the margraves of Meissen had pushed northwards from the March of Lausitz and planted themselves in Mittenwalde and Köpenick, from where they tried to take Lebus and exercise territorial rights in the Barnim and Upper Teltow.

It was not until the period from 1225 to 1240, during the joint reign of John I and Otto III, that the situation upriver along the Spree swung in favor of the Ascertains. A precondition for this was the collapse of Danish supremacy in north Germany following the defeat of King Valdemar in 1227 at the battle of Bornhöved in Holstein, near Kiel.

The death of the Landgrave Louis IV of Thuringia in the same year, who had led the Wettin conquests in the Oder region as guardian of Henry the Gracious and heir apparent of the March of Meissen, also helped the Ascanian case. The situation was decided conclusively by the acquisition of Köpenick and Mittenwalde. The Ascanian program of territorial expansion thus reached its first major phase round 1245.

When their father Albert II died in 1220, the margrave brothers, John I and Otto III, were not of age. The guardianship of the fief lay with the Empire, and was transferred by it to the Archbishop of Magdeburg. And it was through Magdeburg that the late flowering of Hohenstaufen art reached the March of Brandenburg. In 1231, Emperor Frederick II duly granted full rights in the fief and territory to the margrave brothers, at the same time confirming their suzerainty over Pomerania. They also had connections, through marriage, with Denmark and Bohemia. Conditions were ripe for the successful development of a state. The Ascanians thus consolidated their rule by acquiring Uckermark (the area west of the Oder, around Prenzlau) in two stages, around 1230 and then 1250. Advancing into the "land beyond the Oder" (in other words the later Neumark), they drove back the Wettins and had to defend their possession of the Altmark against claims from the Archbishop of Magdeburg. They also withdrew the fiefs of the petty nobility who had seized land in the Prignitz after 1147, during the crusade against the Wendish Slavs. Important too was the seizure of the castle and territory of Lebus, which took place around the mid-13th century. It had been preceded by vain attempts on the part of Magdeburg and Meissen to prize the territory from the Duke of Silos, who had already started populating the area with German settlers and granting territories to Silesian monasteries and the Templars. Following this seizure, the Ascanians refounded the town of Frankfurt an der Oder in 1253. This involved doubling the size of an existing mercantile post, which had been established and endowed with privileges under Silesian and Piast (Polish) rule.

In 1258, and for the purposes of the succession, the joint margraves John I and Otto III split their territory between them, establishing a Johannine and an Ottonian line. In the same year, the margraves founded the monastery of Mariensee on an island called Pehliztwerder in Lake Parstein, endowing it with a *donatio magnifica*, a superb gift. It was the beginnings of the Cistercian monastery of Chorin, the second of its kind in Brandenburg.

Abbeys, Cathedrals, Monasteries

The Ascanians' advance across the Elbe was initially accompanied by the Premonstratensian reformed canons. The order had been founded by Norbert of Xanten, who was appointed as the Archbishop of Magdeburg in 1126. Later, in 1129, he installed Premonstratensians in the collegiate foundation of Our Lady, originally founded in 1015. The abbey in Magdeburg subsequently became the mother church of all Premonstratensian houses founded east of the Elbe in the 12th century. These included not only the convents in Jerichow and Leitzkau, but also the re-occupied episcopal cathedral foundations in Havelberg and Brandenburg.

The Premonstratensian Abbeys of Jerichow and Leitzkau

The choice of Jerichow and Leitzkau for the Premonstratensian houses had an obvious strategic justification. The route to Brandenburg is relatively

Jerichow, choir of former Premonstratensian abbey (second half of 12th century)

The east end, which has three semicircular apses, follows the model of Harzland churches of the Augustinian canons (Halberstadt, Hamersleben), which were in turn based on the churches of the Hirsau reform of the Benedictine order. The delicate brick ornamentation clearly indicates the north Italian origin of the early use of brick architecture in the March of Brandenburg.

Jerichow, former Premonstratensian abbey

The column by the door from the east cloister into the transept of the church is decorated with various ornamental and figured scenes. The section here shows a fox dressed as a monk preaching to geese.

Opposite
Jerichow, former Premonstratensian abbey
Capital in summer refectory (c. 1240)

The groin vaults of the two-aisle refectory in the abbey are carried by monolithic sandstone columns, whose capitals terminate in rich, sinuous, partly *ajour* foliate ornamentation probably derived from Magdeburg, where it appears in the ambulatory.

Brandenburg Cathedral: capital of one of the central columns of the crypt

Much detail work in this brick-built cathedral is made of stone, a typical feature of early brick architecture. This capital shows a hybrid creature consisting of a knight, his sword drawn, and a fabulous beast. The symbolic meaning of this hybrid has yet to be deciphered.

Top
Brandenburg Cathedral, nave
View of choir and east end

free of natural obstacles, and the occupation of Leitzkau by Bishop Hartbert of Brandenburg in the early 12th century and the attested consecration of a stone-built church in 1114 indicate a clear intention to reconquer the episcopal seat on the Havel, which although lost in 983, was not, as we have seen, abandoned institutionally. The Premonstratensian convent, which was established between 1128 and 1138, was to act as a cathedral chapter, and had the right to elect bishops. The patron of the foundation was Albert the Bear, so this was the first time a monastic foundation set up a daughter house in connection with the establishment of Ascanian territorial rule across the Elbe.

This church was the seat of the convent only briefly. Around 1140 or 1142–1145, the convert was moved to high ground north of the settlement, where work began on building a new church and monastery, Sancta Maria in Monte. The church was consecrated in 1155 by Bishop Wigger in the presence of Archbishop Wichmann and Albert the Bear.

The building was a basilica with nave and two aisles in the Lower Saxon style (see page 19). The cruciform eastern end terminates in semicircular apses attached to a rectangular choir and transepts. In the nave, nine bays of irregularly alternating rectangular piers and round columns carry high walls with a clerestory, the number nine being an echo of the mother church of Our Lady in Magdeburg. Two square towers flanking a tall central structure were intended for the west end. The towers were not completed, but a plan based on the model of Our Lady in Magdeburg is nonetheless clearly recognizable. A typical feature is the central tower house projecting forward of the western alignment of the flanking towers, with two round-headed windows above the door. Broad, vaulted staircases lead through the side towers into the gallery in this central structure. As in Magdeburg, this form of west end retains the three-tower feature of older Carolingian westworks, including the central west gallery for the ruler.

The foundation of Jerichow followed more or less the same pattern as that of Leitzkau. In 1144, the place slipped from the grasp of the Count of Stade into the hands of the Archbishop of Magdeburg, who in the same year, at the request of Bishop Anselm of Havelberg, established a Premonstratensian monastery there. Initially, it was situated in the local church of St. Peter in a suburb belonging to the castle, but in 1148 it was moved to land belonging to the Havelberg bishop. The new abbey church was intended to function as an interim cathedral for the bishops of Havelberg. However, as the castle on the Havelberg was recaptured at almost the same time, and as work on the future cathedral already appears to have been under way around 1150, the church at Jerichow never assumed this function in the form it took in the second half of the 12th century and as we know it today (see pages 20–23). As a moderately elongated columnar basilica with transept, nave and two aisles (see page 22, top left), and three-part west tower (see page 21), it is more an abbey or collegiate church than cathedral. Nevertheless, with the use of brick, which probably replaced rubble as a building material during the course of construction, a new note was struck in architecture east of the Elbe, compared with the Marienkirche in Leitzkau and with Havelberg cathedral, both of which are built of dark gray wacke sandstone from the Magdeburg area.

The cathedral foundations of Brandenburg and Havelberg

The Premonstratensian foundations in Leitzkau and Jerichow were established as interim seats for the bishops of Brandenburg and Havelberg. The incumbents moved across as soon as the old episcopal castles had been wrested from the Slavs: Bishop Anselm of Havelberg after 1147 at the latest (though as a diplomat in the imperial service he spent little time in his official residence), and Bishop Wilmar of Brandenburg after 1161 at the earliest.

Wilmar's predecessor Wigger, who died in 1160–1161, was not able to take over the recaptured

Brandenburg Cathedral, crypt

The construction plan for the cathedral was changed several times after the foundation stone was laid in 1165, and the basilican building was completed only in the first half of the 13th century. The crypt, a two-aisle rib-vaulted chamber below the tall choir, was also affected by the delay, which explains why there are both Romanesque features (on the walls) and Gothic features (in the apse). The crypt opens into the aisle via two large arches from the sanctuary, which provide a view into the stately interior.

episcopal castle on the Havel island, but he had made provision for himself and his order in the immediate vicinity, and moreover, during the lifetime of the Slav possessor of the castle. The baptized Pribislav-Henry is supposed to have permitted the founding of a Premonstratensian house in 1147. Selected as a location for the house was a place between the Slav suburb called Parduin and Harlung Hill, on which stood one of the most important pagan places of worship, the Triglav shrine.

Also surviving from the foundations of the Premonstratensians in Brandenburg are the remains of the Gotthardtkirche, which later became the parish church of Brandenburg Altstadt (Old Town). Built of squared rubble, the church had a two-tower west front. The elevation of the St. Gotthard convent to a cathedral chapter in 1161 by Bishop Wilmar, as successor to Wigger, is supposed to have taken place in the expectation of an imminent relocation to the island in the Havel.

It was there, on the spot already allocated to the bishop for his residence in the Ottonian foundation charter of 948, that in 1165 the Premonstratensians started work on the new cathedral of St. Peter and St. Paul. It was built of brick from the foundations upwards, and was of considerable dimensions; it is clear that in building the foundations they had to solve some tricky problems. The Romanesque building can be recognized under the Gothic rebuilding from around 1400 only in the cruciform plan of the eastern half, a semicircular apse in the chancel, an elongated nave (possibly planned as an aisleless church, but in the event endowed with piers and a flat wooden roof), and a two-tower west front. The interior spatial effect of the completed Romanesque cathedral must be imagined as being rather like that of the abbey church in Jerichow.

There was a similar development in Havelberg. Anselm (a Premonstratensian like Wigger and Wilmar) was appointed bishop in 1129. In the course of the imminent expansion eastwards, it must have been his aim to win back the episcopal seat not far from the mouth of the Havel, founded in 948 but lost in 983.

Havelberg Cathedral, tower structure of west front (12th century)

Built of squared gray wacke and coursed rubble in the lower part, the tower structure closes the basilican nave like a crosswork. Its massive fortified appearance had both real and symbolic importance, and the design thus served as a model for church towers in the eastern areas of colonization. The top story of brick and the portal are early 20th-century additions.

After the crusade against the Wendish Slavs in 1147, Havelberg finally fell permanently into German hands. This had been the site of constant conflict and changing fortunes since 1130, and was probably where both the (wooden?) Ottonian episcopal church and the pagan center of worship had been. The understandable assumption that the present cathedral of Havelberg stands on the foundation walls and was substantially erected in the 10th century is in fact incorrect. Nonetheless, the elongation of the unvaulted Romanesque columnar basilica with a flat wooden roof, which was rebuilt as a Gothic church in the late 13th century and around 1400, is unusual for the mid-12th century in Lower Saxony. Particularly striking is its 10-bay arcading, with a dimensional relationship of 1:1.5 aisles to nave; and also, particularly in a cathedral, the absence of a transept. Equally unusual are the two-story chapels that flank the choir bays and are raised like towers. It was certainly no accident that Gothic gables and a saddle roof over them were later to simulate the presence of a transept.

Finally, the 12th-century architects of Havelberg Cathedral also went their own very individual way with the west structure. It constitutes a *querriegel* (crosswork), built like a keep or tower house, and constructed as a refuge in times of danger. Its design and function are clearly explained by the circumstances of its construction, and it served as a model for many church towers, especially in the colonization area east of the Elbe (see left). Today, the west structure clearly shows that the whole Romanesque cathedral in Havelberg was built of a stone known as gray wacke. Brick appears only in the east wing of the cloister, which is said to have been completed for the consecration of the cathedral in 1170.

The Cistercian monasteries of Lehnin and Chorin

The Cistercian order had only two houses of note in the March of Brandenburg, namely Lehnin and Chorin. The monastery of Paradies, founded by the Polish Count Bronisz north of Swiebodzin (Schwiebus) in 1234–1236 and settled from Lehnin, came under Ascanian rule in the second half of the 13th century. However, like the monastery of Himmelpfort, founded by Margrave Albert III only in 1299, it was overshadowed by the two major Cistercian monasteries, both in terms of its significance for territorial policy and in its architecture. There were Cistercian nunneries in the northern frontier areas such as Marienfliess and Heiligengrabe in the Prignitz, and Lindow and Zehdenick in the Ruppin district. Lehnin was founded in 1180.

The monks finally took up residence in 1183, and after the death of Margrave Otto I, who passed away the following year and was buried in the monastery he founded, the house became the family monastery and burial place of the Brandenburg Ascanians.

It is difficult to make definitive pronouncements about the building history and origin of individual features, for the church that survived as a ruin was given an abundance of decoration and over-zealous restoration in 1872–1877. Certainly incontestable is the break in style between the easternmost and four western bays of the nave, indicative of a lengthy interruption in building work.

This is, incidentally, a typical interruption in the building history of Cistercian monasteries: the first part to be built was always the chancel, at the east end; then came the transepts with the side chapels,

Lehnin, church of the former Cistercian abbey
View of the Early Gothic west front, completed 1260–1270 and restored 1871–1878

The Cistercians were not allowed to have towers on their churches, but as this church was clearly intended for show, the buttresses here have been designed to look like towers, as would also happen in Chorin not long after.

and the monks' choir at the crossing into the future nave. Next, the builders would turn to the cloisters, and finally to the western part, which was reserved for the laity.

In Lehnin, this visible seam represents a considerable stylistic change – in fact, the change from Romanesque to Gothic in the history of brick architecture in the March. If we ignore the complicated building history and the often confusing derivation of forms discussed in the literature on the subject, and look instead at the monastic church as a whole as it was consecrated in 1270, the long nave appears, despite the Early Gothic details, as an interior of Romanesque proportions (see page 28). The heavy transverse arches, which have a strikingly rich effect thanks to the shafts that carry them down to floor level, divide up the interior forcefully and span the progress towards the apse like triumphal arches no differently from those in an imperial cathedral on the Rhine. The "closed system" vaulting within the square nave bays, which each cover two square aisle bays, is what wholly determines the character of the interior. An unusual feature is the double row of five windows each (possibly the result of a later heightening) in the apse and the two-story side chapels, the upper floors of which open into the

Lehnin, church of the former Cistercian abbey
View of the nave and east end (begun 1190)

Once construction got under way on this great monastic church around 1190, work started at the east end in the Romanesque style. The western parts are Early Gothic in style, but even so, the great ribbed vaults between broad transverse arches, together with the low double arches of each nave bay, create the distinctive feel of a Romanesque cathedral.

chancel like side choirs or galleries. This serves to emphasize the size and majesty of the apse.

On the west front, the absence of the otherwise usual porch and central portal is very noticeable (see page 27). The porch and the portal are, in fact, on the north side, located in the two westernmost bays of the aisle. A façade as such is formed only by the west wall of the nave. It is three stories high, with blind arcading for the ground floor and two rows of slightly pointed windows above, apparently in counterpart to the apse.

The arrangement of three windows was originally repeated as blind arcading in the gable, surrounded by three blind roundels or oculi, as 18th-century drawings by J. Chr. Beckmann show. The façade is bordered by a pair of buttresses-cum-stair towers (a composite term that is the only way to describe their appearance), and indeed, the stronger northern buttress does contain a staircase.

The joint margraves John I and Otto III divided their territory in 1258. The same year saw the foundation of a new Cistercian monastery, now within the Johannine part, at Mariensee on the island of Pehlitzwerder in Lake Parstein, in the southeast corner of the Uckermark. The first monks were transferred from Lehnin in 1260, along with an already ordained abbot. Among the settlers was one *conradus magister operis*, "Conrad, master of works."

Building work began, and things were far enough advanced in 1266 for the deceased margrave to be buried in the church; but then, in 1273, the monastery was moved. The new establishment was named after the village and lake of Koryn, beside which it was sited. Building work on the church and cloisters at Chorin was already under way in 1275. The plan of the eastern parts followed that of Lehnin, but now in High Gothic style (see opposite). It has a rectangular choir bay with a free-standing projecting apse built as half a 12-sided polygon, and double-story side chapels in the transepts. The chapels were rib-vaulted in four bays over a central support, with the upper floor open to the transept via double arcades.

The building history of church and cloisters in Chorin also ran much as it had in Lehnin. The great structural "seam" that separates the east and western parts of the basilican nave, in other words that separates the monk's choir and the lay area, runs between the fourth and sixth bays from the east.

After the completion of the cloisters, the western part of the nave was built, to a length of 11 bays, in a somewhat lighter material and with a sparser use of architectural decoration. This evident thrift in the building and decoration of the western part of the church in no way affected the design of the façade, on which Chorin's fame in art history rests (see page 31).

The façade of Chorin has often been described and analyzed. To quote first the celebrated German art historian Georg Dehio: "Chorin shares with the usual towerless plan of Cistercian façades only the lack of towers." As the Cistercian ban on towers was to be understood not as a way of avoiding high material expenditure but more as a disapproval of ostentation, the ban was "too narrowly conceived in view of the Chorin façade. Even towers could hardly have created a more majestic impression" (Wolfgang Bickel).

Yet it is not exactly the two stair-tower buttresses enclosing the nave façade that suggested the double-tower element: it is much more, as at Lehnin, the composition based on three (the "the divisor three," as the art historians Pinder and Dehio call it). The central part of the façade is dominated by a row of three tall lancet windows. Two narrow, plain buttresses reaching to the top of the pointed windows articulate the wall area, after which the horizontal dominates: a foliate frieze and a "German band" (a form of nail-head frieze of raked bricks) form both a border and a prelude – a prelude to the gable that crowns the wall like an attic, the central motif of which is a triple blind rosette flanked by triple blind arcades. Above this are three gables framed by upper towers, which are square up to the first gable, then octagonal above that, and crowned with pyramidal helm roofs.

Overall, therefore, it is a three-tower ensemble such as had been developed in imperial architecture since Carolingian days, and had been produced in fully mature form in both Ottonian-Salian and Hohenstauffen days – but here projected onto a flat surface. As in Lehnin, the entrance hall opens onto the aisle, though in this case the south aisle. It also accesses the lay brothers' wing as a two-story rib-vaulted hall of six bays supported on two slender round piers. It is, in fact, not an entrance hall as such, but the "Prince's Chamber," a room with a public function in that, from here, the ruler and his retinue could enter his gallery in the interior of the church.

It comes as no surprise that the portal to this "entrance hall" on the south side of the façade is also gabled. Here the narrow gable wall, articulated by slender blind arcading and topped by gables, repeats the principal motif of the façade at half-height and in simplified form. It has a counterpart on the north side, though this is slightly set back rather than projecting; the matching decorative wall has a window in place of the portal. Thus the façade as a whole is a finely balanced composition, based on "the divisor three," that even takes account of the basilican form of the nave.

Chorin, church of the former Cistercian abbey (after 1273)
View of east end

With its tall, slender tracery windows between buttresses, the polygonal choir follows the standard pattern of High Gothic cathedral architecture, such as that at Amiens or Cologne. But the flanking two-story chapel structures (their arched windows can be seen on the transept) remain wholly in the tradition of an older local version of Cistercian architecture (as in Lehnin, also).

Directly behind the west front there used to be a prince's gallery, though this has not survived. In Chorin, it encompassed the two westernmost bays of the nave, and stood on four piers, supporting rib vaults that divided the under area into three aisles. A gallery of this kind is unusual in a Cistercian church, but can be attributed to the same motives as led to the ostentatious west front – in other words, the need to clearly indicate that this is the ruler's church.

The margrave is represented in his church just as the *imperator* was represented in the westwork of the early imperial period (see opposite). The plentiful natural light streaming through the three windows at the west end of the gallery must have provided a suitably regal radiance. As in Lehnin, the gallery corresponded to the east-end polygon in the form of a west choir. The polypartite rib-vault in the western nave bay certainly created the same impression.

The abbey church of Chorin is a monument of the history of margravial Brandenburg, dating from a period when the margraviate – shortly before the rule of the Ascanian dynasty was extinguished – found itself at the peak of its territorial extent and had therefore found its place in the Empire. The Johannine line, whose family monastery Chorin was intended to be, continued the expansionist ambitions towards Pomerania, the Baltic, and Danzig. Only the confrontation with the Teutonic Knights put a stop to this drive eastwards.

After 1300, Lower Lusitia, the marcher province between Cottbus and Dresden, passed into their hands. Considered the architect of this expansionist policy is Margrave Otto IV, whose 42-year reign from 1266 to 1308 spanned the construction of Chorin. "The idea of the west structure, the 'Prince's Chamber,' prince's gallery, and majestic façade tally with his presence and manner" (Schmoll). But his successor Waldemar also appears to have been yet another ruler in the traditional sense, wreathed in the illusory aura of a surviving culture of chivalry, which invoked everything that could serve as legitimation for a leading princely house. It is only in this connection that the layout of the western part of the abbey church of Chorin makes sense. Work on it must therefore have been completed before the death of Waldemar and the simultaneous end of Ascanian rule in 1319–1320.

Chorin, church of the former Cistercian abbey
Above: West front
Opposite: View along the nave towards the west front

The gable constitutes a masterly compromise between the building rules of the Cistercian order, which banned towers, and the desire for a truly impressive design. The west wall, like the polygonal choir (see page 29), is pierced by tall, traceried windows. The narrow windows below indicate the former presence of the lord's gallery.

Castles

Among the oldest evidence of continuing territorial rule and its defense are castles and aristocratic seats. It is due to the historical development of the March that testimony of this nature – so common in Thuringia or Saxony that every notable hill seems to have a castle – hardly exists there. Yet records referring to them abound. Castles may be presumed to have existed on the west bank of the Elbe, to defend the frontier against the Slavs across the river, as early as the 9th century. Henry I must have renewed and reinforced the chain of castles by 929 at the latest, before his advance into Slav-controlled Havelland and on to Brandenburg, and after the battle of Lenzen. Locations such as Tangermünde, Arneburg, and Werben – notable fortified centers later – can already be named. Otto I added castles east of the Elbe on the site of seats of Slav rule and religious centers, the most significant of which were the episcopal seats of Brandenburg and Havelberg, which were founded in 948.

During the 12th century, after Albert the Bear had been granted the fief of Nordmark, German settlers started building or refortifying castles during the course of appropriating land, often making use of pre-Slav and Slav fortifications. Newly built castles appear to have been constructed only in connection with consolidating German rule in newly captured territory, and as the frontiers continued to be pushed further, they soon lost their value. Thus, substantial remains of the Nuthe castles hardly survive. These were the forts built along the River Nuthe in the second half of the 12th century, the Nuthe rising in Jüterbog valley between the Higher and Lower Fläming Hill ranges and later joining the Havel at Potsdam.

Castles in places that had lasting importance in the growth of the state and its administration fared better. They belonged mostly to the ruling house and stood in strategic locations beside river crossings and passes, where urban settlements later developed. Among these were Spandau, where the Spree runs into the Havel, and Köpenick, besides the confluence of Dahme and Spree – castles and towns with settlements that occupied earlier Slav settlements. Initially, it was the Wettin dynasty that took Köpenick; it passed into Ascanian hands only around 1245, when the latter succeeded in breaking Wettin supremacy in the eastern Mittelmark and thereby opening the way to the Oder. The German castles in these places (if we ignore the work of their Slav predecessors) are therefore not of Ascanian but of Wettin origin. The same applies to the former castles in Strausberg, Wriezen, and Bad Freienwalde: we presume that the margraves of Meissen advanced to the Oder along the Via Vetus and through the Heights of Barnim.

Ziesar, castle chapel (consecrated 1470)
Interior

The vaulting under the gallery and the rib vaults of the roof are covered with painted illusionist decoration that echoes the real sculptural decoration of the exterior.

Ziesar, castle chapel (consecrated 1470)
South side

The side with the entrance from the court has a splendidly decorated façade. The components of the decoration, webs of terracotta tracery, follow the architectural ornament of the school of Hinrich Brunsberg (the Katharinenkirche, Brandenburg).

In the area where the Ascanians then pushed forwards to the northeast (circumventing the Wettin areas in eastern Teltow and the High Barnim in order to reach the Oder and onetime Pomeranian territory) we find early 13th-century castles recorded in the Finow area, in Eberswalde, Hohenfinow, and Oderberg.

The Bärenkasten (Bear's Chest), the ruin of a medieval castle on an island in the old Oder near Oderberg, is possibly of Pomeranian origin but nonetheless a late descendant of 14th-century date, and certainly not a ruler's fortress. The castles along the line of the Havel further north were different: Bötzow-Oranienburg and Liebenwalde were owned by the ruling house, and rebuilt as Renaissance and Baroque structures, although since that time they have disappeared altogether.

Ziesar, castle chapel (consecrated 1470)

The chapel, which was consecrated in 1470, is of considerable significance in art history as it anticipates features of castle chapels built during the Renaissance.

The castles in the Prignitz region in the northwest are a special case. They date from the conquest period and form a chain of frontier castles facing Mecklenburg. As in Putlitz, Freyenstein, and Meyenburg in the Ruppin district, they had long been in the hands of aristocratic families who had moved up from being court officials to being minor barons during the gradual seizure of eastern lands, and had asserted their feudal rights under the margraviate. The medieval fabric is best preserved in the ruin in Putlitz, a burg-ward granted to the Bishop of Havelberg in 948. The most impressive part is the keep, which is of brick.

It is not surprising that Ascanian castles are to be found in the peripheral areas of the margraviate which, even in medieval times, were no longer under Brandenburg rule, such as in the Stargard district (Neu-Brandenburg). What is surprising is the fact that the castle at Stargard is actually the most important example in Ascanian castle history. As a castle in the Gothic style, it fits in perfectly with the post-Hohenstauffen late chivalric culture that the Ascanians had created in their realm by about 1300.

Mention should also be made of the episcopal castles. Of the ones in Brandenburg, we know next to nothing. Perhaps archaeological discoveries will one day tell us more. However, in Ziesar we have a well-preserved castle belonging to the Brandenburg bishops. It is a circular castle with a barbican attached on the north side. The 13th century keep still stands in the bailey; the remaining buildings are much more recent, but no doubt built on the site of more ancient buildings.

Of particular interest in terms of architectural history is the chapel, consecrated in 1470 (see pages 32 and 33), for it can be seen as an anticipation of castle chapels of the Renaissance. It also has rich terracotta ornamentation in the style of Hinrich Brunsberg and his school (see page 42), and the illusionist tracery painting in the interior is a remarkable monument of Late Gothic (see page 33).

Since the 12th century, on the site of a former Slav shrine and ruler's seat in Wittstock, the bishops of Havelberg had a fortified seat that had been made over to them by King Otto I back in 948, when the bishopric was founded. The lower parts of the massive square gatehouse tower on the town side date from the 13th century. Around 1900 it was considered the most important survival of a medieval castle in the March of Brandenburg, and around that time it was used by the architect Ludwig Hoffmann as the principal feature in the construction of his Marcher Museum (see page 442, top left).

A survey of the medieval castle landscape of the March of Brandenburg would highlight the large number of substantial ruins on the periphery of the territory. Of those on the very fringe (such as Rabenstein Castle), those in the Fläming Hills in the southeast belong to the Marcher stock only to a limited extent. They straddle a borderline of interest between land-taking powers (notably the Wettins, Magdeburgers, Ascanians), and from the late 12th century to 1815 were essentially under Saxon influence. They are nonetheless linked to the history of the March and later of Prussia. Belzig belongs to the Zauche area, an allodium (in the feudal system, land held outright and without obligations to an overlord) and therefore was Albert the Bear's territory outright. Yet he bequeathed Eisenhardt Castle (the White Castle in Belzig) to his youngest son Bernhard, the Duke of Saxony Wittenberg), and it later became the foundation of later rule by the Elector of Saxony. In the 15th century, Eisenhardt Castle was rebuilt (see opposite), only the 33-meter (108-feet) high circular granite-built 13th-century keep having withstood the destruction inflicted on the castle by the Archbishop of Magdeburg in the early 15th century.

Early Town Churches

Important as they were in the expansion of the March of Brandenburg, monastic foundations and castles retreat into the background compared with the importance of the foundation of towns. Planned settlements, whether of village or urban dimensions, played a decisive role in the settling of new territories. Slav castle fortifications and marketplaces often formed the basis of new German settlements.

We have town foundation charters from the 13th century that, in order to attract settlers and set up villages and towns, provide the names of those involved in the projects, notably business venturers commissioned by the margrave, and nobles. In the early period of the land-take, village and town were hardly distinct from each other; only the dimensions and, interestingly, the form of church indicated whether a settlement was or was not set up to make a town, with the appropriate powers to grant rights.

Belzig, Eisenhardt Castle
Gatehouse beside the moat (after 1465), altered in late 17th century

The projecting semicircular towers flanking the building were built as defensive features.

Frankfurt an der Oder, the Marienkirche (13th–14th centuries)
View from the north

The history of the construction of the Marienkirche in Frankfurt an der Oder goes back to the 13th century. The first hall (nave and two aisles) with two towers kept its chancel and ambulatory in the 14th century, but was enlarged to a spacious double-aisle church in the 15th century. The choir is covered by a huge saddle roof, while the nave has a gully roof hidden behind the high gable attics. The church is still being restored following serious damage sustained during World War II.

Pre-Ascanian settlement sites were mainly trading posts, and can be recognized even today from the presence of a church dedicated to St. Nicholas. Churches in later town foundations were generally dedicated to the Virgin Mary, and these churches in time became the main civic church of the town. Churches were sited close by marketplaces. Now and then they originally formed a single entity with the market, which would often disappear under later building works. Narrow "church lanes" running between blocks of later buildings are a clear indication of this former connection.

In the development of a town, the construction of houses was a matter for the owners, while the whole town was involved in the construction of public buildings for trade and administration, such as the store-house and town hall, and also for fortifications. The community as a whole was also responsible for churches, which were in fact the first public buildings to be erected. The ruler was entitled to be patron of the church. The appearance of the church thus only gradually came to reflect civic pride, as was the norm with the spacious brick-built hall churches of the later Middle Ages. The older churches in the March, both in town and village, are built of squared granite, using erratics from glacial deposits. The cut of the stone is very precise, and the coursing regular. Overall, the construction is monumental, clearly laid out with permanence in mind. The lack of decorative detail is a result of the unforgiving nature of the material.

Most churches are plain basilicas or simple halls, and up to the end of the 13th century generally terminated in a transverse *querriegel* (crosswork) that was the full width and height of the church. This structure was defensive both in appearance and in function. In the early phases of the settlement of the March, when the settlements possessed no other stone buildings and when towns still bore the character of large castles, the idea of a keep or fortified tower house may have struck them as necessary – the *querriegel* at the west end of the 12th century cathedral in Havelberg obviously served as a model for the design of parish churches in the colonized area (see page 26).

It is noticeable that in some towns the earliest churches were of brick. These were the towns that had particular importance in the political history of the March and therefore enjoyed the protection of the margrave.

Berlin, the Nikolaikirche (13th, 15th, and 19th centuries)
View of west tower and the Lady Chapel

Among the oldest parts of the church is the granite-built lower part of the tower, beneath the much later Gothic Revival upper tower, built of brick. The Lady Chapel, built on the south side in the mid-15th century and featuring an ornate blind stepped gable, was destroyed during World War II and restored in 1986.

Examples are Eberswalde (Maria-Magdalenen-Kirche) and Frankfurt (the Nikolaikirche, and later the Marienkirche, see opposite). These are churches that, in terms of design, can be considered collegiate or cathedral churches rather than civic churches.

In Eberswalde, we have a majestic basilica with Gothic forms related to those of the church of the nearby monastery of Chorin. In Frankfurt an der Oder, the plan is a nave-and-two-aisles hall church with late Romanesque and early Gothic forms. It is remarkable in particular for its transept and double-towered west front, and constitutes a development of the architecture of the monasteries of Lehnin and Chorin. The architecture of both churches thus relates to Cistercian houses that were dynastic monasteries and burial sites of the Ascanian margraves. In all probability it was a team of margravial masons who built the monasteries and then later worked in the towns. Presumably the production of bricks was a privilege of the ruler, and so became a feature exploited most in the towns that enjoyed the margrave's favor.

It was only at the end of the 13th century that brick became widely used; but once it had come into general use, it was used in the rebuilding of many stone churches, though the builders usually retained the stone defensive towers of the original building, probably because they were still needed. Complete rebuilds or over-building took place only in the 19th century, even if not to total demolition, as was the case in Bern. Where such towers have been retained, as in Angermünde (see below) and in the Nikolaikirche in Berlin (see left), we have the survival of a feature from the foundation period of Marcher towns that is of great significance in the art history of the region.

Angermünde, the St. Marien civic church
West tower (mid-13th century)

Following the example of Havelberg cathedral, churches in Ascanian towns founded in the 13th century terminated in a transverse fortified structure called a *querriegel* (crosswork) instead of a tower. This was usually constructed of squared granite and only later furnished with a bell tower of brick, an imposing example of which has survived here.

Briest, parish church (mid-13th century)
View from west

The parish church in Briest consists of a rectangular chancel, a wider nave, and a west tower with a transverse rectangular ground plan. The side gables of the tower flank a square central belfry that also has its own side gables and is topped with a saddle roof.

Opposite
Zinna, church of the former Cistercian abbey (early 13th century)
View of east end

In its almost archaic plainness, this church is the very pattern of Cistercian architecture.

Village Churches

Village churches (of which a considerable number of late Romanesque date have survived in the East Elbe colonization area) are impressive monuments to the early land-take period. They bear witness to the settlers' deliberate and systematic build-up of territorial control that parallels the development of the towns. In the early colonization period, the similarity between town and village applied also to churches. That the earliest churches were built of wood appears to have been established by archaeological finds, mainly in Lower Lusitia, in the south.

The first village churches built of stone were, like the town churches, built of squared granite rubble. There are numerous examples of this Spartan construction technique on the eastern fringe of the Zauche and in the Fläming Hills, in other words in the oldest settlement areas, and it was also used to build the church of the Cistercian abbey at Zinna, near Jüterbog. Like their counterparts in the towns, they were constructed of precisely cut squared granite set in regular courses, as if built to last for ever (see opposite). An early type appears to have been a design that grew progressively larger from east to west, with a semicircular apse attached to a chancel that gave way to a much broader and higher nave. If a tower features at the west end (which was not always the case, towers often being added later), it is mainly to a transverse rectangular pattern. Normally the tower is flush with the side walls of the nave, not projecting beyond the nave, as in town churches. The impression is that this feature, and the actual size of the church, are the two characteristics that allow us to distinguish between town and village church built in the early period.

An area rich in churches of the 13th and early 14th centuries is Uckermark. There they are built almost entirely of rubble, but possess multiple door and window soffits, blind arcading, and gables of brick that give a clue as to the date of foundation.

As time passed, less care was evident in stonecutting, and with it the precision in the bond was lost; in other words, precisely those qualities that clearly characterized the early period gradually diminished. Random rubble was also used, frequently in conjunction with brick. The undivided nave with a set-back, mostly rectangular chancel continued to predominate; in its complete form, it still terminates in a transverse tower that is flush with the outer walls of the nave.

A special case is found in the village of Briest, north of Angermünde (see left). The ground plan is the same, but the tower is vaulted in the lower floor and belfry, while the upper floor has a domical vault set on pendentives and supported laterally on broad transverse ribs. This rather complicated vaulting suggests Lower Rhineland influence, an assumption strengthened by the panel frieze beneath three stepped blind windows on the gable on the narrow side of the upper tower, a feature which crops up on many late Romanesque churches in Cologne.

In this respect, the architecture of village churches shares general stylistic trends that are otherwise found only on larger town churches. As the towns developed, particularly in throwing off their dependence on the patronage of rulers, the similarities between town and country diminished in church architecture as well. Early Gothic village churches, still built of rubble, finally dispensed with the set-back chancel, and were thus reduced to pure halls, while the windows change to slender, pointed Gothic lancets. Further changes in village church architecture after that came only in the modern period, when new Baroque structures were planned to replace medieval churches. This mostly happened only where timber and half-timbered churches, which usually had already been renewed several times, had survived and were now due for replacement. It also happened in

Berlin, the Marienkirche (c. 1300)
View from the southeast

With its six-bay nave and its short, aisleless chancel with a polygonal east end, the Marienkirche in Berlin represents the early form of the urban hall church in the March of Brandenburg such as was used by the friars, especially the Dominicans. The tower was added in the 15th century, while the copper-clad clock tower and lantern were added by the architect Carl Gotthard Langhans in 1790.

the 19th century, when some communities thought that a plain rubble church was out of keeping with their prosperity.

Friary Churches

The mendicant orders arrived while the Marcher towns were still in the early stages of development. Their monasteries were within the town's fortification, even though they could have been fitted in to the broader layout of the town. The land on which they were built usually belonged to the ruler, and often the margrave's official seat was close by; sometimes the monastery itself was built on part of the margrave's seat. In Strausberg (1254) and Prenzlau (1275) the Dominican monasteries were located within the castle district, and the land was actually made over to the order much later. It is therefore no surprise to find that 13th and 14th century friary churches in the March of Brandenburg sport an "Ascanian aspect." The friars, for example, used brick as a general building material, and for vaulting, much earlier than town parish churches did.

The Franciscans seem to have become active in the colonization territories sooner than the Dominicans. In Prenzlau and Angermünde they initially erected large rubble-built halls. The surviving southern wall of the first structure in Angermünde displays pointed lancet windows regularly spaced. On the west front, the pointed doorway with recessed arches also remains, typical of all rubble-built churches in the area of that date (see opposite). But this design, if it ever formed a style, existed only briefly.

In the course of the 13th century, the rubble-built hall here had to merge with parts of the south wall of a brick-built hall. The first ground plan was a two-aisled hall on a rectangular plan, with the two aisles equal in height, length, and breadth. Then the plan was amended once again, and the church ended up as an asymmetrical hall with a broad nave and narrow south aisle. It was already clear, as the details confirm, that the model was now Chorin. Eleven narrow rectangular bays lead on to a polygonal apse, which is in fact half of a ten-sided figure but which, in conjunction with the narrower easternmost bay, clearly betrays a derivation from the 12-sided polygon of the Cistercian abbey church. Rarely has it been so easy to trace the derivation of a building type (the friary church) that is tending towards the secular and destined in every respect for "utilitarian" purposes, back to its sacred, traditional, and authoritarian source. This is the unique interest of the building history of Angermünde's Franciscan church. This High Gothic brick church was built by 1300 at the latest. With its elegant features of Cistercian and Ascanian origin, it must have seemed alien in the young Uckermark town, but all the more frank in its assertion of the ruler's sponsorship.

In Berlin, the land for the Franciscan monastery lay next to the "High House" of the *aula*, the margravial court on the eastern fringe of the town, directly by the borough walls. The Franciscans must have established themselves in the town before the middle of the 13th century. The foundation date is recorded as 1249, and it is assumed that Margrave Otto III was the founder of the monastery. Corroborating this is the fact that a chapter of the order's Saxon province was able to take place in Berlin in 1252.

The Berlin abbey, which has been a ruin since World War II, is supposed to have started out as a flat-roofed, rubble-built hall on a rectangular ground plan, but then to have been very quickly replaced by

Angermünde, church of former Franciscan abbey (second half of 13th century)
West front

The structure here clearly shows that this building was begun as a rubble-built aisleless church with nave and chancel, and yet continued as a two-aisled brick hall church. The asymmetry of the interior in the final development is visible in the external central buttresses, which cut across doorway and window.

Berlin, the Marienkirche
View along the nave towards the sanctuary

As the second and later parish church of Berlin, the Marienkirche was built of brick at the end of the 13th century as a vaulted hall church. Typical of Gothic church architecture in Berlin is the cluster pier, which appeared in Franciscan churches around the mid-13th century and was used elsewhere in the neighborhood (Bernau) up to the end of the Middle Ages.

a brick basilica that in material and appearance – however much it appears to bear the character of contemporary friary architecture – displays an affinity with features of older monastic architecture in the March. One telltale feature is the use of broad arcades carried on bundle piers of different design, a feature derived from the nave of Magdeburg Cathedral, which allows a dating of 1240 to 1274. The details of the Franciscan church in Berlin form part of a link looking back to the cathedral of Brandenburg, and forwards to the abbey church in Chorin.

The Dominican churches in Prenzlau and Brandenburg (there were others in Berlin and Strausberg that have not survived) were constructed as elongated nave-and-aisle hall churches with an aisleless chancel terminating in a polygonal apse. They are plain in the detail, spacious, and on the whole vaulted. This design became popular in Marcher parish churches after the "rubble period" had been left behind and builders were aiming at an independent style. A common plan is a broad nave with transverse rectangular bays and narrow aisles with lengthways rectangular bays. The Marienkirche in Berlin (see pages 40 and 41) is probably the earliest town church with this ground plan. The piers of the church, octagons surrounded by circular half-columns, are based on the example of bundle piers in Berlin's Franciscan church. It was adopted in many churches in the Mittelmark and in Berlin (the Nikolaikirche; see page 44) and Bernau (the Marienkirche), built at the end of the 15th century.

Brandenburg, the Schöppen Chapel on the south side of the Katharinenkirche (early 15th century)
Hinrich Brunsberg

The gable of the chapel, constructed around 1400, is a magnificent example of Hinrich Brunsberg's decorative work in the showpiece style of the time, with lavish *ajour* tracery beneath ornate gables.

Gothic Town Churches in Brick

The end of Ascanian rule also marked the end of the first art-historical period in the March of Brandenburg, a period when works of majestic brick architecture were erected that had echoes of imperial architectural motifs, as in Lehnin and Chorin (west front), or borrowed features from Westphalian and Lower Saxon cathedrals, as in Brandenburg (cathedral), Prenzlau (the first Marienkirche), and Frankfurt an der Oder (the Marienkirche; see page 36). It was also the end of building town churches of granite rubble: at the end of the 13th century, the towns gained access to the sources of raw material (clay bed) and kilns for making bricks.

The use of brick was accompanied by the introduction of vault technology in church architecture. Hitherto, vaults featured only in margravial buildings constructed by the builders close to the Ascanian dynasty, while stone-built basilicas in Strausberg or Altlandsberg, or even the hall church in Angermünde, were covered with flat wooden roofs.

If we compare the first brick-built town buildings of the Ascanian period with present town churches in Frankfurt an der Oder, Eberswalde, and Treuenbrietzen, or with the friary churches, we find a wholly different approach to design that did not depend solely on the prevailing style of the day. For whereas brick architecture sponsored by the margraves endeavored to reproduce the details of their stone-built models in terracotta, especially in the geometric patterns of High Gothic tracery, the town churches dispensed with such complex reproductions and tried from the first to exploit the "rational" building opportunities offered by the serial production of bricks.

The proportion of molded bricks was substantially reduced and the designs simplified. After all, one shape could be used in the most various places in the structure, for example on vertical elements, just as easily as on horizontal cornices. With the advent of brick, geometrical tracery vanished entirely, being replaced by simple stepped lights within a pointed arch field linked by the window jambs. It was only around 1400 that sophisticated forms of decoration made of terracotta reappeared in church and secular brick buildings. Once again, they are linked with a particular school or workshop, in this case that of Hinrich Brunsberg from Stettin, whose work can be found throughout the country, from Tangermünde in the Altmark to the Pomeranian border (Gartz an der Oder). The chef d'œuvre in this style is the Katharinenkirche in Brandenburg, where even the name of the master, Hinrich Brunsberg, is recorded (see left).

In town parish churches, the transition from granite rubble to brick as a building material coincided with the first successes of communal emancipation in the late 13th century. The way was clear for the development of what is now known as the civic hall-church. The first structure of the Marienkirche in Prenzlau, still rubble-built and with transept and double-tower west front, and the Marienkirche in Frankfurt an der Oder, which bears comparison with grand Westphalian cathedrals, do not warrant this description yet. However, towards the end of the 13th century, perhaps under the influence of friary architecture, the first transeptless hall-churches appear, both as reconstructions of older cruciform stone-built churches, for example the Nikolaikirche (see pages 44 and 45), or new churches such as the Marienkirche in Berlin (see page 41).

The most important project in church architecture in the first half of the 14th century was the replacement of the stone church, the Marienkirche in Prenzlau, by a brick hall church of seven bays, the east end being formed by three polygonal apses.

A typical feature of this three-apse east end is the flush alignment of the polygons, so that they appear as part of the articulation of the east façade, which is far more two-dimensional than three-dimensional (see above). The architect was clearly aiming for a unified rectangular structure rather than one that emphasized a stepped, vertical effect. This is emphasized by a huge triangular gable (the end of a large saddle roof) that spans all three apses.

Basically, this is still building in the style of the "chancel-less" hall such as was constructed in the late 13th century in Rostock and Greifswald, or in Neubrandenburg and Friedland. Breaking up the straight east wall of the "chancel-less" hall by giving the aisles polygonal endings may be the result of the influence of cathedral forms. Linking a triple-apse ending of this kind with a gable such as is found, for example, over the east end of the Marienkirche in Greifswald, was first tried out here in Prenzlau, and the result is unique. The application of High Gothic openwork tracery, disengaged from recessed wall surfaces, was never repeated in brick again. The intention to "cathedralize" a civic church was never done so overtly in the March of Brandenburg as in Prenzlau.

Prenzlau, the Marienkirche (c. 1280 to c. 1330)
East façade with openwork gable

This great brick-built hall replaced a structure that was, with the exception of the west towers, built of squared granite. The new building was furnished on the east front (facing the original market place) with a grandiose gable that echoes the great façades of Strasbourg Minster and Cologne Cathedral, but here translated into brick.

Hall Churches with Ambulatories

Two dates from the second half of the 14th century are important for the further development of medieval church architecture in the March of Brandenburg: they are 1367, the year in which the altar of the Marienkirche in Frankfurt an der Oder was rededicated; and 1379, the year in which the construction of a new choir for the Nikolaikirche in Berlin is recorded.

Both dates are connected with construction work in the course of which the churches concerned were given choirs of the hall-church type. In Frankfurt, a simple version was built, without an array of chapels (see page 36), which was copied mainly in the eastern part of the March and in Lower Lusitia. In Berlin, a more complex ground plan with chapels was adopted, but this was followed by only a few churches in the western districts, and even then in strongly adapted form (see this page and opposite).

After the middle of the 14th century, probably even before control of the country was returned by default to Emperor Charles IV, the hall choir with ambulatory entered the grammar of parish church architecture in the March of Brandenburg. It was an adaptation of the cathedral choir, invented and popularized in southern Germany and Bohemia in the mid-14th century.

In churches of this sort, the aisles of a ground plan featuring a choir and aisles are led round the end of the choir to form an ambulatory, the choir and sanctuary being enclosed within a polygonal arrangement of piers. At this date, it was a form of ground plan that had already been in use for a hundred years in European church architecture.

Early examples, which are based on the models of great cathedrals, are not very numerous. The most impressive are the choirs of the episcopal cathedrals in Verden an der Aller and Lübeck, both of which were begun before 1300. Compared with the models they are based on, the scale is altogether reduced both in the height and the ground plan, the most obvious change being the lack of a clerestory.

Despite this early appearance of a modern construction type in northern Germany, there was no line of development from this to the Berlin (Spandau) or the Frankfurt an der Oder type of ambulatory hall choir. Inspiration for the latter came in fact from southern Germany, where a new design became popular in parish church architecture in the mid-14th century. The influence of the cathedral form was still there, but the new ideas of construction and spatial articulation being developed were much more radical. An essential change was that it was no longer considered vital for internal supports and external walls of the east end to be concentric.

In the early examples mentioned above, the polygon around the end of the chancel still had the same number of sides as the outside of the ambulatory. Every external buttress had a corresponding pier inside, and the ground plan was neatly concentric. Now the number of sides on the inside and around the outside of the ambulatory could differ, there being fewer internally than externally. What is important is that the supports outside and inside are no longer linked to constitute a single frame, but instead help to form discrete boundaries that create a subtle visual interplay of forms and space.

This skillful "manifestation" of space is a characteristic of the new type of building, whose creation in the cities of southern Germany is linked with the name of the Parlers, a celebrated family of architects. Even before the middle of the 14th century, a hall choir with an ambulatory containing recess chapels

Berlin, the Nikolaikirche
Above: View from the northeast
Opposite: View from nave into choir

The original basilica, to which the granite part of the west tower belonged, was replaced in the 14th and 15th centuries by a hall church. The final phase in the church's medieval building history was the addition of a sacristy on the north side of the ambulatory. The church was destroyed during World War II, with only the exterior walls left standing, and was rebuilt between 1980 and 1987.

Brandenburg, the Katharinenkirche (after 1395 to 1430)
Vault of the inner polygon of the hall church choir ambulatory

An inscription names Hinrich Brunsberg of Stettin as the architect. However, he built only the nave; the ambulatory choir was added later. The vaulting displays stellar and parallel rib patterns and is richly painted throughout.

(chapels located in the recesses between the buttresses) was erected in the Cistercian monastery of Zwettl in Austria. Formally, this arrangement must derive from Cistercian church architecture, but Zwettl is generally included among the models on which urban churches of this type were based. In fact, in Zwettl we even find the type of vaulting that was subsequently used in the Sebalduskirche in Nuremberg as well as Berlin and Spandau, namely alternating quadripartite and tripartite rib vaults spanning rectangular and triangular fields respectively. Such ribs were the most practical ways of spanning the space between differing polygons of the outer ambulatory wall and the internal nave arcade. In the March of Brandenburg, the most outstanding examples of the hall choir with ambulatory are the Marienkirche in Frankfurt an der Oder, the Nikolaikirche in Berlin (see page 44), the Nikolaikirche in Spandau, and the Katharinenkirche in Brandenburg. The type became very popular, and remained in use until the end of the 15th century. Every self-respecting town built a new church in the style, and particular regions developed their own sub-types, for example in the Altmark at St. Marien in Stendal and St. Stephen in Tangermünde, where the influence of the Mittelmark was strong, especially during the late Middle Ages (the Gotthardtkirche in Brandenburg, Bernau).

The same applies to Lusitia, where of course the proximity to Bohemia played a part once again, but at the same time a surprising similarity with the brick churches of Lower Bavaria and the works of Hans von Burghausen (Landshut) is evident.

The choir built at the Marienkirche in Frankfurt an der Oder around 1367 (as the date recorded for the dedication of the cross altar is interpreted) was based on the Sebalduskirche in Nuremberg, but in fact probably only borrowed its ground plan, because construction work on both must have been approximately simultaneous. The merits of the Frankfurt version can be seen in a comparison of the ground plans. The sequence of the three choir bays is a regular division of chancel and lateral aisles, while the three sides of the polygonal arrangement of piers marking the end of the chancel are in clear correspondence with the seven sides of the outer walls of the ambulatory. The tripartite vault, which blurs the spatial division of bays in the ambulatory, is interrupted only on the apical axis, by transverse ribs. If one adds the octagonal piers inside and the almost totally plain buttresses outside, one can consider the Frankfurt design, in its simplification of form and its taut functionalism of composition, as the very essence of brick architecture.

While we are on the subject of functionalism in building with brick, it should be added that brick is a material that calls for a great consistency of forms. Complicated imitations of models built in stone generally remained unsuccessful. There was a future for brick design only in the simplification of design. It was precisely a simplification of this kind that was achieved in Frankfurt, and it was not long before it was copied.

In the 1370s, the choir of the Nikolaikirche in Luckau was rebuilt following the donation of a holy relic by Charles IV. It appears to have been nearly complete in 1387–1388. The vault of the nave, which replaced a section between choir and west end of a predecessor structure in the early 15th century, has a reticulated pattern that disguises the division into bays through the overlapping of parallel ribs, which pulls the space together into an undivided whole. This type of vaulting was developed by Peter Parler for the choir of Prague Cathedral, which was completed in 1385, and adopted in several places in the brick-building areas of the March of Brandenburg.

After the Hussite wars (1420–1436), the citizens of Fürstenwalde, which had housed the bishop's palace of the diocese of Lebus since 1373, discussed building a cathedral. It was to replace the old parish church, and to perform the functions of both cathedral and civic church. The form chosen was that of the urban parish church. Fürstenwalde Cathedral was therefore built as a hall church, between 1446 and around 1470, with an ambulatory that still carries echoes of the choir of the Marienkirche in Frankfurt.

It is clear that an imported building type could be used over a very long period. Ambulatory choirs on the pattern of the Frankfurt and Luckau civic church models were begun in Mittenwalde and Jüterbog even in the second half of the 15th century, and also in Eisenhüttenstadt-Fürstenberg, where an interesting variant was developed, with six outer ambulatory walls and four internal walls.

The fact that it was no easy matter in the towns of the March actually to carry out expensive building projects is abundantly clear from the building history of the Nikolaikirche in Berlin (see page 45). Work began on a new choir before 1379. On August 11, 1380, fire devastated the town, and subsequent reconstruction consumed so many resources that, for the time being, it was not possible to continue building the new church. At any rate, the old church remained in use for some while. It was only after 1400 that the community had recovered enough to resume work on the choir, and perhaps also to complete it.

What distinguished the ambulatory choir of the Nikolaikirche in Berlin, and set it apart from the Marienkirche in Frankfurt, are the vaulted chapels arranged between the buttresses of the seven-sided east end (see page 45). The array of chapels is continued into the aisles, so that the whole three-bay choir is enclosed in a ring of chapels. This type of ambulatory hall church with a ring of chapels was based on the choir of the Heiligkreuzkirche church in Schwäbisch-Gmünd, begun in 1351, and the somewhat earlier choir in Zwettl. Here again the ground plan is clearly a reduced version of a cathedral choir, but the influence of south German and Bohemian churches on the brick-building areas of the north German coastal areas remains palpable, as was noted even by the celebrated art historian Georg Dehio: "We cannot exclude the possibility of an immigration from Bohemia during the period when Charles IV was lord of the March." Certainly, influences emanating from the architecture of the coastal area of Pomerania (Hinrich Brunsberg from Stettin) cannot be overlooked.

A descendant of the choir of the Nikolaikirche in Berlin is the choir of the Gotthardtkirche in Brandenburg, which was begun in 1456 (see above). However, in this case the chapels are distributed over only five sides of the ambulatory polygon, and instead of the Berlin type of pier, which is octagonal and faced with half columns, in Brandenburg use was made of circular piers with four slender shafts, descendants of the *pilier cantonné* of High Gothic cathedrals, such as were typical of churches in the Altmark in the 15th century. Features that the Gotthardtkirche shares with the Marienkirche in Stendal, where the ground plan still follows the pattern of the early ambulatory choirs of Verden and Lübeck, are the relatively high screen walls above the arcades in the nave, and the canopy-like vault of the internal polygon. A similar form of vault is found in

Brandenburg, the Gotthardtkirche (1456–1475)
View along the nave toward the east end

This hall church was built by Henrik Reinstorp. Typical of the period – and Altmark (Stendal) influence – are the round piers and the spiral decorative motif on them, formed by the insertion of blackened bricks.

several churches of the Prignitz within the Altmark sphere of influence.

The rebuilding, by Hinrich Brunsberg from Stettin, of the Katharinenkirche in Brandenburg created a much more progressive form of building (see page 42).

Brunsberg combined the feature that is found in Uckermark hall churches (such as those in Neubrandenburg and Prenzlau) of a gallery built above wall plinth recesses, with the construction of chapels around the choir ambulatory (probably also to be found in the Nikolaikirche in Berlin, and especially in Königsberg in the Neumark). In the Katharinenkirche, the wall recesses between the buttresses are carried up to room height, so that externally all that remains visible are flat lesenes disguised with rich ornamentation. The continuous parallel rib pattern of the center vault is a palpable effort to achieve a unity of space that, as in the Nikolaikirche in Luckau, can be traced back to the example of the choir vault in Prague Cathedral.

The wall-high recesses of the Katharinenkirche recur in two other churches in the March of Brandenburg, the Stephanskirche in Tangermünde and the Marienkirche in Bernau, which must have followed the same model. Both churches were endowed with choirs (after 1470 and 1485 respectively) consisting of two bays and an ambulatory, with five sides externally and three internally. The ribbed vault is carried on round piers with slender shafts.

In both buildings, the buttresses are moved inside, and wall-high pointed-arch recesses form a surround for the window. The flat lesenes survive as a form of decoration. The forms of the final horizontal frieze of the wall, like the doorway surrounds of the Stephenskirche in Tangermünde, reveal traces of the decorative style introduced by Hinrich Brunsberg.

The sole ambulatory choir in the Prignitz region belongs to the Marienkirche in Pritzwalk. It displays an obvious relationship with buildings in the Altmark and Mittelmark, featuring mostly symmetrical side chapels, wall-high window recesses, and round piers. In character, however, it belongs to the northwestern region of the March, though the umbilical cord culturally attaching Prignitz to the Altmark remains quite evident. The link appears in the former pilgrimage church, now the civic church, of Wilsnack (an exceptional case with a hall and transept and extended undivided choir dating from around 1400); in the cathedral at Stendal; and in the civic churches built from the 14th to early 16th centuries as three-aisle halls with an undivided choir. Further examples can be seen in Perleberg, Kyritz, Havelberg, and Lenzen. Only Wittstock constitutes an exception, where a three-aisle hall choir was built with a straight east end and large blind gable on top.

Templin, city walls (13th century)

The 13th-century city walls of Templin, which have survived almost intact, were built of rubble laid in evened-out horizontal layers. Ornate brick towers over the passageways of the gates (not shown here) were added in the 14th century.

From left to right
Stendal, Üngling Tower (c. 1450–60)
Steffen Boxthude

The castellated appearance of this gate tower, with its rich ornamental detail, is intended to express both prosperity and military preparedness, while at the same time presenting the town as a symbolic fortress.

Frankfurt an der Oder, the south façade of the City Hall (14th century)

The right to construct a market hall that would also accommodate the city council was granted to the burghers in the city charter of 1253. The result was an extended structure in the middle of the marketplace, with the short sides at the north and south ends being given roughly identical flights of gables. With their rows of lancets and their tracery rosettes, the façades clearly display their origin in Gothic church architecture.

Tangermünde, City Hall (c. 1430)

The gables constitute an established architectural tradition, as seen especially in Frankfurt's City Hall, but the staggering of the gables here, with their bar tracery and ornate caps, represents an enhancement, justifying an attribution to the Stettin architect Hinrich Brunsberg.

Secular Buildings

It was the destiny of the March of Brandenburg to change in the course of time from a marginal territory of the medieval German Empire into the heartland of a key state, with Prussia finally coming to dominate German history. Its capital was Berlin, once the principal seat of the Margraves and Electors of Brandenburg, then later the royal, and finally the imperial seat. This afforded no protection for the region: on the contrary, the land and its cities were mercilessly exposed to the ravages of time and, above all, of modern war right down to the 20th century. This is why, with the constantly repeated tide of destruction scarring the towns and cities of the country, hardly any historic private residences from the Middle Ages survive.

The town houses to survive in Berlin (by the late 14th century at the latest, following several great fires, buildings were increasingly built of stone) gave way to more modern buildings even during the Baroque period, though it meant doing without the street-side gables that had till then been customary. Some meager remnants survived into the 1950s in the former Steinstrasse in front of the Rotes Rathaus, only to be flattened by the juggernaut of "socialist" town planning. In Frankfurt an der Oder, gabled Gothic houses fell victim to World War II, leaving intact just a few rib-vaulted cellars from around 1300, probably once communal or private stores. These bear witness to an extremely high level of residential and commercial construction. Things are remarkably similar in the city of Brandenburg, where only the surviving Late Gothic gables of the Ordonnanzhaus still convey an impression of the rows of differently shaped gables that dominated the street scene of medieval cities in the March.

With town fortifications it is different. As with stone-built churches, outbreaks of fire, whatever their cause, usually damaged rather than wholly destroyed them. Moreover, the 19th century's enthusiasm for pulling down medieval city walls was held in check in the province of Brandenburg, with the result that remains of them are found in almost every town or city.

Towns in the March were given permission to build walls relatively early in their history, in fact generally just a few decades after they were founded. The first walls were built of rubble. In Templin, this is done particularly impressively, with layers of hewn stone that are evened out along the top by smaller stones (see opposite). On the wall towers, the layers are formed of large, carefully selected stones. In Fürstenwerder near Prenzlau, though bricks were used for the gateway arches, the walls survive in their early form, without any subsequent richly ornamented superstructures of brick having been added. The amazing feature of city fortifications in the March is that, in the later Middle Ages, the original defensive function was lost and they were increasingly used for effect. City gates were furnished with richly decorated tower and gable superstructures on both city-facing and country-facing façades. Motifs were borrowed from church architecture to give the

Above
Rathenow, communion chalice, civic church of St. Marien and St. Andreas (c. 1260)

This is probably Lower Saxon work. The base is decorated with pictures in relief, the bowl with engraved ornamentation. Inscriptions and rhyming Latin texts explain the iconography, which relates to the Mass.

Top
Brandenburg, the Gotthardtkirche, Late Romanesque bronze font

The font is designed in the shape of a chalice to which four identical support figures have been added. The outside of the bowl is decorated with a foliate frieze of remarkable quality. The piece is assumed to have been made in a Lower Saxon bronze workshop, possibly in Magdeburg.

town as a whole a fortified look. The designs evince considerable architectural imagination, with the best examples being in towns in the Altmark, such as Werben and Tangermünde (see page 49, right), in the Uckermark (see page 48), and also in the Stargard region (Neubrandenburg, Friedland); but there are likewise delightful examples in smaller towns such as Mittenwalde, Jüterbog, and Bernau. Constructing and maintaining city fortifications was a communal duty and an obligation on all citizens.

Another communal duty was the construction of a town hall or a city hall. In the city charter of Frankfurt an der Oder dated 1253, specific provision is made for building a market hall on which the ruler can levy taxes. This store, a large three-story hall, was located in the early city's chessboard-style street layout in a block north of the Marienkirche left vacant for the market (see page 49, center). It involves a single, unified building on a rectangular ground plan, constructed on a north–south axis. Its short sides at the north and south ends have, since the 14th century, been richly decorated with spectacular ornamental gables; the tower on the north gable was added as late as 1609. Gables had a long history in the March of Brandenburg, both in the east (on the town hall of Königsberg in the Neumark) and in the west, on the town hall in Tangermünde in the Altmark (see page 49). The Frankfurt example represents a type of medieval city hall that served both as a council building (city hall) and as a market hall. The larger southerly part is occupied by vaulted two-aisle halls on three floors, but only the bottom hall belongs to the original 13th-century building. The upper stories were refurbished by Thaddäus Paglion in the late Renaissance. The shorter northerly part is three-aisle in structure and contained the "justice chamber" in the lower story, where townspeople could take legal disputes, and council chambers on the upper floors. The southerly commercial part would probably have later acquired a large chamber for council events.

The city hall in Berlin was probably somewhat older than the one in Frankfurt, but only the justice lobby chamber survives, looking somewhat forlorn and out of place in the park of Babelsberg Palace. It probably belonged to the type of medieval city hall that had evolved as a medley of different buildings, as is also the case at Tangermünde. Tangermünde's city hall acquired its fame from its tall, slender ornamental gables pierced with tracery rosettes. The details of the terracotta work show the influence of Hinrich Brunsberg's decorative forms, on the strength of which the design for the entire building is also attributed to him. The gable disguises a two-story vaulted hall structure. The type of vaulting used, with a central support on two or three external axes, carries echoes of the castle architecture of the Lower Vistula under the Teutonic Knights in East Prussia. In Brandenburg, only the city hall of the Altstadt (Old Town) survives. Of the lost

building in the Neustadt (New Town), we have the figure of Roland now displayed there. A comparable figure stands in the marketplace opposite the town hall in Perleberg, as a symbol of civic liberty (see left). The echelon of gables is an Altmark feature, while the tracery decoration is a descendant of the Brunsberg style.

As an example of the late medieval town hall we may mention that of Jüterbog. It is once again of the unified structure type, two-story on a rectangular ground plan, and ornamented with stepped gables on the narrow façades. Facing the market, in the middle of the northern long side, the justice lobby is placed in front. It was endowed with a seven-axis echelon of gables by Master Merten in 1493. A stately Renaissance-style town hall with lucarnes framed in volute gables is found in the small town of Niemegk in the Lower Fläming Hills.

Opposite
Perleberg, figure of Roland in the market square (1546)

A symbol of civic freedom, the armed knight stands in the marketplace opposite the town hall.

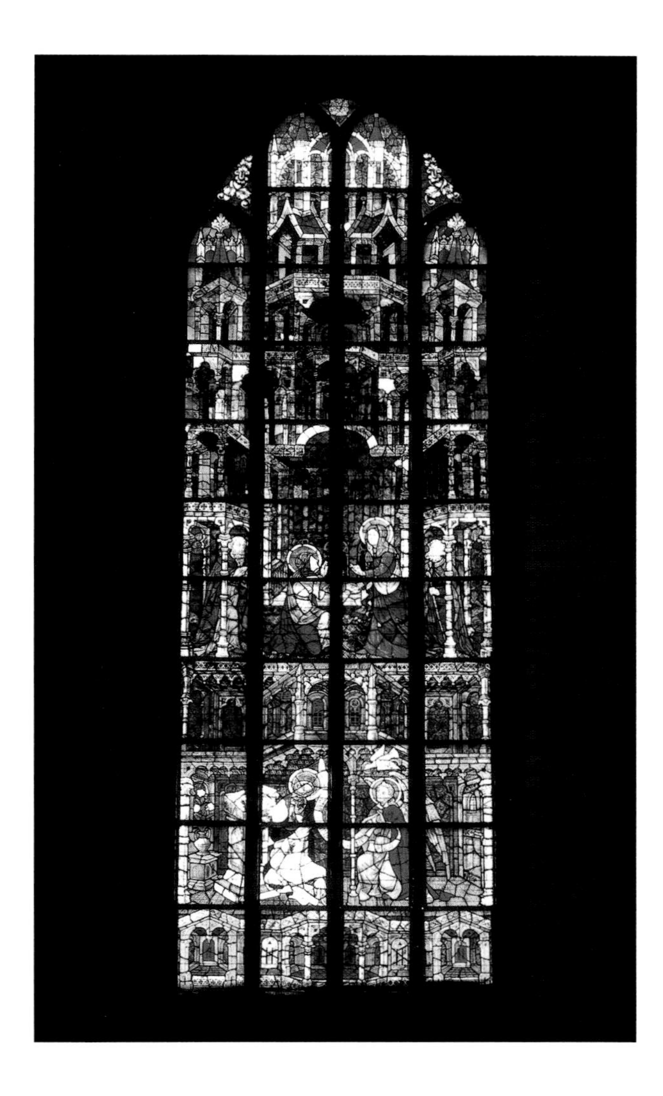

Right
Stendal Cathedral, Annunciation window, east wall of south transept (c. 1430–1440)

The scenes shown include the Annunciation and above it the Visitation, when the pregnant Mary goes to visit Elizabeth, who is also pregnant (with St. John the Baptist). The window suffers from additions and heavy restoration.

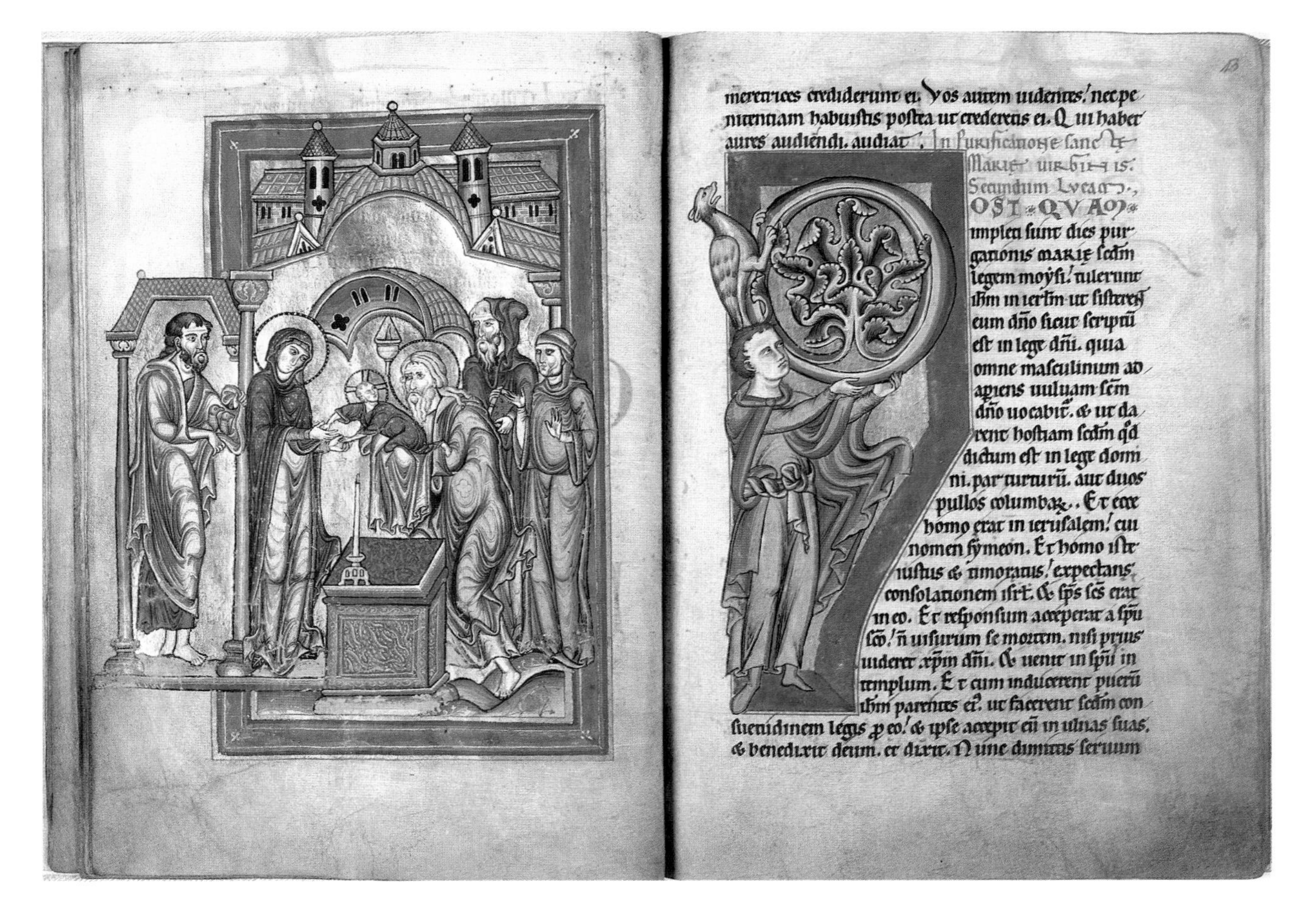

Brandenburg, early 13th-century evangelistary
Lower Saxon work, possibly from Magdeburg

The pages shown are 12r (Presentation of the Christ Child in the Temple, based on Luke 2, 22–32) and 13v (initial of corresponding text from the gospel). This is the reading for Candlemas, in other words February 2. An evangelistary arranges the texts from the gospels in the order of their use on feast days.

The Fine and Applied Arts in the Middle Ages

In the same way as architecture, the arts in the heyday of Ascanian rule (the 13th and early 14th centuries) bear traits inherited from the late Hohenstaufen period. Works of Early Gothic sculpture of German origin reached the colonization areas of the marches via Magdeburg, which constituted a virtual exchange for transmitting western influences to the east. The triumphal cross group from Havelberg and the seated Madonna from Brandenburg are probably the most important pieces, while the Spandau Madonna in the Märkisches Museum (Stiftung Stadmuseum, Berlin) likewise belongs in this group. Plasterwork in the west gable of the parish church at Dolgelin near Seelow in the Lebus region is a particularly rare example of an art form practiced to such splendid effect in Magdeburg. Also possibly of Magdeburg origin are the early bronze fonts in Eberswalde and the Gotthardtkirche in Brandenburg. Both are in the shape of a chalice; the figures that support the Brandenburg font are still in the 12th-century vein. The font in Eberswalde looks no less Late Romanesque, and the armorial eagles of the coats of arms on it and in the church itself prove that both enjoyed the margrave's patronage. The Christ scenes and Virgin subject matter of the terracotta capitals in

Opposite, bottom left
Frankfurt an der Oder, font from the Marienkirche (dated 1376)
Cast by Master Arnold
Frankfurt an der Oder, the Gertraudkirche

The bronze piece consists of a basin and canopy, the overall height being 4.7 meters (over 15 feet). The outsides are richly decorated with reliefs and individual figures.

Above
Font from the Marienkirche (dated 1376)
(Detail) Cast by Master Arnold
Frankfurt an der Oder, the Gertraudkirche

The figure depicts a king in contemporary apparel. The style of the figure clearly shows the Bohemian influence on art in the March of Brandenburg at the time.

Left
Frankfurt an der Oder, the Marienkirche
North (market) doorway (c. 1375)

This is the only medieval church doorway in the March that is decorated with stone figures. The depictions show the Annunciation to Mary and the Adoration of the Magi, in other words the coming of Christ and the Epiphany. This is the iconography of the "Golden Gates" through which rulers entered the church. The arms in the roundels are those of Bohemia, the March of Brandenburg, and the German Empire, indicating that the Emperor Charles IV was patron of the church.

the portals of the church at Eberswalde, which was once perhaps intended for greater things than mere parish church status, pick up on the themes of large-scale Magdeburg sculpture. Similarly unusual is the 13th century sculptural decoration that recently came to light during restoration work on the Marienkirche in Frankfurt an der Oder. Though carved in sandstone, this decoration is nonetheless further evidence of the importance of the church.

The gold work of the late Hohenstaufen era that survives in the March is particularly splendid. The chalices in Rathenow (page 50) and in the Marienkirche in Berlin, for example, are clearly of Lower Saxon origin. Both have rich filigree work on the base and stem boss, plus chased reliefs and engravings illustrating an ambitious pictorial program relating to the Eucharist, the canon of the Mass, and redemption through Christ's sacrifice. The Berlin chalice was possibly a donation intended for a monastery, most probably Chorin. It depicts donors from the margravial house, so the chalice also provides eloquent testimony of Ascanian family history. Also probably of Lower Saxon (Magdeburg?) origin is the Brandenburg evangelistary, which contains whole-page miniatures displaying Byzantine features typical of the first half of the 13th century (see page 51, bottom).

The codex was obviously written for a monastery of Premonstratensian canons, namely the cathedral chapter of Brandenburg.

Extant paintings of this period are not numerous. In Chorin, there are a few murals, and interestingly they are not in the Cistercian church, which, as Cistercian regulations stipulate, contains no pictures, but in the prince's chamber, the antechamber for the ruler's use, where he and his retinue passed into the church beneath a picture of the Adoration of the Magi. The other murals in the Prince's Chamber have turned out to be part of a Christological cycle of 14th century date, and the picture formerly interpreted as a Judgment of Solomon has been shown to be a Massacre of the Innocents.

The retable now preserved in the village church of Rossow near Wittstock is considered to be the former high altar of Havelberg Cathedral. The elegant carvings are thought to be Rhineland work, probably from Cologne, and dated to around 1330. They consist of architecturally designed niches in two rows above each other, and the two groups of figures, a Coronation of the Virgin and below that a Crucifixion flanked by the Apostles, who present the words of the creed on scrolls and hold their attributes in their hands. The paintings in the wings are considered to be Bohemian work of the end of the 14th century. The "Bohemian altar" in Brandenburg Cathedral shows the influence of sculpture and painting from around 1375. The figures depicted include

Bronze candelabra from the Marienkirche
Frankfurt an der Oder, the Gertraudkirche

It appears that the Marienkirche in Frankfurt was extended and refurbished in the 1360s and 1370s under margravial patronage. The two bronze pieces of the candelabra and font date from that time. The status of the monumental Tree-of-Life candelabra as a margravial donation is indicated by the Brandenburg armorial bearings, which hang on the projecting branches as coats of arms.

the patron saints of Bohemia, Wenceslas and Sigismund. Also from the same period is the altar in Rathenow, a shrine with carved figures, female saints beside the Madonna, and two wings, each painted with three saints. These works are considered to be the work of a master working in the 1370s who was influenced by Bohemian painting. The large gilt bronze pieces from the Marienkirche in Frankfurt an der Oder, now preserved in the Gertraudkirche, are thought to have been donated by the ruling family. They include a massive candelabra (see page 53), and a font that, together with its canopy, reaches a height of 4.7 meters (over 15 feet) (see page 52, right; and 53, bottom left). The coats of arms and the eagles on the candelabra are evidence of margravial patronage. Both works are richly adorned with figured decorations, while according to an inscription on the lower edge of the cover, the font dates from 1376, in other words from the reign of Charles IV, and was cast by Master Arnold. The candelabra is possibly a little older.

Top
Havelberg Cathedral, choir screen
(Detail) Coronation of the Virgin, above the north door

Above
Havelberg Cathedral, choir screen
(Detail) Figure of a bishop

Right
Havelberg Cathedral, choir screen (c. 1395 to 1411)
North door

The screen separates the canon's choir from the lay area of the nave. Its sides are richly decorated reliefs. The individual pictures, which are separated by statues, graphically illustrate the Passion in a highly "stagy" way, and in fact medieval religious plays may well have been an inspiration. The scenes in the tympana over the doorways conveys a contrasting, calmer tone.

Right
Havelberg, choir screen
(Detail) Christ nailed to the cross

Below
St. Hedwig's altar in the Schöppen Chapel (c. 1480)
Brandenburg, the Katharinenkirche

The shrine contains three carved figures: St. Hedwig, who was the Duchess of Silesia, and is here shown holding a model of the church, between a knightly saint and a pilgrim saint. The paintings on the wings illustrate the legend of the saints, while the predella contains scenes relating to Christ.

The iconography of the north doorway of the Marienkirche in Frankfurt (see page 52) relates specifically to the ruler of the time. The sandstone figures are unique for the architecture of the brick-building area. The program is that of the Golden Gate through which the ruler passed to enter the church. The Magi scenes refer to the Epiphany, the Magi being witnesses to the arrival of Christ. The arms of Brandenburg, Bohemia, and the German Empire over the doorway proclaim the unique identity of the ruler: Charles IV, German Emperor and King of Bohemia, who since 1373 had also been Elector of Brandenburg. Stained glass, once thought to be lost and now rediscovered, may be connected with this period, for the Bohemian influence in it is very evident.

Stained glass is also found in churches in the Prignitz region (Havelberg and Wilsnack) and the Altmark (Stendal and Werben). Havelberg contains six windows of early 15th century date in the north aisle that illustrate the story of Christ's childhood and the Passion. They are associated with workshops in Stendal, where masters from Halberstadt and Lübeck are supposed to have worked. In Wilsnack, all we have are the remnants of a once much richer series depicting scenes from the legends of the saints, plus the Adoration of the Magi, the Assumption of the Virgin, and two Madonnas. In a crucifixion scene, a princely donor figure, shown below the Cross, has been tentatively identified as Frederick II Irontooth, on which grounds a dating of 1450–1475 is given. The series in Stendal, which are found in the cathedral and in the Jakobikirche, date

Memorial for the Grieben family (early 16th century)
Berlin, the Marienkirche

The scene is the Lamentation of Christ, following the model of Albrecht Dürer's painting for the Dominican church in Nuremberg, now in the Alte Pinakothek, Munich. This is an outstanding example of the influence of Franconia on the art of the March, a development that followed the Hohenzollern takeover of the state. The Hohenzollerns retained the title of burgraves of Nuremburg until the very end of their rule in Prussia.

from the 14th and 15th centuries and are stylistically related to work from north German workshops, as well as from workshops in Erfurt and Halberstadt. The scenes depict the life of Christ and legends of the saints, plus typological scenes (see page 51, top). A convincing impression of a church furnished with stained glass is best obtained in Stendal Cathedral, where all the glass still survives in the choir and transept and fills the interior with radiant colored light.

The churches in the Altmark, and especially the cathedrals of Stendal and Havelberg, have a fine legacy of richly carved choir stalls that bear evidence to typical carving work in the March of Brandenburg around 1400 (see opposite, bottom left). The bench-ends are decorated with both carved reliefs and free-standing figures, and the misericords with fantastic creatures.

A major work, not only for the March but for late 14th-century German sculpture generally, is the decoration of the choir screen in Havelberg Cathedral (see page 54). Some three meters (nearly 10 feet) high, the screen separates the chancel and east end polygon from the rest of the interior. Beneath a tracery balustrade is a frieze carved in relief that depicts scenes from the Passion (see page 55, top). The separate pictorial fields are framed by figures of the Apostles, the Madonna, and a bishop. In front of the wall on the axis of the nave and chancel is the altar for the lay congregation. Flanking it, two entrances with sculptured tympana (see page 54, top) open into the canons' chancel. The wealth of figures on the pictorial wall is reminiscent of the scenes on a stage, and religious drama may indeed have been the inspiration for the carving. Today, this choir screen is unique, yet it could go back to a tradition dating back into the 12th century; it is not out of the question that there was a predecessor. The figures serving as candle bearers in the choir could have formed part of it, as could the late 13th-century Crucifixion group placed high above the screen wall on the triumph bar.

The Bohemian influence persisted until far into the 15th century. Evidence of this includes the ceiling paintings in the civic church at Herzberg and in the Katharinenkirche in Brandenburg (see page 46), the remains of a high altar in the civic church in Jüterbog, and a "Bohemian" panel in the village church of Pechüle. The last of these was probably the predella of a larger altar, and so was surely not produced for a small village church but for a much more important place. It shows 16 scenes from the Passion in two rows, from Christ's entry in Jerusalem until the Ascension, and must have been painted before 1400. In the second half of the 15th century, Low German influence became pronounced principally (but not solely) in the western and northern fringes of the March. An example of this is the St. Hedwig altar in the Katharinenkirche in Brandenburg (see page 55).

Another example is an important wall painting in the tower vestibule of the Marienkirche in Berlin, a *danse macabre* scene illustrating the transience of life, with death coming to all mortals, whatever their rank. Against the background of a hilly landscape, people from all clerical and secular ranks dance in the roundelay, alternating with corpses in shrouds, as they make their way towards their inescapable fate. A text in Low German draws attention to the subject matter, using it as a pretext for moralizing and social criticism. The mural is dated to the 1480s, and it is possible that the events of the plague year 1484 prompted the painting of the work.

Towards the end of the century, Franconian artistic influences become more evident. Again, the trend is detectable in Frankfurt an der Oder, in the high altar from the Marienkirche. Once dated to 1489 on the strength of an inscription, it is considered the

Right
Fürstenwalde, tabernacle (1517) from the cathedral and parish church of St. Marien
Figure of St. Jerome on the tabernacle

St. Jerome is in the act of pulling a thorn from the paws of a lion. Stylistically, this Late Gothic tabernacle of 1517 is comparable with that by Adam Kraft in the Lorenzkirche in Nuremberg.

Stendal Cathedral, choir stall (c. 1430)

The bench-ends of the stalls are decorated with seated figures representing the prophets.

work of Nuremberg masters from the workshops of the artists Pleydenwurff or Wolgemut. The outstanding paintings on the wings of the retable, with which the great shrine, filled with the carved figures of St. Hedwig and St. Adalbert, can be closed, follow graphic works by both Martin Schongauer and Israhel van Meckenem. The pinnacles of the tabernacles in Fürstenwalde and Jüterbog likewise display Franconian traits in their figures (see above, right).

This tendency during the late 15th century to follow Franconia in sculpture and painting must have been a consequence of the arrival of the new ruling dynasty. The incoming Hohenzollerns were burgraves of Nuremberg, and remained so until 1918. Even in Berlin there are works of south German origin.

An altar shrine in the Marienkirche containing the carved and painted figures of a Kinship of Christ group is almost Würzburg Franconian in character. Two painted memorials (for the Grieben family and an unknown donor), which originally came from the Nikolaikirche, even have close affinities with the work of Albrecht Dürer (see opposite). Both panels are attributed to a painter called Nikolaus Winkler, who came to the March from Nuremberg and became a citizen of Frankfurt after 1520 (Berckenhagen). They are among the most important panel painting works to survive in Berlin and the March from the late medieval/early Renaissance period.

The lack of paintings in the March of Brandenburg from the period between the late Middle Ages and the Reformation is probably due to the repeated change of confession; the March was Catholic until 1539 and then Lutheran until 1613, when, for political reasons, it became Calvinist. Because of a general disapproval of religious images within the Reform Churches, individual examples of fine works from the late Middle Ages crop up in places where we would least expect them, mostly in the churches of smaller towns or villages. The only conclusion to be reached must be that artistic works from the leading churches, notably cathedrals and court churches, were spirited away for safe keeping and hidden in obscure churches.

One of these works is the Late Gothic altar in Mittenwalde (see page 59), details of which indicate it came from a Dominican monastery (Berlin – Cölln); another is a Cranach painting in Markgrafpieske near Fürstenwalde showing the martyrdom of St. Sebastian. It is quite possible that the altar in the civic church of Wittstock, where the apostle reliefs clearly show the influence of the Lübeck picture carver Claus Berg, comes from the Bischofsburg. However, the altar in Bernau must have been made for the church there. Its richly painted wings (see page 58) show, like almost all paintings of the period between 1520 and 1540, the influence of Lucas Cranach the Elder. He had worked in Wittenberg from 1505 and did a great deal of work for the Brandenburg electors, including

the furnishings for a Dominican church that was transformed into a cathedral collegiate church in 1536, and the fittings of the Renaissance-style rebuilding of the castle in Cölln, henceforth the official residence of the Hohenzollern capital of Berlin.

Mittenwalde, carved altar (1514), choir of St. Moritz

The central Deposition scene on this lavishly decorated altar is older work of Flemish (Antwerp) origin.

Opposite
Bernau, high altar (c. 1520), civic church of St. Marien

This is one of the largest altars in the March, certainly one with the most figures. Of the six wings, the two outermost are fixed, the rest moveable. The altar opens up to reveal the Coronation of the Virgin in the middle, surrounded by superimposed ranks of saintly figures in both shrine and wings.

Jüterbog, civic church of St. Nikolai, Enthroned Virgin and Child from former high altar (c. 1420–1430),

Although a seated figure is shown, the S-shaped posture is characteristic of standing figures of the time. The faces still shows traces of the influence of Bohemian art from around 1400.

·I·N·R·I·

Protestant Art

An important element in Protestant art was the memorial, which took the form either of a painting or of a sculpture. These memorials came into fashion directly after the Reformation had gained hold in Brandenburg – in other words, during the decades after 1539.

Memorials were, in effect, a replacement for medieval side altars, which had in many cases been removed. Though they are not very numerous and are artistically of little importance, these memorials are remarkably eloquent. They are in fact didactic images composed in accordance with a religious visual language developed by theologians and artists in Wittenberg around 1530, and associated in particular with the Cranach workshop.

Common to them all is an allegorical depiction of Luther's doctrine of the redemption of sinful man by faith, through the crucified and risen Christ. However, although the basic Wittenberg program is always repeated in slightly varied form, many works are stylistically independent of Wittenberg influences and also include a wider range of subject matter.

These works – of which small collections survive in the Marienkirche in Berlin, the Gotthardkirche in Brandenburg (see above), and the Gertraudkirche in Frankfurt (originally in the Marienkirche, Frankfurt) – are connected in particular with the painter Michael Ribenstein and the sculptor Hans Schenk-Scheutzlich.

Hans Schenk-Scheutzlich came from Schneeberg in Saxony, and was obviously brought to Berlin as one of the artists imported from Torgau and Wittenberg for the construction of Joachim II's palace. In 1543 he became a burgher of Berlin, and worked (presumably until his death around 1566) as court sculptor to the Elector, occasionally under-taking commissions from court officials in residence and city dignitaries as well.

Even several mayoral families in Brandenburg ordered their memorials from Schenk-Scheutzlich. He was probably also responsible for the memorial for Caspar Theiss, which was still in the Nikolaikirche in Berlin in the 18th century.

Three tomb-slabs there, made for Gregor Bagius (died 1549), Johann Zeideler (died 1556), and Paul Schultheiss (died 1558), bear the marks of his rather bizarre, quasi-Mannerist style and his unconventional allegorical visual language, which clearly reveals the influence of Luther's doctrine of justification.

About the same time as Hans Schenk-Scheutzlich, Michael Ribestein was also at work in Berlin. Many of his works have survived, and likewise provide an interesting insight into early Protestant iconography. As court painter to the Elector, he apparently acquired burgher status in Berlin in 1539. His signature, the monogram MR on a float stone (*Reibestein* in modern German), crops up initially on graphic prints – woodcut portraits of the Emperor Charles V, of King Ferdinand, and Duke John Frederick of Saxony, executed after the defeat of the Protestant alliance in the Schmalkalden War (1546–1547). It has been assumed that Ribestein was responsible for the portraits in the camp of the victorious army outside Wittenberg.

The only surviving painting on which the monogram MR on a float stone proves the authorship comes from the Marienkirche in Berlin (see right). It is dated to 1562 and is described as a Crucifixion, but unlike the traditional Crucifixion scene does not show Mary and St. John or the soldiers and the three Maries under the Cross.

Here, beside the Cross, which dominates the center ground, we see Moses with the tablets of the Law (an Old Testament prefiguration), and John the Baptist, who points to the Crucified Christ, the "Lamb of God, who takes away the sins of the world," as it says on the scroll in his hand.

This is the same message as is found in allegorical scenes depicting Luther's doctrine of the redemption of man through faith in the crucified and risen Christ, a theme first developed in Wittenberg in the Cranach workshop.

However much Michael Ribestein's message tallies with that promulgated in Wittenberg, his actual style has nothing in common with the Wittenberg style of Cranach. So here we are confronted with the intriguing fact that the Wittenberg subject matter of Protestant art was successfully depicted in a com-pletely different style, whose characteristic feature is a quasi-classical Italianate manner, which was no doubt transmitted by Dutch Mannerist painting.

Memorial for Mayor Joachim Damstorff (died 1572) and his wife Anna During (died 1583)
Brandenburg, the Gotthardkirche

The portraits of the married couple take the form of relief busts at the side of the two-story aedicula superstructure, which contains scenes of Christ being scourged and carrying the Cross. The aedicula is crowned by a delicate model of columnar architecture with a central domed superstructure containing a (now damaged) Man of Sorrows image of Christ.

Opposite
Stained glass in the north window of the transept, with scenes of the Passion (c. 1480)
Stendal Cathedral

This section shows the Lamentation of Christ after the Deposition. The symmetrical composition of the row of figures in front of an architectural background, reminiscent of Flemish painting, is distributed across five lights.

Memorial painting with the Crucified Christ (dated 1562 and signed MR)
Michael Ribestein, Berlin, Marienkirche

With the Crucifixion in the center, Moses on the left, and John the Baptist on the right, the latter pointing to Christ, this picture belongs to a form based on Luther's doctrine of the redemption of man by faith alone, a form that became widespread after the Reformation.

The Elector's Palace in Berlin

When Ascanian rule came to an end with the death of Valdemar in 1319, the March returned to the Empire as a fief, remaining for a time in the hands of the monarch: initially the Wittelsbachs, then the Luxemburg monarchs. After 1370, the Emperor Charles IV had begun work on converting an older fortified seat in Tangermünde into an imperial castle, which, because of its artistic opulence, has been compared with the celebrated Karlstein Castle. After 1412, the castle in Tangermünde became the first seat of the Hohenzollern burgraves of Nuremberg, who were confirmed in the fief in 1417.

In 1443, the Hohenzollerns started work on an official seat at a new site they had selected on an island in the Spree beside Cölln, opposite Berlin (the exact position is shown in a map by Memhardt dated 1650; see page 76). In 1442, Frederick II Irontooth had hived off a large plot of land on the island, on the north side of Cölln beside the Dominican monastery, to develop as a building site that spanned almost the entire breadth of the island. This he surrounded with a rectangular wall, in the northwest corner of which a huge square fortified tower was erected, the predecessor of the Mint Tower. A corresponding tower was constructed in front of the middle of the south wall, roughly on the axis of the Breite Strasse, directly beside the choir of the monastic church. (The south tower was later turned into a church bell-tower after the church was made a cathedral in 1536.) The actual wings of the first Burg (fort) on the Spree island, which Frederick II already described as a *Schloss* (a residential castle or palace), occupied the southeast corners of the block, the chapel being located in the residential wing parallel to the river.

In 1538, the Elector Joachim II began renovation work on the castle on the island of Cölln. The specific reasons which prompted the construction of a Renaissance building as the seat of the Hohenzollerns are not known. Probably the decisive consideration was that, as the official seat of the rulers, its appearance should match its political importance and vie as an equal with the palaces of other German princes. (The process was repeated around 1700, when the Elector of Brandenburg turned himself into the King of Prussia, and the Renaissance building vanished under the newly constructed Baroque Berlin Palace.) That Joachim II was following an established plan can be inferred from his rapid action after coming to power in 1535. The first step he took was to move the cathedral establishment into the church of the Dominican monastery (see the map on page 76, where it is marked F). It is clear that the same plan had been followed by his father, who had taken care to augment the revenues and endowment of the cathedral chapter.

Work was begun by building the city wing. The residential wing beside the Spree came next, after 1540, and is still recognizable in old views and photos. It is recorded that Joachim had Friedrich II's castle totally demolished and rebuilt *a primis fundamentis*, from the first foundations; and indeed, only scant traces of the remains of above-ground walls of the first

Inner court of the Renaissance palace in Cölln, opposite Berlin
Pencil drawing by Johann Stridbeck the Younger, from his sketchbook (1690) Berlin, Staatsbibliothek zu Berlin – Preussischer Kulturbesitz

On the right is the elegant stair tower on the façade facing the town of Cölln. Standing as slender as a column on its high plinth, the tower was modeled on a stair tower at Hartenfels Palace, near Torgau. Another feature similar to one in Torgau is the Reitschnecken (Bridle Stair) in the east wing, a spiral ramp in the octagonal tower (center) leading to the upper floors.

15th-century castle have ever been found. Nonetheless, physical elements of the first building could have been reused or preserved in the Renaissance building, along with the continuity of functions expressed by the structural arrangement. At any rate, the chapel (see right) and its dimensions were retained in the Spree-bank residential wing, in the same place as it had been in Frederick Irontooth's castle. Until its destruction after 1945, the form acquired by the castle chapel after 1540 remained intact, apart from a division of stories – the original height of the two-story space was 13 meters (32.6 feet) – and various new installations. Photos from before the date of destruction show principally the type of vault, a looped rib pattern, whose unifying motion over the whole room is timidly interrupted from vault bay to vault bay by transverse arches springing from armorial consoles decorated with delicate grotesque motifs. The ribs, partly freestanding and fluted with a double groove on both sides, twisted up spirally from the round piers and walls. That the rectangular room once contained galleries all round may be presumed from surviving ground plans showing appropriate supports; that they were also two-story is indicated by Philipp Hainhofer's report from 1617, which mentions that it was furnished "full of paintings and altar panels by Lukas Kronacher and other old painters," which had been returned to the castle chapel after the cathedral chapter had gone over to Calvinism. Cornelius Gurlitt informs us that the design for the palace in Berlin came from the architect Konrad Krebs in Torgau. Supporting this claim are the fact that Krebs was in Berlin in 1537, and an entry in the Torgau building accounts reading: "Item: expenditure for cutting the pattern of the house in Berlin." The actual architect in Berlin is considered to have been Caspar Theiss, who undoubtedly came to Berlin from Krebs's Torgau circle, possibly as early as 1537 and remained in the service of Joachim until his death. It is known that Saxon stone masons and sculptors who hailed from the same group of workshops as Theiss were active in Berlin and the March of Brandenburg until well into the second half of the 16th century. To Caspar Theiss and Hans Schenk-Scheutzlich – whose names epitomize this architectural work in the March, have been ascribed the electoral hunting lodges in Grunewald, Grimnitz near Joachimsthal, Köpenick, Potsdam, Rüdersdorf, Schönebeck, and Zossen. All of these Renaissance lodges of the March of Brandenberg, with the exception of Grunewald (see page 65), have been lost, and therefore we need to study them through 17th-century illustrations, notably the engravings of Matthäus Merian, who recorded such buildings as the significant architectural monuments of his day. The appearance of the Berlin city palace during the Renaissance can be surmised from engravings made before it was comprehensively rebuilt in the Baroque style, which show sports events and festivities on the Stechbahn, the sports area in front of the city wing. There is also a painting from Tamsel Palace near Küstrin which shows the south front of the palace from the Lange Brücke (Long Bridge), later known as the Kurfürstenbrücke (Elector's Bridge) and now called the Rathausbrücke (see page 77). Finally, there are also numerous drawings by Johann Stridbeck, an Augsburg engraver, who during a visit to Berlin in 1690 and 1691 busily filled his sketchbook with views of the palace from several directions and from the garden side.

It is a straightforward matter to reconstruct a palace of the early German Renaissance, whose extended three-story wing facing the city was splendidly enclosed between tall, decorated bay windows. The design bears the stamp of the Torgau master. The double curtain arch seems to be taken directly from Hartenfels Palace in Torgau, which probably also had the same ridge-height transverse roofs with elaborate scrolled gable-ends. In Berlin, however, they seemed to have turned out rather bulky, and their rhythmic

Berlin Palace, Erasmus Chapel (destroyed)
First upper floor
View from west end into choir
(c. 1459–1465)
Historic photograph (c. 1925)

The palace chapel was among the oldest parts of the palace, dating from the 15th century. During the time of Frederick the Great, it was subdivided by a ceiling on wooden joists, at the height of already existing galleries.

View of Palace Island (Schlossinsel) with the towns of Berlin (left) and Cölln (right), seen from the west bank of the River Spree (c. 1650–1655)
Johannes Ruischer
Oil on canvas, 194 x 390 cm
Berlin, Stiftung Preussische Schlösser und Gärten Berlin-Brandenburg, Schloss Charlottenburg

Ruischer was a member of Rembrandt's circle. In this view, he depicts the buildings of the Renaissance palace in the center. To the right are the Late Gothic towers of the cathedral and the tower of the Petrikirche, Cölln, and at the extreme right, the linden trees of the avenue leading from the Von der Hunde Bridge (later called Schlossbrücke), planted in 1647 as a bridle avenue still called Unter den Linden. On the left is Memhardt's summer house and the medieval tower of the Marienkirche in Berlin. The placing of the summerhouse in the pleasure gardens *behind* the medieval city wall is a mistake.

alternation with smaller lucarnes is unusual. The tops of the tall bay windows at the corners, however, in the form of lantern turrets that can be accessed and used like belvederes, are a feature that are not found in the oeuvre of Konrad Krebs. The courtyard façade of this wing facing the city seems in fact to be a copy of the Johann Friedrich building in Torgau, the most notable feature being the great spiral stair tower called the Grosse Wendelstein in front of the façade (see page 62).

The Spree wing is considered the later part of Joachim's palace. Obviously the Elector gave the public part of the building preference before embarking on the renovation of the residential wing, where probably more of the core was retained than was retained during the construction of the new structure on the city side. The palace church was also being constructed at this time. Above its choir a huge tower began to rise, looming over the rest of the buildings. In the drawings, the dominance of the castle tower suggests that it was meant to signal that this was the seat not just of a ruler but also of the head of the Church, and indeed since the Reformation the Elector had been just that (see above). The Renaissance-style electors' palace of Cölln ceased to exist from around 1700. Elector Frederick III of Brandenburg, who from 1701 restyled himself "King Frederick I in Prussia," commissioned Andreas Schlüter to convert it into a grand Baroque palace. In Schlüter's designs, we find an echoe of the 1540 city wing feature, the round corner bays, and the central emphasis in the façade created by the triple axis of the portal frontispieces. It was extensions of this plan, added by Schlüter's successor, that blurred the derivation of the façade composition from its predecessor.

The Hunting Lodge in the Grunewald

Of the electors' Renaissance-period hunting lodges (Caspar Theiss was the most likely architect), only the one in the Grunewald survives. What remains of its Renaissance character was emphasized by recent restoration. Situated 15 kilometers (just over nine miles) west of Berlin's Stadtschloss, it was reached from the latter by a bridle path, later partially planted with linden trees, that passed through the elector's zoo and Spandau Forest. The lodge did not of course survive 1700 unmolested: government architect Martin Grünberg removed gables and modernized windows, but most obviously filled in the moat round the former water-encircled house. However, enough is preserved of the 1542 building for us to get an idea of the original appearance (see page 65). On the courtyard side, which was also the arrival side of the rectangular main building, there is a porch-like structure topped by a roof with an ogival profile. This porch gives access to the spiral staircase of a stair tower (slightly off center), only three of whose eight sides stand clear of the façade. The building was once two-story and had shaped gables fronting a tall saddle roof that had transverse sections; this can be concluded from a report on the lodge by Count

Lynar. Probably these transverse sections, like the two projecting corner wings on the lake front, were also once crowned by gables (there is a reconstruction by A. Geyer). The rich array of gables would thus have matched that of the city palace. Uncertainty as to whether the U-shaped layout leading to the *cour d'honneur* was original led to the conclusion that the projecting wings were former towers, which would have been integrated into a symmetrical three-wing layout in the Baroque style by Rochus Lynar for Elector John George, after Joachim II's death in 1571. In the same interpretation, the bays on the lake front were inserted on early Renaissance consoles. These consoles originally came from the palace stoneyard in Cölln in Caspar Theiss's day and were there intended for the gallery on the courtyard site linking the residential rooms on the second floor. The original impression of the appearance of the hunting lodge, which Joachim II called "Zum grünen Wald" (Greenwood), must have been of a fortified "strong house" rather than a hunting lodge; its later hunting-lodge character was the result of a transformation by Count Rochus von Lynar under John George.

Most of the interior on the ground floor is taken up by the principal room; the western part was divided off by a double arch on a central column like a gallery or lobby (recently reconstructed). In the eastern parts there were service rooms, while the upper floor and attic floor contained living rooms. No architectural decoration from the 1542 building has survived at Grunewald.

Even a relief with the half-length portraits of three revelers, now set into the wall in the vestibule over the door to the former wine cellar, does not prove that such decoration did once exist. The relief must once have been on an external structure, probably the Berlin palace. Here we have the surviving portraits of the three most important men in the building profession of Joachim II's day: the wine waiter (in German *Schenk*), in other words the sculptor Hans Schenk, sometimes called Scheutzlich ("hideous"), who, in the inscription, bids the architect CASPAR THEYS and the clerk of works CONCZ BUNTSCHUG welcome to the *Trunk* (draft). "The relief is among the best to have survived of Renaissance-period sculpture from

Berlin, Grunewald hunting lodge
Courtyard side

Except for the octagonal tower, which contains the spiral staircase, the building does not look like a Renaissance-style building from the days of Joachim II. It was presumably built by the palace architect Caspar Theiss, and much altered in the 18th century. Today it houses a museum.

Berlin … Presumably it was moved here … by Rochus Lynar at the end of the 16th century" (H. Börsch-Supan). Thus, at the hunting lodge of Grunewald, we are clearly presented with a second phase of Renaissance architecture in the Electorate of Brandenburg, a phase that began after the death of Joachim II in 1571 and whose typical representative must be considered Count Rochus von Lynar, an Italian who came to Berlin via Dessau and Saxony.

Country Houses and Mansions

At first glance, it may seem that the Renaissance architecture of the March of Brandenburg was very meager. It takes a more penetrating examination, mainly in investigating the pictorial sources of the 17th century, to establish that Brandenburg was in fact strongly affected by the triumphal march of the Renaissance through northern Europe. There were numerous fine houses in the Renaissance style in town and country, but many shared the fate of the Renaissance palace in Berlin in being replaced by a new building in the succeeding centuries. A number of Renaissance great houses on the periphery of the March are all that remain: these include part of the originally probably much more important building in Freyenstein in the Prignitz region, now a ruin (see opposite); and houses in Meyenburg (not far from Freyenstein) and Boitzenburg in the Uckermark, where the Renaissance element is hidden beneath 19th-century rebuilding.

So the architects and masons from the Electorate of Saxony who came to Berlin with Caspar Theiss and Hans Schenk-Scheutzlich built much more than can be found today. We now have no knowledge of the appearance of the great houses in Schorfheide, Gross-Schönebeck, and Castle Grimnitz, Joachimstal, nor of the residence in Potsdam before it was converted into a secondary residence by the Great Elector. The survey *Topographia electoratus Brandenburgici* (The Topography of Brandenberg), published by Matthäus Merian in Frankfurt am Main in 1652, records the original appearance of the houses in Wolfshagen (destroyed) and Boitzenburg (end of 16th century); of a house in Zehdenick; and (very impressively) of the strong; the one-time appearance of the "strong house" in Badingen (mid-16th century; see below) near Gransee. Also noteworthy are the great houses or mansions in Stolpe an der Oder (1545–1553), Lichterfelde (1565–1567), and Trampe in the Barnim region. The ground plans of these are so similar that an older origin is inferred. Typical features are the main entrance on the long side and a central space acting as an entrance hall, associated with which is the kitchen (which tended later to be moved to another part of the building). Also, the access to the upper floor is via a staircase in an external building, a feature that is no doubt inherited from medieval fortified houses.

Badingen House
Copper engraving, 14.7 x 12 cm, from Topographia electoratus Brandenburgici *(1652)*

Our knowledge of the magnificent Renaissance-style great houses in the March of Brandenburg is derived largely from *Topographia electoratus Brandenburgici* (The Topography of Brandenburg), written by Martin Zeiller and published by Matthäus Merian in Frankfurt am Main in 1652. The core of Badingen (near Gransee) is medieval. This was extended in the 16th century by the addition of an attic story with symmetrically arranged scrolled gables. The house has since been stripped of its gables and looks far less imposing.

Freyenstein, Altes Schloss (Old Palace)
Gable with terracotta decoration (after 1556)

The subdivisions by decorated pilasters and medallion reliefs is related to the Fürstenhof in Wismar. The portrait medallions probably came from the workshop of Statius van Düren in Lübeck.

The houses in Bagow and Demerthin are among the better preserved country houses and mansions of the Renaissance period in the March of Brandenburg. The house in Bagow can, due to the presence of an inscription, be confidently dated to 1545, and the one in Demerthin to 1604, according to an inscription placed over the tower doorway. The strictly symmetrical design of the entrance façade on the courtyard side and the three-dimensional organization of the entire fabric down to the last detail place the house at Demerthin in the late phase of the Renaissance in Brandenburg. It shares the plain gable diagonals of the house in Königs Wusterhausen, which presumably derives from Rochus von Lynar's "Transverse Building" in the Berlin Palace.

Count Rochus von Lynar entered electoral service in Brandenburg in 1578, and took up residence in Spandau, where he was to complete the construction of the fortress begun by Francesco Chiaramella. Although Lynar enjoyed his reputation as a fortifications engineer, he considered himself an architect, indeed an artist, and, like his fellow countryman Giovanni Maria Nosseni in Saxony, it was as such that he headed the building and art industry in Brandenburg until his death. Along with the fortifications at Spandau, he also completed, by 1595, another project begun by Chiaramella, namely the extension of the fortress of Peitz, involving the whole town in the job. Under Lynar's direction, extensions were added to the palace in Berlin that Elector John George wanted for the greater perfection of his official seat.

On the frontier towards Lower Lusitia, on the southeast corner of the Beeskow-Storkow plain, and originally not part of the March of Brandenburg, we encounter in Lieberose in the second half of the 16th century an architect called Thaddäus Paglion (or Paglioni), who was probably of Italian origin. Lieberose was a mesne town (one not directly subject to the Empire but to an estate) that belonged to a minor aristocratic family called von der Schulenburg, In 1557, Joachim von der Schulenburg commissioned Paglion to build a great house with three

wings around a south-facing courtyard. In 1657, this building was reduced to a ruin, then in 1688–1695, rebuilt as a splendid early Baroque house including some major plasterwork ceilings. In the mid-18th century, a fourth side was added on the south, thus totally disguising the Renaissance plan. Only on the north side of the east wing is a Renaissance element recognizable, in the shape of a dove tower, though this was once probably a stair tower. It is round below and octagonal on top, and adjoining it but walled up is the round-arched arcade that once ran round the courtyard as a gallery.

Thaddäus Paglion presumably came to Lieberose via Bohemia. In addition to this, he extended the choir in the civic church to provide a mausoleum for the von der Schulenburgs; until the church was destroyed in World War II, it contained the monumental memorial for Joachim von der Schulenburg, created by the Freiberg sculptors Michael and Johann Grünberger (see right and opposite). From 1607 to 1609, Paglion took up employment with the city council of Frankfurt an der Oder to rebuild the city hall (see page 49, center). What survives of his work there (the interior of the hall and parts of the gable) indicates that he was a capable Mannerist, who was able to give an older building fabric a contemporary appearance, without requiring extensive alterations.

Church Building After the Reformation

Whereas the building of great houses flourished in the March of Brandenburg at this time, as it did elsewhere, church building stagnated. Sometimes repair work is mentioned in the records, and alterations were sometimes made to interiors; but the development of a new type of building to match the order of service after the introduction of the Reformation was not yet in the offing. Admittedly, local lords in some mesne towns made a perceptible effort in the second half of the 16th century to construct memorials to their families by rebuilding or newly building civic churches, churches that were meant to be virtual mausoleums in which stately monuments would preserve the fame of their patrons for posterity. One such family were the Bredows, who in 1568 extended and vaulted the medieval church in Rheinsberg using the classicizing forms of the Renaissance.

Apart from the characteristic aristocratic buildings of the Renaissance period, the real achievement of Protestant church architecture in the March of Brandenburg in the 16th and 17th centuries lay not in the search for novel building designs but in refurbishing buildings that had survived from the Middle Ages. The first move was to replace the existing altars. In place of the medieval carved altars with hinged wings, Renaissance-style retables appeared with a fixed, Protestant iconography. However, eliminating the "Papist" visual images seems not to have been pursued very seriously. In the altar of the Marienkirche in Beeskow (destroyed in 1945), a place was found in the main area of the Renaissance superstructure for the painting and shrine of the late medieval carved altarpiece. Where large medieval altarpieces were in place, as in the Katharinenkirche in Brandenburg, the Marienkirche in Frankfurt, and the civic churches of Wittstock and Bernau (see page 58), respect for artistic quality was probably greater than the desire to illustrate the new doctrine. However, when new pictures where provided, they were intended to be instructive, the pious message being made explicit in the accompanying text. In the fine retable of 1606 in the civic church of Eberswalde, for example, a clear reference can be discerned in the scene to the articles of the Creed.

Above
Detail of the Schulenberg memorial (completed 1597)
Johann and Michael Grünberger
Lieberose, Landkirche

Opposite
Memorial for Joachim von der Schulenburg, died 1594 (completed 1597)
Johann and Michael Grünberger
Lieberose, Landkirche

This memorial was originally in the now destroyed civic church. Each tier of the ornate columnar superstructure contains an alabaster relief with high-quality figured sculptures. The main scene is that of the Crucifixion, and above it the Resurrection.

Nativity scene, memorial for Joachim von der Schulenberg (completed 1597)
Johann and Michael Grünberger
Landkirche, Lieberose

Remarkable Renaissance-style retables are also to be found in village churches in the Barnim region, in Reichenow, Ringenwalde, and Hohenwalde near Frankfurt an der Oder (see opposite).

Another important part of the process of making medieval churches serviceable for the Protestant rite was the installation of newly made pulpits. These were generally of stone, and could be completely plain or richly decorated.

The transformation of medieval hall churches into preaching halls resulted in the construction of galleries, though few of those from before the Thirty Years' War seem to have survived. The galleries of the clothmakers and cobblers in Bernau and Wusterhausen are probably the finest examples, being richly adorned with painted decoration and scenes of biblical episodes on the breast wall.

Even if no new major churches were built between the Reformation and the end of the 17th century, it is evident that the towns and cities of the March of Brandenburg were willing to spend money on fitting out their churches for the new order of service. Moreover, the communal spirit of the burghers was still expressed through their church and its furnishings.

The most magnificent example of this is the reconstruction of the Nikolaikirche in Luckau after the great fire of 1644. Donations for the splendid furnishings continued over two generations for the pulpit, the organ, and the altar, and citizens hung their memorials on the piers and built private pews in the galleries. The result is a grandiose Baroque interior installed in a Late Gothic hall church, as if the intention had been to satisfy the Late Gothic ambition for a spatially unified effect in the interior.

Right
St. Bernardino of Siena (15th century)
Relief from the Marienkirche, Berlin

The saint is wearing the standard Franciscan habit with cincture. In his right hand he holds the orb of the sun inscribed with the Sacred Monogram (IHS), an abbreviation for Jesus popularized by St. Bernardino and later used by the Jesuits.

Parish church of Hohenwalde, near Frankfurt an der Oder, altar

The three-tier superstructure of the altar retable in Renaissance-style architectural frames encloses both paintings and carved figures. The main picture is a Protestant doctrinal allegory relating to the sacrament of communion.

Prussia Becomes a Kingdom

1640–1740

1640–1688 Reign of Elector Frederick William I (1620–1688), the Great Elector. He forms a standing army, initially of 2,700 men, which is later increased to 23,000, and strips the estates of power while increasing the privileges of the aristocracy. By setting up the General War and Domain Directory he creates a single body responsible for the state's financial administration. The country areas are taxed through the Kontribution (a poll tax), the towns by excise (a consumption tax).

1640 Three-quarters of Brandenburg's total expenditure is paid for with income from the domain lands. Besides this, there is also the revenue from the electoral exchequer, which receives the older taxes levied in the March Brandenburg, such as the "old beer money" and tolls, and pays for all the administrative bodies based in Berlin-Cölln. The elector's personal expenditure is covered by the Privy Purse.

1641 Frederick William I agrees an armistice with the Swedes and begins to reduce the size of his army. These are the first signs of Brandenburg following an independent policy in its dealings with the parties to the war.

1642 The town of Neuruppin now has a mere 600 inhabitants living in 150 houses, whereas at the start of the war there were 3,500 in 623 houses.

1643 For the first time, the act of homage by the towns of the March to the new elector, Frederick William, takes place not in the old "electoral and capital city" of Brandenburg, but in the new, official capital and electoral seat, Berlin-Cölln.

1644 Frederick William I launches a new recruitment drive in order to build up a standing army.

1647 As part of the rebuilding of the country following the cessation of the Thirty Years' War, new settlements are founded for migrants from abroad. Among the first to be brought into the country by the elector and accorded extensive privileges are migrants from the Netherlands and Frisian peasants.

1648 Under the Treaty of Westphalia, which brings the Thirty Years' War to a close, Brandenburg acquires Eastern Pomerania, the bishoprics of Halberstadt, Cammin, and Minden, and the reversion of Magdeburg. This represents a gain for Brandenburg-Prussia of about 30,000 square kilometers (11,580 square miles), which is equivalent to more than a third of its previous territory.

1650 An area just north of Berlin, the district of Bötzow, is developed into an electoral residence. Frederick William I gives the new development to his first wife, Louise Henrietta, and it is named Oranienburg in honor of her family (Orange-Nassau).
Among many other new plants in the newly laid out pleasure garden attached to the palace in Berlin, potatoes are experimentally grown for the first time in the March of Brandenburg.

1652 A survey of the country ordered by Frederick William reveals the extent of the devastation and loss of life suffered by Brandenburg in the Thirty Years' War. Certain regions, which were among the worst affected in the whole of the Empire, had lost up to 90% of their population; with the average loss being approximately 50%. The process of making good the damage and rebuilding the country went on into the 18th century.

1654 All political matters concerning the state as a whole are brought before the plenary of the Privy Council, which thereby becomes a central administrative organ of the state of Brandenburg-Prussia.

1657 Frederick William I begins to develop Potsdam as his second residence after Berlin.

1658 Otto von Schwerin, a native of Wittstock, becomes president of the Privy Council, and thus prime minister of Brandenburg. He holds this post for more than 20 years.
At Peitz, the March of Brandenburg's first blast-furnace is built. This ironworks supplies iron mainly to Berlin, Magdeburg, and Silesia.

1660 Increasingly, those appointed to the official bodies of the March of Brandenburg – the Privy Council, the district and court exchequers, the elector's supreme court, and consistory courts – are not drawn from Brandenburg but from other regions: of the 74 privy councilors appointed under Frederick William I, only 20 are from Brandenburg, compared with 24 from the Duchy of Prussia and 20 from the German Empire and from abroad.
Under the Treaty of Oliva, Brandenburg managed to succeed in finally throwing off Polish suzerainty of the Duchy of Prussia.

1661 The first of a total of seven patents of immigration issued up to 1683 ushers in a new phase in Frederick William's population policy. The aim of this is to encourage immigration by foreign settlers, who at this time are chiefly Huguenots, natives of the Palatinate, and the Swiss, in order to revitalise the prostrated economy, and incidentally to strengthen Calvinism, of which the elector himself was an adherent supporter.

1662 Commissioned by Frederick William, Johann Gregor Memhardt begins work on the building of a palace at Potsdam.

The Great Elector and his wife Louise Henrietta, painting by Pieter Nason, 1666

Landing of the Brandenburg fleet in Africa, drawing by Rüter von Langervelt (c. 1690)

1665 At Oranienburg, the March of Brandenburg's first orphanage, endowed by Electress Louise Henrietta, is opened.

1669 After six years of construction work, the Frederick William Canal is finally completed. It provides a fast link, very beneficial to trade, between the rivers Oder and Spree.

1670 An edict issued by Frederick William I announces the admission to the country of 50 Jewish families who have been expelled from Vienna. Only families with a fortune of at least 10,000 thalers are admitted, so that their financial strength can contribute to the rebuilding of the economy.

1675 Brandenburg's troops defeat the Swedes at Fehrbellin. The victory becomes legendary throughout Europe and establishes the reputation of Frederick William I, who is now for the first time dubbed the "Great Elector" in a song printed at Strasbourg.

1678 In Berlin, two officials in the electoral service found Brandenburg's first factory.
At the Hakendamm glassworks near Potsdam, the alchemist/chemist Johann Kunckel invents ruby glass.

1683 On Africa's Gold Coast (Guinea), the colony of Gross-Friedrichsburg is founded. Frederick William I sets up a flourishing trade in slaves.

1685 Frederick William I admits 20,000 French Huguenot refugees.
An edict instructs clergymen not to marry any couples who have not first grafted six fruit trees and planted six oak trees. This regulation is one of Frederick William's measures to raise the general level of land cultivation.

1686 The first tobacco planters come to the Uckermark from northern France.

1688–1713 Reign of Elector Frederick III (1657–1713), who in 1701 will become King Frederick I "in Prussia."
Brandenburg-Prussia has a total area of 111,000 square kilometers (42,860 square miles), with 1.6 million inhabitants.

Roast ox and wine fountains at the public festivities celebrating the coronation of Frederick I at Königsberg on January 18, 1701; copper engraving by Johann Georg Wolffgang after Johann Friedrich Wentzel, 1701

1689 In the following years some 7,000 Calvinist immigrants from the Palatinate are settled in Brandenburg, and about 1,900 come from Switzerland.

1696 In Berlin, the Academy of Arts is founded.

1697 Crown Prince Frederick William receives from his father the estate of Wusterhausen to the south of Berlin, and remodels the Renaissance palace there.

1698 On the instructions of Elector Frederick III, Andreas Schlüter starts to alter and extend the palace at Berlin (until 1707).

1700 At the instigation of the philosopher and mathematician Gottfried Wilhelm Leibniz, Berlin becomes the third city in Europe to acquire an Academy of Sciences.

1701 The sovereign Duchy of Prussia becomes a kingdom. At Königsberg, the elector Frederick III, the first Hohenzollern to gain royal status, places the crown of Prussia on his own head and is known henceforth as Frederick I. This is preceded by a so-called "crown contract," by which the Emperor accords the title of king to the Elector of Brandenburg, but only in the part of Prussia that lies outside the Empire.
Formally, there is no change in the status of the electorate of Brandenburg within the Holy Roman Empire, but in fact from this time onwards Brandenburg is merely the central province of the Prussian state, which is now developing into a major European power.
To mark his new status, Frederick I commissions Jean de Bodt to build the Fortuna Gate (Fortunaportal) at the palace in Potsdam.

1702 Very soon after the coronation, the country finds itself in financial crisis as a result of King Frederick I's desire for outward show befitting his rank. The court alone uses up more than half of the four million thalers of annual revenue.

1710 In Berlin, the Charité Hospital is founded.

1711 Berlin has become Brandenburg's leading economic center.
Of the 6.2 million thalers of excise revenue in the Electoral March of Brandenburg between 1693 and 1712, 42% comes from Berlin.
The French artist Antoine Pesne becomes court painter to Frederick I.

1712 Christian Wolff publishes *Von den Kräften des menschlichen Verstandes* (Of the Powers of Human Reason).

1713–40 Reign of King Frederick William I (1688–1740), the "Soldier King." He enlarges the standing army to 81,000 men, and by placing the army at the center of the whole organization of the state, founds the Prussian military state.
The "Tall Fellows" (a guards unit formed of giants, which also devours gigantic sums of money) are stationed at Potsdam. The new king's bodyguard is his consuming passion. For the tallest of the "Tall Fellows," the Irishman Kirkland, who measures 2.14 meters (about 7 feet), he is said to have paid 9,000 thalers.
In Berlin, the Lagerhaus (Warehouse), the most important German cloth factory of the 18th century, is founded.

1713 King Frederick William I prohibits witch trials in Prussia. Torture and the death penalty may be used only by permission of the king.

1716 A newly formed dike commission for the Oder, under the direction of Lieutenant-General Friedrich von Derfflinger, is charged with the speedy overhaul and extension of the dikes along the Oder.

1717 The Brandenburg colonial bases in Africa (Guinea) are sold.
Tsar Peter I visits Berlin.
Compulsory schooling for all children is introduced in Prussia.
Weavers, mostly from Saxony, are settled at Luckenwalde.
A new regulation confirms a previous order that no church sermon shall last for more than an hour.

1717 Antoine Pesne paints *Self-portrait with Family*.

1718 Frederick William I orders the settlement and agricultural development of areas of Lithuania.

1720 End of the Second Northern War. In the Treaties of Stockholm, Sweden cedes to Prussia Stettin, Western

King Frederick I, by Friedrich Wilhelm Weidemann (c. 1705)

Queen Sophia Charlotte, by Friedrich Wilhelm Weidemann (c. 1705)

Wooden tobacco box in the form of a grenadier, early 18th century

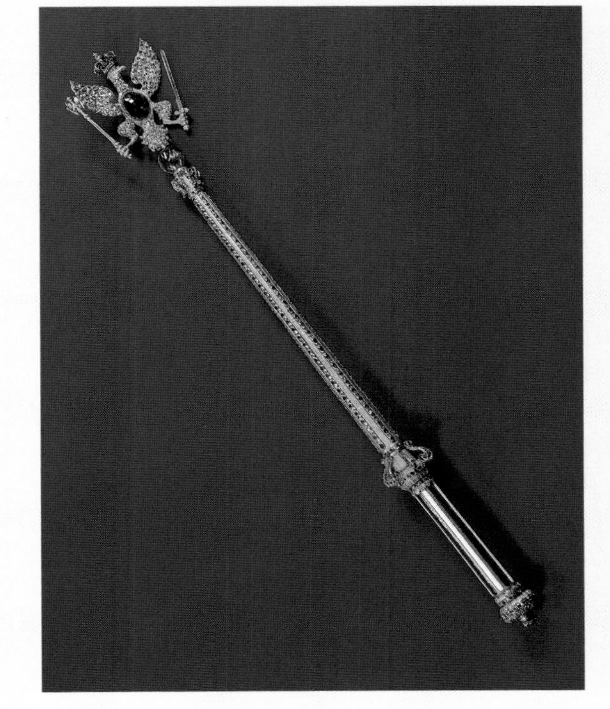

Scepter of King Frederick I, 1701

Orb of King Frederick I, 1701

Pomerania to the area as far as Usedom, and Wollin as far as the Peene.

1723 King Frederick William I founds the General Directory, thus creating the first central administrative body of the Prussian state.
Johann Sebastian Bach writes the *Brandenburg Concertos,* which he composed for orchestra.

1724 Immigrants from Franconia and Swabia are settled in the Uckermark.

1730 To escape his father's despotism, Crown Prince Frederick (II) makes an unsuccessful attempt to flee. He is sentenced to imprisonment in the fortress at Küstrin and is forced to watch the execution of his friend Hans Hermann von Katte, who was party to the plan.
At Potsdam, the Garnisonkirche (Garrison Church) is built to plans by Philipp Gerlach. Its bell tower, 88.40 meters (290 feet) high, rises high above everything around it.

1731 About 20,000 Protestants expelled from Salzburg are settled in East Prussia, which has been depopulated by the plague. Soon afterwards, Bohemian religious refugees are also admitted.

1733 In Prussia, a new recruiting system, the "canton" system, is introduced: each regiment is assigned a district ("canton") from which it can raise conscripts.

1734 Berlin has expanded into a city that now has about 80,000 inhabitants.

1735 Crown Prince Frederick (II) and his wife Elizabeth Christine (of Brunswick-Bevern) move to Rheinsberg, bought for the crown prince by King Frederick William I.
During his years at Rheinsberg (up to 1740), Frederick chiefly pursues his scientific and historical interests. The beginning of his correspondence with Voltaire.

1738 Around about 1738, Crown Prince Frederick (II) writes a symphony in G major for string orchestra and basso continuo.

1739 Having studied *The Prince* (1532) by the Renaissance political theorist writer Niccolò Machiavelli, Crown Prince Frederick (II) responds to it in his *Anti-Machiavelli,* in which he sets out his own ideas about the aims and duties of a ruler.

Queen Sophia Dorothea, by Georg Wenzeslaus von Knobelsdorff (c. 1737)

King Frederick William I, by Georg Wenzeslaus von Knobelsdorff (c. 1737)

ARCHITECTURE, URBAN PLANNING, AND GARDEN DESIGN

Irmtraud Thierse

Rebuilding and Reshaping: the Great Elector Frederick William 1640–1688

The reconstruction of princely seats and pleasure palaces, and the building of new ones; the expansion and embellishment of towns; the refashioning of nature through strictly formal garden design which, spread over the whole country, was intended to demonstrate culture and civilization – these were the architectural hallmarks of the century following the Thirty Years' War in Brandenburg. The three rulers who held power during this time created the basis for a modern state. They brought into the country, which had been depopulated by war, people suffering religious persecution elsewhere who did much to advance crafts, trades, and commerce. Various measures, such as the establishment of a standing army by Elector Frederick William, the proclamation of Elector Frederick III as king of Prussia (Frederick I), the stabilization of the court finances, and Frederick William I's creation of an efficient administrative system all contributed to turning the widely separated parts of the country into a single, functioning state. Unlike the states surrounding it, Brandenburg-Prussia was held together not by adherence to a single religious denomination, but by an officially imposed tolerance that made it possible for Lutherans, Calvinists, and Jews to live side by side. The original Slav population, too, the "Wends," were now accorded rights of citizenship and could thus become members of the craft guilds.

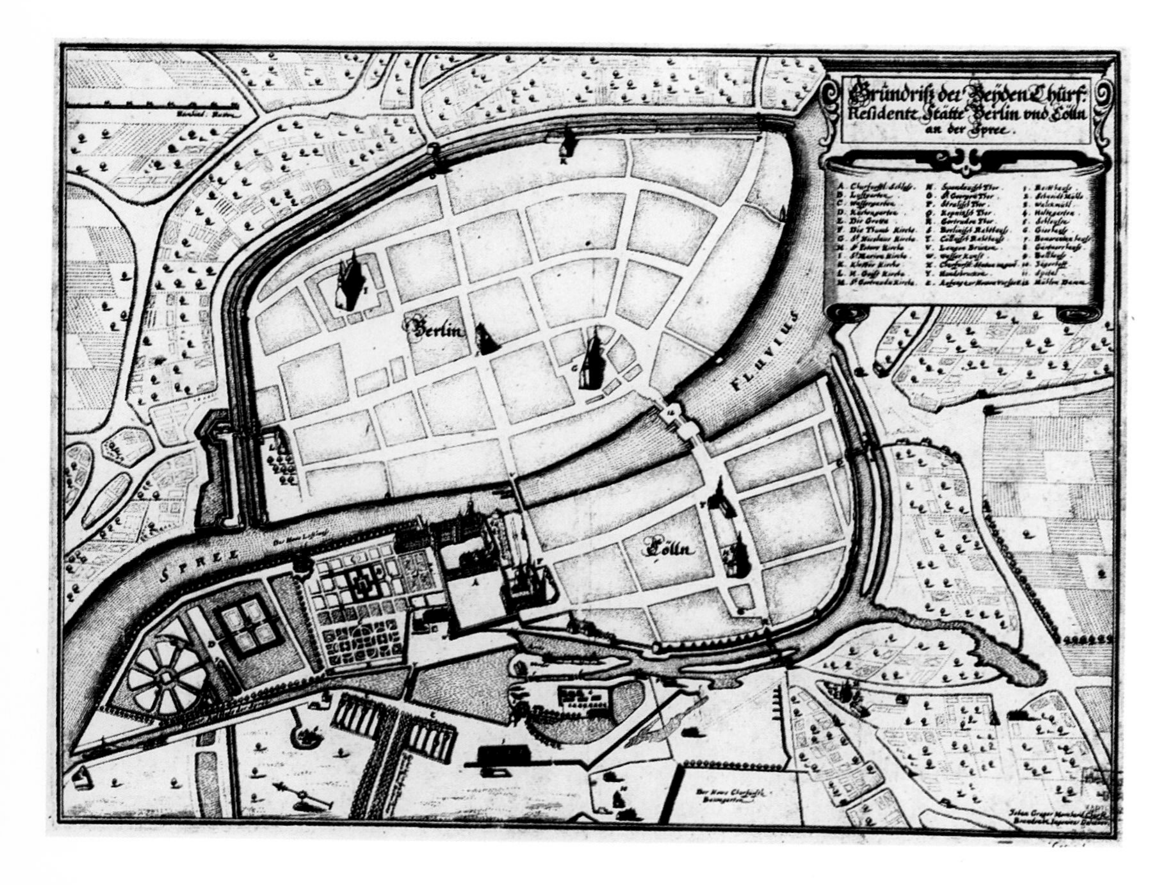

Plan of Berlin and Cölln, detail with the Palace and Lustgarten
Etching by Johann Gregor Memhardt (c. 1650)

Memhardt's plan clearly shows the division of the pleasure garden into three parts: the parterre with the monument to the elector reaching as far as the summer-house; the medicinal herb garden with its pergolas and the pavilion at the center; and the kitchen garden in the form of segments of a circle, which was probably never realized because of the building of fortifications from 1658 onwards.

The situation in Brandenburg after 1640

The Thirty Years' War, which had laid waste large areas of Brandenburg, was not yet over when Frederick William took power in 1640. In other European countries, especially Italy and France, Baroque architecture had been able to develop in a variety of ways, while in Brandenburg both battles and the constant passage of pillaging troops had caused widespread destruction, and generally bled the country dry. It was for this reason that Frederick William attempted to bring the Thirty Years' War to an earlier conclusion, as far as the March of Brandenburg was concerned, by making peace with Sweden.

Of the two main applications of Baroque architecture – the building of churches and the building of palaces – it was the latter that was chiefly promoted by the Elector's court. The Great Elector's grandfather, John Sigismund, had converted to Calvinism in 1613, partly for dynastic reasons. And since in that age, which so delighted in ornament, the followers of Calvin rejected any kind of ornamentation in their churches, it was the building of palaces that played the dominant role in architectural development. In turn, the building of new palaces and the redesigning of existing ones created a network of cultural centers surrounded by artistically designed gardens, and linked to each other by avenues and waterways. The festivities that were organized in the palaces had an impact, not only throughout the realm, but also beyond its borders, proclaiming the aspirations and the status of the rulers of Brandenburg among the princely houses of Europe.

Links with Holland

Frederick William did not take as his model the architecture of the French court, whose brilliance and splendor began, in the course of his reign, to far outshine that of the other European courts, but the more severe, classical forms that were based primarily on the engravings of Andrea Palladio. He had first seen these engravings in Holland during his educational stay at the court of Frederick Henry, stadholder of the Netherlands, in 1634–1638. He also admired the engineering achievements of the Dutch, whose constant battle against the sea had led to land reclamation and also to distinctive styles of garden design. He recognized the similarity of the geographical conditions (flat land, marshes) and later brought Dutch or Dutch-trained experts into his own country. The fact of belonging to the same religious denomination, Calvinism, also contributed to the forming of an especially close relationship, and in 1646 he married the daughter of the stadholder of the Netherlands, Louise Henrietta of Orange.

In 1647 he appointed John Maurice of Nassau-Siegen stadholder of Cleves, Mark, and Ravensberg. John Maurice completely redesigned his seat at Cleves, created a relationship between the palace and the garden buildings, and laid out avenues and vistas. He advised the Elector on his projects, and it was on his recommendation that the avenue was laid out in Berlin in 1647 that now forms the thoroughfare Unter den Linden. So high was Frederick William's regard for his stadholder of Cleves that in 1652 he proposed him for the office of Commander of the Knights of St. John in the Order's Brandenburg province.

John Maurice himself had his palace at Sonnenburg (Neumark) near Küstrin (now Kostrzyn in Poland) built in the years 1661–1668 by Cornelius Ryckwaert, using Dutch craftsmen. It is probable, however, that the plans originated with the Elector and his architect Pieter Post. The result was a severe, classical building modeled on the Huis ten Bosch (1645–1652) near to The Hague that Post had built for Amalia of Solms, the widow of Henry of Orange and mother of the Electress Louise Henrietta. This unique monument to Dutch-style classicism in Brandenburg was destroyed by fire in 1975.

The Berlin Lustgarten

The Elector spent the first years of his reign mainly in Königsberg and Cleves; it was only in the autumn of 1652 that Frederick William moved his court permanently from Cleves to Berlin. However, he started having the Lustgarten (Pleasure Garden) in Berlin redesigned from as early as 1645 (see opposite). The garden's designer, Michael Hanff, had already laid out the garden at Königsberg. Probably, however, Johann Gregor Memhardt was on hand to advise Hanff on the Berlin garden from the beginning. Memhardt, the Elector's builder of fortifications, was ordered to leave Pillau for Berlin in 1650, the very year in which the plan for the garden as a whole seems to have been drawn up. Memhardt's first building in Berlin was the "New Summerhouse" also called the "Grotto," on the Spree. Grottoes had been a part of garden design since classical times (they are mentioned by the Roman writer Pliny), and like the basement of the summerhouse at Berlin, they were usually decorated with shells and branches of coral. Pipes produced melodious sounds, and amusement was provided by fountains that would start to play suddenly, splashing the visitor. In the upper story was a dining room where, up to 1708, the court often dined in summer. The roof, which did not acquire its cupola until later, offered a fine view of the garden, the palace, and the city. This building, designed to enhance the prestige of its owner, also followed contemporary Dutch models, for instance Heemstede Palace in the province of Utrecht. As early as 1685, Michael Matthias Smids, using plans by Johann Arnold Nering, began to build an orangery at the tip of the garden island on the medial axis of the garden opposite the palace. The building nestled inside the bastion begun by Memhardt in 1658, which, completely enclosing Berlin, was intended to protect it from attack. In accordance with the principles of the garden design theoreticians of the day, the orangery building formed a semicircle open to the south.

As the garden was squeezed in between the bastion and the palace, it offered few opportunities for changes that reached out into the surrounding

Berlin Palace (destroyed), view from Burgstrasse (southeast)
Historical photograph (c. 1870)

In the foreground is the former Lange Brücke (Long Bridge) – later known as Kurfürstenbrücke (Elector's Bridge) and now known as Rathausbrücke – with Schlüter's equestrian statue of the Great Elector. On the right, along the river Spree, are the older parts of the palace, the Chapel Tower and the Duchess's House; on the left are Entrances I and II.

countryside, like those undertaken after the death of the Great Elector by his son in the other gardens at Oranienburg, Schönhausen, Friedrichsfelde, and above all Charlottenburg. The Berlin garden enjoyed one more short-lived period of improvement, when the royal palace was redesigned by Schlüter in the years leading up to 1706, though this meant that the upper part of the garden, with its statue of the Great Elector, had to make way for the garden wing. The palace acquired a garden room as well as a garden gateway, and palace and garden could now be felt to be spaces that actually related to one another. The Renaissance principle that favored the juxtaposition of different parts of a work of art (such as palace and garden) on equal terms had finally given way to the Baroque system of a hierarchy of component parts. The thrifty Frederick William I changed the pleasure garden, which was expensive to maintain, into a *place d'armes*, a parade and drill ground.

The Berlin Palace under the Great Elector

When, in 1643, the Great Elector traveled to Berlin to receive the homage of the estates, the palace in Berlin, which had suffered badly during the Thirty Years' War, was greatly in need of repair; to begin with, he merely had it made habitable (see page 77). Only when the Elector visited Berlin with his wife in 1650 did he order an extension to be built in the chapel courtyard of the palace; it was to adjoin the Duchess's House alongside the Spree, next to the "Green Hat," a tower forming part of the Cölln town wall and incorporated into the palace (see right). The small oratory by Memhardt on the upper story was the first in the palace to be decorated in the Baroque style (see opposite). Although this room continued for a long time to be known as the "old chapel" – the Electress Louise Henrietta is described as having been a strictly pious Calvinist – its function is not wholly clear. The ornamentation shows no religious symbolism, and the original paintings from the oval stucco frames have been lost. At some time before 1893 the ceiling was lowered, so that we may assume that the room was lit from above. If so, this would have given the electress a very fashionable room with a lantern and dome *à l'italienne*, of which there were many examples in Holland, such as the one created in the Mauritshuis at The Hague, and the Orange Hall in the Huis ten Bosch.

Only after the conclusion of an external peace (the alliance with France, Saint-Germain 1679) and the internal consolidation of power against the influence of the estates (among other things by the establishment of a standing army and the creation of a centralist administration), did Frederick William set about altering the palace of his ancestors to make it suitably impressive. But he deliberately opted for historical continuity and, like them, contented himself with extending the existing building. He had his own residential apartments in the Spree wing enlarged and a corridor created to connect them with the apartments of the electress: the so-called Brunswick Gallery (see page 81). These extensions, carried out between 1679 and 1681, provided a sequence of rooms that enabled him to present himself more advantageously to the nobility. Alongside the old and the new private apartments there was now a state apartment consisting of three magnificent rooms, creating the first example of an *appartement double*, a double series of rooms side by side. The deliberate separation of private from ceremonial apartments distinguishes the Elector's residence from the arrangement of rooms created at almost the same time by Louis XIV at Versailles, in which the "public nature" of the monarch – Louis placing himself on show before the nobles he had divested of power – was the determining principle of the architecture. The Elector lived close to his family and his favorite occupations (books, collections, and alchemy): his life was not led, as yet, in the midst of courtiers, advisers, and administration, as was the case at the French court, which was soon to become the model for all absolutist courts.

Consolidating the absolute power of the ruler demanded on the one hand a reduction of the power of the estates, and on the other the integration of the nobility into the life of the court. The banqueting hall in the tilt-yard wing on the south side of the palace (see below) was over one hundred years old

Opposite
Berlin Palace (destroyed during World War II), Spree wing of the Duchess's House, so-called Chapel of Louise Henrietta of Orange on the second upper floor
Historical photograph (c. 1927)

This internal room without windows, but receiving light from a lantern above it, was one of the first Baroque rooms in northern Germany. It was strictly articulated by an interplay of the vertical elements, like pilasters and bands of stucco work, and the horizontal cornices. This geometrical order was made somewhat less severe by the addition of heavy stucco ornamentation in the form of leaves and hanging fruits.

The Electoral Palace at Berlin (1650)
Anonymous
Oil on canvas, Berlin, Stiftung Stadtmuseum, Märkisches Museum

This view of the palace from the southeast shows the Spree side with the "Green Hat" and the Palace Square side with the vendors' arcade by Johann Arnold Nering. In the background by the Spree, the cupola and two turrets of the summerhouse can be seen.

Berlin Palace (destroyed), Alabaster Hall
Copper engraving by C. F. Blesendorf and J. C. Schott, in Lorenz Beger, Thesaurus Brandenburgicus III *(1701)*

The engraving shows how this great hall, which owes its name to its marble statues, was used. It shows the Order of the Garter being presented to the Elector Frederick III. The room was articulated by pilasters, each pair framing a niche in which there was a statue of an elector or an emperor.

and was not higher than the rooms adjoining it. However, during the Baroque period it was not only the size of a room but also its height that was a measure of its dignity. The relationship between height, length, and width were to be determined by considerations of beauty, suitability, and function. Frederick William therefore felt it necessary to have alterations made in order to create a room befitting his status for the necessary festive occasions, acts of state, and receptions. The building that separated the inner and outer courtyards of the palace was lengthened and the extension containing the new room was built on top of an existing side building (see above). One could call the Alabaster Hall a hall for the estates, since it was the place of assembly for the estates of the Electoral March and also the place for acts of homage by all the estates. The subjection of the estates to the authority of the Elector was a matter of prime political importance for Frederick William in establishing absolute rule in Brandenburg. The position of the Alabaster Hall made it a "place where the inner and the outer courtyards met," at some distance from the state rooms and from the living apartments of the Elector; his rooms were also situated a story higher than the hall, an expression in architectural form of his superior rank. But the hall also occupied a position in between the apartments of guests and those of court officials, and was thus a place representing the disempowerment of the estates. In addition, it served as a festive room for all occasions of state and court celebrations.

The character of the Alabaster Hall was determined by its statues of electors which, together with figures representing the emperors, showed the Elector's ancestry stretching back to the Roman Empire, and thus asserted the legitimacy of his power. The hall with its 12 statues of electors, representing the political history of Brandenburg since Frederick I (1415–1440), could be described as "Brandenburg's hall of fame"; through the presence of the statues of emperors it embodied a still more ambitious dynastic claim.

A building project to extend the palace, which was begun shortly before the death of the Great Elector, was to be executed in the latest, this time French, architectural style, and to be almost 140 meters (about 458 feet) long. The lower story was to contain the picture gallery, while the apartments of state were to be above. The roof story, with horizontal oblong mezzanine windows, was to accommodate the library, which gave its name to the whole building.

Baroque town planning and town expansion

The Baroque architectural "art of persuasion" is characterized by symmetry, axiality, and the subordination of parts to the whole. Visitors to a building or a town were to be firmly convinced of the power and importance of the owner and ruler. This is why in gardens the wildness of nature was tamed, trees were pruned and cut into ornamental shapes, routes led to particular features in the garden or in the town (*points de vue*) or radiated from a center into the countryside in order to demonstrate the latter's subordinate status. The best-known example of this is provided by the three roads that went out from the palace of Versailles, the middle one of which led to Paris.

During the reign of the Great Elector, existing roads were made more prominent and new avenues, like the one which became Unter den Linden, were laid out; these provided the structure for Baroque town layouts and also determined the town's future development (for instance westward development in the case of the avenue of linden trees later called Unter den Linden). The Berlin palace, as a monument to absolutism (one of the earliest in Germany, according to Peschken), was to be the focal point (the *point de vue*) of the electoral seat of Berlin and Cölln, with the major streets oriented in relation to it. The palace became the destination of the ceremonial processions that had been traditional since the late 15th century; in the late Middle Ages they had culminated in knightly contests in the tilt-yard (on the southern side of the palace, later known as Schlossplatz, Palace Square). It was only under the Great Elector that these triumphal processions acquired a Baroque character through the erection of temporary triumphal arches or gates of honor made of wood or papier mâché. He no longer chose the direct route from the nearest city gate, but sometimes made detours in order to enter through Königsstrasse (King's Street), which, as a result, gained the enhanced status of being Berlin's main axis.

The ceremonial entry of the new king Frederick I in May 1701 also led through Königsstrasse and then across the Lange Brücke (Long Bridge), which Nering had built in 1692 as part of the Via Triumphalis, and to provide the transition from the bourgeois city to the palace precinct – a stone bridge for the first time, since a place on it was reserved for a monument to the Great Elector. Until 1747,

Königsstrasse was terminated at its western end by the cathedral, unless one had turned aside earlier to go through the gates to the palace. Since 1536, the former Dominican church had been the cathedral, the court church, and also the burial place of the Brandenburg electors and kings, and it was therefore a very suitable feature to catch the eye on the triumphal route.

The other street that led directly to the palace was the Breite Strasse (Broad Street). Unlike Königsstrasse, it did not begin at the edge of the town, but it did run straight towards the gateway Memhardt had built in 1659 next to Joachim II's palace building. This gave access to the outer palace courtyard and there was a way through to the inner one, where a celebrated spiral stair-tower (see page 62) led to the Elector's apartments. These, on the northern side of the palace, seemed as though raised up on a pedestal (the upper terrace) above the pleasure garden. The geometrically arranged garden was laid out wholly in relation to the palace. The main path, in particular, led to the point on the palace building where Schlüter's entrance, the later Portal V, was added. From here there was also a visual link with the linden tree avenue,

Berlin Palace (destroyed), Brunswick Gallery on the second upper floor, view looking southwards
Historical photograph

The Great Elector had this gallery built to form a link between his new private apartments and those of his wife. Originally there were windows on the west side of the gallery too.

which was laid out at almost exactly the same time as the garden (see below). From his residence at Cleves, inspired by the garden landscape commissioned there by John Maurice of Nassau, the elector issued a written order on April 16, 1647, for the "planting of walnut and lime trees to create an avenue from the Hunde Bridge to the Game Park" (where today Schadowstrasse meets Unter den Linden). From 1695, this carriage-way, planted with six rows of trees, was the connecting route used by the court between the city palace and the summer residence of the Electress Sophia Charlotte at Lietzenburg, which from 1705 onwards, was systematically developed into the town of Charlottenburg. When the court was at Charlottenburg, King Frederick I ordered the road to Berlin to be decked with lanterns, which formed lines like "threads of fire" across the nocturnal landscape.

At the beginning of the linden tree avenue between the Hunde Bridge and the Neustadt Gate, the building of the Arsenal created the Platz am Zeughaus (Arsenal Square), bounded on the opposite side by the crown prince's palace (built by Johann Arnold Nering in 1687, modernized and extended in 1732–1733, and reconstructed in 1969 on the basis of old engravings after being destroyed during World War II). To the west, similarly, the avenue ended, up to 1734, at a square. Because this was designed to form a true square it was called simply the Karré (Square); it was only from 1814, after the victory over Napoleon, that it was named Pariser Platz (Paris Square). In 1738, the first Brandenburg Gate was built there, on the western edge of this royal capital city; it consisted of Baroque gateposts, gateways at the sides, and two sentry-boxes. In the east, the development of the avenue into a road of Baroque splendor began at the Arsenal. In the west, next to the Brandenburg Gate, the Saldern Palace, and Villa Kamecke (see page 128) towered up above other buildings that were uniformly two stories high. Thus, at each end of the avenue of linden trees, there was a place where one could linger a while before strolling along the avanue.

Along this westward axis new districts came into being, still within the lifetime of the Great Elector, which were treated as separate towns. Already in 1641 Frederick William had issued new building regulations in order to improve the city's infrastructure. Streets and squares had to be surfaced, and in the evenings the city was to be illuminated by lanterns. But it was only with the economic upturn around 1670, a result of the introduction of an excise tax, which affected all equally, including the clergy, the aristocracy, and the estates, that building activity showed a marked increase. In due course not only was the war damage made good, but also to the west of Cölln the district of Friedrichswerder grew up (see opposite). In 1670, the elector gave this district, inhabited mainly by court officials and other employees of the court, its charter as a town.

As the third town forming part of the electoral seat, Friedrichswerder possessed an administration with a town hall (built in 1673 on the site of the later Mint) and had its own civic rights and municipal privileges; for instance, it could hold fairs and have guilds of its own. The fortifications architect Johann Gregor Memhardt became the first mayor of this

The Linden in Berlin
Colored drawing by Johann Stridbeck the Younger (1691), 16.8 x 25.4 cm; Berlin, Staatsbibliothek zu Berlin – Preussischer Kulturbesitz

This traveler's sketch, the earliest view of the Linden (an avenue lined with linden trees), looks from the Neustadt Gate (now between the Opera and University) towards the west, where the drawbridge belonging to the fortifications looms up (now close to Schadowstrasse).

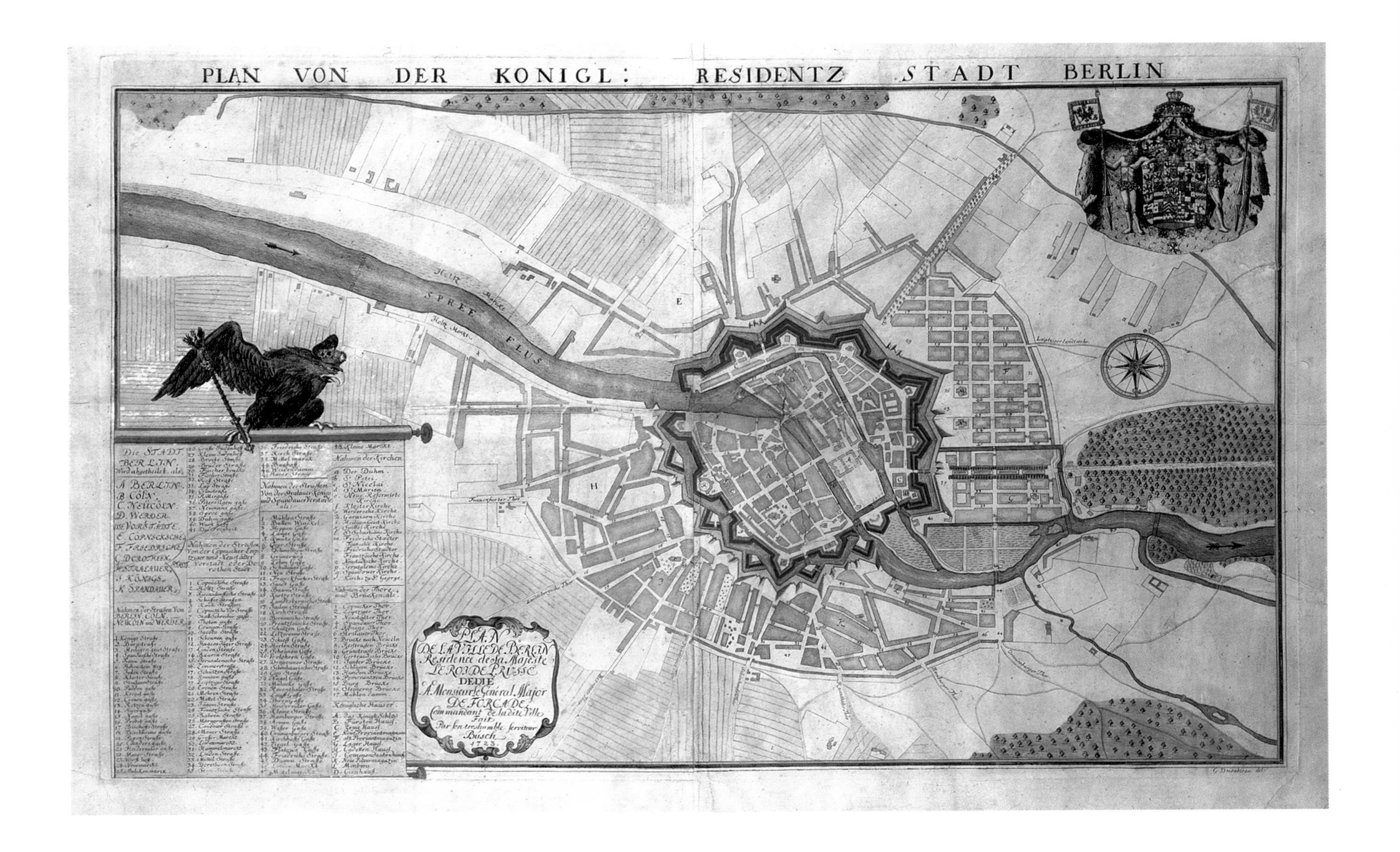

new town. Outside the fortification walls, to the north of the avenue of linden trees and on the land that the elector had presented as a gift to his second wife, Dorothea, there grew from 1674 onwards the fourth component of the electoral capital, named Dorotheenstadt after its founder. This too obtained its own administration and its own rights of jurisdiction. Within its network of straight streets at right angles to each other stood Berlin's first shared church, used equally by Lutherans and Calvinists. To the south, also parallel to the road Unter den Linden, the fifth in the cluster of towns began to grow. Immediately upon his accession in 1688, Elector Frederick III (King Frederick I from 1701 onwards) had founded the new town that was named after him, Friedrichstadt. After the 1685 Edict of Potsdam, Huguenots were beginning to come in larger numbers. In overall charge of the development of the new town were Johann Arnold Nering and Michael Matthias Smids. A regular grid of streets was created around what is today the Gendarmenmarkt. In 1709, Frederick issued a cabinet order in which the hitherto independent towns of Berlin, Cölln, Friedrichswerder, Dorotheenstadt, and Friedrichstadt were joined together into a single political unit that was to be called Berlin. This gave the absolutist Prussian state, which had gained in prestige as a result of Frederick's self-proclamation as king, a larger and more weighty center, a capital from which the administration of the state could operate.

The expansion of Potsdam

"The whole island must become a paradise," wrote Prince John Maurice on August 20, 1664, to Frederick William. He knew the area around Potsdam, having stayed there several times between 1652 and 1658. From 1646 onwards the elector had been trying to gain possession of the palace and the district of Potsdam, and after several failed attempts he had finally succeeded in 1660. The elector's persistent efforts to acquire the district of Potsdam were inspired not only by his passion for hunting and the possibility of reaching many destinations by water, but above all by his plan to turn the island of Potsdam into an artistically designed garden. Like Cleves, it was planned that Potsdam would become the focal point for a comprehensive reshaping of the surrounding landscape.

Plan of the electoral seat of Berlin in 1723 by G Dusableau, viewed from the south
Colored engraving on paper by Georg Paul Busch, 45.1 x 74.9 cm; Berlin, Stiftung Stadtmuseum Berlin

The ring of fortifications begun in 1658 encloses the towns of Berlin, Cölln, and Friedrichswerder, which was founded in 1662. Both Dorotheenstadt, which was built from 1674 onwards north of the Linden, and Friedrichstadt (1688 onwards) to the south of it, have a grid of streets at right angles to each other.

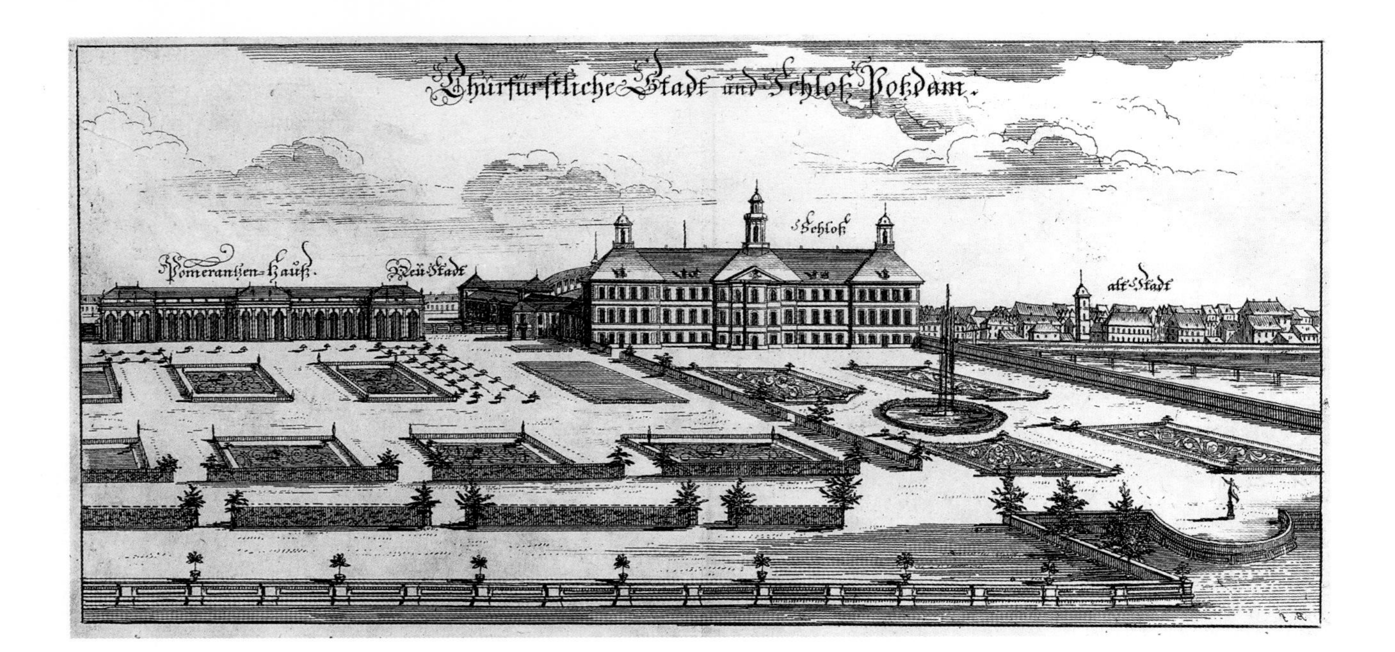

Potsdam Palace, garden front
Etching by Samuel Blesendorf (c. 1695), 17.7 x 26.1 cm

This etching shows the palace complex as it was in the lifetime of the Great Elector. The Pomeranzenhaus (Orangery, left) was built in 1685 to plans by Johann Arnold Nering.

The Catherine Palace on the Havel (named after Electress Catherine of Brandenburg, 1559–1602) was by 1660 in a state of disrepair, and Memhardt had first of all to renovate it to a more or less acceptable condition (see above). From the correspondence between the elector and his stadholder from the middle of 1664 onwards, we can gain a good impression of the former appearance of the palace. In its general layout, with a main building articulated by pavilions and low side wings, it showed similarities to the Dutch palace of Honselaarsdijk built by Jacob van Campen for Frederick Henry of Orange. It was also similar to Campen's Amsterdam City Hall, from the rear façade of which the form of the projecting sections and the arrangement of the rooms was copied here. In the same way as the city hall, the palace at Potsdam had a belvedere tower, with an encircling balustrade, which admitted light to the room below. The design of this building is often attributed to Philipp de Chièze, but he, as the Elector's quartermaster-general (from 1664), was probably the organizer of the building operations. Engravings deriving from Memhardt make it seem more likely that he was in fact the architect responsible for the design.

The façade was rendered and painted white; on the ground floor and at the corners of the projecting sections it was rusticated, which gave it a livelier appearance. This rustication was complemented by the red-tiled roofs. The courtyard side of the three-story *corps de logis* had a tri-axial central projection that jutted far forward because it contained the double wooden staircase that went up to the second upper story (see opposite). A similar staircase still exists today in Oranienbaum Palace near Dessau, which was built after 1683 for Princess Henrietta Catharine of Nassau-Orange (a sister of the Brandenburg Electress Louise Henrietta, who in 1659 married John George II of Anhalt-Dessau). From the staircase one passed through a narrow gallery to the Elector's apartments in the west and the rooms of the electress in the east, which were on the first floor. They were magnificent, with gilded and silvered leather wall-hangings on a red, blue or white background, woven tapestries, and costly furniture. On the garden side, in front of the electress's suite, was the great hall, which was 22 meters (72 feet) long, 13 meters (42 feet) wide, and 20 meters (65.5 feet) high, and which reflected the latest ideas on palace design. This hall, which, like Amalia of Solms's Orange Hall in the Huis ten Bosch, received additional light from the belvedere above, was meant to glorify the Great Elector, just as the Orange Hall was intended to enhance the prestige of Frederick Henry. Essentially, the electoral palace at Potsdam conformed to the type of the *maison de plaisance* created in France (Vaux-le-Vicomte, 1656–1660), which could be used both as a pleasure palace and as a main residence. But this was not the only way in which the palace at Potsdam fulfilled the most modern architectural requirements. It possessed the first enfilade in Brandenburg, and thus one of the first in Germany: in other words, in the main story the doors were arranged in a sequence, so that when they were all open they created a long vista through all the rooms. The palace had not enough rooms, given that from 1671 onwards the elector stayed at Potsdam more and more often, in winter as well as in summer, with his whole court. With this in mind, he decided in 1679 to extend the side wings to twice their existing length and to add a further story. A semicircular gallery with a portal section facing towards the town linked the two wings. The old transverse building remained, so that two courtyards were formed. This enlargement gave the palace its final dimensions (the later changes made by

Frederick II did little to alter the ground plan), and the palace held its place as a symbol of absolutist power set right among the ordinary citizens in the town center, on the Alter Markt (Old Market).

Hanff, the garden designer, was already living at Potsdam in 1658, but in laying out the pleasure garden there he was probably following plans by Memhardt, as in Berlin. The proximity of the bank of the river Havel and the wooden Lange Brücke built in 1662 made it impossible for the garden to be laid out in a symmetrical fashion. It therefore stretched out to the west, in front and to one side of the palace. There were only flat *parterres de broderie*, in order to give an unimpeded view from the palace to the countryside and vice versa. In this respect, the Potsdam palace garden was more up-to-date than the pleasure garden in Berlin, with its pergolas and rows of trees. The Potsdam garden of 1664–1669 was laid out at almost the same time as the park created by the celebrated garden designer, André Le Nôtre, for Louis XIV at Versailles, which became the model for the whole of Europe. In 1685, Nering was given the commission of designing an orangery for Potsdam, too. It was to be built by Michael Matthias Smids against the northern perimeter wall of the pleasure garden to the west of the palace. In summer, the orangery was used for festivities, theatrical performances, and concerts.

The flat and open pleasure garden gave an uninterrupted view of the Havel and the Brauhausberg behind it. This was part of the Grosser Tiergarten (Great Game Park) the elector had ordered to be created on the model of the game parks at Cleves, and about which he had written proudly to John Maurice as far back as 1665. The Kleine Tiergarten (Small Game Park) was on the Babelsberg and belonged to the Glienicke hunting lodge. Because all the countryside around Potsdam was a hunting area, it was criss-crossed by rides and paths. A number of these were made into broader avenues and were thus used for the purpose of opening up the countryside, as the elector had previously seen it done in Cleves.

From the western corner pavilion of the palace, a visual axis led (from the middle window, not from

Garden front of the Potsdam Palace
Etching, 29.5 x 45.3 cm; in Jean Baptiste Broebes, Vues de Palais et Maisons le roi de Prusse, *Augsburg 1733, fol. 2*

This etching shows the palace as it was in 1698. The central tower has been removed for reasons it is no longer possible to determine. An innovation is that two ramps in front of the central section lead from the garden directly up to the level of the great hall.

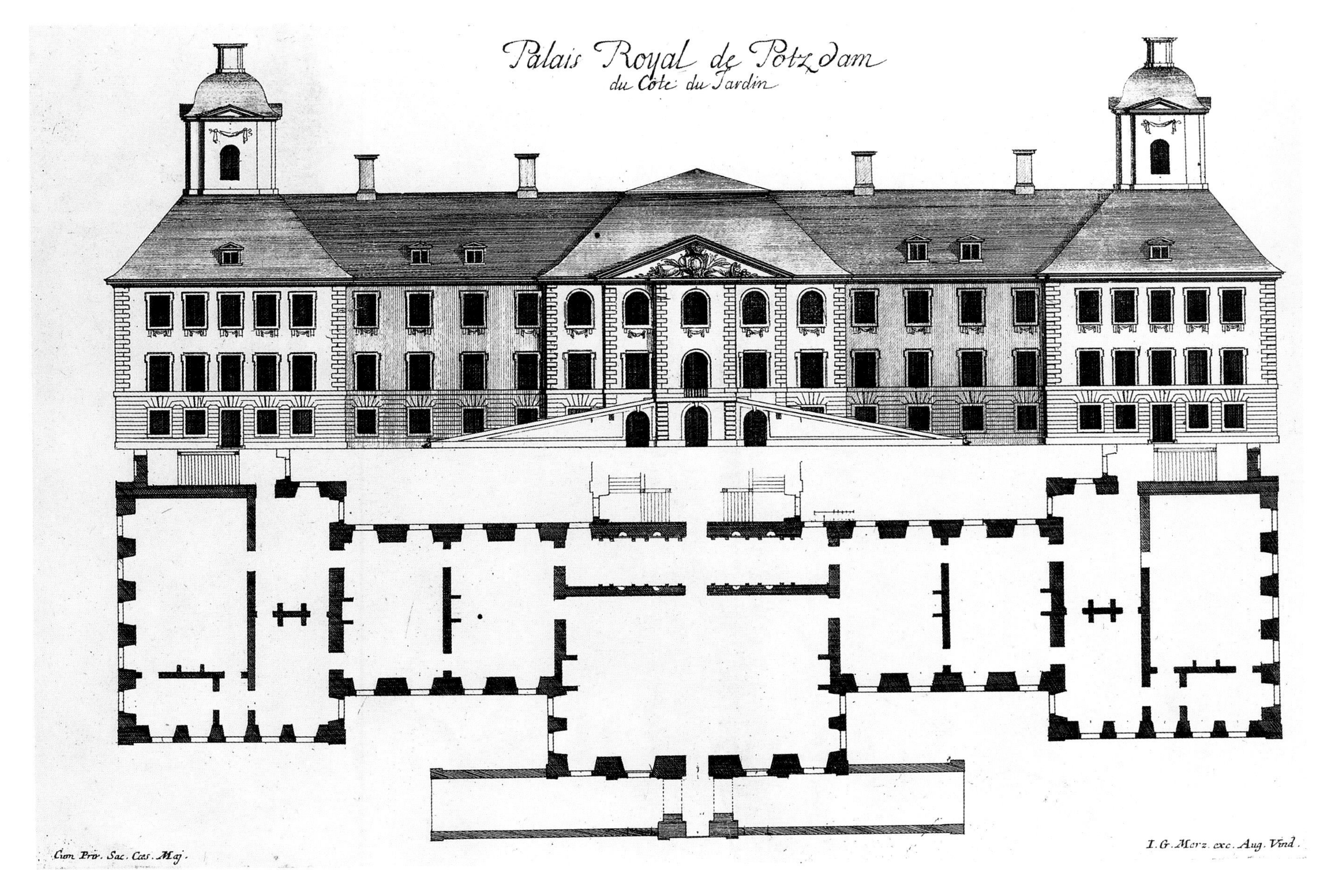

Caputh, palace and garden

With its brightly painted exterior, the palace, on the bank of the Havel, was a conspicuous landmark. The river formed a visual link between it and the Potsdam Palace.

the one at which the enfilade ended) to Caputh Palace; another was formed by the avenue going towards the Pannenberg and the site of the later New Palace (Neuen Palais), and branching off from this was another which crossed the pheasant garden and led to the Eichberg (Pfingstberg). On the Pannenberg stood a mighty tree as a *point de vue*, and later there was a gateway of honor (Ehrenpforte), which gave this hill near Golm its present-day name of Ehrenpfortenberg, and from which one could see an emblem with the golden rays on top of the central tower of the palace. Putting up gateways of honor as *points de vue* was a very common practice. A third ride went from the corner pavilion to the Grosser Tiergarten which was on the far side of the Havel and formed, together with two others which had no particular landmarks, what was apparently the earliest six-pointed star in Brandenburg, with a shooting-lodge at its center. In 1701, the game park was moved to the Pirschheide on the other side of the Havel.

A piece of paradise: palaces and gardens in the country

The Great Elector surrounded his new seat of Potsdam with a ring of pleasure palaces in splendid parks, close to which vineyards, fishponds, and hunting areas were created. To the west, visible across the Havel from the palace at Potsdam, was Caputh; to the north were Bornim and Fahrland; and to the north-east Glienicke.

Caputh is the only one of the electors' country seats to has survived largely unchanged from the time of Frederick William (see below). This small country estate had been the property of the electors since the mid-16th century. Frederick William gave the building, which had fallen into disrepair during the Thirty Years' War, to his chamberlain, Philipp de Chièze, a Dutchman who was employed at the court of Brandenburg as quartermaster-general and as an engineer (on the building of the palace at Potsdam, among other things). Philipp de Chièze reshaped the ruined palace into a rectangular

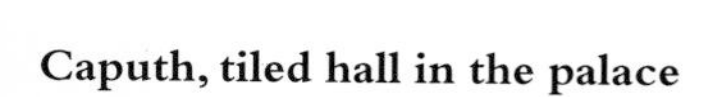

Caputh, tiled hall in the palace

The tiled hall, used in summer as a dining room, is one of the few surviving examples of the widely adopted fashion for this kind of decoration. King Frederick William I had the walls covered with over 7,500 Dutch faience tiles in about 1720.

building with nine axes. After Chièze's death in 1673, Frederick William gave the estate to his second wife, Dorothea of Holstein-Glücksburg, for her lifetime. She retained de Chièze's two-story, stuccoed building as a seven-axis *corps de logis*, but added two corner pavilions that projected beyond the end axes, so that on the courtyard side it looked like a building with three wings. On the garden side, facing the Templiner See (Templin Lake) to the north, a curved external staircase in front of a shallow central projection with a portal led into the garden. The main path in the garden led to a small peninsula that was the landing stage for the princely pleasure-yachts, and also the focus of the vista from the palace at Potsdam.

The façades have survived almost unchanged from the time of the electors. So have the original stucco work and ceiling paintings inside, and their quality suggests that the furnishings, too, were magnificent, more so than at Bornim or Glienicke. The inventory of the property left by Electress Dorothea at her death lists leather wall-hangings, valuable furniture, and some 300 paintings. On the central axis is the staircase, around which the rooms are not yet grouped strictly symmetrically. In the eastern part of the main story are the great hall and the former apartments of the Elector, and in the west the Electress's apartments, with a porcelain room in the western pavilion.

After the death of the Electress Dorothea, her stepson, Elector Frederick III, continued to make improvements to the palace, which he gave in 1690 to his second wife, Sophia Charlotte. The ceiling painting in the great hall shows the Triumph of the Arts over Ignorance. In the basement a vaulted grotto was made, which may have been used in summer as a dining room.

In 1699 Sophia Charlotte gave up her summer palace at Caputh, choosing instead the newly built Lietzenburg Palace (from 1705 onwards called Charlottenburg). Caputh was the scene of one more outstanding festive occasion, the meeting of three kings, when on July 8, 1709, Frederick I of Prussia, Augustus the Strong of Saxony, and Frederick IV of Denmark, came from Potsdam on the royal pleasure-yacht Libornica and landed at Caputh. Later, Frederick William I, despite his thrift in all other matters, kept this palace, for he was an enthusiastic huntsman and the palace was close to the Grosser Tiergarten. Around 1720, he even had the walls of the summer dining room covered with about 7,000 blue and white Delft faience tiles, following a widespread fashion (see opposite).

This well-preserved room is one of the few surviving examples of its kind, and the only one in Brandenburg (there are others at Oranienbaum and Brühl). In 1764, Frederick II leased both the palace and its grounds to a dye works. Today, with the palaces in Berlin and Potsdam lost, this small palace is an important monument of the court culture of the time of the Great Elector.

While the Great Elector made these changes to the surroundings of Potsdam, his first wife, Louise Henrietta, changed the landscape of the March of Brandenburg in a different way. In 1651, Frederick William had given her the district of Bötzow to the north of Berlin. It was no doubt the similarity of the countryside to that of her native Holland, and also the discomfort of the Brandenburg palaces, dilapidated as a result of the Thirty Years' War, that led her to create a modern country seat on the Dutch model, which, like the whole district of Bötzow, was called Oranienburg in her honor. She included the whole surrounding area in her project, bringing Dutch colonists into the countryside that had been depopulated by the war and urging the native population to set up model agricultural enterprises or to improve the old estates and farms to a similar standard. The aim was to create a "New Holland." In Memhardt she found an architect who understood what she wanted, and starting in 1651 he built a three-story, cube-shaped main building with two-story pavilions on three sides, linked by galleries (see below). The simple design of the façades, the tall roofs, and the platform that afforded a view all followed the severely classical model of Dutch buildings, while the tower at the back owed more to local tradition (Grunewald, Königs Wusterhausen). In the first year of building, Memhardt began to lay out the pleasure garden, which was not related to the palace in the French manner but, following a common practice in Holland, was largely independent of the palace and indeed lay at an angle to it. It is probably safe to

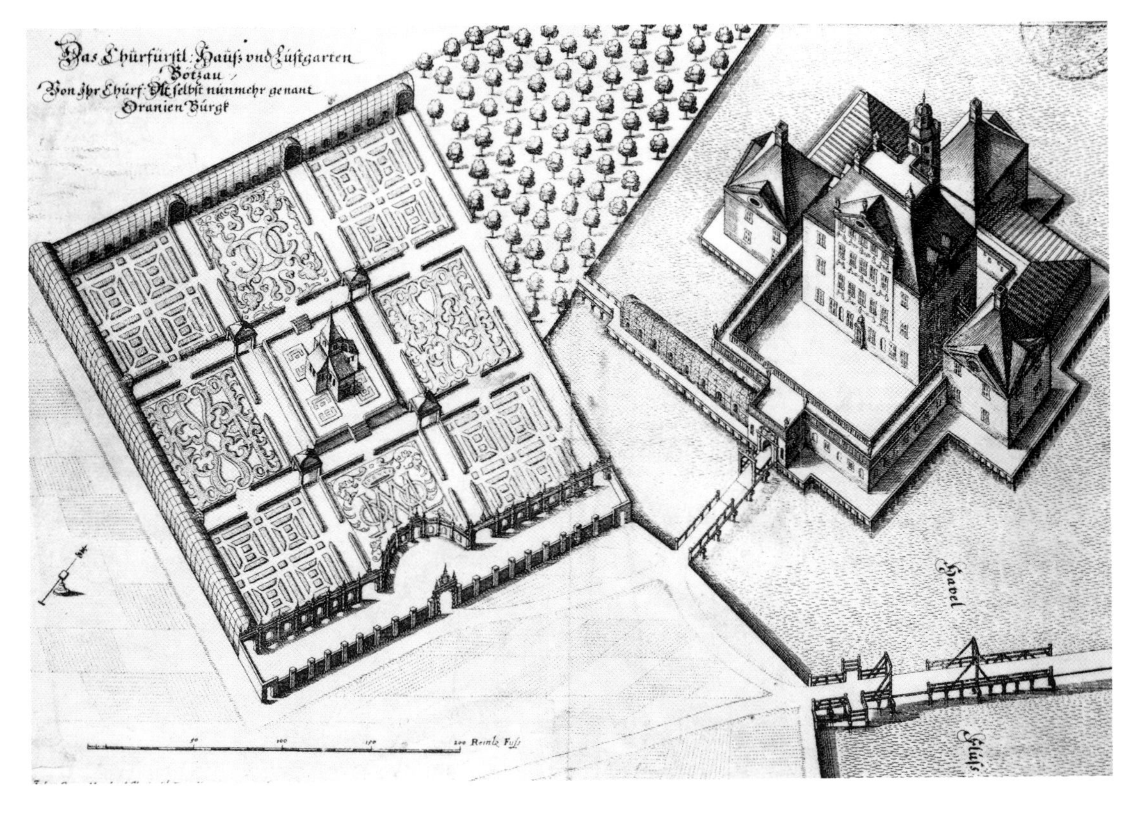

Oranienburg (previously Bötzow), Elector's house and pleasure garden
Copper engraving by Johann Gregor Memhardt, 27 x 33.5 cm; in Topographia electoratus Brandenburgici, *(1652)*

This engraving shows the palace building erected in 1651–1655, following Dutch models, for the Great Elector's first wife, Louise Henrietta. The palace, which stands on an island in the Havel, and the geometrically designed pleasure garden divided into small sections are not yet related to one another.

Berlin, Köpenick Palace, chapel
Johann Arnold Nering

In 1682 the Elector's daughter, Princess Elizabeth Henrietta, laid the foundation stone for the palace chapel, which had been designed by Johann Arnold Nering. The central section has a dome-like roof with a drum, bearing a crown that embodies the Elector's aspiration to royal status.

assume that the interior decoration and furnishings of the palace were just as strongly influenced by Dutch taste. As early as 1652, Merian reports that "the rooms and hall are excellently adorned with extremely rare paintings and precious tapestries and other furnishings." Around 1662, Louise Henrietta created a porcelain room, the first in a Brandenburg palace.

A ceremony took place at Oranienburg in June 1655 to mark the completion of the palace (the main building and galleries), but the work continued under Michael Matthias Smids until 1661. Around 1660, the Elector's interest began to focus itself on Potsdam, and the Electress too found little time to relax at Oranienburg.

The Great Elector's second wife, Dorothea, also had a suitably impressive palace complex built for her children. She too engaged a Dutch architect, Cornelius Ryckwaert, a follower of Pieter Post, who between 1670 and 1688 built for her at Schwedt on the Oder an elongated building, the garden front of which was enlivened by a gabled central projection and dainty corner turrets. These features made it reminiscent of the palace of the Teutonic Knights at Sonnenburg (Neumark), near Kostrzyn, built by John Maurice. The palace at Schwedt influenced the design of the new palace at Köpenick, which was begun in 1677 (see below).

Frederick III, as heir to the electorate, chose Köpenick as his residence. From 1677, if not before, he lived in the old Renaissance palace at Köpenick and had a new building designed by the Dutch painter Rutger von Langerfeld. To what extent Nering was involved in the design is uncertain, since from September 1677 he was on a three-year study tour. However, it is thought that the gateway, which was executed in 1682, was his work, since it showed strong similarities to the Leipzig Gate in the Berlin fortification wall, which he built a year later. Also in 1682, the foundation stone was laid for the palace chapel, which was built to his design opposite the palace (see left).

On an island in the Dahme (where the Dahme flows into the Spree) stands the broad, stuccoed building of the palace, articulated by central and side projections. The central projections have richly ornamented round gables surmounted by the electoral hat and decorated with hunting motifs. The mansard roof, which has a French air, is flattened by a roof terrace, a feature that had already appeared, though in a less perfected form, at Oranienburg and Potsdam. The arrangement of the rooms inside appeared especially modern. The rooms are arranged in a regular series on either side of an oak staircase that was very imposing for those days and consisted of a double flight of stairs and a balcony. On each floor is a vestibule in which the walls are richly articulated and the ceiling is decorated with stucco.

Still more important, because they are preserved only here, are the stucco ceilings, dating from the early days of the building, which formerly framed

Berlin, Köpenick Palace
Begun in 1681 by Rutger von Langerfeld

Originally a Renaissance palace, Köpenick was remodeled as a residence for the Elector's son, the future Frederick III, who as king planned to enlarge it into a building with three wings.

ceiling paintings (in oil on plaster) that were mainly on hunting themes. Some of these, which were painted by Jacques Vaillant, who died in 1691, can still be seen. The stucco work, too, was completed in about 1690, showing that the building was finished at around this time. One is struck by two different forms of decoration, which consist either of very three-dimensionally worked garlands of fruit and laurels or of acanthus leaves in less high relief (see below). Giovanni Carove, who had previously worked in Thuringia (at Friedenstein Palace at Gotha, in 1683), was employed at Köpenick from 1694 onwards; so, probably, was the electoral court stucco artist Giovanni Simonetti, who had already worked on the stucco in the palace in Berlin and at Schwedt. Since stucco artists at that time worked from engravings (by Daniel Marot and Jean Lepautre in particular) it is difficult to make stylistic attributions. Excavations made in 1938, but also historical travel accounts and above all sketches by the Weissenfels architect Christoph Pitzler, who visited Köpenick in 1695, suggest that there were plans to build, opposite the gateway building, a garden wing with a curved external staircase, as at Caputh. The building that exists now would then have formed an asymmetrical side wing, like the chapel opposite. In 1688, the year of Frederick's accession, Nering also started to build the two-story gallery extension next to the palace moat. This extension might have closed off the three-winged building on the town side and linked the existing palace with the chapel wing. This building by the heir to the electorate still reflects the period of the Great Elector. A variety of Dutch architects, painters, and sculptors were chosen to design the buildings, their furnishings, and their surroundings, especially the gardens. Classical severity and elegance were combined with the simplicity characteristic of the March of Brandenburg.

Berlin, Köpenick Palace, armorial hall (1685–1690)

Pairs of herms support coats of arms, some framed by acanthus leaves, of the territories of the Electoral March of Brandenburg. The electors' intention was to glorify the state that they ruled. The coat of arms of the March of Brandenburg was given a central position above the fireplaces on the long sides, supported by "savages."

Oranienburg, royal pleasure palace, viewed from the garden
Copper engraving by Johann David Schleuen (c. 1750)

In 1688–1709 the palace was made by Johann Arnold Nering and Martin Grünberg into an H-shaped complex. The garden was altered for the sake of the palace forecourt: as at Versailles, three axes converged on the garden front.

A Suitably Regal Display of Magnificence: Elector Frederick III/ King Frederick I (1688–1713)

Elector Frederick III inherited an efficiently functioning state from his father. He was therefore able to devote far more attention than his father had to modernizing and embellishing his country and his capital city. He loved impressive ceremonial and outward show, and used them to further his ambition to achieve royal status.

As a cousin of the King of England, William III of Orange, he felt that he belonged to a royal family, and accordingly determined to raise his own rank, using both political and artistic strategies in order to acquire the royal crown of Prussia; he attained his goal in 1701. The founding of the university of Halle, the creation of an Academy of Arts (1696) on the French model, and the formation of the Society of Sciences (1700) were all part of this strategy.

He also increased the amount of building activity, since fine buildings are a permanent testimony to a ruler's status and the economic strength of his country. It was through his generous support that for the first time architecture, art, and culture in Berlin achieved European stature.

Electoral and royal pleasure palaces: centers of court culture in the countryside

Soon after his accession in 1688, Elector Frederick III embarked on further alterations to his mother's country seat at Oranienburg (see opposite). The austere severity of the palace seemed to him insufficiently impressive, and so he commissioned the architect Nering to modernize the building. Architectural ideas from Köpenick were introduced here, too. In order to give a greater horizontal emphasis, Frederick removed the tower and had the pointed gable demolished and replaced by a tall attic story.

The façade was probably covered in white and pale gray stucco, and the roof, unlike that of Memhardt's earlier building, was of slate. Altogether, the alterations gave the *corps de logis* an Italianate and more imposing character (see left); they reflected what Nering had been able to observe during his travels in Italy in 1677–1680. After an interval, he began in the spring of 1694 to build the eastern and western extensions to the *corps de logis* – the two pavilions in the front courtyard and the two courtyard wings. After Nering's death in 1695, these were completed by Martin Grünberg and linked by a gallery that was similar to the one at Houselaarsdijk Palace in Holland, a place where the father of the Electress Louise Henrietta was fond of staying. This created a *cour d'honneur* on the northern side, facing away from the town. It was only in 1706–1709 that Johann Friedrich Nilsson Eosander von Göthe also built side wings linking the two kitchen pavilions with the central building, thus creating a *cour d'honneur* on the town side too, and giving the complex as a whole an H-shaped ground-plan.

Writing in 1695, the chronicler Christoph Pitzler mentions oriental decor and furnishings inside the palace, but like other visitors (for instance John Toland in 1702) he reserves his highest praise for the rich decoration of the Porcelain Room in the northwest pavilion. Today, only the ceiling painting by Augustin Terwesten is still preserved. It is an allegorical representation of the introduction into Europe of Far Eastern porcelain and shows many individual pieces from the collection, which has now unfortunately been lost.

The model for the great hall built by Eosander von Göthe, which was also used as a dining room, was Amalia of Solms's Orange Hall, which had already been imitated in the palace at Potsdam. In the Berlin palace, too, Frederick had created an "Orange Hall," in which there were tapestries portraying the history of the House of Orange. On the ceiling, William III of Orange was depicted on horseback, and his coronation of 1689 formed the main theme of the room. What was pictorially represented at Oranienburg was not the coronation of Frederick I in 1701 but his claim, following the death of William III on March 19, 1702, to the title of Prince of Orange. Alterations were made to the garden, as well: Nering had already begun on this in 1690. The first part of the garden to the point as far as the summerhouse was removed to make way for the forecourt, but towards the west it was made both longer and wider. Today, Nering's garden gateway is all that remains of Elector Frederick III's splendid pleasure garden, the central axis of which led to a summerhouse called "Favorite," built in 1699 by Eosander von Göthe as a focal point, just as in Berlin the visual end-point of the garden was the Orangery. As at Versailles, three roads radiated from the palace square, here the central one leading to Berlin. The main axis of the garden ran westwards from the square formed by Nering in 1685–1695. On the other side, to the northeast, an avenue led to the subsidiary palace of Friedrichsthal, which was designed by Nering in 1692 and demolished in the 19th century, and from which the Oranienburg Palace could be seen.

Like his father, Frederick enlarged his collection of residences by extending and improving small country palaces. Thus in 1691 he bought the "petit palais" at Schönhausen (Niederschönhausen), which had been built between 1662 and 1665 by Countess Dohna (see page 92). It was probably Nering who gave it a more strongly articulated façade by emphasizing projecting sections in the middle and at the sides. The three middle axes were framed by pilasters, as at Köpenick, but again only the central one was surmounted by a round gable. Each of these two palaces has a balcony at the level of the main story

Oranienburg Palace, middle section of the side facing towards the town

This impressive Italianate façade, which still survives, was created in the course of the alterations made by Elector Frederick III after 1688.

and an entrance portal with a round arch. In this way Frederick copied at Schönhausen, his preferred summer residence at this period, elements from Köpenick, which had been his seat prior to his accession. On the symmetrically positioned chimneys were two electoral hats, as at his father's pleasure palace at Bornim. In 1704, Eosander von Göthe enlarged the complex of buildings still further by lengthening the single-story extensions at each side. The estate also included a large garden, which ended with a semicircular boscage that, like other parts of the garden, was reminiscent of the Dutch garden of Het Loo. As at Oranienburg, Berlin, and Potsdam, here too on the parterres close to the palace building low shrubs and flowers were laid out in the shape of the elector's initials. The central axis of the garden led, in the form of an avenue of linden trees, to Blankenburg. This main axis leading out into the countryside linked this French-style garden motif with the canal marking the end of the garden, another feature showing Dutch influence.

Frederick's love of magnificently laid out gardens, which he used for short stays in summer, led him in 1693 to obtain country mansions and estates at Tegel, Hermsdorf, Rosenthal, and Blankenfelde and transform them into small pleasure palaces with appropriately splendid gardens. Just as his father had surrounded his favorite residence of Potsdam with pleasure palaces, so he too created a ring of Baroque palaces with gardens around his capital, Berlin. These also included Altlandsberg, adapted by Eosander von Göthe as late as 1709–1713, and the new garden at Ruhleben dating from 1708–1710.

In 1698, he confiscated the properties of Admiral Raule, his director-general of the Fleet, and took over his garden and palace of Rosenfelde, which he promptly renamed Friedrichsfelde, early in 1699, in order to set his own mark upon it. Raule, a Dutchman by birth, had, as Pitzler reports in 1695, created a country seat and garden in the Dutch style. The two-story building was articulated by massive Ionic pilasters and had a double external staircase and a balcony above the entrance. The central axis was surmounted by a triangular pediment, which may point to the chief court architect, Nering, as its designer (as at Niederschönhausen). In 1705, single-story extensions were added on each side of the building, which had five axes. The gardens, on the northern side, are particularly interesting: reconstructed in 1987, they give a clear impression of a Dutch-style garden. The building was later enlarged, so that one can now only guess at its appearance around 1700 (see opposite). From Friedrichsfelde, avenues led to Köpenick (there, too, rides led into the nearby game park) and also to Berlin.

Berlin becomes a royal seat

When the Great Elector developed the fortifications of Berlin in 1658–1683, he planned from the outset to build an impressive arsenal (see pages 94 and 95). The Elector Frederick felt that executing this plan would be a fulfillment of his father's legacy, and, naturally enough, he planned to build it as a monument to the Great Elector's military achievements. But the foundation stone was not laid until as late as May 28, 1695.

On October 21, 1695, Nering died, and Martin Grünberg took over the direction of the building, but was instructed by the elector to make no alterations to the plans. Nering's design revealed his extensive knowledge, acquired both at first hand on his Italian tour and from theoretical writings, especially those of Nicolaus Goldmann and Charles Philippe Dieussart. From 1696 onwards, as well as Grünberg, Andreas Schlüter was already working on the Arsenal, as a sculptor. In 1698 he also took over as director of the building works. Before long he had developed ideas of his own for the sculptural decoration of the building and had departed from Nering's plans. But he retained the design of the façades, which were to have a finely rusticated base with round-arched windows and an upper story articulated by Doric pilasters. He also kept the central projecting sections on each front, with, on the Unter den Linden side, an arc above the entrance reaching up into the next story, as on the east front of the Louvre in Paris. But he wanted further to emphasize that main entrance by adding a massive, apparently unattached cartouche. Furthermore, he planned a broad attic story ornamented with reliefs, and on top of it a number of gigantic statues to crown the building. His brilliant ideas would have given the building "a magnificent Italianate note of

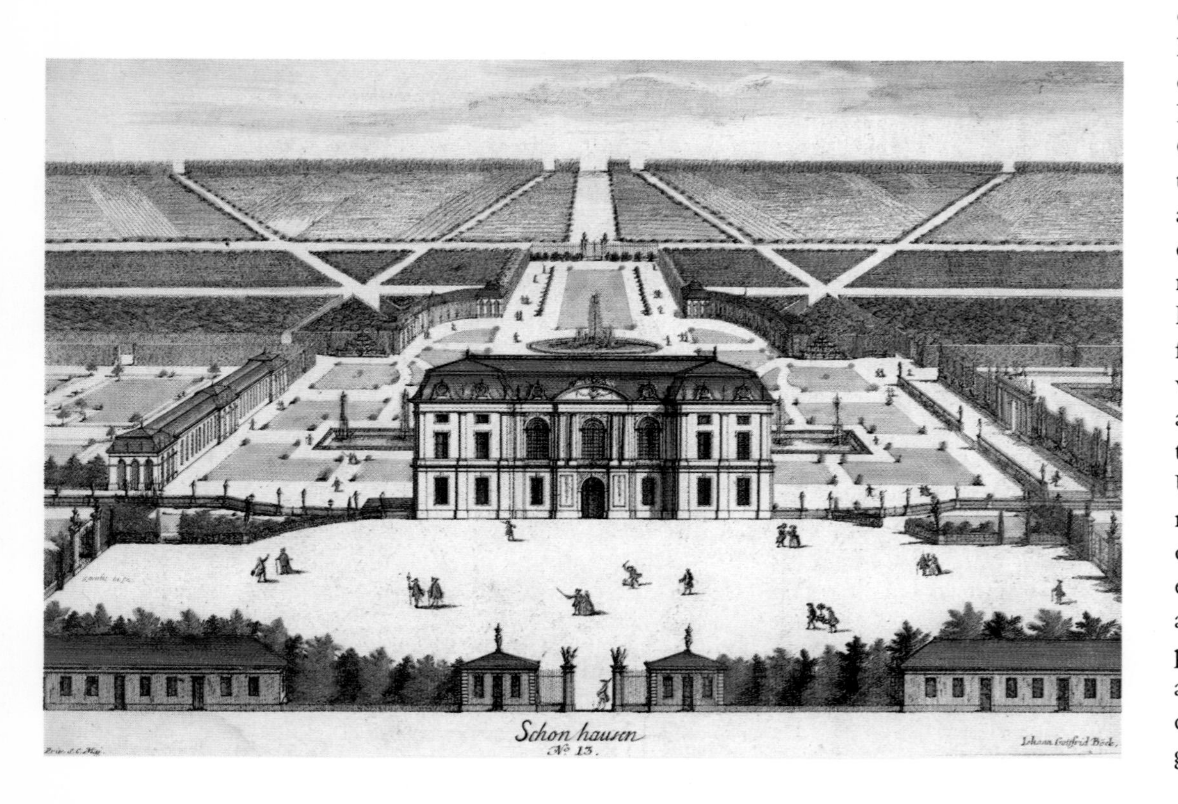

Berlin, Niederschönhausen (Schönhausen) Palace
Colored etching by Jean Baptiste Broebes (after 1733), 28.4 x 44.5 cm; Berlin, Stiftung Stadtmuseum Berlin

Both the Great Elector and his son built pleasure palaces around their main residences (Berlin and Potsdam), creating a network of gardens and palaces, many of which were linked by vistas.

celebration." But technical flaws and poor materials (on the ground floor a load-bearing pillar collapsed) prevented Schlüter's plans from being realized. Jean de Bodt was brought in to make the building safe and in 1699 he took complete charge of the project. He changed the design of the façade (substituting a balustrade for the attic story) and commissioned the French sculptor Guillaume Hulot, who had been in the service of Brandenburg since 1700, to execute the crowning statues and the cartouches. The bronze relief of King Frederick I that was placed above the south portal on the Unter den Linden side (see page 94) was also Hulot's work. It bears a gilded bust portrait of Frederick, who is wearing a laurel wreath, and above this is an armorial cartouche on which the royal crown is flanked by two goddesses of victory. A Latin inscription celebrates Frederick as king and as the builder of this arsenal and bears the date 1706. This gives the impression that the building was finished by then, but in fact the construction work continued and was only finished under Frederick William I in 1729.

Berlin, Friedrichsfelde Palace
(Begun 1695, extended 1719), north front with the parterre reconstructed in Baroque style

In 1698, the elector took over the summer palace of his Dutch director-general of the Fleet, who had also laid out the garden in the style of his homeland. Avenues linked this small palace with Köpenick Palace and with Berlin. The core of the building is still there, its original five axes now linked by a gable.

IVSTITIAE·ARMORVM·TERRORI·HOST·
TVTELAE·SVORVM·POP·ET·FOEDERAT·
FRIDERICVS·I·
REX·BORVSS·P·P·P·AVG·INV·
HOC·ARMAMENTARIVM·OMNI·INSTRVM·BELL·
NEC·NON·SPOLIOR·MILIT·
AC·TROPHAEOR·GENERE·REFERTVM·
A·FVNDAM·EXTRVENDVM·CVR·M·DCC·VI·

Opposite
Berlin, Arsenal, central projecting section with the Unter den Linden entrance

The bronze relief above the entrance with the portrait of Elector Frederick III is by Guillaume Hulot, who also created the female figures next to the entrance. They represent pyrotechnics, arithmetic, geometry, and mechanics.

The *Schloss:* the symbol and monument of the Prussian monarchy

Frederick's aspiration to royal status found many critics, his grandson Frederick II among them, who saw in it little but personal vanity and a love of ostentation. The critics also included his second wife, Sophia Charlotte, who was influenced by the ideas of the Enlightenment. However, such criticism overlooks the political constellations and developments among Brandenburg's neighbors, which necessarily had an important impact on Prussia. In 1689, William of Orange gained the crown of England. Hanover, an electorate from 1692 onwards, aspired to the English succession, and the elector of Saxony, Augustus the Strong, was elected King of Poland in 1697.

The position of the Emperor, Leopold I of Habsburg (1658–1705), had been strengthened by the victory over the Turks at Vienna in 1683; and France, during the long reign of Louis XIV (1661–1715) was continually striving for European dominance. So Brandenburg-Prussia found itself involved in a political contest in which it needed royal status in order to hold its own against its rivals. Using art to glorify himself and the power of his state was the most effective way for a ruler to give tangible expression to his political stature. Thus the aim of the celebrated architect Johann Bernhard Fischer von Erlach at Schönbrunn near Vienna (from 1692 onwards) was to outdo the French Sun King with his vast palace and grounds at Versailles. As late as 1704, while visiting Berlin, Fischer von Erlach offered Frederick his design for a "counter Versailles" (though this was never realized in the proposed form).

It is in this context that Frederick's wish for a new residence to enhance his prestige, one which would make a stronger impression on the outside world than his father's "adaptations" has to be seen. The Great Elector had carried on the tradition of his dynasty and tended merely to add to the existing building of the Berlin Palace. The French kings, too, had extended existing palaces (Versailles, the Louvre, Fontainebleau). Frederick I, on the other hand, wanted to refashion the existing building in such a way as to obtain the attention and admiration of his neighbors. He therefore favored plans that would give the building a symmetrical, block-like, and positively imperial form. In France, too, there had been attempts to give the Louvre and Versailles (the garden side) a unified appearance.

The precise course of the alterations to the palace in the first decade of the rule of Elector Frederick III is not known; this is especially true of the years 1690–1696, during which Nering, the court architect, had to give his attention to many other projects apart from the palace. Nicodemus Tessin, who stayed in Berlin in 1688, spoke of courtyard arcades, which were to have massive columns in front of them, an "imperial-style motif" that was intended to express Frederick's determination to put his *palais royal* on a par with those of other European rulers. In the Louvre projects of both Giovanni Lorenzo Bernini (1665) and Pietro da Cortona, the courtyard was surrounded by massive columns that were intended

Berlin, the Arsenal seen from the southeast
(Built 1695–1729), now Deutsches Historisches Museum

The main fronts of the Arsenal were the east front facing towards the palace and the side containing the entrance on Unter den Linden. The oldest building on that road, it survives to bear witness to the high quality of Baroque architecture in Berlin around 1700.

to evoke a classical peristyle. However, it seems that the building work was halted after the completion of the arcades in the southeastern corner, especially as the presence of the old Renaissance towers containing the staircases made it difficult to continue.

After Nering's death in October 1695, Frederick entered into negotiations with foreign architects (Domenico Martinelli and Nicodemus Tessin) with whose help he intended to make his palace into a building of European stature. A plan dating from 1697, showing a "city palace in the Italian manner," is variously attributed to Tessin (according to Peschken) or to a different architect, perhaps even Schlüter (according to Keller). This so-called second plan was succeeded by a model of the palace that Schlüter offered to the elector as a counter-proposal. Johann Friedrich Wentzel depicted this model on the ceiling of the Knights' Hall (see right), which was formally opened on January 19, 1703, the feast-day of the Order of the Knights of St. John. This representation of the model was positioned opposite the royal throne and was thereby accorded outstanding importance. The palace building had become a monument to the founding of the royal house by the Hohenzollern dynasty.

It has not so far been possible to determine exactly when Schlüter was brought into the building process. After Nering's death, Martin Grünberg had carried on with the alterations from November 1695 to March 1699, directing the works with care but taking little interest in the artistic design of the façade. It was this, however, that Schlüter, as a sculptor, was especially interested in. Alongside Grünberg, Schlüter began, even before he was officially appointed director of works on the palace on November 2, 1699, to execute the second plan according to his own ideas.

His intentions could not be fully carried out since owing to the "Mint Tower affair," of which more later, he worked on the palace only until 1706. But his overall conception – the shape of a regular cube enclosing a magnificently ornamented courtyard – was retained by all the building directors who succeeded him. On to the four-winged complex of the old Renaissance palace, he added, in the manner of Roman *palazzi*, further wings of the same height enclosing a rectangular inner courtyard with façades all designed in similar style (see page 99, bottom). Central projecting sections jutting noticeably forward both in the courtyard and on the outer façades gave rhythm to each section of the building and created the emphasis on the center that is an indispensable feature of the Baroque style. The garden front and the façade on the town side were intended to be the main sides viewed by observers; they had been designed in relation to their respective surroundings and therefore were conceived in different ways (see page 77). The projection containing the entrance portal on Palace Square had a commanding appearance because it was designed as a triumphal arch for the ceremonial entry of the King on May 6, 1701. Above a base with smooth, horizontally banded rustication there were four massive Corinthian columns without fluting, which bore a complete entablature (architrave, frieze, and cornice) of a kind found nowhere but here, and not extended to the sides. The roof balustrade was crowned, above the projection, by four statues. The whole portal stood on a protruding podium and

Berlin Palace (destroyed), second upper story, state rooms, Knights' Hall
Historical photograph

This detail from the ceiling painting by Wentzel shows *Fame Proclaiming the Glory of the Prussian King*. His fame is also enhanced by his palace, to which a Muse is pointing while looking towards the figure of a man who represents the architect Andreas Schlüter.

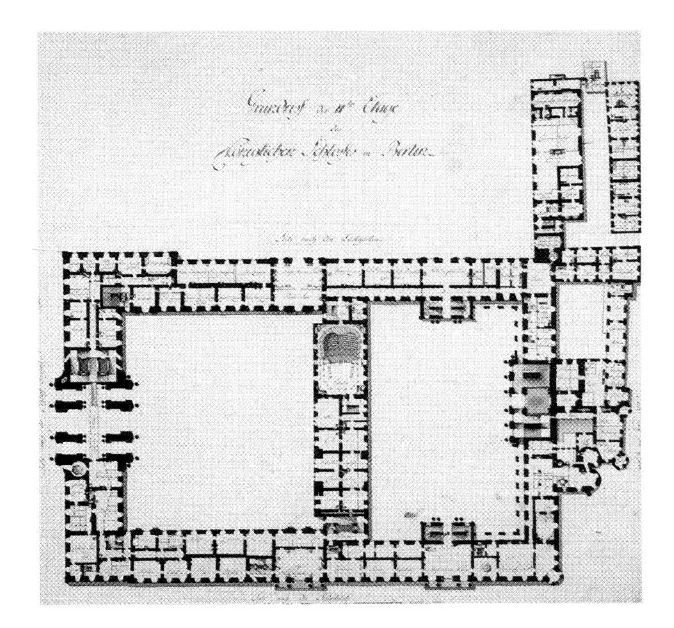

Berlin Palace (destroyed), plan of the second upper story
Pen and ink on parchment (1794); Potsdam, Stiftung Preussische Schlösser und Gärten Berlin-Brandenburg, Plankammer

The second upper story was the real *piano nobile*, the main story. This is where the main rooms and state rooms were.

could only be reached by a number of steps. This reinforced the effect of the portal as a monument. Schlüter was at the time in competition with other architects who were also preparing for Frederick's entry by designing temporary triumphal arches representing the districts of the city and the guilds. Schlüter's portal was the last on Frederick's route to the palace. Although he would not pass through it (the procession took its usual route through Memhardt's gateway into the outer courtyard and from there into the inner one), it would, as a permanent gateway, continue to serve as a memorial to Frederick's entry. For with it, the new king took possession of his residential city and at the same time received the homage of its citizens.

The entrance portal on the garden side, on the other hand, had none of this solemn monumentality; it had, by contrast, a more light-hearted and festive air.

The monumental and refined design of the façades reveal a thorough knowledge of Roman Baroque architecture, including Bernini's designs for the Louvre. With it Schlüter had brought Berlin into the mainstream of European architectural development.

Because the palace has been lost, it is no longer possible to study the thematic content of the sculptural decoration of the façades. But it was not only in the statues or individual parts of the building that the significance of the building expressed itself: every aspect of the decoration contributed. Thus the gilded eagles all around the palace pointed emblematically to the Olympian sovereignty of the newly crowned king, just as in many places inside the palace he was identified with Jupiter (in the same way that Louis XIV chose to be celebrated as Apollo, and Augustus the Strong as Hercules).

The garden wing formed an addition to the old, still-existing ceremonial apartments and the elector's private apartments in the Spree wing (see above). As at Versailles, anyone seeking access to the king had to pass through successive suites of rooms, creating the sense of a hierarchical distance. This second audience suite was symmetrically arranged; at its centre was the Knights' Hall of the Order of the Knights of St. John, in which the king's throne stood (see page 98). Schlüter's interior decoration reached its height in the sculptural representation of the four continents

Eduard Gärtner
Schlüter Courtyard of the Berlin City Palace (1830)
Oil on canvas, 98 x 155 cm; Berlin, Stiftung Preussische Schlösser und Gärten Berlin-Brandenburg, Schloss Charlottenburg

The painting shows the warm coloring of the sandstone of which the palace was built. On the left, behind the huge, magnificent columns, is the main staircase; to the right is the central projecting section of the south wing. In between these one is looking at the arcades that Schlüter refashioned.

Berlin Palace (destroyed), second upper story, state rooms, Knights' Hall, view looking westwards towards the wall with the silver service
Historical photograph

The Knights' Hall (Rittersaal) in the garden wing is an outstanding example of Schlüter's sculptural decoration and interior design. The stucco ornamentation in the corners breaks through the several levels of weighty cornice and, by the movement of the figures rising from cartouches and over volutes, establishes a link with the painting on the ceiling vault.

on the *sopratortà*, and in the fusion of sculpture and painting in the richly ornamented ceiling moldings (see page 96). The main means of access to the state rooms was still from the Spree wing via the great staircase by Schlüter (replacing a spiral staircase), which led to the antechamber of the Swiss Hall, where the palace guards stood (see opposite, above). This enormous staircase, ornamented with herms, consisted of two flights of stairs that ascended around a square well. As one either climbed up, or rode up (one flight was actually a ramp), one was greeted by a figure of Jupiter hurling lightning bolts. Since these stairs did not lead directly to the state rooms, Schlüter had built separate staircases into the two courtyard projections, so that the Knights' Hall in the garden wing and the Elizabeth Room in the Palace Square wing could be reached directly from below (see page 97). Schlüter's main staircase is among the earliest of all the magnificent Baroque staircases in Central Europe, and is comparable to those at Würzburg and Pommersfelden. At the northwestern corner of the old, low outer part of the palace, Frederick wished to replace the old Mint Tower with a new one that was to accommodate a water tank (to supply the fountains in the gardens) and also, in the Dutch manner, a carillon, which had been bought in the Netherlands. There is in existence a sketch plan by Johann Arnold Nering that must date from before 1695. The other plans are by Schlüter, whose first design is likely to date from 1702.

The building work on the tower started in 1704, but for technical reasons Schlüter had to draw up a second plan taking into account the boggy nature of

Berlin Palace (destroyed), main staircase (so-called "Giants' Staircase") by Schlüter
Historical photograph

The main staircase of the Berlin Palace is one of the earliest German Baroque staircases: two flights of stairs each ascended in a narrow shaft, offering views with surprising perspectives.

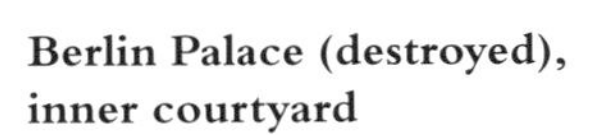

Berlin Palace (destroyed), inner courtyard
Historical photograph (1942)

Through Portal I, which led out towards Palace Square, one reached the gateway on the left side of this courtyard. Schlüter's sculptures of Roman kings and allegories of the virtues of a ruler celebrated the royal status that Frederick I had acquired in 1701. The gateways were the main means of access to the royal apartments.

Earliest view of Lietzenburg Palace (Charlottenburg; courtyard side), after a design by Johann Arnold Nering
Engraving in Lorenz Beger, Thesaurus Brandenburgicus III, *c. 1696*

The palace was built as a summer palace of the *maison de plaisance* type. Sophia Charlotte did not have her rooms in the main story, as prescribed by court custom, but transferred her apartments to the ground floor in order to be close to the garden.

Andreas Schlüter
First design for the Mint Tower (1702)
Copper engraving

The tower, resting on a supporting building, has three stories open at the sides; it was the king's wish that they should contain bells and a carillon.

the site and the existing masonry of the old tower (see left). The walls were reinforced and the upper stories were altered by the addition of tapered corner ties. Architectural engineering, worked out in practical, three-dimensional terms, had replaced the playful elegance of the first design. But ominous cracks in the walls led Frederick to order that the tower, a cherished project of his, should be pulled down.

Schlüter attempted to rescue the idea of the tower by presenting a third plan, but his plans all lacked a continuous vertical structure necessary to ensure stability; he placed the stories, clearly separated, one above the other, which shows that his intention was to use Roman Baroque forms to give the tower an austere, solemn, indeed majestic character.

A commission of enquiry found that Schlüter was to blame for the likely collapse of the Mint Tower, and as a result he was dismissed from his post as director of building works. His rival, Eosander von Göthe, took over the direction of building work on the palace from 1707 to 1713. The king now wished a number of official bodies to be accommodated in the palace, in order to centralize them as part of the royal household, close to the throne. He therefore wanted the palace to be extended to the west by twice as much as Schlüter had envisaged. In all essentials Schlüter's balanced, rhythmical articulation of the façades was retained, but Eosander von Göthe moved the main entrance to the new west wing and so gave the palace a new orientation to the west, towards the new districts of the city. The motif of the Roman triumphal arch, inspired by the arch of Septimus Severus in the Forum in Rome, gave emphasis to the position of the entrance on the central projecting section, which was linked to the west front with a concave curve at each side. The plan for a tall cupola was not carried out until 1845–1852, when a somewhat altered version of it was built by Friedrich August Stüler.

Charlottenburg: a pleasure palace becomes a residence

Sophia Charlotte, Frederick's second wife, had in 1694 given up the palace in Caputh, the gift made to her by her husband on the day after their marriage, and received in its stead a building close to the village of Lietzenburg (Lützelburg). There, starting in the spring of 1695, she had a pleasure palace built for her by Nering. This palace, like Friedrichsthal near Oranienburg, wholly conformed to the highly fashionable type of the *maison de plaisance*, and was in fact the first example in northern Germany (see above). Since Nering died on October 21, 1695, only a few months after the start of the project, the history of the building of the palace is somewhat complicated. First Martin Grünberg continued to build, following Nering's plans, so that the building was ready to be ceremonially opened on July 1, 1699. This original core of the building is still easily recognizable within the complex that was enlarged by Eosander von Göthe from 1701 onwards. The oval *salle à l'italienne* (Italian room) situated in the central pavilion, which curved out into the garden, was a standard feature of the *maison de plaisance*, of which Louis Le Vau had built the first example at Vaux-le-Vicomte in 1661. But Bernini's Louvre project of 1665 also had a similar middle section curving far forward, and Fischer von Erlach's pleasure palaces contained many variations of this kind of garden room. Anyone entering the courtyard would immediately gain a view of the garden through large glazed doors. Above this garden room was the great

hall, the walls of which were articulated by pilasters; large niches with mirrors caught the light of the windows opposite.

Sophia Charlotte did not live in the *piano nobile* in the upper story but on the ground floor, in order to be close to the garden (see above). This made it necessary to change the plans, because now the main royal apartments were now on the ground floor and the upper story of less importance. A report by a member of the Berlin Academy, Abraham d'Humbert, in the second half of the 18th century confirms that major alterations were indeed carried out by Schlüter from 1698 to 1701.

After the coronation at Königsberg (January 18, 1701), Frederick entrusted Eosander von Göthe, who had been his court architect since 1699 and whom he had previously sent on study tours of Italy and France, with the task of extending the palace (see page 102). Eosander von Göthe's plan envisaged a three-winged complex, with the *cour d'honneur* closed on the fourth side by a wrought-iron screen. He used projecting sections to articulate the transverse wings and the pavilions terminating them, and also the garden front, which extended beyond the transverse wings situated on the courtyard side. A balustrade ran right around the roof. The four projecting sections and the garden pavilion had massive columns, the vertical line of which was reinforced by the statues on the roof. They gave the façade rhythm and showed an unmistakable affinity with the garden front at Versailles. With the help of the Duchess of Orleans (Lieselotte of the Palatinate was a cousin of Sophia Charlotte), Eosander von Göthe had had the opportunity to study it closely during his stay in France.

Berlin, Charlottenburg Palace, apartments of Sophia Charlotte, dressing room

The wall-covering, gold, red, and green *brocatelle*, is not original.

Berlin, Charlottenburg Palace, courtyard side

The core of the building with its 11 axes, the work of Nering, is still easily recognizable. A roof on which one could walk about was very popular in the Baroque period; Köpenick Palace also has this feature.

Berlin, Charlottenburg Palace, Frederick I's audience chamber

Here one can see how the architect Eosander von Göthe raised the ceiling for the royal suite. The generous dimensions of the room and the fact that the walls are faced with marble also underline the room's importance. The walls are hung with Brussels tapestries of about 1730.

After the death of Sophia Charlotte (February 1, 1705), Frederick changed the name of Lietzenburg to Charlottenburg. It was only then that he finally resolved "to make Charlottenburg, as an eternal memorial to Her Majesty the Queen, of most blessed memory, into a place of incomparable beauty." The queen's pleasure palace was to become a country palace with the character of a royal residence. To assert this character to all who saw the palace, the king pursued another project involving a tower, since the Mint Tower had had to be demolished because of its inadequate foundations and Eosander von Göthe's plan for a tower above the west portal of the Berlin City Palace was not carried out.

A tower was designed for Charlottenburg about 1706 by the Hanover court architect Charles Louis Remy de la Fosse. It was very similar to the cupola that featured in the earliest plan for the palace, but the 1706 plan also envisaged a pavilion projecting out into the courtyard. Eosander von Göthe's solution, which was carried out in 1710, was based on de la Fosse's proposals, but he placed the circular room beneath the cupola within a rectangle, so that the projection into the courtyard could still have a straight rather than a curved front. On top of the commanding tower, which had an arcaded story and an attic story, was a weather vane in the form of a gilded figure of Fortuna; such a figure had in fact been envisaged for the Mint Tower and for the

Berlin, Charlottenburg Palace, audience chamber (reconstructed 1958–1959)

Shown here is a cartouche with a figure of Pegasus above the crowned monogram of Sophia Charlotte. It is surrounded by allegories of music.

Berlin, Charlottenburg Palace, chapel with crown and canopy by Eosander von Göthe (1704–1708, reconstructed after World War II)

The chapel is a high-ceilinged room lit from above by a lantern; its walls with their rich sculptural ornamentation, some of it gilded or colored, create an extremely impressive effect.

Berlin, Charlottenburg Palace, Porcelain Room, reconstructed after World War II

In 1695, Frederick III had the shelves and porcelain moved from Oranienburg to the corner room at Lietzenburg. Mirrors greatly enhance the effect of the light.

planned portal tower at the Berlin Palace. The tower at Charlottenburg now also acquired bells, which it retained until 1940.

In late 1706, Frederick was able to move into his royal suite to the west of the garden room. Inside, Eosander von Göthe had dispensed with the mezzanine story in order to make the royal apartments taller (see page 103). From 1707 onwards, ceremonies which had previously been possible only in Berlin or Königsberg, and for which the king had to leave his pleasure palaces and return to his main residences – for instance the reception of foreign ambassadors, knighting ceremonies, and so on – now increasingly took place at Charlottenburg (see opposite).

For a long time there had been talk of building an external staircase similar to the one planned for the garden wing at Köpenick. As early as 1698, Nikolaus Tessin the Younger had presented a design for one. In 1704, Eosander von Göthe built a hanging staircase to the west of the vestibule. Following the French pattern, it consisted of a flight of stairs without supports ascending a square stairwell. A ceiling painting by Anthonie Coxie, which was destroyed during World War II, depicted Apollo among the Muses. The king regarded this staircase as "the most beautiful ornament of the whole house." In conformity with the status of this palace as a royal residence, Eosander von Göthe had planned an *avant-cour* similar to the one at Versailles, a great front path which was to be bordered by some single-story buildings by Tessin. The narrow opening would then have emphasized still more strongly the axial nature of the road running up to the palace. This road met at right angles the axis which, coming from the city palace via Unter den Linden and the game park, had been laid out long ago, in 1647, by the Great Elector.

Berlin, Charlottenburg Palace, garden front

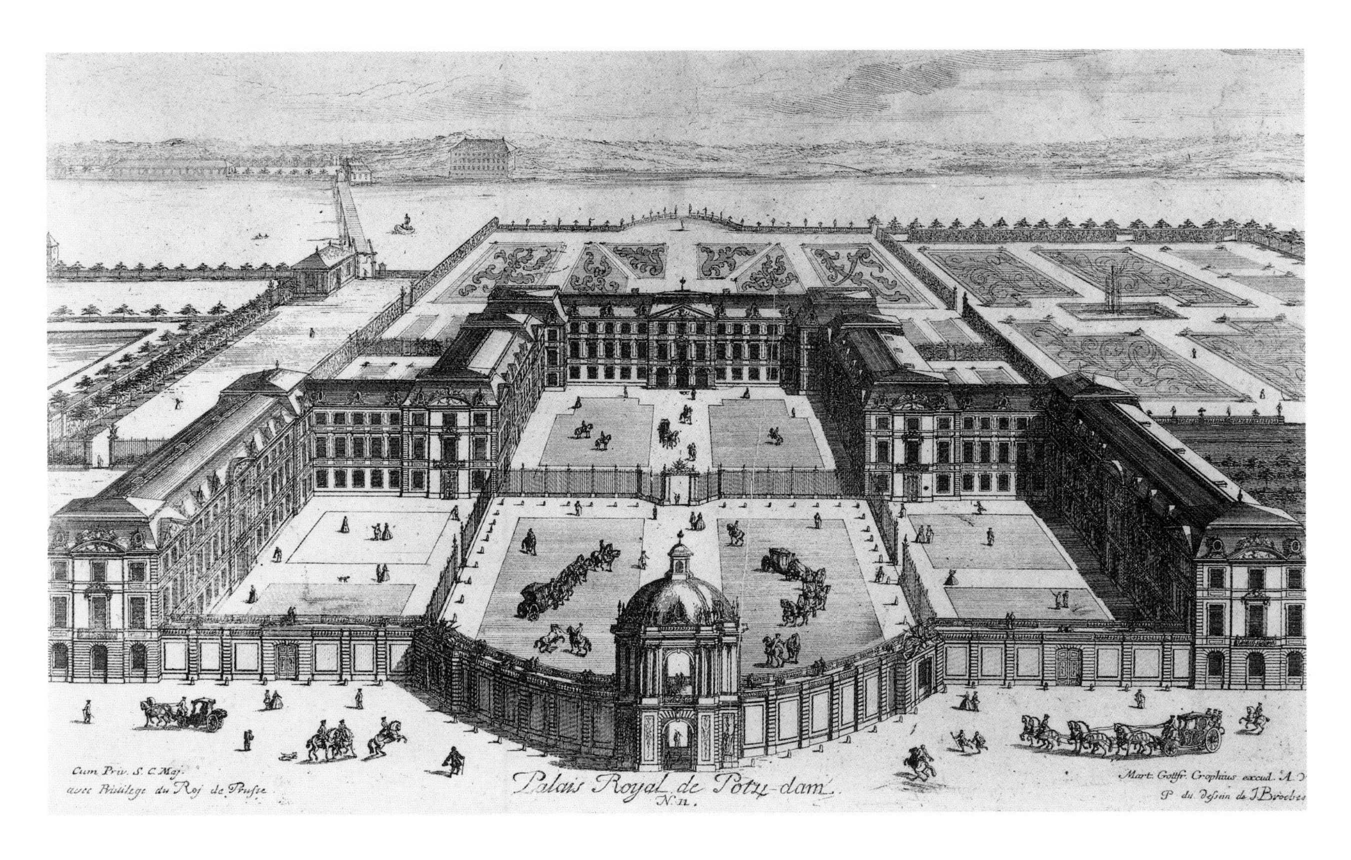

Artist's view of Potsdam Palace
Palais Royal de Potzdam
Etching by Jean Baptiste Broebes, 42 x 53 cm, in Broebes, Vues de Palais et de Maisons le roi de Prusse, *Augsburg 1733*

Michael Matthias Smids was in charge of the alterations made to the palace in 1679–1682; the plans were probably by Memhardt or Nering. The Fortuna Gate, by Jean de Bodt, was not built until 1701.

This palace complex was also reachable by water, by the river Spree. In addition, the proximity of the river was very useful for providing water for the garden planned by Sophia Charlotte. As she herself had visited many of the gardens of her day (the Hortus Palatinus at Heidelberg, a garden laid out by her grandfather, Frederick of the Palatinate; and in France Fontainebleau, St. Cloud, and Versailles), she had high ambitions for the design of her new garden (see left), especially as her mother, Sophia, had had a vast garden laid out at Herrenhausen starting in 1696. With the support of her cousin, the Duchess of Orléans, she consulted the creator of the park at Versailles, André Le Nôtre, who sent her his pupil Simeon Godeau. Godeau's plan gave the garden an orientation at right angles to the palace, and incorporated three visual axes (westwards to the citadel of Spandau, northwards to Tegel Palace, and northeastwards to Niederschönhausen Palace). He also wanted the garden to extend further northwestwards beyond the Spree. But because of the Spree, a layout with a lengthwise orientation was adopted; however, the visual axes were included as planned. From the palace a broad central path led through *parterres de broderie* to a pond that flowed into a canal leading to the Spree. On the axis of the jet of the fountain on the parterre, Godeau created an artificial island in the Spree, on which he placed an obelisk as a focal point.

In front of the garden façade there was a terrace, separated from the garden by a wall with flower borders, a central staircase, and with side ramps. This area was ornamented with sandstone statues, vases, and orange trees in tubs. On the western side, the enfilade inside the palace was continued into the garden by pergolas (*berceaux de treillage*) running parallel to the planned and executed orangeries.

The conversion of Potsdam into a royal palace

Between 1690 and 1694, following the death in 1689 of his stepmother, the Electress Sophia Dorothea, Frederick bought back the palace and district of Potsdam from his stepbrothers and stepsisters, to whom the Great Elector had bequeathed them in his will of 1686. From now on, Frederick began to plan alterations, which were to continue until his death in 1713. Despite the building works, he often chose to stay at Potsdam.

Frederick now wanted to give this essentially Dutch-style building, like his mother's palace at Oranienburg, a more modern character, which at this time meant a French character (see above). After Nering's death in 1695, the managing of building works was taken over first by Martin Grünberg, but then from December 4, 1700, by the Frenchman Jean de Bodt, who had come to Berlin in 1698. The old wing separating the two courtyards was pulled down in order to create a larger *cour d'honneur*, fronted by a portal with a dome, topped by a statue of Fortuna. This gateway by de Bodt faced towards the town, and its creation is to be viewed in the context of Frederick's coronation in 1701. As in Berlin, after his coronation Frederick made a ceremonial entry into his palaces at Oranienburg, Köpenick, and Potsdam.

The dainty and delicate design of the walls of the gate with their plain surfaces, in combination with harmonious proportions and sculptural decoration, are evidence of de Bodt's French sense of form, which was favored by the king. Frederick II evidently still saw this gateway as a visible manifestation of royal status, for he forbade Knobelsdorff to alter it.

On the main wing of the palace the towers (belvederes) placed on the roof in the Dutch manner were removed, and the windows were enlarged and made more ornate (with ear-shaped ornamentation, as at Caputh), to give the palace a "French look." But probably the most effective features were the raised stucco decorations by Andreas Schlüter, which are thought to have been executed as early as 1694, and which Frederick II respectfully retained when having the palace decorated anew by Knobelsdorff. Between 1705 and 1706, Schlüter was responsible for directing the building works alongside de Bodt. Groups of allegorical figures, placed at cornice level and above the central doorway, were intended to glorify the Great Elector.

Thrift and severity: Frederick William I (1713–1740)

In the years before his accession, Frederick William I had already lived in the west wing of the town palace at Potsdam. His rooms (anteroom, living room, and bedroom) were different even then from his parents' magnificent rooms. As king, too, he continued to have plain white walls, decorated only with portraits of his officers or pictures he had painted himself, and simple furniture. In the corridors hung portraits of his "Tall

Palace at Königs Wusterhausen
Historic photograph

This palace, a 16th-century building, was adapted to be a royal hunting lodge by Frederick William I in 1717–1718. He had lived here before his accession, and later Königs Wusterhausen continued to be one of the places where he most enjoyed staying.

Potsdam, Jägertor (Hunter's Gate)

This is Potsdam's oldest surviving gateway; an inscription bears the date of 1733. It was built in the course of the second phase of expanding the town. The square pillars with their pilasters and the rusticated bands going round them support an architrave with a hunting scene framed by hunting trophies. The buildings attached to each side were demolished in 1907.

Fellows," his personal guards. Frederick William I had inherited a kingdom, but the territory was widely scattered and had few economic resources. He intended that the army should demonstrate power and strength to the outside world and underpin his planned reform of the state administration. He cut down on every aspect of court life, and dismissed many artists in order to save money and restore his country's finances, which were in a desperate state. He discontinued the upkeep of many of the palaces and gardens, and retained for his use only a few of his father's numerous palaces. Yet he was not actually hostile to art (he was even a painter himself) but on the whole he wanted art to serve specific purposes, for instance to enhance the standing of the monarchy. Thus he commissioned Andreas Schlüter to make the magnificent tomb for his father, King Frederick I (in the cathedral in Berlin). But the pleasure garden, which had only just been modernized, probably by Simeon Godeau, was leveled in 1714 to provide a drill ground, and the orangery was used as stables. The palace was no longer the venue for court celebrations on special occasions, but became the permanent residence of the king, who had come to regard himself as a citizen of Potsdam.

A second royal seat is created: the expansion of Potsdam

On July 3, 1713, the king had marched into Potsdam with more than 600 of his tall Red Grenadiers from Königs Wusterhausen (see opposite). He needed quarters for the soldiers, and each household in Potsdam was expected to take in two or three grenadiers. Whereas his grandfather had wanted to turn Potsdam into a paradise, Frederick William I wanted it to be the permanent home of his guardsmen, in other words a garrison town, and this was to determine the town's structure and appearance for the next two hundred years.

However, the capacity of the available houses was limited, and the town's inhabitants were soon unable to meet the demand. Tax concessions and the offer of free houses for new citizens started a great influx of people to Potsdam, and it soon became essential to enlarge the town. In 1722, Frederick William I gave instructions to this effect.

Only 11 years later, in 1733, the second phase of expansion began. The new land that was added to the town on each occasion was enclosed by a wall, in order to prevent soldiers from deserting (see page 110, bottom). The soldiers' accommodation was

Potsdam, Dutch houses in Mittelstrasse

Jan Boumann built the Dutch quarter in 1737–1740 with the help of the fortifications engineers Pierre de Gayette and Andreas Berger. A small range of variations in the design gives the façades of the houses a rhythm that subtly enlivens their appearance.

governed by strict regulations, which had to be observed when new houses were built. The rooms intended for the soldiers had to be the "regulation size" – in other words, big enough to accommodate four soldiers and their spinning-wheels (each soldier was expected to spin wool). This regulation size room (20.5 square meters: 208 square feet) was next to the front door, which was in the middle of the house-front. For the sake of symmetry, not for functional reasons, there was a room of the same size on the opposite side of the central passage.

In order to create a large amount of accommodation as quickly and cheaply as possible, only timber-framed houses were built at first. These were grouped around the Neuer Markt (New Market), reaching as far as Charlottenstrasse. Pierre de Gayette had been placed in charge of the building of this first new district. But Frederick William I also attached importance to "embellishing the town."

Although the frontages of these terraced houses were very simple and austere, some decorative motifs (shells, palmettes, and acanthus leaves) were used sparingly, but in such a way as to allow for considerable variation. The availability of a choice of decorative motifs, however modest, shows that the strictly prescribed design did leave scope for some individuality. A few years later, under Frederick II, such individual expression would no longer be possible.

The second phase in the expansion of the town (1733–1740), which was actually a further northward extension of the first, encompassed the area from Charlottenstrasse to Kurfürstenstrasse and from the Brandenburg Gate to the square by the "Bassin" (see right). Here, heavy stuccoed façades, painted yellow and articulated by four white pilaster strips, were the norm.

The two-story houses, generally with five axes, varied chiefly in the dormer windows (topped by a rounded or triangular pediment) above the main entrance on those houses that stood with their eaves fronting the street (see opposite). What is particularly interesting is the rhythmic increase in the number of individual features towards the middle of a row: this, and the fact that the opposite side of the street was deigned in corresponding fashion, were typically Baroque features.

Thus, for instance, in Nauener Strasse (now Friedrich-Ebert Strasse), the number of window axes to each house shows the sequence 5-7-9-7-5. In the Dutch quarter, a rhythm was created by the alternation of gable-end and eave fronts, or by having houses of corresponding dimensions on opposite sides of the street, for instance in Mittelstrasse nos. 14–22 and 23–31.

Frederick William I had encountered the Dutch manner of building in brick on his educational visits in 1700 and 1704–1705. On his visit to Amsterdam in 1732 the king was so impressed by the neat appearance of the house-fronts – he placed an extremely high value on clarity, simplicity, and cleanliness – and by the expertise of Dutch engineers in building on marshy terrain, that he hired Dutch builders to build a district in their native style.

The first house in the "Dutch style," which contemporaries also called "the big Dutch house," was built 1733–1737 for the commander of his bodyguard. His Stern Hunting Lodge, on the former Chase, had just been completed (1730–1732; see page 112), and he deliberately chose to build the first town house in his preferred style for the commanding officer of his "Tall Fellows." The years from 1734 to 1736 saw the building of the first experimental houses in

Opposite
Potsdam, Dutch house in Mittelstrasse

This house, with its gable end towards the street, is typical of the style of building in this district. The curve of the gable ends on each side with volutes, which adjoin those of the neighboring houses.

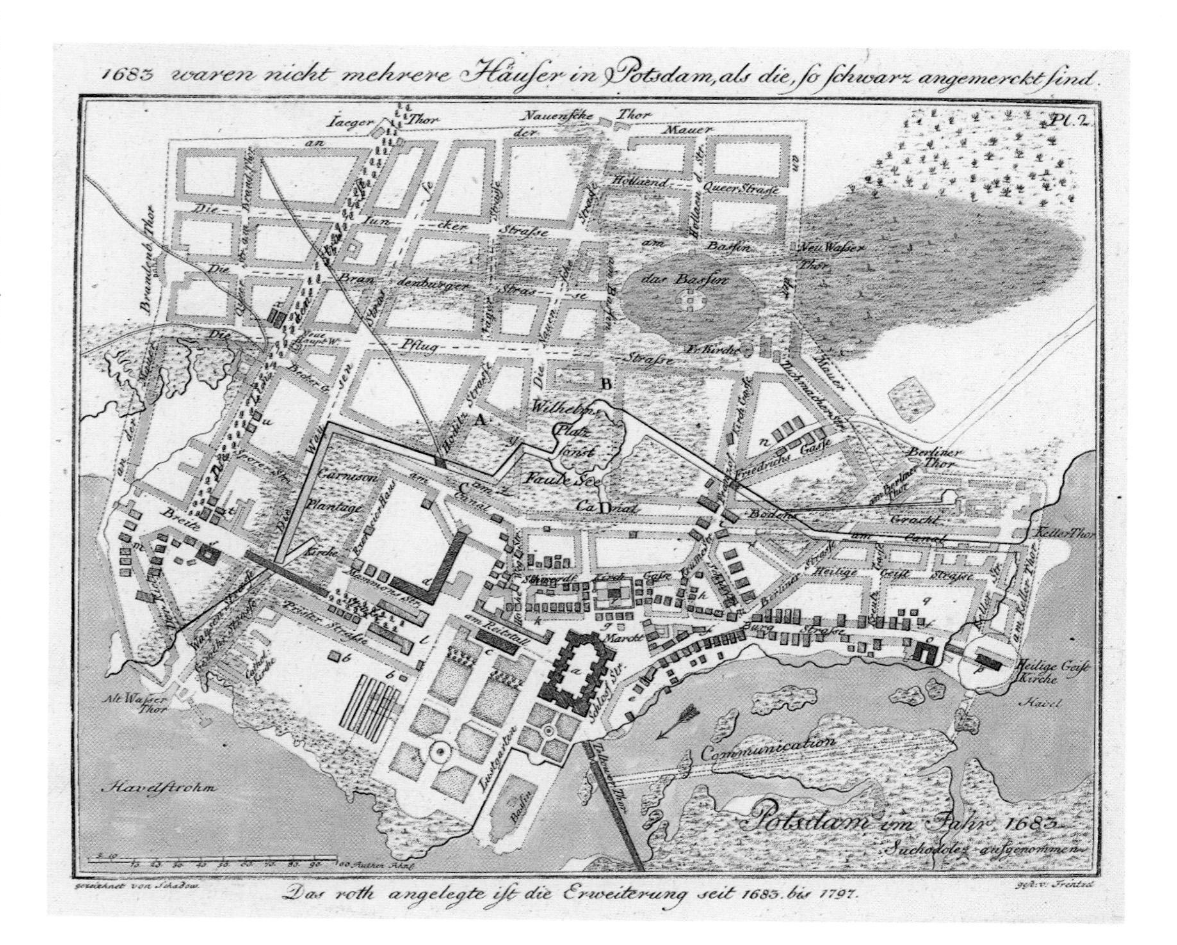

Town plan of Potsdam showing the expansions of the town up to 1797
Drawing by Samuel von Suchodelez (1683), with additions by Friedrich Gottlieb Schadow, engraving by G J F Frentzel, 18.4 x 22.5 cm

Potsdam was designated a garrison town by King Frederick William I. In order to have sufficient quarters for the soldiers, the town had to be enlarged. The first phase of expansion around the Neumarkt took place 1722 onwards, and the second began in 1733, while the Dutch quarter was built from 1737 onwards.

Potsdam, Stern Hunting Lodge

This lodge is in what used to be the Parforceheide (Chase). It was built 1730–1732 for King Frederick William I, who was an enthusiastic hunter. The largest room is the main hall with wood-paneled walls painted a yellowish color. The sash windows show Dutch influence.

the north of the town, on the area of land that was to be the Dutch quarter, and from 1737 building proceeded systematically, with 134 houses forming four squares (see page 110, top left). The Holländische Querstrasse (now Mittelstrasse) ran parallel to the main streets of the second extension of the town, Junkerstrasse (now Gutenbergstrasse), Brandenburger Strasse, and Charlottenstrasse.

The Holländische Strasse (later Kreuzstrasse, now Benkertstrasse) cut across what is now Mittelstrasse at right angles. It ran from the northern city wall (built from 1733 onwards) southwards to a marshy area that was later filled with water to form the "Bassin," or Pond (1737). At the center of this artificial lake, at the crossing of the present-day Benkertstrasse and Brandenburger Strasse, an artificial island was created, on which Jan Boumann built a pavilion as a focal point in 1739 (see opposite, bottom). This small square summerhouse, with its strongly curved roof culminating in a sort of lantern with a weather-vane, could be reached by a ferry. In 1825 the lake was filled in, and in 1925 the Gloriette, the little pavilion, was also destroyed.

Landmarks for the town: church building under Frederick William I

Only one medieval church, Katharinenkirche, stood on the Alter Markt (Old Market Place), and in 1721 the king ordered it to be demolished because it was in a dilapidated state. It was probably Philipp Gerlach who built the new church, dedicated to St. Nicholas, between 1721 and 1724. The ground plan of the church was in the shape of a Greek cross, like the Garnisonkirche (Garrison Church) in Berlin built by Grünberg in 1701–1703. Centralized designs were much favored in both the theory and practice of Protestant church building, since the church was primarily intended to be a place for preaching. An early Dutch example is the Norderkerk in Amsterdam, built 1620–1623.

It was chiefly the tower of this new church, the Nikolaikirche, that made its mark on the appearance of the town of Potsdam. The position of the tower did not actually accord with the principle of the centrally focused design, as it was built above the northern arm of the church and so created a T shape in the interior. The entrance was on the south side,

Potsdam, Grosse Stadtschule, 17 Friedrich-Ebert-Strasse

Built, probably by Pierre de Gayette, in 1738–1739. King Frederick William I had a school built for every parish. This elegant but simple building, the Grosse Stadtschule (The Great School), housed a grammar school.

Potsdam, the Gloriette on the "Bassin"

Colored engraving by Johann Friedrich Nagel (c. 1790)

Potsdam, Stiftung Preussische Schlösser und Gärten Berlin-Brandenburg, Plankammer

Jan Boumann built this small summerhouse in 1739 on an island in the artificial lake, the "Bassin," that had been created 1737–1739 in connection with the draining of the land. In 1825, the lake was filled in, and in 1945 the Gloriette was destroyed.

opposite the Fortuna Gateway. The church burned down in 1795. Under the reorganization of the parish in 1722, the island in the Havel – where up to the 12th century a Slavic castle had stood, and where the Great Elector had had built an administrative building with a wine cellar and grain store – was made a district of the town and was given a permanent link with the land. It was here, in 1726, that Pierre de Gayette started work on the building of the Heiliggeistkirche (Church of the Holy Spirit), which was completed in 1728 with the tower by Johann Friedrich Grael. The church was severely damaged in World War II; the ruin was demolished in 1960, and the remains of the tower in 1974.

As early as 1720, Frederick William I had a new church built for his garrison on the former "Kurfürstliche Freiheit" (electoral land) between the "Kiez" (the old fishing settlement) and the town. Like the other buildings, it was a timber-framed structure, but it was given a carillon, brought from Amsterdam, which was accommodated in the roof-space. Since it also served as the court church, Frederick William I allowed the French community to have the palace chapel. The garrison church collapsed after only ten years, in 1730, and had to be demolished. Philipp Gerlach now designed a new church that fully matched up to European standards of Baroque church architecture. The tower (1732–1735) was built on the long side of a transverse rectangular nave opposite the pulpit, the altar, and the crypt, which was to become Frederick William's burial place (see below). The tower has often been compared with Schlüter's designs for the Mint Tower. But Gerlach's tower grew from the bottom upwards and the division between stories did not detract from this upward thrust, especially as the stories became progressively narrower. After its destruction in World War II, what was left of the tower remained standing until 1969, when the church was demolished. In 1729, Friedrich Grael had designed for Frederick William I a similar tower for the new church outside the Spandau Gate in Berlin (see opposite). The foundation stone for this church had been laid by Queen Sophia Louise who was the third wife of Frederick I, on June 11, 1712, and the church, which was later called the Sophienkirche after her, was consecrated only a year later, on June 18, 1713. The tower, added 1732–1734, stands on the end of the nave as though on a massive fluted pedestal. Above a pediment two stories rise up, united by pilasters. Above these, Ionic columns placed across the corners give the two tapering stories containing the bells an extraordinarily delicate appearance. On top of the copper cupola, with its bold curves and obelisk-like point, was a Prussian eagle.

In his tower for the Potsdam garrison church, Johann Philipp Gerlach was even more successful in creating a unified composition. He avoided abrupt transitions, opened up only the topmost story as a section for the bells, and capped the whole tower with a convex dome. Now three towers almost 90 meters (about 295 feet) high stood out against the Potsdam skyline. Standing almost in a straight line,

Left
Berlin, the Parochialkirche (Parochial Church), by Philipp Gerlach
Engraving by C. H. Horst, 41.2 x 25.6 cm

For Berlin's Calvinist church, Nering had wanted to combine a centralized space in the style of the early Italian Renaissance with a tower on the model of Roman High Baroque. Jean de Bodt then designed a tower to be placed in front of the church, to house the carillon that had originally been intended for the Mint Tower.

Opposite
Berlin, Sophienkirche (tower by Johann Friedrich Wilhelm Grael, 1729–1735)

As far back as 1712, the third wife of King Frederick I, Sophia Louise, after whom the church was named, had laid the foundation stone. It was only under Frederick William I that the tower was built by Johann Friedrich Wilhelm Grael.

Hof und Garnisonkirche (Court and Garrison Church)
Historical photograph

The church was consecrated in 1732, but the building of the tower dragged on until 1735. With the tower of the Garnisonkirche, Johann Philipp Gerlach created the western, dominant accent in the town's skyline.

Berlin-Buch, Schlosskirche (Palace Church)

This church was built in 1731–1736 by Friedrich Wilhelm Diterichs for the government minister A. O. von Viereck. Above a centralized space was an octagonal drum to support the tower, which was destroyed during World War II. The design of the façade and the well-shaped main body of the church undeniably owe something to Schlüter's buildings.

they clearly marked the extent of the town. It was town-planning considerations that led to their being built, for the actual houses of worship were, in accordance with Calvinist beliefs, of very simple design. The artistic embellishment of the towers began above the roofline of the houses, in order to enhance the existing silhouette of the town. The placing of the tower of the Nikolaikirche was predetermined by the previous church on the site. But in the case of the Garnisonkirche, Gerlach was able to plan for a particular effect. The church was not to disturb the visual axis, created by the Great Elector, to the Ehrenpfortenberg (the hill with the gateway of honor), but the tower could be placed slightly in front of the church, thus creating a visual link with the *corps de logis* of the town palace. The side aspects of the two buildings were in line with each other, while their main aspects were turned towards other specific areas in the layout of the town.

In Berlin, a church building had been started even before 1700 that had significance beyond the boundaries of Brandenburg. In 1694, Elector Frederick III had commissioned Nering to prepare a design for a parish church for the Calvinist community. The reason for his great interest in this building was that only the princely house and a small community were Calvinists. For this reason, Elector Frederick III arranged for the laying of the foundation stone on August 15, 1695, to be marked by a particularly splendid ceremony.

For his design, Nering chose a form of centrally designed space, the tetraconch, since a room built around a center suited the style of worship of the Calvinists, in which the sermon is at the heart of the service. The interior was similar to designs for sacred buildings drawn in the Renaissance by Leonardo da Vinci and Bramante. The church of Santa Maria della Consolazione at Todi (built from 1508 onwards), which Nering may have seen during his visit to Italy in 1677, has the same layout. The architect Johann Jacob Küchel, who in 1737 was rather critical of the Berlin churches, describing them as "of no very great worth," praised the Parochialkirche (Parochial Church), the main church of the Calvinist district, as having "an interior of incomparable beauty." Since the parish was constantly short of money, in 1696, just after Nering's death in the previous year, Elector Frederick III approved a second plan by Martin Grünberg that reduced the dimensions envisaged in Nering's plan. In 1698, the roof vaulting caved in, but the building work was continued, to Grünberg's design, because Frederick wanted the dedication of the church to take place on the second anniversary of his coronation, January 18, 1703; in the event, however, it could not take place until July 8 of that year.

Very shortly before his death, in February 1713, he instructed Jean de Bodt to produce a design for a tower to hold the carillon that had been intended for the Mint Tower. For the top section of the tower, de Bodt took over the design first made for the cathedral project that had been favored by the king but had come to nothing. The more austere version carried out by Philipp Gerlach under the new king was still based on de Bodt's design and was completed in about 1714 (see page 114, top). As with the other towers, one can recognize the influence of the towers, designed by Francesco Borromini, of the church of Santa Agnese on the Piazza Navona in Rome. The concave curves of the façade also derive from Borromini, so that High Baroque motifs mask a Renaissance-style interior. The Parochialkirche is thus the earliest church in Brandenburg to have been built on the Italian model. Since Jean de Bodt's designs for the cathedral were never realized, this church was the first to have a dome above a centralized interior space. From the 1730s onwards, centrally designed buildings with domes became characteristic of church architecture in Berlin. The Böhmische Kirche (Bohemian Church, 1735–1737), the Dreifaltigkeitskirche (Church of the Holy Trinity), the cathedral by Jan Boumann (from 1750 onwards), Stüler's palace chapel (1845), and also Raschdorff's new cathedral (begun 1905), each had a dome (see opposite).

For his own use, Frederick William I built only the small Dutch-looking Stern Hunting Lodge; otherwise he merely remodeled palaces, such as Königs Wusterhausen, or bought them from his landed aristocracy, as in the case of Kossenblatt (see below). His real significance as a promoter of building was that through the churches he built, and particularly their towers, he gave a highly visible shape and order to his towns.

Kossenblatt Palace

This palace was built 1699–1712 on an island in the Spree for Field-Marshal Johann Albrecht von Barfuss. In 1736, King Frederick William I bought it from his widow, with the intention of staying there to hunt, paint, and cure his gout. It is rare for country palaces in the March of Brandenburg to have three wings, and in addition, the delicate rustication gives the building a very elegant appearance.

SCULPTURE

Sepp-Gustav Gröschel

Gottfried Christian Leygebe
Equestrian statuette of the Great Elector Frederick William (1680)
Iron, height with base 27.7 cm; Berlin, Staatliche Museen zu Berlin – Preussischer Kulturbesitz, Skulpturengalerie (on loan to the Kunstgewerbemuseum)

This sculpture, which shows great technical virtuosity and was a showpiece of the elector's art collection, represents the Great Elector in classical-style armor as St George. Shown on horseback, he is defeating the dragon, which is modeled on the Chimera of classical antiquity, and he thus embodies those virtues that defeat evil.

When dealing with the subject of Baroque sculpture in Brandenburg-Prussia, one immediately thinks of the greatest architect-sculptor of that period in northern Germany, Andreas Schlüter, known as the "Michelangelo of the North," whose works represent a high point of formal technique and artistic invention. One would hardly expect this in a country whose economic resources were limited and whose cultural achievement rested to a very considerable degree on the contribution of immigrants or of artists and craftsmen temporarily hired from abroad. In this area, sculpture was no exception. In Protestant Brandenburg-Prussia, ecclesiastical institutions made virtually no contribution as independent patrons of the arts, nor was the aristocracy in a position to set standards of taste. The rise, flowering, and then decline of Baroque sculptural art were thus almost entirely determined by the patronage of the country's rulers.

The Rise of Sculpture: Frederick William, the Great Elector

After the Thirty Years' War, the Great Elector succeeded in stabilizing his country both politically and economically, and within the context of this policy he also promoted the arts. As a result of his education in Leyden, he saw the Netherlands as the model to follow in the arts as well as in other areas.

At Leyden University, a center of classical studies, the Great Elector's interest in classical times had been awakened. Objects from antiquity were among the first he collected in order to replace the art collection that had been lost in the war, and he preferred classical motifs and styles even when the subject-matter was Christian.

A characteristic example is the statuette group, made of iron, representing the Great Elector as St. George slaying the dragon (see left), executed between 1678 and 1680 by Gottfried Christian Leygebe. On a galloping horse the figure of the elector, wearing classical-style armor and holding a spear in his raised right hand, tramples the monster, which, with its lion, goat, and snake heads, is intended to recall the Chimera of antiquity that raged in Lycia and was slain by the hero Bellerophon.

Earlier, in 1672, Leygebe had made a statuette, now lost, of the Great Elector as Bellerophon on the winged horse Pegasus, fighting the Chimera: so the two statuettes had the same theme, namely the victorious battle fought against evil by the ruler as the heroic champion of virtue, in the one case in the form of the Christian knight, though wearing the garb of antiquity, and in the other case as a classical demigod.

In 1671, Leygebe created a portrait of the 51-year-old ruler, a bronze relief showing a life-size bust of the elector in profile, which was held to be a particularly good likeness (see opposite page). It was intended for the Marble Hall of the palace in Potsdam.

The ruler's features are represented almost hyper-realistically, and yet the setting, the laurel wreath framing the oval relief, the semi-naked bust with an antique-style cloak and the wreath tied with a bow, is so much in the style of classical antiquity that the portrait itself reminds one of the portraits on classical coins and of Baroque series of portraits of Roman emperors. There is no mistaking the intended resemblance between this portrait of the Great Elector

François Dieussart
Portrait of the Great Elector Frederick William (1651)
Marble, height 190 cm; Potsdam, Stiftung Preussische Schlösser und Gärten Berlin-Brandenburg, Skulpturensammlung

and those of the Roman emperors, and hence his claim to be their successor.

Alongside works in iron and bronze, precious metals and amber, the elector's art collection included a particularly large number of contemporary works in ivory. In 1648, the Great Elector succeeded in attaching one of the most renowned miniature sculptors of the day, the southern German Leonhard Kern, to the Brandenburg court for a year. Kern may well have created works for the court at Berlin in later years too. He preferred biblical, especially Old Testament subjects, as in the signed ivory group of Adam and Eve (see page 120, right). Because of a certain facial resemblance between Adam and the Great Elector, and also the numerous allegorical elements referring to married life – for instance the dog (faithfulness), the tortoise (domestic propriety), the plantain (fruitfulness), and the water-lily leaf (mourning turning to joy) – it is generally thought that this work is to be understood as an allegory on the elector's marriage to Louise Henrietta of Orange in 1646. Adam's stiff, even hesitant posture is in deliberate contrast to Eve's lively movement as she tries to tempt her husband into eating the apple.

The Great Elector had a strong feeling for his works of art, and Joachim von Sandrart records that the Elector "did not neglect to gladden his heroic

Gottfried Christian Leygebe
Portrait of the Great Elector Frederick William (1671)
Bronze relief, height 72 cm; Potsdam, Stiftung Preussische Schlösser und Gärten Berlin-Brandenburg, Skulpturensammlung

This image in profile is thought to be a faithful portrait of the Great Elector at the age of 51. Through the use of the bust format, the antique-style cloak fastened with a clasp, the laurel wreath with the bow at the back of the neck, and the Roman-style profile, the artist has succeeded in placing this portrait in the tradition of classical portraits on coins and medallions.

spirit with this virtuous pleasure." Particularly suited to this purpose was the ivory group of Hercules fighting the Hydra of Lerna and the Nemean lion (see below, left), executed by Christoph Maucher, very probably in 1682.

Maucher specialized in ivory and amber work, and preferred classical and historical themes. His depiction of Hercules fighting both monsters at once, and moreover not in the traditional order – his Hercules first kills the Hydra and then throttles the lion – is unique in Baroque art and has no model in antiquity. Formally, too, this small group, with its finely nuanced treatment of the surface and its expressive plasticity, is of uncommonly high quality.

Hercules, the virtuous hero of antiquity, whose labors freed the world from evil, was the model of the ruler in the Baroque period, so that in contemporary eulogies both the Great Elector and Frederick III (I) are likened to Hercules. For works intended directly to express the dignity of himself and his family, the Great Elector preferred sculptors from the Low Countries, like the Walloon François Dieussart, who was probably in the elector's service from about 1647 to 1655. Unlike the pronounced realism of an artist such as Leygebe, Dieussart's observation in his portraits is exact, objective, but restrained.

This is also true of the seated statue made in 1648, when the elector and his family still lived mainly at Cleves, of the elector's first son, Prince William Henry of Brandenburg, at the age of seven months (see opposite page, bottom); he was to die in 1649 aged 17 months. The chubby baby with his rounded cheeks is shown, despite his tender age, sitting with great dignity on an animal skin, holding in his right hand the electoral hat as a sign of his status and resting his left on a cornucopia, a sign of the welfare and prosperity that he is expected to bring; among the things tumbling out of it is a medallion bearing the likeness of his parents.

Below left
Christoph Maucher
Hercules Defeating the Nemean Lion and the Hydra of Lerna (probably 1682)
Ivory, height 28 cm; Berlin, Staatliche Museen zu Berlin – Preussischer Kulturbesitz, Skulpturengalerie (on loan to the Kunstgewerbemuseum)

Hercules, the greatest hero of antiquity, who as a paragon of strength and virtue was the model for rulers in the Baroque period, is here, contrary to classical tradition, overcoming two monsters simultaneously, the Hydra of Lerna and the Nemean lion, whose head he has in a stranglehold. For its formal qualities, this group attributed to Maucher is rightly regarded as one of the outstanding achievements of late Baroque ivory work.

Far right
Leonhard Kern
Adam and Eve (c. 1646)
Ivory, height 23 cm; Staatliche Museen zu Berlin – Preussischer Kulturbesitz, Skulpturengalerie (on loan to the Kunstgewerbemuseum)

This work, fashioned with immense skill from the upper end of an elephant's tusk, is thought by most experts to allude in biblical-allegorical terms to the marriage of the Great Elector and his first wife Louise Henrietta of Orange in 1646. It was probably a gift from the Great Elector to his bride.

Right
Bartholomäus Eggers
Portrait of the Elector Joachim II of Brandenburg (1685–1687)
Marble, height 204 cm; Potsdam, Stiftung Preussische Schlösser und Gärten Berlin-Brandenburg, Skulpturensammlung

This over-life-size statue is one of a series of 11 statues of electors of Brandenburg from Elector Frederick I to the Great Elector Frederick William. The Great Elector had ordered them to be made for his great hall in the Berlin Palace, the Alabaster Room created in 1685. The figure, with its static, almost classical stance, clothed in knightly armor and an ermine cloak, does not attempt actual portraiture.

François Dieussart
Portrait of Prince William Henry of Brandenburg (1648)
Marble, height 49.5 cm; Potsdam, Stiftung Preussische Schlösser und Gärten Berlin-Brandenburg, Skulpturensammlung

This image of the Great Elector's eldest son, Prince William Henry, is a characteristic example of the realistic portraiture practiced by sculptors of the Dutch school. According to the inscription on the cornucopia, the prince is seven months old.

In 1651–1652 Dieussart was commissioned by the Electress to make an over-life-size portrait-statue of her husband, the first of its kind in Berlin (see page 119). The sculpture of Frederick William in contemporary dress formerly stood on a tall pedestal, adorned with putti and dolphins, in a pond in the Berlin pleasure garden. A sculpture in modern dress was an exception in this garden, which was created in the years following 1645, since its design, under the controlling influence of Johann Gregor Memhardt, was wholly in the spirit of antiquity, following mythological models and descriptions by classical authors. It therefore featured 47 statues of gods and heroes of antiquity, as well as putti representing the signs of the zodiac, the seasons, and the five senses. They also included copies of ancient statues of the Apollo Belvedere and the Diana of Versailles. The garden at Berlin was thus in the tradition of the classically inspired gardens of the Italian Renaissance. But the statue of the Elector, too, shows classical influence: the stance, body posture, and position of the arms recall the statue of the Ares Borghese, which in the 17th century was thought to be a portrait of Alexander the Great. Thus the Great Elector in his contemporary armor is in effect admitted, as an Alexander of his time, to the company of the heroes of antiquity.

In 1685, the Great Elector commissioned from the Dutch sculptor Bartholomäus Eggers portraits of his ten predecessors in the office of elector as well as of himself, to adorn the so-called Alabaster Hall, the room for official celebrations and receptions which had been completed that year (see page 80). The statues of the electors were to document the dynastic continuity of the house of Hohenzollern. The sculptures were delivered and set up in 1686 and 1687, but this speed was achieved at the expense of intellectual content, though the portrait of the Great Elector himself forms an exception. The statue bearing the name Joachimus II on its base (see left) may be seen as a typical example of the series. In a frontal pose, with no additional ornamentation, the statue of Joachim (which gives the impression of wanting to occupy a large space) in knightly armor and with an ermine-lined cloak acting as a background foil, is in a static, contrapostal pose, extending the right hand as though speaking. This representation, conservative for its time and following a classical type of figure, makes no attempt at actual portraiture.

A third major Dutch sculptor worked in Berlin also – Artus Quellinus the Elder, who between 1660 and 1664-1665 created for the Great Elector's field marshal, Otto Christoph Freiherr (Baron) von Sparr, the splendid tomb monument, with its many figures, which is in the choir of the Marienkirche in Berlin. This work too shows both down-to-earth realism in its portraiture and a certain classicistic use of types.

The age of the Great Elector proved to be a highly productive period in both small- and large-scale sculpture. Frederick William was an acclaimed patron of sculpture as of other arts, and in 1679 Joachim von Sandrart dedicated to him Volume II of his work *Teutschen Academie der Edlen Bau-, Bild-, und Mahlerey-Künste* (German Academy of the Noble Arts of Architecture, Sculpture, and Painting). The factors that determined his choice of artists and works were his piety, a determination to assert his status, his love of classical antiquity, and his special affinity with the art and culture of the Netherlands.

The Flowering: Elector Frederick III/ King Frederick I

At his accession in 1688, Elector Frederick III was able to build upon what his father had achieved. Some among his own positive political achievements were that he overturned his father's will, thereby preserving the unity of the state, and that in 1701 at Königsberg he crowned himself king of Prussia, taking the name Frederick I. From the economic point of view he brought his country almost to financial ruin, but his reign saw a tremendous cultural flowering that showed itself in the founding of cultural institutions like the Academy of Arts (1696), where Andreas Schlüter was dean of the department of sculpture and then director from 1702 to 1704.

Gabriel de Grupello
Portrait of the Elector Frederick III (1692)
Marble, height 202 cm; Stiftung Preussische Schlösser und Gärten Berlin-Brandenburg, Skulpturensammlung

This statue is without any of the usual allegorical attributes, its objective portraiture placing it in the Dutch tradition of artists like Dieussart. A more modern aspect is the elaborate treatment of the armor and clothing, which are intended to convey princely magnificence and contribute to the monumental appearance of the statue. The holes in the head are from a metal wreath which the statue, set up at Oranienburg, wore on the occasion of Frederick's coronation in 1701.

Opposite
Andreas Schlüter
Equestrian statue of the Great Elector Frederick William (1696–1700; the slave figures completed by 1708)
Bronze on a marble base, height of the statue 290 cm, or with base 560 cm; Berlin, court of honor, Schloss Charlottenburg

The equestrian statue of the Great Elector, in classical-style armor and with somewhat idealized facial features, which stood on the Lange Brücke (Long Bridge) from 1703 until the end of World War II, faced towards the Berlin Palace. With his right hand outstretched, he greeted his subjects as they stepped on to the bridge from the Berlin side. This statue, which combines the assertion of absolute power with consummate artistry, is considered to be the most significant equestrian statue of northern European Baroque. The figures of slaves, which were part of Schlüter's first design and were carried out by his workshop, were placed on the base in 1709.

At the court of Frederick III (I), who himself spoke fluent Latin, classical antiquity played an even greater role than it had under his father, thanks to his advisers such as the diplomat and numismatist Ezechiel von Spanheim and the antiquary Lorenz Beger, chief curator of the court art collection and author of the monumental three-volume catalogue of it, *Thesaurus Brandenburgicus selectus*. Classical art was by no means simply an abstract field of research: artists took it as their model, imitated it, and aspired to surpass it. From contemporary panegyric writing about the ruler, we know that Berlin was to be made into a new Rome, and it was in the reign of King Frederick I that for the first time it was also called the "Athens on the Spree." Because of his strong wish, under the influence of Louis XIV, to be glorified by art, and the aspiration to be king which he had probably already conceived at the time of his accession as elector, the arts were promoted on an unprecedented scale.

Frederick III (I) retained contact with the artists who had been engaged by his father. Thus Christoph Maucher of Danzig delivered two amber reliefs with classical motifs that are still in the Berlin sculpture collection; and in 1688 Eggers was commissioned to complete the decoration of the Alabaster Hall with a portrait statue of Frederick III (I) and figures representing Caesar, Constantine, Charlemagne, and Rudolph of Habsburg, to be ready by 1689. The 12 statues of electors were then placed along the long sides of the room, and the statues of emperors placed against the end walls. Through the inclusion of medieval and classical emperors in the series of statues, the dynasty's claim to rulership was derived from the Middle Ages and, going further back still, from ancient times.

However, the elector also attracted new artists to his court. Consequently, as early as 1688 he brought from Sweden the medallion-maker, wax modeler, ivory carver, and goldsmith Raimund Faltz, who had previously worked in Paris for Louis XIV and in Sweden for Charles XI. Faltz is considered "probably the most significant of the medallion-makers working in Germany around 1700" (C. Theuerkauff). He made many medallions in elegant classical style celebrating the expansion of Berlin and the new buildings commissioned in Berlin by Frederick III. The prize medal of the Academy of Arts engraved in 1700 bears on its reverse a depiction of Hercules with the apples of the Hesperides beneath the legend "Virtuti praemia ponit," an allegory of Frederick III (I) and his liberality towards the arts. As well as pictures on wax executed in extremely fine relief, Faltz also produced ivory statuettes in the antique style, as well as a series of medallions worked in relief bearing bust portraits of members of the house of Hohenzollern.

The important Dutch sculptor Chevalier Gabriel de Grupello evidently also worked for Frederick from 1690 to 1695. In his statue of him (see left) he rather conservatively follows Dieussart in the stance and the down-to-earth portraiture. On the other hand, he tries to give the figure a degree of monumentality by means of the elaborate clothing; the old-fashioned armor is probably meant to suggest knightly virtues. Executed at Cleves around 1692, the statue was only erected in 1701 and at Oranienburg, not Berlin, since it depicted Frederick as an elector and so was no longer up to date after his coronation as king.

In 1694 a man was established as court sculptor in Berlin who "in just two decades transformed the electoral and then royal seat into an artistic metropolis which was for a time of European rank" (J. Rasmussen). This was Andreas Schlüter of Danzig. He had been trained in Danzig, where the arts were very much subject to Dutch influence, and then worked from 1681 to 1694 in Poland, mainly in Warsaw. After returning from his travels – probably to France and then to Italy, where he obtained plaster casts of antiques for the Academy of Arts – Schlüter worked tirelessly as an architect and sculptor in

Berlin from 1696 until his dismissal as court sculptor in 1713, when he left for St. Petersburg.

Schlüter's sculptural work included not only free-standing sculptures such as the monuments to the Great Elector or Frederick III (I), or reliefs like those on the tombs of members of the royal house, but also all the architectural sculpture, both internal and external, on the buildings for which he was responsible as architect. This included the ornamentation in stucco and wood, and even the subjects of the wall and ceiling paintings, for instance in the Berlin Palace. His position required not only the genius of the artist designing and executing the *bozzetti*, but also an outstanding organizational talent to coordinate the many projects taking place in parallel, and to oversee and, where necessary, correct the individual artists and craftsmen (from the sculptor and stucco artist to the carpenter and bricklayer); it also required the desire to put across his own ideas. This immense task could not have been performed without a drawing office of his own and a well-functioning workshop. Furthermore, Schlüter was not simply an inspired creative artist drawing upon his own imagination and feelings, but, as was the ideal at that time, very much an intelligent artist fully aware of international developments. He was not only a teacher at the Academy of Arts, where he based his teaching on the art of antiquity, but was also a member of the Academy of Sciences. He had a considerable library, and made an intensive study of the scientific problems of mechanics. For all his individuality, his outstanding knowledge of the art of classical antiquity as well as of the works of the French and especially the Italian masters, notably Michelangelo, Bernini, Pietro Algardi, and Pietro da Cortona, exerted an influence over his style, which went as far as quotation and direct borrowing. Schlüter's work is one of the outstanding examples anywhere in Europe of classically inspired art of the Baroque period.

The best known of those works by Schlüter of which the originals have survived is undoubtedly the equestrian statue of the Great Elector Frederick William (see page 123), which was created as a plaster model in 1697 but was cast, by the "court and artillery founder" Johann Jacobi, in a single cast using the lost wax technique, only three years later, in 1700. In the eyes of contemporaries, the masterly technical feat of the casting appeared more spectacular than the work itself. In 1703 the statue was ceremonially unveiled on the Lange Brücke (Long Bridge), incidentally as a substitute for an equestrian statue of Frederick III (I), which had originally been planned for that position. This bridge, linking Berlin and Cölln and built between 1692 and 1694, was intended, with its statuary, to rival the Ponte Sant'Angelo in Rome, and the monument itself was to rival the source of its inspiration, the equestrian statue of Marcus Aurelius on the Capitol in Rome. In formal terms, though, the statue owes more to the equestrian statue of Louis XIV by François Girardon, or to that of Alessandro Farnese by Francesco Mocchi in Piacenza. The four slaves on the base were already part of the plan of 1696 and Andreas Schlüter made the *bozzetti* for them. They were executed by members of his workshop, Friedrich Gottlieb Herfert, Johann Samuel Nahl, Cornelius Heintzy, and Johann Hermann Backert, and added to the base afterwards, the last of them in 1709. The statue is regarded as an expression of "absolutist self-assertion" made "with consummate artistry" (E. Fründt).

Schlüter's second important bronze statue, the portrait of Elector Frederick III (see above), which was designed in 1697 and cast by Jacobi in 1698, was intended for the inner courtyard of the Zeughaus (Arsenal). Schlüter has Frederick III not standing, as in the portrait statues by Eggers and Grupello, but in a walking pose like the Apollo Belvedere, his head turned forward, wearing classical-style armor with his clothing and cloak swaying as he strides ahead, his feet on a shield: an embodiment of strength as both a ruler and a warrior. This, the most elegantly conceived of all the portraits of Frederick as a ruler, fell from favor after his coronation as king in 1701 because of its electoral insignia. It was not until more than a century later in 1802 that the statue found its permanent place, at Königsberg.

The tomb of Queen Sophia Charlotte (see page 125), made in 1705 of gilded tin, is intended to be viewed from the left, which suggests that it was expected to stand alongside a future tomb for Frederick I. It rests on the Queen's armorial beasts,

Andreas Schlüter
Portrait of the Elector Frederick III of Brandenburg (1697–1698)
Bronze, height 213 cm; (lost, photograph dates from 1913), secondary casts survive

This work, intended for the Berlin Zeughaus (Arsenal) is artistically the most important portrait statue of Frederick III. Wearing antique-style armor and a long cloak, he strides forward confidently: this movement is intended to express his dynamism as a ruler and a warrior, and is influenced by the ancient Greek statue, the Apollo Belvedere. Because of its emblems of electoral rank, the statue was no longer appropriate after the coronation in 1701 and therefore only found a permanent place at Königsberg in 1802.

Andreas Schlüter
Tomb of Queen Sophia Charlotte (1705)
Gilt tin; Berlin Cathedral,
Hohenzollern crypt

This tomb, created in collaboration with the metal-caster Johann Jacobi, has at the head end a medallion with a portrait of the Queen, supported by two female spirits. Death, sitting in front of the tomb, is inscribing the Queen's name in the book of eternity. The theme of the contrast between the young women and majestic Death has been brilliantly executed by the artists, making this an outstandingly successful work.

Prussian eagles and Hanoverian half-horses. At the head end a female guardian spirit holds a medallion with the portrait of the deceased; on the other side a second, still supporting the medallion, has fallen asleep. The conception of the work leads from the idea of Sleep, the brother of Death, to Death himself, who, sitting before the tomb majestically clothed in a voluminous cloak, is inscribing the Queen's name in the book of eternity. In what must be one of the greatest Baroque works on this subject, Death is here represented not as a demon who robs people of life but as a governor of destiny.

Among Schlüter's earliest Berlin works are the reliefs created between 1696 and 1699 on the keystones of the portals and windows on the ground floor and upper story of the external and courtyard façades of the Arsenal, of which he was the director of works from late March 1698 to autumn 1699. It was Schlüter who made the designs and *bozzetti* for the sculptures, which were executed in stone by his workshop under the direction of Georg Gottfried Weyhenmeyer. On the outside there are 73 richly ornamented Baroque ceremonial helmets and on the north front cartouches with two heads of Medusa and a coat of arms with two winged female spirits of death. In the courtyard, the keystones of the ground floor windows bear 22 cartouches with severed heads of warriors (see page 126), mostly in groups of three. The expressive and exact way in which Schlüter reproduces the suffering of young and old,

Andreas Schlüter
Masks of dying warriors (1696)
Sandstone, keystones of window arches; Berlin Zeughaus (Arsenal), ground floor of inner courtyard

The 22 masks of slain warriors in the inner courtyard of the Arsenal are among the most moving of Schlüter's works. Although, as trophies of victory in the wars against the Turks, they are part of the triumphal symbolism of the Arsenal, their forceful expressiveness makes them appear to us today as a protest against war. The terracotta models for the masks, which were then executed in stone by his workshop, were among Schlüter's earliest works in Berlin.

"barbaric" and "classical" warriors in death, and the extraordinarily high quality of the work, have raised the question of whether Schlüter was here trying to portray the negative side of war, as a warning. But for Schlüter's contemporaries, these severed heads, like the helmets on the outside, were considered "trophies of victory." Of the *bozzetti* of the warriors' heads, a few 19th-century plaster casts have survived, having subsequently been used for teaching purposes in the Academy of Arts.

From 1698 onwards, the most outstanding artists in Brandenburg-Prussia were all brought together to work on the alterations and new building at the Berlin Palace. Schlüter worked here, as a sculptor but chiefly as an architect, at least from the time of his appointment as Director of Palace Building on November 2, 1699, until his dismissal on January 28, 1707, following the Mint Tower affair (see page 100). According to his model of the palace, made probably in the winter of 1698–1699, the roof balustrade of the outer façades was to be adorned with figures alternating with vases and trophies. Only five figures have survived; of these, two naked male figures represent Spring and Autumn, and a female one Philosophy, while the other two remain unidentified. The figures of Spring and Autumn are by Balthasar Permoser and were therefore placed on the garden front; only the other three figures can probably be attributed to Schlüter's workshop.

The inner courtyard of the palace, also known as the Schlüter courtyard, represents a particularly successful combination of architecture and architectural sculpture. The sculptures fall into two phases. The first phase, from 1698 to 1701, produced the eight female statues, allegories of the virtues of a ruler, and the reliefs of the first four Roman kings (Romulus, Numa, Tullus, and Ancus) on the shorter sides (see right). The second phase, probably from 1703 to 1706, saw the creation of the eight statues of the projecting section that contained the spiral staircase on the eastern side of the courtyard, allegories of Prussia and of Peace, and two groups of three consisting of Apollo, Jupiter, and probably Mars, and Meleager, Hercules, and Hermes. The pictorial program of the courtyard is supposed to glorify the newly won monarchy of Prussia, to celebrate the kings of Rome as predecessors and models, to extol the virtues of leadership and to praise the monarch (represented by the images of Jupiter and Hercules) on the one hand as a patron of culture (Apollo) and as a warlord (Mars), and on the other hand as a promoter of commerce and animal husbandry (Hermes) and a leader of the hunt (Meleager) – all in all, as the protector of the kingdom and guarantor of peace. Here the influence of antiquity is especially strong: thus, for instance, the portraits of the kings are based on what were, or were thought to be, coins of the Roman Republic, while one of the Virtues is an imitation of the Flora Farnese and another is modeled on the St. Susanna by François Duquesnoy (see below, figures on the far right and far left).

Schlüter's sculptural work for the interior of the palace was no less extensive, especially in the state rooms and the Queen's apartments on the third floor; in Giovanni Simonetti of Tessin Schlüter had an artist of comparable stature to himself to carry out the sculptures in stucco. Of particular note from Schlüter's early phase, 1698 to 1699, are the Atlantes seated beneath half-arches on the end walls of the Elizabeth Room, which is the main room on the Palace Square side (see opposite). These are modeled entirely on the figures of slaves which were painted by Michelangelo on the ceiling of the Sistine Chapel in the Vatican. Their most notable characteristics are their powerful build and the extremely antithetical, almost awkward movements of the body, arms, and legs.

Architectural sculpture reached the highest point of its development in 1711–1712, in the roof statues on the central section of the villa, now destroyed, of the president of the court treasury, Ernst Bogislav von Kamecke. The statues on the street and garden fronts continue upwards the line of the pilasters articulating the building. There were four pairs of statues, of which Apollo and Daphne in particular (see pages 128 and 129), show Schlüter's style reaching a new level of achievement – this can be seen clearly in their slender figures, which seem almost to float upwards as if borne by the wind, their fluttering hair, and the strong lines of the folds in their garments.

Two special instances among Schlüter's works in Berlin are the family tomb he created in 1700 for the court goldsmith Daniel Männlich (who died in 1701) in the Nicolaikirche (his only known work

for an ordinary citizen of Berlin), and the pulpit of the Marienkirche, executed in 1702–1703, his only religious work in Berlin. The monument (see page 130) actually takes the form of the ornate entrance to the family vault, with the funeral urn resting on the architrave. Concealing the urn, and backed by some drapery held by guardian spirits, is a medallion with a double portrait of Männlich and his wife, executed in the style of a cameo. Behind it lurks Death, who is snatching a child, a scene that is observed by a horrified young man. In contrast to the portrayal of Death on the tomb of Queen Sophia Charlotte, Death here is a sinister, aggressive demon who robs people of life. Schlüter formed the death's head in an expressive way in order to convey the horror of death, while giving the portraits classically serene expressions, thereby seeking to convey the idea of eternal remembrance of the dead.

To instal the pulpit (see page 130), which as an aside he partly paid for himself, in the Gothic Marienkirche, Schlüter had to cut off one of the pillars of the central nave at a height of 6.5 meters (21 feet) and underpin the upper section with four Ionic columns each topped by a sandstone slab. The canopy is attached to this slab and the body of the pulpit to the columns by iron clamps, but it is supposed to appear to the observer as though the angels beside the pulpit were carrying it supported on consoles. The canopy is richly decorated with a Heaven populated by cherubs, at the sides of which one can see the tablets with the Ten Commandments and the open book of the Gospel of St. John, while the three reliefs on the faces of the pulpit – in the middle John the Baptist with the Lamb of God (John 1, v29), at the sides the personifications of Faith and of Charity – are probably meant to represent the three Christian virtues of faith, hope, and charity. Even if this work was influenced by Bernini, the manner of representation here is strangely restrained, especially if one compares the angels with the far more lively figures of Fame or Victory at the Berlin Palace.

One of the sculptors who played an essential role in the artistic flowering of Berlin was Balthasar Permoser, who from 1689 onwards had been court sculptor at the Saxon court, where he created the so-called Zwinger style. Like Schlüter, he too was strongly influenced by classical antiquity and by Italian sculpture. While working in Berlin between 1698 and 1708, he is said to have had some part in the interior decoration of the Berlin Palace, for instance in the Drap d'Or room, one of the state rooms, but especially in the work on the garden front, where the herms on Portals IV (see page 131) and V, dating from the years 1706 to 1708, are attributed to him. While the slightly earlier herms of Portal V representing Spring and Summer are still very much influenced by Schlüter, the herms of Autumn and Winter on Portal IV, on the wing of the palace already built by Johann Friedrich

Opposite, right
Andreas Schlüter
Allegories of the virtues of a ruler and portraits of the Roman kings Romulus and Numa (1698 to 1701)
Sandstone; Berlin, Schloss, projecting bay of Portal V in the Schlüterhof (destroyed, photograph taken in 1943), reliefs in Märkisches Museum, Berlin

This sculptural decoration ranks among Schlüter's most important designs that express a political program. The statues, reliefs, and architectural decoration all have the purpose of glorifying Frederick's new status, gained in 1701, of Prussian king. The reliefs with depictions of Roman kings point to the Roman monarchy as the forerunner and model of that of Prussia, while the female figures represent the virtues of a ruler. The statues and reliefs date from the second phase of alterations made to the courtyard up to 1701; the second figure from left is a 19th-century replacement.

Andreas Schlüter
Atlantes supporting architectural arches (1698–1699)
Stucco; Berlin, Schloss, Elisabethsaal, east wall (destroyed, photograph taken in 1943)

The Atlantes, in the style of Michelangelo, on the end walls of the Elizabeth Room in the Palace Square wing, are among Schlüter's earliest sculptural designs for the interior architecture of the Berlin Palace. Executed by the stucco artist Giovanni Simonetti, these demigods, a young and an old one in alternation, sitting apparently unattached to the wall on pillar imposts, support the semicircular tympana above the doors and the fireplace alcove.

17 12
FREI HAUS
2
Droschken I. Cl

Eosander, called von Göthe, are clearly independent works by Permoser.

Three sculptors from the colony of French artists in Brandenburg-Prussia deserve to be mentioned: Guillaume Hulot, Charles Claude Dubut, and René Charpentier, who all came to Berlin after 1700. Jean de Bodt, architect in charge of the Arsenal from 1699 onwards, had engaged Hulot from Paris for the sculptural work on that building. The quantity of work undertaken by Hulot and his workshop was considerable: he was responsible for the 12 large groups of figures and 44 trophies on the roof balustrade, the reliefs on the pediments and on the main portal, the four allegorical figures representing engineering, geometry, arithmetic, and pyrotechnics, as well as the medallion, cast by Jacobi, with the bust portrait of Frederick (see pages 94 and 95). When this portrait was set in place in 1706, the building was regarded as complete. Other works of Hulot's included a large number of oval reliefs on mythological themes, in a style of polished classicism, in the destroyed Berlin Palace and in the Charlottenburg Palace. Charpentier and Dubut worked under Eosander in the Berlin Palace, notably in the picture gallery. Charpentier created the architectural sculpture in the court of honor of the now destroyed town palace in Potsdam.

Contemporary panegyric literature celebrated King Frederick I as the creator of a new Rome, and indeed placed him above the Roman rulers, since it had taken them centuries to build Rome while he, on his own, had attained his goal in Berlin in only a few years. There can certainly be no doubt that there was an extraordinary flowering of the arts and especially of sculpture during his reign, mainly thanks to the work of Andreas Schlüter. Schlüter's genius produced such a powerful effect that less gifted sculptors also created great works under his direction. However, the artistic endeavors placed a great strain on the limited financial resources of the state; this, and the fact that this blossoming depended so heavily on a single individual, were bound to lead to a decline when he was no longer there.

The Decline: Frederick William I

Frederick William's first action as a ruler was to take gold medallions from the art collection to be melted down. In 1726 he gave away the greater part of the antique collection, and in 1715 he made the pleasure garden, laid out by his grandfather, the Great Elector, as a garden of classical sculpture, into a drill and parade ground; most of the statues that had stood there have been lost as a result. Unlike his father and grandfather, he cannot therefore be credited with a special love of classical antiquity.

Upon his accession in 1713 he dismissed most of the sculptors, or halved their salaries. Anyone with any self-respect as a sculptor left Berlin: Schlüter in that same year, Dubut in 1716, and Hulot in 1720. Hardly any new free-standing statues were made; instead, the existing ones were recycled. Thus in 1728 Eggers's statues of electors and emperors were removed from the Alabaster Hall and set up in the newly created White Hall. For the visit by August II the Strong of Poland in 1728, Schlüter's standing figure of Frederick III was erected on the Molkenmarkt in Berlin, with plaster figures of slaves on the base; these were not replaced by bronze figures until 1733. In 1739, the statue was removed again, apparently with the intention of setting it up it on Unter den Linden, but because of the king's death on May 31, 1740, this never happened.

Andreas Schlüter
Apollo and Daphne (1711–1712)
Sandstone, roof statues on the street façade of the Villa Kamecke, Dorotheenstrasse, Berlin-Mitte (photograph c. 1925); Staatliche Museen zu Berlin – Preussischer Kulturbesitz, Skulpturengalerie

The central section of the Villa Kamecke, now destroyed, was crowned by roof statues at both the front and the back (see opposite). These represented four pairs of classical gods and demi-goddesses, including (above) Apollo with Daphne. The slender figures with their lively movement and lightness mark a new stylistic phase in Schlüter's work.

Above
Andreas Schlüter
Family tomb of the court goldsmith Daniel Männlich (1700)
Marble, gilded stucco relief; Berlin, Nikolaikirche (pre-war appearance, photograph taken in 1919)

The Männlich family tomb is Schlüter's only known sculptural work carried out for an ordinary citizen of Berlin. Above the entrance to the crypt is the funeral urn. Concealing it, and backed by drapery, is the medallion with the portraits of the deceased couple in gilded stucco. The figure of Death stretched out behind the urn is snatching a small child, watched with horror by a young man. The scene symbolizes the baneful power of Death.

Andreas Schlüter
Pulpit (1702–1703)
(Original position, photograph 1919)
Marble, sandstone, oak; Berlin, Marienkirche

In order to erect the pulpit, Schlüter cut off the base of the pillar 6.5 meters (21 feet) from the ground, replacing it with four columns of sandstone topped by a slab. To this construction he attached the canopy with its Heaven populated by cherubs, and the body of the pulpit with reliefs depicting Charity, Faith, and St. John the Baptist. To the observer the two angels standing at the sides appear to be supporting the pulpit.

Among the few monuments erected during his reign, we can mention the statue at Rathenow of Frederick William, the Great Elector. This had been designed by Bartholomé Damart, appointed court sculptor in 1716, but was then executed between 1736 and 1738 by Johann Georg Glume – a pupil of Andreas Schlüter's who was court sculptor from 1713 to 1736, and additionally the father of a more gifted son. It is decidedly the work of imitators. The statue itself is a reworking, as a mirror image, of Schlüter's portrait of Elector Frederick III; at the corners of the base, with its two steps, sit four figures of slaves which are rather unsuccessful copies of the slaves on the base of the equestrian statue of the Great

Balthasar Permoser
Herms of Autumn and Winter
(1706–1708)
Sandstone reliefs from Portal IV (built on the former Staatsratsgebäude, Schlossplatz); Berlin, Schloss

Permoser's sculptural forms, with their multiplicity of small components, are in marked contrast to Schlüter's sculpture.

Elector. Frederick William I was at that time making a genuine effort to restore the economy of his country and, alongside this, build up its military strength; culture, therefore, had to take second place to this ambition. This attitude had a devastating effect on sculpture, and the consequence was that Schlüter had no direct successors.

PAINTING

Gerd Bartoschek

In the field of painting, as in sculpture, architecture, and the decorative arts, the reign of the Great Elector represents a new beginning. Reflecting a situation where the distribution of political power was leading towards the absolutist state, the development of painting took place largely within the court's sphere of influence, or was directly dependent on it. After the Thirty Years' War, the middle classes in the towns, who had grown in influence in the 15th and early 16th centuries, played only a minor role in the cultivation of the arts, while the aristocracy was defined more and more by its closeness to the electoral court.

Nor was art able to develop independently in the ambience of the Church, for the state was now Protestant. Michael Conrad Hirt was the only painter of any significance who chose to work in the field of religious art. Through the influence of Heinrich Bollandt, who was both his teacher and his father-in-law, his painting was rooted in the art of Cranach the Elder and Younger, who continued to exert a dominant influence in central Germany right into the 17th century, not least because of the superbly organized production of paintings by their workshop. Their influence also extended to the Franconian territories of Ansbach and Bayreuth, the margraves of which were members of the Hohenzollern family, and this was Bollandt's and Hirt's native region. Bollandt may have come to Berlin in 1631 to paint a portrait of the Swedish king Gustavus Adolphus (at Grunewald Hunting Lodge, Berlin). Hirt worked for some years in Lübeck, where the patrician and middle classes were the main patrons of art, before being appointed court painter in Berlin in 1645. There and at Frankfurt an der Oder and at Stendal he produced memorial paintings with biblical subjects for churches. He also painted portraits of members of the clergy, outstanding among which is a portrait of the musical director of the Nikolaikirche (St. Nicholas Church) in Berlin, Johannes Krüger, painted in 1663. In this work, meticulously executed, Hirt's finely nuanced handling of light achieves the intensity of one of Rembrandt's portraits of scholars. He was the first artist whom the Great Elector had taken into his service, but he appears to have received very few commissions from him, as his art was clearly not suited to promoting a ruler's ambition.

A picture painted immediately after the end of the Thirty Years' War by Mathias Czwiczek does have a programmatic character of this kind. In an allegorical scene with numerous figures, it represents the alliance, underpinned by dynastic links, between the electoral house of Brandenburg and other rulers who supported Calvinist doctrine (see opposite). A religious refugee from Bohemia, he had become the court artist of Elector George William, the Great Elector's father, in 1628. He then made a study tour of England, France, and Holland lasting several years, but the merely additive composition of this small-scale allegorical picture shows that he gained only limited benefit from this tour. In his life-size portraits of the elector's family, his artistic weaknesses are even more evident. Czwiczek spent the rest of his life at Königsberg, which had become the main electoral seat during the Thirty Years' War, but afterwards had to cede this function to Berlin once again.

In 1646, the Great Elector married Louise Henrietta of Orange, after which the couple spent long periods in the elector's territories adjacent to the Netherlands, especially Cleves, and he used this opportunity to make systematic attempts to attract Dutch artists to Brandenburg. However, the artists with the most outstanding talent were not prepared to spend years in a country both ravaged and depopulated by war in order to provide the basis upon which an indigenous flowering of the arts could take place. Several painters – such as the highly regarded Govert Flinck, a pupil of Rembrandt, who was born in Cleves and was now working in Amsterdam – accepted commissions from the elector but carried out the work in their own studios. Others came to Berlin, but only for short periods. The most significant of these was undoubtedly Jan Lievens, who shared a workshop with Rembrandt in Leyden and who, after visits to England and Antwerp, modeled his style on that of Antony van Dyck. In 1653 and 1654, Lievens painted pictures in Berlin to be placed above the fireplaces of Oranienburg Palace, which was then in the process of being built (see page 135). At the same time, Adam Pynacker supplied, from Lenzen on the Elbe, where he was a guest of Gysel van Lier, a Dutch admiral in the service of the elector, a large landscape in the Italian style which

also found a prominent place above a fireplace at Oranienburg (now in the Gemäldegalerie, Berlin). As well as Gysel van Lier, Prince John Maurice of Nassau-Siegen also probably played a mediating role.

The use of paintings to decorate rooms in the electoral palaces was often directly influenced by models that the Great Elector knew from his stays in the Netherlands. Foremost among these were the residences of the stadholder's family, the splendor of which reached its highest level in the Orange Hall of the Huis ten Bosch near The Hague. The Great Elector's mother-in-law, Amalia of Solms, had had this room decorated with allegorical historical paintings, making it into a temple glorifying both her late husband, the stadholder Frederick Henry, who had died in 1647, and also the House of Orange. Jan Lievens was among the many artists engaged for this work. In 1649 Gerard van Honthorst, who had attached himself to Caravaggio in Rome and after his return from Italy had become one of the most prominent members of the Utrecht school of painting, created an allegory on the marriage of the Great Elector for the Orange Hall. He never traveled to Berlin. But already in 1647, almost as his representative, his younger brother and pupil Willem van Honthorst accepted the elector's offer of a post as court painter. The importance of the tasks to be undertaken by the artist was reflected in the generous remuneration of this position: 1,000 thalers, equivalent to a year's salary for a privy councilor. The most significant of Honthorst's works still in existence today, a picture executed in 1660 as a ceiling painting for the audience room in Oranienburg Palace, is an allegory on the re-founding of the town of Oranienburg, with portraits of the elector and his wife in the roles of the Trojan hero Aeneas and of Queen Dido, who, according to legend, founded Carthage (Kreismuseum, Oranienburg).

Mathias Czwiczek
Glorification of the Dowager Electress Elizabeth Charlotte of Brandenburg as the Queen of Sheba (c. 1649)
Oil on wood, 33 x 44.5 cm; Berlin, Stiftung Preussische Schlösser und Gärten, Berlin-Brandenburg, Charlottenburg Palace

The Electress is surrounded by rich material possessions and by her family, led by her son, the Great Elector, his wife Louise Henrietta, and Prince William Henry, who died at a young age. A panel in the background shows deceased relatives lined up in a similarly old-fashioned cumulative manner.

Willem van Honthorst
Margrave Christian Ernst of Brandenburg-Bayreuth (1657)
Oil on wood; Plassenburg ob Kulmbach

This portrait of the Margrave, who was born in 1644 and succeeded to the title at the age of only 11, is characterized by a simple, Dutch-influenced style that aimed to convey the sitter's personality. The blackened armor and the dark background help to focus attention on the youthful face.

Willem van Honthorst also produced a large number of portraits, some of them for other patrons, such as the Dohna and Lynar families, who had close links with the electoral court. These were standardized pictures in the rather unambitious format of bust portraits (see above). Their simplicity indicates that court society at that time had not yet developed a strong desire for ostentatious display. To Honthorst we may also attribute a series of knee-length portraits of Brandenburg military commanders that the Great Elector kept in the palace at Potsdam. The immediate model for the series, of which only the portrait of Field-Marshal Sparr survives (in private ownership), was clearly a series of portraits of officers which Jan Antonisz. van Ravesteyn had painted between 1611 and 1624, probably for the Dutch stadholder Maurice of Orange.

It is not known whether Willem van Honthorst also did some of the painting of the Great Hall at Oranienburg, which lost its function as a result of the remodeling of the palace around 1700 and was finally destroyed by a fire in the 19th century. Unlike the allegory of the founding of Oranienburg, which was painted as though on an easel and was not intended to be viewed from below, the vaulted ceiling of this hall included, as well as personifications of the four seasons, portrait-like figures positioned behind a trompe l'oeil representation of a roof balustrade.

It is hard to think of an artist living in Berlin during the lifetime of the Electress Louise Henrietta who would have been capable of carrying out such a difficult and complex task. A possible candidate might be Michael Willmann, the greatest German painter of the 17th century. He was born, a Brandenburg subject, at Königsberg, and after studying in Amsterdam and Antwerp, where he became familiar with the painting of Rembrandt and Rubens, he worked at the electoral court in Berlin for a short time around 1657. However, not one work of this period can be attributed to him with certainty. In 1660, he went to Silesia and there placed himself at the service of the Catholic Counter-Reformation. It has rightly been observed that his painting, impassioned and filled with inner ecstasy, lay outside the limits of artistic appreciation in Berlin at that time. Later, however, though from a distance, Willmann painted an impressive allegorical picture paying tribute to the Elector's achievement in the cultural development of his country (Charlottenburg Palace, Berlin). Some letters contain evidence that the Venetian painter Pietro Liberi applied, also in 1657, for an appointment in Berlin. He was to decorate a room with Old Testament scenes. However, there was some delay in concluding the agreement, and nothing came of the commission. It therefore remains an open question whether this cosmopolitan artist, whose works continue and develop the tradition of the great Venetian painters of the 16th century, might have steered the development of painting in Brandenburg-Prussia in a different direction.

Also at a relatively early date, in 1652, the landscape painter Johannes Ruischer, who may be counted among the circle of artists around Rembrandt and who was influenced by Hercules Seghers, was appointed court painter. It is difficult to gather much information about this artist, and apart from a painting of the town of Brandenburg (Brandenburg Museum) and two drawings – one of which shows the village of Trampe near Eberswalde, the property of Field-Marshal Sparr (Kupferstichkabinett, Berlin) – the only work painted in Berlin that can be attributed to him is his view of the Berlin Palace, which is remarkable for its monumental dimensions (see page 64). He possibly also painted a series of landscapes for a coffered ceiling in the palace at Königsberg. Isolated from the vigorous artistic life of

Right
Jan Lievens
Mars and Venus (1653)
Oil on canvas, 146 x 136 cm; Berlin, Stiftung Preussische Schlösser und Gärten Berlin-Brandenburg, Jagdschloss Grunewald

Despite its obvious eroticism, this painting has a serious message. Venus submits to Mars, the god of war, so that Cupid may take his weapons from him. Lievens, who shared a studio with Rembrandt at Leyden, was thus painting an allegory of peace for Oranienburg Palace, where the picture originally hung and where, after the Thirty Years' War, the Electress Louise Henrietta worked in exemplary fashion to create prosperity for the nation.

Above
Nicolaus Wieling
Venus and Adonis (c. 1670)
Canvas, diameter 83.5 cm; Caputh, Stiftung Preussische Schlösser und Gärten Berlin-Brandenburg, Schloss Caputh

Disregarding all the goddess's warnings, Adonis goes hunting and is killed by a wild boar. In his portrayal of the farewell scene, designed like a relief, the painter, who was much admired by the Great Elector, adopts the classical ideal of beauty, which was known above all through sculpture, and which academic doctrine had established as the only acceptable model.

Gedeon Romandon
Queen Mary II of England (1690)
Oil on canvas, 121 x 98 cm; Berlin, Stiftung Preussische Schlösser und Gärten Berlin-Brandenburg, Schloss Charlottenburg

Together with his father Abraham, Gedeon Romandon introduced to Berlin in 1686 the style of Baroque portrait of a ruler that at the court of Versailles had reached the highest degree of grandiloquence. In 1690 he was sent to London to paint the reigning queen, Mary II, who was married to King William III of Orange, and her sister Anne.

Opposite
Ottmar Elliger the Elder
Garland of Flowers and Fruit with the portrait of the Electress Dorothea of Brandenburg (c. 1670–1675)
Oil on canvas, 140 x 114 cm; Caputh, Stiftung Preussische Schlösser und Gärten Berlin-Brandenburg, Schloss Caputh

A still-life painting of flowers in its own right is a rarity in the 17th-century art of Brandenburg, though sometimes portraits are framed by flowers and fruit. It is possible that the small portrait of the Electress was not painted by Elliger himself. The luxuriant garland, which was painted by him, symbolizes the continuing flourishing of the dynasty thanks to the Great Elector's second marriage.

his homeland, Ruischer could not sustain his artistic momentum for long. He finally worked for the court of the Elector of Saxony at Dresden.

To supply works designed in a further genre, in 1661 the Elector engaged Frans de Hamilton, a painter of animal and still-life pictures, who was probably a Scot and was trained in Holland. The only painting that survives from his Berlin period is distinguished by its reproduction of objects with such exactness that they actually appear real (see page 138). Here, as in Ruischer's view of Berlin, the artist's main concern is faithfully to record what is before him.

The year 1666 seems to have given the Great Elector a new impetus to deploy the arts in the cause of glorifying his power. At this time he was at Cleves again, negotiating the peace agreement between the Dutch States-General and the Prince-Bishop of Münster, an achievement that brought him great prestige and numerous honors. He commissioned from Theodor van Thulden, a pupil of Rubens, two gigantic allegorical paintings celebrating his political successes (destroyed by fire in the Potsdam Palace in 1945). At the same time, Jan Mytens and Pieter Nason, two portrait painters favored by the court of the stadholder at The Hague, created life-size paintings of the elector's family (in New Palace, Sanssouci, Potsdam), which reflect the influence of the great Fleming, Antony van Dyck, and his style of portraiture designed to convey the dignity of his princely sitters.

In 1667, the historical painter Nicolaus Wieling from The Hague, took over the position of court painter in Berlin, which had been left vacant by Willem van Honthorst. His too was not an outstanding talent, although in his *Teutschen Akademie* (German Academy) Joachim von Sandrart praised him as a successor to van Dyck. In his many-figured compositions, highly prized by the Great Elector (Wieling was given a rise in salary after two years), one is struck above all by his close adherence to the rules of composition laid down by academic doctrine, of which Paris was by now the center. In Wieling's works, which soon fell into oblivion after his death, a French element for the first time becomes perceptible in the art of Berlin (see page 135). In 1772, Jacques Vaillant was appointed alongside him, a painter with a far more forceful artistic temperament, reflecting his Flemish origin, and one who was evidently also far more productive and better able to decorate the growing number of electoral palaces with wall and ceiling paintings. In Samuel Theodor Gericke of Spandau, he had an able pupil and colleague who was a native of the country. Although most of Vaillant's works have been destroyed, a whole cycle of rather crudely executed ceiling paintings from his workshop has survived in Köpenick Palace and bears witness to the important role of Elector Frederick III as a patron in the period before his elevation to the throne. The architect of Köpenick

for the materiality of things. It was also in 1670 that Ottmar Elliger the Elder came to Berlin. He specialized in depicting flowers and fruit, and his work catered for the increasing demand for paintings to delight the eye (see page 137). Elliger was a pupil of the famous Antwerp Jesuit father Daniel Seghers, whose decorative still-life paintings were much sought after by the Great Elector.

There are few records of the activity of the Great Elector as a collector of paintings; seen in the international context, he probably played only a very minor role. However, compared with the meager beginnings in the 16th century, he did lay the foundations, in this area too, for the splendors of later times. Without a doubt he made use of his contacts with Holland for this purpose, and he also benefited from inheritances from his Orange relatives. From 1682 onwards, his court painter Fromantiou paid visits to Holland, London, and Danzig to buy pictures on his behalf. The part of his collection of paintings that passed into the possession of his widow, the Electress Dorothea, itself comprised more than 1,200 "depictions." However, when they were valued by Fromantiou and Vaillant after her death, they were worth only just over a quarter of the value of her jewelry. But the paintings that were most valuable – and which were reproduced by Johann Gottfried Bartsch (the first court copper engraver, appointed in 1674), in a set of engravings, never completed, intended for display in a gallery – were not among these. They included such treasures as two male portraits by Titian and Palma Vecchio (Gemäldegalerie, Berlin). Finally, with the purchase of a number of drawings by Old Masters which had belonged to Matthäus Merian the Younger, who spent some

Willem Frederik van Royen
Menagerie of the Elector Frederick III (I) of Brandenburg (1697)
Oil on canvas, 232.5 x 190.5 cm; Berlin, Stiftung Preussische Schlösser und Gärten Berlin-Brandenburg, Jagdschloss Grunewald

Like the collecting of Far Eastern porcelain, the keeping of exotic animals also contributed to a ruler's prestige. The stuffed animals themselves and paintings of animals were included in art collections. Van Royen's main task as court painter was to depict zoological and also botanical curiosities faithfully.

Palace was Rutger van Langerfeld from Nijmegen, who was appointed court painter in 1678 and who produced portraits as well as architectural paintings. In this country of Brandenburg, where expertise was in short supply, versatility was an especially welcome attribute. A probable compatriot of Vaillant's was Daniel du Verdion, who in 1674 decorated the newly built shooting lodge in the Potsdam game park with landscape paintings, thus becoming a successor to Ruischer. He was not appointed a court painter until 1682. Of his work there is only a single idealized landscape bearing his signature that survives (Gemäldegalerie, Berlin), so we are hardly in a position to assess his talent. In Frans de Hamilton's genre of still-life, the Dutch painters Willem Frederik van Royen and Hendrik de Fromantiou came to Brandenburg in 1669 and 1670. The latter, in particular, stands out as having an especially acute eye

Abraham Jansz. Begeyn
The Elector Frederick III hunting by the Havel (c. 1695)
Oil on canvas, 216 x 307 cm; Berlin, Stiftung Preussische Schlösser und Gärten Berlin-Brandenburg, Jagdschloss Grunewald

At the elector's behest, this Dutch landscape and still-life painter traveled the country to capture views of the most important towns belonging to Brandenburg. This piece of open, unidentified stretch of countryside by the Havel was considered worth painting because it was the scene of a hunt led by the elector.

months in 1673 at the Great Elector's court carrying out portrait commissions, the core of the Berlin Kupferstichkabinett (Cabinet of Engravings) was established. Such collections always did more than merely give pleasure to princes and provide a visible expression of their power; additionally, they had a stimulating effect on the local cultural climate and set artistic standards.

The skillful copper engraver Samuel Blesendorf, a native of Berlin, never obtained a court appointment (see page 84). He is thought to have been the first artist in the electoral city to try his hand at miniature painting. In this genre, however, which presupposes a highly refined cultural environment, the two Swiss brothers Jean-Pierre and Amy Huaut became the leaders. They were among the first refugees to come to Berlin in 1686 following the revocation of the Edict of Nantes, and were followed by Abraham Romandon and his son Gedeon, who were both portraitists. In them, the Great Elector acquired two artists who had mastered the formulae of the Baroque official portrait, which had been perfected at the court of Louis XIV. However, their type of portraiture, in a cool, distanced style, which emphasized the social status of the sitter by means of significant gestures and attributes, only gained general acceptance under the Elector Frederick III (see page 136).

He too, from the time of his accession in 1688, used well-established Dutch artists when an accurate depiction of reality was required. Thus in 1689 he expressly renewed the appointment of van Royen, who possibly only moved at this point to Berlin (see page 138, left). Abraham Jansz. Begeyn of The Hague was engaged as early as 1688 as a painter of landscapes and hunting themes (see above); he died while making a journey through the western parts of the Elector's territory in order to record it in painting. His successor was Michiel Carree of Amsterdam, a pupil of Nicolaus Berchem. From 1698 onwards, Frederick III also had in his service a specialist in marine painting, Michiel Maddersteg, another native of Amsterdam. This painter was also an expert on shipbuilding, and built frigates and opulent pleasure yachts for the Elector. The pictures of landscapes and of animals painted by Peter Caulitz for the electoral court also had a decidedly Dutch character, although he was a Berliner who had trained in Rome.

One of the earliest important commissions given by Elector Frederick III was for the production of a series of tapestries glorifying the achievements of the Great Elector (Charlottenburg Palace, Berlin). They were made from 1690 onwards in the manufactury of the tapestry-maker Philippe Mercier, who had come to Berlin as a refugee. They were designed by the brothers Joseph Franz and Alexander Casteels from Brussels, Rutger van Langerfeld, Abraham Jansz. Begeyn, and Paul Carl Leygebe, who had been appointed court painter in 1696 and was a son of the sculptor and iron chiseler Gottfried Leygebe, an immigrant from Nürnberg (see page 140). This combining of many talents on one project was one of the ways of realizing the ambitious artistic projects that

Frans de Hamilton
Hunting Still-Life (c. 1670)
Oil on canvas, 150 x 126 cm; Berlin, Stiftung Preussische Schlösser und Gärten Berlin-Brandenburg, Jagdschloss Grunewald

Aiming at a trompe l'oeil effect, Hamilton depicted hunting implements hanging from a painted wooden wall, among them a cage with a decoy bird and a hunting pouch bearing the monogram of the Elector George William, father of the Great Elector. This still-life reflects an approach to reality based on the objective examination of things that was typical of the period of development following the Thirty Years' War in Brandenburg.

the Elector set in train in order to further his aim of achieving royal status. In these matters he was advised in the most part by his minister Eberhard von Danckelmann, who also played a very active part in the founding of the Berlin Academy of Arts in 1696. It was created in imitation of the Paris Academy as an institution which was designed to develop but also to exercise control over a body of artists, who should as far as possible be natives of the country, and who would be charged with carrying out vast projects in connection with the ornamentation of the electoral, later royal, residences. Historical and allegorical paintings were intended, in close association with the architecture and architectural sculpture, both to trumpet the fame of the ruler and to further his political aims. These two genres were the most highly esteemed in the academies' scale of values, and in the study of them the obligatory guideline that had to be followed was, as it had been since the Renaissance, the conception of the human being that was expressed in the art of antiquity.

The founders of the Academy were able to induce the Swiss painter Joseph Werner, one of the most highly regarded artists of his day, to come from Paris in 1695 to be its organizer and first director. From today's standpoint, his best work was as a miniaturist. It was other artists who shaped the character of the Academy in its early years and at the same time raised the quality of painting in Berlin, though this could not keep pace with the outstanding artistic achievements of Andreas Schlüter. In 1690, Augustin Terwesten came to Berlin and was appointed in 1692 court painter in place of Jacques Vaillant, who had died in the previous year. He had grown up in The Hague, and his first teacher had been Nicolaus Wieling. After journeys to Italy, France, and England he had risen to become, in his homeland, a much sought-after representative of the international academic style. In 1694, the Elector sent him, together with Samuel Theodor Gericke, whom we have already mentioned, to Rome to make plaster casts of sculptures from classical antiquity for the Academy. It was also these two painters who arranged the purchase of Pietro Bellori's collection of antiquities for the Academy. Gericke used his stay in Rome to study under Carlo Maratta, the most important painter working there at the time. Once back in Berlin, he was appointed court painter in 1696. In his capacity as a professor at the Berlin Academy he became known as the editor of important writings on the theory of art. The Berliner Johann Friedrich Wentzel also trained under Maratta from 1698 to 1700 at the Elector's expense. It was these three painters who were entrusted with the

Paul Carl Leygebe
King Frederick I's Tabakskollegium in the Drap d'Or Room of the Berlin Palace (c. 1710)
Oil on canvas, 130 x 166 cm; Berlin, Stiftung Preussische Schlösser und Gärten Berlin-Brandenburg, Schloss Charlottenburg

Following the Dutch fashion, Frederick I introduced the Tabakskollegium (smoking circle) to the Berlin court. Leygebe's depiction of it also shows Dutch influence in its objective approach. The future Soldier King, who is shown sitting to the left of the king and his third wife Sophia Louise, used this institution, which was not bound by strict court protocol, for informal meetings where differences of rank could be set aside.

Samuel Theodor Gericke
Allegory of King Frederick I of Prussia as Prince of Orange (c. 1710)
Oil on canvas, 67 x 86 cm; Berlin, Stiftung Preussische Schlösser und Gärten Berlin-Brandenburg, Schloss Charlottenburg

This picture is the cartoon for a ceiling painting that was probably never carried out. Its subject is the king's claim, which he was not able politically to realize, to the succession of the House of Orange after the death without issue of his cousin, the Dutch stadholder William III. The illusionistic composition of the picture shows Gericke's preoccupation with questions of perspective.

Augustin Terwesten
Europe (1694)
Oil on canvas, 289 x 203 cm; Berlin, Stiftung Preussische Schlösser und Gärten Berlin-Brandenburg, Schloss Charlottenburg

This painting is one of a four-part cycle of allegories of the Continents; its original positioning as part of the decoration of a room is unknown. The attributes accompanying the main figure include the classical head of Laocoön. The composition of the picture, which is full of movement and is designed to be viewed from below, breathes something of the same spirit as works by Andreas Schlüter.

execution of most of the ceiling paintings in the Berlin Palace when it was being converted into a royal palace. In painting the ceiling of the Knights' Hall, Wentzel showed himself to be almost the equal of Schlüter, who provided the sculptural decoration of that room. This outstanding work combining the different arts was lost during World War II, as were most of Augustin Terwesten's monumental paintings. Only one cycle of allegories of the continents by him (see right) and the ceiling painting, executed in 1697, in the Porcelain Room of the Oranienburg Palace have survived. The same fate befell the ceiling paintings by his younger brother and pupil Matthäus, who was involved particularly in the decoration of the Charlottenburg Palace. There the only painting to survive the war was the ceiling painting in the Porcelain Room, a notable work by the Fleming Anthonie de Coxie, who worked in Berlin from 1705 onwards. Apart from an early work in Caputh Palace, all that remains of Gericke's work in this field is a design for a ceiling; where it was intended for is unknown (see above).

By the time Frederick I died, painting in the capital of the new kingdom presented a varied aspect. Even so, it did not experience a flowering comparable to that which took place in Holland in the 17th century. The extensive building programs and the ruler's desire for magnificent display were the major factors which attracted artists to Berlin; but the Baroque splendor with which the king surrounded himself was not matched by general prosperity, so that the group of potential patrons outside the court and in the country as a whole remained small. Significantly, it was still the case in this period that many painters stayed only briefly in Berlin, leaving their mark on the city to a greater or lesser extent through the works they had created and the impression they had made. The portrait painters Anton Schoonjans and Adam Mányoki may be cited as examples of this. The style of Schoonjans, who worked in 1702–1703 chiefly for Queen Sophia Charlotte, combined, with great bravura, elements of his native Flemish idiom and that of Rome; the same is true of his compatriot, de Coxie. Schoonjans's memory has been kept alive in Berlin primarily by his portrait of Crown Prince Frederick William I as David. The Hungarian Mányoki, who become a skillful portrait painter under Andreas Scheits in Hanover, worked at the Berlin court for various short periods between 1702 and 1710. He is thought to be the painter of a series of portraits of officers carried out for the crown prince that reveal a productive talent (at present in Charlottenburg Palace, Berlin).

The works of these two painters seem like forerunners of the portraits by the French artist Antoine Pesne (see page 142), who was invited to Berlin in 1710 and a year later became the successor to Augustin Terwesten. He was born and trained in Paris and continued his studies in Italy. His range as a painter was comparable to that of Schoonjans and Mányoki, and was enriched above all by his skill as a colorist. Thanks to his perseverance and his remarkable ability to influence others and so establish a

school, he succeeded in becoming, and remaining for decades, the leading painter in Berlin and hence in Prussia as a whole. When the economies of the "Soldier King" ushered in a period of stagnation for the arts and thus also for the Academy, which was still in its early years, he remained in place and was soon without any competition. Frederick William I gave him special functions that obliged him occasionally to carry out ceremonial duties, and made him an ambassador in artistic matters. In this way Pesne's influence extended as far as the court of Augustus the Strong in Dresden. In Berlin, it was not least the favor of Queen Sophia Dorothea, who remained firmly attached to French taste, that ensured his artistic survival.

Apart from Johann Harper, who was appointed court painter in 1716 (see opposite, above), the only painter whom the "Soldier King" himself engaged to work at his court, was, significantly, a painter of battle scenes, Dismar Degen. The king had encountered him while on his campaign in southern Germany in 1730 (see opposite, below, right). Otherwise he contented himself with artists of modest abilities, artists such as Friedrich Wilhelm Weidemann and Johann Christof Merck, who had previously served his father. They were required above all to paint portraits of his officers and the most physically impressive members of the Potsdam "guard of giants," a task which clearly served to reinforce the apparent naivete and uniformity of their style. The king himself was a painter of naive pictures (see opposite, below, left). In the final decade of his life, which was overshadowed by serious illnesses, this activity afforded some distraction from his unendurable pain.

Antoine Pesne
Margrave Philipp Wilhelm of Brandenburg-Schwedt (c. 1711)
Oil on canvas, 153 x 117 cm; Berlin, Stiftung Preussische Schlösser und Gärten Berlin-Brandenburg, Schloss Charlottenburg

King Frederick I's half-brother, who died on December 19, 1711, at the age of 42, appears in the pose of a triumphant military commander. In the first period of his work for the Berlin court, Pesne brilliantly demonstrated his ability to combine the form of the French-style Baroque portrait of a person of rank with his gift as a colorist, which he had perfected in Venice.

Opposite, below, left
Frederick William I, King of Prussia
Self-portrait (1737)
Oil on canvas, 81 x 65 cm; Potsdam, Stiftung Preussische Schlösser und Gärten Berlin-Brandenburg, Jagdschloss Stern

That the "Soldier King" was himself an amateur painter is a rather touching aspect of his personality. The paintings, with their somewhat awkward, naive appearance, were done during the last years of his life, especially during periods of severe physical pain. They prove that he did have a feeling for art, which, however, he always subordinated to the interests of the state.

Johann Harper
Marquard Ludwig, Baron von Printzen and his Family (c. 1720)
Oil on canvas, 251 x 300 cm; Berlin, Stiftung Stadtmuseum Berlin

The Prussian Chief of the Royal Household obtained his influential position under Frederick I and was able to retain it under the "Soldier King," Frederick William I. This large family portrait, which radiates self-confidence, is inspired by works by Pesne. The precision with which the details are executed derives from Harper's training as a miniaturist.

Bottom right
Dismar Degen
Houses Being Built in the Friedrichstadt District of Berlin (c. 1735)
Oil on canvas, 101 x 135 cm; Berlin, Stiftung Preussische Schlösser und Gärten Berlin-Brandenburg, Jadgschloss Stern

Under the "Soldier King," Frederick William I, houses conforming to specific types were built in the southern part of Friedrichstadt. This schematic view is complemented by a detailed portrayal, in the foreground, of the actual processes of building and of laying foundations. This form of presentation is analogous to that used by Degen in his battle paintings, which depict the slaughter of battle but at the same time accurately show the troop formations.

THE APPLIED ARTS

Burkhardt Göres

Medallion tankard (c. 1657)
Attributed to Daniel Männlich the Elder
Silver; Berlin, Stiftung Preussische Schlösser und Gärten Berlin-Brandenburg, Schloss Charlottenburg (on loan from Deutsche Bank)

The Applied Arts Under the Great Elector Frederick William, 1640–1688

When Elector Frederick William of Brandenburg, later known as the Great Elector, came to power in 1640, the Thirty Years' War (1618–1648) was still raging. The applied arts, consequently, were in a poor state. Although one may assume that his father's court, which was established in Königsberg for some years, had managed to save many objects that were part of the splendor of court life, the Electoral March of Brandenburg had been heavily plundered, despite its attempted policy of neutrality. When in the 1640s the electoral palace in Berlin was to be renovated, it became apparent that there were hardly any craftsmen left who would have been capable of carrying out the necessary work. Still less, one may imagine, had crafts dedicated to the production of luxury goods remained viable. This was to change in the course of the ensuing decades, when there was increasing demand for such crafts. However, later losses prevent us from gaining a clear idea of the early development of the applied arts in Brandenburg-Prussia.

The young elector certainly returned from his educational stay in prosperous Holland (1634–1638) filled with a desire to surround himself with objects of artistic beauty, but the desperate situation of the country meant that this had to wait for the time being. He did, however, have his electoral residence in Berlin restored from 1640 onwards, and engaged court painters and also, from the 1650s onwards, Dutch sculptors. As early as 1642 there is a record of a collection of objects from antiquity in Cleves being purchased for the elector's own art collection. His marriage to Louise Henrietta of Orange in 1646 obliged him at least temporarily to display a degree of pomp appropriate to his rank. For his own wedding apparel and as a gift for the bride he ordered valuable jewelry from Hamburg, and the most significant recent creations of applied art in this early period came to Brandenburg-Prussia as part of his wife's trousseau; probably the most noteworthy of these were items of silverware. Certainly after his wedding, if not before, the elector increasingly engaged practitioners of the applied arts, as well as other artists, in connection with the alterations to the Berlin Palace prior to the court's move from Cleves to Berlin in 1650, the building of the summer house in the pleasure garden, and the building of Oranienburg Palace, following Dutch models, between 1651 and 1653. Already in 1652 we read that at Oranienburg "the rooms inside and the hall are excellently adorned with extremely rare paintings and precious tapestries and other furnishings." In the years following 1660, Oranienburg acquired a portrait gallery and the first porcelain room in any of the Prussian palaces, with leather wall hangings with gilded decoration on a blue background and a rich gilded ceiling into which were set oil paintings of "Indian" scenes in gilt frames. The already considerable collection of Japanese and Chinese porcelain was later divided up among the porcelain collections that resided in the other palaces.

From 1661 onwards, the elector devoted himself to altering and adding new extensions to the palace at Potsdam, closely following Dutch models. This work continued right into the 1670s – as late as 1674 the stucco artist Giovanni Baptista Novi and a painter named Marini were working in the great hall of the palace. The result was the largest secular complex built by the elector, which was extended again in 1679–1682 and was decorated and furnished, we may be sure, in suitably magnificent style from the outset. Gregorio Leti mentions in his *Historia della Casa serenissima et Elettorale di Brandenburgo* (History of the Electoral Houses of Brandenburg) of 1687 the unusual lavishness of the palace, "with halls and splendid rooms which are all fitted out with the most magnificent furniture, but especially with paintings of high quality." After the Great Elector's death in 1688, the Electress Dorothea received this palace as her widow's portion. She evidently assembled all her greatest treasures here, for the 1690 inventory of her estate tells us of gilded leather wall hangings, series of tapestries, splendid furniture, and a wealth of objects in silver. It lists no fewer than 26 parts of a set of gold tableware, 252 items of "jewels, precious objects, and all kinds of rarities," various pieces of silver furniture, and 196 silver utensils not including the tableware. Silver, in the form of impressive ornaments and of tableware, played an important part in demonstrating a ruler's wealth, but when the state fell on hard times it would frequently also prove to be a useful reserve and was often unhesitatingly sent off to the mint. Of the collection of silver owned by the elector, Leti writes in 1687: "There are few princes in Europe who are provided and endowed with tableware in such quantity, or with such a wealth of sideboards full of silver utensils for everyday use, surpassing that of many great men in both quality and quantity, most of it of silver gilt." There is so much tableware that one could "entertain two great lords lavishly with silver at the same time ... quite apart from the many silver objects that serve only as decoration."

The quantity of outstanding works in silver grew as a result of gifts of homage from the elector's territories, official gifts from other rulers, and items that he himself commissioned from Augsburg (see page 144). In addition, the Great Elector in the course of his reign appointed a succession of Berlin craftsmen as court goldsmiths to provide his silver tableware. As early as 1673 we find a mention of "the gold tableware, the Augsburg white silver tableware, the travel silverware, the Potsdam silver, and the tableware of the heir to the Electorate."

Since most objects in precious metals had been lost during the Thirty Years' War, the items in the newly amassed collections in Brandenburg-Prussia, as elsewhere, were mainly "modern," and their ornamentation reflected the contemporary stylistic development in Germany, especially southern Germany, since most of the silver designed for show came from Augsburg. The development was given impetus by the many graphic designs that were used as models. Bizarre, knobbly decoration gradually gave way to acanthus-leaf decoration mixed with bunches of fruit. The surfaces decorated with pictorial reliefs made the leap from late Mannerist forms to the dynamic forms of the high Baroque.

In the mid-17th century the furniture in the palaces was probably for the most part simple and functional. The tables, benches, and stools mentioned in inventories are often made of the most ordinary kinds of wood. The plain wooden tables were completely hidden by rich cloths. There were also tables made for show, with turned columnar or carved legs, which, as the 17th century progressed, were more elaborately decorated with three-dimensional sculptural work in the form of heraldic beasts, "savages," fettered slaves, gods, or putti. Stylistically, Holland provided the dominant influence in northern Germany, but in the furniture with sculptural decoration one can also detect the influence of the work of the Italian stucco artists employed in the palaces of Brandenburg-Prussia. Examples can still be seen today in Köpenick Palace, where Giovanni Carove

Bench in the style of a throne (c. 1690)
Wood, gilded; Berlin, Staatliche Museen zu Berlin – Preussischer Kulturbesitz, Kunstgewerbemuseum

This bench, made about 1690, and now completely gilded, is decorated with all the symbols of the state (electoral hat with arched crown, scepter, initials of the reigning elector, and the star and motto of the Order of the Garter), and is a prime example of painted Berlin carved furniture. Prestige pieces like this were obviously designed to go with the silver furnishings. Originally, the acanthus leaves were silvered and the laurel branches and palm fronds gilded, the ribbon with the motto of the order was painted blue, the cross within the silver star was red, and the frame was pink.

Table and two gueridons
Berlin, Stiftung Preussische Schlösser und Gärten Berlin-Brandenburg, Schloss Charlottenburg

The painted and gilded table frame, supported by four putti, has large-leaved acanthus foliage out of which grow two kissing putti. On the stretcher reclines a (perhaps Hessian) lion. It may have been made in about 1679–1680 on the occasion of the marriage of Prince Frederick to Princess Elizabeth Henrietta Maria of Hesse-Kassel.

and other stucco artists decorated the walls and ceilings in the main hall and the vestibules (see page 89). For this palace, which is one of the most significant to have survived from that period, an inventory of 1682 from the building it replaced gives us a good idea of the furnishings of a princely residence. Köpenick was at that time the chief seat of the Great Elector's son Frederick, who loved outward show, and his first wife, Princess Elizabeth Henrietta Maria of Hesse-Kassel. The furnishings were probably very similar to those of the elector, apart from the lack of particular showpieces. The list of tables and gueridons of walnut or olivewood, with black or red-painted feet and initials, shows considerable variety (see above).

Writing in 1687, Gregorio Leti, who has already been quoted, is especially enthusiastic in his praise of the furnishings of the electoral palaces. The country seat of the Electress Dorothea, Caputh Palace, where he particularly draws attention to the good internal disposition of the rooms, contained among other things a "room full of the rarest curiosities that one could wish to see, be they miniatures, objects made of coral, or embroideries ... Altogether, the rooms are furnished in a most refined manner, adorned with mirrors, pictures, and expensive porcelain and vases in all sizes." The writer describes the Berlin Palace in great detail and is quite carried away by the electress's apartments: "Very few queens in Europe have even one set of living apartments of the kind of which the most noble electress has several, but in particular few apartments can compare with those in Berlin, where even the most exalted queen would be magnificently accommodated." Leti remarks on the wall hangings, pictures, tables, clocks, and chairs, and then turns to the furnishings of the bedroom. The room has an alcove, as is usual in France, before which stand "two splendid tables, each furnished with a very fine upper part containing various pieces made of silver or heavy gold, and holding the implements used in dressing ladies and attending to their hair, and the whole is covered by a broad, overhanging cloth wonderfully embroidered in gold. There are, further, silver tables, splendid mirrors, valuable paintings, a clock of enormous size in the form of a cabinet, wholly of silver and studded with

Armchairs
Berlin, Staatliche Museen zu Berlin – Preussischer Kulturbesitz, Kunstgewerbemuseum

In about 1670–1674, the Great Elector commissioned from David I Schwestermüller in Augsburg a pair of armchairs with silver mountings that are still preserved in the Berlin palaces. As the only surviving pieces of silver furniture at the Prussian court, these chairs were later used as thrones.

jewels ... and a cabinet with two crystal doors such that one can see what is inside, in short rare objects of every kind (whether made of gold, silver, the finest porcelain, or precious stones) and other curiosities and conveniences." We can be sure that Leti is not exaggerating: the silver furniture from the trousseau of the Electress Louise Henrietta, and the pictorial tapestries and set of silver furniture she received in 1666 as a gift from Louis XIV, are enough to lend credibility to his account. To these possessions were added a silver toilet set and two series of tapestries, also given by Louis XIV to the Electress Dorothea. In addition, the electress had in 1684 inherited the famous Pomeranian collector's cabinet and an ebony table with silver mountings made in Augsburg. We may probably identify the two collector's cabinets mentioned as being in her bedroom with the so-called "small Muscovite cabinet" with a clock and a "large Muscovite cabinet" made of ivory, ebony, colored enamel, and glass.

Other items that were also very much sought after at that time for use in the furnishing of the electoral residences were Far Eastern lacquered cabinets, of which some examples still remain in the palaces. In 1687, towards the end of the Great Elector's reign, Gerard Dagly came from Spa to Berlin, and through him the city became, until 1713, a leading center of lacquer work. As early as 1689 there are records showing that Caputh Palace possessed a number of such pieces of furniture, among them a mirror, a table, two pairs of gueridons, and writing-tables "with blue and white figures in the style of porcelain decoration, and half gilded," which probably came from Dagly's workshop. Naturally, under Frederick III (I) he also supplied pieces to Oranienburg, Potsdam, Berlin, and Charlottenburg (see right).

Highly prized because of the rarity of the material, objects worked in amber were among the most popular items to be displayed in the art collections. They were also of special interest to the Great Elector for economic reasons, since the extraction of amber in Prussia had always been one of the rulers' most important sources of income. In 1641, the elector finally permitted the establishment of a guild of workers in amber at Königsberg, which had long been the center of this craft. In the latter half of the century, however, Danzig took on the leading role in the working of amber. Official gifts in this material made by the elector to other European courts – mostly vessels, bowls, caskets, reliefs, and often, later on, unusually large objects such as mirror frames, cabinets, and even a throne-like armchair – also stimulated demand (see page 149). Such items were sought after particularly for art collections, and so amber workers were employed at the courts of other rulers, and they too imported the amber they used from Prussia.

The elector also took a great interest in the production of glass. After all the destruction that had occurred during the Thirty Years' War, there was an urgent need for glass vessels and window glass to be produced for the elector's use. Another reason for strengthening this craft was the wish to keep money within the country. The elector assisted the development of the glass works at Marienwalde (Neumark), Grimnitz (Uckermark), and Drewitz near Potsdam. In a few years, as a result, this branch of applied art was destined to enjoy a flowering that was to continue for the first half of the 18th century. The Great Elector also initiated the production of faience wares on the Dutch model, having become familiar in

Cabinet for a collection of coins and medallions (c. 1695–1701)
Gerard Dagly
Berlin, Staatliche Museen zu Berlin – Preussischer Kulturbesitz, Kunstgewerbemuseum

This type of cabinet, made to contain items in the Berlin art collection, was based on Far Eastern lacquer cabinets and was made by the workshop of Gerard Dagly even before the rooms themselves were refashioned by Andreas Schlüter.

One of a series of tapestries celebrating the Great Elector
The Battle of Fehrbellin
Cartoon: attributed to Abraham Cornelisz Begeyn
Pierre Mercier (Berlin c. 1695)
405 x 435 cm; basse-lisse (low-warp) technique
Berlin, Staatliche Museen zu Berlin – Preussischer Kulturbesitz, at present in Schloss Charlottenburg

Holland with Delft faience wares that were imitations of Chinese porcelain. In 1678, the "porcelain maker" Pieter Fransen van der Lee was brought from Delft to found a factory for "Delftish porcelain" in Berlin. The earliest records of Dutch-style products of the Berlin faience factory date from the 1690s. The trade in luxury products of the applied arts, especially in textiles, received an enormous boost in Brandenburg-Prussia with the influx of the Huguenots. After the revocation of the Edict of Nantes by Louis XIV, which led to their expulsion from France, they were invited to Brandenburg-Prussia by the Edict of Potsdam issued by the Great Elector in 1685, and they came and settled in large numbers. A particular piece of good fortune for the elector was the arrival of two tapestry makers and their assistants. In November 1686 Pierre Mercier from Aubusson was appointed court tapestry maker

Amber chandelier
Berlin, Stiftung Preussische Schlösser und Gärten Berlin-Brandenburg, Schloss Charlottenburg

Large objects in amber, which was known as "Prussian gold," were frequently presented as official gifts from the Great Elector to the courts of Moscow, Paris, and Vienna. Chandeliers, like this one, which was probably made at Königsberg about 1660-1670, were among the extraordinary items created in this material. Such artifacts reached their culmination in the amber room made for Frederick I, which Frederick William I presented in 1717 to Peter I of Russia.

with a fixed salary for himself and his assistants, to run the new electoral factory that was set up on the model of the French royal manufactury. The tapestries were designed by painters attached to the court (see opposite). A second workshop was founded by Jean Baraband the Elder, Mercier's brother-in-law. His main artistic models were tapestries produced by the factory at Beauvais in France.

In the field of work in metals, too, the arrival of the Huguenots brought new impetus. Here, the name that stands out is that of Pierre Fromery, whose richly ornamented weapons, steel caskets decorated with gilt bronze, and gold-decorated steel chandeliers made Berlin a renowned center for such work.

The Applied Arts Under Frederick III (I), 1688–1713

With the accession of the Elector Frederick III in 1688, who crowned himself "king in Prussia" at Königsberg in 1701, the applied arts in Berlin became even more important. This follows from the fact that at the end of his reign this ruler left behind, in and around Berlin, no fewer than 25 palaces which he had either inherited, bought, remodeled, extended, or built. The extensions carried out at Oranienburg Palace from 1688 until after 1700, the building of Charlottenburg Palace, and the remodeling and extension of the Berlin Palace deserve special mention. Most of the workshops and enterprises that had been set up by the Great Elector now entered their period of greatest success. This applies especially to the production of tapestry, glass, faience (see below), and lacquer. There was even a plan for an amber gallery in Oranienburg Palace – intended to present a comprehensive collection of the finest amber work – though the gallery was later reduced to a room and incorporated in the palace in Berlin. The founding of the Academy of Arts in 1696 brought benefit to all the arts. But above all it was the new ruler's desire for lavish display, and the practical need to decorate and furnish his many palaces, that challenged artists and craftsmen to produce outstanding works.

As early as 1694, Frederick succeeded in attracting an artist of the stature of Andreas Schlüter to the Berlin court, first as court sculptor and later as architect supervising the building work on the palace.

Multi-sectioned serving-dish (between 1690 and 1701)
Faience; Berlin, Staatliche Museen zu Berlin – Preussischer Kulturbesitz, Kunstgewerbemuseum

This object can be dated by the insignia of Frederick III that it bears. It was among the grand tableware at Oranienburg Palace and is one of the earliest surviving examples of Berlin faience ware. It was produced in the factory of the widow Molin, or that of her subsequent husband Gerhard Wolbeer.

Philipp Wilhelm Marggraf zu Brandenb: in Schwedt, geb:1669. gest:1711.

Through his versatile talent and his position at court he influenced every branch of the arts. "As Schlüter was full of invention and was also very ready to be of service to others, he was happy to help all other artists with his drawings, whether for weaving tapestries or for making chairs, for work in precious metals, wood or inlaid, and in this way he brought great improvement to this city, and gave even the coaches a better form and appearance, so that they were sought after by many from elsewhere," reports an 18th-century source.

It was now the goldsmith's art that produced the most spectacular works. To the silver that he had inherited, Frederick continually added new items, many of which he bought on his constant journeys; in particular, he placed many large-scale orders with goldsmiths in Augsburg. In the years up until the mid-1690s, in connection with Frederick's royal ambition, plans were made for a splendid silver service, with Schlüter making a major contribution to the design. Once completed, this silver service took pride of place at all the various court festivities, and after being given a permanent place in the Knights' Hall, which was also the throne-room, of the Berlin Palace, it was the centerpiece and the most glorious of all the silver treasures assembled there (see right and page 98). But in the other palaces too, huge amounts of new silverware (the quantity is recorded in old inventories) were added to inherited silver.

The art collection of those years housed famous masterpieces of the goldsmith's art by Christoph Jamnitzer, Hans Straub, Jonas Silber, and Matthias Wallbaum. Even in the last decade of his life, Frederick retained his passion for collecting large silver items. By 1713, as inventories of the Berlin and Charlottenburg palaces testify, the quantity of silver owned by the king was many times greater than it had been in 1702.

With the appointment of Charles King as court sculptor in 1703, a virtuoso of woodcarving in the naturalistic style of Grinling Gibbons came to Berlin. King made superb pieces that were received into the art collections of rulers with whom Frederick was on friendly terms. At first, King was probably deployed by Eosander to work on the decoration of rooms in Oranienburg Palace; but at Charlottenburg he was able to engage in more varied work. Accounts show that throughout his time there he made exquisite pieces of furniture, picture frames (see opposite), and also smaller items.

The Applied Arts Under the "Soldier King," Frederick William I, 1713–1740

The scaling down of the court lifestyle which began upon the accession of Frederick William I in 1713, one of the measures by which he hoped to restore the state finances, involved the dismissal of all the applied artists who had held court appointments. However, not all of them left Berlin. From 1713 to 1716, the completion of the Berlin Palace by Böhme and its interior decoration and furnishing, though no doubt carried out as inexpensively as was possible, still provided sufficient earnings for a few craftsmen. Moreover, despite the austerity adopted by the young king, the country's aristocracy continued to obtain luxury goods from the Prussian capital. Thus Berlin's transition from being an "Athens" under Frederick I to a "Sparta" under the Soldier King affected the applied arts only to a limited extent, and only in the early years.

Opposite
Showpiece picture frame (early 18th century)
Charles King
Wood, carved, gilded; Berlin, Stiftung Preussische Schlösser und Gärten Berlin-Brandenburg, Schloss Charlottenburg

Silver service (1695–1698)
Made by Ludwig Biller in Augsburg to designs by Andreas Schlüter
Berlin, Staatliche Museen zu Berlin – Preussischer Kulturbesitz, Kunstgewerbemuseum

At first the king was by no means the chief patron of the applied arts, but later he readily allowed his wife, Queen Sophia Dorothea, to furnish her personal surroundings in a luxurious manner. It was only after the finances of the state had been restored, in the late 1720s, that the king himself earned a place in the history of the applied arts in Germany by commissioning magnificent silverware, and this in quantities unmatched by any other German prince.

Among the most significant branches of the luxury applied arts in Berlin was tapestry making, which after the departure of Mercier was carried on by Baraband the Younger and the brothers Jacques and Siméon Coullodon. It was still fashionable for walls to be hung with tapestries. Besides models from Beauvais, which the Berlin masters were able to obtain through a French branch in Leipzig, Baraband and Charles Vigne also used designs by painters resident in Berlin, among them Antoine Pesne.

In Berlin, the art of furniture making was for a long time very much undervalued and was recorded only fragmentarily, at a late date, in connection with certain pieces that can be dated with certainty. From about 1720 onwards, however, its development in Berlin achieved a first great flowering that made the city an important center of furniture making in Germany even before the advent of Frederician Rococo. Artistically influenced by England and by Brunswick, where English influence was also strong, there appeared – attested with certainty for the first time – cabinets decorated with "all manner of inlaid work in brass, tortoiseshell, cedar, and similar woods, as well as French and English cabinets, also bureaux or writing-desks with lockable compartments and mirror doors." As this shows, craftsmen in Berlin had mastered boulle work.

Armchair (Berlin, c. 1740)
Friedrich Christian Glume (?), Wood, carved, silvered

This armchair was used by Frederick the Great as a desk chair, together with a set of upholstered chairs designed by Nahl in 1745–1746, in his bedroom and study in Potsdam Palace. The wings were certainly added later. It is a chair of a type probably still being made as late as the 1730s, possibly for Rheinsberg Palace, or in 1741 for Potsdam Palace. Such chairs represent a cumbersome, backward-looking tendency that was superseded in the 1740s by the superb chairs produced by Nahl and the Hoppenhaupt brothers.

Queen Sophia Dorothea's court cabinet maker, Martin Böhme, is recorded as having been in Berlin from 1723 onwards, and over the following decades he became the most important figure in his craft; it is possible to trace the commissions he carried out for the Queen up to the mid-1740s. He evidently also made furniture to designs by Knobelsdorff, Nahl, and the Hoppenhaupt brothers. Many other master craftsmen, about whom we have less information, worked alongside him in the 1720s and 1730s. Two years after the new imperial regulation of guilds of 1734, the King had issued a new "General Privilege and Guild Charter of the craft of cabinet making ... most particularly ... in Berlin," which made it easier for a craftsman to gain the status of a master. This was very opportune, given the many new tasks that craftsmen were now to perform.

When Frederick William I took all the silver from the various palaces he had inherited from his father and gathered it together in the Berlin Palace, he was probably concerned for the safety of the state reserves. But the concentration of more than 900 items of goldsmith's work, including some large pieces, crowded into little more than a dozen rooms in the state apartments of the palace, was certainly also intended to proclaim the wealth of the state.

Shortly after 1719, Johann Christian Lieberkühn the Elder was commissioned by Frederick William I to make, as a curiosity, the great coin tankard. This tankard, covered with 688 thalers and 46 medallions – an ancestors' gallery of the Brandenburg-Prussian dynasty – was used in his "smoking circle" (an informal gathering of the court) as a beer keg (capacity 135 liters, nearly 30 US gallons). When the

Covered pâté dish (1732–1733)
Silver gilt; Berlin, Staatliche Museen zu Berlin – Preussischer Kulturbesitz, Kunstgewerbemuseum

The few surviving examples of silverware commissioned by Frederick William I include two heavy pâté dishes made by Ludwig II Biller in the style of grandiose decorations by Schlüter. After Frederick the Great had melted down most of the silverware, these dishes were incorporated into the silver service in the Knights' Hall.

state finances had been restored, in the last ten years of his reign up to 1740, the commissions given by the king to goldsmiths in Berlin and Augsburg were probably the largest in volume ever given by a German ruler within so short a time. Impressed by the splendor of the Dresden court while on a visit there in 1728, he went so far as to have an unfinished room in the Berlin Palace made into a ceremonial hall for the promised return visit by Augustus the Strong. That silver should have a prominent place in its furnishings went without saying. The lavishness of the new furnishings of this room went far beyond anything previously known.

In 1731, the enormous service of silverware consisting of 247 items (with sets of identical pieces counting as one item) was assembled here out of the existing stocks of silverware. Then there were large orders for new items, which included five very heavy chandeliers. Equally overwhelming is the volume of the other orders placed in these few years, which were almost exclusively for the state rooms in the Berlin palace. The complete inventory, made by Paul Seidel, of the silver purchased by the Soldier King lists, among other things, 12 heavy chandeliers made by Berlin goldsmiths, four large tables and mirrors from Augsburg, and 38 gueridons from Berlin workshops. Johann Elias Riedinger is thought to have played a major part in designing the Augsburg pieces. Johann Ludwig II Biller, Johannes Biller, Philipp Jakob VI, Emanuel and Abraham III Drentwett, Johannes Engelbrecht and Georg Lorenz II Gaap were responsible for the execution. Except for three pairs of items – two covered pâté dishes, two tureens, and two candelabra – nothing remains of all these treasures (see opposite, below). The royal mints turned them into thalers during Frederick the Great's Silesian Wars and in 1809 into monies to fight Napoleon. But those few surviving masterpieces enable us to judge the decorative vigor and the artistic quality of the lost treasures. The Soldier King's last major commission is like a triumphal closing fanfare for his obsession with silver. In 1738, he commissioned from Christian Lieberkühn the Younger a musicians' balcony for the Knights' Hall (the throne room) of the Berlin Palace; the balcony was completed the following year. Its lavish monumentality and its iconographic program, determined by the king himself, make it a unique expression of the spirit of the time. In its ornamentation, the first hints of Rococo herald the next stylistic phase in the art of silver work in Berlin.

Large goblet with lid (Potsdam, c. 1715)
Colorless glass, intaglio and relief engraving with polished and matt finish.
Berlin, Stiftung Preussische Schlösser und Gärten Berlin-Brandenburg, Schloss Charlottenburg
(on loan from the Freunde der Preussischen Schlösser und Gärten e.V.)

Under Frederick William I, the Potsdam glassworks continued to operate at the same site until 1737, producing further outstanding items for the new king. This goblet, superbly engraved and polished, and bearing the coats of arms of the royal couple (those of Prussia and Hanover), was probably made soon after Frederick William's accession to the throne in 1713.

Prussia Under Frederick the Great
1740–1786

1740–1786 Reign of King Frederick II, the Great (1712–1786). Making use of the politically unstable situation created in Europe by the death of Emperor Charles V, Frederick invades Silesia, occupies Breslau, and pushes his way as far as Bohemia and Moravia; this initiates the First Silesian War (to 1742). Frederick enacts an order for wide-ranging restrictions on the use of torture in Prussia.
Frederick consolidates the machinery of state with the foundation of the so-called V Department, a ministry of trade and industry.
The average population of the cities of the March of Brandenburg is only 2,647; the economy is based chiefly on agriculture, brewing, and distilling. Meanwhile, in the capital, Berlin, there are already factories and a comparatively high rate of employment. For economic reasons, recruitment of troops has come to a halt in Brandenburg on the Havel, as well as in Berlin and Potsdam.

1741 The Pragmatic Sanction (succession in the female line in Austria), agreed in 1713, is rejected by Saxony, Bavaria, Spain, and France. The result is the Austrian War of Succession (to 1748): Bavarian and French troops march on Prague, and Prussian wins a victory over Austria at Mollwitz. Following the foundation of the Berlin Academy, the mathematician Leonard Euler and the French mathematician and physicist Pierre Louis de Maupertuis visit Prussia. The Berlin Opera House is built by Georg Wenzeslaus von Knobelsdorff. The Forum Fridericianum (Friedrichforum) is built in its first form; in 1780 it is extended to include the Hedwigskirche, the Prinz-Heinrich-Palais (Prince Henry Palace, now Humboldt University), and the Royal Library.
Johann Joachim Quantz becomes court composer to Frederick II. The interior designer and sculptor Johann August Nahl comes to Berlin and is appointed *directeur des ornements*.

1742 Battle of Chotusitz is fought, a Prussian victory over Austria; the Peace of Breslau between Prussia and Austria is agreed. As a result of the First Silesian War (1740–1742), Prussia acquires Upper and Lower Silesia, thereby enlarging its territory by one-third.
Frederick II acquires Cardinal Polignac's collection of antiquities for 36,000 thalers.
Introduction of Italian opera to Berlin; the Opera House opens with a performance of Johann Gottlieb Graun's opera *Cäsar und Kleopatra*.
Frederick II compiles the first version of his work *Denkwürdigkeiten zur Geschichte des Hauses Brandenburg* (Memorabilia of the History of the House of Brandenburg).

1743 Official opening of the Berlin Opera House with Johann Adolf Hasse's opera *La clemenza di Tito*. The painter and engraver Daniel Nikolaus Chodowiecki comes to Berlin.

1744 Second Silesian War begins (to 1745): in view of Austria's military success in the Austrian War of Succession, Frederick II begins to suspect anti-Prussian objectives. He enters upon an alliance of aggression with France, and renews the war.
Architect Georg Wenzeslaus von Knobelsdorff begins rebuilding of the City Palace of Potsdam (to 1752). Work begins with the layout of the terraced vineyards at Sanssouci. The Italian dancer Barbara Campanini, known as La Barbarina, comes to Berlin. Cotton manufacture begins in Berlin.

1745 The Peace of Dresden brings about the end of the Second Silesian War: Silesia is once again awarded to Prussia. On the title page of a publication about the celebrations of the end of the war, Frederick is for the first time described as "the Great." He is now 33 years old.

King Frederick II (the Great), by Antoine Pesne (c. 1745)

On the instructions of Frederick, Samuel Freiherr von Cocceji, the minister of justice, undertakes judicial reforms in Prussia. Sanssouci Palace in Potsdam is under construction by Georg Wenzeslaus von Knobelsdorff (to 1747).

Queen Elizabeth Christine, by Antoine Pesne (c. 1740)

1746 Frederick II prepares the second version of his work *Denkwürdigkeiten zur Geschichte des Hauses Brandenburg* (Memorabilia of the History of the House of Brandenburg).
About 1746, Frederick II writes his symphony in D major for two flutes, two oboes, two horns, string orchestra, and basso continuo.
Johann August Nahl leaves Prussia.

1747 In the course of reclamation of inland waters, Frederick has the Lower Oder dam drained (to 1753), and further tracts of land follow in subsequent decades. Johann Sebastian Bach applies for a position with Frederick II, and the king decides on a theme for the composer. Bach then composes his chamber work *Musikalisches Opfer* (*Musical Offering*), dedicated to the king.

1748 Austrian War of Succession ends (from 1740). Marie Theresa of Austria has shown her ability as a major European leader, but has lost Silesia to Prussia. The German writer Gotthold Ephraim Lessing and the French philosopher Julien Offray de La Mettrie visit Prussia.
In order to improve wool production, specially bred Spanish fine-wooled sheep, the so-called merinos, are introduced into Prussia.

A Peasant Reading, copperplate engraving by Daniel Chodowiecki, 1757

1749 Frederick II publishes his work *Über die Gründe, Gesetze einzuführen oder abzuschaffen* (On the Reasons for Introducing or Repealing Laws).

1750 Frederick II founds a weaving colony outside the gates of Potsdam for Bohemian religious refugees. The colony, named Nowawes, is now known as Babelsberg.
Voltaire visits Prussia as a guest of Frederick II (to 1753).

1751 G.E. Lessing contributes to the newspaper *Berlinische privilegierte Zeitung* (later *Vossische Zeitung*). The merchant Wilhelm Caspar Wegely founds the first porcelain factory in Berlin.

1752 Frederick II writes his first *Testament Politique* (Political Testament), in which he describes the development of military affairs as the most important task for the prosperity of Prussia. He recommends the conquest of Saxony in order to extend the borders of the Prussian state. A royal iron and steel industry grows up near Luckenwalde. Factories are also created in other locations to produce pig-iron and ammunition.

1754 Frederick II's speech in memory of Georg Wenzeslaus von Knobelsdorff (died 1753) is read out in the Academy of Sciences in Berlin.

1755 First performance of the opera *Montezuma*, with music by Carl Heinrich Graun and libretto by Frederick the Great. Gotthold Ephraim Lessing publishes his play *Miss Sara Sampson*. Christoph Friedrich Nicolai publishes *Briefe über den itzigen Zustand der schönen Wissenschaften in Deutschland* (Letters on the Present State of the Humanities in Germany). Immanuel Kant publishes *Allgemeine Naturgeschichte und Theorie des Himmels* (General History of the Nature and Theory of the Heavens).

1756 Seven Years' War (Third Silesian War) begins (to 1763). In order to forestall an attack by a coalition of Austria and France, which is soon joined by Russia and Sweden, Frederick II occupies neutral Saxony and pushes forward as far as Bohemia.

1757 Frederick the Great is forced to conduct a war on several fronts, which drains his military power and, despite a few significant victories (Rossbach, Leuthen) fails to improve Prussia's position decisively.

1758 A supplementary treaty concluded between England and Prussia. Frederick the Great is put more and more on the defensive. The East Prussian states pay homage to the Russian Empress Elizabeth.

1759 Prussia experiences a crushing defeat in the battle of Kunersdorf at the hands of an alliance of Russian and Austrian troops. Losses on both sides total 35,000. For a short time Frederick the Great relinquishes supreme command of the Prussian army.
Gotthold Ephraim Lessing publishes *Fabeln* (Fables). In Berlin, Christoph Friedrich Nicolai and Moses Mendelssohn found the journal *Briefe, die neueste Literatur betreffend* (Letters Concerning the Latest Literature).

1760 Victories of the Prussian army over the Austrians in the battles of Liegnitz and Torgau. Frederick the Great is able to hold his ground in Saxony and Silesia. Russians and Austrians temporarily occupy Berlin.

1761 Prussian military power finds itself in a near-hopeless situation. The fortresses of Schweidnitz and Kolberg are both lost, Russian troops are able to capture Pomerania, and Austrian troops occupy Silesia and Saxony.

Soldier's Wife Begging, etching by Daniel Chodowiecki, 1764

Punishments: Running the Gauntlet and Public Whipping, etching by Daniel Chodowiecki (c. 1777)

Frederick the Great encourages the re-foundation of the Berlin porcelain factory by the merchant Johann Ernst Gotzkowsky.

1762 Peter III, the heir to the Russian throne, reputed to be an admirer of Frederick the Great, concludes a peace treaty with Prussia. Subsequently, Sweden too retires from the war. The Prussian army regains Silesia and once again occupies Saxony.

1763 Peace of Hubertusberg between Prussia, Austria, and Saxony: the prewar *status quo* is restored. Prussia keeps Silesia and is decisively established as a European great power.
Introduction of general educational regulations, which include compulsory school attendance between the ages of five and 13. The Prussian national educational system becomes the model for most German and several European states until the end of the century.
Frederick the Great gives orders for the abolition of serfdom, but is thwarted by resistance on the part of the nobility.
Frederick II takes over Gotzkowsky's porcelain factory, which now receives the title of Königliche Porzellanmanufaktur Berlin (KPM) (Royal Porcelain Factory of Berlin).
Work begins on the New Palace (Neues Palais) in the park at Sanssouci in Potsdam and is undertaken by Johann Gottfried Büring, Heinrich Ludwig Manger, and Carl Philipp von Gontard (to 1769).

1764 Alliance of Prussia with Russia against Poland. Because of the economic crisis caused in Prussia by the Seven Years' War, Frederick the Great devotes his main attention to the economy and financial affairs. The internal land reclamation activity begun after the Second Silesian War is continued and improvements are introduced into agriculture. Frederick II sets up a weaving and spinning colony for 200 immigrant families from Saxony at the Zinna monastery on the Jüterbog-Luckenwalde road.

1765 A bank is founded in Berlin.

1766 In Frankfurt an der Oder, the Gelehrte Gesellschaft der Wissenschaften und Künste (Learned Society of Sciences and Arts) is founded.
Frederick II summons French financiers to Prussia and founds a new tax system, the so-called *Regie*. The purpose of alterations to the state administration in the years after 1766 is the rationalization of the administrative apparatus.
Gotthold Ephraim Lessing publishes *Laokoon, oder, Über die Grenzen der Malerei und Poesie* (Laocoön, or, Beyond the Limits of Painting and Poetry), and his play *Minna von Barnhelm*.

1768 Frederick the Great writes his second *Testament Politique* (Political Testament). He describes Prussia as a "military state," which must conduct an appropriate internal and foreign policy. As before, he considers the first priority to be the conquest of Saxony. For the first time, Frederick expresses the idea of a partition of Poland.

Allegory of the First Partition of Poland between Catherine II of Russia, Joseph II of Habsburg, Stanislaus II Poniatowski, and Frederick II of Prussia, etching by Johannes Esaias Nilson, after 1773

1769 Frederick the Great and the Austrian emperor, Joseph II, meet in Neisse.
Daniel Nikolaus Chodowiecki produces 12 engravings for Lessing's play *Minna von Barnhelm*. In Berlin and Potsdam there are 150 silk factories with 1,335 looms.

1770 Frederick II engages in dispute with two works of the late French Enlightenment, both by Paul-Henri Thiry d'Holbach and this year: *Essai sur les préjugés* (Essay on Prejudices) and *Systém de la nature* (System of Nature). He consistently rejects their demands for the general education of the people. Immanuel Kant becomes a professor at the University of Königsberg.

1772 First division of Poland by the Russo-Prussian Treaty of St. Petersburg, which is joined by Austria. Prussia acquires West Prussia, apart from Danzig and Thorn, as well as Ermland and the Netze district – a total area of 36,000 square kilometers (13,900 square miles), with a population of 580,000. Frederick the Great gives himself the title of "King of Prussia," with immediate effect.
Frederick II publishes *Über den Nutzen der Künste und Wissenschaften im Staate* (On the Uses of the Arts and Sciences in the State).

1778 Bavarian War of Succession begins (to 1779): Frederick II, fearing the growing power of Austria, marches with his army into Bohemia. No open battle takes place, but the king exhausts all of his powers in the strategic operations.
Frederick II writes a commemorative speech in honour of Voltaire and has it read at the Academy of Sciences in Berlin.

1779 Peace of Teschen between Prussia and Austria, which is allotted the Inn valley. The Prussian succession in Ansbach and Bayreuth is guaranteed, and the right of inheritance of the house of Wittelsbach in Bavaria is assured.
There are 30,713 houses in the March of Brandenburg. This makes it clear that the number of houses is not significantly greater than before the Thirty Years' War.

1780 Frederick the Great disciplines Prussian judges in favor of Arnold the Miller (Müller Arnold case). Under the newly appointed minister Johann Heinrich, Count von Carmer, the judiciary reforms are continued with a view to drawing up a general statute book.
A book by Frederick, probably written much earlier, *Über die deutsche Literatur* (On German Literature), is published.
Frederick II orders the building of the domes of the Deutsche Kirche and the Französische Kirche (German and French Churches) on the Gendarmenmarkt in Berlin, to the designs of Carl Philipp von Gontard (1785).

1781 Immanuel Kant publishes *Kritik der reinen Vernunft* (Critique of Pure Reason).

1782 In order to stifle the expensive importation of coffee beans, Frederick the Great bans the private roasting of coffee. So-called "coffee sniffers" were appointed to supervise the implementation of the ban, to general ridicule.
Frederick the Great publishes *Über den politischen Zustand Europas* (On the State of European Politics).

1783 Johann Erich Biester and Friedrich Gedicke become editors of the newly founded *Berlinische Monatsschrift* (Berlin Monthly), which becomes the most important organ of the Berlin Enlightenment.

1784 Publication of selected parts of the draft General Common Law.
Immanuel Kant publishes *Was ist Aufklärung?* (What is the Enlightenment?)

1785 Frederick II initiates the foundation of the German *Fürstenbund* (Alliance of Princes), as a riposte to Austria's attempts to gain greater power in the German Reich.
Trade and friendship treaty between Prussia and the United States of America.

Improvement of Manners, etching by Daniel Chodowiecki, 1786

ARCHITECTURE, URBAN PLANNING, AND GARDEN DESIGN

Hans-Joachim Giersberg

Potsdam, Palace of Sanssouci, east latticed pavilion
(Detail) Sunburst

In the extension of the round library tower on the east side of the palace of Sanssouci stands the latticed pavilion with the sunburst decoration. A matching latticed pavilion on the west side bears a representation of a moon.

Architecture under Frederick the Great, 1740–1786

No Prussian king showed as much concern for architecture and building in Prussia, and particularly in the two royal capitals Berlin and Potsdam, as did Frederick the Great. His father, Frederick William I, had in fact designed rows of streets and made architectural plans; nor was he as negative in his attitude to artistic matters as is usually maintained. It was just that for him the principles of utility and order took priority. Frederick the Great's search for individual artistic solutions is comparable rather with the efforts of his great-grand-nephew Frederick William IV, a great number of whose architectural design sketches are known. But the latter never intervened in actual architectural work, nor attempted to supervise its administration according to his own ideas, as fully and as energetically as Frederick the Great did. In this respect he is placed at the end of a development that originated in France in the mid-17th century. The example of Louis XIV, in particular the concentration of power in one person, and his passion for building, spread his influence to almost all the princes of Europe.

At this time the *Schloss*, or palace, the precondition for a lifestyle befitting members of the nobility, became the prime symbol of princely power. Thus the European princes, and to some extent even the Catholic Church, became gripped by a building fever that reached its climax in the first quarter of the 18th century and began to subside only after the middle of the century.

Royal palaces of colossal proportions were projected, inspired by Versailles; we need think only of Schönbrunn, Karlsruhe, Mannheim, Ludwigsburg, Würzburg, Düsseldorf and, last but not least, Berlin. Not all were built in the form originally conceived, and often an heir inherited an unfinished building and a mountain of debts.

A keen delight in building and planning, above and beyond considerations of necessity and function, are characteristic of the whole era. Louis XIV's artistic advisor, Jean-Baptiste Colbert, told him that a prince could leave no greater memorial to posterity than architectural monuments. Moreover, the ruler should aim to be remembered not merely as the commissioner of a building, but also as someone who had exercised a direct influence on its planning and building. This was perfectly consistent with absolutist thinking: it is natural that a princely client should influence a project's artistic direction through his choice of the architect, the location and the size of his palace, and the disposition of the rooms. To take part in decisions over the execution of the project, and to make sudden alterations to plans and arbitrary interventions in the building work, were rights claimed as a matter of course by the absolutist client. Financial considerations played only a limited part.

So with respect to administrative and artistic participation in building matters, Frederick the Great was directly in the tradition of princely absolutist

rulers. But there is hardly any parallel for the intensity that the king brought to his decisions over building activities. The "chief and royal capital cities of Berlin and Potsdam" are, as they presented themselves at the end of the era of Frederick the Great, products of a royal client who enforced his own ideas resolutely and with great personal commitment. It was not least for this reason that the two cities developed into the artistic centres of Prussia during the second half of the 18th century.

"Here everything took place under his direct orders, supervision and execution," wrote Heinrich Ludewig Manger in his architectural history of Potsdam. In this account, published in 1789, Manger, who worked in the Potsdam building office from 1753 up until his death in 1790, not only informs us of the yearly building activity in Potsdam during the rule of Frederick the Great; above all he provides us with an invaluable insight into the activity of the king as client cum architect.

The king's interest in building work and how much it cost

Heinrich Ludewig Manger's testimony clarifies the way in which the king took an interest in every detail of the building work throughout the 40-odd years of his reign. His decisions, once taken, were immutable and had to be followed to the letter, even if they subsequently turned out to be mistaken. For every building project, a plan and estimate of costs had to be prepared, and only when these were approved by him was building allowed to begin. The building program was linked to a calendar year, and if a project overran (as happened particularly with the construction of palaces) it was resumed the

Potsdam, Sanssouci Palace
View of vineyard

The palace of Sanssouci, situated on the topmost terrace of the vineyard, built from 1745 to 1747 from plans by Georg Wenzeslaus von Knobelsdorff, was the summer residence of Frederick the Great until his death in 1786.

following year. Paramount in all cases was the king's personal plan, which included not only the building itself but also all the artistic contents, such as furniture, ceramics, paintings, sculpture, wall coverings, and so on.

On the king's direct orders, sums of money were transferred from the treasury to the director of the building office, who entered them in the income section of the accounts for the project in question, and then passed them to the accountant for the builders' pay office. The latter was responsible for supplying receipts to the king, paying the bills and, again after confirmation from the office director, preparing the final accounts.

An important function was performed by the treasurer, who acted as middleman between the royal client and the building office. He often had to pass on orders regarding building work to the architect concerned, and as he was not an expert in building matters, there were often misunderstandings.

The king's interest in building matters embraced not only the general design but also the details. He replied "immediately, on the day they were handed in, to all reports, proposals and queries concerning building projects, either in his own hand or through Cabinet documents which he signed," reports Manger. Even when he was out of the country he wanted to be kept informed at all times.

"Tell Knobelsdorff to write to me about my buildings, my furniture, my gardens and the opera house, to distract my mind," he wrote to Jordan, his secretary and trusted adviser. And further, to the same man, on May 8, 1742: "I have received a letter from Knobelsdorff, with whom I am very satisfied; but everything in it is too dry, there are no details. I would like the description of each part of a column at Charlottenburg to occupy four quarto pages, that would entertain me greatly." And soon afterwards: "Tell that fat Knobelsdorff to write to me about how things are looking at Charlottenburg, in my opera house and my gardens. I am like a child in these matters; these are the dolls I play with."

Apart from the king's intensive involvement, these passages from the king's letters reveal something else: as if he were at the theater, he wants to be "distracted," "entertained," wants to "play" with these things, just as he played on his flute. Despite all the seriousness that he brings to his building, and to surrounding himself with works of art, these activities are never free of Baroque capriciousness. It is a sort of leisure activity for him ... though a very expensive one.

All this stands in marked contrast to his thriftiness, which was heightened in the later years of his reign into a positive miserliness; he was continuously distrustful of all officials concerned with building, and indeed of all persons with whom he was involved in the most various of business relationships, whether they were actors, merchants, or goldsmiths. Voltaire reports: "In Potsdam, the utmost thriftiness was the guiding principle in all the king's inclinations."

He saw many estimates of costs as being too high; and so, to be on the safe side, he had those supplied by the Potsdam building contractor revised by the builder in Berlin, and vice versa. If necessary, repairs had to be carried out in the course of building, the builders had a constant battle to obtain authorization for the necessary funds. "It only needs to last as long as I live," he commented to an inspector; repairs, therefore, were not necessary.

Admittedly, the king's mistrust did have a certain justification. In the regulations for the Potsdam building office for 1752, he had specified that a detailed journal had to be kept, in which all deliveries to the building sites were to be recorded, and that this journal should be checked weekly. But in spite of such instructions, the reality was very different, as Manger writes: "Also, it was well known, and certainly the case, that no such quantities of materials as were bought and paid for were used for any building, and this was denied by no one. Just as well known is the cause for this, namely theft. For theft takes place from the ships which bring the materials; from the warehouses where they are stored; in the course of delivery; and at the building site itself; and this in so many different ways and by different people, that guards with the eyes of Argus could not manage to discover everything. On average, one-sixth must always be allowed for theft, and in some years the same proportion is accounted for by breakages, particularly when there are late frosts in the spring, which cause the building materials to crumble. It is quite possible that at times only two-thirds of the materials are to be found in a finished building, because the rest was unfit to be used."

Certainly the building contractors could not be held primarily responsible, but the mistrustful royal client always took action against them first when something was wrong with the building or when thefts took place.

King Frederick II, His Architect Knobelsdorff, and His Artistic Adviser Algarotti

As early as the year of Frederick's accession to the throne, 1740, Georg Wenzeslaus von Knobelsdorff was entrusted with the most important building contracts and thus *de facto* took over the direction of all Prussian building projects.

De jure, a Cabinet regulation of July 31, 1742, defined his position as "superintendent of all royal palaces, houses and gardens as well as *directeur en chef* of all structures in the various provinces." He was in charge of all building workers, and the employment of new staff depended on his decision. He was granted a seat and voting powers on the governing

Potsdam, Sanssouci Palace, central building
Garden side

At the summer residence of Frederick the Great, in the center of the side facing the vineyard is to be found the name of the palace, which is a motto: *sans souci*, without a care.

Opposite
Potsdam, Sanssouci Palace, colonnade on north side
Left side

The *cour d'honneur* on the north side of the palace ends in a colonnade of slender Corinthian columns, which forms a boundary to the courtyard but at the same time allows a view of the surrounding landscape.

Rheinsberg Palace, south and west sides

The west side of the palace, facing the lake, marked out by the two towers joined by a colonnade, is today practically a symbol of the architecture of Brandenburg-Prussia in the 18th century. No trace remains of the modest structures of its late medieval predecessors. The motif of the tower with the adjoining south wing, broken up by an unpretentious central projection, formed the basic principle of the three-winged arrangement whose courtyard opens onto the lake. In 1802 the towers, formerly flat-topped and intended as lookout points, were provided with conical roofs.

board, and in 1748 even acquired the rank of minister. Construction drawings were made as fair copies from Knobelsdorff's designs, and so-called *polierrisse* (polished versions) were produced, which formed the basis for the construction of the building. Among his immediate collaborators were Andreas Krüger, Johann Füncke, C. H. Horst, and perhaps also Johann Friedel.

During his time as crown prince at Neuruppin and later at Rheinsberg, Frederick had still allowed himself to be advised and directed in all artistic matters by Knobelsdorff.

Between Frederick, who was preparing to take up his royal role, and Knobelsdorff, until recently an army officer, and now undertaking his first ventures into architecture and garden design, there existed a teacher–pupil relationship that continued even during the first years after the prince's accession to the throne. It would appear that the relationship between Frederick and his chief architect was still untroubled at the beginning of his reign. This certainly applies to the time when planning was still taking place in Rheinsberg.

In the dedication portfolio of the plans for the Berlin opera house, Knobelsdorff commented that the king himself had produced the designs and passed them on to him to be executed. Since Knobelsdorff was far from being a court flatterer, his claim should be taken seriously. But there is evidence that the further realization of the plans for a Forum Fridericianum – of which, of course, the opera house was intended to form part – led to the first disputes between the client and the architect.

More and more, the king was freeing himself from Knobelsdorff's influence. Frederick proved that he was by no means an orthodox follower of the French academic school; as early as with the Berlin Opera House, then with the Potsdam Palace and other buildings, he had adopted the British version of Palladianism. The prints in his five private libraries were an important source of ideas; these libraries were in his palaces in Potsdam, Sanssouci, the New Palace, at Charlottenburg, and Breslau.

In these libraries nearly all the most important architectural works of the time were represented. These included literature about buildings of classical antiquity, in Rome, Paestum, Baalbec, Greece; important works on French architecture by Jacques François Blondel, Jean Mariette, Robert Pitrou; various editions of the works of Andrea Palladio as well as his Italian and British followers such as Vincenzo Scamozzi and Colen Campbell; and architectural prints from Vienna and Stockholm.

"The King had the works of Piranesi and Panini constantly lying on the table in his room, and it was from these that he drew the instructions he gave for the construction of buildings in Berlin and Potsdam," reports a contemporary.

The king obtained the books from his agent in Paris. As far as Palladio is concerned, the most influential intermediary was the Venetian patrician Francesco Algarotti. Algarotti was one of the king's most important advisers in artistic and particularly architectural matters. The crown prince and the count had met as early as September 1739, at Rheinsberg. Algarotti was, as Voltaire reports, "a most amiable Venetian and the son of a very rich merchant, had traveled throughout Europe, knew about everything and lent charm to all things."

In a relationship that lasted 25 years, and which was predominantly cordial, this amiable Venetian influenced the king's architectural ambitions to an extent not to be underestimated. On June 2, 1740, only a few days after his accession, Frederick the Great summoned him to Berlin, where he arrived on June 28. Algarotti soon won a position of trust.

In April 1747 he received both the Ordre pour le Mérite and the title of chamberlain. On February 2, 1753, Algarotti, with the king's permission, traveled to Italy – he had already spent some time there at the end of 1748 – and in July 1754 he was granted the discharge he had requested. He lived first in Venice, then in Bologna, and from 1762 in Pisa, where he died in 1764. Frederick II had a monument set up to him at the cemetery there.

During his stay in Berlin and Potsdam, and also later from Italy, Algarotti made every effort to supply the king with new works of architecture in the form of prints and drawings. On August 4, 1751, he wrote to the king: "In accordance with your Majesty's wishes, I have written concerning the Pitti Palace and the new Palladio, which is being printed in Venice and I hope your Majesty will accord the same honour to the architects of Venice as you have done to those of Rome and Versailles, namely to give a new home to some of their creations and to mingle them with your own. Potsdam will become a school of architecture, as it is already a school of the art of war."

The practice of building by starting from the façade – and it was only this that interested the king – resulted in inadequate living conditions for town houses. Not infrequently, the front views of palaces, or buildings resembling palaces, with a striking first floor, had to be combined, as far as possible, with plans for an appropriate bourgeois lifestyle.

Thus there were particularly high-ceilinged rooms, while the floors in between were correspondingly low-ceilinged, and badly lit, with some windows at floor level. These houses were built partly at the king's expense and donated to the owners, who received a document signed by the king recording the gift, with the obligation not to alter the façade in any way. In this way the uniform, mansion-like character was preserved.

Georg Wenzeslaus von Knobelsdorff
Temple of Apollo in the Amalthea Garden, Neuruppin

Built in 1735, this temple was the first work of the celebrated architect Georg Wenzeslaus von Knobelsdorff. The structure (a round building formed by single columns) was strongly influenced by the forms of classical antiquity, and was the first of its kind in Prussian architectural history; it was much imitated in the 18th century, notably in the Temple of Friendship at Sanssouci. A statue of Apollo originally stood on the flat cupola roof. The appearance of the temple has been materially changed by the walling-in of the spaces between the columns in 1791.

The term *Fassadenzwang* (façade requirement) was employed, but looked at in a positive way, it was perhaps the beginning of the concept of the preservation of historic buildings.

The beginnings: Neuruppin and Rheinsberg

New developments often take place in the provinces, far away from the main cultural centres and undisturbed by official developments. And this was the case with the architecture of the age of Frederick the Great, which had its roots in a little temple in the town of Neuruppin, some 80 kilometers (50 miles) northwest of Berlin. It was there, incidentally, that one of the most important German architects, Karl Friedrich Schinkel, was to be born at the end of the 18th century, as was similarly the poet of the March of Brandenburg, Theodor Fontane, at the beginning of the 19th century.

In 1732, Crown Prince Frederick, after agreeing to a marriage with Princess Elizabeth Christine of Brunswick-Bevern, had become commander of a regiment stationed in Nauen and Neuruppin, and had set up a modest establishment in two simple houses in Neuruppin. The gardens extended as far as the city wall and the ramparts in front of them, which, following the orders of Frederick William I, had already, between 1726 and 1730, been partially levelled and transformed into gardens for the middle classes. The crown prince was well aware of the regional characteristics of the ramparts with their distinctive trees, and not only refused to have the trees felled, but also had more trees planted and paths laid for the citizens' use. He himself acquired a small section of the rampart area in direct proximity to his home and had a garden designed – perhaps by Knobelsdorff – for vegetables and fruit, but also with decorative hedges. Frederick named it Amalthea, probably after the country residence of Atticus, a friend of the Roman orator Cicero. This is the first example of Frederick's principle of combining function and decorative qualities in one garden, which was soon to be expressed in more striking form at Rheinsberg and later at Sanssouci. The creative focus of the garden was a round building surrounded by single columns (see page 163), designed by Knobelsdorff and erected in 1735. On August 24, 1735, Frederick wrote to his favorite sister, Wilhelmine, in Bayreuth: "I am also occupying myself with gardening, and beginning to design a garden for us. The garden house is a temple with eight Doric columns bearing a cupola. A statue of Apollo stands upon it. As soon as it is finished we will offer sacrifices – to you, of course, dear sister, the protectress of the fine arts."

It is the first work by Knobelsdorff, who had since 1732 belonged to the closest and most intimate group around the crown prince. Under the influence of the artist and architect Antoine Pesne, he at first

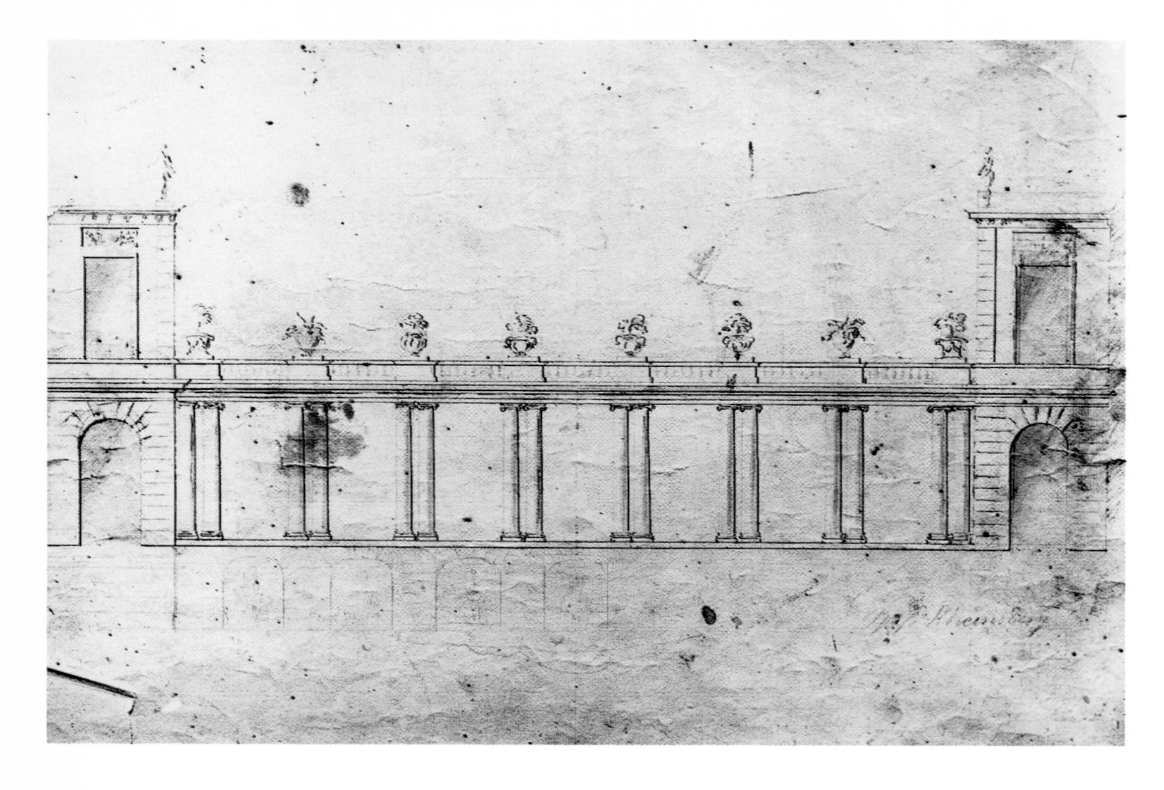

Top
Georg Wenzeslaus von Knobelsdorff
Rheinsberg Palace, elevation of the colonnade (c. 1735)
Pencil and brown ink with gray wash
34.2 x 48.2 cm; Potsdam, Stiftung Preussische Schlösser und Gärten, Berlin-Brandenburg, Plankammer

Up to 1736, the royal building director J. G. Kemmeter had been rebuilding the old palace complex, on a provisional basis, so that the crown prince and his consort could occupy. Knobelsdorff took over the direction in 1737, extending the building into a three-winged design with the colonnade closing off the courtyard.

Above
Georg Wenzeslaus von Knobelsdorff
View from Rheinsberg (c. 1745)
Chalk on black paper with white highlights
25.7 x 42.8 cm; Potsdam, Stiftung Preussische Schlösser und Gärten, Berlin-Brandenburg, Plankammer

The drawing shows the garden portal with the obelisk in front and the completed palace behind.

Opposite
Rheinsberg Palace, Tower Cabinet

The motif of the round room, like this one at Rheinsberg, was also Frederick's model for the library at Sanssouci.

inclined more towards art, and provided evidence of his skill in both portraits and the representation of the local landscape in the manner of Claude Lorrain. He received his architectural education and instruction from Johann Gottfried Kemmeter, A. von Wangenheim, and Christian Friedrich Feldmann, who were very much in the post-Schlüter tradition of Böhme, Gerlach, and Grael.

The new, conscious orientation looking towards classical antiquity and the architecture of the late Renaissance – particularly that of Palladio – is already stated in the temple of Apollo. The preserved drawing by Knobelsdorff, showing the ground plan and elevation, not only suggests the double-column motif which he later used over and over again, but above all his intense preoccupation, after the journey to Dresden of 1732, with the proportions and arrangement of columns of classical qrchitecture. The motif and intellectual content were taken up again by Frederick in the temple of friendship at Sanssouci, which was erected in 1768 to the memory of his sister, Wilhelmine, who had died in 1757. It is thus evident even in this first temple, which is modest by comparison with later architectural productions under Frederick the Great, that the buildings created in close cooperation with Knobelsdorff left their mark on the king for the remainder of his life. This is also clear from the relationship between Rheinsberg and Sanssouci; from the marble hall and theater in the Potsdam Palace and the corresponding rooms in the New Palace at Sanssouci; and finally from the city gates of Potsdam and Berlin.

Rheinsberg

From his seat at Neuruppin, the crown prince discovered Rheinsberg, only a few miles away, which his father, Frederick William I, acquired for him from the former owner, Beville. The rebuilding of the moated castle, which dated back to the 16th century, was entrusted to Johann Gottfried Kemmeter. The so-called Klingenberg wing was

Rheinsberg Palace, Mirror Room

The Mirror Room, situated on the upper floor of the north wing, was the banqueting hall of the palace. The large ceiling painting by Antoine Pesne shows Aurora, the goddess of the dawn, driving away darkness. This theme is taken to be an allegorical reference to the impending accession of Frederick II.

Opposite
Rheinsberg Palace, Shell Room

Prince Henry received Rheinsberg as a gift from his brother in 1744. From 1766, he had alterations made to the decoration of the rooms after drawings by Carl Gotthard Langhans. Situated next to the stairwell, the Shell Room acquired its present size and decoration with shells and coral in 1769.

Right
Rheinsberg, view from the obelisk to the palace

In 1790–1791, Prince Henry had an obelisk set up on the rise opposite the palace in place of a column of Trajan, which had been erected in 1765. He dedicated the obelisk to the heroes of the Seven Years' War, who in his opinion had not been sufficiently honored by Frederick the Great. From the obelisk, the view is across the lake of Grienerick to the waterfront of the palace. The pavilions built by Georg Friedrich Boumann the Younger in 1786, turned towards the town, are clearly outlined.

extended, and the apartments of the crown prince and his consort were set up in the added upper story. The *corps de logis* was created at right angles to this, using the older foundations. In 1736, after a period of building that lasted several years, the crown prince was able to move into the apartments with his wife, who had lived in Berlin since their marriage in 1733.

The latest research takes as its starting point the fact that the plan, with its three wings, two round towers, and connecting colonnade, can be traced back to Kemmeter and is not, as has previously been assumed, the work of Knobelsdorff. This also explains the partly traditional division of the façade. The colonnade motif, which forms the end of the courtyard, can be traced back to the arcade between the side wings at the palace of Oranienburg (see pages 162, 164). Knobelsdorff, on the crown prince's orders, had been in Italy in 1736–1737, and only after his return did he take up the direction of the building, which was then progressing only slowly because of the economical policy that had been laid down. The motto in the cartouche above the main entrance on the city side – *Friderico tranquillitatem*

Rheinsberg, view from the palace colonnade towards the obelisk

This view clearly shows the close connection between architecture and garden at Rheinsberg. From the palace courtyard the outlook traverses the flat island with the figure of Apollo, created by the Italian sculptor Giovanni Antonio Cybei and set up here in 1769, and passes across the water of Lake Grienerick to the obelisk erected in 1790–1791.

Opposite, below
Rheinsberg, pavilion in the orangery in the palace park

In the center of the great orangery roundel, which interrupts the diagonal avenue, stands a pavilion, the remains of an orangery designed by Knobelsdorff, but never completed. When the roundel was first planned in 1753, parts of the side wings were already being dismantled, and in 1790 the remaining cabinets were also removed. After the glass doors had been taken out in the mid-19th century, and the balustrades decorated with putti and vases had also been removed, the roof acquired its present form. Even though only the shell of the original building is left, it remains an example of Knobelsdorff's architectural language.
The four marble statues by Giovanni Antonio Cybei, placed here in 1769, represent the four seasons.

colenti MDCCXXXIX (dedicated to Frederick, who cultivates leisure here) – states the date of completion of the exterior building work, 1739. The interior work had still not been completed by the time Prince Henry took over the palace.

Johann Karl Scheffler's decoration, which sometimes has a rather heavy effect, becomes somewhat looser and livelier under Knobelsdorff in the north wing. Few experienced artists were as yet available. Johann Christian Glume was employed as a sculptor and Antoine Pesne as a painter; Pesne's ceiling paintings in five of the rooms, still preserved today, reflect the crown prince's intellectual world, influenced as it was by classical antiquity (see pages 165 and 167). Frederick's time at Rheinsberg was the happiest and most unconstrained period of his life. The stay was characterized by a close artistic cooperation with Knobelsdorff, which resulted in design models such as the colonnade, the library in the tower, scenes from Ovid for the music rooms, and the garden portal with the obelisks. Later, these models were to be repeated at Sanssouci on a higher artistic level. The garden, too, with its avenue starting from the south wing, with hedged areas, and a large diagonal avenue, can be traced back to Knobelsdorff's influence. But it was only to receive its definitive form under Prince Henry (see above and opposite).

Building in Berlin and Potsdam Under Frederick the Great

Over 40 years of architectural activity (1740–1786) under the rule of Frederick the Great left a deep impression on Berlin and Potsdam. Their architectural development had begun with the rise of Brandenburg-Prussia as a political power under the Great Elector Frederick William, and had reached a high point under the first Prussian king, Frederick I. Andreas Schlüter and the Huguenot Jean de Bodt understood the art of giving due architectural expression to the demands of the king. However, there was a clearly evident awareness of France and Louis XIV. "Under Frederick I, Berlin had been the Athens of the north; under Frederick William it became the Sparta of the north," was how Frederick the Great described the artistic turnabout. Frederick William I, "who loved useful and feasible projects," did indeed extend both cities, but this took place without great architectural extravagance, with the exception of the case of churches. But the development of middle-class buildings for Berlin and Potsdam, which today appears thoroughly modern, was perceived by the next generation as "monotony," and the neat, newly

Johann Michael Hoppenhaupt the Elder
Design for the wall decoration of the Great (Golden) Gallery in the New Wing of Charlottenburg Palace (1742–1743)
Pencil and pen, brown India ink and wash, 31.8 x 45.8 cm; Potsdam, Potsdam-Museum

In this drawing, which is attributed to the elder Johann Hoppenhaupt, various alternative suggestions are presented for the decoration of the wall-piers and the window niches in the gallery.

Berlin, Charlottenburg Palace, south side of the New Wing

Soon after Frederick the Great's accession, in July 1740, work began on a counterpart to the orangery, created on the west side by Eosander von Göthe after 1700. In the structure of the building, Knobelsdorff makes a reference to the architectural system of the orangery by the insertion of a five-axis central projection. Work on the exterior and on the dining room cum throne room (today called the White Room) on the upper floor of the central projection was completed in all essentials by 1742. Work on (and in) the New Wing, by contrast, was not concluded until 1746.

laid-out streets were seen "as though their houses represented a line of soldiers, with the bay windows in the roofs above the second floors resembling grenadiers' caps." However, only three years after the accession of Frederick II, no less a person than Voltaire remarked on his visit to Berlin: "His [the king's] concern is now totally directed towards beautifying the city of Berlin, building one of the finest opera houses in Europe, and bringing artists of all kinds to the city. For he wished to gain fame by all means and as cheaply as possible ... things changed visibly: Sparta became Athens."

Berlin 1740–1753: Monbijou and Charlottenburg

After Frederick II's accession, one of Knobelsdorff's first commissions was to extend and convert the palace of Monbijou, as the home of the widowed Queen Mother, Sophia Dorothea, adding two wings on the east side. Knobelsdorff himself carried out this project, to the Queen's satisfaction, and the work was completed by the middle of 1742. Although there are no accounts of Frederick's influence that have been recorded, the king must certainly have discussed his wishes and proposals with the architect, especially considering the young monarch's veneration of his mother.

In the very same year of Frederick's accession, Knobelsdorff also received the commission to build the New Wing at the palace of Charlottenburg (see opposite, below). The palace had been built by Johann Arnold Nehring between 1695 and 1699 for the Electress Sophia Charlotte, and in 1701 it was extended by Eosander von Göthe. However, the east side lacked a counterpart to the orangery on the west side.

Knobelsdorff found an excellent solution: he gave an unpretentious though stately character to the long-drawn-out structure by emphasizing the center by means of a shallow, five-axis central projection. For a princely residence it has an unusual form. The official opening of the building took place on August 29, 1742, although the Golden Gallery (below and opposite, above) was not completed until 1746 and the "apartments of three salons and a chamber," the second residence of Frederick the Great, not until 1747. It has not been possible to ascertain with what degree of precision the king conveyed his artistic ideas to the architect,

Berlin, Charlottenburg Palace, Golden Gallery

The Great Gallery in the New Wing (known since the mid-19th century as the Golden Gallery), is one of the most splendid creations of interior decoration under Frederick the Great. The large windows on the two longer walls of the 42-meter (138-feet) room not only create a connection with the garden, but also enable a diverse play of light over the green of the stucco marble and the gilded ornamentation. The original decoration of the room also included gilded benches and classical busts on tall pedestals. The gallery was burnt out in 1943, with the exception of a few remains of decoration, and it was restored between 1961 and 1973.

Berlin, Charlottenburg Palace, White Room in the New Wing

The White Room, built in 1742 as the dining room cum throne room of Frederick the Great on the upper floor of the New Wing, was burnt out in 1943. Only the reliefs above the doors, which represent the four seasons, were substantially preserved. The reconstruction repeated the division of the walls with pilasters, but of the ceiling decoration, only the ornamental part could be copied from old designs. In 1972–1973, the artist Hann Trier created a modern variation in place of Antoine Pesne's ceiling painting *The Marriage of Peleus and Thetis*.

Opposite
Berlin, Charlottenburg Palace, library of Frederick the Great

This narrow, gallery-like room, with its silver-plated decoration on walls and ceiling, was restored in its essentials after being destroyed in 1943. However, both the ceiling paintings are missing. Although the six cedarwood bookcases belong to the original scheme of the room under Frederick the Great, they were probably created as early as 1735 for the Potsdam Palace or Monbijou. Today, they contain the books from the library of Frederick in the Potsdam Palace. The console table, one of the finest of its genre, is attributed to Johann Michael Hoppenhaupt the Elder.

though letters survive that show how much interest he took in the progress of the building work. In the early 1740s Frederick did not yet manifest his later stubborn insistence on architectural solutions formulated by himself, but even then he had very clear notions as far as his own immediate living space was concerned.

Thus his study, bedroom, and library (see opposite) lie next to each other, facing the garden side, positively modest in their proportions, "but very personal in the fusion of the artistic and intellectual content" (Kühn). By contrast, there has never, in later times, been a grander staircase than that at Charlottenburg Palace. In the White Room, the king's dining room and the throne room (see above), Knobelsdorff's classicism is combined with Antoine Pesne's artistic flair in the ceiling painting. The high point of Rococo under Frederick the Great is undoubtedly the Golden Gallery, a creation of Knobelsdorff's.

Berlin, Opera House Unter den Linden, side view

The Opera House, built between 1741 and 1743, and according to Knobelsdorff's designs, was burnt out in 1843 and was reconstructed by Karl Ferdinand Langhans the Younger with late-classical interior decoration. Destroyed by bombing in 1941, it was rebuilt in 1943, only to become a victim of bombing for the second time soon afterwards. Its rebuilding between 1952 and 1955 to a design by Richard Paulick to a great extent preserved the appearance of the exterior, but a tall structure was added above the extended stage area.

The Forum Fridericianum

With the Opera House, built by Knobelsdorff between 1741 and 1743 (see above), a new architectural era began in Berlin. The king, in Silesia while building went on, requested its completion "within two months." This was impossible. Even on Frederick's return and the provisional opening on December 7, 1742, in the king's presence, there was scaffolding everywhere, and of the Apollo Hall only the foundation walls were to be seen. Only in the following year was the building finally completed, and a second ceremonial opening took place. Contemporaries were full of praise; they found the building to be imbued with the spirit of classical antiquity, and constructed in the manner of the "great Palladio." It is undoubtedly the result of the close cooperation between Knobelsdorff and the king during the king's Rheinsberg period. The king had contributed his share to the design, as remarked by Knobelsdorff in the dedication folder containing the plans for the Opera House (see opposite). The Opera House was part of a grandiose forum, which provided for the construction of a palace with side wings on the street called Unter den Linden, and also, opposite, the Opera House and the Academy of Sciences (see page 177). Thus the Opera House was setting new directions for architecture and town planning. But the king had already made corrections to the plan, which had probably been created in Rheinsberg before 1740, which clarify his stubborn insistence on his own involvement.

This unique idea of the Forum Fridericianum, which would have created a town-planning connection with the Gendarmenmarkt in addition to the Markgrafenstrasse, was not realized. From 1744, the king turned his attention to Potsdam. Nevertheless, during the 1740s Berlin acquired a few more monumental buildings to underlined its character as the capital: in 1747–1750, the Dome at the Lustgarten (a pleasure garden), from 1747 the Hedwigskirche behind the Opera House, and in 1748–1753 the palace of Prince Henry, the substantially reduced variant of the previously planned royal palace. For all these projects the king had prepared sketches and chosen

Below
Georg Wenzeslaus von Knobelsdorff
Royal Opera House, Unter den Linden, Berlin, elevation of column (1742)
Brown ink and brown wash, painted in polychrome watercolor, 61 x 90 cm; Potsdam, Stiftung Preussische Schlösser und Gärten, Berlin-Brandenburg, Plankammer

On his journeys to Italy and France, Knobelsdorff had become familiar with both classical and contemporary architecture. But his greatest teacher was undoubtedly Palladio, whose rules he applied with respect to the relationship of the individual architectural parts. His starting-point is the diameter of the column, divided into 60 parts, each part called a module. From this he also obtains the height of the column and the space between two columns.

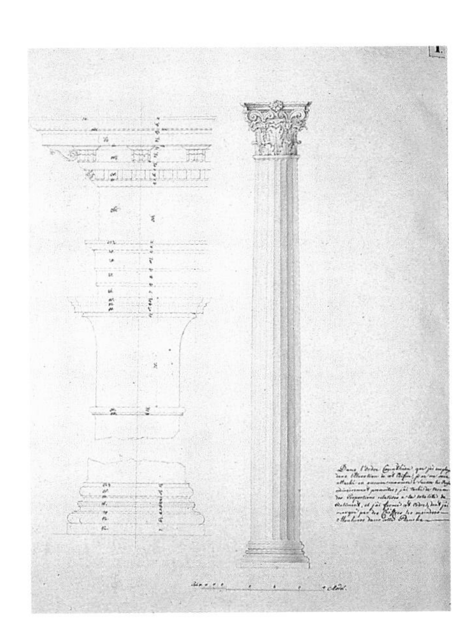

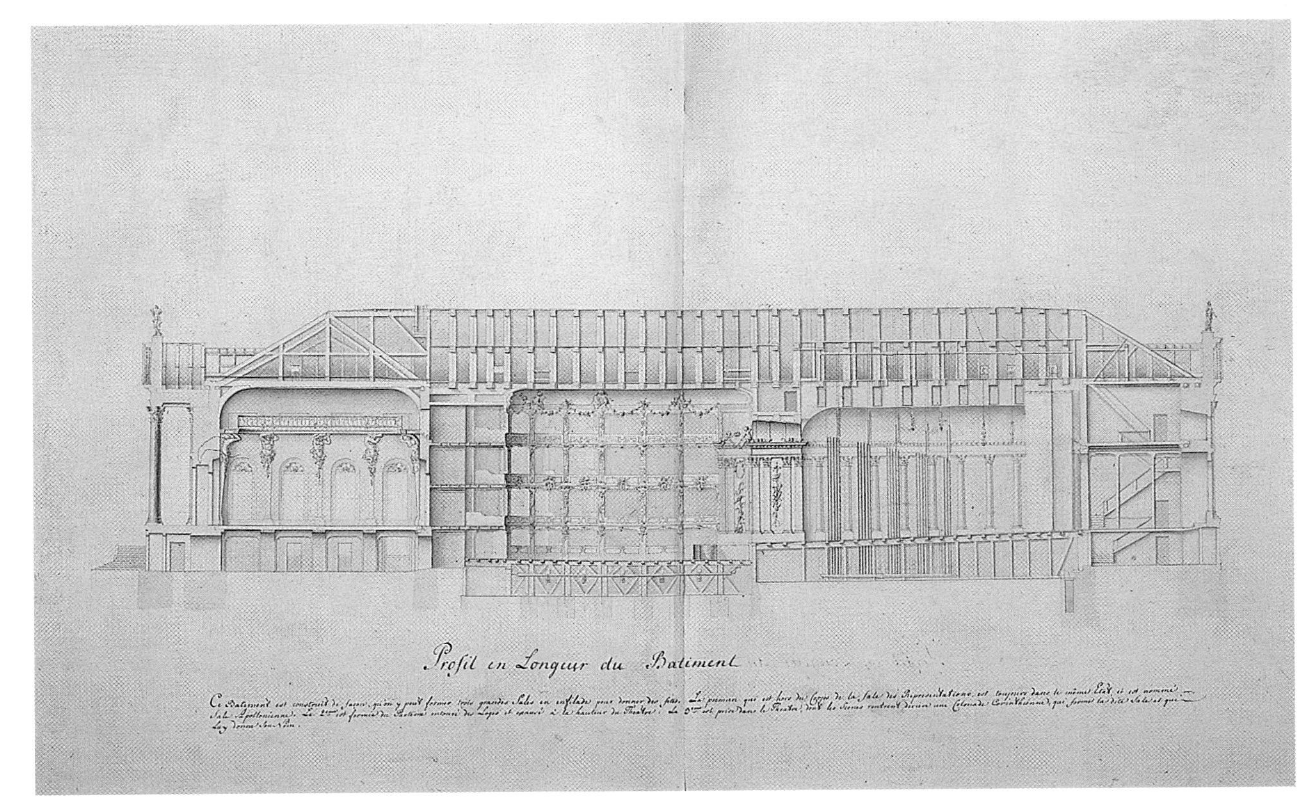

Above
Georg Wenzeslaus von Knobelsdorff
Royal Opera House Unter den Linden in Berlin, elevation of a column (1742)
Brown ink, brown wash, polychrome watercolor, 61 x 90 cm; Potsdam, Stiftung Preussische Schlösser und Gärten, Berlin-Brandenburg, Plankammer

The architecture illustrated by this column was admired by contemporaries for its classicist language of forms, which was strongly influenced by British followers of Palladio.

Above
Georg Wenzeslaus von Knobelsdorff
Royal Opera House Unter den Linden in Berlin, longitudinal section (1742)
Brown ink, brown wash, polychrome watercolor, 61 x 90 cm; Potsdam, Stiftung Preussische Schlösser und Gärten, Berlin-Brandenburg, Plankammer

This drawing shows the longitudinal section through the Apollo Room, the auditorium designed as a theater with boxes, which could be transformed into a banqueting hall by means of a technique that increased the area of the stalls and the stage area. The sculptural programme was dedicated to Apollo and the Muses.

the location. The Hedwigskirche (see page 178) was not originally part of the forum plan; it is an addition that the king undertook for political reasons. The intention was to provide a spiritual home for the Catholics of Berlin, and particularly those subjects who came from Silesia, which had been conquered in two wars. Dedicated to St. Hedwig, the patron saint of Silesia, the building was modelled on the Pantheon in Rome, the temple of all the gods, which gave it the character of a token of tolerance; the

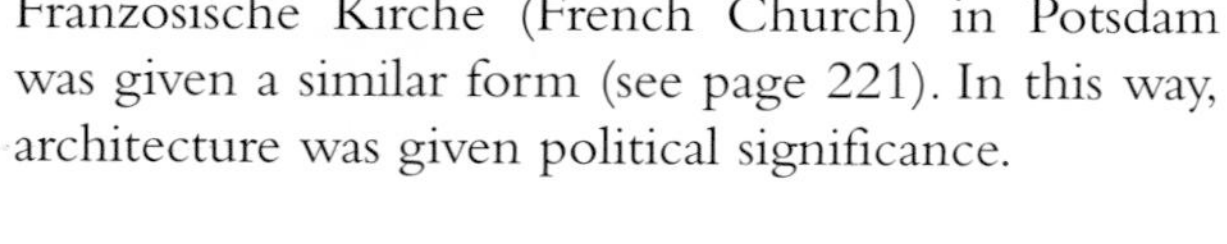
Französische Kirche (French Church) in Potsdam was given a similar form (see page 221). In this way, architecture was given political significance.

Opposite, below
Carl Friedrich Fechhelm
Berlin, view along Unter den Linden (1755–1765)
Oil on canvas, 62 x 94.7 cm; Potsdam, Stiftung Preussische Schlösser und Gärten, Berlin-Brandenburg

From the Opera House square one looks westward along Unter den Linden. The Opera House is on the left. On the right is Prince Henry's *palais*, and beyond it, Jean Boumann's Royal Academy of Sciences and Arts, built in 1748. The plan for a Forum Fridericianum was carried out only in a restricted form, but the newly created buildings show that Unter den Linden had developed into a street of great splendor.

Left
Johann Georg Rosenberg
View of the Berlin Opera House (1782)
Etching, 48.2 x 71.5 cm; Berlin, Stiftung Preussische Schlösser und Gärten, Berlin-Brandenburg, Plankammer

The Platz am Opernhause (Opera House Square), leading off from Unter den Linden, was bounded on the east side by the Opera House and the Hedwigskirche (far left) standing at an angle behind it, with the houses of the Behrenstrasse adjoining on the south side. Opposite stood the orangery of the Bredow Palace, hardly an appropriate structure for this square.

Johann Georg Rosenberg
View of the Berlin Opera House (1782)
Etching, colored, 48.2 x 71.5 cm; Berlin, Stiftung Preussische Schlösser und Gärten, Berlin-Brandenburg, Plankammer

Having acquiring the site in 1744, between 1775 and 1780 Frederick the Great had the Königliche Bibliothek (Royal Library) built, after a design by Fischer von Erlach for the Michaeler wing of the Hofburg in Vienna. The return to Baroque forms of architecture forms a singular contrast to the nearby Opera House, which had an even more modern appearance at the time.

Right
Berlin, Platz am Opernhause
Potsdam, Stiftung Preussische Schlösser und Gärten, Berlin-Brandenburg

Together with Knobelsdorff, Frederick the Great planned a forum on Unter den Linden that was to consist of an opera house, a large town palace, and a building for the Academy of Science. However, only the royal Opera House was built according to this plan. The place of the town palace was taken after 1748 by the smaller *palais* for Prince Henry, and it was not until 1775 to 1780 that Georg Christian Unger built the Königliche Bibliothek (Royal Library), colloquially known as the "chest of drawers," from a façade design by Fischer von Erlach for the Michaeler wing of the Vienna Hofburg. Not originally included in the forum plan, the Catholic Hedwigskirche (far right) was built south of the opera house.

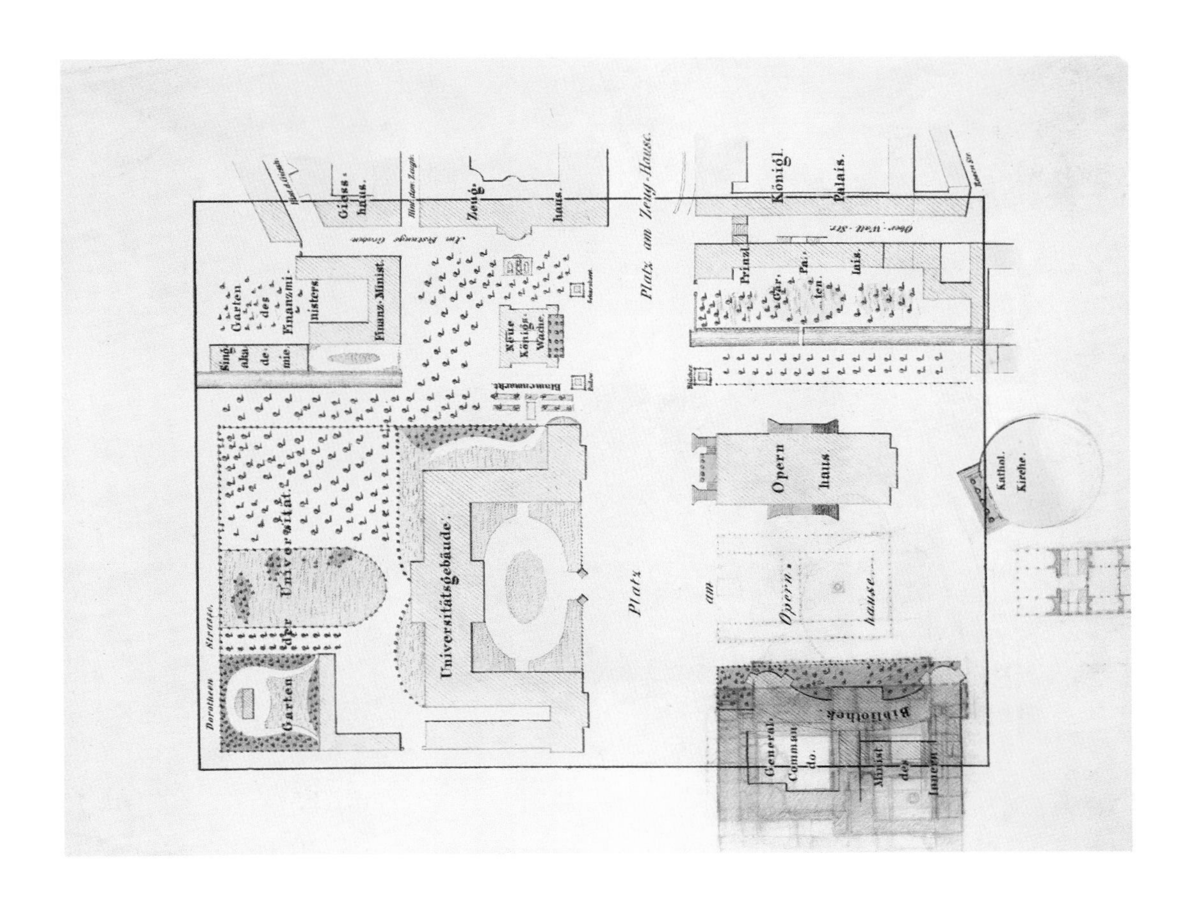

Jean-Laurent Legeay
(also called Le Geay)
Longitudinal section of the Hedwigskirche with sacristy (1748)
Etching; Staatliche Museen zu Berlin-Prussischer Kulturbesitz, Zupferstichkabinett

As Legeay's etching shows, the interior of the Hedwigskirche was to have been richly furnished. Double Corinthian columns support a broad cornice, above which rises a cupola, completely covered with painted scenes. Here there are saints floating on clouds, and scenes of Baroque trompe l'oeil decoration. However, the painting was abandoned for lack of funds. It was not until 1773 that the stage painter Bernardino Gagliari executed a simple decorative scheme at his own expense.

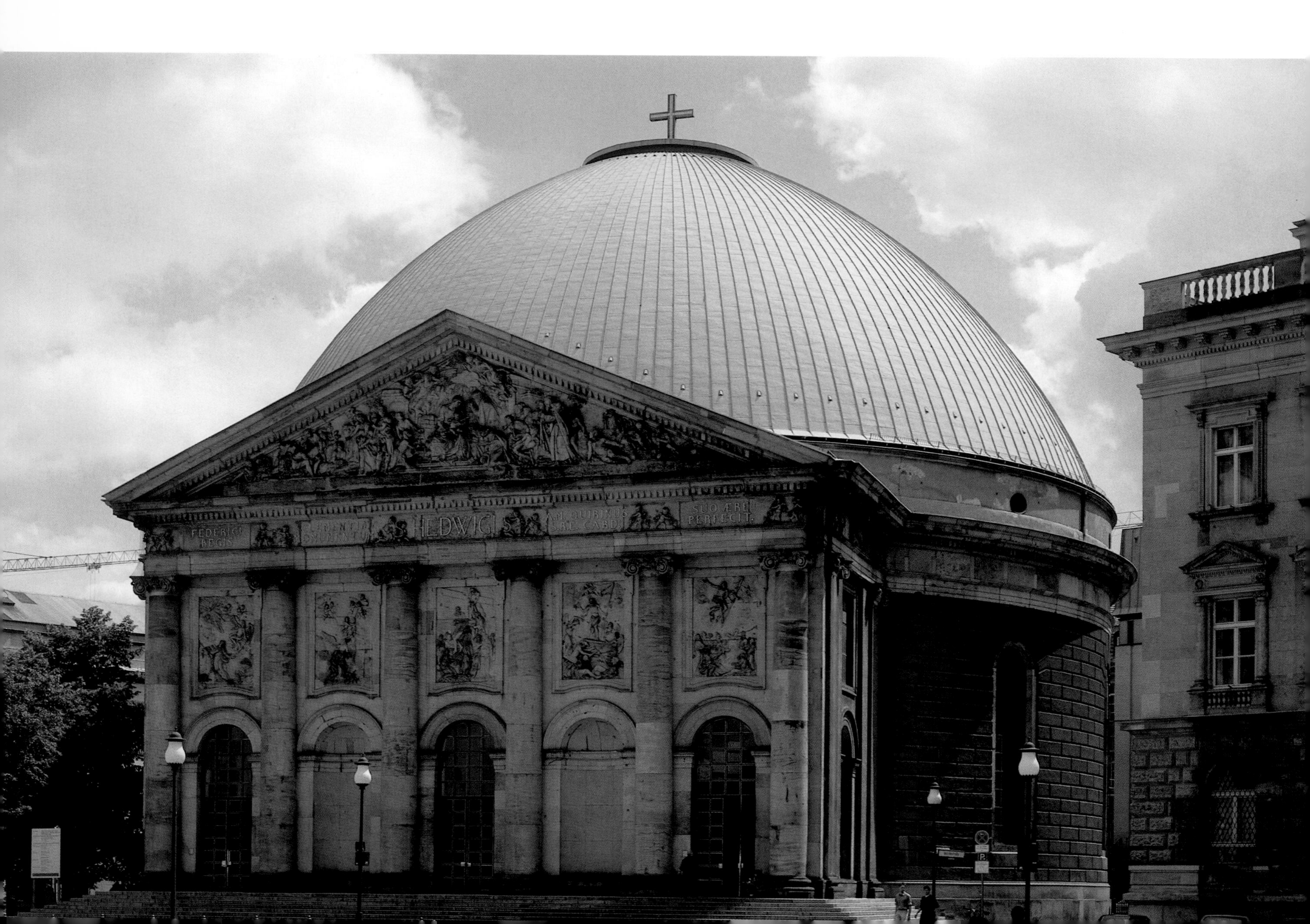

The town palace in Potsdam

While work was still proceeding at Charlottenburg, a new project had already been conceived: the extension of Potsdam to form a new royal capital, which was soon to take priority for Frederick over Berlin and Charlottenburg. How this came about cannot be precisely determined. Perhaps Charlottenburg was too close to Berlin and the king did not enjoy the seclusion there that he desired.

However, one cannot exclude the fact that the surrounding landscape – hilly, wooded countryside, with the lake-like course of the Havel – was similar to that of Rheinsberg, and that Potsdam was closer to the capital, Berlin, than Rheinsberg.

Soon after his accession, Frederick the Great had begun to undertake alterations to the interior of the town palace of Potsdam. The building – which had been constructed between 1662 and 1669 under the Elector Frederick William on the site of an old castle complex and a later Renaissance structure, and extended further between 1679 and 1682 – had experienced a whole series of internal and external alterations under the first Prussian king, Frederick I. When Frederick II (the Great) first came to power, the palace consisted of a three-story *corps de logis*, emphasized by central and corner projections, and two side wings of lower height, which again ended in three-story structures. The court room was closed off by a flat gallery building, projecting in an arch towards the Alter Markt, with the Fortuna Gate, built in 1700–1701 by Jean de Bodt, in its center (see below and page 180).

As early as 1740–1741, Frederick the Great had chosen for his own use the rooms in the southeast corner of the main building on the first floor, which had formerly been occupied by the Electress Dorothea and Queen Charlotte.

In 1744, Johann August Nahl designed the six rooms west of the Marble Hall, which formerly had been occupied by Elector Frederick William and then later Frederick I, so that some rooms for the use of Frederick the Great adjoined the banqueting room. However, the king very soon relinquished these rooms to his guests, and extended his eastern residential suite (see page 180). Apart from this internal redesign and rebuilding, the same year also saw work take place on the exterior, which by now hardly harmonized with the more and more grandiose interior.

The external rebuilding of the Potsdam town palace was carried out in three stages. The first stage in 1744 included renovation and cleaning; the second, in 1745–1746, involved more thorough rebuilding, according to a plan by Knobelsdorff; and the third, which began in 1747 and ended in 1752, led to the completion of the whole building – at this stage, the intensive involvement of the king himself is shown by the plans.

Opposite, below
Hedwigskathedrale, Berlin

From 1747, Frederick the Great had the Catholic Hedwigskirche (which is now a cathedral) built according to his own sketches and Knobelsdorff's plans, south of the Opera House on the site of an old fortress bastion. The building of the church dragged on until 1773, and of the sacristy until 1779. The building, modelled on the Pantheon in Rome, the classical temple of all the gods, gave architectural expression to the King's principle of tolerance. The Hedwigskirche was the largest church built in Berlin under Frederick the Great.

Potsdam, Alter Markt
Aerial view (c. 1935)

The Alter Markt (Old Market Square) was Potsdam's urban and artistic center. It is dominated by the Nikolaikirche (right), built between 1830 and 1850 from plans by Carl Friedrich Schinkel; and by the town palace (left, now destroyed), which occupied the south side of the square, and which was closed off by the Fortuna Gate with its circular arch. On the east side stands the Rathaus (City Hall), with its small cupola. All three buildings were aligned with the obelisk designed by Knobelsdorff, which stands in the center.

Potsdam, entrance to the town palace on the Alter Markt (destroyed)

The south front of the Alter Markt is determined by the entrance side of the town palace. Between the tall side wings of varying size, each of which ends in a portico, there extends the gallery, lower in height, at whose center stands the semicircular Fortuna Gate. While the Elector's palace was rebuilt between 1744 and 1752 according to plans by Knobelsdorff and the ideas of Frederick the Great, it was the king who decided that the Fortuna Gate, erected on the occasion of the coronation in 1701, should not be altered.

Potsdam, south and east side of the town palace (destroyed)

From the southern point of the Freundschaftsinsel (Island of Friendship), the entire size of the town palace becomes evident. The east front stretches along Humboldtstrasse as far as the Alter Markt and is divided by shallow projections. Behind the Havel colonnade, built by Georg Wenzeslaus von Knobelsdorff in 1745–1746, and still preserved today, the splendid garden side of the building emerges. The central projection stands out with its ramp, which leads into the great Marble Hall. In front of the apartments of Frederick the Great, which were located in the first upper story of the southeast corner building, stood the so-called Bittschriftenlinde (Petitions Linden), a linden tree to which anyone could attach a petition addressed to the king.

Frederick the Great
Potsdam, Palace
Sketch in the king's own hand of the central projection on the garden side of the corps de logis (end of 1746)
Pencil drawing; Berlin, formerly Hohenzollernmuseum, Schloss Monbijou; missing since 1945

Knobelsdorff had planned only a division by means of pilasters or half-columns for the stairwell on the north side of the *corps de logis*. This must have pleased the king so much that in the sketch shown here he recorded his impression of the side of the building facing the garden. It formed the basis for the alterations to Knobelsdorff's plans, and the proposed structural scheme remained definitive for the further extension of the palace up to 1752.

The building measures for the Potsdam Palace must be considered in conjunction with the building work at Sanssouci; a comparison of the king's individual Cabinet orders clarifies their striking parallelism. On August 2, 1744, the order is given for the cleaning and painting of the town palace; on August 10, the architect Friedrich Wilhelm Diterichs receives the directive for the construction of the six terraces at Sanssouci; on December 29, 1744, the order is given to build the two colonnades in the pleasure garden; on January 13, 1745, the building of the palace of Sanssouci is ordered; and on January 27, the order is given for the building of the new east wing at the town palace.

It is clear that Potsdam had now, for all practical purposes, become Frederick's royal capital, while Berlin and Charlottenburg had taken second place. Up to the time of his death in 1786, the king lived at the palace of Sanssouci during the summer months, and the town palace became his winter residence. Furthermore, the town of Potsdam became the king's sphere of artistic activity.

Frederick appears to have been in agreement with the plan produced by Knobelsdorff, which preserved the basic original structure of the palace and merely provided the *corps de logis* with a balustrade adorned with figures. A sketch by Frederick, probably made at the end of 1746, of the central projection on the garden side (see above), with the uniform division by means of pilasters, was undoubtedly the incentive for a new language of architectural forms, which was probably inspired by Perrault's façade for the Louvre in Paris.

The division by means of Corinthian pilasters or half-columns that was proposed by Knobelsdorff for the stairwell projection built in 1746 now became obligatory throughout the palace. After the building of the central projection on the garden side in 1747, there followed in 1748 the external rebuilding of the side projection of the *corps de logis*, with the extension of the "machine table" in the corner between the eastern corner projection and the side wing. This machine table, a kind of dumb waiter, was a table with a special mechanism for transporting dishes upwards from the space underneath, so that the King and his guests would not be disturbed by servants.

In 1749, the two sides to the right and the left of the stairwell projection on the court side were given a new Corinthian division. In 1750, a story was added to the east wing and in 1751 one to the west wing. Temple-like façades, which consisted of four columns with a triangular pediment, were placed in front of the two main buildings on the Alter Markt. Heymüller's pediment reliefs indicate the intended use of the rooms that lay behind them: on the east building, which contained the theater, the subject was Apollo with the Muses, while on the west building, which was called the Chapel Pediment, where until 1752 the palace church was located, there was a representation of the "Sacrifice of Peace" with ten figures.

As early as 1750, accommodation had been provided for the palace guards in the two semicircular structures that formed the conclusions to the court, and certain architectural alterations were now necessary here, too.

When this work had been carried out, all that remained of the former palace structure was the Fortuna Gate, which had hitherto been erected on the occasion of the coronation of the first Prussian king in 1701, and which was preserved on the express wish of Frederick the Great as a symbolic entrance structure.

After the eight years of building, from 1744 to 1752, the outwardly not very attractive Potsdam

Johann Friedrich Meyer
View of the Potsdam Palace from the Brauhausberg (1772)
Oil on canvas, 77.2 x 110 cm; Potsdam, Stiftung Preussische Schlösser und Gärten, Berlin-Brandenburg

About 1770, Frederick the Great gave the painter Johann Friedrich Meyer the commission of portraying certain houses, streets, and squares in Potsdam. This included this view of the town center from the Brauhausberg, on the far side of the Havel.

Potsdam Palace, bedroom cum study in the eastern apartments of Frederick the Great (destroyed)

View of the room from the bed alcove, with the opened balustrade. While the window and alcove walls, as well as the area over the fireplace, display a very delicate silver-plated ornamentation, the other two walls were given a covering with silver lace. Instead of the usual gilding, this room exhibits the king's preference for silver, which is to be found 20 years later in the New Palace at Sanssouci.

Opposite
Potsdam Palace, stairwell (destroyed)

Contemporaries greatly admired this stairwell, which was constructed after designs by Georg Wenzeslaus von Knobelsdorff between 1746 and 1748. In the extended oval space, the staircase is inserted in a bold curve. The walls, which were clad with green Swedish marble, were divided by white Ionic pilasters. Together with the caryatids in the corners, they supported a cornice on which were placed six allegorical groups carved by Johann Peter Benckert. They were connected by their subject-matter with the ceiling painting by Antoine Pesne, which made symbolic reference to the peace achieved after the Second Silesian War.

town palace had been transformed into an imposing structure. It now presented a magnificent sight, largely as a result of having a uniform architectural structure, rich sculptural decoration, and, not least, a striking color scheme – red-painted walls, yellow architectural features, blue-lacquered copper roof with golden lambrequin motifs, and green Fortuna Gate (see page 181).

As far as the internal arrangement of the palace is concerned, here too the king undoubtedly brought his artistic intentions to bear. Certainly the division of the rooms is to be attributed to him.

The center of the main building was taken up by the stairwell (see opposite), the Marble Gallery, and the great Marble Hall, with decorations by Schlüter (see page 185), which Frederick had Knobelsdorff transform into the Hall of Fame for the Great Elector. To its east on the first upper floor lay the king's apartments; to the west was the Bronze Hall (which was the dining room), and the audience room. These were adjoined by rooms for "foreign dignitaries." This was also the purpose of the rooms on the first upper floor of the west wing, where among others Prince Henry, the brother of Frederick the Great, had an apartment.

The rooms in the east wing, apart from the theater, were designated for administrative purposes and for the staff. Apart from Knobelsdorff, it was above all August Nahl and the brothers Johann Michael and Johann Christian Hoppenhaupt who were responsible for the exquisite decoration, particularly that of the rooms of Frederick the Great.

Knobelsdorff's contribution is noticeable, above all, in the Marble Hall and in the theater, which was removed as early as 1801. These rooms, like the king's bedroom (see above and page 184), effectively became the models for rooms bearing the same names at the palace of Sanssouci and the New Palace.

Left
Johann August Nahl
Design for the decoration of the alcove wall for the bedroom cum study in the eastern apartments of Frederick the Great at the Potsdam Palace (1744)
Ink with pink and gray-blue wash, 16 x 19 cm; Berlin, Stiftung Preussische Schlösser und Gärten, Berlin-Brandenburg, Plankammer

After 1744, Frederick the Great had an apartment built for himself in the Potsdam Palace; its individual interior decoration was for the most part created by the *directeur des ornements*, Johann August Nahl. The few designs that have been preserved include the alcove wall in the king's bedroom cum study. The design for this room must have corresponded entirely with the king's wishes, for in his sketch for the palace of Sanssouci he expressly notes that the bedroom there should be constructed to the exact proportions of the bedroom in the Potsdam Palace.

Right
Georg Wenzeslaus von Knobelsdorff
Ground plan and three elevations of the Marble Hall in the Potsdam Palace (c. 1748)
Pencil, gray ink, gray wash, 49.5 x 56.8 cm; Potsdam, Stiftung Preussische Schlösser und Gärten, Berlin-Brandenburg, Plankammer

Apart from the ground plan, which had not been altered since the building of the palace between 1662 and 1669, three sides of the Marble Hall are shown in these drawings. Above the ground plan, the north wall is shown, with a door leading to the Marble Gallery, with two blank areas left for the two large paintings. Below is the window wall, divided by long continuous pilasters as well as double windows and wall surfaces with trophies between them. The shorter east front wall has a fireplace in the center and, above, a space for a painting. The king's agreement to the design is shown by the note at bottom left: "This page has been approved by your Royal Majesty."

Opposite
Potsdam, Palace, Marble Hall

From 1749 to 1752, Frederick the Great had the central banqueting hall transformed into a hall of fame in honor of the Great Elector. Sketches and designs provide evidence of Knobelsdorff's substantial part in this project. The decoration included large-scale paintings from the late 17th century that glorified the deeds of the Great Elector by means of allegories. When Frederick had it redesigned, the cornice designed by Andreas Schlüter, probably in 1706, with its rich sculptural ornamentation and painting, was preserved, but with the addition of the large ceiling painting by Charles Amédée Philippe van Loo, *The Elevation to Olympus of the Great Elector.*

Potsdam, Sanssouci Palace, garden side

With its caryatids – the companions of Bacchus, the god of wine – framing its windows, the south-facing garden side of Sanssouci Palace alludes to the vineyard that lies in front of it. The palace was the summer residence of Frederick the Great. The center is emphasized by the cupola of the dining hall; to the east (right) are the apartments of the king, and to the west those of his guests. Only three steps lead from the parquet or marble floor of the interior rooms to the gravel surface of the garden.

Sanssouci: the terrace and palace

To an even greater extent than the rebuilding and extension of the city palace in Potsdam, after 1744 the design of Sanssouci became the favorite object of Frederick the Great's artistic passion (see above and pages 187 and 188). The city palace was, after all, intended for winter occupation; but at Sanssouci, his summer residence, he planned to follow his personal inclinations and interests, "undisturbed" by affairs of state. In Sanssouci, again, Frederick declined to entrust the design of his refuge to the architect, but intervened in the plans and sketches in the minutest detail.

"This much is certain," wrote Manger, "that the first idea for it was given by the king to Baron von Knobelsdorff, and that it had to be built just as it stands now, despite all the latter's objections." This sentence was indeed written about the palace of Sanssouci in retrospect, but its first part may be taken to apply to the whole complex. Continual attempts have been made to find out what sort of "idea" it was that the king had, and what the relationship was between the client and the architect during the practical planning stage in view of such basic dependence.

Evidence of what this "first idea" looked like is provided by two drawings by the king: one shows the parterre or ground floor, the terrace complex with the ground plan of the palace, the other only the ground plan of the palace. The king had been familiar with the site from his youth. His father, Frederick William I, had had a modest garden with a dairy laid out in front of the Brandenburg Gate at Potsdam, and had mockingly called it "my Marly." At that time, the nearby mountain was still wooded with oak trees, which were felled in 1729, and as a result was known as the Wüste Berg (Wild Mountain).

Wine-growing had also been a local industry in the March of Brandenburg since the 13th century, and many of the hills around Potsdam were used for this purpose. Thus, in the second half of the 17th century, vineyards had been attached to the summer residences near Potsdam, Bornim, Caputh, and Glienicke, as well as Rheinsberg. These vineyards, however, had never been in a central position, but had always lain at the edge of the summer residence. In Sanssouci, by contrast, a vineyard was now to become the focus, indeed the very heart of a princely garden complex.

Georg Wenzeslaus von Knobelsdorff, building office of J. C. Berger (?)
Ground plan and elevation of the court and garden side of the Sanssouci Palace, Potsdam, (c. 1744–1745)
Pen and pencil in gray, 57.6 x 78.8 cm; Potsdam, Stiftung Preussische Schlösser und Gärten, Berlin-Brandenburg, Plankammer

As Frederick's signature attests, this plan was intended to be executed. In the course of realization of the project, however, alterations were undertaken: thus, for example, the access from Frederick's bedroom cum study to the library was altered, and the drive up to the palace was widened by shortening the colonnade by two bays.

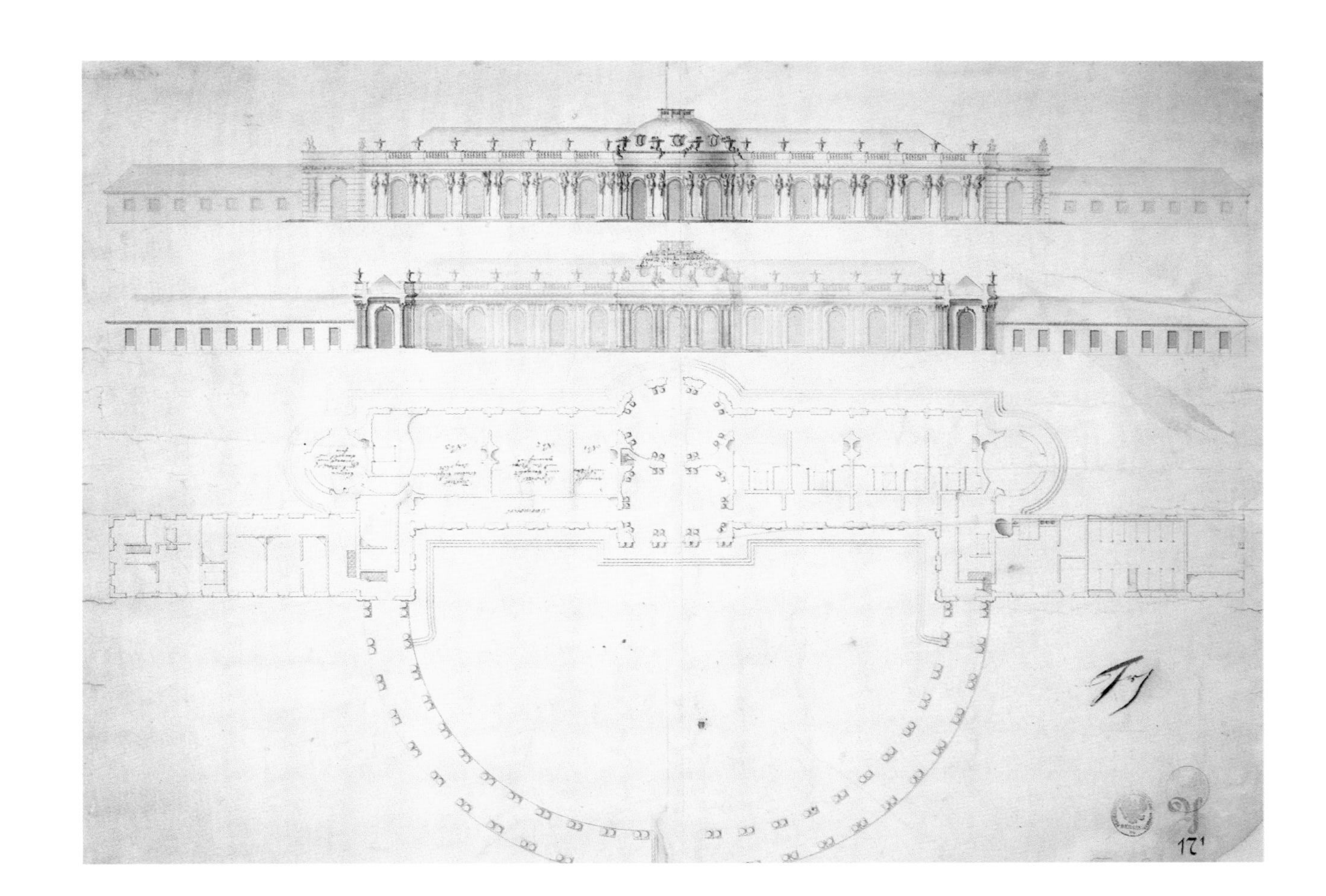

Potsdam, Sanssouci Palace, drive to the *cour d'honneur*

To the north, the *cour d'honneur* is surrounded by a colonnade with access by means of a steep ramp leading to the open center of the colonnade.

Opposite
Potsdam, Sanssouci Palace
View through the colonnade to the Ruinenberg

Between the columns of the colonnade, the view is of the Ruinenberg north of Sanssouci Palace. In 1748 Frederick the Great had had a pool built at the top of the hill to supply water to the fountains, and had mock "classical ruins" arranged around it. Knobelsdorff's design was modified by the Berlin stage designer Bellavite. That these ruins, which were intended to evoke the buildings of Rome, should have been placed at the highest point of the surroundings of the palace shows that classical art had supreme status for the king and was enthroned, as it were, above all else.

Potsdam, Sanssouci Palace, library

The library at Sanssouci is without doubt one of the most outstanding rooms there. In his sketch, Frederick the Great had already referred to the corresponding room at Rheinsberg as a model. Thus the circular form is again adopted here, but larger and in the ideal proportions, that is, with the diameter the same as the height. Situated to one side of the actual suite of rooms, the library is only to be reached through a concealed door (seen to the left in this illustration) and was thus the most private room in the palace.

On May 25, 1744, the last ruler of the principality of East Friesland died. The state thus became the property of Prussia, bringing unexpected income to the king, so that the financial conditions for the realization of bigger projects now arose. At the end of June, the king's brother, Prince Henry, received Rheinsberg from him as a present. During the same month, Diterichs was summoned to the king and on August 9 he received the commission to lay out a vineyard. On August 10, the Cabinet order was issued, and on August 13, 1744 work commenced on the six terraces. The terrace form of the vineyard, which had the walls curved in the form of a segment of a circle, was recommended by theorists of the time for the design of an orangery and the growing of fruit and vines. Cherry, apricot, and plum trees were planted on the terraces, and in the niches and on the espaliers grapevines from Portugal, Italy, France, but also from Ruppin. There were also fig trees, and the strips of land beside the ramps were planted with walnut and

Potsdam, Sanssouci Palace, Marble Hall
View of the cupola

The Marble Hall is documented as a work by Knobelsdorff in a eulogy written by Frederick the Great on the death of his favorite architect.

Potsdam, Sanssouci Palace, Marble Hall

The motif of the double Corinthian columns introduced in the colonnade and the north side is continued via the vestibule in the Marble Hall, which was not completed until 1748, and thus links the interior and exterior structure. The choice of Carrara marble lends a festive elegance to the room, which was the dining room of the palace. This room was the setting for the famous round table of Sanssouci, where the king held open discussions with friends and guests, who on occasion included Voltaire.

chestnut trees. In addition, the curve indicated a point of reference in the plain. Here, extending the "central line of this new symmetrical arrangement" (Manger), at the end of the old kitchen garden, stood a little pleasure house from the time of Frederick William I. It was demolished in 1745 (according to Manger, as early as 1744) and set up again in the Deer Park as a pheasant-keeper's hut. With the building of the vault on the topmost terrace, it had become clear that the king gave at least the same importance to this new complex as he did to Rheinsberg, which was hardly the equivalent of a small half-timbered building. On January 13, 1745, the Chamber of War and Demesnes of the March received the royal Cabinet order "to deliver … the necessary materials for the projected building of a pleasure house at Potsdam." From April 3, the trenches were dug for the foundations, on April 14 the foundation stone was laid, and by the end of 1745 the shell of the palace was complete. After the estimate of costs had received the approval of the king on 18 July, 1746 the interior building was completed; on May 1, 1747, the building was officially opened with the addition of a dining

table, even though the Marble Hall and the colonnade were not yet complete. The impatient king could never wait for a residence to be completed in all respects before he occupied it; he always took possession in advance. At Rheinsberg he was practically living on a building site the whole time, though "with certain inconveniences," as he admitted; the Berlin Opera House, at the time of its official opening, was still full of scaffolding, with only foundation walls to be seen in some parts, and things were not very different later at the New Palace.

An idea of the vineyard and palace is conveyed by the *sopraporta*, painted presumably in early 1747 by Charles Sylva Dubois, in the concert room of the palace of Sanssouci: the view across the Havel is of the palace with its terraces, while the figures of two shepherdesses and a shepherd stand or sit in the foreground with their herds near a classical tombstone with the inscription *Et in Arcadia Ego* ("I, too, was once in Arcadia"): Sanssouci is the new Arcadia in which, despite all its bliss, death still has its place. At Rheinsberg the crown prince and his court lived according to "the taste of Watteau," and attempted to turn the French artist's *fêtes galantes* into reality. The *View of Rheinsberg*, which was painted by Knobelsdorff in 1735 (compare the drawing on page 164) is also a view across the water, but has a group of courtiers enjoying themselves in the foreground. Here the motif was a carefree life among friends. Later, during the course of two Silesian wars, the king had looked into the face of death; it had become part and parcel of the life of the philosopher of Sanssouci.

Potsdam, Sanssouci
Palace, vestibule

As in the Marble Hall, so in the vestibule the overall impact of the room is determined by double Corinthian columns, which lend it a festive character.

The building of the palace in the vineyard places the latter, with its curved terraces, in a new relationship with the garden and the landscape. It is no longer a conclusion, but a link between the palace and the parterre, and serves to open up to the landscape, which in moving down to each gradation is seen and experienced in a new and a different way. The stimulus for the division of the palace into rooms was inspired by a treatise of 1737 by the French architectural theorist Jacques-François Blondel, *De la distribution des maisons de plaisance et de la décoration des édifices en général* (On the Siting and the Decoration of Pleasure Houses and of Buildings in General), which the king, however, modified according to his own ideas and requirements. There are precise details in his sketch on the use of the wings, on individual rooms, and also on the arrangement of columns. The notes, in addition, clarify the individuality of the king with regard to reusable architectural and spatial forms: the bedroom was to have the same proportions as the one at the city palace in Potsdam. "Commes à Reinsberg" was his intention for the colonnade and library (see page 189), which corresponded to a guestroom of the same circular form found on the west side of the palace. At Rheinsberg, Frederick had had his library in the medieval-style round tower, while in the palace in Berlin his study, completed in 1745, was of almost the same diameter as the library at Sanssouci. Only Knobelsdorff alone could have an understanding of such references. It was

Johann August Nahl the Elder
Potsdam, Sanssouci Palace, design for the decoration of the west wall of the Concert Room (c. 1746)
Pencil, pen, with gray wash, 16 x 26.3 cm; Berlin, Staatliche Museen zu Berlin – Preussischer Kulturbesitz, Kunstbibliothek

Official accounts show that the wall decorations were carried out between the summer of 1746 and the spring of 1747 by Johann Michael Hoppenhaupt the Elder. For this reason the drawing shown here has always been regarded as a design by this master's own hand. However, by means of a comparison of styles, recent research (Eggeling) has now ascribed the drawing to Johann August Nahl the Elder.

Potsdam, Sanssouci Palace, Voltaire Room

Among the guestrooms in the western part of Sanssouci Palace, the Voltaire Room, furnished with sculpted flower and animal decoration, is the most unusual.

Opposite
Potsdam, Sanssouci Palace, concert room

As had already been done at Rheinsberg and later at the Royal Opera House in Berlin, the theme of Ovid's *Metamorphoses* was also used in the Concert Room for the wall decorations. Pesne's paintings lead visitors out of reality into the dream world of transformation. Not only the floral and abstract ornamentation, but also the mirrors arranged opposite the windows, transported them, as it were, into nature. It was here that the famous Sanssouci flute concerts took place, which are known, certainly in an idealized form, from the painting by Adolph Menzel.

undoubtedly he who translated the king's guidelines into artistic forms. This is proved by his drawings in the sketchbook preserved in the plan room of the palace, and their conversion into the plan approved by the king. In the center are the two rooms, the vestibule (see page 191) and Marble Hall (see page 190), whose architectural division by Corinthian columns is a continuation of the same structure of the north side of the palace. The rooms situated to the east of these demonstrate the development of Rococo under Frederick the Great at its highest point. The same artists worked at the same time at Sanssouci and the city palace: notable names, apart from Knobelsdorff, are those of Johann August Nahl, who was *directeur des ornaments* until his hasty departure from Prussia, Johann Michael and Johann Christian Hoppenhaupt, Antoine Pesne, and Georg Franz Ebenhech. The Marble Hall, whose creation the King himself attributed to Knobelsdorff in his eulogy of the architect, who died in 1753, the concert room (see pages 192 and 193), and the library will together probably be counted in the future among the outstanding works of interior design of the mid-18th century. Of the four guest rooms west of the Marble Hall, with their uniform basic structure, it is important to mention the so-called Voltaire Room (see page 193), with its naturalistic flower and animal decoration, as a special feature of the Rococo of the age of Frederick the Great.

The garden and its buildings

As early as 1745, a year after the laying out of the vineyard, the idea developed of extending the garden to east and west, while the palace with the terrace retained its dominant position. To the east, at half the height of the hill, a hothouse was built, which was replaced after 1755 by the picture gallery, and also, at the foot of the mountain, the Grotto of Neptune. The corresponding structures to the west were the Orangery (later called the New Chambers), built in 1747, and once again a grotto. This five-part arrangement, with a conscious orientation to the water, is drawn together by means of a continuous east–west axis connecting the buildings. This produces a series of images that allows the palace to appear as a prospect among prospects, though clearly the most important of these. The main avenue no longer leads to a palace, but is, in its extension to east and west, parallel to the Sanssouci hill, the artistic backbone of the garden (see below). The obelisk portal, after a design by Knobelsdorff, is a reminder of Rheinsberg and forms the eastern conclusion of the garden. At half the height of the wing, the palace of Sanssouci is flanked by two outwardly similar buildings, the Orangery and the picture gallery. Single-story and broad in structure, both buildings have large windows opening onto the park. As with the palace of Sanssouci, the center in each case projects slightly and is emphasized by a cupola.

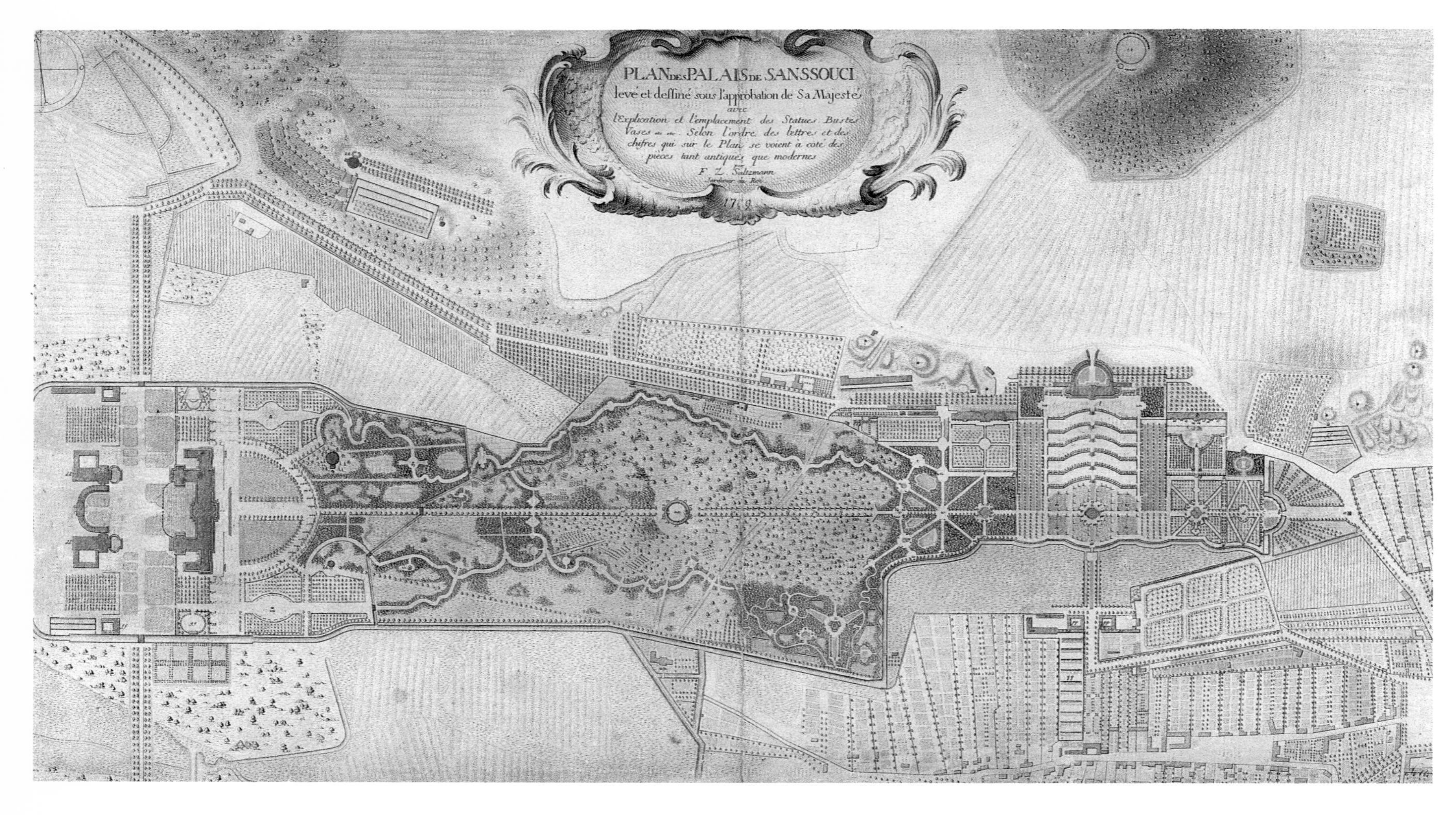

Johann Friedrich Schleuen, after Friedrich Zacharias Saltzmann
General plan of Sanssouci Palace (1772)
Etching, colored, 46.1 x 82.2 cm; Potsdam, Stiftung Preussische Schlösser und Gärten, Berlin-Brandenburg, Plankammer

In an impressive east–west extension, the narrow park of Sanssouci stretches from the east (right) entrance area to the New Palace. The main axis that runs through the whole park is, as it were, its backbone. The palace of Sanssouci with its terraces and parterre in front is clearly outlined, as are the side buildings known as the New Chambers (to the west) and the picture gallery. Next to the actual pleasure garden is the forest-like Deer Park to the west, and this is enclosed by two winding paths running north and south of the main avenue. A colonnade designed by Knobelsdorff occupies the center. The New Palace with the Communs forms the conclusion to the west.

The Orangery had been built to the west of the palace, according to Knobelsdorff's plans, in 1747, in order to accommodate the potted plants that adorned the garden during the summer months (see above). While the caryatids at the south front of the palace of Sanssouci are a fixed component of the structure of the building, here the figures, brought from Carrara in 1749, were placed in front of the façade, so that they became a link between the building and the garden. When the guestrooms in the palace of Sanssouci were no longer adequate, Georg Christian Unger, who was a pupil of Gontard's, transformed the building into a residence for guests (1771–1774) that was given the name of the New Chambers (Neue Kammern). In a reference to the picture gallery that had been built in the meantime (compare the illustration on page 199), Unger added a cupola to the New Chambers. The central hall, in addition to three rooms in the eastern part, was left as seen in the ground plan, and transformed into reception rooms according to designs by Johann Christian Hoppenhaupt the Younger (see right and page 197). Once again, the Rococo of Frederick the Great demonstrates its creative power in the oval Buffet Hall and the Ovid Gallery, with its gilded stucco reliefs referring thematically to the *Metamorphoses* of Ovid. In the west part of the building, seven gentlemen's rooms were added, in which the two intarsia cabinets by the Spindler brothers (see page 196) are among the most important achievements.

The place of the old hothouse, which was built in 1746 on the east side of the palace, was taken up from 1755 by the picture gallery (see page 199). The country architect Johann Gottfried Büring had prepared the design in order for it to match the

Potsdam, New Chambers in the park of Sanssouci

In 1747 Frederick the Great had an orangery built by Knobelsdorff to the west of the palace at a somewhat lower level, and this was later rebuilt as the guest accomodation, the New Chambers.

Johann Christian Hoppenhaupt the Younger
Designed for the ceiling decoration and the narrow west side of the Ovid Gallery in the New Chambers (1773–1774)
Pencil, pen in gray, painted in watercolor, 43.8 x 52.1 cm; Berlin, Staatliche Museen zu Berlin – Preussischer Kulturbesitz, Kunstbibliothek

After 1770, the Oangery was converted into a guesthouse, the exterior by Unger and the interior according to designs by Hoppenhaupt the Younger. The building was now given the name of the New Chambers.

Potsdam, New Chambers in the park of Sanssouci, Intarsia Cabinet

The gentlemen's rooms situated in the west part of the New Chambers are all grouped two to an "apartment," consisting of a bedroom and living room. Among the furnishings, two intarsia cabinets (rooms decorated with intarsia) have a particular nobility. They were produced by Heinrich Wilhelm Spindler the Younger and Johann Friedrich Spindler the Elder, who had come from Bayreuth in 1764.

Orange House. However, because of the Seven Years' War, the completion of the work was in fact delayed until 1764.

The figures, once again placed free-standing in front of the wall surfaces between the large windows, like the keystones, made thematic references to the character of the house. The picture gallery is the first building in museum history to have been dedicated exclusively to the display of paintings. Until then it was usual to allocate certain rooms inside the palace complex for this purpose, such as can be seen in the Little Gallery at the palace of Sanssouci. The extraction of a certain type of room out of the palace domain in order to make it structurally independent had already been achieved by Knobelsdorff with the building of the Opera House in Unter den Linden in Berlin between 1741 and 1743.

The interior of the picture gallery (see pages 198 and 199) extends over almost the whole length of the building, except that at the east end there is a cabinet for "small portraits," and at the west a stairwell which creates a direct connection to the topmost palace terrace.

In its well-balanced proportions, this gallery is among one of the finest of German museum spaces.

Opposite
Potsdam, New Chambers in the park of Sanssouci, Jasper Room

The Jasper Room is the central room in the New Chambers. Its name is derived from the use of this hard and costly material for the wall mirrors and the floor. For the king, this room offered a further opportunity to display on the consoles busts from the Polignac collection, just as he had done in the style of a museum a few years earlier, in 1768, in the Classical Temple near the New Palace.

Opposite
Potsdam, Palace of Sanssouci, picture gallery

The picture gallery in the palace in Berlin, created by Eosander von Göthe between 1707 and 1710, was the model for this long inner room.

Below
Potsdam, Palace of Sanssouci, picture gallery
View of the inner room

In the picture gallery, it was predominantly large-format paintings by Flemish and Italian Baroque masters that adorned the walls opposite the windows.

Johann Friedrich Schleuen
Garden side of the picture gallery at Sanssouci (c. 1770)
Etching, 20.9 x 32.2 cm; Potsdam, Stiftung Preussische Schlösser und Gärten, Berlin-Brandenburg, Plankammer

Between 1755 and 1763, Frederick the Great had a picture gallery built east of the Palace of Sanssouci, after a design by Johann Gottfried Büring. In obedience to the rules of Baroque symmetry, the façade of the gallery is based on the Orangery, later New Chambers, built in 1747 after plans by Knobelsdorff, on the west side of the palace.

Potsdam, Chinese House in the park of Sanssouci

Among the special testimonies to the fashion for chinoiserie is the Chinese House, erected by Büring between 1754 and 1757 in the southeast area of the former Deer Park, after a design sketch by Frederick the Great. The exotic impression is evoked not only by the lavish use of gold but also by the figures on the cabinets and in the anterooms, the tent-like painted roof, and the columns in the form of palm trees. Originally the surrounding garden was also divided by winding paths and screened by hedges; in the 19th century, Lenné made the house into a focus of attention in an extended landscape garden.

The Deer Park and the New Palace

The great main avenue had also been extended after 1748 with the so-called Deer Park (Rehgarten). At its central point, Knobelsdorff erected a colonnade after 1751, but this was demolished again as early as 1797 because of its bad state of dilapidation. In this area of the park the beginnings are clearly evident of a new type of garden design which, diverging from the geometric system, had its origins in England. Until 1772, the existing forest was "only slightly aired and put into order by artistic means." Two winding paths enclosed the whole area from north to south. This "forest" was given a particular accent in its southeast corner after 1754 by means of the Chinesisches Haus (Chinese House) (see below). Again, it is not to be discounted that the first idea for this came from Knobelsdorff. At any rate, the choice of a building in the fashionable Chinese style seems to have been influenced by Knobelsdorff, even if the king employed the provincial architect Büring in 1754 to construct a building according to a sketch Frederick himself had produced. Frederick had allowed himself to be inspired by a similar arrangement which the Polish king Stanislas Leszczynski had had constructed in Lunéville near Nancy by the architect Heré. In 1753, Heré had published an engraving of his building, which the king had in his library in the city palace of Potsdam. The Chinese House is a perfect example of the Chinese style in architecture. Here, building and nature enter into a close connection, and the imaginatively created life-size gilded Chinese figures and groups on the cabinets and in the entrance halls strengthen the bizarre impression. The interior decoration as well as the ceiling painting *à la chinoise* by Thomas Huber, from designs by Blaise Nicolas Le Sueur, also contribute to the playful nature of this building (see page 201). In 1763, somewhat to the side of this, Büring built the

Below
Potsdam, Dragon House in the park of Sanssouci

With the building of the "Dragon House," the workers' residence in the nearby vineyards, the fashion for chinoiserie was taken up again in 1770. The design was prepared by Gontard. He found his inspiration in Chambers' works about Chinese houses (1757) and in the buildings of Kew Gardens near London (1763), designed by Chambers.

Potsdam, Chinese House in the park of Sanssouci, Cupola Room

The interior of the Chinese House is dominated by the central Cupola Room, from which the low-ceilinged cabinets branch off. Round-arched windows and the lantern in the cupola supply light to the room, whose center is occupied by a sumptuous chandelier. The paintings by Thomas Huber are based on designs by the Frenchman Blaise Nicolas Le Sueur. Above the painted balustrade, Chinese figures observe the presumed bustle of activity among the courtiers.

kitchen building belonging to the Chinese House. Outside the actual garden area of Sanssouci, on the Klausberg, Gontard built in 1770 a "little Chinese house" for the vineyard workers, the Dragon House (see above right). English influences, particularly that of the Pagoda built in Kew Gardens by William Chambers, probably stimulated the revival of the fashion for chinoiserie.

The New Palace at Sanssouci

After the end of the Seven Years' War, the New Palace was created between 1763 and 1769 at the west end of the main avenue of the Sanssouci park (see pages 202 and 203). It is the last and at the same time the most extensive palace building by Frederick the Great at Sanssouci, and was intended for the relatives and guests of the king when they came to stay during the summer months. The plan for this building goes back to the prewar years of 1755–1756. At first it was planned to build a southern extension to the terrace axis of Sanssouci on the Havel. There is much evidence that ideas for Frederick's forum in Berlin as well as for Rheinsberg were adopted here. It is possible that the plan for the New Palace, in its position by the water, may still have been the result of discussions between Knobelsdorff and the king. After all, following a period of coolness in the relationship after 1746, there was a rapprochement around 1750 between the king and the architect, which lasted until the death of Knobelsdorff in 1753 and found expression in numerous buildings at Sanssouci and Potsdam.

The first plans were worked out by Johann and Gottfried Büring as well as Heinrich Ludewig Manger. The first of these was also responsible for the supervision of the building work until 1764, and from 1765 it was taken over by Carl von Gontard, who had meanwhile arrived in Prussia (see page 204). Quite

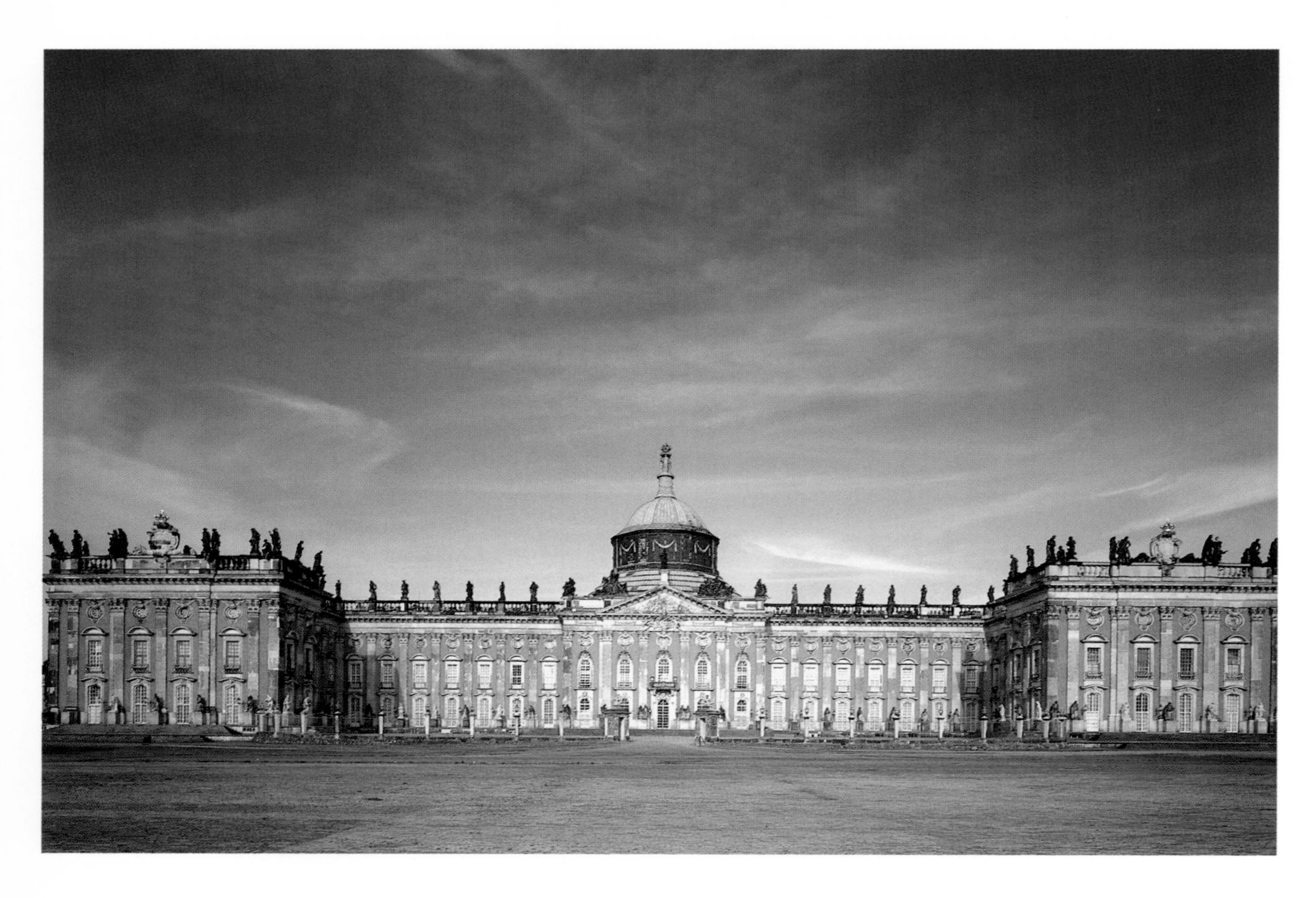

Potsdam, New Palace at Sanssouci, *cour d'honneur*

To the west, two large side wings act as boundaries to a *cour d'honneur* that is divided by a semicircular fence. The light-colored sandstone dividers (formerly painted yellow) contrast effectively with the red of the walls. At first, it had been the intention of Frederick the Great to construct the whole building so that the stonework was visible. This was in fact done in the little south wing in which his apartments were located. Since the building work had to go on at a brisk pace, the masonry was rendered, and gaps were painted onto the red paint to suggest lines of mortar.

undoubtedly, even though the conception of the New Palace goes back to the prewar years, as an architectural monument to the victorious conclusion to the Seven Years' War it has its parallels in the palace-building in Berlin built by Frederick I. Both complexes were intended as architectural expressions of royal dignity achieved or asserted. A similar expression of self-satisfaction is found in the project of the Forum Fridericianum, which was intended to proclaim the new position of Prussia as one of the established political powers.

The enormous building is structured by means of projections and colossal pilasters made in the Palladio tradition, and crowned by a cupola (compare page 204, below). Its counterpart, opposite, is the superb architectural scenery of the Communs (see page 204, above right). These buildings included kitchens and administrative offices as well as accommodation for staff and the royal household. But the architects also had the task of supplying an effective separation of the total palace complex from the rather unattractive uncultivated land that lay behind it. The two Communs, which are reminiscent of Palladio's villas, are linked by a widely curved colonnade with a triumphal arch in the center. The design by Gontard, who directed the work between 1766 and 1769, was already based on plans by the French architect Jean Legeay. The conventions of French Baroque continued to be applied to the interior arrangement of the New Palace. Corresponding to its function, the house is divided into individual apartments, which are approached via four staircases (see page 204, center). There is no ostentatious main staircase. The apartments include bedrooms (see page 207), writing rooms, and reception rooms (see pages 205 and 208), to which are added great banqueting halls (see page 209) and a theater (see page 206). For the interior decoration, the designers relied on the stylistic elements of Rococo. Even more strongly than in the Voltaire Room at Sanssouci Palace, the special characteristics of Rococo under Frederick the Great are

Potsdam, New Palace and Communs at Sanssouci

Aerial view (c. 1935)

The magnificent design of the New Palace becomes all the more evident from a bird's-eye view. The Communs (the administration buildings), linked by a colonnade, are opposite the palace.

noticeable in the effective contrast between smooth wall surface and rich ornamentation. Flowers, fruit, animals, putti and all sorts of adornments are interspersed with the rocaille work in sometimes almost bewildering variety. Admittedly, the imaginative and creative talent is no longer as powerful as before, so that existing models are drawn upon: in the Marble Hall (see page 209), for example, the design of the corresponding room in the Potsdam city palace is repeated, and in the Lower and Upper Concert Rooms, and also in other rooms, the designs created in 1754 by Hoppenhaupt the Elder were again brought into service. The younger Hoppenhaupt, who was probably entrusted with the direction of a major part of the interior decoration, was assisted by a multitude of sculptors, stucco artists, and varnishers.

The banqueting rooms, by comparison with the reception rooms, have a more strongly architectural emphasis in their construction and are therefore probably to be attributed to Gontard for the most part. The Marble Gallery (see page 209) and Marble Hall (compare page 209) appear cool and dignified, while the Upper Gallery (Dance Hall) displays a warmer quality. To what extent the garden architecture also had an influence on the interior decoration is demonstrated by the Shell Hall, with its large windows which open out onto the park (see page 210), and the oval Small Cabinet with its bower-like room structure and decoration.

The New Palace with the attendant Communs were also the stimulus for the building of two more temples in the immediate vicinity. The Classical Temple, built by Gontard in 1768 after a sketch of the king's, is, like the picture gallery, a building solely dedicated to the collection and preservation of works of art, namely Frederick's collection of classical antiquities. Its counterpart, the Temple of Friendship (see page 211) was created at the same time in memory of Frederick's sister, Wilhelmine, Margravine of Bayreuth, who had died in 1758. At Voltaire's suggestion, medallions of famous classical pairs of friends adorned the Corinthian columns. The seated

Potsdam, New Palace at Sanssouci, garden side

The wide front of the main building with its cupola as well as the lower side buildings dominate the garden space in front of it. The division of the façade by the pilasters linking the stories is a reference to the English version of Palladianism. Still totally Baroque, however, is the series of figures on the balustrade and in front of the pilasters on the ground floor.

Immediately below
Carl von Gontard
Ground plan of the first and second floors of the New Palace at Potsdam (c. 1765–1766)
Black and brown ink, gray and pink brush, 58 x 91.5 cm; Potsdam, Stiftung Preussische Schlösser und Gärten, Berlin-Brandenburg, Plankammer

The basis for the interior division of the palace was a design by Heinrich Ludewig Manger of about 1755. Gontard, who was entrusted with the supervision of the work in 1764, had taken into account Frederick the Great's wishes for alterations.

Right
Carl von Gontard
Elevation of the side façade of the northern Communs of the New Palace at Potsdam (c. 1766)
Gray ink with gray wash, 47.4 x 67.8 cm; Potsdam, Stiftung Preussische Schlösser und Gärten, Berlin-Brandenburg, Plankammer

Opposite the New Palace lies the magnificent architectural backdrop of the Communs, the administration buildings, which were built by Gontard between 1766 and 1769 with the use of a design by Jean-Laurent Legeay.

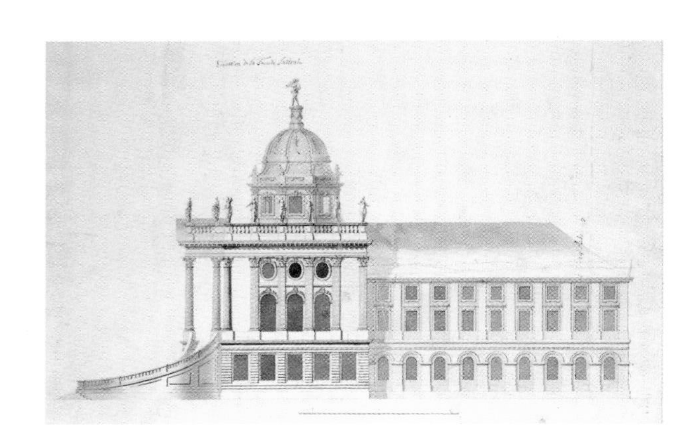

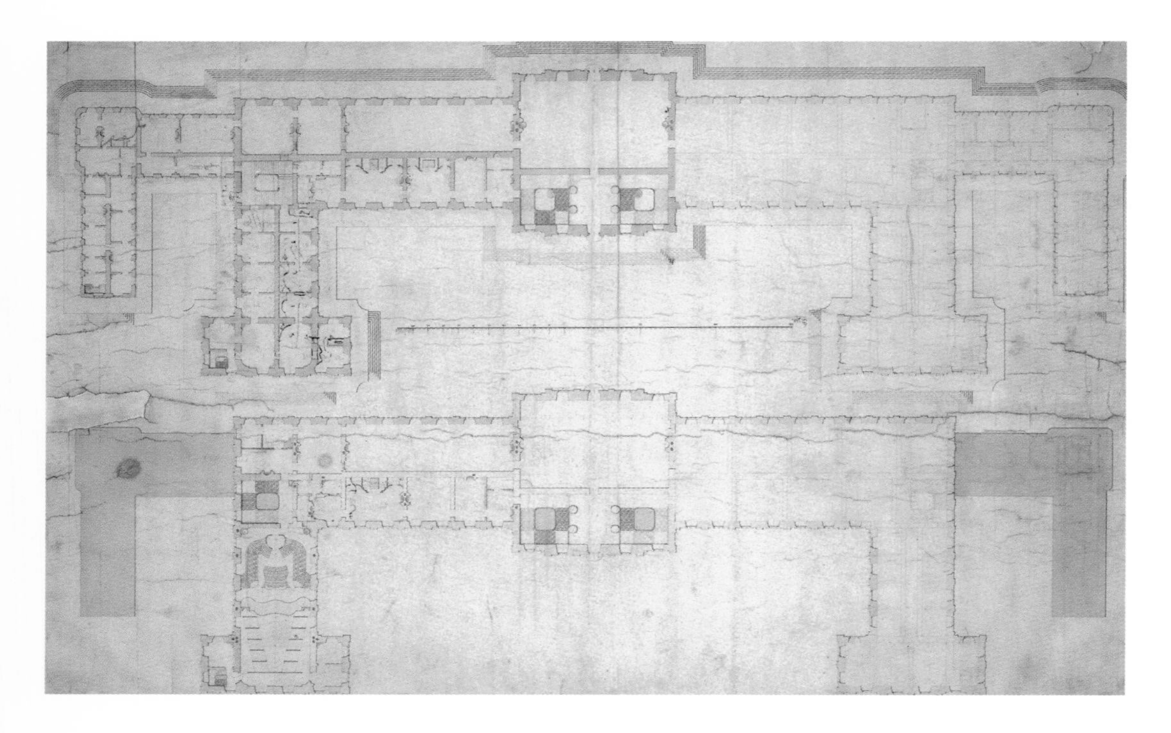

statue of the Margravine in a niche within the temple was created by the Räntz brothers in 1772 after a painting by Antoine Pesne.

A positively triumphal effect is created by the final building at Sanssouci, the Belvedere on the Klausberg (see page 211), built by Georg Christian Unger between 1770 to 1772. The Macellum of Nero in Rome, reproduced in the book of prints *Palazzi dei Cesari* (The Palaces of the Caesars) by Francesco Bianchini (Verona, 1738), served as a model for this final and at the same time so pleasing 18th-century building at Sanssouci. From here there is a superb view across the entire park. Inside the Belvedere there are two round rooms, one above the other. The lower one is adorned with precious jasper and the upper with marble stucco. As at the Communs, at the New Palace an extensive two-level staircase leads to the upper story. It was undoubtedly at the suggestion of Frederick the Great that Unger made use for his design of the reconstruction of the Macellum of Nero in Rome, which Francesco Bianchini had reproduced in his *Palazzi dei Cesari*; a copy of the book was in the king's library at Sanssouci Palace. The Belvedere is the final and at the same time one of the most pleasing 18th-century buildings in the park of Sanssouci.

Opposite, bottom
Carl von Gontard
Elevations of the garden and courtyard façades of the New Palace at Potsdam (c. 1766–1767)
Pencil, black ink and gray brush, 58.5 x 93 cm; Potsdam, Stiftung Preussische Schlösser und Gärten, Berlin-Brandenburg, Plankammer

The plan, which was created only during the course of building work, corresponds to the early design by Büring. The broadly based main building is crowned at the center with a cupola. On each side is a low, one-story building that again is surmounted by a cupola and softens the massiveness of the building.

Potsdam, New Palace at Sanssouci, Blue Room

The Blue Room is the first antechamber to the apartments of Frederick the Great. Since anterooms are mostly furnished as cabinets of painting, this purpose also defines the architecture. Thus the paneled, blue-painted walls are divided by gilded vertical panels with putto figures and consoles, with the free spaces in between used to accommodate the paintings.

Left
Johann Christian Hoppenhaupt the Younger
Longitudinal section of the theater of the New Palace at Potsdam (1766)
Graphite, gray and black ink, gray wash, 53.2 x 78.7 cm; Potsdam, Stiftung Preussische Schlösser und Gärten, Berlin-Brandenburg, Plankammer

Apart from the rooms, the princely occupants of the New Palace in the 18th century also had a theater at their disposal, indispensable for Baroque courtly life. The banqueting hall situated in the south side wing was officially opened in 1768 after a building period of two years.

Right
Potsdam, New Palace at Sanssouci, bedroom of Princess Henry

In accordance with its status as a palace for princely guests, the interior of the New Palace is divided into separate apartments. Thus the king's brother, Prince Henry and his wife were allocated an apartment on the ground floor of the north side wing, which includes two bedrooms as well as an anteroom and cabinets.

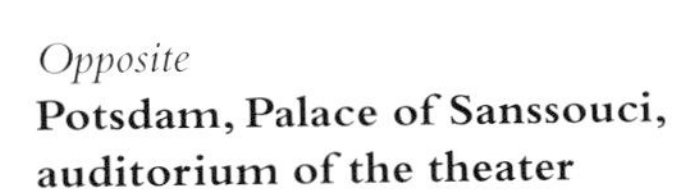

Opposite
Potsdam, Palace of Sanssouci, auditorium of the theater

In the front area only, a semicircle is formed by the rising rows of seats in the auditorium, while the next rows form a flat curve and the topmost rows are shortened because of the oblong ground plan, so that a good view of the stage is possible from all the seats. In 1856, the auditorium of the theater was altered: the two staircases leading to the dress circle were removed, and the front stalls were broken up. Festoons were also added to the lower circle. The otherwise customary royal box is absent from this theater: the monarch usually sat in the fourth row, which corresponded to the eye-level of the actors.

Opposite
Potsdam, New Palace at Sanssouci, study of Frederick the Great

In order to avoid drafts, the king had ordered that the doors in his apartment should be staggered. Thus an excellent position was created in his study for his desk, where the light fell upon it through a large window. As at the city palace of Potsdam, the king preferred silver-gilding of the ornamentation here, as well as a wall-covering of silver brocade. The decoration of the stucco ceiling, with its naturalistically painted flowers, is also in harmony with this color scheme.

Left
Potsdam, New Palace at Sanssouci, Marble Hall

The Marble Hall is the main hall of the palace and was designed by Carl von Gontard with reference to the room of the same name at the city palace in Potsdam. It takes up the whole width of the central projection and extends over two stories. The inlaid marble floor is the work of Johann Melchior Kambly.

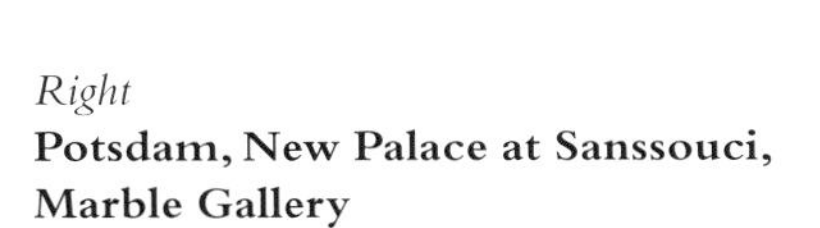

Right
Potsdam, New Palace at Sanssouci, Marble Gallery

The creator of the Marble Gallery, which sometimes served as a dining room, was Carl von Gontard. The shape and design of this ceremonial room is comparable to the French mirror galleries. As in the Little Gallery of the Palace of Sanssouci, the three ceiling paintings by Bernhard Rode – *Morning*, *Noon*, and *Night* – are set in an undulating, gilded mirror. Undoubtedly this design was carried out at the request of Frederick the Great himself, who was once again using the stylistic trademarks of the Knobelsdorff era.

Potsdam, New Palace at Sanssouci, Grotto Hall

The furnishing of the Grotto Hall, designed by Carl von Gontard, with indigenous, less costly minerals (glass slag, shells, and limestone formations) was enriched at the end of the 19th century with polished gemstones, rare minerals, fossils, and shells, including snails' shells, from all over the world.

Right
Potsdam, Temple of Friendship in the park at Sanssouci

In 1768, in memory of his sister, Wilhelmine of Bayreuth, Frederick the Great had this small, elegant temple built by Gontard according to his own sketches and plans. It was modelled on the Temple of Apollo in the Amalthea garden at Neuruppin, Knobelsdorff's first work.

Below
Potsdam, Belvedere on the Klausberg
Destroyed, rebuilt in the 1990s

Between 1770 and 1772, Georg Christian Unger created a belvedere on the Klausberg, near the New Palace, which allowed a view of the whole park.

Potsdam under Frederick the Great

The rebuilding of the Potsdam city palace and the design of the summer residence of Sanssouci entailed in addition an alteration to the appearance of the city, in accordance with its status as a royal seat. It was probably no longer consistent with the building ambitions of Frederick William I, who had as much accommodation as possible provided for soldiers, but also for new inhabitants. The simplicity of the architectural development – modest decor and rows of similar houses differentiated only by subtle differences – was no longer suitable for an era that was intent on creating splendid effects. With the houses built by Knobelsdorff from 1748 for the middle-class citizens, one admittedly does not yet observe the structure based, like a stage backdrop, on the form of the façade. In their unpretentiousness and simplicity they are models of a classicist sensibility of form. This is particularly evident in the two houses at the entrance to the Breite Strasse and those in the Schlossstrasse (see above).

The effectiveness of the bourgeois structures depends on the clear relationship between opened and closed parts, of door and window openings to the wall. The wall is consciously included as a medium of design. All superfluous decoration has been omitted, for "his sensitivity rejected all inappropriate adornments," as Frederick the Great wrote in his eulogy of the architect who died in 1753.

In this, Knobelsdorff was ahead of his time, for this manner of construction did not become fashionable until 1800. His successors would not tolerate a blank surface and overloaded it with rich decoration, imposing cornices, and pilasters.

Following Knobelsdorff's death in 1753, the influence of Palladian classicism became noticeable in Potsdam, undoubtedly encouraged by Francesco

Below
Andreas Ludwig Krüger
Potsdam, view of the Breite Strasse to the west (c. 1772)
Colored India ink drawing, 49.3 x 145.8 cm; Potsdam, Stiftung Preussische Schlösser und Gärten, Berlin-Brandenburg, Plankammer

The view is dominated by the massive pile of the Great Military Orphanage (Grossen Militärwaisenhauses) designed by Gontard. Left, the view leads to the Neustadt Gate by Knobelsdorff, which formed the conclusion of Breite Strasse, beginning at the palace west front.

Algarotti. But it was not only copies of Palladio's buildings that were produced; Piranesi's engravings and the façades of Roman architects of the late Renaissance and of the Baroque also served as models. The houses, some 20 in number, and built according to foreign models, are a typical peculiarity of Potsdam, and not to be found elsewhere. The king selected specific locations for them that would be effective in terms of urban planning. But they were not effective as models, as Frederick had hoped, in the manner of Algarotti. They fitted in only with difficulty, even when, diverging from their models, they were brought into line with the proportions of Potsdam. However, it would be wrong to dismiss these buildings as eclectic in the manner of the second half of the 19th century. These are showpieces created by an absolutist monarch, who wished to see his glory reflected in his architecture and who was prepared to allow himself the costly pleasure of collecting not only paintings, sculptures, and books, but also buildings.

The adornment of the city with impressive buildings, which had begun in the immediate vicinity of the palace at the entrance to the Breite Strasse, was continued in the Alter Markt. Out of this simple old city center, the Alter Markt, a Roman square was created (see page 215). The Baroque city church built by Gerlach between 1724 and 1727 was given a new façade on the model of Santa Maria Maggiore (1741–1743) in Rome (designed by Ferdinando Fuga). The city hall resembles Palladio's design, never executed, for the Palazzo Angarano, and the preachers' and school house resembled the palace of Cardinal Querini (1732–1737) in Rome (Palazzo della Consulta, also by Ferdinando Fuga). In 1771, Gontard built the Barberini Palace after the building of the same name in Rome. This particular example illustrates for how long Italian architectural designs continued to be transplanted to Potsdam. It was not until the late 1770s that the influence of Frederick the Great on architecture began to lessen and Italian models to lose their appeal. But until about the mid-1760s, foreign copies were more greatly prized in Potsdam than native German architecture.

The Seven Years' War (1756–1763) interrupted building activity in Potsdam. Carl von Gontard had come to the city from Bayreuth in 1764. With his followers, he determined the course of building activity for decades to come in Potsdam and Berlin, and left his mark on the last part of the era of archi-

Opposite
Potsdam, Schlossstrasse 1

The private residence Schlossstrasse 1 was built by Knobelsdorff in 1748 and with the building opposite forms a gate-like starting point for the Breite Strasse. Frederick the Great had begun to rebuild the city palace in 1744, and as its new outlines began to appear, he also began to contemplate the improvement of the immediate surroundings.

Potsdam, Hiller-Brandt house in the Breite Strasse

This double-fronted house, built by Unger in 1769 on the instructions of Frederick the Great, after a design by the English architect Inigo Jones for the palace of Whitehall, originally belonged to the merchant Hiller and the tailor Brandt. The lower intervening building served as quarters for billeted troops. This building is one of the few surviving examples from Ferderick the Great's era of a building clearly based on a foreign model.

GUILLERMO KAHLO
TINA MODOTTI

Potsdam, Alter Markt, obelisk and City Hall

The Potsdam City Hall on the east side of the Alter Markt was built between 1753 and 1755 by Boumann and Hildebrandt after an unexecuted design by Palladio for the Palazzo Angarano in Vicenza, Italy. Of the original five copies of Palladio in Potsdam, only the City Hall has been preserved, after being destroyed in World War II and later rebuilt.

tecture under Frederick the Great, "a late-Baroque architecture which retrospectively refers to older stylistic elements, and combines the powerful, picturesque, sculptural feeling for architecture of the Baroque with the strict language of forms of the classicist tendency" (Drescher, 1996). His activity in Potsdam up to 1779 was very extensive, and it was actually through him and his school that the image of the city under Frederick the Great came into being. The middle-class houses for which he created the designs, over 70 in all, give clear evidence of his feeling for picturesque effect. Gontard often linked two or three houses with one façade, which linked them with palace architecture, and this resulted in building fronts with as many as 27 axes. The wall is no longer apparent as a surface; it is only the basis for the most diverse decoration. Gontard's most important work in the city is the large military orphanage built between 1771 and 1777 (see page 212) with its crowning cupola supported by eight free-standing columns on the west side (destroyed in 1945).

A year before Gontard, another southern German had also come from Bayreuth to Potsdam: Georg Christian Unger. He had studied architecture under Gontard at the Bayreuth Academy and in 1763 he began his activity in Potsdam as *conducteur* (director of building). At first, entrusted with the execution of Gontard's designs, he developed a style that still shows his debt to Gontard.

The combination of several houses behind one façade, the architectural division by means of rustic columns on the ground floor, pilasters and powerful window frames in the upper stories, along with the use of rich decoration hardly differentiate his early work from that of his master, Gontard. Like Gontard, Unger also had to copy well-known foreign buildings according to Frederick's designs, for example the so-called Hiller-Brandt houses in Breite Strasse (1769), which were based on designs by Inigo Jones for the palace of Whitehall in London (see page 213). Apart from the three-story houses that Unger built under the influence of Gontard, he also created a new type, the two-story middle-class house. This is an independent achievement on Unger's part.

In Unger's later creations the influence of the *Zopfstil* (the plain style of the late 18th century), which was even more strongly evident in the work of his successors, was already becoming noticeable. The *Zopfstil* (the "pigtail style," named after a fashion of the day) was a name given to the transitional phase (1760–1780) between Baroque and Rococo on the one hand, and classicism on the other. In Potsdam, however, this style did not set in until the end of the 1780s. It becomes noticeable in the waning of the lively spatial and structural forms, and in the intrusion of classicist elements of decoration.

For the division of façades, plain strips of wall begin to be used in place of the customary pillars and columns of the Baroque. The framing of windows and impressive roof cornices begin to lose their prominence, and horizontal divisions become more common. The resulting façades, which often have a rather dry and sober effect, are characteristic of the late works of Unger and his followers.

Karl Christian Wilhelm von Baron
Potsdam, Alter Markt, view of the Schlossstrasse (1772)
Oil on canvas, 64 x 93 cm; Potsdam, Stiftung Preussische Schlösser und Gärten, Berlin-Brandenburg

Potsdam's urban and architectural center, until its destruction in April 1945, was the Alter Markt. Surrounded by stately middle-class residences built under Frederick the Great, the city palace with its Fortuna Gate (center), the Nikolaikirche, and the City Hall formed the main architectural features of the square. The central point is formed by the marble obelisk built 1753–1755 after a design by Knobelsdorff. The Nikolaikirche is visible at the right-hand edge of the picture; in 1753, on the orders of Frederick the Great, it had been given a showy façade on the model on that of the church of Santa Maria Maggiore in Rome.

Johann Friedrich Meyer
View of Sanssouci from the Brauhausberg (1772)
Oil on canvas, 77 x 110 cm; Potsdam, Stiftung Preussische Schlösser und Gärten, Berlin-Brandenburg

This view, from the Brauhausberg, situated south of the Havel, covers the whole park of Sanssouci. On the right is the palace at Sanssouci with the terraces that lie in front of it, flanked by the New Chambers (left) and the picture gallery. At the left-hand edge of the picture the New Palace, which had just been completed at this time, is to be seen. In the center, above the green of the park, rises the Belvedere. Meyer had painted a three-part panorama of the city seen from the Brauhausberg for the New Chambers.

When the new appearance of Potsdam became evident to view and the biggest building project at Sanssouci, the New Palace, had been completed in 1709 as well, the king had a painting made of the city from the surrounding hills (see below), and also of its streets and squares, and presented these views to his guests at the former Orangery, which was converted in 1771 to become the New Chambers at Sanssouci.

With some justification, a certain pride is reflected here in the works that had been created, so different from those of the king's father and so widely admired. The "smoking party" of Frederick William I in the city palace, where the guests drank beer and entertained each other with coarse jokes, had been transformed into the "round table" of Frederick the Great in a palace where the king led philosophical discussions with Voltaire and his other friends over glasses of wine.

This general shift from "Sparta" to "Athens" had already been noticed by Voltaire on his first short visit to Berlin in 1743. When he came for a longer stay in Potsdam, from 1750 to 1753, he expressed himself with characteristic succinctness: "There are a surprising number of bayonets and very few books." The king had beautified Sparta to a great extent, but brought Athens only into his cabinet. The opposition of Sparta to Athens was a current concept in the mid-18th century, when Sparta in general referred to the Berlin and Potsdam of Frederick William I, and Athens to the same cities during Frederick the Great's reign. For contemporaries, it must have been above all the difference in architecture and art that were so generally noticeable that they repeatedly made use of this comparison.

The military forces had not diminished; on the contrary, their strength in the city had increased. Potsdam under Frederick the Great was probably Athens and Sparta at one and the same time, as Winckelmann observed on his stay in Potsdam in 1752, and it was again Voltaire who summed it up most tellingly: "Athens and Sparta, military encampment and Epicurean garden, trumpets and violins, war and philosophy."

The city gates

Under Frederick William I, the city had been given an outer wall, as had Berlin, in order to prevent not only the desertion of soldiers, but also the smuggling of dutiable goods. The city gates were simple structures, consisting of two pillars with the two doors between, which were closed at night, or, like the Jägertor (Hunters' Gate), which was built in 1733, with an architrave over the pillars concluded by a simple sculptural decoration. On both sides of the gate were houses for the guards and also for toll-collectors.

Frederick the Great retained the walls, but replaced four of the six gates with new structures. Although they also had to fulfill the original function of an entrance to and exit from the city, their main objective now was to act as showpieces as well. Here again we observe the broad palette of architectural motifs under Frederick the Great, of which the king was the final arbiter, from obelisks through triumphal arches, to Neo-Gothic elements.

Potsdam, Neustadt Gate

The gate built by Knobelsdorff formed a visual conclusion to the Breite Strasse. The gate was destroyed in World War II, all that remains being this obelisk, which is covered with hieroglyphics.

The Neustadt Gate

While the process of rebuilding the Potsdam City Palace was still under way, a start had been made in 1748 on providing Breite Strasse with new buildings and transforming it into a boulevard. Four years later a certain finality had been achieved in the section of street between the pleasure garden and the city canal that crossed the street, so that a worthy conclusion could be given to it. This was done in 1753 with the building of the second Neustadt Gate, after a drawing by Knobelsdorff.

The first gate had been built in 1722 in the course of the first program of city extension, and had consisted of a gate structure with a half-timbered tower above. But since the second extension of the city, after 1733, traffic had been passing only through the new Brandenburg Gate (see page 219). Neustadt Gate, robbed of its function, now lay within the city, and the new structure served only as a visual prospect by which the palace area was concluded (compare page 212). The decision as to its location was certainly made by Frederick.

The gate, destroyed during World War II, was formed by two obelisks with hieroglyphs made from blocks of Pirna sandstone. On the tops of the obelisks were stone eagles, which had to be replaced in 1776 by copper substitutes. The two iron doors had only symbolic value and were never closed. On each side were low-level wings that represented the old tollhouses and guards' lodges, but now had no function. Each wing had three round-arched openings with keystones, and four trophies on the low concluding top stories.

For Knobelsdorff, the building of obelisks was not a new concept. As early as the days of Rheinsberg, he had placed in front of the portal of the Ruppin road a wooden obelisk that was adorned with hieroglyphs, which was rebuilt in stone in 1761. As the motif of the Rheinsberg portal was taken up again at Sanssouci, here too an obelisk of sandstone announced the beginning of the royal terrain; and as at Rheinsberg, hieroglyphs were used in the decoration of the shaft. During his journey to Italy in 1736–1737 Knobelsdorff had become familiar with the original stone examples of Egyptian culture, which had been set up since the Renaissance in squares and gardens, particularly in Rome.

If the form of the single obelisk was not new for Prussia – Frederick William I had already set up obelisks as milestones, as in Saxony – the use of double obelisks as gates was undoubtedly influenced by the second project of Fischer von Erlach for

Potsdam, Nauener Gate (1755)
View from the city side

The Nauener Gate, standing in the field of vision of the Friedrich Ebert Strasse, built by Johann Gottfried Büring in 1755, is the first example of the Neo-Gothic influence on the continent of Europe, a style emanating from Britain. The side buildings were intended for the toll-collector and the guards. It is difficult to say what persuaded Frederick the Great in favor of this "modern" building.

the entrance to the Schönbrunn Palace in Vienna. Knobelsdorff, whose design must be considered as emanating from Frederick, made use of the Schönbrunn motif, perhaps even with a political intention after the Second Silesian War, but at the same time gives a specifically Egyptian character to the individual forms.

The motif of the gate, formed by two obelisks, was taken up again by Frederick at the end of his reign in the construction of the Hamburg Gate in Berlin. The design, which presumably was created by Unger in 1786, took its origins from a royal Cabinet order of January 13, 1786, which ordained that the existing gates with their guards' and toll-collectors' buildings should be redesigned as monumental groups of buildings, and thus would give an imposing conclusion to the streets.

The actual building, diverging slightly from the original design, was not carried out until 1789, when the Brandenburg Gate, heralding the new classicist style, was already under construction.

The Nauener Gate

At the time when Winckelmann published his *Gedanken über die Nachahmung der griechischen Werke …* (Thoughts on the Imitation of Greek Works …) the Nauener Gate was being built in Potsdam (see above). The structure, erected in 1754–1755, was based on a sketch of the king's, from which Büring had to make his drawings. In contrast to other gates in Potsdam, the Nauener Gate, like the Neustadt Gate, was not intended to be impressive when seen from the outside, but when seen from the city. The new structure was therefore placed in the position of the existing gate of 1733, on the city side. As a result, it was considered unnecessary to follow through the design on the external, country side of the gate, and the wings were given their new height and concluding battlements only on the city side. The gate consisted of two round gate towers flanking the passage through it, with a door with pointed arch at ground level, and with three similar windows above, as well as a tall cone as conclusion. The side buildings for the guards (right) and the toll collectors (left) were given three arcades with pointed arches, concluding with a cornice that matched those of the towers. On the pillars of the arcades, there were placed grotesque heads, which were similar to gargoyles, with copper rings through their mouths.

In 1867, after more than a hundred years, the Nauener Gate was rebuilt. The 1733 gate was dismantled and an opening was inserted with a pointed arch crowned by battlements. The gatehouses were now added on the country side too, at the same height as on the city side. Beyond this one senses the desire to appear "purely Gothic," particularly in the alterations to the architectural details, such as the cornices, wall conclusions, window locations and shapes. But as a result the building lost much of its original charm.

According to Frederick, the Nauener Gate was to be built "in the Gothic taste." "Gothic taste" was a well-established idea in the 18th century and denoted general irregularity; the term "Gothic" was thus a negative concept. In 1757, Eggers wrote in his *Kriegslexikon* (Lexicon of War): "By Gothic in architecture is meant everything which is carried out without taste, without rules, without proper ordering of profiles and without proportion"; and in his *Theorie der schönen Künste* (Theory of the Fine Arts), Sulzer wrote in a similar vein: "The Gothic is in fact a display made in works of art without any taste at all, lacking not only what is great and splendid, but also what is beautiful, pleasing and fine. Since this lack of taste may be apparent in many various ways, the Gothic style may also appear in different guises." While in many cases he was conservative in his thinking and building, with the Nauener Gate Frederick the Great proved himself to be "modern" and in advance of his time. The Gothic Revival in England had taken place shortly before the middle of the 18th century. The Nauener Gate became the first example of the Gothic Revival in Europe, where a serious interest in the Gothic did not awake until decades later with the early Romantics. The basic form, with two tall verticals that flanked the passage through and gatehouses with arcades to the sides, was predetermined by Knobelsdorff's Neustadt Gate and was part and parcel of the fundamental attitude of classicism. This system was "Gothicized" by means of towers, arcades with pointed arches and windows, and a battlement-like top story.

The Brandenburg Gate

The gate of this name at Potsdam, erected at the exit to the city in the direction of Berlin in 1752–1753, took up the motif of the classical triumphal arch. The side designed for display, with the double columns flanking the entrance and the surmounting figures, offered the traveller arriving from the capital a triumphal reception. It led directly to the city palace, whose extension and rebuilding had been completed in 1752. Thus the building of the Berlin gate of the same name (demolished in 1952), undertaken in the same year in the form of a triumphal arch as an entrance to the city, may be understood to have a symbolic significance.

To the west, the Brandenburg Gate (see below) was the exit gate of the city. It had been planned in 1733, in the course of the second extension of the city, as the focal point of the Brandenburger Strasse, and existed until 1769 as a very simple structure in the manner of the Jägertor. A year later it was replaced by a new, significantly larger gate building in the form of a classical triumphal arch with a large central opening. The low side openings were formerly the windows of the guards' rooms, and were only later opened to pedestrians. At the sides, in a quarter-arch, the guardhouse and the quarters of the guard and toll-collector were added. On the country side, which, as with the Berlin gate, is more richly

Potsdam, Brandenburg Gate

The exit from the city towards Brandenburg, but also to the park of Sanssouci, is formed by the Brandenburg Gate, which was built in 1770 in place of an old gate of 1733. The form is that of a Roman triumphal arch, and it stands at the end of the Brandenburger Strasse. The more richly decorated country side, shown here, was designed by Unger, and the city side by Gontard.

ornamented with architectural features than the city side, four pairs of linked Corinthian columns are placed on pedestals at the front. The top story is crowned by a large cartouche flanked by figures of Mars and Hercules. Above the pairs of columns the top story is adorned with trophies; two trumpet-playing figures flank the cartouche above the central portal. The city side is decked out in a considerably more restrained manner.

Here the triumphal architecture, for which Gontard, Unger, and Frederick himself are believed to have provided designs, is found in a richer rendering than with the Berlin gate. Apart from the classical arch, its predecessors also include French triumphal arches of the 17th and 18th centuries, and not least the gates of honor that were erected on ceremonial occasions. It must be assumed that the Brandenburg Gate does not, as has always been believed in the past, celebrate the victorious conclusion of the Seven Years' War, but instead the completion of the New Palace in 1769. Potsdam was to have been given a third triumphal arch with the building of a new gate on the Lange Brücke (Long Bridge), but this was never built. As illustrations show, the triumphal arch motif was to be taken up again, as with the Oranienburg (1768–1788) and the Rosenthal gates (1781–1788), neither of which has been preserved.

Palaces and gardens, middle-class houses and city gates, yet only one church, the Französische Kirche (French Church) (opposite), gave Potsdam its special character in the reign, which lasted over 40 years, of Frederick the Great. Through his almost uninterrupted presence in the city, the passionate royal designer of Potsdam impressed his personal mark upon it deeply, even more deeply than on Berlin.

Berlin after 1769

After 1769, the year of the completion of the New Palace and the Communs at Sanssouci, Berlin again began to attract the attention of the king, though he did not care to spend time in the city and therefore rarely did so. Once more, intensive building activity began, its main object being to lend Berlin the aspect of a European metropolis by means of new splendid façades in its main streets. Thus there were created in Unter den Linden, the Leipzig Strasse, and the Königsstrasse (today the Rathausstrasse) so-called royal personal buildings – that is, "houses built in part or whole at the expense of the king, for private persons, whether officials, court suppliers, or others granted this favor through other recommendations, for which considerations of the expectations or convenience of the occupiers were less decisive than those of the beautification of the city for the royal builder" (Borrmann). As at Potsdam, along Unter den Linden several house façades and properties were linked. The pace of building was hectic; between 1769 and 1777, 149 new houses were created, and as many as 421 between 1778 and 1785.

In the early 1770s, the king manifested a special interest in the Gendarmenmarkt in Friedrichstadt. Here, once again, he seems to have attempted to create a new closed urban ensemble with a strongly expressive architectural character. Perhaps the Gendarmenmarkt could be seen as the late variation of his failed forum plan? The quarters of the regiment of "gens d'armes," which had been built in 1736, vanished in 1773, and a year later the Frenchman Bourdet submitted a design which provided for a uniform rebuilding of the square. According to this plan, street junctions were replaced by triumphal arches, and even the churches built in the early 18th century were to be concealed behind similar façades in the north or south wall. It is not known why, but Frederick rejected this plan, and instead, after 1774, realized his own building plans. According to designs by Unger, Jan Boumann the Elder built the French Komödienhaus (House of Comedy) between the Deutsche Kirche (German Church) and the Französische Kirche. Again, as with the Forum Fridericianum, it was a theatrical building that formed the prelude to a planned ensemble whose ground plan, admittedly, had been fixed since the end of the 17th century, and which Frederick the Great himself did not alter. Between 1777 and 1785, Frederick, through Gontard and Unger, had the boundaries to the square marked by 20 three-story residential houses. The square, however, attained its architectural dominance in the city between 1780 and 1785 by means of the two towers built by Gontard "according to the King's own notions" (see page 223). As early as the 18th century, the Piazza del Popolo in Rome was seen as a model because of the

Opposite
Potsdam, the Französische Kirche on the Bassinplatz

The Französische Kirche (French Church), designed as a circular building with a portico with four Tuscan columns, and built by Jan Boumann in 1753, presumably according to plans by Knobelsdorff, once again takes up the motif of the classic Pantheon, already used for the Catholic Hedwigskirche in Berlin and the Marble Hall at Sanssouci. As a church for the French community, it is an architectural expression of the politics of tolerance practiced by Frederick the Great. It is the only church building commissioned by Frederick in Potsdam.

Berlin, Gendarmenmarkt, Deutscher Dom (German Cathedral)

The two complementary towers, built by Gontard for the Deutsche Kirche (German Church) and Französische Kirche (French Church), are not actually connected to the churches themselves, but serve purely as part of the design of the square.

MDCCLII.

similarity of its tower to those in Berlin. But there are also relationships with the dome plans of Frederick I and with the Hospital at Greenwich, near London, by Inigo Jones, and thus with English Palladianism, to which Frederick had already paid homage in his earliest buildings. Planned at first as church buildings, they soon became simply towers, without interior features; but in the similarity of their positions in front of the German and Französische Kirche and in their sculptural program, oriented towards the Enlightenment, they became a symbol of religious tolerance. "The whole makes a highly original impression," observed the writer and critic Christoph Nicolai, full of admiration, in 1786.

The plan for the forum, too, was now taken up again. Opposite the Opera House, instead of the formerly planned Academy of Sciences, Frederick, between 1775 and 1780, had Unger build a library (see page 176, bottom). For this the architect followed the design of Johann Fischer von Erlach for the Michaeler section of the Vienna Hofburg. The Baroque architecture, long out of fashion by this time, makes a somewhat singular impression opposite the classicist Opera House, then quite modern in its effect. How are we to explain this reversion to a building begun in 1735 in Vienna, whose construction was however halted after two years because of lack of funds, and was not completed until 1890? What remained a mere shell in Austria was completed in Prussia! In fact, the king's decision to create this building at this location seems to have been political rather than architectural. The reversion to the architecture of Fischer von Erlach had already been established in the Neustadt Gate in Potsdam. Berlin was now given stone bridges, for until now the only large bridge had been the Lange Brücke (Long Bridge). As a decoration for this bridge in the Leipzig Strasse, which crossed over the city moat, Carl von Gontard built the Spittel colonnades in 1776. In connection with the new structure of the Königsbrücke (King's Bridge) over the moat, near the present-day Alexanderplatz, Frederick the Great between 1777 and 1780 also had colonnades built to right and left of the Königsstrasse to designs by Carl von Gontard. They helped to beautify the city, formed an entrance gate for travelers who came to Berlin from the eastern parts of the country, and also served an extremely practical purpose: they housed 26 antique shops, lottery offices, tailors, clothes and food shops. Before the colonnades had been built, individual wooden booths had stood in this place on the bridge, making a far less pleasing impression (see below). With its triumphal character, the architecture here went far beyond its task of providing fixed shops rather than wooden stalls. In the year of the king's death, the command was issued for the rebuilding of the Oranienburg and Rosenthal gates as triumphal arches, as well as the Hamburg Gate with two obelisks. The capital city now presented an imposing appearance to the arriving visitor. Its population had risen from 90,000 in 1740 to 145,000 in 1786. By comparison with the Berlin of the "Soldier King," Frederick William I, the Berlin of Frederick the Great had not actually grown larger, but had become, with its deliberate interior consolidation, the most densely populated German city after Vienna: a European metropolis.

Berlin, Royal Colonnades in the Kleist Park

In connection with the rebuilding of the Königsbrücke over the moat near the present-day Alexanderplatz, between 1777 and 1780 Frederick the Great also had colonnades constructed to right and left of the Königsstrasse after designs by Carl von Gontard. They served to beautify the city and also had a very practical purpose: they housed shops, lottery offices, and workshops. After the royal moat was filled in (1878) and the newly built bridge, constructed between 1871 and 1873, had been removed, the Royal Colonnades also had to go. They were set up in the Kleist Park in the Schöneberg district.

Closing remarks

Two architects left their mark on the architecture of the time of Frederick the Great: first, up to the beginning of the Seven Years' War, Georg Wenzeslaus von Knobelsdorff, who rose from being a dilettante army officer to being Prussia's building supremo; and, after him, Carl Philipp Christian von Gontard, who in 1765 came from Bayreuth to Potsdam and later to Berlin. Their achievements were closely linked to the basic direction predetermined by Frederick the Great, which led in the first years of his reign to a distinctive style of his own. Later, the longer Frederick clung to his ideas of style, which had been formed before the Seven Years' War, the more his absolutist and unchanging building principles stood in the way of the further development of architecture.

This had an effect on both politics and architecture. Frederick's teacher was Knobelsdorff, and the architectural solutions not infrequently reached in consultation with him were repeated a great many times, even after the architect's death. These repetitions become evident when the palaces of Rheinsberg and Sanssouci are compared. In the same way, the shapes of rooms and decorative details of the palace at Sanssouci and the city palace are adopted yet again

Berlin, view of the Gendarmenmarkt

The Gendarmenmarkt is named after the stables of the regiment of "gens d'armes," which were built in 1736 and demolished in 1773. They were flanked by the Deutsche Kirche (German Church, 1701–1708) and the Französische Kirche (French Church, 1701–1705), built for the Huguenots. Between the churches, the French theater known as the Komödienhaus (House of Comedy) was built in 1774–1775; in its place there stands today the theater built by Schinkel between 1818 and 1821. In addition to this, a uniform rebuilding program for houses was undertaken. The square acquired its dominant character when the towers that stand in front of both churches were built by Carl von Gontard between 1780 and 1785.

in the New Palace. A significant feature of building activity under Frederick the Great was its political prestige. This becomes most evident in the middle-class houses built on foreign models or after Frederick's own drawings. Specially favored locations in Berlin and Potsdam were given middle-class houses that looked like palaces, so that they were immediately noticeable to every foreigner. The new city gates, too, above all those in the form of triumphal arches, are attempts to gain prestige.

While his father, Frederick William I, significantly enlarged the cities of Berlin and Potsdam, and filled them with a number of simple middle-class houses that also served as barracks, the architectural and artistic achievement of his time actually consisted in the numerous church buildings. During the reign of Frederick the Great, on the other hand, the two cities became the architectural centers of Prussia as a result of innumerable new houses, city gates, but also public buildings such as opera houses and libraries. The two royal residences thus corresponded to the status that Frederick had achieved for Prussia in Europe.

SCULPTURE

Saskia Hüneke

Sculptors From German States

Immediately after the accession of Frederick II (the Great) in 1740, it became clear that the king's artistic and creative needs would lead to a new era in building and the patronage of the arts. In an appeal dated September 1, 1740, published in the journal the *Berliner Priviligierten Zeitung*, which was followed by others, "merchants, manufacturers and artists who are prosperous, or else useful in other ways because of their skill are invited to Berlin," with the assurance of special privileges.

In this way the king was continuing his efforts, begun in Neuruppin and Rheinsberg, to create garden designs and palaces. There, as crown prince, he had begun his collaboration with Georg Wenzeslaus von Knobelsdorff, who had decided to abandon a military career in 1729 in order to devote himself to the arts and architecture, and with Friedrich Christian Glume, who came from a Berlin family of sculptors, and who initiated the development of Prussian Rococo.

The building projects of the first ten years of Frederick II's reign were particularly extensive: new rooms were created in the Berlin Palace, as were the Knobelsdorff wing of Charlottenburg Palace and the Opera House in Unter den Linden in Berlin. The palace in Potsdam was given a whole new façade, and in its interior, important room decorations were created for Frederick II's apartments.

Within a brief space of time, the summer palace of Sanssouci and its vineyard were completed. This was the beginning of the transformation of the park of Sanssouci, which continued up to the 1770s, into one of the most splendid and costly estates of the 18th century. Until the Seven Years' War, there was ample employment for the artists who streamed in from all districts of the group of small states, but only projects that had already begun, such as the Picture Gallery, the Chinese House, and the Marble Colonnade, were to be completed.

In his building projects, Frederick II drew upon the great cultural models of Europe, above all those of Italy and France. Despite the multiplicity of artists who were emerging from various artistic regions in the German-speaking area, there developed in Prussia a language that was common to all the arts: that of Prussian Rococo. There had been many sources of inspiration: architectural works by Vitruvius and Andrea Palladio as well as vivid engravings such as Piranesi's *Vedute di Roma* (Views of Rome) were represented in the libraries of Frederick II. Contemporary travel accounts, particularly that of Knobelsdorff, but also those of the numerous guests, acted as stimuli.

Not the least influence was exerted by works of art such as the paintings of Watteau or, in the case of sculpture, the collection of antiquities which were acquired in 1742 from the estate of Cardinal Melchior de Polignac, and the French sculptures which came to Potsdam as presents from Louis XV. Again and again, Frederick II's personal aims are evident.

Over the last 200 years, the work of many of the sculptors represented in Prussian collections has been decimated, partly by natural weathering, but also by bombing during World War II, so that their development and their effect on the art of their contemporaries can no longer be fully grasped. For example, the versatile artist Johann August Nahl, who was active in Berlin and Potsdam, exercised a

Friedrich Christian Glume
Bacchante herms at Sanssouci Palace (1746)
Sandstone; Potsdam, Stiftung Preussische Schlösser und Gärten, Berlin-Brandenburg, Schloss Sanssouci

The extended south façade of Sanssouci Palace, built between 1745 and 1747 to plans by Knobelsdorff, is adorned with 36 male and female Bacchantes. The figures, full of energetic movement, entwined in flowers, vines and other fruiting plants, which are repeated in the decorations of the interior, refer to the underlying theme of the palace vineyard. Contemporaries report that in 1746 Glume "carved the figures right out" of the sandstone blocks *in situ*, after they had been moved there in 1745.

profound influence in the early years of his work on the development of Prussian Rococo, which reached far beyond the period of his activity. The son of a co-worker of Schlüter's, in 1741 and then again in 1745–1746 Nahl visited Berlin and Potsdam, where not only decorative designers, but clearly also sculptors such as Friedrich Christian Glume, Johann Storch, Georg Franz Ebenhech, Johann Peter Benckert, and Johann Gottlieb Heymüller worked to his designs.

Among the new artists, the Berlin artist Christian Friedrich Glume attained an exceptional position, as can be gauged from the contract for 36 sandstone herms on the south-facing garden façade of Sanssouci Palace, one of the most important locations in the whole complex.

The multifarious, strongly expressive movement of the individual herms lends an unexpected dynamism to the restrained façade, which is varied only by the great projecting vault of the Marble Hall (see page 224). As with other preserved herms – such as the pre-1740 statues of Flora and Pomona at the Rheinsberg garden portal, or the horse-tamers that surmount the Potsdam royal stables, rebuilt by Knobelsdorff in 1746 (see above) – the Bacchantes point clearly to Glume's origins, through his father Johann George Glume, in the school of Andreas Schlüter. It is quite possible that Frederick II was drawing a deliberate contrast between this tradition and the modern masterpieces of French sculptural art.

In 1746, Frederick II founded his own French sculpture studio in Berlin. This was in order to have decorative pieces sculpted for both his buildings and gardens, and at the same time to encourage the development of the art of sculpture in Prussia.

Frederick II had evidently adopted Knobelsdorff's respect for French sculpture, in particular the classical tendency in French Baroque, based on models of antiquity, which was transmitted to Brandenburg Prussia through the work of the French sculptors Jean Baptiste Pigalle and Lambert Sigisbert Adam. The stylistic flair and the technical perfection of their marble works posed a corresponding challenge to German sculptors, who at this time worked mainly in sandstone. Glume too was faced with this challenge, as can be seen from his development. Around

Friedrich Christian Glume
The Horse-tamers, Sandstone; Potsdam, Stiftung Preussische Schlösser und Gärten, Berlin-Brandenburg, Marstall

The Royal Stables at Potsdam had originally been built (in 1685 by Johann Arnold Nering) as an orangery in the pleasure garden of the palace. When it was rebuilt by Knobelsdorff in 1745, the top part, in accordance with its new function as royal stables, was decorated by Glume on the central projection and at the sides with very lively groups of horse-tamers. Although these sculptures were partially replaced from the mid-1970s by copies, they still give an impression of the extent to which Glume, particularly in his younger years, remained in the powerful tradition of the Berlin Baroque of Andreas Schlüter.

Friedrich Christian Glume
Roundel of the Muses (before 1752)
Marble, height c. 190 cm; Potsdam, Stiftung Preussische Schlösser und Gärten, Berlin-Brandenburg, Sanssouci

The Roundel of the Muses lies in the west of the pleasure garden along the main avenue of the park of Sanssouci. Of the nine Muses, in classical mythology the daughters of Mnemosyne, the guardian of memory, eight are represented here: Calliope, Clio, Erato, Thalia, Melpomene, Terpsichore, Euterpe, and Polyhymnia. This work is based on a design drawing by the architect Knobelsdorff. The Muses are the last surviving works by Glume, who died in 1752 at the age of 38.

1750, his models for statues of Flora and Pomona were executed in marble by Ebenhech for the pleasure garden of the palace in Potsdam. The most important works of his last years, the marble statues for the Roundel of the Muses, were apparently carried out by Glume himself (see below). In his attempts to achieve greater elegance in composition, we find indications of a new, French-influenced style, though its further development was prevented by Glume's early death in 1752.

The ability of Franz Georg Ebenhech to work in marble was particularly admired by his contemporaries, as was his work in the French sculpture studio run by the Adam brothers. Ebenhech, who had come from Leipzig in 1746, must however have worked as an independent artist, since he became an honorary member of the Berlin Academy of Arts in 1751. To what extent he worked from his own designs, from those of Johann August Nahl, or to the commission of the French Studio, run by the Adam brothers, is difficult to determine today.

It is possible that he carried out the few independent groups for the west pleasure garden and the marble copy of the Dresden Vase (see page 227) as part of his work with the French Studio. The two marble sphinxes in the park of Sanssouci (see page 227) and the apostle figures in the Hedwigskirche in Berlin are among his independent works, and place him in the first rank of sculptors of the reign of Frederick the Great.

In 1747, both Johann Peter Benckert and Johann Gottlieb Heymüller came to Potsdam together from Bamberg. They worked in the same studio and often on the same building project – in 1760, for example,

Left
Georg Franz Ebenhech
Dresden Vase (c. 1750)
Marble, height 229 cm; Potsdam, Stiftung Preussische Schlösser und Gärten, Berlin-Brandenburg, Sanssouci

In his free rendering of Antonio Corradini's vase, dated 1734–1735, from the Great Garden of Dresden, Ebenhech proves himself the perfect sculptor in marble. With this vase, a work of Baroque luxuriance took its place in the park of Sanssouci. The Neo-classic relief *Alexander the Great and the Wives of Darius* runs around the body of the vase and is set between strongly projecting mouldings. The fully sculptural decoration, with the putti and the group *Sensuality Confronting Innocence*, appears to be quite independent of the body of the vase.

Right
Georg Franz Ebenhech
Sphinx with two putti (1755)
Marble, height 126 cm; Potsdam, Stiftung Preussische Schlösser und Gärten, Berlin-Brandenburg, Sanssouci

Two groups, female sphinxes with playing putti, form the prelude to the second main north–south axis of the park of Sanssouci. The composition of both groups shows the influence of models such as the groups of marble sphinxes with putti of 1660 by Jacques Sarrazin in the gardens of the Palace of Versailles in France. Ebenhech's close connection with the French sculpture studio is evident here, even though in this case the work is based on Ebenhech's own design.

they worked together on the Neptune group in the pleasure garden of the palace in Potsdam; in 1755 on the Chinese House; and from 1758 to 1760 on the Picture Gallery in the park of Sanssouci.

Nevertheless, each retained his own distinctive character, deriving from his own artistic background. Benckert had received his education in Munich and had then gone to Bamberg. A characteristic of his work is the sweeping movement of the south German Baroque, whose rich detail lends something at once splendid and fantastic to his figures.

His works were very much in tune with the exotic costumes and musical instruments of the Chinese figures at the Chinese House, or the allegories of the arts on the façade of the Picture Gallery.

At both buildings his figures stand side by side with works by Heymüller (see page 228), which radiate classical calm with an elegance derived from ancient models and at the same time include, as a matter of course, the necessary intellectual content. In Vienna, Heymüller had come under the influence of the work of Georg Raphael Donner, which was characterized by a classically schooled feeling for form.

The work of Heymüller and Benckert, both of whom were involved in the rich sculptural ornamentation of the Marble Colonnade in the park of Sanssouci and the Potsdam Palace, has suffered great losses.

A happy exception is the preservation of two tympanum reliefs by Heymüller, *Apollo Among the Muses* from the theater wing, and *Sacrifice of Peace* from the chapel wing of the city palace in the Alter Markt (Old Market) in Potsdam, which were created in 1750–1751, works rescued from the palace before it was demolished in 1960.

The great artistic wealth of the Rococo under Frederick II is conceivable only with the collaboration of a great number of artists, who in addition were very versatile. Apart from the "figurists" they included the "decorative sculptors": the modeller and bronze-caster Benjamin Giese, who created bronze reliefs and marble herms for Potsdam Palace and bronze reliefs for the library of Sanssouci Palace; sculptors and decorators such as the Hoppenhaupt brothers, who, along with Knobelsdorff and Nahl, supplied important designs for interior decorative schemes at the palaces of Rheinsberg, Charlottenburg, and Monbijou, at the town palaces of Berlin and Potsdam, and even the New Chambers at Sanssouci; the versatile Swiss Melchior Kambly, whose preserved works include bronze-decorated stone vases and furniture with tortoiseshell inlay; stucco workers such as Merck and Sartori; and marble workers such as the Calame brothers, without whom the treasures of interior decoration under Frederick the Great would be unthinkable.

Right
Johann Gottlieb Heymüller
The Horn-player (1755)
Sandstone, gilded, height 207 cm; Potsdam, Stiftung Preussische Schlösser und Gärten, Berlin-Brandenburg, Schloss Sanssouci, Chinesisches Haus

Johann Peter Benckert
Dancer with Castanets (1755)
Sandstone, gilded, height 216 cm; Potsdam, Stiftung Preussische Schlösser und Gärten, Berlin-Brandenburg, Schloss Sanssouci, Chinesisches Haus

The richly gilded sculptural decoration of the Chinese House, built 1754–1755 to plans by Johann Gottfried Büring, combines the exotic Far Eastern elements with the carefree, fantastic manner of Rococo. In the costumes and musical instruments there is a colorful mixture of Far Eastern cultures as seen by 18th-century Europe.

The French Sculpture Studio in Berlin

The sculpture collection of Cardinal Melchior de Polignac, which was acquired by Frederick II in 1742, included, in addition to numerous classical works, some modern ones as well, among them the busts of a Neptune (see page 231) and an Amphitrite by Lambert Sigisbert Adam, the most important member of a family of sculptors in Lyons. The bust of Neptune, above all, which is of finer quality, may have given Frederick II an individual insight into French sculpture and also an idea of the importance of this sculptor. It was also known that Adam had restored and completed the classical works in the collection.

In 1748, when the French king, Louis XV, offered Frederick II a present of his own choice, the latter decided in favor of sculpture. Altogether, five particularly valuable marble works came to Potsdam. Three are by Adam: *Le retour de la chasse* (see page 230), *La pêche dans la mer*, and the marble copy of the Ludovisi Ares, which Adam had made in Rome in 1726–1730 for the French king, and which stands in the vestibule of Sanssouci Palace to this day. There are also two works of 1748 by Jean Baptiste Pigalle representing Venus and Mercury, which were highly regarded in France as masterworks of the French classical period. The execution of these works in marble took Adam some time, so that the transport of all the pieces to Potsdam did not take place until 1752.

Meanwhile, Frederick II had founded his own French sculpture workshop, in order to be able to furnish his own buildings and gardens with statues. Its first director was the youngest of three sculptor brothers, François Gaspard Adam, who came to Berlin in 1747. Through his work with Lambert Sigisbert Adam in the same studio, he was well prepared for this task. He had certainly collaborated in Rome in 1730–1733 on the restoration of the Polignac collection, and later, in Paris, had taken part in the execution in marble of the two hunting scenes which were destined for Potsdam. In 1742, as a recipient of a scholarship from the king of France, he was able to return to Rome for three years, before continuing to Berlin via Paris.

The king supported the studio, which had been set up in the former garden house in the pleasure garden of the Berlin Palace, by means of exceptional privileges. In contrast to the German sculptors, who had to meet all their own expenses out of the fee paid for the works, the French sculptors, including the journeymen, received a fixed annual wage, with additional payments for the works, as well as money for the marble and equipment. The king entered into the contracts, gave out the commissions in person, and visited the studio to inspect the works in progress; the designs had also to be approved by him. The French sculptors received the commissions for the individual figures that were displayed in the interior rooms and garden complexes. The first commissions given to François Gaspard Adam were for the statues of Venus and Apollo (see page 231) for the Marble Hall of the palace at Sanssouci, which were followed in 1749 and 1750 by the Flora and Cleopatra for the topmost terrace of the vineyard at Sanssouci. After the arrival of Lambert Sigisbert Adam's large groups for the park, a start was made on the extension of the Roundel by the Great Fountain in the parterre of the palace (see page 232).

François Gaspard Adam's work must have been to Frederick's satisfaction, for in his eulogy on Knobelsdorff, read in 1753 at the Academy of Arts, Frederick compared him with the classical sculptors Phidias and Praxiteles. But a closer examination of his work reveals that his strength lay less in figure composition than in technical execution. In his early work, which in its elegance still appears to be influenced by that of his elder brother, François falls back on a composition by Antoine Pesne, that of Galatea in the wall painting *Pygmalion and Galatea* in the Concert Hall at Sanssouci. The groups of the elements of Fire and Earth, too, with their many figures, despite their technical perfection do not achieve the great vitality of the work of his brother Lambert. For the furnishing of the Picture Gallery with French works of art, at any rate, Frederick did not commission his own studio, but again tried to procure

Lambert Sigisbert Adam
Air (Return from the Hunt) (1749)
Marble, height 140 cm; Potsdam, Stiftung Preussische Schlösser und Gärten, Berlin-Brandenburg, Schloss Sanssouci

The large marble groups *Le retour de la chasse* (Return from the Hunt) and *La pêche dans la mer* (Sea Fishing) are among the most important works of the eldest of the Adam brothers, all sculptors. Their wide-ranging compositions, crowded with figures, seem in their vividness to belie the qualities of stone; the wealth of perfectly worked detail enriches without endangering the clarity of the total impression. Carved immediately after Adam's return from Rome, they clearly demonstrate the influence of his collaboration in Bernini's workshop. Originally destined for the garden of the French king Louis XV at Choisy, they were completed in 1749 and reached Potsdam in 1752, a gift from Louis to Frederick II, the Great. When they were set up at the Great Fountain, the groups were reinterpreted as allegories of the elements of Air and Water, and between 1756 and 1758 they were supplemented by François Gaspard Adam's allegories of Earth and Fire, to complete the four elements.

Opposite, below left
Lambert Sigisbert Adam
Bust of Neptune (1724)
Marble, height 70 cm; Potsdam, Stiftung Preussische Schlösser und Gärten, Berlin-Brandenburg, Schloss Sanssouci

This bust of Neptune was carved in Rome, where the sculptor, who came from Lyons, was active from 1723 on a scholarship from the king of France. In its vitality and loosely structured silhouette it clearly shows the influence of Bernini. The French envoy in Rome, Cardinal Melchior de Polignac, acquired the bust, which came to Paris as part of his possessions, and after his death became the property of Frederick II, who bought the collection in 1742. The king placed them in the Small Gallery of Sanssouci Palace, where other pieces, above all classical ones, from the Polignac collection were displayed. Put into storage during World War II, they ended up in the Charlottenburg Palace, and in 1991 they were returned to their original location.

first-class sculptors in France, though he ran into difficulties because of the deaths of Lambert Sigisbert Adam and Michel-Ange Slotz. In the end, important French works once again reached Potsdam: the Apollo of Jean Baptiste Lemoyne, the Venus and Mars of Guillaume Coustou the Younger, and a Diana by Jean-Pierre Vass.

François Gaspard Adam returned to Paris in 1760 and, unusually, left several uncompleted contracts behind. One cannot escape the impression that he wanted above all to withdraw from the portrait commissions to which he was unaccustomed. His nephew, Sigisbert Michel, who took over the direction of the studio in 1764, completed the work on the Mars for the Roundel by the Great Fountain, the bust of the judicial reformer Samuel von Cocceji, as well as one of the two statues commissioned for the Wilhelmsplatz in Berlin, that of General Field Marshal von Schwerin (see page 233). For the statue of General von Winterfeld, there was not so much as a sketch that Sigisbert Michel could have used. He, too, fled from the implementation of the memorial contract and in 1771 was back in Paris.

With his contract for the monuments to the outstanding generals of the three Silesian Wars, Frederick had beaten a new path towards the personal memorial, in which achievements were honored irrespective of the origins of those portrayed. Admittedly, the dynamic composition of the Schwerin statue by François Gaspard and Sigisbert Michel still owed everything to the 18th century. Only with the statues by Jean-Pierre Tassaert and the Räntz brothers do we observe the development of a new concept of the monument. Jean-Pierre Tassaert, who through the good offices of D'Alembert came to Berlin in 1774 and in 1775 was made the new director of the French Studio, was able within a short time to execute the contracts for the monuments to General von Seydlitz (see page 233) and Marshal Keith. But even Tassaert found little appeal in these lifesize portrait statues. Born in 1727 in Antwerp, he had studied in Paris with Michel-Ange Slotz, one of the old masters of French classicism, and in his statuettes, which make up the greater part of his work, he had trodden an intermediate path between Rococo and early Neo-classicism.

In portraiture, too, as for example in the bust of Moses Mendelssohn (see page 234), he sought a connection with the realistic portrait developed by Anton Graff in the painting of Berlin at the time, from which Tassaert was also able to benefit in his designs for monuments.

Wilhelm von Humboldt informed Johann Gottfried Schadow of the death of his teacher Tassaert in 1788, and later demanded that the Schadow, who had immediately returned from Italy, should be appointed as the new director of the studio. The studio was later absorbed into the Academy of Arts as a result of the Academy's revival and reorganization. Schadow's report that German sculptors still lacked some essential skills, particularly in the carving of marble, makes clear the role of the French Studio in the development of the art of sculpture in

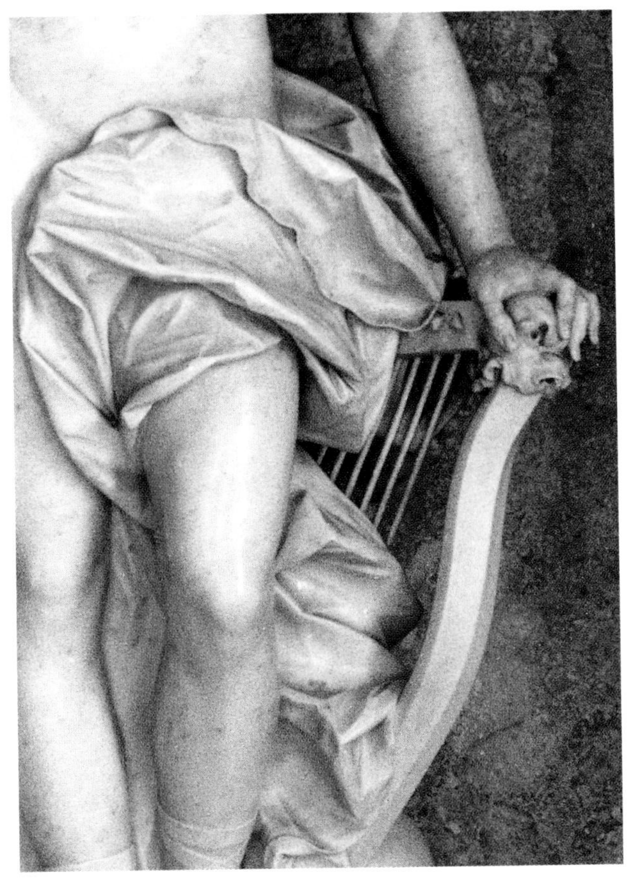

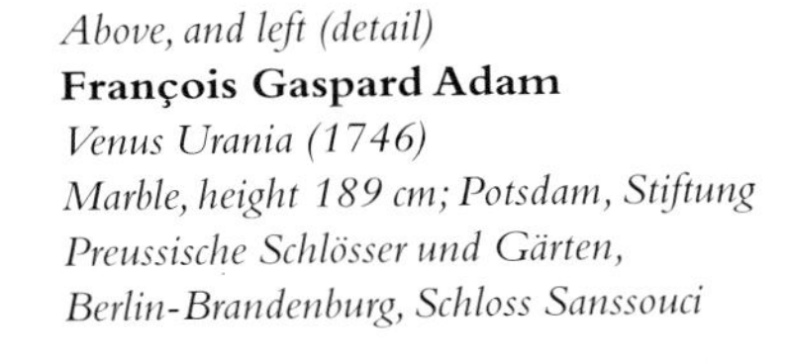

Above, and left (detail)
François Gaspard Adam
Venus Urania (1746)
Marble, height 189 cm; Potsdam, Stiftung Preussische Schlösser und Gärten, Berlin-Brandenburg, Schloss Sanssouci

The creation of a Venus and an Apollo for the Marble Hall of Sanssouci Palace was the first commission that François Gaspard Adam received as head of the newly founded French Studio in Berlin. In this hall, in which Frederick II conducted philosophical conversations with his friends, they represented the twin concepts of Art and Nature. Venus could stand for the artistic inspiration that comes from Nature.

Brandenburg-Prussia, though his judgment proves to be correct only to a limited degree when one observes the marble works of Ebenhech, Benckert, Heymüller, and later of the Räntz brothers. The significance of the studio goes far beyond technical proficiency, however, since it brought to Berlin both the stylistic influence of classical French sculpture and also a wide range of skills from the great art centers in France and Italy. It influenced contemporary sculptors to a marked degree and left a major legacy.

The Bayreuth Sculptors and Their Generation

About 1760, the change in the artistic climate in Brandenburg-Prussia also began to affect sculpture. Artists who had determined the course of the first fruitful decades in Prussian Rococo had died: Glume in 1752, Knobelsdorff in 1753, Benjamin Giese in 1755, Ebenhech in 1757, Benckert in 1763, and Heymüller in 1764. The decline in the French Studio after the departure of François Gaspard Adam was obvious, and the Seven Years' War of 1756–1763, with the resulting sharp decrease in commissions, had led to the departure of a number of artists.

For the major assignments after the war, the Prussian envoy Buchholz succeeded in attracting several outstanding artists and craftsmen from Bayreuth to Potsdam, where the efforts of Wilhelmine, the favorite sister of Frederick II, to create a rich cultural climate were not continued after her death in 1758 and that of her husband, Margrave Frederick, in 1763. Again immigration to Prussia was encouraged by means of privileges, to such an extent that this period was named by the Potsdam architect Heinrich Ludwig Manger, not without bitterness, as "the time of the Bayreuthers." The architects Carl von Gontard and Georg Christian Unger, with their designs for palace buildings in Potsdam and

Opposite, left
François Gaspard Adam, Sigisbert Michel Adam
General Field Marshal Kurt Christoph von Schwerin (completed 1769),
Marble, height 213 cm; Berlin, Staatliche Museen zu Berlin – Preussischer Kulturbesitz, Skulpturensammlung

Frederick II wanted to erect a memorial in honor of the field marshal who, with General von Winterfeld, had drawn up the plans for the beginning of the Seven Years' War. Adam withdrew from the commission, which he had received in 1759, by suddenly returning to Paris, and it was completed by his nephew, Sigisbert Michel, who succeeded him as head of the French Studio. The extremely wide-ranging movements and the sweeping, restless folds of material are a conscious link with Baroque sculptural traditions.

Opposite, center
Jean-Pierre Tassaert
General Friedrich Wilhelm von Seydlitz (1781)
Marble, height 245 cm; Berlin, Staatliche Museen zu Berlin – Preussischer Kulturbesitz, Skulpturensammlung

Tassaert completed the commission for a statue of General von Seydlitz within 18 months, so that the monument could be set up on May 2, 1781. Von Seydlitz was a legendary cavalry general whose reputation was based particularly on his new, highly disciplined training of the Hussars and on his strategically difficult deployments in the Second Silesian War and the Seven Years' War. In 1757 Frederick II bestowed on him the Order of Merit.

Left
François Gaspard Adam
Minerva (1760)
Marble, height 183 cm; Potsdam, Stiftung Preussische Schlösser und Gärten, Berlin-Brandenburg, Schloss Sanssouci

The statue of Minerva and its companion piece, Mars, form a conclusion to the Roundel at the Great Fountain on the parterre of the Sanssouci Palace. Minerva is a work by the younger Adam, who also began work on Mars before returning to Paris in 1760. Mars was completed by his nephew and successor, Sigisbert Michel.

Above
Johann David Räntz and Johann Lorenz Wilhelm Räntz
Lieutenant General von Winterfeld (1777)
Marble, height 248 cm; Berlin, Staatliche Museen zu Berlin Berlin – Preussischer Kulturbesitz, Skulpturensammlung

Hans Karl von Winterfeld had already served in Grederick II's regiment "Tall Fellows" (personal guards), and later, through his achievements in the Silesian War, came into the close circle around Frederick, who entrusted him with several very difficult military tasks. The Räntz brothers took over the commission for his monument from Sigisbert Adam after the latter's return to France in 1771. In this work they were clearly alluding to the tradition of the classical military statue, in conscious contrast to the exaggerated dynamism of the statue of Schwerin (above, far left).

bourgeois houses became the leading architects of the latter part of the reign of Frederick II. Among the decorators, it was the Spindler brothers who created outstanding achievements with their intarsia work on furniture, floors, and wall panelling for the later palace buildings, the New Palace and the New Chambers, and thus left their mark on the late style of the period.

The most important of the Bayreuth sculptors were the two brothers Johann David and Johann Lorenz Wilhelm Räntz, together with Johann Schnegg, who, coming from the Tyrol, was active in Bayreuth before moving on to Potsdam. In this phase of a new influx of talent, sculptors also arrived from other areas: Joseph Joachim and Rudolf Kaplunger both from Bohemia, Friedrich Elias Meyer from Erfurt, and the Wohler family of sculptors from Magdeburg. It was also customary for the widows of sculptors such as Benckert, Heymüller, and Johann Wohler the Elder to continue running their studios. Thus it was possible for the great new buildings to be richly decorated with sculptures – this included the New Palace and its administrative buildings, the Communs, in 1763–1769; the Belvedere on the Klausberg near the New Palace in 1770–1772 (see page 211); and the rebuilt New Chambers in 1771–1774 (see page 195). The New Chambers was first built as an Orangery that was rebuilt at the orders of Frederick II as a guest house with banqueting halls. The Räntz brothers supplied the Concert Hall, the Green Gallery, with gilded reliefs including large figures (see pages 236 and 237). They also represent transformation scenes from Ovid's *Metamorphoses*, and for this reason the hall is also known as the Ovid Gallery. The stories of the Roman poet, in which humans are transformed into plants and animals, were among Frederick's favorite reading matter. Both in painting and in sculpture they were frequently used for the decoration of concert halls – in the ceremonial hall at Rheinsberg, created by Johann Carl Scheffler to designs by Knobelsdorff

Below
Jean-Pierre Tassaert
Moses Mendelssohn (1785)
Plaster, tinted, height 50 cm; Berlin, Staatliche Museen zu Berlin Berlin – Preussischer Kulturbesitz, Alte Nationalgalerie

Twenty friends and admirers of the great Berlin writer and philosopher Moses Mendelssohn subscribed to a bust for the Free School of the Berlin Jewish community. Apart from the original, now preserved only in a fragmentary state, Tassaert supplied a plaster cast for each subscriber. The portrait was considered very lifelike by contemporaries.

Right
Jean-Pierre Tassaert
Female Bacchante Playing the Tambourine (1775)
Marble, height 180 cm; Potsdam, Stiftung Preussische Schlösser und Gärten, Berlin-Brandenburg, Sanssouci, Neue Kammern

Frederick II had the orangery at Sanssouci rebuilt as the New Chambers, a mansion for his guests, with banqueting halls and living quarters. For the Buffet Hall, Jean-Pierre Tassaert, the director of the French Studio, newly appointed in 1775, received his first commission: for four marble sculptures, a male Bacchante, a dancing faun (see far right), a female Bacchante with tambourine, and a Maenad with thyrsus, all of whom in classical mythology formed part of the entourage of Bacchus.

Far right
Jean-Pierre Tassaert
Dancing Faun (1775–1779)
Marble, height 180 cm; Potsdam, Stiftung Preussische Schlösser und Gärten, Berlin-Brandenburg, Sanssouci, Neue Kammern

or Glume; in the Concert Hall of Sanssouci Palace; and in the New Palace. The stucco reliefs of the Räntz brothers, despite their splendor, cannot belie the loss of energy of the late period, in which the need for new developments had already come to be felt. At the same time as they were creating sculptures closely linked with specific buildings, the Räntz brothers were also sculpting outstanding individual works, such as the seated statue of Wilhelmine of Bayreuth (see page 236), in the Temple of Friendship built in 1768–1770, or the monuments on the Wilhelmsplatz, which represent the only great project for Berlin of the late period under Frederick II.

While the first early Neo-classicist palace and garden complex was coming into being in Wörlitz, in the small state of Saxony-Anhalt, with the New Palace Frederick II was consciously using the influences of the language of forms of the Baroque.

Johann Christoph Wohler, and his sons Johann Christoph and Michael Christoph (and the Räntz brothers?)
Neues Palais, central projection on the garden side (1766)
Sandstone; Potsdam, Stiftung Preussische Schlösser und Gärten, Berlin-Brandenburg, Sanssouci

In the surmounting groups and the pediment relief, the dramatic deeds of Perseus are presented as equivalent to the glorification of Frederick II's acts of war and heroism. A goddess of victory surmounts the pediment, and the crowned cartouche with the fanfare-blowing figures announces victory.

In the profusion of sculptural decoration, the center is emphasized by dramatic groups of figures and reliefs in the triangular pediments. The reliefs of the central projection on the garden and court side (see above) have been ascribed to the Räntz brothers and Johann Christoph Wohler the Elder. His sons, Johann Christoph and Michael Christoph Wohler, were not identified by name at this time, but may already have been working in their father's studio. It was not until the 1770s that they continued their training with the Räntz brothers. Like Ebenhech, Benckert and Heymüller, the Räntz brothers left important marble works behind in Berlin and Potsdam, for example the monument of Lieutenant-General von Winterfeld by Johann David and Johann Lorenz Wilhelm on the Wilhelmsplatz in Berlin (see page 233) and the statue of Wilhelmine of Bayreuth in the Temple of Friendship in the park at Sanssouci (see page 236). Here the leading role is attributed to the younger brother, Johann Lorenz Wilhelm, since in 1756 he had already won a prize from the Copenhagen Academy of Art for a marble relief. Although a rapid transformation in style took place after the death of Frederick II in 1786, the style of the sculptors associated with the late period of his reign is still discernible in some later works – a notable example is the sandstone coach over the portal, reminiscent of a Roman triumphal arch, at the coach stables built by Andreas Ludwig Krüger in 1787 at the Neuer Markt (New Market) in Potsdam.

Johann Lorenz Wilhelm Räntz
Wilhelmine of Bayreuth (1772–1773) (modern copy)
Marble, height 149 cm; Potsdam, Stiftung Preussische Schlösser und Gärten, Berlin-Brandenburg, Sanssouci

In 1770, Frederick II had a temple built that was to be dedicated to his sister, Wilhelmine Margravine of Bayreuth, and, in a wider sense, to the concept of friendship. The life-size seated statue of Wilhelmine is ascribed to the younger of the Räntz brothers. In its portrayal of the well-educated Wilhelmine, who was a lover of the classics, the combination of human intimacy and delight in Rococo detail results in one of the masterpieces of the period.

Johann David Räntz and Johann Lorenz Wilhelm Räntz
Jupiter and Danae (opposite), and Bacchus and Ariadne (below) (1774)
Stucco, gilded; Potsdam, Stiftung Preussische Schlösser und Gärten, Berlin-Brandenburg, Sanssouci, Neue Kammern

The Concert Hall of the New Chambers is also known as the Ovid Gallery, for the Räntz brothers here created stucco reliefs illustrating scenes from Ovid's *Metamorphoses*. An example (see opposite) is the scene in which Jupiter approaches Danae in the form of a shower of golden rain and makes her the mother of Perseus. The gilded reliefs stand out exquisitely from the background of stucco marble, originally a greenish shade but now faded, which was to represent the semi-precious stone chrysoprase.

PAINTING

Gerd Bartoschek

Opposite
Antoine Pesne
Court Lady in Black (c. 1745)
Oil on canvas, 144 x 107 cm; Berlin, Stiftung Preussische Schlösser und Gärten, Berlin-Brandenburg, Schloss Charlottenburg

In a series of paintings executed over several years – works that represent a high point of his late style, which was strongly influenced by Watteau and Lancret – Pesne portrayed eight ladies-in-waiting to Queen Elisabeth Christine, grouped in pairs. Among the series are two portraits of court ladies in black gowns, each posing with a mask in her hand, the backdrop being a garden scene.

By far the most important influence on the Rococo painters of Brandenburg-Prussia was French artist Antoine Pesne. The court painter of Frederick I and of his son, the "Soldier King" Frederick William I, Antoine Pesne, together with Georg Wenzeslaus von Knobelsdorff, to whom he had taught painting at the beginning of his artistic career, became the co-creator of a style that was perfectly tailored to the personality of Frederick the Great. It was so well suited to him that at first it was restricted entirely to the court of the Crown Prince. Of French birth, Pesne had settled in Prussia, and about 1735, when living in Rheinsberg, he entered a field to which he was unaccustomed, that of ceiling painting, but with which he soon familiarized himself. At the age of 50, he was still able to benefit from his openness to new artistic currents. It is presumed that he contributed significantly to introducing Crown Prince Frederick to the artistic world of the French painter Antoine Watteau, who became much imitated in Rheinsberg. Pesne cannot have been personally acquainted with the creator of the genre of *fêtes galantes*, who died in 1721, but he enjoyed a close friendship with the latter's follower, Nicolas Lancret. Together with other artists, Pesne profited from the mood of dissolution that prevailed at the court of Rheinsberg and colored the early years of the reign of Frederick the Great. His style increasingly loosened up, and his palette became brighter. Only now could he give full proof of his gift for coloring and his talent for decoration. Of his mythological wall and ceiling paintings, which in their content provide more or less lightly veiled references to the function and location of their spatial surroundings, original evidence of major works can now be found only at Rheinsberg and Sanssouci (see below). Among the most brilliant examples of Pesne's late portraiture are the full-length portrait of the legendary dancer Barbarina

Antoine Pesne
Apollo and the Muses (c. 1742)
Oil on canvas, 56 x 81 cm; Berlin, Stiftung Preussische Schlösser und Gärten, Berlin-Brandenburg, Schloss Charlottenburg

It was only under Frederick the Great that Pesne was able to develop his decorative talent, Frederick commissioning him to carry out wall and ceiling paintings in his residence. For the stage curtain, now lost, of the Berlin Opera House, which opened in 1742, Pesne created a portrayal of Parnassus, the home of Apollo and the Muses. The effect of this surviving oil sketch derives from the shimmering colors, broken up by areas of delicate shadow.

from Frederick the Great's study in the Berlin Palace (now in the Charlottenburg Palace) and a series of portraits of court ladies (see page 239). The charm of these paintings is unthinkable without Watteau. The closeness to reality that they nevertheless possess is an element that characterizes not only the work of Pesne, but also the best examples of Berlin art in general. At that time the search for the ideal based in reality also led to the discovery of the landscape of the March for painting. The Rheinsberg view by Knobelsdorff is the earliest example (see below). In 1745, a journey that was taken together by Pesne, Knobelsdorff, and Charles Sylva Dubois resulted in landscape paintings that show the marshes of the Oder at Freienwalde as well as the district around Schwedt. Dubois had come from Brussels to Berlin as a dancer under King Frederick I and it was only at the court of Frederick the Great that his artistic talent developed. The court painter Johann Harper too, in his late period, painted Arcadian landscapes in the style of Claude Lorrain and Watteau, as well as ceiling paintings in the palaces of Charlottenburg and Sanssouci. Pesne's pupil Johann Gottlieb Glume, the flower painter Augustin Dubuisson, a brother-in-law of Pesne's, the architect and painter Andreas Krüger, and the versatile decorative painter Friedrich Wilhelm Höder are also associated with the Rococo period under Frederick the Great in its most creative phase, which came to an end with the departure of Johann August Nahl (1746) and the death of Knobelsdorff (1753).

As is well known, Frederick the Great had no great confidence in the abilities of his native artists. This prejudice also determined his attitude towards the Berlin Academy. The fire in 1743 at the Academy building in Unter den Linden, in which the majority of the collections and archives were destroyed, also contributed to the crippling of the institution. Following the death in 1750 of Friedrich Wilhelm Weidemann, who had been appointed director of the Academy by Frederick, it was only after an interregnum of several years that Blaise Nicolas Le Sueur was appointed as his successor in 1756. This rather unproductive painter, who did not achieve much either as an official, had been summoned to Berlin in 1748 with Charles Amédée Philippe van Loo, after Frederick's efforts to obtain the services of François Boucher as his court painter had failed. Van Loo, a member of a important French family of painters, was to take some of the burden from Pesne, but was not able adequately to replace him as an artist. His activity is recorded by a series of portraits, which in their soulless, stereotyped character typify the end of Prussian portrait art, which was dominated by the court (see opposite, above right), by a few conversation pieces and smaller historical paintings, and the enormous ceiling painting, executed on canvas, in the Marble Hall of the New Palace at Sanssouci. The painter, who obtained leave of absence in France during the Seven Years' War, said his final farewell in 1769 after completing this commission. Apart from him, after Pesne's death in Berlin, there was hardly sufficient talent available for tasks such as those that were created by the decorating of the New Palace. Christian Bernhard Rode (see opposite, below) and his pupil Johann Christoph Frisch (see opposite, above left), who followed Pesne in this field, were hardly able to disguise their inadequate academic education. Both worked for Frederick the Great at the New Palace at Sanssouci. In addition, Frisch created a great ceiling painting in the New Chambers at Sanssouci Palace, whose brilliant colors betray his preoccupation with the classical technique of encaustic painting. In this

Opposite, above left
Johann Christoph Frisch
Psyche Being Received into Olympus (1770)
Oil on canvas, 110 x 142 cm; Potsdam, Stiftung Preussische Schlösser und Gärten, Berlin-Brandenburg, Neues Palais

This painting is one of a four-part series of illustrations of the classical story of Eros and Psyche. Frisch, like his teacher, Rode, attempted to bring new life to historical painting in Berlin according to the principles of Neo-classicism and of the Enlightenment. He made up for his lack of creative power with his experiments for reviving the ancient encaustic technique, in which wax is used as a medium.

Georg Wenzeslaus von Knobelsdorff and Antoine Pesne
View of Rheinsberg (c. 1737)
Oil on canvas, 82 x 163 cm; Rheinsberg, Stiftung Preussische Schlösser und Gärten, Berlin-Brandenburg, Schloss Rheinsberg

In this painting the two artists brought Watteau's dreamlike world of images into the real landscape of the March of Brandenburg. Knobelsdorff's view is a document of the carefree days that Frederick the Great spent at Rheinsberg as crown prince. He is shown on the right among the figures added by Pesne, accompanying his mother and his consort.

Above right
Charles Amédée Philippe van Loo
Princess Louise of Anhalt-Dessau as Diana (1765)
Oil on canvas, 145.5 x 111 cm; Hamburg, Kunsthalle

When choosing an artist to succeed Pesne as court painter, Frederick the Great once again decided on a French artist. However, there was a shortage of talent among the principal exponents of court portrait painting. Van Loo attempted to make his mark by means of portraits in mythological disguise. The faces are always depicted in a formulaic manner and show little individuality.

Left
Christian Bernhard Rode
The Empress of China Picking the First Mulberry Leaves (c. 1770)
Oil on canvas, 91 x 103 cm; Berlin, Staatliche Museen zu Berlin – Preussischer Kulturbesitz, Gemäldegalerie

This painting was created as a *sopraporta* for the Britz Palace near Berlin, the country seat of the minister von Hertzberg, which had been developed into a "showhouse." In the spirit of the Enlightenment, the decoration of the palace glorified agriculture as the basis of all culture. In his efforts to revive the arts in Berlin, Rode was here able to dedicate himself to new pictorial themes.

Joachim Martin Falbe
Portrait of an Old Lady (c. 1755)
Oil on canvas; Nuremberg, Germanisches Nationalmuseum

Falbe surpassed his teacher Pesne in his power of characterization, above all in his portraits of old people. In this portrait of an unknown woman, whose face exercises a compelling effect on the observer, realism combines with the middle-class principle that the status of a person should not be defined by his or her origins.

area he rivalled Benjamin Calau of Leipzig, who carried out experiments at the Berlin Academy from 1771. Friedrich Reclam, who died early, was also a member of the circle of painters in Berlin who after the Seven Years' War devoted their limited powers of portrayal to revive the portrait in the manner of the newly developing Neo-classicism. At Rheinsberg, Reclam created interior decorative paintings for Prince Henry, who was the brother of Frederick the Great, which have been preserved, although they have been partly overpainted. In Prince Henry's Palace in Berlin (the present-day Humboldt University), the king engaged the Roman painter Gregorio Guglielmi to carry out the most important frescoes to have been created during the latter part of Frederick's reign. This fashionable painter moved on immediately afterwards to Augsburg, Warsaw, and finally to St. Petersburg. The fresco in the stairwell of Henry's palace fell victim to building alterations, while that in the hall was destroyed during World War II.

For portrait painting, which occupied only a subordinate position in the academic order of precedence of painting genres, Pesne had been able to lay down much more solid foundations. Joachim Martin Falbe, who gave the number of Pesne's pupils as 38, must himself qualify as probably the best of them. Like most other Berlin portraitists, he was dependent on the demand for portraits among the nobility and middle classes, which was gradually beginning to become emancipated and played a growing part in the patronage of the arts (see left). In addition, he worked from time to time at the court of Anhalt-Köthen. The regents of the other Anhalt states, the semi-sovereign margraves of Brandenburg-Schwedt and dukes of Brunswick-Wolfenbüttel and Mecklenburg-Schwerin, also made use of the artistic talent that was developing in Berlin. At their courts one might encounter members of the related artists' families of Lisiewski and Matthieu. Their clan leaders, the Pole Georg Lisiewski and the Huguenot David Matthieu, had already been active as portrait painters in Berlin under Frederick the Great, and were only indirectly influenced by Pesne. The siblings of the next generation, Anna Rosina de Gasc (born Lisiewska, first married to David Matthieu), Anna Dorothea Therbusch (born Lisiewska), and Christian Friedrich Reinhold Lisiewski, as well as their nephew Georg David Matthieu, each left behind unrelated works, though they did not, in fact, work independently of each other. A certain fame was achieved by Anna Dorothea Therbusch (opposite left), who was for a time protected by Diderot during her courageous stay in Paris, then the artistic metropolis of Europe. It may have been for this reason that Frederick the Great also gave her some commissions. She and her sister Anna Rosina, who became court painter in Brunswick, may be described as the first notable women painters in Berlin. Christian Friedrich Reinhold Lisiewski, intermittently court painter at Dessau and Ludwigslust, created probably the most artistically ambitious portraits during the second half of the 18th century in Berlin (opposite right), apart from the work of Anton Graff, who from 1771 regularly visited the Prussian capital from Dresden. Between 1777 and 1779 Johann Heinrich Wilhelm Tischbein, known as "Goethe-Tischbein," was also active in Berlin. His great success as a society portrait painter, achieved through routine and flashy superficiality, was one of the reasons for him to seek a new basis for his artistic creativity in the classical works of Italy.

Many portrait painters active in Berlin are known today only for single works, such as Heinrich Christian Friedrich Franke for his powerful portrait of Frederick the Great of around 1763, which has contributed substantially to the still prevalent image of "Old Fritz" (copies in Charlottenburg Palace, Berlin, and in the New Palace, Potsdam).

The human image of the Enlightenment was most enduringly represented in the art of Berlin by Daniel Chodowiecki. Born in Danzig, he came to Berlin in 1743. His uncle, whose luxury goods business he entered, at first had him trained in miniature painting. Soon he was able to compete on technical terms with the works of other miniature painters active in Berlin, the most outstanding of whom were Anton Friedrich König, Karl Friedrich Thienpondt, and later Nathanael Diemar. Chodowiecki achieved artistic independence when he took up oil painting. His most important achievement was probably the sympathetic depiction of the middle-class life in his immediate surroundings, mostly in very small format (see page 244). In the years around 1765, he began to make his name in the field of etching, in which his activity became as tireless as it was successful. Apart from single sheets, he produced above all series of illustrations for calendars and almanacs, which made his name known far beyond Berlin. With scenes such as those for Lessing's play *Minna von Barnhelm* he contributed substantially to the popularization of the literature and thought of the classical period. Chodowiecki himself lived in an exemplary manner, maintaining the moral aspirations that are embodied throughout his etchings. In Berlin, with all his unpretentiousness, he represented a new type of artist, equally associated with the crafts and guilds and independent of the court. Constantly in correspondence with his friend Anton Graff in Dresden, he devoted himself to the reform of the Berlin Academy in an attempt to make it into an institution of professional training in all genres of art,

Below
Christian Friedrich Reinhold Lisiewski
Friedrich Balthasar Schönberg von Brenkenhoff (c. 1775)
Oil on canvas, 77.5 x 65 cm; Berlin, Stiftung Preussische Schlösser und Gärten, Berlin-Brandenburg, Jagdschloss Grunewald

The subject of this portrait went down in Prussian history for his reclamation of the Netze and Warthe marshes. By means of slight foreshortening, the artist has given a monumental effect to the portrait. The intense quality of the drawing and painting captures in equal measure the character of the face and the materiality of the clothing.

Above
Anna Dorothea Therbusch
Julius Vieth von Golssenau (1771)
Oil on canvas, 141 x 107.5 cm; Berlin, Staatliche Museen zu Berlin – Preussischer Kulturbesitz, Gemäldegalerie

The artistic sophistication she had gained in Paris secured the success of Therbusch as a portraitist of Berlin society. Her attempts in the realm of historical painting, however, aroused pitying smiles. In this portrait she produced a warm-hearted image of the Saxon statesman Vieth von Golssenau amidst his collection of works of art.

Daniel Chodowiecki
Domestic Lesson (1773–1774)
Oil on wood, 23 x 19 cm; Darmstadt, Hessisches Landesmuseum

Chodowiecki's work as draughtsman, engraver, and painter represents the first high point of middle-class art in Berlin. He dedicated himself intensively to the study of everyday life, and found the subjects for his not very numerous paintings above all in his personal surroundings.

a development that was in keeping with the spirit of the times. The realization of this project, shortly before the death of Frederick the Great, was to the credit of the minister von Heinitz. Rode, who had succeeded Le Sueur as director, remained in that position, in which he was succeeded, only after his death in 1797, by Chodowiecki.

In 1762, Jakob Philipp Hackert, born in Prenzlau, undertook a journey to Stralsund with his friend, the portrait-painter Georg David Matthieu (see opposite, right), a journey that took him to the island of Rügen and to Stockholm. Thus began an international career as a landscape painter, which culminated in his appointment as court painter to the King of Naples. In Italy, Hackert, whose artistic beginnings are documented by views from the Berlin zoological gardens (Stiftung Stadtmuseum Berlin and Burg Hohenzollern), formulated the principles of Neo-classical landscape painting in an exemplary fashion. His admirers included renowned personalities such as Catherine the Great and Goethe, who as a landscape draughtsman was Hackert's pupil and honored his memory with a short biography. Hardly less gifted was his younger brother, Johann Gottlieb Hackert, who died in Paris. An early work of his, a view of Charlottenburg, has been preserved (Charlottenburg Palace, Berlin).

After the brilliant new awakening in the field of landscape painting involving Knobelsdorff and Dubois, and the departure of the Hackert brothers, it was the painting of *vedute* above all that developed in Berlin. Around 1760, still in the manner of conventional perspective views as practiced in 18th-century central Germany above all by Johann Alexander Thiele, Gottfried Hempel, an artist who had arrived from Silesia, painted views of Rheinsberg, Magdeburg, and Schöneberg on the Elbe (Rheinsberg Palace; the view of Rheinsberg has been missing since 1945). In Berlin at the same time, several members of the Fechhelm family of painters from Dresden, who had come to the Prussian court as theatrical decorators, became active in the field of *vedute*. Carl Friedrich Fechhelm, his younger brother Carl Traugott, and his son Carl Friedrich transmitted to Berlin, though admittedly with far less virtuosity, the landscape style that Bernardo Bellotto (sometimes known as Canaletto, after his famous uncle) brought from Venice to late-Baroque Dresden. The special quality of Venetian *vedute* painting of the 18th century is found in the subtly nuanced reproduction of everyday urban scenes, in the use of light to convey mood and atmosphere, and not least in the portrayal of the everyday citizens who enliven the streets and squares. The Fechhelms' works were satisfying a growing interest in urban views, which had developed both from an increase in the population and also from the interest now taken in architecture and in city life generally (see opposite, bottom).

A further center for *veduta* painting was found in Potsdam under Frederick the Great, and here it was personally encouraged by the king himself. For the guest apartments in the New Chambers, the neighbor to the west of his favorite residence, he commissioned views of the city from Carl Christian Wilhelm Baron and Johann Friedrich Meyer, which were above all to demonstrate the extensive architectural improvements instigated by him. Baron took part as a decorative painter and gilder in the later building projects of Frederick the Great at Sanssouci. Meyer, also born in Dresden and, following the example of Bellotto, came to Potsdam as a stage decorator. Independent contributions to the development of painting in Brandenburg-Prussia would not originate in Potsdam, either then or in later times. The court and the capital were too near.

Right
Jakob Philipp Hackert
The Palace of Niederhof, near Stralsund (1762)
Oil on canvas, 60.5 x 74 cm; Berlin, Stiftung Preussische Schlösser und Gärten, Berlin-Brandenburg, Schloss Charlottenburg

At the beginning of his career as a landscape painter, Hackert went to stay in Western Pomerania, where he was inspired in particular by the flat landscape, particularly when it was suffused in glow of evening light. The palace is seen behind trees in the background. It provides a reason for the presence of the splendid coach, which sets off the foreground of the painting.

Carl Traugott Fechhelm
The Neuer Markt in Berlin (c. 1785)
Oil on canvas, 78 x 113 cm; Berlin, Stiftung Preussische Schlösser und Gärten, Berlin-Brandenburg, Schloss Charlottenburg

During the later part of the reign of Frederick the Great, members of the Fechhelm family of painters from Dresden familiarized Berlin with urban views in the style of the Italian artist Bernardo Bellotto. This view of the Neuer Markt (Old Market), with the Marienkirche in the background, shows the square, surrounded by both splendid and more modest houses, as the focus of the many different aspects of city life.

THE APPLIED ARTS

Wasilissa Pachomova-Göres

Opposite
Library in Sanssouci Palace (1746–1747)
Johann August Nahl, Johann Heinrich Hülsmann and others; Cedarwood, fire-gilded bronzes; Stiftung Preussische Schlösser und Gärten, Berlin-Brandenburg

The magical appeal this temple had for those of Frederick's era lay not least in its all-embracing, airy decoration, full of enchantment and mystery.

Ceiling of the concert hall in Sanssouci Palace (c. 1746–1747)
Johann Michael Hoppenhaupt the Elder, Johann Michael Merck, and Georg Franz Ebenhech, gilded stucco; Stiftung Preussische Schlösser und Gärten, Berlin-Brandenburg

Real elements observed from nature, displayed with wit and high spirits, crowd into the magical world of ornamental fantasy of the age to Frederick the Great. The result is a poem that captures the enchanting mood of the Rococo period.

The contemporaries of Frederick II who gave him the title of "the Great" had good reason to do so. In an astonishingly short time the young king had grasped how to transform his country into one of Europe's great military and political powers, but also to let it blaze in unwonted cultural splendor. He turned his court into a unique realm of the Muses, which yielded in no respect to the principal European capitals, and was capable of producing extraordinary and highly individual things. Not only history but also art – and above all applied arts, the major sphere of Rococo – has him to thank for one of the most exciting of their chapters. No less, and perhaps even more clearly and more intimately, than his politics and philosophy, the interior decoration that was created according to his will, and with his unparalleled involvement, tells us about the personality of this lonely philosopher of Sanssouci. That the young king was concerned about an appropriate framework for his political and military triumphs was by no means unusual. Since Louis XIV had infected all of Europe with his grandiose lust for magnificence, the clothing of absolutist claims to power in imposing garments was, rather, a "must" for every potentate who thought anything of himself. "Nothing gives a kingdom more brilliance than when the arts flourish under his protection": it was with this conviction, already formulated in his *Anti-Machiaveli*, written when he was still crown prince, that Frederick II ascended the throne in 1740. For the new Prussian king, however, the arts meant more than the customary instruments of a ruler's self-image; art created at his bidding was more than the wish "that everything the wide world produces should also be found in his kingdom" (which, according to the poet Goethe, has been seen as the main driving force of Frederick the Great's enthusiasm for art).

Surrounding himself with beautiful things fulfilled an inner need in Frederick. The rebuilding and extension of his palaces, and their design – from the ceiling to the vase on the chimney piece and the cup on his breakfast table – were also matters that concerned him, but not by any means only for the sake of ostentation. Sarcastic by nature, he set very little store by etiquette and fashion, and did not hesitate to ignore current trends if they contradicted his personal tastes and habits. Any craving for luxury was totally foreign to him, and in his everyday life was unpretentious to the point of asceticism. But if the pocket of the shabby uniform worn by this man, who reminded his contemporaries of a Spartan in the ragged cloak of Diogenes, never failed to contain a snuffbox set with diamonds; if he would not give up until he had, at great expense, tracked down exactly the right shade of his favorite color for a porcelain service – then clearly such things meant a great deal to him. This was a question of his station in life, his inner home; it was not by chance that he was particularly authoritarian, not to say dictatorial, when it was a question of the design of his private apartments. Just as his books, his essential spiritual nourishment, had to be within reach at all times and places; just as he, according to his own statement, needed "for the soothing of his cares and sorrows" a daily dose of music and to have his "best friend," his flute, close at hand – so it was important for his eye continually to slake his aesthetic thirst with a world

Ceiling of the Voltaire Room (1752–1753)
(Detail) Johann Christian Hoppenhaupt the Younger (design), Karl Joseph Sartori the Elder (execution), Augustin Dubuisson (painting)

In its almost naturalistic execution, this delicate garland floating in the air, which seems to have blown into the room from the garden, is full of the poetic charm of Prussian Rococo. Painted, carved, shaped, and chased, such flowers, with their special "Prussian perfume," are ever present in Frederick's palaces and are among their trademarks.

of forms that were in perfect harmony with his spiritual world. Where his glance rested, his soul needed to rest too, and free itself from the bonds of his "abominable work," as he himself described his duties as a monarch. In order to carry out these duties, the great king required a counterbalance, his realm of Sanssouci, even if it was only an illusion. This was to be supplied by the Muses. And they did so, obediently following his wishes and his will. For the king of the Prussians not only had unerring taste and an innate instinct for the beautiful – he also had artistic visions no less exacting than his political ambitions, both of which he sought to realize with astonishing persistence and obstinacy. If, in his liberal state, everyone might "be happy after his own fashion," the art that was created according to his bidding still had to be tailored exclusively to his personal measurements. The involvement of absolute rulers in the affairs of the artists of the time was admittedly nothing new in itself; one has only to consider the court of Louis XVI, the influence of Saxon Baroque on Augustus the Strong, or the enormous part played by Peter the Great, in the Europeanization of the arts in Russia. What was unusual, if not unique, was the degree and, above all, the personal character of Frederick's interventions in all questions relating to art. He determined not only "what," but he also, rigorously and inexorably, determined "how." The intensive nature of his commitment, which ranged from detailed specifications to sketches by his own hand, suggests that Frederick might have become an artist if fate had not, "by a blind accident of birth," condemned him to his "abominable work." To do justice to the enormous demands of such a client, artists needed not only a huge amount of imagination and an acute sensitivity to his wishes, but also a large measure of real talent. These qualities were possessed in full measure by the men whom Frederick employed. The architect Knobelsdorff, the creators of interior decoration Johann August Nahl, and the brothers Johann Michael and Johann Christian Hoppenhaupt, transferred to paper the visions of their sovereign and the ideas that shaped the style of the entire reign of Frederick II. And others, who from time to time did honor to their craft, took up the ideas of these four and developed them, as if in a fugue for several voices, into a decorative polyphony of unique beauty. Thus there came into being, with the collaboration of the royal "artistic director" (a collaboration that sometimes subsequently became an authoritarian reaction against those "of a different persuasion") the phenomenon of Frederician Rococo – a world of unique charm and expressive power, one of the most delightful versions of all European Rococo. What, then, is the special nature of this phenomenon?

Is it simply a tendency towards naturalism, which is usually regarded as a Prussian characteristic? Or is it the wondrous mingling of the real and the fantastic, the irrational and the logical, the light-hearted and a hint of melancholy? Or perhaps it all depends on the way in which everything fuses together so loosely and spontaneously, entwining and clinging, each element flowing into another? How naturally do amusing inconsistencies blend together, perfect elegance with the freshness of a diverting improvisation? Or is it colors, forms, rhythms, everything so delicate and dainty, carefree and weightless? Or is it that feeling for measure and discretion that protects even the boldest artistic acrobatics of form from exaggeration, and which preserves balance and inner discipline; that feeling which, together with liveliness of sensibility, produces such different forms as the exuberance of southern Rococo and the comparative abstraction of French Rococo? Or is it, finally, a hidden meaning which wafts through this apparently frivolous, carefree decorative style with a similar spirit to that which dwells in the lyrical fantasies of Frederick's beloved Watteau (see pages 246 and 247)? To uncover the secret of this phenomenon, one must walk through the rooms of Frederick's palaces, for only from the entire ensemble created there does it seem possible to grasp to its fullest extent the meaning of the individual genres of art.

No style has produced more architecture-related craftwork than the Rococo style. This is particularly true of the Rococo of Frederick the Great, thanks largely to the strong personal involvement of the king himself. Here it is difficult to tell where the wall ends and the carved console begins, for it is not a piece of furniture placed against the wall, but seems to grow out of it. The mirror, too, does not hang on the wall; the delicate edges of its frame are no more than the continuation of the decorative structure of the wall and ceiling. The sofas and chairs, with their slender legs dancing on tiptoe, must also stand by the wall, where a predetermined place is often reserved for them, crowned by ornamentation. The silk fabric with the same pattern for both furniture and wall coverings forbids any separation between them, for such a separation would disturb the balance of this apparently arbitrary room arrangement (see page 251). For from the ceiling of a palace to the snuffbox in the king's pocket, all this was a closed world, a wondrous theater of dreams, which could be harmonized only by a uniform regime. The main role here is given to the décor. Carved in wood, shaped in stucco, cast in bronze, gilded or silvered, expressed

Armchair from the bedroom of Frederick II in Potsdam Palace (1745)
Johann August Nahl
Wood; Potsdam, Stiftung Preussische Schlösser und Gärten, Berlin-Brandenburg, Neues Palais

This armchair is an eloquent example of the playful grace of Rococo sculpture under Frederick the Great. In the contours of the arms, the delicate "dancing" legs, and the silvered carving, and even in the bold quadruple C-curve of the arms, the daring acrobatics of Rococo form are tempered by a moderation that is typically Prussian.

Desk from the study of the royal apartments in the New Palace, Sanssouci (c. 1765)
Johann Melchior Kambly
Tortoiseshell, cedarwood, silvered bronze; Stiftung Preussische Schlösser und Gärten, Berlin-Brandenburg

In no way inferior to their Parisian contemporaries in their artistic perfection, Kambly's works, particularly in the individuality of their exquisite bronze compositions on the fiery tortoiseshell veneer, demonstrate the unmistakable handwriting of this gifted master of the art of furniture making.

Marble Hall, Sanssouci Palace, Allegory of Music (c. 1747)
Georg Franz Ebenhech
White stucco; Stiftung Preussische Schlösser und Gärten, Berlin-Brandenburg

With spontaneous informality, these chubby-cheeked putti, together with their allegorical playthings and their charming female guardians, make themselves comfortable on the cornice of the hall. The ceremonial severity of the architectural design is immediately relaxed by the Epicurean cheerfulness, a typical feature of the age of Frederick the Great.

in colors, it casts its magic net over walls and ceilings, furniture, and carpets. Rocaille formations in C- and S-curves, dominating everything, here pass through typically Prussian metamorphoses. Here they grow into a palm twig, there into a stalk of vegetation with great sagging leaves, or are transformed into a delicate rose or a juicy grape; sometimes they frame airy ironwork, sometimes they shelter a great melon and a bursting pomegranate, or suddenly change into an elegant heron (see pages 246, 247, 251, and 256). Potsdam birds of paradise feel at home everywhere in this enchanted world. Lightly they flutter from the mirror to the back of the sofa, from the wall to the foot of the console. Here one, with its inquisitive pointed beak, pecks at the overturned "Prussian" flower-basket above the mantelpiece; there another, with the same indescribable grace, curves its long neck to catch the flower-garlands coming loose from the mirror. And the roguish, plump little putti among them know no mercy and no limits; they romp and tumble with hunting-nets on the ceiling, paint pictures and play their games on the cornices with attributes of the arts, clamber up clock cases, cupboard pediments, and the lids of the soup tureens, hide behind console tables and gather in clouds on the porcelain cups (see page 246 and above).

Ever present, too, are the flowers of Frederick's Edens. Delicate tendrils climb over the cornices and chair-legs, entwine around the mirror frames, panel mouldings, and console frames; combine into colorful carpets in the furniture intarsia, silk wall coverings, and wallpaper; and form into wreaths on stucco ceilings and snuffboxes (see page 248). If this craftwork, so closely interwoven and interdependent, is torn from its setting and placed in the glass case of a modern museum, it still remains a masterpiece of its genre – but it loses its soul, that indefinable *esprit* that perhaps represents the actual nature of Friderician Rococo. Seeking out the French, English, Dutch influences in Prussian craftwork is therefore, with all its importance, hardly very revealing when it comes to trying to understanding it. The independence of the objects that have been created from all possible influences transcends their foreign sources.

Three names are definitive in the furniture production of the early part of Frederick's reign. The general responsibility for the decoration of the royal palaces belonged to the interior decorator of the early period, the Berliner Johann August Nahl. After him comes his successor, Johann Christian Hoppenhaupt the Younger, who in 1763 was also entrusted with the interior decoration of the last

Opposite
Concert Hall of the Upper Princely Quarters, New Palace, Sanssouci (1768–1769)
Johann Christian Hoppenhaupt the Younger, from a design by Johann Michael Hoppenhaupt the Elder
Silvered wood sculpture and stucco decoration, floor marquetry by Johann Friedrich and Heinrich Wilhelm Spindler; Stiftung Preussische Schlösser und Gärten, Berlin-Brandenburg

Like a fugue for many voices, in the "total art work" of the age of Frederick the Great, the theme announced by Frederick of a "longed-for paradise" was played through in many variations and inversions. In later years, in the guest rooms of the New Palace, it admittedly has a more impersonal and heavy sound, and acquires more splendor, but loses its original freshness and transparency.

great palace, the New Palace, at Sanssouci; and his brother, Johann Michael Hoppenhaupt. In the uniformity of the Prussian style they created, however, it is possible only in rare cases to distinguish the personal contribution of each one, usually with the help of preserved design sketches and accounts. At the same time, with the high standard of craftsmanship of Berlin furniture making during this period, each individual who produced designs was able to introduce many a personal note. In this splendidly coordinated "orchestra" under the direction of Nahl and Hoppenhaupt the Younger, there were also outstanding soloists. One of them was the multitalented Swiss-born Johann Melchior Kambly. He made his name above all with the high quality specialities of furnishing art he supplied for decades to the Prussian court: commodes, desks, corner cupboards, longcase clocks, and music stands, all adorned with flaming tortoiseshell that stands in elegant contrast to the unusually sumptuous gilded and silvered sculptural bronze mounts. Ornamental additions include ruined buildings, gambolling putti, and inquisitive female heads, all of which suggest elegantly amusing Rococo stories.

Quite different "stories of furniture," only to be compared with the stories from *1001 Nights*, were brought to Berlin from Bayreuth in 1764 by the representatives of a famous family of cabinet makers, the brothers J. F. and H. W. Spindler. They won their supreme position in Prussian furniture making at first with their sumptuous floral marquetry. In their hands, the floral inlays that had come into fashion in the 1760s in Germany blossomed into the most beautiful examples of this genre. Already established as renowned masters in Bayreuth, the Spindlers not only adopted Prussian decorative motifs in their work, but also totally acclimatized themselves to this style. Their richly decorated furniture, such as wall panelling and floors, covered with lustrous flowery carpets and made of colored woods, resembled the sumptuous carpets of the Prussian palaces and the embroidery on the clothing in this age of gallantry.

Detail from the Intarsia Cabinet in the New Chambers, the park of Sanssouci (1772–1773)
Johann Friedrich Spindler and Heinrich Wilhelm Spindler
Marquetry of colored woods; Stiftung Preussische Schlösser und Gärten, Berlin-Brandenburg

Commode
Johann Melchior Kambly
Wood, lapis lazuli; Stiftung Preussische Schlösser und Gärten, Berlin-Brandenburg, Neues Palais

Exquisite combinations of dark, flaming tortoiseshell veneer, with its magical inner life, and powerfully modeled, silvered or gilded sculptural mounts are the trademarks of Kambly's magnificent furniture. Above all, however, as with this commode with lapis lazuli panels, the observer is captivated by the bronze work, executed with a jeweler's delicacy.

The elegant bronze fittings of Kambly completed the aristocratic brilliance of such works (see pages 249 and 253).

The splendor of the commodes, however, with their inlays of shimmering mother-of-pearl and ivory, embedded in dark tortoiseshell, outshone all else. Two of these chests, which could compete with the most costly of Frederick's snuffboxes, were created by H.W. Spindler the Younger in happy collaboration with M. Kambly for the New Palace at Sanssouci, works of breathtaking virtuosity that must be numbered among the miracles of the art of furniture (see below).

While the fabulous "furniture snuffboxes" of H. W. Spindler the Younger and Kambly were a costly exception even among Frederick's furniture, the real snuffboxes of gold and precious stones in his possession were to number some 300 by the time of his death. His passion for these small boxes can perhaps be compared only with Catherine the Great's obsession for cameos, or with his own passion for porcelain. These fascinating little treasures were always within his reach, accompanied him on journeys, and one, in his breast pocket, actually saved him from a bullet on the battlefield. Snuffboxes, above all those *à portrait*, bearing enamel portraits of the giver, were part of a long tradition in which presents of very high distinction were exchanged, equal to decorations such as medals or medallions. The production of snuffboxes was not a new departure for Prussia: Frederick's mother, Queen Sophia Dorothea, owned 372 of them, many of which originated in Berlin. This probably explains the high standard of these exquisite boxes, even in the early period of Frederick's reign, a standard that forced even visitors from Paris to declare that Berlin jewelers were equal to their Parisian counterparts, indeed even surpassed them. The Berlin makers were, nevertheless, schooled in the French style, at least at first, since in Berlin this was almost exclusively dominated by Huguenots coming from France. Among the multiplicity of jewelers who, under Frederick's fostering care, brought the art of making these boxes to its highest flowering in Berlin, he particularly favored Daniel Baudesson, the Jordan brothers, and Jean François Reclam II. Apart from goldsmiths, engravers and chasers, there were also many miniature and enamel painters (Daniel François Chodowiecki

Commode from the study of Frederick II, New Palace, Sanssouci
Heinrich Wilhelm Spindler the Younger and Johann Melchior Kambly
Wood, tortoiseshell, mother-of-pearl, ivory and silvered bronze; Stiftung Preussische Schlösser und Gärten, Berlin-Brandenburg, Neues Palais

Like a story from *1001 Nights*, this truly royal commode captivates the imagination. Here both masters have surpassed themselves. The breathtaking virtuosity of their handling of the precious materials makes them marvels of the art of furniture making. Only two examples of this kind are known.

Longcase clock
Johann Friedrich and Heinrich Wilhelm Spindler and Johann Melchior Kambly
Wood, gilt bronze; Stiftung Preussische Schlösser und Gärten, Berlin-Brandenburg, Neues Palais

This magnificently shaped and decorated longcase clock may be justifiably regarded as a highpoint in the Prussian arts of furniture, sculpture, and jewelry. The sophisticated Berlin clock mechanisms of this period, already highly regarded by contemporaries, acquire a truly majestic aura from the colorful marquetry of Johann Friedrich and Heinrich Wilhelm Spindler, and the enchantingly beautiful gilded bronze ornamentation by Kambly.

is the most important name among these), who conjured up a miniature dreamlike world of great charm. The warm glow of gold in conjunction with the restless sparkle of diamonds, the mysterious shimmer of mother-of-pearl, and the shining lustre of enamel, the play of colors of vitreous paste, and the endless diversity of the semiprecious stones from the Silesian mountains, with the chrysoprase, Frederick's favorite stone, at their head – all these live in lively interplay and endless change, and dissolve into an enchanting harmony (see page 254).

The degree of concern shown by Frederick for his silver could not compete with that for his snuffboxes and porcelain, but one can hardly say that he neglected it. He undoubtedly preferred his "white gold" (his porcelain) at the table, but he was able to enjoy this in the grand style only 23 years after his accession, as owner of his own porcelain factory. In any case, according to tradition, a prince's table was unthinkable without the gleam of silver. Thus one of his first decisions when he became ruler, soon after the decisive victory in the First Silesian War (1741), was to commission from Christian Lieberkühn the Younger, his father's goldsmith and a man of outstanding talent, a full-scale service of massive gold. "Because," according to Frederick, "they had been of no use," he had the old gold treasures of the Great Elector and Frederick I melted down – something that had been done many times before at princely courts, and not only in times of need, thus

Corner cupboard (1768)
Heinrich Wilhelm Spindler and Johann Melchior Kambly
Stiftung Preussische Schlösser und Gärten, Berlin-Brandenburg, Neues Palais

In their close and congenial collaboration, Spindler combined the luxuriance of his floral marquetry, full of contrast and color, with the exquisite splendor of Kambly's fire-gilded bronze decoration. Such works by these two gifted furniture-makers, distinguished by their accomplished elegance, contributed greatly to the fame of Prussian Rococo.

depriving posterity of much of the aesthetic riches of this branch of craftsmanship. As early as December 2, 1743, the new gold service of Frederick the Great was already proudly displayed on the royal dinner table.

To this, in every sense massive tribute to princely splendor, which by no means every court could afford in such abundance, there were added several silver services in the years that followed. Of these gleaming treasures, only a fraction has survived until today. The usual fate of so many generations of craftwork in precious metals also befell Frederick's silver tableware: in 1809 it was for the most part melted down as a contribution to Napoleon coffers.

So today we lack the basis for a comprehensive assessment of these pieces. Although Frederick himself, as was to be expected, checked and approved the designs and models for his silver, and Knobelsdorff in the 1740s supervised the entire work, the preserved pieces are at first glance not easily identifiable as Prussian, or as dating from Frederick's reign.

May the reason perhaps be that for Frederick silver tableware, though an important status symbol and a capital investment, was never viewed as one of his "favorite children"? Admittedly, this does not apply to his feeling for silver as a material. The unusually important place it occupies in his room decorations is positively striking – from silvered

Decorative snuffbox of Frederick the Great (c. 1765)
Chrysoprase, gold, diamonds, 5 x 9.7 x 7.6 cm; Stiftung Preussische Schlösser und Gärten, Berlin-Brandenburg, property of the House of Hohenzollern (formerly Hohenzollernmuseum, Monbijou Palace)

In the wide repertoire of the decorative snuffboxes of Frederick the Great, those made of chrysoprase were his particular favorites. Because of the magical attraction of his favorite stone, with the mysterious inner life of its changing green tones, it shines out with new enchantment in every possible setting of gold and diamonds. Made with colored gold, diamonds, and chrysoprase of a misty green, these exquisite objects convey a special charm.

wall boiserie panelling, stucco ceilings, furniture carving, wall lamps and chandeliers, to furniture mounts and the silvered bronzes of Kambly (see pages 251 and 252).

Not to be ignored in Frederick's décor is the chandelier, which, with its glow of candles, scintillating in the facets of a thousand festoons of glass, multiplied many times the magic of the dream world of Frederick's era. Over the decades, the king repeatedly acquired chandeliers of rock crystal, together with longcase and console clocks, in Paris.

As early as the 1740s, important domestic branches of these crafts were beginning to develop in imitation of these models. Most of the wall lighting and chandeliers for Frederick's palaces were then supplied by Potsdam and Berlin bronze masters and glass cutters. They are a further credit to craftsmanship under Frederick the Great and are among the most beautiful objects to have been created in this field in Germany.

But the king's particular pride, with justification, was in his porcelain. Out of a desire, common in the 18th century at the European courts, to be at the forefront of the production of fine porcelain, Frederick developed an exceptionally intense passion that went far beyond mercantilism. In the age of "white gold," porcelain was for all rulers a question of luxury and the prestige of the state. But for Frederick the Great alone, it became an affair of the heart.

The beginnings of Berlin porcelain were not easy, despite Frederick's energetic support. The first factory, founded in 1751 by the wool merchant W. C. Wegely, lasted no more than six years. Meanwhile, the opportunity during the Seven Years' War to become thoroughly familiar at first hand with the famous Meissen factory reawakened Frederick's appetite for porcelain of his own. In 1761, the daring entrepreneur J. F. E. Gotzkowski declared himself ready to assuage that appetite. Although his factory, too, was to be short-lived, in his case lasting less than three years, it laid the foundations for the later flourishing of the art of porcelain on Prussian soil.

The most important precondition for this was the outstanding artistic talent which Gotzkowski was able to acquire from Meissen. These were the most gifted colleagues of the chief craftsman of the Meissen porcelain factory, J. J. Kändler, namely the modeller F. E. Meyer, the figure and landscape painter K. W. Böhme, the painter of landscapes and views J. B. Borrmann, and the mosaic painter C. J. C. Klipfel.

Hardly, however, had this experienced team, under the direction of another Saxon, J. G. Grieninger, got the production at the factory on its feet, when Gotzkowski too became a victim of the industrial crisis of 1763. Frederick himself now bought the whole factory, with its fittings and equipment, a staff of 146 and its entire stock of porcelain.

The generous sum of 225,000 thalers, which he paid out of his private purse, was probably money well spent in his opinion. Princely ambition and the industrial considerations, which also played a part, appear to have been his strongest motives. There was certainly more to it, however. This was not just a refined aesthete sheer delight in the exotic material. Having his own factory offered the creative urge of the Prussian king a new field of

Silver tableware
Silver, property of the House of Hohenzollern; Stiftung Preussische Schlösser und Gärten, Berlin-Brandenburg, Schloss Charlottenburg

These pieces are among the few preserved from the extensive silver tableware owned by Frederick the Great. The distinctive style of Rococo under Frederick is hardly to be recognized in its restrained elegance, unless the vines with their finely worked leaves and shoots, which form the handles, forming almost the only sculptural decoration of the unpretentious forms, are to be interpreted as a reference to the vineyard of Sanssouci. Clearly, the first delivery of this service on May 2, 1747, adorned the first round table of Sanssouci at the ceremonial opening of the palace.

"First Potsdam" table service (1765–1766)
Porcelain, Berlin, Staatliche Museen zu Berlin – Preussischer Kulturbesitz, Kunstgewerbemuseum

One of the most delightful creations of European porcelain art, the "First Potsdam" table service was the first great commission of Frederick the Great for the New Palace of Sanssouci. With its "Relief Decoration" model and delicate, almost sentimental painting, of all the royal services it was, in form as well as in spirit, the one most intimately bound up with the room decoration of Frederick's age.

development, the opportunity to express his artistic concepts in the language of porcelain. Frederick, according to his own statement, became not only "my own factory's best customer," but additionally an enthusiastic co-creator of his porcelain, whether it was a matter of technical questions, work processes, or the whole scope of a project, from the choice of themes to the nuances of color.

Only the fire and drive of his own artistic vision will explain how in an unbelievably short time the KPM (Royal Porcelain Factory) freed itself from the overwhelming influence of the Saxon model, which until then had outshone all else and attained convincing supremacy – and this with a staff almost exclusively originating from Meissen and burdened by tradition. As early as April 1764 the new, extremely critical factory owner at the KPM was convinced that the "good things" that were made there were "more beautiful than had ever been imagined at Meissen." This conviction was confirmed by even biased observers. "They may indeed have learned much from us," commented the widowed Electress of Saxony on her visit to the KPM in 1769, "but it seems to me as though the pupil is trying to surpass her governess."

As early as in the first service, the First Potsdam Service (see above), the individual poetry of the palaces of Frederick the Great revives (see page 246). In the 1760s, the creations of the interior decorators directly also inspired porcelain chandeliers and pillar mirrors (see page 256). But such costly objects remained the exceptions. Fashionable accessories of all kinds and even sculpture, which found gifted creators in Friedrich Elias and Wilhelm Christian Meyer, were of marginal importance in Frederick's day.

The king, on the other hand, loved to create tableware along with his skillful porcelain masters. He had 21 dinner and dessert services that had been alternating since the 1760s on his tables of the palaces for which they had been specially designated. Parallels between porcelain design and room decoration are thus compelling.

But even more essential seems to be the key in which the theme of Rococo under Frederick was interpreted in the language of porcelain. Every piece

Breakfast service with Watteau painting (c. 1767)
Porcelain; Berlin, Staatliche Museen zu Berlin – Preussischer Kulturbesitz, Kunstgewerbemuseum

All the charm and grace of the porcelain of Frederick the Great radiates from this KPM breakfast service with virtuoso iron-red painting by Watteau and delicate gold-decorated edges. General de la Motte-Fouqué, Frederick's old friend, to whom the service was presented in 1767, rightly described it as a "perfect creation, whose beauty and taste surpass all that can be seen in this genre."

was created in its own fashion, imaginative, fresh, and highly accomplished, exhibiting supreme confidence in the mastery of sculptural form and brilliance of the painting, a fine sense of the potential and the limits of the material, and an understanding of the relation of parts and the whole – all skills characteristic of the Berlin masters and evident over and over again in the magical harmony of the services of Frederick the Great. But there were also the usual Rococo themes: "gallant" fantasies by Watteau (see page 255, below), Boucher, and Teniers, "flying children" on clouds, mythological deities, and above all the fragrant flowers of Berlin, carelessly scattered, woven into floating, random garlands, or bound up into splendid formal arrangements – and all have their unmistakable Berlin character. The names of the models in their chronological order – "Relief Decoration," "New Decoration," "Classical Decoration," "English Smooth" – point to the stylistic changes and the sources of inspiration for Berlin porcelain between 1763 and 1786.

From the 1760s onwards, the decoration loses the spontaneous vitality and the capricious originality of the Rococo, the wavy lines become calmer, the whole system of ornamentation becomes tighter and more disciplined. The breath of approaching Neoclassicism is most clearly to be felt in the works carried out for clients and as gifts. For Frederick, porcelain works were an important instrument of his diplomacy, fragile but reliable ambassadors and transmitters of his politics and friendship (see right and page 255).

In such matters he had, even if hesitatingly, to make concessions to the new spirit of the times. But he kept his Rococo for himself to the end of his days. His attitude is usually described as conservative. Was it really the caprice and obstinacy of an old king? Is not the expression "loving constancy" perhaps more appropriate? Like Pygmalion, Frederick the Great fell in love with his own creation, and never tired of adorning it with new garments and jewelry.

What particularly suited his taste was repeated again and again: cedarwood for the furniture and wall panelling of his apartments, carved and arranged according to his wishes; the delicate green of chrysoprase in the color scheme of the room; the stone itself in ever more variations of his luxurious snuffboxes; silver decoration for everything that could be decorated; and, in the paradise gardens of Sanssouci, flowers blooming and filling the air with their unique Prussian perfume – flowers carved in wood, shaped in stucco, cast in bronze, displayed with diamonds on gold snuffboxes, or painted in brilliant porcelain colors.

Following his inner dictates, he occasionally tried new clothing for his Galatea: and her dress in its more severe cut and calmer décor acquires a hint of the new spirit of the times (see page 249). But even in her new adornments she does not lose her old charm and youthful freshness, and just as she was at the beginning, that is how the aging Frederick still loves to see her, even if the whole world already finds her old fashioned. For this was his pride, his consolation, his dream, and his love, of which so little in real life fell to his share.

Dessert service for Catherine the Great of Russia
Königliche Porzellanmanufaktur Berlin (1770–1772), St. Petersburg, Staatliche Ermitage

Among the gifts of porcelain made by Frederick the Great, this legendary service had no equal for significance. The allegory, executed according to Frederick's own concept, with its costly epergne, became in equal measure a hymn in porcelain to the Russian Empress, and to the mastery of the Berlin porcelain artists.

Opposite
Porcelain mirror in the study of Frederick the Great in the New Palace (1767)
Johann Christian Hoppenhaupt the Younger (design), Königliche Porzellanmanufaktur Berlin (execution)
Porcelain, white-glazed, mirror glass; Stiftung Preussische Schlösser und Gärten, Berlin-Brandenburg

The graceful movement and every lovingly formed flower of this mirror convey the enthusiasm of the porcelain masters for their conquest of the material and their respect for its precious whiteness.

Sedan chair of the Prussian Queen Sophia Louisa (1708–1713)
175 x 76 x 98 cm; Potsdam, Stiftung Preussische Schlösser und Gärten, Berlin-Brandenburg

The Prussian eagle and the Mecklenburg ox's head, the monogram "SL" on the gilt bronze handles, and the embroidered covering of the back wall refer to the fact that the sedan chair belonged to the third consort of Frederick I. The roof was folded back to allow the passenger to get in.

Carriage Building at the Prussian Court in the 18th Century

Splendidly accoutred state coaches were among the most distinctive images of the great capital cities. The importance they had in the magnificent courtly display of the early reign of the first Prussian king, Frederick I, can be clearly gauged by the many surviving accounts of ceremonial processions. State coaches were ordered to be made in France and Holland, and these, together with the rapidly circulated engravings of carriage designs by the French decorative masters Jean Bérain and Daniel Marot, formed the basis for local carriage building. The artist and architect Andreas Schlüter was also said to have given design and form to the Berlin state coaches. According to contemporary descriptions, royal coaches were mostly gilded, lined with carmine velvet, and adorned with gold and silver braid and heavy gold fringes. With their carved and painted heraldic decoration, they clearly expressed the rank and dignity of the owner. Even though on official occasions the ruler often went on horseback, in the traditional manner, driving in carriages had long been considered a means of transport befitting to the station of a member of nobility. The brother of Frederick I, Margrave Albrecht, was considered the most skilful carriage driver of his day; he was supposed to have brought into fashion a new carriage with a canopy supported by four poles. The coach of the electoral prince Frederick William is documented as a carriage of this kind, at whose corners we can imagine the diagonally set roof supports (see below). The trapezoid shape, as well as the hanging of the body of the coach from straps between the framework bridges over a pole that connected the two axes, are both characteristic of the state coach of the 18th century. Presumably this small coach was constructed by Dutch carriage builders resident in Berlin, if it was not actually brought from Holland.

As a light and convenient form of transport that also demonstrated the owner's status, sedan chairs were also to be seen in Berlin from the last third of the 17th century. The earliest preserved such *porte-chaise* of the Prussian royal house belonged to the third consort of Frederick I, Sophia Louisa of Mecklenburg-Schwerin (see left). The influence of graphic models by Bérain is clearly to be seen in the painting of grotesques and banding.

In 1713, the very first year of his regency, Frederick William I had a large area of the existing carriage park and the "considerable supply of costly horses and magnificent harnesses" put up for sale. Only when demanded by protocol, at weddings or the visits of foreign rulers, was there an ostentatious display at court. For these occasions, the king acquired from Holland in 1718 a golden *carrosse de parade* together with the harnesses for eight horses. A decisive, primarily technical innovation had resulted

Garden carriage of the Electoral Prince Frederick William (c. 1690)
103 x 77 x 250 cm; Potsdam, Stiftung Preussische Schlösser und Gärten, Berlin-Brandenburg

That this carriage was intended for the first-born son of the Elector Frederick III is shown by the carved and painted coats of arms and the eagles crowned with the electoral headdress on the open face-to-face body. The coach could be drawn by two ponies.

in the invention of the "berline" (so called because it was made in Berlin). According to written documentation, the berline, designed by the architect Philipp de Chièze, who was in the service of the Great Elector, and manufactured by Berlin cartwrights, created a great stir in Paris. By means of supporting the framework on broad leather straps between two poles, designers had finally achieved a higher degree of safety in driving and steering. Whereas this chassis construction was at first used in Prussia for travelling chaises, hunting and garden barouches, in Paris berlines were designed as early as the beginning of the 18th century as elegant city carriages. It is documented that in 1733, on a ceremonial procession in the Prussian capital, Frederick William I led the way in a berline. The ladies followed in phaetons, which were open carriages often covered by a canopy. Coaches and designs for them are not preserved from the Berlin of this period. The economy measures laid down by the Frederick I, the "Soldier King," had first affected the arts that served display and ostentation, and many artists and craftsmen had left the country. According to contemporary travellers, Berlin now seemed entirely "martial," and no splendid equipages with lackeys in costly livery were to be seen, such as were found at other courts.

This was to change, however, when Frederick II, the Great, ascended the throne in 1740. It was precisely the luxury trades that the new king encouraged, in order to keep funds in the country, and no object of luxury combined the products of so many trades as did carriage building. The newly appointed court architects and decorators Johann August Nahl, Georg Wenzeslaus von Hoppenhaupt, and Johann Michael Hoppenhaupt the Elder all created designs for berlines, state coaches, and phaetons that exhibited extravagant curvature and a great delight in structural details. Like "sculptural furniture," carriage bodies took on elaborate forms. Out of the frameworks sprouted fantastic shell formations, leaves, and blossoms. The accounts preserved from the first decade of the reign of Frederick II, for royal coaches almost without exception show Hoppenhaupt the Elder as the sculptor responsible for their design and execution. In December 1745, Frederick had Hoppenhaupt construct a "golden coup" state coach that cost 10,733.23 thalers (see top of page). A year later the Russian tsarina Elizabeth received a similar "gala coup" as a present, which is preserved to this day in the armor room of the Moscow Kremlin. The accounts show in addition that Frederick took a keen pleasure in silver for his carriages as well as for the interior decoration of his palaces.

When a new carriage was required, the order was taken by the saddler. He prepared the "specification" or estimate of what the coach would cost, had the body constructed by the cartwright and fitted with metal mounts by the blacksmith, and then commissioned all the other work that he could not carry out

Top
Design for a state coach-coup, after a drawing by Johann Michael Hoppenhaupt the Elder (1745)
Etching by Johann Wilhelm Meil (1755), 36.4 x 61.2 cm; Berlin, Staatliche Museen zu Berlin – Preussischer Kulturbesitz, Kupferstichkabinett

The design for this coup, with eagles under the corners of the roof and the royal crown on the rear chassis bridge was made by Hoppenhaupt the Elder for Frederick II, the Great. A similar very ornate carriage was sent as a gift to the court of the Tsar of Russia.

Above
Design for a phaeton with canopy after a design by Johann Michael Hoppenhaupt the Elder (1745)
Etching by Johann Wilhelm Meil (1755), 31.9 x 46.4 cm; Berlin, Staatliche Museen zu Berlin – Preussischer Kulturbesitz, Kupferstichkabinett

Playful ornamentation characterizes the little "pleasure carriages" of the Rococo, which their owners liked to use for informal outings. The canopy (originally a sign of high status) is no more than a parasol that is here held by a squatting Chinese figure.

Left

State Berline of Frederick II, the Great (c. 1780)

245 x 170 x 490 cm; Potsdam, Stiftung Preussische Schlösser und Gärten, Berlin-Brandenburg

Because of the need for comfort, the demand for an ornate carriage had changed in favor of technical perfection. Steps for getting in and out were now folded out from the high, spring-mounted body. The side steps were for pages to stand on for a ceremonial entry.

Above

The Coaches in the Carriage Hall of the Hohenzollern Museum at Monbijou Palace

Historical photograph (1927)

Of the 11 carriages shown here, only five survived World War II, though with severe damage. They include the berline-coup, of the Saxon envoy Freiherr von Ende (1750–1765), after a design by Hoppenhaupt the Elder (left), and the state coach of Frederick William II (right background), built in Strasbourg by August Christian Ginzrot (1789).

Garden Carriage with Canopy (c. 1750–1765)
220 x 150 x 320 cm; Potsdam, Stiftung Preussische Schlösser und Gärten, Berlin-Brandenburg

A comparison with the designs of Hoppenhaupt the Elder shows the relationship between this carriage, from the coach-houses of Sanssouci, and the splendid phaetons of the Prussian court. The broad wheels, covered with leather, are particularly unusual; they were probably to protect the lawns and paths.

himself. Velvet and silk fabrics were delivered by the Berlin factories of David Hirsch, and David Girard & Pierre Michelet. This business was particularly lucrative for the haberdasher Christian Friedrich Blume, who as a court supplier delivered all sorts of braid, tassels, and trimmings for the coaches. The embroidered work was made by the embroiderers Elli Pally and Matthias Heinitschek. If the carriage body was to be painted, Friedrich Wilhelm Höder, who was active as a decorative painter in the palaces of Berlin and Potsdam, was called in. By the mid-18th century the art of carriage building in Berlin had achieved artistic independence and a widely admired quality. One surviving example, made in 1765 to a design by Hoppenhaupt the elder, is the berline coup, of the Saxon envoy Freiherr von Ende (see opposite, above). The body of the carriage shows the curvature typical of the late Rococo period. Painted on a gold ground, Aurora and Aphrodite appear as symbols of light and fertility, surrounded by a wreath of flowers and shells. Similar motifs are found in the interior decoration of Frederick's time. Related to the phaeton in form, construction and furnishings is a garden carriage with a canopy (see above and page 259). When the encyclopedist Georg Krünitz dealt with the subject of carriage building in 1792, he remarked that tastes had changed in Germany to an incredible degree during the last 20 years. "Our state and city carriages were enormously heavy, large, gilded, ornate and strangely shaped machines ... In the end, England improved our taste in this respect as well." He describes as typically English the flat roof of the carriage body, and its lack of curves on the sides. For a state carriage it was enough in the way of display to have a coat of arms painted on top of the gilding, slender decorative moldings and a crowning gallery. Frederick the Great had remained committed to the Rococo style all his life, and for a long time had also given preference to it in carriage building. The state berline made a few years before his death (see opposite, bottom left) no longer shows any return to outdated style, but rather an adaptation to the new taste. It seemed that the time when foreign rulers would place orders for coaches in Berlin was over. In 1789, Frederick William I ordered his state carriage from the renowned Strasbourg carriage maker August Christian Ginzrot (see opposite, above right). This berline remained the official ceremonial coach of the Prussian royal house well into the 20th century.

Claudia Meckel

Textile Furnishings in the Palaces of Potsdam and Berlin

Frederick William of Brandenburg, the Great Elector, can be regarded as the founder and first patron of the textile arts in the March of Brandenburg. In the course of the rehabilitation of his country, which had been so heavily devastated in the Thirty Years' War, his interests included the textile industry, which even then was of importance to the economy. From the outset, the energetic young elector had made efforts to acquire foreign specialists from progressive countries such as Holland and Saxony in order to set up textile factories in his underdeveloped state. It was only shortly before his death in 1688 that he experienced the greatest success of his settlement policy: the immigration to Brandenburg of almost 20,000 French refugees on religious grounds – the Huguenots. In the welcoming "Edict of Potsdam" of 1685, manufacturers of cloth, fabrics, and hats were expressly invited to settle in the state. Indeed, more than half of the immigrating tradesmen came from the textile and clothing industries, including more than 25 trades which had previously been unknown there. The refugees brought with them their knowledge of new products, tools and production processes as well as actual patterns and dyes. This widened the range and improved the quality of textiles. There were also new artistic achievements: in 1686, as a prestige enterprise of the elector's, Pierre Mercier's tapestry factory was founded in Berlin, as well as the workshop of the Barrabands, father and son. For one hundred years the production of the world-famous Berlin picture carpets and rugs was in the hands of the Huguenots. Their works adorned the elector's palaces in Berlin and Potsdam, where a few are still preserved to this day. The first silk factories were also founded by Huguenots. It was typical of the politics of the Great Elector that in this issue he considered both the industry's economic impact on the country as a whole and the quality of the textile products; in other words, he was just as concerned about the production of simple mass products for the needs of the population as he was with the satisfaction of his own artistic requirements.

As supporters of mercantile industrial politics, all the rulers of Brandenburg-Prussia in the 17th and 18th centuries strove to become independent of luxurious imports from France and Italy, and to have the costly picture carpets and silk fabrics, for extravagant use in their palaces after the Thirty Years' War, produced in their own country.

Frederick William's son and successor, Frederick III (I), was concerned above all for the satisfaction of his desire for an appropriately regal lifestyle. After

Potsdam, New Palace, anteroom of the Prince of Prussia

This room is decorated with celadon-colored silk damask with a symmetrical lacy band pattern after a French design. The damask was used in all the rooms of the Prince's apartment and served to unify and differentiate his private living quarters.

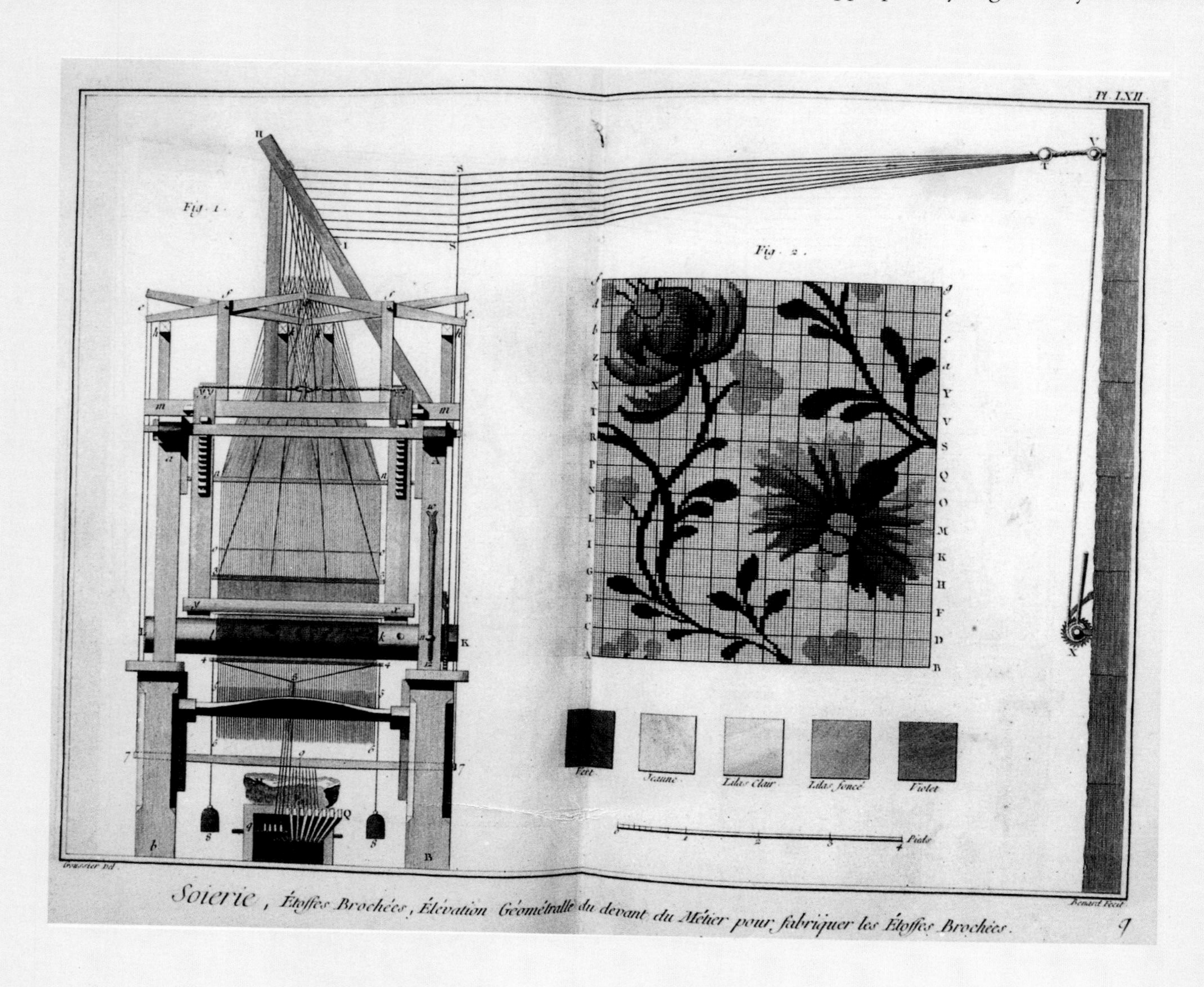

Right
Illustration of a loom for the production of a brocaded silk fabric, with a point-paper plan and color information
From Encyclopédie des Sciences, des Arts et des Métiers *by Diderot and D'Alembert, Paris 1751*

This loom, which needed two people to operate it, was used to produce silk fabric with complicated patterns.

Opposite
Potsdam, park of Sanssouci, Chinese House, wall covering in northeast cabinet

This silk wall covering, with its distinctive painted flower pattern, is a reconstruction from 1991–1993 of a covering originally produced in 1760 which had survived only in fragments.

Right
Potsdam, New Palace, part of the wall covering in the Hunting Room

The letters FBF A BERLIN woven into this silver brocade probably stand for "Frères Baudouin Fils" ("Sons of the Baudouin Brothers"). Signed fabrics were very rare in the 18th century.

Opposite
Potsdam, New Palace, lady's bedroom in the lower princely quarters

The multicolored brocaded silk fabric and the carpet come from a Berlin factory. The matching patterns of the wall hanging, with flowers in their natural size, and the furnishings lead one to suppose that the designs all originate from the same hand.

Potsdam, New Palace, Hunting Room in the upper princely quarters

The Hunting Room, shown here, is decorated with a signed Berlin silver brocade and a carpet from the tapestry factory in Berlin.

all, these precious decorative textiles were admirably suited for the demonstration of the wealth and importance of a princely court. He also brought to completion his father's plans by setting up, among others, a Gobelins Gallery in the Berlin Palace, according to the French model, for a series of eight large picture carpets ordered from Mercier between 1693 and 1699, showing "the actions of the Elector Frederick Wilhelm of most blessed memory." With the naturalistic depictions of his success in the war against Sweden, in which the Great Elector is always placed at the center, the memory of this patron of the textile arts was fittingly preserved.

King Frederick William I, his grandson, placed little value on textiles in home furnishings, but was not oblivious to the importance of the textile industry of his country. For this reason, he demanded above all the production and processing of indigenous raw materials, such as wool, and attempted to introduce silkworm breeding (sericulture) as a national industry. His successor, Frederick II, the Great, continued to encourage the textile industry in a more systematic and comprehensive way, although with regimentation down to the last detail. In this way, under him this craft attained its greatest prosperity in Brandenburg-Prussia and wide international admiration.

Frederick encouraged the textile arts on the basis of solid knowledge. Soon after his accession he had had precise studies prepared, for example of the silk factories. According to these, in 1744 in Potsdam there were 32 masters with a total of 144 looms; and in 1748 in Berlin there were 13 factories with 124 looms, on which 564 people worked, including 50 orphanage children. Twenty years later, in 1769, there were in Berlin and Potsdam together 150 silk factories with more than 1,335 looms, on which more than 1,457 people were working. The figure rose steadily and reached its highest point in 1796 as a result of the lack of French competition after the Revolution, when 2,886 looms for pure silk wares were being operated. This induced the successor to Frederick the Great, Frederick William II, to terminate state subsidies, whereupon the number of looms promptly decreased, and by 1800 there were only 12 factories for pure silk goods left in Berlin. From luxury industries such as silk production, Frederick hoped not only for a favorable balance of trade, but also an increase in state reserves. In a Cabinet order of 1746, he remarked that the silk factories, their setting up and their increase in numbers, was the main object of his attention. On the other hand, it was his aim, through a national product, to satisfy his own desire for an appearance of princeliness, and also the needs of the nobility and upper middle classes. After all, the money that went out of the country to be spent on French, Dutch, Saxon, or Swiss silk wares was the largest single item among all his imports. But for Frederick the provision for his population for the time being took priority over major artistic and technical achievements, such as woven furnishing goods

Potsdam, Sanssouci Palace, alcove niche of the Voltaire Room

The fourth guest room, the so-called Voltaire Room, is decorated with jonquil-colored atlas. The alcove decoration is richly trimmed with so-called "ballet" fringes made of silk.

tended to be. Thus he ordered the Berlin and Potsdam silk production between 1746 and 1748 to restrict itself to damask, atlas, and *gros de Tours*, until favorable developments around 1748–1750 made it possible also to create "rich stuffs" such as brocade or brocaded silk weavings.

The king subordinated his personal artistic wishes to his economic policy in using almost exclusively home-produced silk weavings in his apartments. He had otherwise grown increasingly conservative in artistic matters, but remained strikingly modern in his attitude to textiles. He always used the latest fabrics and patterns supplied to him by the silk industry, even if these were sometimes a few decades behind French fashions (see page 262). Thus the interiors of the Prussian palaces impressively mirrored both the artistic and the technical stage of development that had been reached by the Prussian silk factories. At the same time, it turned out that each palace had its own special character. At Sanssouci Palace, atlas, glazed fabrics, and damask were primarily used; at the New Palace at Sanssouci, the finest Rococo brocades in the king's apartments and those of his most important guests, and also brocaded silk fabrics and damask, and, finally, in the most lowly rooms of the Palais (as well as in the Communs and in the Chinese House), the "Pekings" (silk wallpaper painted on a light-colored ground), which were very popular at the time.

An example of Frederick's "modernity" is supplied by his order for the New Chambers: on the recommendation of the Berlin manufacturer, instead of the intended damasks, the king now bought the very fashionable watered silk taffetas (in the form of preprinted patterned lengths of inexpensive woven silk fabric). Frederick had sent Berlin entrepreneurs to England to find out about the production process for these taffetas. His supportive measures included above all the acquisition of skilled workers (through offering credit, accommodation, and so on) from the more progressive foreign countries; the setting up of a savings bank and a commissioning office for the silk factories; the establishing of a warehouse for raw silk (1750); and also the issuing of a set of regulations for silk manufacture and a guild for manual workers (1766). In sericulture, courses in silkworm breeding and a training scheme at Frederick's own expense were created, particularly for the pupils of the Potsdam military orphanage. They provided an inexhaustible and inexpensive reservoir of workers for the Prussian textile industry, just as did the inmates of the prisons, workhouses and poorhouses, and the Potsdam garrison.

But the greatest support of all was given to the silk factories by the great royal commissions, mostly in connection with the furnishing of the palace rooms, which ensured the stability and improvement of the textile factories. This can be seen even during the crisis that followed the Seven Years' War: many industries were suffering badly, but in the renowned Baudouin factory in Berlin during the interior decoration of the New Palace (1766–1769) the processing of gold and silver fabrics increased threefold by comparison with earlier years, and fourfold by comparison with the years that followed.

Smaller entrepreneurs were also given consideration, such as Puis, who supplied the red-gold brocade, hardly suitable as a furnishing fabric, for Frederick's dining room in the New Palace. The use of such high quality brocades was attentively observed by contemporaries. In the descriptions of the palaces of that period, these textiles are mentioned along with details of their Berlin provenance and even the names of the factories. It was particularly stressed that Frederick chose them

Right
Potsdam, New Palace, silver brocade in the reading cabinet of Frederick II, the Great

The reading cabinet of Frederick II is decorated with crimson silver brocade. The pattern for this *drap d'argent* was among the asymmetrical lace edgings that were typical of the 1760s and the Rococo style under Frederick.

Potsdam, New Palace, study in the apartment of Frederick II, the Great

Pink silver brocade (*drap d'argent*), brocaded with chenille, adorns Frederick's study at Potsdam. A factory for the production of chenille yarn was founded in Berlin as late as 1764. The pattern is formed asymmetrically from lace edgings and imitation fur.

himself and paid for them from his own private purse. For almost 50 years Frederick also determined the color palette for the silks, preferring above all light Rococo shades, dyed in the skein with natural colors.

That the factory owners were aware of the value of their own products is shown by the woven signature FBF A BERLIN on the edges of two lengths of silver brocade for the Hunting Room in the New Palace, something very unusual at that time. Presumably the initials stand for "Frères Baudouin Fils," a particularly capable factory (see page 265). The pattern of this brocade seems to be an independent Prussian design. Just as "Prussian" – as can be presumed from their origin and Rococo pattern – were the rugs, favored by Frederick, from the Berlin tapestry factory Vignes Erben, which he supported. They take their place in the "complete work of art" created by interior decoration. The silk fabrics, too, were restrained enough to be incorporated into the ensemble character of a room. With their sheen and the delicate play of reflected light called up by their

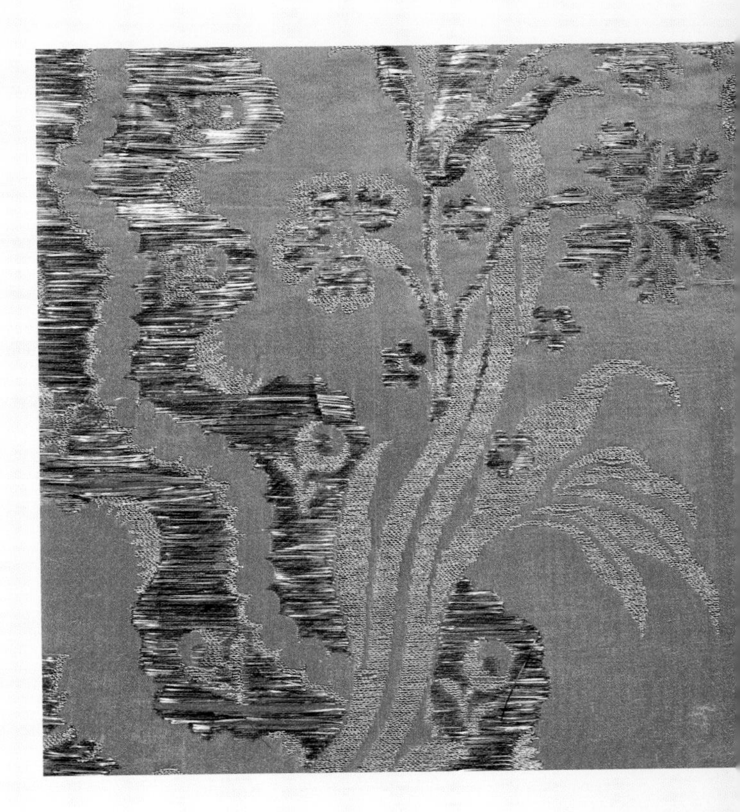

patterns, they were suitable as was no other textile for achieving that elegant effect that was aimed for in the palace rooms of the 18th century. Today, the palaces of Potsdam and Berlin still display a large number of original examples of their textile furnishings. They represent outstanding tributes to the Prussian silk industry, particularly that of Berlin and Potsdam manufacturers, and give us a vivid picture of the princely style of interior furnishing of their time.

Karola Paepke

The Age of Revolutions

1786–1871

1786–1797 Reign of King Frederick William II (1744–1797).

1787 Frederick William II commissions Carl Philipp von Gontard and Carl Gotthard Langhans to build the Marble Palace on the banks of the Heiliger See near Potsdam (completed in 1791). In Berlin, Luigi Boccherini becomes court composer to Frederick William II.

1788 The Minister of Justice, Johann Christoph Wöllner, later to be head of the Rosicrucians in Berlin, and the Minister of State, Johann Rudolf von Bischoffswerder, issue their anti-Enlightenment *Edikt, die Religionsverfassung in den preussischen Staaten betreffend* (Edict Concerning the Religious Constitution of the Prussian States).
Immanuel Kant publishes *Kritik der praktischen Vernunft* (Critique of Practical Reason).

1791 Daniel Itzig becomes the first Jew to hold civil rights as a citizen of Berlin. Carl Gotthard Langhans completes the Brandenburg Gate in Berlin.

1792 Beginning of the Coalition Wars against Revolutionary France (to 1797), with France fighting Austria and Prussia.

1793 The Second Partition of Poland between Prussia and Russia; Prussia receives Posen.

1794 The Allgemeines Landrecht (General Code of Law) of Prussia, drawn up by the Minister of Justice, Johann Heinrich Count von Carmer and his colleague Carl Gottlieb Svarez, comes into force. It imposes a single judicial code on the whole of Prussia.

1795 The Third Partition of Poland, which is between Prussia, Austria, and Russia: Prussia receives New Silesia and Warsaw.

King Frederick William II, by Anton Graff (c. 1788)

1797–1840 Reign of King Frederick William III (1770–1840).

1799 Prussia remains neutral in the Second Coalition War against France (to 1802).

Wilhelmine Encke, by Anna Dorothea Therbusch, 1776. Encke was later Countess Lichtenau, mistress and artistic adviser of Frederick William II

Alexander von Humboldt sets out on a journey of exploration to Central and South America.

1800 The population of Berlin rises to 172,000. By comparison with 1680, when Berlin had about 16,500 inhabitants, the number has increased by over tenfold. The city has the fastest growth rate of any European metropolis. There are 112 printing works in Prussia. Karl Friedrich Schinkel erects his first building, the Temple of Pomona, on the Pfingstberg in Potsdam.

1803 As compensation for the loss of territory in the west, Prussia receives the bishoprics of Hildesheim and Paderborn, together with parts of the bishoprics of Münster and Mainz, and some smaller imperial estates.

1804 Founding of the Royal Ironworks in Berlin.

1806 Prussia declares war on France and subsequently suffers a crushing defeat at the battle of Jena and Auerstedt. French troops occupy Berlin. Napoleon has Schadow's quadriga removed from the Brandenburg Gate and taken to Paris.

1807 The Peace of Tilsit: Prussia loses the territory between the Elbe and the Rhine, Lower Lusatia, and the Altmark. The Grand Duchy of Warsaw is created out of the larger part of the Polish territories. Danzig acquires the status of a free city for the first time. Prussia has to pay 400 million talers in war contributions to France. Reform of the army begins. Under Baron von und zum Stein, fundamental reforms are introduced into Prussia (including the rescinding of hereditary serfdom for the peasants and the privileges of the nobility).
Georg Wilhelm Friedrich Hegel publishes his *Phänomenologie des Geistes* (The Phenomenology of Mind) and Johann Gottlieb Fichte his *Reden an die deutsche Nation* (Speeches to the German Nation).

1808 The Municipal Statutes introduce a new form of communal self-administration. Citizens owning property and pursuing a trade acquire the right to elect an assembly of municipal deputies, who in turn elect the city council as their executive organ. In imitation of the French model bureaucracy, a single ministry consists of five specialist ministerial departments.

1809 Wilhelm von Humboldt becomes the Minister of Culture.

1810 The introduction of freedom to trade finally leads to the abolition of the guilds.
The University of Berlin is founded.

1812 The edict on the "civil constitution of the Jews" makes about 30,000 "protected Jews" citizens with equal legal and economic rights.

1813–1815 The Wars of Liberation against Napoleon.

1814 Army reforms conclude with the Military Service Act, establishing the principle of military service for all.
Rahel Levin marries the diplomat and writer Karl August Varnhagen von Ense and founds her famous salon.

Hussar on Crutches, pen and ink drawing by Friedrich August Calau (c. 1800)

King Frederick William III and Queen Louise at Charlottenburg Palace, by Friedrich Georg Weitsch, 1799

1814–1815 After the defeat of Napoleon, and in the reorganization of the European territorial and political order negotiated at the Congress of Vienna, Prussia receives West Prussia, Posen, North Saxony, the Rhineland, and Westphalia. Russia, Prussia, and Austria form the "Holy Alliance" against liberal and revolutionary movements.
Frederick William III rejects the introduction of a Prussian constitution.

1816 The Regulation Edict on the compensation of lords of the manor favors large landowners.
E. T. A. Hoffmann publishes his novel *Die Elixiere des Teufels* (The Devil's Elixirs). He also composes a Romantic opera.
The *Prinzessin Charlotte von Preussen* is the first steamer on the Spree.

1818 The Tariff Act abolishes all internal tolls and excise; they are replaced by a border tariff system.
Georg Wilhelm Friedrich Hegel succeeds Johann Gottlieb Fichte at the University of Berlin.

1819 On the basis of decrees promulgated in Karlsbad, a movement known as the "prosecution of demagogues" begins in Prussia.

1821 Carl Maria von Weber's opera *Der Freischütz* has its première at Schinkel's new theatre in Berlin.

1823 Prussia is divided into eight provinces.

1825 Pension rights for civil servants are introduced. The first horse omnibuses come into service in Berlin.

1827 Alexander von Humboldt delivers his lectures on the cosmos in Berlin.
At the instigation of Frederick William III, a Russian settlement, which is named Alexandrovka, is constructed in Potsdam for use by former Russian soldiers.

The steamer Prinzessin Charlotte von Preussen *on the Spree, near Bellevue Palace, colored etching by Friedrich August Calau, after 1815*

1828 At the urging of Karl Friedrich Schinkel, systematic preservation of the ruins of the monastery of Chorin begins.

1829 The Old Museum (Altes Museum), built to plans by Schinkel, is opened in Berlin.

1831 Schinkel starts work on the Architectural Academy (Bauakademie) in Berlin (completed in 1836).

Hegel Lecturing, lithograph by Franz Kugler, 1828

1833 The Deutscher Zollverein (German Customs Union) is founded under the leadership of Prussia.

1834 Hermann, Prince von Pückler-Muskau publishes his *Andeutungen über die Landschaftsgärtnerei* (Hints on Landscape Gardening).

1835 Karl Blechen completes his painting *The Ironrolling Mill at Eberswalde*.

1837 The building of the first railroad in Prussia, the line between Berlin and Potsdam.
In Berlin, August Borsig starts up an iron foundry and engineering works. Prussia has 423 steam engines, amounting in all to 7,523 horse power.

1839 In the Havel area of Brandenburg the army is called on for the first time in the history of the province to put down a strike by workers, who are in dispute with a silk goods factory.
To improve fitness for military service, children under nine are banned from employment in factories. Death sentences are passed on journeyman artisans in Berlin who have joined illicit journeymen's unions.

Alexander von Humboldt in his Library, lithograph after a watercolor by Eduard Hildebrandt, 1856

1840–1861 Reign of King Frederick William IV (1795–1861).

1842 Frederick William IV lays the foundation stone for the resumption of building work which will take place on Cologne's medieval cathedral.
Karl Marx works as editor on the newspaper the *Rheinischen Zeitung* in Cologne, before being forced to emigrate to Paris in 1843.

1843 Bettina von Arnim publishes *Dieses Buch gehört dem König* (This Book is for the King).

1844 A revolt of Silesian weavers' is suppressed.

1845 Repeated calls for political reform are heard at public and citizens' meetings.
Alexander von Humboldt publishes his five-volume work *Kosmos. Entwurf einer physischen Weltbeschreibung* (Cosmos: Outline of a Description of the Physical World).

King Frederick William IV, painting by Franz Krüger, 1846

1848 The March Revolution: unrest in France spreads to Germany. There are demands for national unity, freedom of assembly and freedom of the press, assize courts, and a people's militia. In March, after street fighting in Berlin, Frederick William IV appoints the liberal Camphausen ministry (which lasts only until June) and promises a national assembly. At the end of the year, conservative forces regain the upper hand. The king dissolves the remnants of the Prussian National Assembly and "imposes" a constitution for the Prussian monarchy.

1849 The German National Assembly, meeting in the Paulskirche in Frankfurt, draws up a constitution and elects the king of Prussia Emperor. Frederick William IV refuses the title. Prince William of Prussia puts down the revolt in Baden with great violence.

1850 The Treaty of Olmütz restores the German Confederation under Austrian leadership. The population of Berlin is 412,132.

Queen Elisabeth, painting by Joseph Stieler, 1843

1851 Otto von Bismarck represents Prussia at the assembly of the German Federal Diet.

1852 Adolph Menzel completes his painting *Flute Concert at Sanssouci*.

1858 William (I), Prince of Prussia, becomes regent for his sick brother Frederick William IV.

1859 In Berlin, construction work begins on the Rotes Rathaus, built of red brick to plans by Hermann Friedrich Waesemann. The construction is eventually completed in 1870.

1861 Accession of King William II (1797–1888), who also becomes Emperor of Germany in 1871.

1862 After a governmental crisis, Otto von Bismarck becomes Prime Minister of Prussia.
Theodor Fontane writes his book entitled *Wanderungen durch die Mark Brandenburg* (Walks through the March of Brandenburg).

Rail station in Berlin, etching (c. 1840)

1864 Prussia and Austria go to war with Denmark for possession of Schleswig-Holstein. At the Peace of Vienna, Denmark cedes Schleswig, Holstein, and Lauenburg to Prussia and Austria. The administration of Schleswig is transferred to Prussia.

Karl Marx as the "Prometheus of the Rhine," an allegorical allusion to the suppression of the newspaper the Rheinische Zeitung *on which Marx worked, lithograph (c. 1843)*

1866 At the battle of Königgrätz, Prussia wins the war with Austria for supremacy in Germany. Austria agrees to the dissolution of the German Confederation at the Peace of Nikolsburg. Prussia annexes Schleswig-Holstein, Hanover, the Electorate of Hesse, Nassau, and Frankfurt am Main.

1867 Otto von Bismarck founds the North German Confederation and becomes chancellor.

1869 August Bebel and Wilhelm Liebknecht found the Social Democratic Workers' Party in Eisenach.

1870 The railroad network in Prussia now covers 11,523 kilometers (7,160 miles).

1870–1871 The Franco-Prussian War, with the North German Confederation and the allied South German states in opposition to France.

1871 King William I of Prussia becomes Emperor of Germany on January 18 in the Hall of Mirrors at Versailles. The imperial German Reich is a confederation of states under Prussian hegemony, with the Emperor as supreme military commander. Otto von Bismarck, Prime Minister of Prussia, is also Chancellor of the Reich.
Some 62.8% of the population of Prussia live in communities of less than 2,000 persons (in the Rhineland province, the figure is only 42.7%).

"To my Beloved Berliners," a caricature of King Frederick William IV, 1848

Baron Rothschild's ironworks at Wittkowitz, colored lithograph (c. 1850)

ARCHITECTURE AND URBAN PLANNING

Heinz Schönemann

Potsdam, Sanssouci, Frederick the Great's study and bedroom

A Change of Style: The Age of Frederick William II

The date of the transition from Baroque to Neo-classicism in Europe differed from region to region; in Prussia the transition can be dated to the year of Frederick the Great's death, 1786. And nowhere was this change more obvious than in architecture. A general sense of stagnation in public affairs towards the end of Frederick the Great's long reign now offered scope for new ideas. Frederick himself had begun to feel that everything was coming to a standstill. As work on the late Baroque building of the New Palace at Sanssouci approached its end, he complained rather fretfully of the "house at Wörlitz" that there seemed no other subject of conversation except that "the Prince of Dessau has built himself a new palace." Even the deliberate asymmetry in the design for the surroundings of the New Palace, the commissions given to the British architect Sir William Chambers, and the laying out of winding paths in the Anglo-Chinese style in the deer park of Sanssouci brought little sense of freshness or real innovation to architecture; only Prince Henry's new designs for the palace and park at Rheinsberg were really in touch with contemporary trends.

The 11 years during which Frederick the Great's nephew reigned as King Frederick William II have almost vanished from sight, squeezed as they are between two long reigns, each lasting over 40 years: that of his uncle, Frederick II the Great, and that of his son, Frederick William III. However, those 11 years are of the utmost importance for the development of art in Prussia, a period when styles changed almost overnight, and not just in the two residences in Berlin and Potsdam. The new king strongly encouraged this development by employing outstanding artists. Of all the visual arts, his preference was for classical architecture and the beginnings of landscape gardening, where he probably derived his ideas not so much from Britain itself as from the example of Anhalt-Dessau. The gardens of Wörlitz in Dessau had set an influential fashion since the late 1760s, and that fashion had been noted in Prussia. As Prince of Prussia, Frederick William II had stayed at Dessau and Wörlitz quite frequently, and his artistic tastes were formed there. When he succeeded to the throne, indeed as early as the later months of 1786, he recruited the architect Friedrich Wilhelm von Erdmannsdorff from Dessau and appointed him consultant at his own residence. Erdmannsdorff's function was not so much to work as an architect as to advise on questions of art and style in all cultural and educational matters. His position as an arbiter of elegance enabled him to exert a benign influence over customs and manners in general. He gave the new king guidance, breathed life into the architectural activities of the time, corrected his colleagues' plans, acquired works of art dating from classical antiquity, and supervised the training of craftsmen. He was also the first choice for architectural commissions that would set new standards, for instance in the Palace in Berlin (Stadtschloss), and in the vineyard palace of Sanssouci.

Changes in artistic attitudes became evident directly after the death of Frederick the Great: posterity ignored his dislike of portraits of himself and even his express wish that there should be no monuments to set up to him. The demand for some memorial to a national genius, one popularly seen as the father of his people, outweighed any compunction over the dead man's wishes. Frederick William II decided "to arrange everything as it had been done at the exequies of King Frederick William I." Carl von Gontard was commissioned to provide the funeral decorations at the palace in Potsdam, and a circular structure was erected in the Garnisonkirche (Garrison Church) to figure as a Temple of Immortality for the display of the state coffin. It was designed by the painter Bernhard Rode. This rotunda was understood as an allusion to Knobelsdorff's Temple of Amalthea, built for the young Crown Prince Frederick in Neuruppin, and a counterpart to Gontard's temple buildings for the New Palace, constructed at the end of the Seven Years' War. At the same time, it was a step towards the symbolic architectural forms that would be developed in the future.

The change of attitude was very obvious in the proposals put forward for a memorial to the late king; there could be no question of using the Rococo forms of Friderician art to express the now generally expected themes of commemoration and admonition directed at both the new king and his people. Frederick himself had been interested in classicism only in its picturesque, Neo-Gothic

Opposite
Potsdam, Sanssouci, Frederick the Great's study and bedroom
Renovated by Friedrich Wilhelm von Erdmannsdorff (1786)

When Frederick William II came to the throne he wanted the palaces and gardens of Potsdam converted to the new style of architecture and design. Even in the year of Frederick the Great's death, Erdmannsdorff had begun renovating his bedroom and study at Sanssouci in the Neo-classical style. The bedroom was set apart like a temple, and the decorative themes referring to Frederick himself created a memorial to the great man.

aspect, as a variant on the exoticism of the Rococo style. He regarded Neo-classical forms in themselves with suspicion, because of their inherent relationship with the Enlightenment and its influence on social conditions, commenting that "the forms of government in all the states of Europe would have to be modified first ..." The sober mood with which the old king's death was received, as noted by the French writer Mirabeau ("The solemnity of death rather than mourning"), was typical of a profound change in social concepts occurring in Prussia, as elsewhere. The accession of a new king was not expected to provide continuity, but to usher in a new age. In architecture, the new ideas took a form that, while it could not of itself change society, embodied the nation's self-image and served as an institutionalized representation of democracy until almost the end of the next century. When news of Frederick's death arrived in Rome, for instance, the architect Hans Christian Genelli and the sculptor Johan Gottfried Schadow designed a classical temple intended to serve as both a funerary monument and a memorial to the king. As a whole and in every detail, it entirely rejected everything that was familiar in the art of Frederick's own age: it at once paid tribute to the king, and expressed a total change of style.

The first architectural work carried out by Friedrich Wilhelm von Erdmannsdorff, in Potsdam, adopted the same approach. Frederick William II obviously intended to retain Sanssouci as his summer residence, and commissioned Erdmannsdorff to modernize it. The architect began with the old king's study and bedroom, which after 40 years of use were the parts that most needed renovation. The project, undertaken only a few months after Frederick the Great's death, could not be simply a matter of just redecoration. Erdmannsdorff had in mind a place that would be a fitting memorial to the venerable king, who was now beyond raising any objections or distancing himself critically from such a plan (see page 273). With this end in view, Erdmannsdorff began by making the two parts of the room separate entities, whereas before they had been linked in a manner typical of the Rococo interior, with a putti-crowned balustrade projecting from the bedroom into the study and a vault connecting the ceiling and walls. Erdmannsdorff designed the two rooms in different styles, the most striking feature being an imposing temple façade for the room in which Frederick had died. An outer pair of columns and an inner pair of pillars stood at the entrance, with high breastwork and a molded cornice running around the area. Erdmannsdorff decorated the plinths of the pillars and columns with laurels and lyres, and the capitals of the columns with pairs of griffins. A sense of opulence and contrast is created by the juxtaposition of the fluted columns and the gilded faces of the square pillars, decorated with fruit and sprays of acanthus leaves. The architect used a sketch he had made in Italy of a horizontal Renaissance architrave, which he arranged vertically. Erdmannsdorff turned the alcove where the king had died into a shrine, in an area that was set apart like the inner chamber of a temple. He emphasized this effect with the ceiling paneling, on which are displayed 15 heraldic eagles contained in wreaths of oak leaves on large circular fields, interspersed by eight lion's heads in smaller circular areas to symbolize the sovereign, while poppy capsules in the border spandrels convey notions of peaceful slumber. By contrast, Erdmannsdorff designed the larger part of the room, the study, to suggest a place of assembly and sacrifice outside the temple. The open sky on the ceiling is covered by a round velarium, its outer area bearing the signs of the zodiac as symbols of time and eternity (see opposite). Moving inward on the velarium, the zodiac is followed by scenes of sacrifice alternating with depictions of the gods, which may also be interpreted as symbolizing the course of the year and of human life. The four female spirits shown against clouds in the spandrels relate directly to Frederick's character: they are allegorical figures influenced by the figures of Victory on the spandrel reliefs of classical triumphal arches. They personify Poetry (the figure with the lyre), History (with the quill and the scroll), War (holding a standard surmounted by an eagle), and Wisdom (with the globe of the earth and a palm frond). They link with scenes of sacrifice placed above the carefully aligned doors as *sopraporta* reliefs. These too refer directly to the character and life of Frederick: the relief above the door to the music room, decorated by Knobelsdorff as a hunting chamber, shows a sacrifice to Diana, the goddess of the hunt, and the relief above the false door beside it depicts a sacrifice to Apollo, god of light and the arts. Opposite, over the false door on the garden side of the room, a sacrificial scene set between warlike emblems emphasizes the connection between Victory and Courage. Finally, the scene above the door to the library shows a sacrifice to Hercules, in reference to the classical cult of the emperor as bringer of peace. By placing the tributes to Apollo and Diana opposite the symbols of the ruler's virtues, the two sides of the room play on ideas of the contrast between the king's person and his office – between "business and ... hours devoted to the Muses" – an idea already suggested by Frederick himself in the decoration of his palace.

Seen as a whole, Erdmannsdorff's design sets out a clear iconographic system honoring Frederick the Great, and it is his first memorial, created in what was both the most private and the most official room of his favorite residence. A very similar iconography appears in the plans for a memorial drawn up in collaboration by the architect Genelli and the sculptor Schadow under the motto "Friderico Magno Victoriae Musagetae Patri Patriae Sacrum," which

Potsdam, Sanssouci, Frederick the Great's study and bedroom

Opposite
Potsdam, Sanssouci, Frederick the Great's study and bedroom, detail of ceiling
Redesigned by Friedrich Wilhelm von Erdmannsdorff (1786)

After the death of Frederick the Great, Erdmannsdorff redesigned the study as a memorial to him. The symbols of time and eternity (the signs of the zodiac and sacrificial scenes in the manner of classical antiquity) are framed by allegorical figures referring to the late king's character as a ruler: the themes are the art of war, the writing of history and poetry, and wisdom.

Carl Gotthard Langhans
Design for the tower of the Marienkirche in Berlin (c. 1789)
Pen and ink with water color, 63.4 x 44.3 cm; Berlin, Stiftung Stadtmuseum Berlin

Langhans replaced the old tower of the Marienkirche, demolished in 1788 because it had fallen into disrepair, with a two-story structure in a very ornamental Gothic style deriving from British examples. His contemporaries saw a clear connection between this tower and the Brandenburg Gate, and interpreted it as a reference to the king's paternal care for his country.

was to appear as an inscription on the architrave of the temple. A comparison with this design makes it clear that Erdmannsdorff was not at ease with the radical nature of the independent architectural and sculptural methods developed in Rome by Genelli and Schadow, who took their ideas from ancient monuments and young French architects. However, Erdmannsdorff himself had a free hand in making discriminating use of spatial proportions and sculptural and artistic elements, and in determining his own range of iconographic expression. Both styles anticipated the Romantic Neo-classicism of the future architecture of Berlin.

Under Frederick William II, Prussia established a reputation as a country where the arts flourished. The king acquired the services of three major architects – Friedrich Wilhelm von Erdmannsdorff, Carl Gotthard Langhans, and Carl von Gontard – and appointed the young Johann Gottfried Schadow his court sculptor. He revived the Academy of Arts (Akademie der Künste), which had been in existence since 1696, and in the Minister of State whom he appointed its curator, Friedrich Anton, Baron von Heinitz, he found a skillful reformer who in addition bridged the gulf between the arts and industry, since he was President of the Royal Porcelain Manufacturing Commission. In 1790, new regulations made it possible to build up a collection of models and found a school of draftsmanship for craftsmen. The royal collections were open to members of the Academy and their pupils, and methods of architectural training were updated. From 1786, the Academy held its regular exhibitions in Berlin, providing a survey of the state of artistic development in Prussia and at the same time stimulating artistic activity throughout Germany.

The exhibition of 1789 was dominated by architecture, in particular by the work of Carl Gotthard Langhans, who had come from the provinces a year earlier to be appointed director of the new Supreme Royal Planning and Building Department. He had made his name with the work he carried out for Prince Henry in Rheinsberg in the 1760s, and Erdmannsdorff, who thought highly of him, had probably given Langhans financial support on the study tour that took him from Anhalt to England, France, and Holland in 1775. Until his appointment to Berlin, however, Langhans's activities were confined to the provinces, in Silesia and in Greater Poland. He presented himself to the public at the Academy exhibition with plans and also with three models for the pioneering buildings of the new Berlin: the Brandenburg Gate, the tower of the Marienkirche, and the Veterinary School.

It was already obvious at the time of this exhibition that the Brandenburg Gate would "mark the beginning of a new epoch in the history of style" (see below). Langhans's design of 1788 for the first monumental gate in the new style was undoubtedly suggested by the plans of Claude Nicolas Ledoux for the saltworks town of Chaux. The main gate of that town, completed by Ledoux in 1776, is a structure in the rustic manner, consisting of a low, round-arched portal, a Doric colonnade of six smooth columns and two corner columns beneath a frieze, which is shared by both parts of the building, and an upright,

Carl Gotthard Langhans
The Brandenburg Gate, Berlin (1789), picture by Ludwig E. Lütke, aquatint, 41.8 x 67.4 cm

To replace the Baroque gate dividing Unter den Linden from the zoological gardens, Langhans designed a new structure incorporating as much open space as possible, to give views from the city to the zoological gardens. Langhans designed the sides facing the city and the country as a Doric colonnade, each side having six fluted pillars set on plinths. The colonnade is flanked by adjoining wings to accommodate the guardhouse and the customs office, giving the impression of a three-winged building and thus opening up the area of the square.

self-contained attic story. Each group of three columns and one corner column stands on a base that consists of two steps shared by both groups, with a broad access road to the round-arched gate in the middle. Although Ledoux and Langhans both cite the Propylaea in Athens as their model, their buildings could not be more different. Ledoux gives his entrance gate for the model town of Chaux the forbidding character of a fortress. The Brandenburg Gate designed by Langhans, on the other hand, opens the city up to the country around it. It is a magnificent structure, standing at the end of Unter den Linden and giving a view of the Zoological Gardens beyond. Langhans's reference to his classical model could be called merely the citing of authority in justification, as might be expected when something in so new a style was being built in such a prominent place.

The "Hellenic" Brandenburg Gate is matched by the tower of the Marienkirche in the New Town on the other side of the Spree island, for which Langhans provided a "Gothic" superstructure built in 1789–1790 (see page 276, above). Constructed on two levels – the lower consisting of columns in the style of classical antiquity, curving walls, and windows with pointed arches, the upper level of free Gothic forms – it meets the requirements both of classical proportions as well as the Gothic theories of its period. The two poles represented by the Brandenburg Gate and the Marienkirche tower are comparable to the contrast between the Marble Palace (see page 281) and the Gothic Library (see page 280) in the New Garden, or between the place and Gothic house in the park at Wörlitz. The typical contrast between classical and picturesque elements immanent in the new style is illustrated here in the very center of Berlin. It was a contrast that could equally well represent south and north, classical antiquity and the present, the Neo-classical and the Gothic, cosmopolitanism and patriotism, discipline and liberty.

Even before he designed the Brandenburg Gate and the tower of the Marienkirche, Langhans introduced a new architectural form into Berlin. This form ultimately derived from the medical theaters of antiquity, and in the form of a plenary lecture hall is still an architectural expression of the supremacy of democracy. The Anatomical Theater of the Veterinary School was built in Berlin in 1789; it is a scientific center in a predominantly agricultural country where the horse was the main means of transport (see page 279). Projections form a Greek cross on the basic square ground plan of the building and surround the circular lecture hall, which resembles an amphitheater. The shallow dome is in the new timber truss structure first tested out in France and then introduced for agricultural buildings by David Gilly. The Veterinary School, situated in the Prussian capital, was a model for new forms of architecture that were meant for new purposes. They also included theaters, stud farms, and, at a later date, buildings for stock exchanges and factories (see above). In line with contemporary ideas, the model road in the New Garden set an example for new roads linking the whole country, and the model village of the Dutch Establishment, also in the New Garden, was followed by the new plan for Neuruppin, rebuilt as a model town after its devastation by fire in 1787 (see page 278). The design shows handsome squares standing out from the grid plan of the housing areas, with the church and the school (see page 278) prominently placed as institutions guaranteeing both patriotic morality and good standards of education.

Karl Friedrich Schinkel
National Theater in Berlin, built by Langhans 1800–1802, pen and black ink, color wash, 13.1 x 21.1 cm; Berlin, Schinkel-Museum

This drawing shows the theater for which Schinkel designed state sets. When it burned down in 1817, he replaced it with the Schauspielhaus.

Glogau, the State Theater (c. 1800; destroyed)
Berlin School of Architecture

The State Theater (Stadttheater) in Glogau clearly shows the influence of contemporary Berlin architecture.

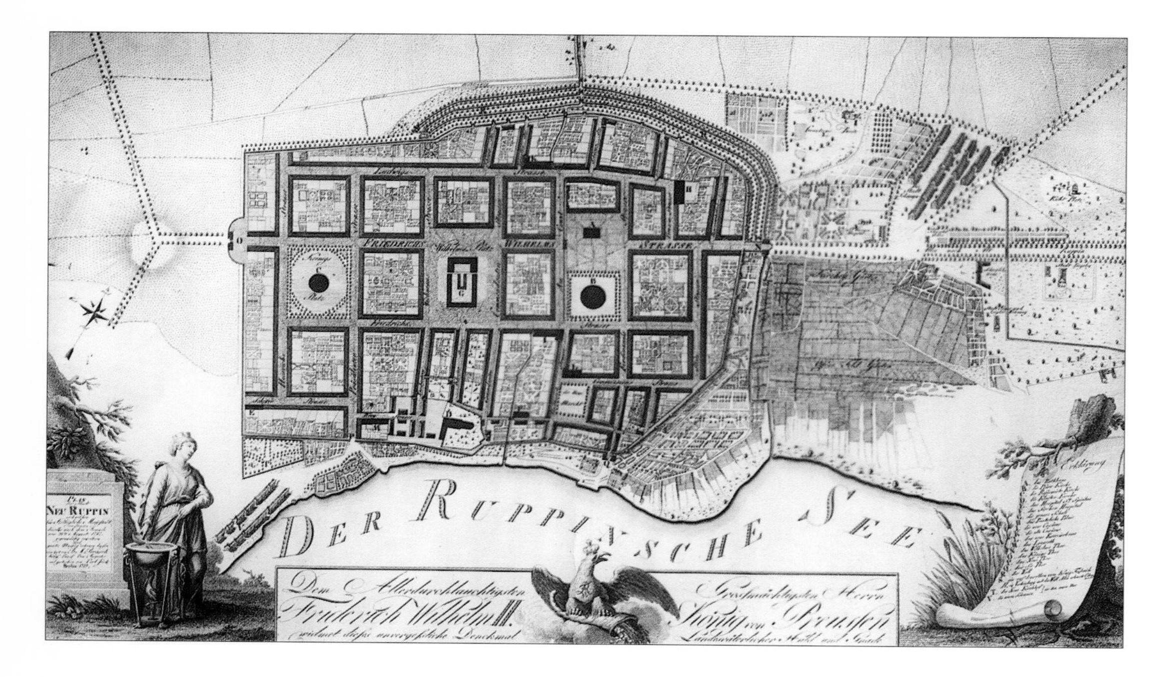

Bernhard Mattias Brasch
Plan of the town of Neuruppin (1789), engraving, 61 x 93 cm

Neuruppin was rebuilt after the great fire of 1787. The aims of Prussian urban policy in the 18th century are summed up here in a bold piece of town planning. The plans presented a simple basic structure still perceptible today: the town is planned on a strict grid pattern, with precisely marked boundaries to each area.

Carl Gotthard Langhans
Berlin, the Anatomical Theater in the Veterinary School (1789–1790)

Within a shallow convex dome resting on a drum, Langhans placed a semicircular inner cupola spanning the entire central area of the Anatomical Theater. Recessed windows and the skylight at the top of the dome provide ample light. Christian Bernhard Rode added painted scenes fitted into the trompe l'oeil Gothic architecture; the subjects refer to the work of the Veterinary School and show typical breeds of livestock reared in Prussia.

Opposite, below
Philipp Bernhard François Berson and Bernhard Mattias Brasch
The Schoolhouse, Neuruppin (1789–1791)

Detailed plans were made late in 1789 for the Schoolhouse, which later accommodated one of the outstanding schools of Prussia. It was centrally placed in the grid system of the town, and dominates the square where it stands.

Potsdam, the Gothic Library in the New Garden (1792–1793)
Carl Gotthard Langhans

Langhans built the king's private library as a Neo-Gothic octagonal tower on two floors. On the ground floor, the tower is surrounded by a square structure of massive dressed sandstone with pointed arches.

Carl Gotthard Langhans
Design for the Moorish Temple in the New Garden in Potsdam (1792), pen and ink with watercolor, 59.5 x 42.1 cm; Potsdam, Stiftung Preussische Schlösser und Gärten Berlin-Brandenburg, Plankammer

The "Moorish Temple" stood beside the Hasengraben linking the Heiliger See to the Jungfernsee, and balances the Gothic Library on the side of the Heiliger See nearer to the town. The Moorish Temple fell into disrepair and had to be demolished in 1869.

Under Frederick William II, art in Prussia became a subject of public interest, and was to remain a major intellectual and social force for the following generations. Both through direct contacts and also through the appointment of people of proven ability (even if, like Langhans, they came from the provinces) the king laid claim to the position of artistic leadership then occupied by Anhalt-Dessau.

It was from Dessau that Frederick William II brought first Erdmannsdorff and then the landscape gardener, Johann August Eyserbeck the Younger, to the Prussian court. This act demonstrated Frederick William II's feelings for the new style when he entrusted his most important project – the layout of the New Garden – to Eyserbeck. The very name of the New Garden (Neuen Garten) in itself distinguished it from the old gardens of Sanssouci. It was laid out around a lake, the Heiliger See, as a landscape garden very much in the Anhalt style.

The buildings in the New Garden in Potsdam and on Peacock Island (Pfaueninsel) made extensive use of architectural forms of all periods and all lands in a manner typical of the new style. From the tower of the Gothic library (see opposite) situated where Potsdam comes down to the Heiliger See, there was a view over the royal gardens to the Palladian rectangle of the Marble Palace (see below), to its kitchen, designed as a ruined Roman temple, the Green House, modeled on a Baroque farmhouse, and then the Moorish Temple at the eastern end of the lake (see above). Finally, the ruined castle on Peacock Island (see page 292) rises above the wide expanses of the lake called the Jungfernsee, the Maiden's Lake.

Ancient Egypt is represented by a pyramid and the façade of the Orangery, inspired by Ledoux (see pages 282 and 283); and Holland by a model village consisting of dwelling houses, the royal stud farm and carriage houses, and a nobleman's house that was originally to have had a bell tower. This "Dutch Establishment" stands with its show side towards the Heiliger See on the road laid out as a model avenue between the porter's lodge and the Marble Palace. As a village where real people lived, it was one of the series of model villages built around 1800 and including the hamlet at Versailles (a plaything for the queen) and the layout of the real village of Paretz (see page 284, above). The Marble Palace itself (see below) had its precursors in the work of Palladio and the English Neo-Palladian style (a style that also spread, by various routes, to Poland and Russia); in 17th-century German Palladian buildings; and the Petit Trianon of Louis XVI at Versailles, together with the buildings all over Europe influenced by it. Its "marble" hall, overlooking the Heiliger See, looks across to the ruined castle on Peacock Island. Just as the Marble Palace rose above a model village, this castle, built of "native timber" and containing a room designed to evoke Tahiti (see page 293), rises above the utilitarian buildings of the island like a citadel above its village. There is a dairy farm built as a ruined Gothic abbey at the other end of the island. The local and familiar stood in close proximity to the exotic and dreamlike: all kinds of experiments

Potsdam, the New Garden, Frederick William II's Marble Palace

The Marble Palace is one of the earliest Neo-classical buildings in Berlin and Potsdam, and was built in 1787–1792. The cube-shaped Palladian central building by Carl von Gontard stands above a projecting terrace on the banks of the Heiliger See. Side wings with galleries designed by Carl Gotthard Langhans were added in 1787 to create more space inside the Palace.

Potsdam, Orangery, New Garden (1791)
Carl Gotthard Langhans

With its statues, pillars, and sphinx, the Neo-classical false façade of the Orangery, facing the Dutch Establishment, was intended to suggest Egypt. Langhans took the inspiration for his design from the works of the French architect Jean-Nicolas Ledoux.

Potsdam, icehouse in the form of a pyramid in the New Garden (1791–1792)
Andreas Krüger

Andreas Krüger built the icehouse near the Marble Palace on the model of the pyramid known as "La Glacière" in the garden designed by Désert de Retz, published by Le Rouges in his volumes on *Die Neue Garten-Kunst* (The New Garden Art). The hieroglyphs on the sides represent the planetary symbols of Rosicrucian tradition. On a clear day, the pyramid can still be seen in the middle of the New Garden from the Babelsberg.

were permissible in these garden buildings, though it would be misleading to speak of a plurality of styles. Instead, the buildings provided a general foundation for the architect's cosmopolitan creativity. Here, it was possible to dispense with the ideal types of classical antiquity and introduce rustic features, creating norms that would become part of the new style.

The architect Carl von Gontard set the Marble Palace, with its terrace projecting above the lake, at the center of the panoramic view of the New Garden as seen from the Heiliger See. Gontard had been the most prominent of the old king's architects. In the New Palace, and even more markedly in his later buildings in Potsdam and Berlin, he had already shown leanings toward a kind of architecture moving on from the late Baroque to Neo-classicism. Frederick William II valued Gontard most highly among all the Berlin architects, and had entrusted to him the building of this summer palace on the Heiliger See. Gontard's plans for the Marble Palace (see page 284) are in the tradition of Palladian "cubes," modeled on a series comprising the Queen's House at Greenwich, begun by Inigo Jones in 1616; the Petit Trianon at Versailles, begun by Jacques-Ange Gabriel in 1762; and finally the pavilion built by Ledoux for Madame du Barry at Louvenciennes in 1771. A characteristic of these classic rectangular Palladian buildings is a central area, usually round or polygonal, with the stairway to the upper floor concealed in the spandrels. Gontard's Marble Palace is very different. It is organized around a central stairwell on a square ground plan

that was designed to direct the course of the stairs up to the belvedere on the roof. German Palladian designs of the 17th century do, of course, sometimes have square ground plans and a central spiral staircase, but there are other precursors of Gontard's plans for the stairs leading to the belvedere. Domenico Merlini's designs for the palace on the Lazienki island in Warsaw had more influence on Gontard than any French or English buildings, and those designs include ground plans comparable to the Marble Palace. Gontard's royal patron had himself directed the architect's attention to Merlini's works. Frederick William II's ideas for the buildings in the New Garden were strongly influenced by his own experiences: for instance, his one journey of any great length, to the court of Catherine II at St. Petersburg in 1780, had made a lasting impression on him, and he is known to have seen the residences outside the city as well as St. Petersburg itself. It may be assumed that he also spent some time at the court of King Stanislaw August Poniatowski of Poland on his way back to Prussia. Architectural developments at the Polish court, in particular the building work on the royal baths in Warsaw, were widely admired throughout Europe, and around 1780 Domenico Merlini, who at this time was preparing for the extension and renovation of the royal baths at Lazienki, was incorporating more classical elements into his work. Even the planning stages of the conversion of the 17th-century bathing pavilion into a palace on the island attracted a great deal of attention, as did the completion of the project in 1784.

Frederick William II must have seen a parallel between the site at Lazienki and the Heiliger See, and no doubt formed his own ideas of a palace on the water from the Warsaw model. The concept of the Marble Palace as a lakeside palace determined both Gontard's plans and the first stage of the building work itself (see page 284). However, Gontard's Marble Palace provided relatively little space for practical use, and in its original form would not have been adequate for long summer visits by the king: it could not have accommodated even a modest court. The architectural concept as a whole was obviously

Potsdam, Palm Room in the Orangery, New Garden (1791–1793)
Carl Gotthard Langhans

This winter garden, where naturalistically ornamented palm trees stand above short sections of fluted column, was also used as a concert hall. Flowering potted plants were arranged all around the room on brackets and rostrums, in porcelain containers specially designed for the setting. The hall was heated by two large cast iron stoves shaped like full-length female figures in the form of ancient statues.

Heinrich Ludwig Manger
Design for a castellan's lodge and other domestic buildings (1788) in the New Garden in Potsdam, pen and brown ink with water color, 25.7 x 61.7 cm; Stiftung Preussische Schlösser und Gärten Berlin-Brandenburg, Plankammer

The design shows the building, which resembles a grotto, at the end of the long path to the New Garden and directly opposite the porter's lodge. The single-story building was intended to support the level upper terrace with a wall and a stairway for the guards. It was altered around 1845, when another floor was added.

The village of Paretz, view of Paretz Palace and the manor house from the park (c. 1800)
Unknown artist
Gouache, 21 x 30.4 cm; Potsdam, Stiftung Preussische Schlösser und Gärten Berlin-Brandenburg, Plankammer

The history of the designing of model villages in the 18th century concludes with the building of the summer residence for the crown prince, later Frederick William II, as a model design for a real village. At the same time it looks forward to planned improvements in agriculture.

less important than the provision of a fine vantage point from which to see the view. At first Frederick William II probably intended the Marble Palace only as a pavilion for occasional visits, a place where he could stop when he traveled by boat between Berlin and Potsdam. His route passed from the belvedere built in 1788 by Carl Gotthard Langhans in the park at Charlottenburg and on along the river Spree to the Havel lakes and the Heiliger See, ending in the center of Potsdam. But soon after building work began, the intended function of the Marble Palace changed. It was no longer to be just a place where the king could stop briefly on a boat journey, but his favorite place to stay. A more extensive spatial plan than Gontard's original design was now required. Such a building, moreover, could not relate exclusively to the water, but had also to be more closely linked to the surrounding gardens.

After consultations between the king and Erdmannsdorff, Carl Gotthard Langhans took charge of the building work and saw the new project through. We may assume that the casting vote over the change of concept was Erdmannsdorff's. His objections to Gontard's designs must have gone into the details; Langhans mentions one such detail in a letter to Erdmannsdorff later. Gontard had intended to place chimneys between the windows on the outside walls, but Erdmannsdorff thought them inappropriate for a building north of the Alps. As they had to be present to accommodate the flues fitted between the pillars of the roof balustrade, they did not disappear from the design until the belvedere was raised above the roof on a stepped platform. Then the flues (like the obelisks serving the same purpose on the roofs of the English buildings derived from Palladio's Villa Rotonda in Vicenza) could be fitted in the string boards of the steps, and the chimneys themselves were moved to the interior of the building.

The idea of a magnificent main façade looking out on the water was abandoned, and the main façade was now to be the plainer one facing the land, and not raised on a base but set on the same level as the garden. This change meant that the entire interior design of the building had to be turned around: the hall leading to the garden now became the main entrance. The new staircase designed by Langhans began at floor level in this vestibule, and the pairs of pillars already erected to support the side of the stairwell facing the land were subsequently standing on disproportionately tall plinths (see opposite). Gontard's design for the stairway had taken it from the lakeside entrance to the upper part of the building in four flights of steps running clockwise. The stairway designed by Langhans, by contrast, passes from the vestibule to the upper story with only three flights of steps, running counterclockwise. Gontard's stairway, in the tradition of Palladian design, was set against the outer walls of the building alone (the closest comparison is to the stairway of the École Militaire in Paris, begun by Ange-Jacques Gabriel in 1751). The staircase designed by Langhans, on the other hand, follows English examples, the most similar being the staircase built by James Stewart for Montague House, Portman Square, in London (1777–1782). The new design for the stairwell, with the alterations it entailed to those parts of the building that had already been constructed, must account for the slow progress made in completing the palace, a delay that is otherwise difficult to understand.

The open rotunda of the temple on the roof above the stairwell was a feature that Gontard himself had already abandoned. The walls of the stairwell were above the height of the attic story, so that a plinth formed the substructure. Above it, the Marble Palace is now crowned only by a raised wooden belvedere with windows filling the walls of its eight sides. Large semicircular windows in the platform below the belvedere illuminate the stairwell, and flights of steps with gilded rails lead up the outer sides of the platform to the belvedere itself. The

Carl von Gontard
Plan of the site of the Marble Palace, New Garden, Potsdam (c. 1786–1787)
Pen and gray ink, color wash, 43.1 x 98.6 cm; Potsdam, Stiftung Preussische Schlösser und Gärten Berlin-Brandenburg, Plankammer

The site plan shows the Marble Palace from the lakeside, raised above the great flight of steps and the palace kitchen, which is designed as a ruined temple to Mars. At this early stage of planning, the belvedere was still a round, open temple on a flat roof. The rooms are arranged around the new type of central stairwell.

Potsdam, the stairwell in the Marble Palace (1787–1792)
Carl von Gontard and Carl Gotthard Langhans

When the design of the interior of the Marble Palace was changed and enlarged, the hall looking out on the garden became the main entrance. The new staircase designed by Langhans begins on the level of this vestibule. The pairs of columns already erected by Gontard and supporting the landward side of the stairwell remain in place, but standing on disproportionately tall plinths.

Marble Palace had been converted, in effect, from a feature dominating the lakeside panorama (see opposite) to part of a garden laid out according to the contemporary concept of "sensibility," being made subordinated to the landscape (see pages 281, 299 and 300).

This change of basic concept had an immediate bearing on the internal architecture of the building. The height of the floor on the side of the vestibule facing land was the important factor: only the tripartite area facing the lake still retains its lower level. Once intended as the main entrance area, it became an elegant and intimate dining room, with large mirrors on the walls making it look like a lakeside grotto (see page 286). Two of the antique classical statues acquired by Erdmannsdorff in Italy were destined for the Grotto and installed there as fixtures: one is a nymph rising from the water, the other the Greek mythological figure Thetis with a dolphin. They heighten the intentionally atmospheric and magical effect of this low-lying room, which is filled with the reflected light of the lake.

Not only changes in taste and fashion but also the increasingly introverted style of Frederick William II's court influenced the structure of the palace. Only the Grotto and the Great Hall retained their original links with the lake; all of the other rooms turned inward, so to speak, and hardly related at all to their surroundings any more. This is particularly evident in the side wings built by Langhans (see page 281), designed to increase the space available in the palace. The independent rectangular buildings were linked to the cube of the original building by galleries.

With the form taken by the alterations, the position of the palace in the entire Potsdam ensemble is a good illustration of what could be called an architectural generation gap. However, there is more than one way of looking at this artistic development: the original Marble Palace, which faced the lake, could have been seen in relation to the historic system of waterways laid out between Berlin and Potsdam for economic reasons. Thus the first palace may have expressed Frederick William's wish to follow the example of Anhalt-Dessau and introduce agricultural improvements linking the surroundings of his two residences. On the other hand, the second design's concentration on the New Garden can be interpreted as a gesture of resignation. Political and economic contradictions were opening up, separating dream and reality, and causing the king to lead an increasingly reclusive life in his *hortus conclusus*. Situated between the Jungfernsee and the Heiliger See, the Marble Palace assumed the character of a Utopian island.

Considering the importance it has in architectural history, the Marble Palace did not become as well known as it might have done. But it gained greater significance when another great work of the royal architects, the royal apartments in the Berlin Palace, was destroyed in World War II.

Unlike Frederick the Great, who had avoided the Berlin Palace and at most spent a few months there in winter, Frederick William II had new apartments designed in the palace for himself and his second wife, Frederica Louisa of Hesse-Darmstadt. Working in parallel, Erdmannsdorff and Gontard began planning the royal apartments in 1787. The reconstruction was finished in November 1788, and the decoration and furnishing of Queen Frederica Louisa's apartments by Carl Gotthard Langhans followed at the beginning of 1789. Although Langhans was moderate in his expenditure, he provided the requisite magnificence and made varied use of his favorite theme, the oval room, as both a cabinet and a fine pillared hall in a suite of rooms that display a wealth of diversity (see right). Since Gontard and Erdmannsdorff were obviously under no compulsion to design and furnish the royal chambers as a consistent whole, the attraction of the separate groups of rooms consisted in their constant variety. Gontard designed the audience suite and the throne room together (see page 289); Erdmannsdorff worked on the state rooms of the apartments, including the Pillared Hall, the Parole Hall, the dining room and the library (see page 291); Gontard again was responsible for the series of rooms lying between them and consisting of anteroom, concert room, the bedroom and study looking out on the courtyard, and the lacquer cabinets leading to the pleasure garden. The relationship between the two architects was one of direct and stimulating rivalry, which lead them to create independent works of extremely high quality – the ensemble was probably the finest early Neo-classical suite of rooms in Germany. Erdmannsdorff, however, was the driving force. In consultation with the king and with von Heinitz, the minister responsible for the Academy of Arts, he hoped to help raise the general standard of arts and crafts in Berlin. Erdmannsdorff's achievements represented an artistic advance that would have many consequences, while Gontard, then approaching the end of his professional life, had an extraordinary opportunity to prove his worth again for a new patron with very different tastes in architecture, under new conditions and in a new style.

In the process, he successfully combined elements of Frederician art with contemporary themes in his own unique style and with a sure touch. He too was aiming ultimately for a high standard of arts and crafts executed to specifications of the utmost quality, a

Opposite
Potsdam, the Grotto Hall in the Marble Palace (1787–1792)
Carl von Gontard and Carl Gotthard Langhans

The earlier entrance hall on the lakeside was still at a lower level, and with its wall mirrors this room resembles a grotto beside the water. The reflections of the light produce magical effects.

Berlin Palace (destroyed), Pillared Hall in the apartments of Queen Frederica (1789–1791)
Carl Gotthard Langhans

The busts of famous Roman women and the columns of the Ionic order in the banqueting hall of the queen's apartments were intended to refer to the queen herself.

Berlin Palace (destroyed), Marble Hall in the apartments of Queen Frederica (1789–1791)
Carl Gotthard Langhans

The ceiling of the Marble Hall was surmounted by a vaulted dome with a trompe l'oeil effect showing the sky, putti, and the signs of the zodiac. Semicircular niches were recessed in the walls to display white marble statues. Stucco reliefs on a blue background, to designs by Johann Gottfried Schadow, showed mythological scenes with dancing Maenads.

requirement that spurred on his colleagues and pupils. Among them was the outstanding figure of the young Friedrich Gilly, who with his father, David Gilly, had been summoned from Stettin by the king.

The well-preserved interiors of the castle on the Peacock Island and the rooms in the Marble Palace are the only extant examples of the outstanding quality of interior design at the Prussian court toward the end of the 18th century. The special charm of the little castle on the Peacock Island (see page 292) lies in the fact that most of its architectural components are made of wood.

The idea was to show what beauty could be achieved using material naturally present in Prussia. Frederick William II had acquired the Peacock Island in 1793 as a place to visit on his boating excursions from the belvedere in Charlottenburg and the New Garden. The court master carpenter, Johann Gottlieb Brendel, built a small castle in the form of a ruin on the island, at the end nearest Potsdam and within sight of the Marble Palace. It had a counterpart to balance it at the other end of the island: a dairy in the Gothic style, with rustic outhouses, and also built to simulate a ruin; it was intended to suggest a place of high-minded rustic simplicity in contrast to the worldly palace. The surroundings of both buildings, like the New Garden itself, were designed by Johann August Eyserbeck the

Berlin Palace, Green Damask Chamber in the Royal Chambers of King Frederick William II (1787–1789)
Carl von Gontard

This chamber was the second room in the audience suite of Frederick William II's apartments. The richness of the design – the generous decoration of the wooden panels, the ornaments above the mirrors, and the figural painting of the ceiling fresco – led to even richer ornamentation in the throne room next door.

Berlin Palace (destroyed), Throne Room in the Royal Chambers of Frederick William II (1787–1789)
Carl von Gontard

The throne room was the last in the audience suite. The heraldic decoration, heavy sculptural demarcations, rich gilding, and the deep red of the velvet wall covering all imparted a note of solemnity to the room. Erdmannsdorff acquired the white marble chimney-piece in Rome in 1790.

Younger on the principles of the "sentimental" landscape garden. The original oak trees were left growing on the island, so that this garden of sensibility, when seen across the water, looked like a land of dreams; and such dreams were given unique expression by Peter Ludwig Lütke, when he decorated the Tahitian Cabinet in the tower of the castle to suggest a bamboo hut (see page 293). Lütke painted four murals between the windows, which are framed by the trunks of palms trees: a view of the Peacock Island and the castle itself as seen from Potsdam; a view of the Marble Palace on the Heiliger See; the Gothic dairy standing on a peninsula of land; and finally an imaginary South Sea island complete with palaces and exotic trees. Dreams merge with reality in this castle of dreams. Similarly, memories merge with real life in the Marble Palace, where the educational tour of Italy undertaken in 1795–1796 by Countess Lichtenau, who was the king's life-long companion, is called to mind by various pictures by Jakob Philipp Hackert, who had taught Lütke in Rome, the Italian views on the ceiling frescos created by Johann Christoph Frisch, and relief work copied from models in the Vatican.

Probably the most influential artistic event of the period was the planning of a memorial to Frederick the Great in 1796–1797. It is impossible to overestimate the effect on classical architecture in Germany of the various plans submitted. The design proposed by young Friedrich Gilly in particular, and the stimulus it gave Karl Friedrich Schinkel, were to usher in another change of architectural style at the end of the reign of Frederick William II.

The experience and skills acquired in the development of early Neo-classical architecture culminated in the two competitions held in 1796 and 1797 to design the memorial. Those who submitted plans included Langhans, Gentz, and Friedrich Gilly. Langhans's design kept to the conditions of the competition published in 1796. He planned a round building supported by 12 columns, standing at the junction of Unter den Linden with the axis of the Friedrichforum and thus providing a pendant to the Brandenburg Gate. In the text accompanying his plans, Langhans cites his imspirations: he had taken "the city gate of Athens as the model" for the monumental gate structure, while the columns were "designed after the portico of Philip of Macedonia on Delos," and as for the memorial itself, the dome was "modeled on the Pantheon in Rome." "The dome will be open at the top, allowing light to fall on the bronze statue of Frederick II standing in the middle of the temple, illuminating it to the best advantage and imparting the solemnity of an antique temple to the whole." A design now in the Engravings Collection in Berlin shows variant designs for the temple with Ionic or with Doric columns; it was to stand on a base consisting of eight granite steps. In the Ionic version, four iron lions set at a diagonal

Opposite, above
Berlin Palace (destroyed), Blue French Room in the Royal Chambers of Frederick William II (1787–1789)
Friedrich Wilhelm von Erdmannsdorff

The Neo-classical forms used by Erdmannsdorff in the rooms of the audience suite were more severe and rigid than Gontard's decorations. The rigorous rectangular segmentation of the walls, mirrors, and *sopraporta*, and the absence of a vault show no trace of any lingering Rococo influence. Erdmannsdorff consistently pursues the early Neo-classical decoration he had developed in Wörlitz.

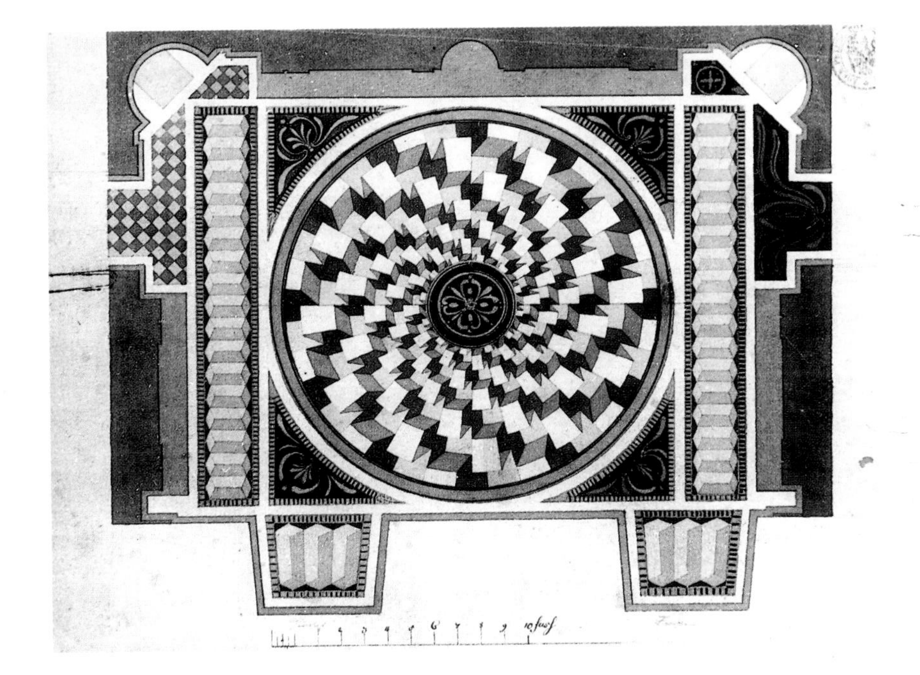

Friedrich Wilhelm von Erdmannsdorff
Design for the library floor in the Royal Chambers of Frederick William II (1787–1788) in the Berlin Palace
Pen, color wash and watercolor, 32.7 x 38 cm, Potsdam, Stiftung Preussische Schlösser und Gärten Berlin-Brandenburg, Plankammer

Frederick William's reference library was designed by Erdmannsdorff, and lay west of the French Room, the first room in the projecting pleasure garden wing. It had two windows looking out on the garden. The drawing for the design records the plan of the magnificent parquet pattern, which consisted of concentric parallelepipeds in dark, medium, and pale woods.

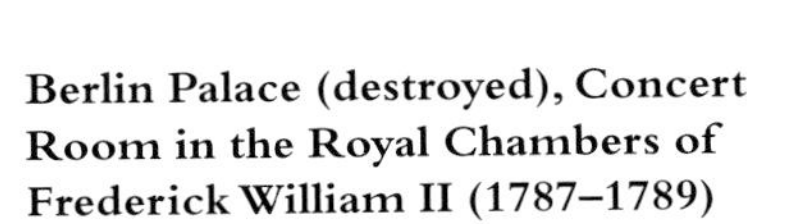

Berlin Palace (destroyed), Concert Room in the Royal Chambers of Frederick William II (1787–1789)
Carl von Gontard

The Concert Room is regarded as Gontard's major contribution to the Royal Chambers. His characteristic fusion of styles – the straight lines of the wall decoration, and the ornaments above the mirrors and doors on the one hand, the festoons of the veduta decoration on the other – derived from publications illustrating the works of the Scottish architect Robert Adam.

Opposite, below
Berlin Palace (destroyed), Dining Hall in the Royal Chambers of Frederick William II (1787–1789)
Friedrich Wilhelm von Erdmannsdorff

The king's rectangular Dining Hall adjoined the great Pillared Hall. Erdmannsdorff's ornamental scheme covered three walls, the ceiling and the richly inlaid floor, while the window wall had mirror glass from ceiling to floor between the jambs. The mural paintings imitated a room looking out on views of a summer landscape. Erdmannsdorff's composition, in his free combination of Raphael's subjects in the loggias of the Vatican, created a new and entirely coherent scheme.

Berlin, the castle on Peacock Island (1794)

The Peacock Island castle was commissioned by Frederick William II as a place to which he could go on long boating excursions. It was made entirely of "native timbers," and looked like a romantic ruin that combined local and exotic elements.

angle stood on the granite steps, and the statue of the king was to wear antique robes. The Doric variant showed the king in his historical uniform, with sphinxes. According to a letter from Carl August Boettiger to Goethe, a Cabinet decree of Frederick William II had already been issued for the execution of the "Ionic proposal," but was canceled shortly before the king's death in favor of a design by Aloys Ludwig Hirt.

Heinrich Gentz submitted a design for a round temple that would have meant rebuilding the Lindenforum entirely. It resembles the monumental Altar to the Fatherland seen in depictions of the French declaration of national unity on the Champs de Mars in Paris in 1790. The round structure was to stand on a massive, oblong base through which traffic could pass in the direction of Unter den Linden. Imposing flights of steps were to lead up to the temple on all sides of the platform, which would be flanked on both sides of the road by subsidiary buildings: four square corner pavilions accommodating a guardhouse, a coffee house, a restaurant, and a store. The idea was to make the memorial a focal point in the life of the city.

In October 1796, Konrad Levetzow describes Friedrich Gilly's reaction to the announcement of the competition. "It was on a fine summer's evening in the month of July, 1796, that I visited Gilly at his father's country house in Schöneberg, and found him in the garden there, with the communication he had just received from the Academy in his hand. With a cheerful expression, he told me of the Academy's decision to make this memorial a subject of competition between a number of artists.

The enthusiasm that took hold of him during this conversation increased at every moment, now and then heightening the animation of the interview, in which he set out his great design to me in ever more extensive detail. We soon agreed that a mere statue alone would not suffice, and it must be linked to some work of architecture that would serve as a national shrine, uniting all the greatness and majesty that could possibly be achieved, and at the same time making it a means of promoting great moral and political ends, in the same way as the great public buildings and monuments of the ancients had done."

In the early stage of his thinking, Gilly rejected the round temple design as Gentz had planned it and drew a rotunda modeled on the tomb of Cecilia Metella in Rome, which dates from around 50 BC and is a round structure on a square base. Gilly's temple was to bear the inscription: *Divo Friderico SPQB* – in the manner of a Roman emperor, Frederick the Great was to be deified by "the Senate and people" of Prussia, by the nation and also by its representative body.

Gilly's final design for the temple

Gilly's final design (see page 294) also owed something to Gentz, from whom he took the massively vaulted lower structure and the monumental flights of steps. However, he moved the planned location to the outskirts of the city and the octagonal Leipzig Square outside the Potsdam Gate, where the street carried vehicles and pedestrian traffic. It was to be made a "true promenade," running from Leipzig Strasse past couchant lions and tall obelisks, as if in a hippodrome of classical antiquity, beneath rows of trees surrounding the dark, massive base of the memorial, and finally ending at a new city gate crowned by a quadriga.

Arched passageways were to provide a view of the mausoleum within the lower structure, which contained Frederick's sarcophagus, and a radiantly white Doric temple was to stand above it. Gilly's plans included altars on raised terraces in front of the narrow sides of the temple: the altar facing the city was

Above and right
Berlin, Peacock Island, the Tahitian Cabinet in the north tower of the castle

The early Neo-classical design and furnishings of the castle on Peacock Island are extent in their original form, and include the Tahitian Cabinet. The internal design of the room imitates a bamboo hut. Views of the castle's real surroundings as seen through the windows are linked to painted views both of these very scenes and also tropical landscapes.

Heinrich Gentz
Architectural model of the New Mint in Berlin (1800–1802)
Model: Schulz, Breiden, and Ruckenwiener (Berlin 1979)

This model, made in modern times, shows the Mint building (now demolished), and still conveys a sense of its dignity and importance. The building housed the Department of Mines, the Supreme Royal Planning and Building Department, and the newly founded Architectural Academy as well as the mint. Its relief frieze depicted the mining and refining of metal, minting coins, architecture and the visual arts, agriculture, and civil engineering.

dedicated to "the protector" and the altar facing the gate to "the peaceful ruler."

By linking the theme of an ascent with the image of a shrine raised aloft in the light, Gilly associated death with transfiguration: the heavy, dark burial chamber would be down below in the dark, though there was to be a view of it through vaulted passages intersecting beneath the central skylight; but the temple would stand above, in dazzling light, reached by mighty stairways with flights of steps running in opposite directions.

The model for this combination of stepped pyramid and temple was a building in Pasargadai in the highlands of Iran. It has been recognized as the monument of Cyrus, king of Persia; the account of his life by the Greek historian Xenophon was the first description of an ideal prince, and it has been frequently quoted.

Carl Haller von Hallerstein and Leo von Klenze took Gilly's plans as the starting point in working out the architectural program of their Valhalla; Klenze made drawings from Gilly's design. In 1814, at the end of the Wars of Liberation, Klenze proposed a "monument à la pacification de l'Europe": a Tuscan temple with the tomb of the fallen heroes in its terraced base. The allusion to the fate of the nation itself that Gilly had already indicated took shape more clearly in this new proposal: the upward climb now led from the nation's prehistory to its free and enlightened present.

This idea for a national monument entered into Schinkel's proposal for a memorial to Frederick on the site of the palace pharmacy; his design for the Berlin Schauspielhaus (theater); his plans for a palace on the banks of the Havel in Potsdam; and his projected monument to Frederick on the Mühlenberg at Sanssouci.

From Sanssouci the idea returned to Berlin in a suggestion by Frederick William IV for the extension of Museum Island (Museuminsel), and was finally realized by Friedrich August Stüler and Johann Heinrich Strack in the National Gallery (Nationalgalerie) (see page 431) built from 1862 to 1876. As late as 1872, Georg Adolph Demmler submitted a plan that owed much to Friedrich Gilly in the competition to design the Reichstag building. He too proposed to build a massive substructure, with entrances on all four sides providing access for the deputies, the court, and the public through passages forming a cross and meeting in the center beneath the plenary hall, which was to be the central building, decorated in a light color and standing on the base platform.

Recovery in status of Prussian architecture

Prussian architecture recovered its status in Europe during this period, and assumed a leading role in the German-speaking countries. The distinction between royal and non-royal buildings in town and country largely disappeared. Similarly, architectural styles in the provinces and in the residence cities drew closer

Friedrich Gilly
Design for a temple as a monument to Frederick the Great in Berlin (1797)
Pen and black ink, watercolor and opaque paint, 58 x 130 cm; Berlin Staatliche Museen zu Berlin – Preussischer Kulturbesitz

Friedrich Gilly's participation in the competition to design a monument to Frederick the Great was of the greatest significance for the development of Neo-classical architecture in Germany.

together. Architects came to the capital from the provinces, bringing new ideas and breathing new life into the architectural profession. State architecture as a whole was reorganized, and the Supreme Building Department ceased to be a branch of court administration and became a public authority.

Institutionalized training for architects, on the French model, united the aesthetic and technical aspects of the profession. As well as the course set up on the basis of a memorandum written by Friedrich Becherus in 1790 at the Berlin Academy of Arts, itself founded as early as 1696, there was also the Architectural Academy (Bauakademie) under David Gilly, which finally became independent in 1799. The new Academy, where Friedrich Gilly taught after 1798, moved into the building of the Royal Mint, which also accommodated the Mines Department of the Supreme Building Department. Preliminary studies were made from 1795 for this exemplary work of Neo-classicism in Berlin, and it was built by Heinrich Gentz between 1798 and 1802 on the site of the Werdersches Rathaus, which had been destroyed by fire.

The relief frieze above the rusticated ground floor referred to the building's function and so depicted mining and metal refining, the minting of the state's coinage, architecture and the visual arts, agriculture, and civil engineering. Gentz recorded his opinions of architecture in a comment on the depiction of that subject in the frieze: "A little way removed from them [the arts] stands Architecture, grave, simple and firm, compasses leaning on an area which shows the plumbline, the symbol of all that is fine, straight and upright in architecture."

The new generation of architects

The competitions for architectural plans held by a private society and organized by Friedrich Gilly also molded the ideas of the younger generation of architects, particularly Friedrich Schinkel. The competitions were for model projects to develop new state and industrial buildings (see above).

The journal founded as a central organ for architecture, the *Sammlung nützlicher Aufsätze, die Baukunst betreffend* (Collection of Useful Essays On Architecture), served architects, master builders, civil engineers, hydraulic engineers, and road builders alike. Intended as a means of communication and education, it was edited by members of the Supreme Royal Planning and Building Department from 1797, and was initially published by Johann Friedrich Unger.

David Gilly was undoubtedly the leading figure behind this journal, and consequently it focused mainly on technical questions of architecture, providing information and discussing modern technology. Gilly was impelled by a "conviction founded on long experience of the necessity of thorough instruction, to be as complete and practical as possible, particularly with respect to the proper construction of buildings."

Essays on hydraulic engineering occupied a good deal of space, since the subject was of particular importance in Prussia, with its many rivers, lakes, and stretches of coastline. In a related subject area, bridge building was also covered, and the improvement of the quality of building materials, as well as Friedrich Gilly's favorite theme, "building with wood, and timber roof-construction." Other subjects included building in wattle and daub, and technical means of providing protection against fire when constructing a building. New aesthetic principles were also discussed, as well as model estates and villages, the development of buildings of importance to the economy – saltworks, factories, agricultural buildings of all kinds – and the knowledge brought back from France by Friedrich Gilly and imported form Italy by the young Schinkel.

Friedrich Gilly
Title page vignette for Sammlung nützlicher Aufsätze, die Baukunst betreffend (1804)

Gilly's design for an iron foundry was created in the context of a competition held for his private society of young architects. He was very influential in the development of industrial architecture in Prussia in general, particularly the designs of Karl Friedrich Schinkel.

The Schinkel Period

Karl Friedrich Schinkel made his deepest impression on the architecture of Prussia when he finally succeeded the outstanding representatives of the new European style – that is, Friedrich Wilhelm von Erdmannsdorff, Carl Gotthard Langhans, Johann Gottfried Schadow, and David Gilly. These men had dominated Prussian architecture, and were still very influential figures, when the young Schinkel came to Berlin to begin his architectural training. No city in Europe could have offered more to an ambitious student of architecture at this period than the Prussian capital.

Gransee, Memorial to Queen Louise Henrietta (1810–1811)
Karl Friedrich Schinkel

A memorial was erected in memory of the queen's lying in state in Gransee on the night of July 25 to 26, 1810; it was made by the royal iron foundry to a design by Schinkel. Its form is related to his previous Gothic design for Queen Louise's mausoleum at Charlottenburg.

Frederick William II had promoted the new style of architecture and new departures in art; his son Frederick William III did not require or encourage further stylistic change. Father and son alike, however, encouraged creative talent and enlisted artists and scholars, hoping to change the predominantly military image of Prussia and its capital, and lend Berlin fresh intellectual and artistic luster. There followed a period when the people of Berlin could once again feel justified in calling their city the "Athens on the Spree." An influential circle of outstanding artists, architects, and educationalists gathered in the Prussian capital, putting their knowledge and skills to the service of an intellectual revival. In 1794, when Schinkel left Neuruppin, the "model town of the Enlightenment" (see page 278), and came to Berlin, where he was to begin his studies in 1799, he found a city that was open to new ideas, and he was able to benefit directly from the expertise of the brilliant architects David and Friedrich Gilly. He entered the General Architectural Training Institute founded by David Gilly, and became one of the circle of architects around Friedrich Gilly. The Gillys gave him a feeling for building in brick and for the aesthetics of the Gothic style (see left and opposite, above), and passed on to him the ideas of the French architects of the Revolutionary period, Claude Nicolas Ledoux and Jean-Nicolas-Louis Durand. Schinkel's first design for a museum, dated 1800, shows him applying his knowledge of French Revolutionary architecture. The plan is of a rectangular cube, square in effect and also comprising the elements prescribed by Durand – in other words, a rotunda, long exhibition halls with their accompanying galleries and square inner courtyards, with the whole building raised on a platform. Durand had specified that the design for a museum building should be a cube with a dome of moderate size rising above it. At a later date, Schinkel was to create the lofty yet practical design of his museum in the Berlin Lustgarten from the combination and interpenetration of circles, squares, and rectangles (see page 284).

Schinkel's earliest building, the Temple of Pomona in Potsdam, also dates from around 1800 (see opposite). It already displays the essential qualities that are to be found in his later architectural work: once more, the interpenetration of cubes and cylinders clearly demonstrates its close relationship to French Revolutionary architecture. The placing of the triangular gable on the front of the south façade and the round tower to the north illustrates Schinkel's instinctive feeling for the symbolism of architectural elements, while his keen sense of the functional shows in the design of the roof, which could be used as a viewing platform as well as protected from excessive sun and prying eyes by a simple structure of canopies and blinds. The Temple of Pomona was built while Schinkel was still training; a year later, in 1801, he set up independently as an architect.

Besides producing some designs, he took over some commissions already begun by Friedrich Gilly, who died in 1800, and began work on new commissions of his own. Schinkel thus embarked upon his own career in the tradition of Friedrich Gilly.

But the new construction work on the residences and in the country as a whole, a project upon which Frederick William II had embarked with such a level of enthusiasm and which his son Frederick William III continued, was interrupted when "the old Prussia" came to an end with the country's defeat by Napoleon's troops in the battle of Jena and Auerstedt in 1806.

Without commissions, Schinkel, like a great many of his colleagues, could no longer work as an architect and master builder. Instead, he painted Romantic landscapes and architectural fantasies, providing a diorama theater with scenes of famous places and historical events. He also brought his literary and philosophical education, his proliferation of ideas, and his depth of feeling to bear on stage sets, using themes that were to recur again and again later in the atmosphere and ideas conveyed by his architectural works. In 1810, at the prompting of Wilhelm von Humboldt, Frederick William III appointed Schinkel to a position in the service of the state. His really productive period, however, began only after the Wars of Liberation against Napoleon (1813–1815). He celebrated the end of the war with a design for a memorial, referring back to medieval German history (in the shape of Strasbourg Cathedral) in a modern and national architectural form.

Frederick William III's way of life was plain and thrifty even before the conflict with France, and even more so afterwards – during the whole of his 43-year reign, for instance, he did not add a single building of his own to the Potsdam Palace, but was content to use the buildings already in existence. During the same period, however, the face of Berlin itself was greatly changed, and the second great phase of planning began in Potsdam, where Frederick William III allowed his sons Frederick William (the later Frederick William IV), William (the later Emperor William I), and Carl to build. The landscape designer Peter Joseph Lenné and the architect Karl Friedrich Schinkel worked together on these projects in congenial collaboration, introducing far-reaching innovations.

It seems likely that Chancellor Karl August von Hardenberg had met the young Lenné at the Congress of Vienna, and persuaded him to enter the service of the Prussian Landscape Gardening Department. At any event, Hardenberg arranged a meeting between Schinkel and Lenné in 1816 during renovation work on his castle at Glienicke. Their subsequent collaboration must have proved fascinating for both men, and produced what could be called joint works in which it is not always easy to distinguish their individual contributions. A unique partnership developed, one comparable only with the brilliant years of the collaboration between

Friedrich Gilly
Entrance to Marienburg Castle (1794)
Pen and brush in brown ink, 37.8 x 34.2 cm, Potsdam, Stiftung Preussische Schlösser und Gärten Berlin-Brandenburg

In 1794, the architect Friedrich Gilly accompanied his father on a journey from which he brought back drawings of the castle at Marienburg, drawings that led to a revival of the appreciation of Gothic forms.

Karl Friedrich Schinkel
Design for the Temple of Pomona in Potsdam (1800)
Pen and black ink with watercolor and pencil, 19.4 x 26.3 cm; Berlin, Stiftung Stadtmuseum, Märkisches Museum

Schinkel built the Temple of Pomona in Privy Counsellor Karl Ludwig Oesfeld's vineyard on the southern slope of the Pfingstberg in Potsdam, which at the time still bore the name of the Judenberg. The "temple," completed in 1801, is Schinkel's first entirely independent design. The drawing shows the façade with its Ionic portico, set in rural surroundings. It was rebuilt in the 1990s from the fragments that had survived.

Berlin, casino in the park at Glienicke
Karl Friedrich Schinkel

The structure of the small casino on the bank of the Havel was made by extending the old billiard house that had stood there earlier. Schinkel did not demolish the old walls, but instead added another floor to the building itself as well as two pergolas, giving it an entirely different appearance in a manner extremely new for its time. The garden lies on one side of the Casino, and a wide expanse of lake and landscape on the other.

Humphrey Repton and John Nash in Britain. Garden designer and architect inspired each other to create an entire and consistent system, defining the structure of the environment with buildings and at the same time incorporating "natural elements" into architecture. Their system, in both regular and open planning schemes, is based on a grid pattern. Schinkel and Lenné followed philosophical ideas of the "enhancement" of nature and society, striving to convert the natural, moral, and political theories of the great thinkers of their time into model landscapes, towns, and villages. The fundamental pattern of French Revolutionary architecture, passed on to Schinkel by Gilly and acquired by Lenné from Durand himself at a seminar on design in 1810–1811, was the point of departure to which the artists constantly reverted: it featured the hippodrome as a favorite outdoor area and the exedra as a place for meditation.

The work at Glienicke came to a sudden end when Hardenberg died in 1822. However, it was resumed two years later when Prince Carl acquired the property for himself and his future wife, Marie of Saxe-Weimar. From the beginning, it was Prince Carl's aim to convert Glienicke into a vast landscape garden. The castle seemed ideal for just such a purpose, with its beautiful situation in the surrounding countryside as well as extensive views over the Havel, which broadened out like a lake at this point, and with its proximity to the main Berlin road.

Schinkel began by converting an old billiard house on the banks of the Havel into a casino (see above). The billiard house ran parallel to the lake, and he extended it by adding pergolas at the sides, thus employing "natural objects in architectural composition." Lenné created the first of the terraced gardens that were to feature prominently in his later work, using pergolas and terrace walls with slight differences of height. Another pergola on the downward slope of the bank in front of the building completed a design that was reminiscent of an Italian Renaissance garden.

The idea of providing an entrance to the garden from the old billiard house was abandoned during the planning stage, and a trompe l'oeil effect was substituted. The new casino thus became an enclosed "pleasure ground," and its effect is of a stage set obstructing the view. It looks out over the lake, and the pergolas seem to embrace the landscape. A pretend frigate anchored by the bank completed this "Italian scene."

Access to the interior of the building could be gained only through the pergolas at the sides and from the terrace in front. As a result of this, the landscaping follows a very unusual course, with sudden changes of views reflecting each other and creating an intriguing fusion of reality and illusion.

The manor house at Glienicke was built for Prince Carl between 1824 and 1827. As with the rebuilding of the Humboldt family's palace in Tegel (see above), Schinkel put into practice the insights he had acquired both during his studies and in collaboration with Gilly on the renovation of country houses in the March of Brandenburg; he also profited by his experiences during a study tour of Italy in 1803 to 1805. He wrote to the Berlin publisher, Unger: "On a journey through the mainland of Italy and its islands, I had the opportunity of collecting impressions of a number of interesting works of architecture which have not been either much regarded or much employed before … I intend to select items of a distinguished kind, reflecting the true nature of their country and their purpose, and as a consequence of this aim I will take the liberty of replacing individual features that in the original object may appear commonplace and without real character, by other and better features found in the same locality, in order to heighten the interest of the item." Describing and analysing a country house in Syracuse, he expressed his opinions on the free spatial composition of plants and buildings for the first version of his *Architektonisches Lehrbuch* (Manual on Architecture), which he was then planning to write.

Schinkel's aim at Glienicke was to build a villa rather than a palace (see page 300). He and Lenné therefore avoided the grandeur imparted to a building by great height or such features as axial symmetry between palace and garden. The charm and the extent of the entire complex was to reveal itself

Berlin, Tegel Palace (1820–1824)
Karl Friedrich Schinkel

Schinkel wrote of his plans for renovating the 16th-century castle: "The parts of the old tower that can still be used are the reason for providing the building with a tower at each corner, thus bringing out the character of the little castle. These small towers, their upper areas linked by galleries, contain rooms made very pleasant and comfortable by the many different views of their surroundings to be obtained from their windows."

naturally, as if in passing, as the visitor followed the garden's winding paths (see opposite).

Two drawings made by the later King Frederick William IV, and reminiscent of the plans for Glienicke, are evidence of his interest in the undertaking. When the small farm of Charlottenhof in the southwest part of Sanssouci park came up for sale in 1825, the crown prince was able to realize a similar project there.

Working in remarkable harmony, Schinkel and Lenné had the best possible conditions in which to draw up their plans to build Charlottenhof on the not very productive arable land and pastures of the small farm. Since their patron's nostalgic desire for surroundings expressive of humane ideals was combined with an ability to play a knowledgeable part in planning the design, both landscape gardener and architect had unique opportunities open to them. Their task was not so much the planning of a house for Frederick William as seeking "the architectural ideal ... whereby a building wholly fulfils its purpose in both concrete and intellectual terms, in all its parts and as a whole," as Schinkel put it. Lenné commented: "I was pleased to hear that the crown prince does not actually mean to reside permanently in the newly laid out property of Charlottenhof ... which is the site of an imaginative creation ... with the city of Potsdam behind it, so that the eye ... comes to rest on the magical atmosphere of a strange, dreamy world, an object of yearning."

In speaking of this "object of yearning," the crown prince almost always used the term "Siam" rather than the place's official name of Charlottenhof. He took a close interest the creation of the castle and park there, recording its progress in an unusually large number of sketches and designs.

At the time, he described himself as an "architect from Siam," even signing himself thus on a souvenir picture from Venice in 1829. There was more behind this whim than an affectation related to exotic architectural versions of China (Frederick II's garden pavilion) or Tahiti (the Tahitian Cabinet on Peacock Island). To the crown prince, Siam was a synonym for a better world. He wanted to realize his ideas of

Opposite
Berlin, the Grosse Neugierde, (1835–1837), Glienicke Palace
Karl Friedrich Schinkel

The Grosse Neugierde (Great Curiosity), was built on an artificial hill above the road between Berlin and Potsdam. Sitting on the bench that runs around it, visitors could take their ease and contemplate the changing views of the landscape through the spaces between the columns.

Berlin, Glienicke Palace (1824–1827)
Karl Friedrich Schinkel

Prince Carl of Prussia acquired the Glienicke estate in 1824, and Schinkel completed the extensive rebuilding of the castle to form a palace in 1827. The south side, shown here, is the main façade but does not contain the entrance.

Potsdam, Charlottenhof Palace
Karl Friedrich Schinkel
East side

From the east, the raised garden terrace makes the building look as if it were on a single floor. The portico has rather grave Doric columns rather than the delicate Ionic columns that might be expected in a garden façade.

a well-ordered community on his own estates, and his aim was to depict the nature of his future rule: it would derive from Romantic theories of the ideal state, and would achieve harmony between all interests and between people of all ranks.

The exotic imaginary location of "Siam" enabled the team planning it to apply architectural metaphors freely, without feeling compelled to conform to a distinct formal canon. Schinkel, Lenné, and the crown prince could draw on the entire cultural inheritance of their period in an iconographic program expressing both Frederick William's wish to harmonize political and social opposites and his understanding of practical solutions. The situation itself imposed certain constraints on them: these constraints included the boundaries of the site itself, the presence of existing farm buildings dating from the middle of the previous century, and the limited extent of the crown prince's purse. These constraints ultimately turned out to be an advantage.

The area was combined with the old deer park between Sanssouci and the New Palace (see page 194) to create an impression of "infinity," with views running from north to south; but trees were also planted to shield it from the neighboring road, fields, and gardens, so that only "slight suggestions of the city of Potsdam" remained visible.

The existing eastern boundary of the property, where the Schafgraben flowed into the Havel, was converted into a picturesque watercourse and widened to look like a lake. Cleverly varied effects created by excavation and the addition of material to improve the soil gave the flat land the charm of a hilly landscape. The dense wood on the game park side of the property remained, and the landscape's own unique dynamic was revealed by emphasizing the contrast between areas of open water and meadowland to the east and the dark woodland to the west.

The axial design of the palace

The logical architectural structure of the castle axis, running east to west, was used to create an image of the course of the day and the "course of the world," an allegory of eternity. This axial design was constructed in several phases of development. A crucial phase was Schinkel's decision to situate the steam engine house, later demolished, at its eastern end. The "fiery machine" symbolized the origin of all life: it could stand for sunrise, and it also pumped the water that the garden needed.

The view concluded with the last part of the garden to be laid out, a hippodrome at the western end.

Potsdam, Roman Baths (1829–1836), Charlottenhof
Karl Friedrich Schinkel

The group of buildings now known as the "Roman Baths," consisting of the court gardener's house, the house for his assistant, the tea pavilion and the baths themselves, was built to accommodate the court gardener of the park at Charlottenhof. In its structure and details, the court gardener's house follows the type of post-classical free-standing farmhouse, built of horizontal and vertical stone blocks with shallow penthouse roofing over open roof trusses, and surrounded by summerhouse arbors of the kind that fascinated northern visitors to Italy.

Lying beyond the dark woods into which the setting sun disappeared, this was to be a place suggesting both liberty and the long duration of time. The palace terrace stood at the center of the axis (see page 302), and was a place where the king, a "man raised by fate to eminence," could show himself to his people in a "natural" resolution of the conflict between rulers and subjects and an expression of "the all-embracing principle" (Novalis). Thus, the intellectual world of the natural philosophers assumed architectural and landscape form.

As with the casino at Glienicke, the funds available meant that when the manor house was converted into a villa for the crown prince and his wife, as much as possible of the existing building had to be retained. Schinkel and Ludwig Persius, the architect who executed the project, succeeded in creating a new building by radically simplifying the old one. The original manor house stood on a suitable enough site for the new castle. The old court gardener's house (the dairy) near the stream was redesigned to make a welcoming entrance to the palace, and a new gardener's house was built by the open water of the pool and pumping station for the steam engine, with the buildings known as the Roman Baths grouped around it (see page 302).

The court gardener's house follows Italian models and offers an ideal picture of a carefree lifestyle, removed from both the formal conventionality of the "rich and idle" and the uncultured boorishness of the "laboring poor." Open and enclosed areas, both outside and inside, are linked together around the vertical axis of the tower which, as it is also a water reservoir, represents the life-giving focal point of the

Potsdam, Charlottenhof Palace (1826–1829)
Karl Friedrich Schinkel
View from the northwest

In rebuilding the manor house at Charlottenhof, Schinkel gave the building a raised transverse axis with a portico to both west and east. The western façade is on two floors and has an enclosed appearance. It is set against a grove of dark chestnut trees. The more open, eastern side faces the exedra, where visitors could sit as if in a theater and watch the world go by.

Carl Grael
View of the Glienicke Bridge from Babelsberg Palace
Watercolor, since 1945, lost in the war

Schinkel always included designs for the fittings and furnishings. This watercolor by Carl Graer shows Schinkel's delicate ironwork, scarcely interrupting the views of the expansive landscape seen through the large windows. The view here is of the Glienicke Bridge linking the Berlin bank with the Potsdam bank of the river. The Grosse Neugierde (Great Curiosity) and Glienicke Palace are visible on one side, and the Villa Schönigen on the other.

entire complex and is a practical counterpart to the "fountain of life" on the castle terrace (see page 305).

The court gardener's house and the buildings that are grouped around it are in marked contrast to the palace of Charlottenhof, imparting new significance to the dichotomy between the grandeur of a palace and the picturesque nature of its auxiliary buildings, an idea familiar since the Renaissance and late Baroque. Setting palace off against cottage had once been a frivolous game, but here the unequal partners stand side by side on equal terms, acquiring profound social significance in the architects' artistic program.

The difference in architectural styles: its impact

The contrast inherent in the architecture of the palace and the gardener's house was not glossed over; in fact the differences resulting from their different purposes were emphasized and exploited, their mutual dependency was visibly expressed as a principle of the design.

The official and private relations between the crown prince and the court gardener, aristocratic guests and ordinary wayfarers, masters and journeymen, domestic households and the social authorities were presented in an idealized version of the hierarchical society, showing the evolution of its traditional rules in harmony with eternal progress and constant change.

The system created here out of elements of landscape design, architecture, and horticulture, with their visual and functional interaction, appears like a proposal for the harmonious co-existence of members of society in a changing world.

This new theory stemmed from France and the large claims made by Ledoux's tract on *L'Architecture considérée sous le rapport de l'art, des mœurs et de la législation* (Architecture Considered with Respect to Art, Customs, and Legislation). In 1820, Gabriel Thouin had submitted plans for a huge park of over 2,500 hectares (6,180 acres), to enclose the palace of Versailles with its Baroque park and the smaller château buildings as historical monuments. Lenné had worked with Gabriel Thouin during his visit to Paris in 1811, and many aspects of his plans for Sanssouci after 1816 show Thouin's influence. It may be assumed that the inclusion of the New Palace in the plans for Charlottenhof derives from Thouin's plan for Versailles.

Even while he was working on Glienicke, Lenné was already thinking of bringing the Babelsberg, rising to 44 meters (144 feet) above the Havel, into the Potsdam landscape of castles and gardens (see above). When Prince William expressed a wish for a summer residence of his own, Lenné drew his attention to this site at the eastern end of the Potsdam lakes. Early sketches by Crown Prince Frederick William of a long, low building like an Italian villa with features of a Norman castle show that he took a keen interest in his brother's project. King Frederick William III hesitated for some time before allowing his son, later Emperor William I, to build here, and did not give his permission for the purchase of the site until 1833.

Schinkel's best pupil, Ludwig Persius, had already been commissioned to draw up the first plans in 1831. Following the wishes of the princely couple, he designed a building in the Gothic style. Augusta of Saxe-Weimar, who had married Prince William in 1829, was particularly fond of the British Gothic style and had her own clear ideas on the building of the palace. The final plans were entrusted to Schinkel in 1833, and were influenced by the wishes of his patron, the limitations of the budget, and the difficult terrain.

Schinkel proposed to construct a long building running from the pergola to the east, by way of the octagonal tower, in a gently rising line culminating in the tall flagpole tower (see below). The front of the building is set back from the octagon to enhance the spatial effect of the façade as a whole. During Schinkel's lifetime, only the part from the pergola to the octagon was completed, in 1835.

Schinkel had planned to build a corridor along the slope of the hillside next, and a start had already been made on it, but this feature, an important one in terms of utilizing the space available, was omitted from the revised plans drawn up by Persius in 1844 so as to create more space at the back of the building. Today, the general impression of the palace is determined largely by the revision of Schinkel's plans, carried out first by Persius and then by Strack, when work on the building continued between 1844 and 1849.

Schinkel's role with the Prussian state

Schinkel first entered the service of the Prussian state in 1810, and until his death in 1841 held state appointments of increasing importance. In the

Johann Heinrich Hintze
Charlottenhof, view from the arcaded hall of the Roman Baths (c. 1845)
Watercolor (now lost)

Hintze's watercolor shows the view of the park at Charlottenhof and on into the distance, as seen from the arcade above the Romano-Pompeian baths. The towers of the city of Potsdam and the mountains on the far side of the Havel are visible in the background.

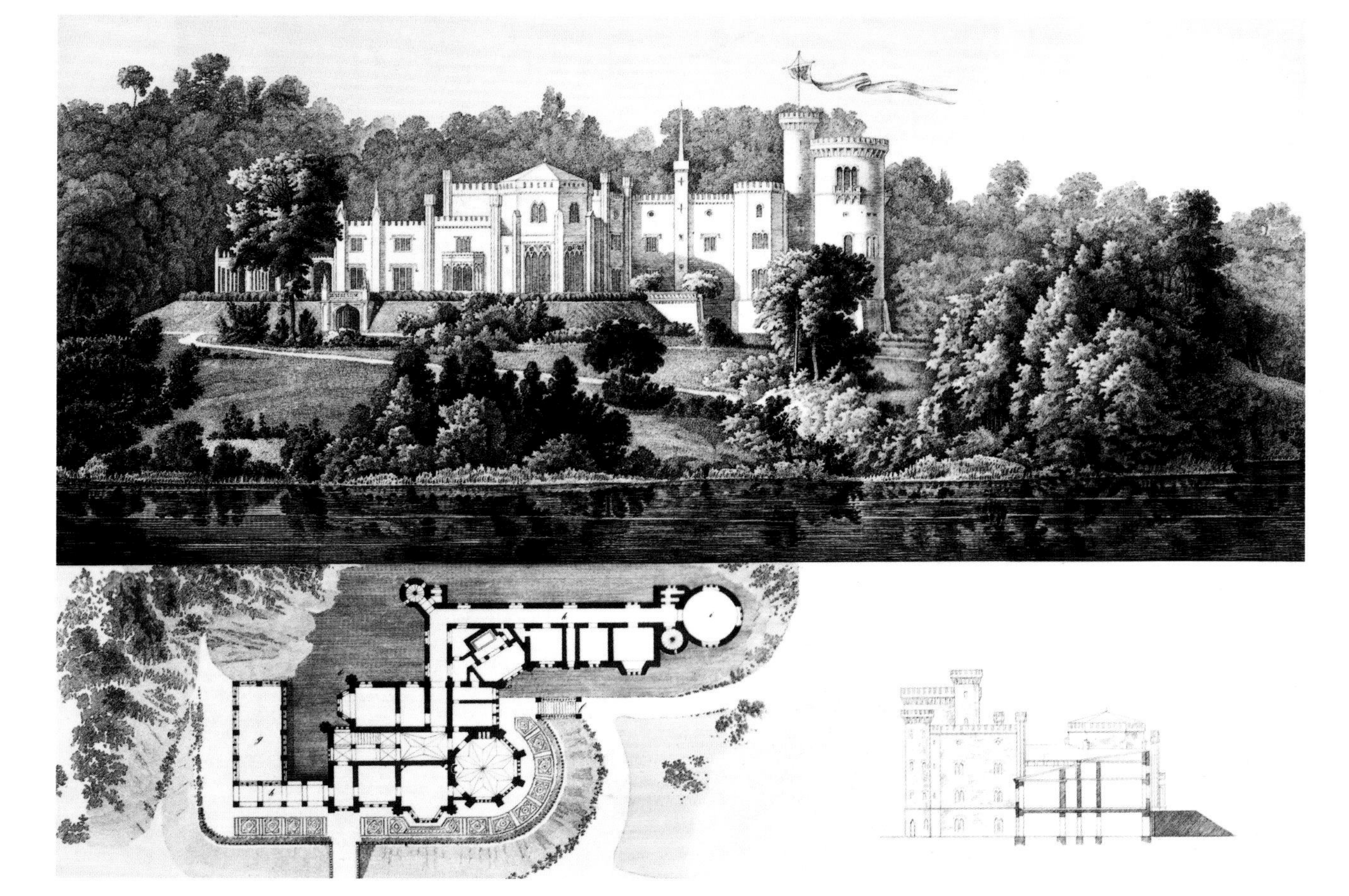

Karl Friedrich Schinkel
Design for Prince William's palace on the Babelsberg, near Potsdam
Engraving, 41 x 52 cm; Potsdam, Stiftung Preussische Schlösser und Gärten Berlin-Brandenburg, Plankammer

Schinkel provides a view, ground plan and cross section of Babelsberg Palace as he intended to build it. In accordance with Prince William's wishes, the palace was to be built halfway up the slope of the hillside above the Havel. Schinkel suggested a building complex resembling a medieval castle, only a part of which, for financial reasons, was to be built at first. Changes were made to Schinkel's design by his successors, and determined the eventual appearance of the building.

capacity of an administrator, he showed a remarkable talent for organization and an ability to reconcile aesthetic requirements with the budget available. Besides his designs for palaces in Potsdam, he was much involved with the construction of a whole series of new buildings in the center of Berlin, bringing order and harmony to the heart of the city as it took its place among the great capitals of Europe.

Schinkel had planned a well-ordered, harmonious urban design that would meet all the legitimate demands of its inhabitants. Schinkel was not solely concerned with the buildings that gave the center of the growing city its character; he also turned his attention to streets and squares, bridges, waterways, and promenades, sometimes designing and executing them himself, sometimes providing ideas for their conversion and extension. Even to his contemporaries, it was obvious that the new urban structure of the city center was one of his major achievements. He made the inner city of Berlin an integrated work of art, and he can take his place among the great architects of the 19th century who were active in town planning and urban building.

Schinkel's initiation of new projects in Berlin

In 1818, Schinkel initiated several projects of importance for Berlin. First was the reconstruction of the Schauspielhaus (theater) in the Gendarmenmarkt. The National Theater (Nationaltheater) built in 1802 by Carl Gotthard Langhans (see page 277) had been destroyed by fire in July 1817, and only the shell was left standing; Schinkel was commissioned to rebuild the theater.

The opportunities open to him were considerably restricted by the circumstances: the foundation walls of the old building had to be used again, and he had to coordinate the various parts of a very extensive plan. He converted Langhans's long rectangular building into a cross-shaped complex looking out over the square (see top, right). The exterior was classically designed, with verticals and horizontals forming a pattern on the walls, and only the portico consisting of the traditional pilasters and columns.

The king had wanted a harmonious exterior, and Schinkel complemented it with a functional design for the interior; he divided the building into three main areas, with the theater in the middle (see below, right), flanked by a concert hall with its foyer (see page 307), and by wardrobes and rehearsal rooms.

On May 21, 1821, the Schauspielhaus in the Gendarmenmarkt was opened, with a prologue by Goethe, as below:

> "So for your sake the architect has striven,
> And with rare skill to these fine rooms has given
> A harmony that minds and hearts will cheer,
> And you yourselves will feel well ordered here."

On this occasion, Schinkel had a view of the theater itself painted as a backcloth for the stage. "The curtain went up, and we saw before us, faithfully and correctly painted by Gropius, the magnificent theater in which we were sitting, and the two stately towers between which it stands on the great square," wrote the correspondent of a contemporary journal, the *Nachrichten von Staats- und Gelehrtensachen* (News of State and Scholarly Affairs).

The new structural organization of the exterior of the theater pointed to the future; it was a system that could be applied to other building projects, and served Schinkel's pupils and successors for the whole of the next century.

In the Casino he built in Potsdam at the same time, Schinkel himself showed that it would also suit buildings that were not symmetrically designed around an axis. Throughout his architectural career, Schinkel worked on the principle of the balanced composition of spatial and architectural components around horizontal and vertical coordinates. What is more, he did this without feeling any obligation to observe axial symmetry.

In the same way as when he built the Berlin Schauspielhaus, Schinkel used the cruciform interpenetration of a long, low shape and a short, tall shape in his rebuilding of the main house and the court gardener's house at Charlottenhof – in the one case converting what appears on the outside to be an axially symmetrical building, in the other creating a structure of irregular shape.

Opposite
Berlin, the Schauspielhaus in the Gendarmenmarkt, foyer of the concert hall
Historical photograph (c. 1935)

Schinkel ornamented the concert hall and adjacent rooms more lavishly than the auditorium of the theater. They had artificial marble on the walls and columns, white and gold ceilings, coffering with brightly colored figural ornamentation, and busts of famous composers, actors, and dramatists in the niches.

Karl Friedrich Schinkel
Perspective view of the Schauspielhaus on the Gendarmenmarkt, Berlin
Pen and black ink, brush and brown ink, color wash, highlights in white, 47.4 x 74.5 cm; Berlin, Staatliche Museen zu Berlin – Preussischer Kulturbesitz

Schinkel was commissioned to rebuild Berlin's main theater when the National Theater burned down. Here he describes the exterior of the new building to the king: "The central placing of the theater, as the essential part of the building, produces an effect of height interrupting the long and uniform mass of the old building, and gives a pyramidal shape to the whole. Flat roofs, and frontispieces above the entrances, endow the building with nobility of style after the manner of Greek architecture."

Karl Friedrich Schinkel
Perspective view of the auditorium in the Schauspielhaus on the Gendarmenmarkt in Berlin, from the Sammlung Architektonischer Entwürfe (1826)
Pen and ink, 33.3 x 42.4 cm; Berlin, Staatliche Museen zu Berlin – Preussischer Kulturbesitz

Schinkel describes the way in which the auditorium was laid out, "so that for the most part the boxes have the stage almost directly in front of them, and even the worst seat in the house provides a full view of the front of the stage and over half the back of it. In the manner of many French theaters, there is a gallery which provides very agreeable seating in front of the boxes."

Friedrich Hebbel

The call for a public art collection and a building in which to house it

Ever since the end of the 18th century, Prussian scholars and artists had been calling for a public art collection. Only after 1815, however, did these demands take concrete shape. The first stimulus came with the return of some of the works of art removed to Paris in 1806, and museums in the great capitals of Paris, Vienna, and London provided inspiration. But the real turning point did not come until January 1823, when Schinkel submitted his designs and a report on the building of the Berlin Museum (which would later be known as the Old Museum).

His plans were for a large, handsome building looking out over the Lustgarten and facing the royal palace. Work began on the foundations in 1824, and the museum was opened six years later (see opposite, and pages 310–311). Schinkel had found a forward-looking style for his task, and the situation of this museum (which was an expression of middle-class culture) opposite the castle made the Lustgarten the real center of the city. The museum façade now occupied one side of the square, adjoining the sides where the armory and cathedral stood, and the castle façade formed the fourth side. Schinkel's proposals for the reorientation of the center of Berlin were completed later, when the rectangular building of the Architectural Academy (see page 312) was built from 1831 to 1836, forming a perfect visual relationship with the museum building seen across the Spree.

The open stairway of the museum, one of the most effective such designs in modern architecture, gave visitors many different views of the city (see page 313). They could feel raised above the square and at their ease, as if on a large, roofed platform on the same level at the staterooms of the royal residence. This platform design is an explicit expression of the growing confidence of democratic forces during this era. Schinkel always tried to combine the functionality of a building with the dignity of its appearance, to reinforce and foster the values and positive emotions of those who used it, and he successfully achieved that effect in the Berlin Museum.

While the museum was under construction, the prolonged building projects drawn up for the Friedrichwerdersche church entered a new phase: a decision was taken on the church's design and a plan to integrate it into the Werderscher Markt. After several alternative proposals for a building in the form of a Roman or a Doric Corinthian temple had been put forward, the plans drawn up in 1823–1824 were adopted. As with the castle at Babelsberg, British models were the inspiration for these plans.

Both the Gothic design of the whole and its Gothic details were incorporated into the rationalist structure of Neo-classical thought. The simplicity of the building called for particularly careful treatment of the exposed brickwork, and had to be handled in a manner appropriate to each part of the building.

In the lowland plain of northern Germany, an area where there is little stone, building in brick had already reached a high standard of expertise in the Middle Ages. Like Friedrich Gilly, Schinkel restored this traditional material to a position of importance in architecture.

In 1819, he designed his first entirely brick building, the military guardhouse in Berlin, explaining his ideas in a detailed report. Schinkel found a remarkably able ceramic artist to assist him with his brick buildings in the person of Tobias Christoph Feilner. A handsome house was built for Feilner to plans by Schinkel in 1829. The façade on the street had courses of colored brick and terracotta ornamentation in many shades, made by Ludwig Wichmann from Schinkel's designs.

The Architectural Academy

Schinkel's achievements in this field were put to good use in the planning and building of the Architectural Academy (see page 312). It was to stand on the vacant site of the former Packhof, between the Werdersche Mühlen on the Spree and the Friedrichwerdersche church. The site formed a long triangular shape running along the left bank of the Spree, with the point of the triangle extending to the Schloss Bridge in the north.

The free-standing building (demolished in the 1960s after suffering war damage) was intended to accommodate the Architectural Academy and the administrative headquarters of the Supreme Planning and Building Department. The plans also provided for shops that could be rented out in the lower parts of the new building.

As early as 1827, Schinkel had the idea of a large store that would serve as both a commercial center and a place where Berliners and visitors to the city could meet. "At present, one may seek such a place in vain." He designed a building with three wings, apparently on two floors as seen from the outside but with four floors inside. It was to be surrounded by a low courtyard planted with trees (see page 312). A system of uprights and cornices was to divide the face of the building. A balustrade, a flat roof and a tent roof of painted sheet metal running round it in front of the lower floor gave the structure additional horizontal emphasis.

There was provision for over a hundred separate shops on the first floor and third floor, with the apartments in which their tenants would live on the second and fourth floors. The interior of the building, to be visible in part from the outside, was to have interconnecting vaulted ceilings.

The Architectural Academy, on the other hand, was built to a square ground plan with four façades of equal proportions and an internal courtyard. The façades of the building, which was four floors high, each had eight sections. With the exception of the

Lighthouse on Cape Arkona (1836–1827)
Karl Friedrich Schinkel

This functional building followed a clear principle of construction, linking it, in Schinkel's design, to the Neo-classical approach. The division of the walls into separate areas, with recessed windows and a clear emphasis on the divisions between the floors, makes the building resemble Schinkel's plan (never realized) for a large Berlin store. The lighthouse was built by the Supreme Planning and Building Department of Berlin, under Privy Chief Architect Günther, and still stands today.

Opposite
Berlin, Rotunda of the Old Museum (Altes Museum) in the Lustgarten (1823–1830)
Karl Friedrich Schinkel

Schinkel's ground plan for the Berlin Museum in the Lustgarten is brilliant in its simplicity. The central rotunda is set in the transverse rectangular building, which has four wings. The rotunda, its circular shape accentuated by the pillars running around it, forms the architectural center and focus of the building, and gives access to the great halls containing the collections.

Berlin, Old Museum (Altes Museum) (1823–1830)
Karl Friedrich Schinkel

In the memorandum on his plans for the Berlin Museum, Schinkel writes: "The beauty of the surroundings is perfected by this building, which for the first time encloses the beautiful square of the Lustgarten in an appropriate manner on its fourth side." The architect opposed suggestions for alterations: "The design forms a unified whole, its parts connecting in such a way that nothing essential can be changed without distorting the structure."

GENAE ET ARTIVM LIBERALIVM MVSEVM CONSTITVIT MDCCCXXVIII
Antiken
sammlung

Eduard Gaertner
Architectural Academy, Berlin (1869)
Oil on canvas, 63 x 82 cm; Berlin, Staatliche Museen zu Berlin – Preussischer Kulturbesitz, Nationalgalerie

The painting shows the colorful appearance (resulting from the brick) of the Architectural Academy built by Schinkel 1831–1836 on the site of the old Packhof. Its exterior is divided into separate areas by vertical pillars with cornices between floors. In the use of the lowest floor for shops, the commerce of the city was integrated with administrative and educational buildings.

north side, where the two main entrances were situated, they were all identical.

A framework structure visible from the outside (unlike that of the design for the store) with load-bearing pillars, their vertical direction in contrast to the horizontal cornices between all four floors, divided the building clearly. The pillars rose from the basement story of the building and up to the main cornice running along the roof. They were built separately and linked only by arches and iron stays, a new method anticipating future developments. Only when the skeleton was in place were the walls in between then added. The exterior had a cladding of smoothly-laid, and carefully-chosen, sharp-edged courses of colored brick. Finally, the larger ornamental panels were fitted from top to bottom.

In his work *Sammlung Architektonischer Entwürfe* (Collection of Architectural Designs), Schinkel wrote: "The building is in brick, and the exterior is neither whitewashed nor plastered. The material has therefore been worked with particular care. All the structural elements and cornices, all the ornaments and bas-reliefs, the uprights (in the nature of herm pillars) in the broad windows, and the infilling of the arches they support are constructed with great precision in brick," as also were the richly ornamented windows and the courses of brickwork glazed in different colors. The fantastic plants on the reliefs of the gateways were suggested by the poet Goethe's treatise *Metamorphose der Pflanzen* (The Metamorphosis of Plants), in a Romantically enigmatic style symbolically alluding to humanity. A different association of ideas seemed to be indicated by the figural depictions at each gateway (for instance, architecture as science and architecture as art), while the window breasts of the second floor illustrated the history of the development of architecture.

The master architect

Schinkel was one of the master architects of the city of Berlin. During his lifetime, the old 18th-century residence and capital city of Prussia became an international metropolis, the third largest in Europe. The number of inhabitants, which had been around 200,000 in 1800 and had then decreased considerably during the years of Prussia's misfortunes, quickly rose again after the Wars of Liberation, so that by 1819 the population count was over 200,000. In 1830, Berlin had a population of 245,000, and by 1840 about 350,000. Architecturally, Schinkel gave Berlin a European stature.

However, his buildings and his achievements in urban design were not the sum total of his influence:

Michael Carl Gregorovius
View of the Lustgarten from the stairway of the Berlin Old Museum
Watercolor (1843), 30.9 x 50.9 cm; Potsdam, Stiftung Preussische Schlösser und Gärten Berlin-Brandenburg, Plankammer

A stairway stands in front of the rotunda, its initially narrow steps opening out to the wide space on the second of the upper floors. Exterior and interior are directly related to each other by the double row of columns.

Opposite, below
Karl Friedrich Schinkel
Design for a store in Unter den Linden, Berlin (1827)
Watercolor and pencil, 18.7 x 55.4 cm; Berlin, Staatliche Museen zu Berlin – Preussischer Kulturbesitz

In his plans and report for a large store near the Academy in Unter den Linden, Schinkel submitted an architectural idea entirely new to Berlin and to Prussia. The proposal was turned down by the king for reasons of expense and the building's situation.

his theories, his principles of form, and his practical example molded an entire generation of the Berlin School of Architecture, so-called after Schinkel. His talents and achievements also had an inspiring influence on other parts of Germany and Europe, and do so to this day.

Schinkel's artistic universality and his interest in technical progress are also evident in the design and making of furniture and craftworks. He himself personified the idea of the combination of architect and designer, a concept not generally current until the 20th century.

Schinkel's part in the industrialization of Berlin

Schinkel played a large part in the rapid industrialization of Berlin and the intensive encouragement of commerce in the city. In his view, this encouragement of trade and industry should include the thorough training of craftsmen both in technology and in style. He wanted craftsmen to work as far as possible to historical and more particularly classical models, but with the aid of the latest technical processes, most of which had been imported from Britain and France.

In 1837 he wrote: "Finally, I hope I may be allowed to remark that recent inventions and improvements enabling works of art to be duplicated faithfully, easily, and safely may properly be used to give industry a direction in which beauty is as important as utility. I cannot, as many do, regret the mechanical progress that turns the artist's attention increasingly towards the intellectual element in the production of works of art, something that no machinery can replace. Anything that a machine can imitate and duplicate perfectly is no longer in the realms of art. But if a work of art can be mechanically duplicated both faithfully and with ease, and thus distributed to all classes of society, if the knowledge of that work need no longer be acquired solely in museums or in those private collections to which access is difficult, then we may hope that here and there one of the seeds thus broadcast will take root and eventually bear fruit."

Architecture under King Frederick William IV: The Period after Karl Friedrich Schinkel

"Don't lose heart, Schinkel, we'll build together some day!" Crown Prince Frederick William had told his architect in the lean years of the early decades of the 19th century. However, not long after the crown prince came to the throne as King Frederick William IV in June 1840, Schinkel fell sick. He did not survive the year.

The new king, who as crown prince had taken a passionate interest in architectural projects and produced drawings as well as ideas of his own as work progressed, now wanted to build in both town and country, but particularly in his capital, Berlin, and in his favorite residence, Potsdam. After Schinkel's death, he felt the lack of the great architect's restraining influence and guiding genius. Moreover, it was now out of the question for him to keep the promises he had made as crown prince to his architect and respected teacher. Frederick William's political principles had changed: the idea of "kingship for the people" expressed in the "Siam" project realized at Charlottenhof Palace in the collaboration between Schinkel, Lenné, and the crown prince gave way after his accession to a policy of restoration and the conviction of his divine right as king.

After 1840, the direction taken by architecture in Prussia was largely determined by Schinkel's former pupils and colleagues. There were a great many good, well-trained architects: prominent among them were Ferdinand von Arnim, Ludwig Ferdinand Hesse, Eduard Knoblauch, Ludwig Persius, Albert Dietrich Schadow, Johann Heinrich Strack, and Friedrich August Stüler. They had at their disposal the freedom of method devised by Schinkel, and a knowledge of both traditional architecture and the work of their European contemporaries; they possessed sound building skills and the ability to make technical innovations. But they lacked Schinkel's authority in his dealings with the king: to Frederick William, they were there simply to carry out his ideas rather than their own.

The leading architects of the period – among whom Friedrich Ludwig Persius and August Stüler occupied leading positions as the royal architects – therefore continued to develop architecture in line with the king's new concepts rather than those he had entertained while he was still crown prince. Fundamental changes took place both in Berlin, where Stüler (born in 1800) was particularly successful, and in Potsdam, where the leading architect until his premature death was Persius (born in 1803), working in collaboration with Lenné.

In Berlin, Schinkel's museum building, the Old Museum (Alte Museum), soon proved too small,

August Stüler
Design for Museum Island (Museumsinsel) in Berlin (1841–1846)
View of the front (top left), view of the rotunda in the 3rd courtyard (top right), view looking out on the Spree, lithograph, 1862 (from the 1841 watercolor); Potsdam, Stiftung Preussische Schlösser und Gärten Berlin-Brandenburg, Plankammer

Stüler's first plans for Museum Island showed the New Museum, consisting of a tall temple-like structure among a series of buildings arranged around three courtyards, housing collections, workshops, and the Academy of Art.

New Museum, Berlin, Hall of Western Art on the second upper floor, Cabinet of Engravings
August Stüler
Photograph of 1920

Here Stüler used the new method of building in iron to construct the framework of the building and also to create different spatial impressions. He emphasizes the constructional forces brought into play by using decorative openwork elements, with figural ornamentation illustrating the purpose for which the area was designed. The building was destroyed in the World War II, but is to be rebuilt as a museum and will retain its character as a memorial.

and shortly after his accession to the throne Frederick William IV decided to "convert the whole of the island in the Spree behind the Museum into a shrine of art and science." In 1841, Stüler was commissioned to draw up plans. He created a structure in clearly distinct sections to stand behind Schinkel's museum, with buildings rising to different heights and grouped around courtyards of three different designs (see opposite). The New Museum (Neue Museum) followed the Schinkel tradition, and was a plain building with little ornamentation. The interior was dominated by new technology and science, its plain decoration helping in effect to interpret the exhibits to the visitor and reflecting the current state of scholarship in the presentation of art and history.

In a very limited sense, the royal plans for this shrine of art and science as a contrast to the Berlin Palace realized Schinkel's design of 1835 for the "residence of a prince." At that time, Schinkel's vision of an ideal state reconciling the aristocratic and middle-class spheres had been created not least at the crown prince's suggestion and with his sympathetic interest.

Despite the great respect he felt for his principal architect, however, the crown prince did not pass this idealistic plan for publication in the proposal Schinkel intended to write, and after he came to the throne as Frederick William IV such innovative ideas of kingship for the people stood no chance of architectural expression in the context of town planning. Even Schinkel's own ideas were now becoming increasingly misinterpreted.

Potsdam, the New Orangery at Sanssouci (1851–1864)
View of the landscape over the park of Sanssouci from one of the two belvedere towers

The two towers, the portico between them, and the upper viewing platform provide a wide view over the landscape. The uneven number of columns counters any sense that the center dominates the building, and visitors walking in the portico can view the landscape without being drawn to a specific focus.

Lenné must have anticipated this development in 1839 when he published a colored lithograph showing an ideal view of the recently completed "Charlottenhof, or Siam." When he became king, Frederick William IV abandoned his former plans for realizing a better world, and showed it by moving the pheasantry from the animal park in Berlin to the game preserves of Potsdam: Lenné's plan for a complex in natural surroundings to the southwest of the New Palace was rejected, and the pheasantry complex, designed by Ludwig Persius, with its farmhouse, carriage house and stables, yards, and enclosures, was situated on a newly created axis west of the Charlottenhof hippodrome. To provide areas for rearing and feeding game, and for the benefit of the Royal Hunt Department, the hippodrome was separated from the Charlottenhof land by a woodland ride and a fence.

However, Lenné still retained his influence over the king. It was he who created the image of the surroundings of Potsdam as a diverse but perfectly harmonious landscape, in contrast to the disordered and unchecked growth of the metropolis of Berlin.

This period, when living space was constantly being extended, saw the emergence of the concept of the "concentrated image" of a given subject, to employ Lenné's phrase. The idea was to focus the viewer's eye and so encourage a more perceptive

response to landscape. To this end, buildings providing good views were erected on the hills around Potsdam. The old town ramparts that had once served defensive purposes now had a new function: in their free time the citizens could leave the narrow streets of the town to walk on the ramparts, looking out over the surrounding countryside and into the distance.

Potsdam, the New Orangery at Sanssouci (1851–1864)
August Stüler and Ludwig Ferdinand Hesse
View from the north

A large tea-room on the north side of the New Orangery gives a view of the landscaped area in front of it, the land around Bornstedt, and the lake. In the foreground, a stele dedicated to the Roman goddess Juno presides over a semicircle sunk in the turf, perhaps to suggest a classical amphitheater.

Changes to the palace at Sanssouci

Frederick II himself had taken meditative walks along the upper terrace of his palace at Sanssouci, looking out over the beautiful landscape of the glacial valley where Potsdam lay. At the end of his life he had a belvedere constructed at the western end of the range of hills, on the Klausberg. Its sole purpose was to provide a good view. This was the first of many similar buildings erected on the hills around Potsdam. Frederick William II provided his new Marble Palace on the Heiligersee with a belvedere on its roof, and a Gothic tower on the Brauhausberg followed around 1800.

Crown Prince Frederick William planned an entire promenade above the gardens of Frederick II, the Great, to reveal a series of changing views. He dreamed of a *via triumphalis*, a triumphal way in honor of his celebrated ancestor and for the contemplation of his legacy.

After many drawings and imaginative sketches had been made, the first step was taken with the building of the triumphal gate at the foot of the royal vineyards in 1851. Frederick William's ideas at this time had been formed by real buildings in Italy, and Stüler and Hesse built the New Orangery (1851–1864) in imitation of an Italian villa to suit the king's new tastes (see right). Its two towers, like those of the Villa Medici, could now preside over the landscape rising naturally above the village of Bornstedt, while terraces in Frederick II's gardens ran down the slope to the south in the same way as those of the Villa d'Este in Tivoli, near Rome. Here Lenné created the Sicilian Garden, still bright in summer today with container-grown southern flora. Palms and agaves mix happily with casts of classical statues on a marble wall surmounted by a fountain. Lenné designed the Northern Garden, which was dominated by evergreens, to face the Sicilian Garden.

The central hall of the New Orangery contains copies of works by Raphael, and on both sides of it there are long, high-ceilinged rooms for growing southern plants, with corner pavilions copied from the Uffizi in Florence. The two towers are linked by a portico with an open viewing platform above it; visitors walking here have an almost uninterrupted view of the various landscape views (see opposite). Although the rest of the building was designed with axial symmetry, the portico has an uneven number of columns, without any focal point at the center.

An open tea-room on the northern side once linked the rooms of the central building with the garden (see page 318). It was one of the many charming tea-rooms situated by Frederick William in various parts of the Potsdam landscape.

The light falling in from the south directs the eye to the farmland around Bornstedt, which seen from this vantage point appears to have been transformed into an Italian view. Subsequently, and in line with these ideas, other buildings were erected to provide fine views. Frederick II's Ruinenberg (Hill of Ruins) had a Norman tower added to it.

Lenné provided a new version of Frederick's prospect on this hill, making the temple on the southern side resemble the Temple of the Sibyl in Tivoli, with

Potsdam, the New Orangery at Sanssouci (1851–1864)
August Stüler and Ludwig Ferdinand Hesse
View from the north

Long halls containing plants stand on both sides of rooms for the king's guests, which are arranged around a picture gallery. The central part of the building looks out on a large courtyard to the south, which has terraces and fountains, and which slopes down to the park like an Italian Renaissance garden.

Franz Michelis
Belvedere on the Pfingstberg (1861)
Oil on canvas, 138 x 223 cm;
Potsdam, Stiftung Preussische Schlösser und Gärten Berlin-Brandenburg, Plankammer

Franz Michelis shows that the belvedere on the Pfingstberg was built to provide a view of Potsdam as an "ideal landscape." His painting depicts the lakes, woods, and parks, and the eye is drawn to the main buildings, including the engine house and casino in Glienicke; the castle, court ladies' house, and Flatow Tower in Babelsberg; the Moorish Temple, Marble Palace and Gothic Library in the New Garden; the Heiliggeistkirche (Church of the Holy Spirit), Old City Hall, the Nikolaikirche, and Garnison Kirche (Garrison Church) in the city; the Norman tower on the Ruinenberg, with the Alexander Nevsky Chapel and Temple of Pomona in the middle ground of the picture.

a waterfall on the slope below and a view of Sanssouci, like another Hadrian's Villa, above. On the other side of the hill the new tower, together with the old round wall and the road lined with oaks and pines on the north slope of the Ruinenberg, looked like a medieval ruined castle from a northern land.

These buildings reached their culmination with the Belvedere on the Pfingstberg. Work on it began in 1847, but it could not be completed until 1863, after a ten-year interruption, and even then the whole plan was not executed (see above). In its fragmentary form, this building served no purpose but to afford fine views, and it satisfied the hunger for such views by allowing visitors to climb different ascents of varying gradients, rising higher and higher until they reached the top platforms of the towers, which offered the most extensive view of the landscape; if they looked downward, they would look into the profound and mysterious depths of the dark pool in the inner courtyard.

If this kind of architecture was the expression of private sensibilities, the many churches built by King Frederick William IV are the "public" statement of his divine right. The king aimed to create a new religious basis for state and society modeled on the Early Christian community, and felt the architectural expression of this intention was best realized in the form of Early Christian basilicas.

The rebuilding of the Nikolaikirche

The rebuilding of the Nikolaikirche in Potsdam began as a collaboration between the crown prince and Schinkel (see page 320). This church had burned down in 1795, and Schinkel was commissioned to rebuild it in 1826.

Years before, Friedrich Gilly had planned to rebuild it in the form of a rectangular cube – to contrast with nearby buildings, notably Jean de Bodt's Fortuna Gate, and the Potsdam Palace as renovated by Knobelsdorff – in accordance with the architectural idiom of the French Revolutionary architects. Schinkel took account of this radical design in his plans, and in 1837 the cubic shape of the building was covered by a broad saddleback roof. Both Schinkel and the crown prince thought that a dome similar to the one Brunelleschi (1377–1446) had designed for Florence Cathedral would be appropriate in this civic church, but work on it did not actually begin until 1843. It was carried out by Persius and then completed by Stüler, though it can be thought of as Schinkel's legacy.

The Friedenskirche

On the eastern border of the park of Sanssouci, the Friedenskirche (Church of Peace) was built as the new parish church for the Brandenburg suburbs, to provide a symbol of the union between the king and his subjects (see page 321). Frederick William wished to place his divine right in the care of Christ, the Prince of Peace, not in some remote court chapel but in an assembly room of an Early Christian type, to be modeled on the church of San Clemente in Rome. This was a church that could not have been built as part of the crown prince's "Siam" even if land prices had not been so high there, for its location was part of the king's decision to make his summer residence in the palace of his ancestor Frederick the Great. The foundation stone was laid on April 14, 1845 – a hundred years after building had begun at Sanssouci.

Opposite, above
Potsdam, the Friedenskirche (1845–1854)
View down the nave

Italian buildings gave Frederick William IV the idea for the Romantic architecture of the Friedenskirche (Church of Peace). The interior of the basilica, with its main nave and two side aisles, is impressive in its costly materials, particularly the original Venetian mosaic in the apse of the choir, which dates from the 13th century.

Potsdam, Nikolaikirche (1830–1843)
Karl Friedrich Schinkel

Influenced by his teacher Gilly, Schinkel began planning this church in 1826 as a rectangular building. Persius added the dome that was part of the plans after Schinkel's death.

The Heilandskirche

Four years earlier, the Heilandskirche (Church of the Redeemer) had been built at the Sacrow harbor basin (see page 323). Once the estate of Sacrow had been acquired late in 1840, it was then possible to integrate the banks of the Havel at that point into the picturesque structure of the Potsdam landscape gardens, opening up the entire panorama from Glienicke to the Pfingstberg with a path along the bank. At the king's wishes, a church on the Early Christian model was to be built here, with the side facing the lake extending far out over the water (see page 322). Persius designed the church, which has a single nave and a free-standing campanile.

In much the same way as the royal gardens created model landscapes for general projects of land improvement, the architectural form and the siting of utilitarian buildings provided models for future industrial and urban design. The Army Commissariat Department, with its steam-driven flourmill built by Persius on the Havel in Potsdam, will serve as an example (see page 324).

The two rectangular buildings where the administrative staff lived are in a quiet location, their façades on the street, and linked by a gateway, a triple archway set back from them (see page 324, left). The entrance itself is the central arch; the two side arches stand above the outside steps leading up to the doors giving access to the main floors of the two buildings. On the opposite side of the courtyard, and in contrast to the quiet façade facing the street, there is a dynamic series of buildings arranged according to their functions – the engine room, the mill, the granary, and the silo – forming an irregularly shaped ensemble like a medieval castle and reaching their culmination in the chimney of the engine house, which suggests the tower of an urban Italian palazzo.

The whole building looks out on the water like a classic three-winged complex, and also includes – in the manner of a dock – a yard for the landing and onward transport of produce. There is also a small harbor basin at the mouth of the Schafgraben, which here flows into the Havel from the park of the Charlottenhof Palace. The effect is of an impressive conclusion to the city streets as they come down to the river, while the functional buildings are accessible from the bank, where work actually went on, and from the waterway that was the traffic link.

Modern elements, in the shape of the smoking chimneys of engine houses and workshops, were included very much as a matter of course in landscape design. Contemporary depictions show that these new technological verticals still had to conform to the ideals of Schinkel's Florentine vedutas. However even in those buildings Persius designed in accordance with Schinkel's principles, it is clear that the significance of their architecture had changed. This change parallels the social change from a rigidly hieratic to a class society.

The Roman Baths

When Schinkel built the Roman Baths he meant the court gardener's house and the adjacent stable (with

Potsdam, the Friedenskirche (1845–1854)
View over the Friedensteich (Pool of Peace) showing the nave, bell tower, pillared walk and mausoleum of Emperor Frederick III

The Friedenskirche (Church of Peace) was built at the eastern boundary of the park of Sanssouci, between the gardens and the city. Frederick William IV himself made many drawings of the structure it should have. Persius began work on the plans and was succeeded by August Stüler. Ludwig Ferdinand Hesse and Ferdinand von Arnim then took over, and created the building as a unique synthesis of many stylistically different historical elements, consisting of a basilica, bell tower, and adjoining buildings resembling a monastery.

Potsdam, Heilandskirche at the Sacrow harbor basin (1841)
Ludwig Persius
View from the south

From this view point, the well-proportioned church, clad in brick, suggests a ship at anchor, a symbolic effect achieved by making the building project out into the lake.

the quarters for the gardener's assistant or his likely successor to the post above it) to relate the crown prince's own Tea Pavilion. Such grouping of buildings expressed a patriarchal approach that was taken for granted.

Persius was still thinking in these terms when he converted the "dairy" (see page 329); but his first entirely independent design, for the pheasantry, was entirely different (see page 325). Here again the assistant gamekeeper's accommodation is above the stable, to the east, but it is no longer related to the main building. In terms of composition, it echoes the hayloft over the horses' stable to the west, and its outward appearance hardly differs from the cowshed under it. However, the tower now clearly relates solely to the main building, serving the function of entrance and stairway. The stable building with the assistant's quarters above it is marked off by a courtyard containing a well, connected with the main building only by an arcade of three arches.

In the same way as Schinkel had developed the graphic and symbolic expression of his own architectural ideas on the basis of Durand's system, the structural methods he had enriched were now handled with freedom by other architects. Like the pheasantry building, for instance, town villas were constructed as groups of buildings, with or without towers, standing in gardens or by the roadside. These new houses were not expected to have symbolic significance. They were simply intended to adorn their surroundings, provide focal points in the landscape, and form an urban street landscape interspersed with green plants.

Potsdam, Heilandskirche at the Sacrow harbor (1841)
Ludwig Persius

For the Heilandskirche (Church of the Redeemer), King Frederick William IV wanted an Italianate church with a campanile. Persius built a tall, single nave encircled by an open ambulatory of round arches, producing the effect of a basilica with three naves.

Villa Jacobs and Villa Persius

Ludwig Persius built two private villas of the new asymmetrically composed, free-standing type: the Villa Jacobs (1835–1836), a building with its component parts loosely grouped around a tower and visible from some distance away as a distinctive feature in the landscape; and his own house, the Villa Persius (1836–1837), consisting of almost unadorned rectangular components in an austere ensemble designed as part of an urban landscape (see page 324).

Persius also designed the Villa Illaire (1844–1846) in severely rectangular forms like those of his own house, but adding a considerable amount of varied architectural decoration (see page 325). The southern side of this villa gives character to the chestnut-lined avenue leading into the park of Sanssouci. The northern side, a composition of several small architectural elements, looks out on the ornate Marly Garden. Schinkel's own urge toward innovation laid the foundations upon which his successors could build, creating a number of different architectural types in extremely varied forms. Nonetheless, there were challenges – particularly when the architectural task related to machinery, still a new and unfamiliar element of design. It is true that Schinkel had already shown the way with his own buildings to accommodate machines, but the demands made on the next generation went much further.

In 1824, the first steam engine installed in a royal garden, to work the mechanism of the fountains and the irrigation system, was concealed rather than housed in a low, inconspicuous building with a hipped roof, similar to the farmhouses of the March of Brandenburg. Pride in man's mastery of the new element of steam was expressed not in a new type of architecture, but in an iron candelabra-like structure with water cascading down from it, which was installed at the highest point of Peacock Island. Schinkel's first plans for the water supply to the park at Charlottenhof were in fact technologically out of date, since they provided for the water to be pumped by a large tread-wheel worked by animals.

After Schinkel's visit to England and Scotland in 1826, however, he abandoned the tread-wheel as a driving force. The productivity of English factories had convinced him of the benefits (as well as the dangers) of steam and the potential that it offered mankind. The construction of suitable buildings to accommodate this new force, a "fifth element" devised by human ingenuity, was an entirely new architectural task.

Precedents of a kind existed in the many depictions of volcanic eruptions made in contemporary research into volcanism, and the theme of fire rising vertically from the cone of a mountain had already been used as an artificial image of incalculable natural forces in the landscape design at Wörlitz. French Revolutionary architects had also made use of the phenomenon of volcanic eruptions: Jean-Nicolas Ledoux, designing a cannon foundry as an extended factory complex of buildings within a square, had placed the smelting furnaces with their fiery emissions in pyramids at the corners. Boullée combined this image with the monumental structure of a sacrificial altar in his plans for museums, using a rectangular platform with a drum shape containing the eternal flame on top of it.

Friedrich Gilly showed that he had been influenced by these architects when he drew up a plan in one of the monthly competitions held by his private association of young architects, on this occasion to design an iron foundry (see page 295); he saw the smelting furnaces as pavilions flanking the central building; they were rectangular in form and crowned by cylindrical chimneys.

On the whole, both Ledoux and Gilly turned to traditional forms in compiling their plans for these new requirements, but Schinkel was able to build directly on their experience when he had to design his first steam engine house. The boiler, steam cylinder, and pump had been made by the Berlin engine builder Egells (probably in consultation with the architect) in cast iron sections of Gothic design. Schinkel designed a rectangular building to house this engine, with a tall chimney resembling a candelabrum and ornamented in high relief. The chimney of the "fiery machine," spouting sparks, clearly echoed the candelabrum from which water cascaded on Peacock Island.

Potsdam, the Steam Mill (1841–1843)
Ludwig Persius
Yard on the side facing the street

Divided into false arcades with round arches, the sides of the courtyard offer a view that changes as the perspective shifts diagonally. The complex has been almost completely preserved, and is now used for cultural events and as a restaurant.

Left
Potsdam, the Steam Mill (1841–1843)
Ludwig Persius
View through the arcade leading to the administrators' living quarters

The living quarters for the administrative officials form a self-contained unit. Seen from the street, it conceals the yard of the complex behind, which consists of three wings (two storehouse buildings and the central mill). The central arcaded hall glimpsed here, with its stairs leading to the living quarters at the sides, provides a view of the buildings outside.

The engine house in Glienicke

When the next steam engine was installed in a royal garden, in 1837, Persius built it an engine house in Prince Carl's garden in Glienicke (see page 327). Rather surprisingly, he based his design on Schinkel's old plans, which included a tread-wheel.

The building has been set on rising ground above the Jungfernsee, looking down on the water of the lake. Additionally, it contains almost all of the elements that would be expected in what was also the court gardener's house: for example, a small front structure resembling a temple to house both the steam engine and the pump; a tower for the cistern with a floor below it providing a view from a balcony; a tall gate with a rounded arch leading to the living quarters for the man who tended the engine and the court gardener; and finally the house itself, a narrow structure clearly influenced by the parallelepiped that would have accommodated a tread-wheel. A loggia in front makes the building broader, and a pergola lying parallel extends it into the garden. The self-contained rectangular structure of Persius's early buildings is some way from Schinkel's designs for Charlottenhof ten years earlier, but there is obviously a basic relationship.

The engine house for the fountains at Sanssouci

Ludwig Persius did not design another engine house until after Schinkel's death, this time at the Neustadt basin on the Havel in Potsdam, on the site of what

Ludwig Persius
The Villa Persius, Potsdam (1837)
From: Allgemeine Bauzeitung 4, 1839, plate 306; Berlin, Staatsbibliothek zu Berlin – Preussischer Kulturbesitz

In villas such as his own home, Ludwig Persius devised a new type of asymmetrically composed, free-standing house. The villa is an ensemble of severe rectangles with almost no decoration.

had once been the contractors' yard for the castle. The engine here was to operate the fountains of Sanssouci park on the Ruinenberg north of the castle, where Frederick II had never succeeded in maintaining a constant water supply, a problem that was now solved with the aid of steam power and reliable cast-iron pipelines.

The king had considered the creation of an engine house by making a Moorish ensemble out of the contractors' yard on the Havel basin, with its picturesquely aging half-timbered buildings, piles of marble, remnants of building materials, stores of stone and workshops. Influenced by this idea, Persius built an engine house in the form of a mosque (see page 326). The engine, made by August Borsig, was intended from the outset to be on view.

The idea of displaying the steam engine and pumps seemed appropriate for the new force created from the natural element of water in combination with man-made fire – an idea that had already been given expression at Charlottenhof, where the encounter of fire and water was also given explicitly oriental associations. Once subjected to the rigors of technology, however, the water was sent on its way to Western and indeed classical architectural features, passing from the Moorish mosque on the riverbank to the heights of the Ruinenberg behind Sanssouci with its buildings in the Roman style.

The engine house itself unites symmetrical and asymmetrical features that clearly derive from the functions of the parts of the building. The imposing façade consists of the three upright parallelepipeds of the engine room, which is crowned by a dome, and the flat-roofed pumping rooms beside it. From the street, the picturesque reflection of the building in the water could be glimpsed only on the right. A large gateway leads into the engine room with its exotic ornamentation.

Potsdam, the Villa Illaire (1844–1846)
Ludwig Persius

Counsellor Illaire's house at the southeast corner of the park of Sanssouci displays Persius's typical rigorously rectangular form, but is enriched by a variety of ornamental architectural motifs, notably the classical columns.

Potsdam, the pheasantry in Sanssouci park (1842–1844)
Ludwig Persius

This complex, dominated by the master gamekeeper's house and its tower, is really a utilitarian building, and was meant to serve as the model for country farms or for factories. The various functions of the separate parts of the building set each other off well, and are combined to very good effect.

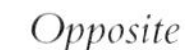

Persius used ornamental forms derived from Moorish models such as the Alhambra of Granada and the Mosque of Cordoba to create an almost fairy-tale atmosphere in which visitors could admire the cylinders arranged in pairs, for producing high, medium, and low steam pressure (see opposite). The Prussian eagle hovered over the balancing valve on the dome above, and to good symbolic effect, since it flew up when the steam valves opened and came down again when centrifugal force closed them and the engine slowed down.

The boiler house where the fire was stoked to generate steam was a long, low parallelepiped next to the engine room. The chimney was placed to one side, behind the dome, providing a vertical axis. The rather larger parallelepiped of the workshop building, a plain structure that also had living quarters on the upper floor for the man who tended the engine, stood beside the engine room and boiler house, so that the building presented an asymmetrical composition on the side facing the water, where a terrace stood in front of the boiler house. The king could display the new technology to his guests from this terrace, which seems to hover above the surface of the water.

Persius combined the various parts of the building to create an interesting outline in which the slender chimney, designed as a minaret, contrasts with the dome of the engine room. The walls of yellow brick have decorative colored horizontal banding, friezes, and crenelations, and there is a clear crescendo of effect beginning with the plain living quarters and passing on to the boiler house and then the engine room, the most important part of the building. The bank where the contractors' yard stood, still in its original condition at that time, was dominated by the three massive parts of the building, forming an interesting whole with its reflection in the water on the other side. The amazing new force of steam was thought obviously worthy of a shrine – a shrine in oriental form.

The pumping station in the New Garden

Of all the engine houses in the Potsdam gardens, the pumping station in the former dairy in the New Garden gave least indication of its true function. Langhans's picturesque stable building was converted into a Norman fortress to house it. There were plans to build the chimney in the shape of the Sibyl's tripod, thus comparing the smoke of the "fiery machine" with the mist of Apollo's oracle, and emphasizing the sense of mystery that steam power still evoked.

However, the idea was not put into practice; instead, the theme to which the designs adhered was that of mountain and valley, the conveying of water from a lake or river to the reservoir on top of a hill, which was seen as symbolizing the passage from morning to evening, from east to west, from activity to contemplative reflection.

The pumping plant for the park at Babelsberg represented a high point of technical development.

Opposite
Potsdam, engine house at Sanssouci (1841–1843)
Ludwig Persius

The construction of the pumping station at the Neustadt Havel basin, with its efficient steam engine, guaranteed a constant supply of water to the park of Sanssouci for the first time. Its oriental forms and the illusion produced by its reflection in the water gave it the exotic image required by Frederick William IV.

Berlin, the gardener's house and engine house in Glienicke (1837)
Ludwig Persius

The mighty tower of the building contains a cistern; the floor below provided visitors with a view of the landscape. The tall gate with its round arch leads to the house for the court gardener and for the man who tended the steam engine.

Carl Graeb (c. 1844)
Engine House in Babelsberg Park, Potsdam, Stiftung Preussische Schlösser und Gärten Berlin-Brandenburg

The painting shows the view from the engine room over the Havel to Glienicke and the Glienicke Bridge.

Opposite, above
Potsdam, the engine house in Babelsberg park (1844–1845)
Ludwig Persius

Walks laid out high up on the hills of the park offer a good view of the severe architectural form of the engine house, which resembles a medieval castle. The major-domo's quarters on the top story gave visitors a chance to admire not only the landscape, but also the new force that human ingenuity had devised through the union of fire and water.

Opposite, bottom
Peter Joseph Lenné
Ornamental Features and Boundaries of Berlin (1840)

Lenné submitted this plan, with an explanatory text, to the Ministry of the Interior. He had developed this ideal design for Berlin in consultation with the king.

Outwardly, this engine house also resembles a medieval castle: the rectangular, crenelated main building, accommodating the engine, living quarters, and workshop, has a square tower with oriels above it at one corner, the official residence of the major-domo, and small turrets at the others (see above and opposite). Diagonally opposite the square tower the chimney, built in the powerful shape of a round tower, reaches to the sky.

On the side of the building facing the water, there is a gallery around the boiler room, ending with a pergola that extends three-quarters of the way around the shaft of the tower. This feature is reminiscent of the terrace of the engine house of the Mosque on the Havel basin (see page 326), but it is also related to Schinkel's Grosse Neugierde (see page 301), where the form of a temple is transformed into a rustic feature from which one could observe the road between Berlin and Potsdam in the same way as boats moving on Lake Glienicke at this point could be seen from as far away as the Tiefer See and the Glienicke Bridge. The cylindrical engine itself stood in the middle of the building and was lit from above, very much on display: an open gallery from the living quarters led to it and provided a view of its moving parts in action. Visitors could see the crankshaft with its connecting rods and the flywheel that they drove, almost 6 meters (about 19.5 feet) high, a quarter of its height reaching into the roof space, so that the disappearance and reappearance of its spokes through the narrow opening especially made for it in the ceiling was a particularly impressive sight.

The camshaft and centrifugal mechanism of the balancing valve passed through the ceiling as well, directly below the octagonal skylight, providing the movement of the centrifugal regulator with a very theatrical setting. The rapid movement of the iron ball bearings for the control valves merged under the central source of light in the engine room into a new dynamic form.

The importance of the engine houses

It would be wrong to think of the engine houses of the Potsdam gardens as mere royal or private whims. Rather, they illustrate the way in which architects were tackling an entirely new kind of task, and their efforts to include industrial building in the field of architectonic design.

The developments Schinkel had seen in England and Scotland, where purely utilitarian buildings were simply traditional functional buildings reproduced on a larger scale, contrasted with an attempt to express the nature of the new technology in the best possible way. It was important to show its significance. In Germany, there was an idealistic respect for the creations of this new technology, and a desire not only to explain how they worked but also to show how they could be mastered.

While Potsdam was being enhanced by buildings providing good views, churches, palaces integrated into parks, and symbolic structures housing new technology, Berlin was growing, unchecked, into a city with a huge population; here the Industrial Revolution, coupled with flight from the land, led to a huge boom in building.

The garden designer Lenné, also a town planner, tried to impose some order on the developments. His partnership with Karl Friedrich Schinkel had included urban planning projects; he was familiar with Schinkel's skills and ideas, and had to deputize for him during his sickness and replace him after his death. Most of the energy he expended on Berlin was devoted to his attempts to create a well-ordered city organism. Lenné could be called the real planner of the modern city. His project, which he submitted to the Ministry of the Interior in April 1840, *Schmuck-u. Grenzzüge v. Berlin mit nächster Umgegend* (Ornamental Features and Boundaries of Berlin and its Immediate Surroundings) was intended as the point of departure for all future planning in the city (see page 329).

The proposal envisaged a semicircular boulevard, which established the extended boundary of the city to north and east. At this time, Lenné envisaged the Landwehrgraben waterway as the city's boundary to the south, set among green spaces, and planned to enlarge it to take shipping. Lenné suggested parceling out the Köpenicker Feld in between these areas and thus opening up a link between the Landwehrgraben and the Spree through the Luisenstadt Canal.

It is clear that he was attempting to ensure good communications between the city and the country

surrounding it, in order to satisfy both economic and aesthetic requirements. The growth of the city was to be guided in certain directions by the traffic routes, while green spaces among the existing dwelling and working areas of the city would provide for relaxation.

In spite of the increase in private building, Frederick William IV and Lenné tried to control disorganized growth by purposeful planning. The plans – for the capital and for other Prussian cities, as well – were intended to reconcile the technological requirements of traffic in the growing metropolis with the social needs of its inhabitants.

In Berlin, the building of the Landwehr Canal in 1845 and the Luisenstadt Canal in 1848 opened up the new industrial areas to water traffic. Harbor basins in large squares were intended to provide aesthetic enrichment of the environment and green spaces where people could take their ease. The bend in the canal, with its wide expanses of water, was the site of monumental churches – for instance, the

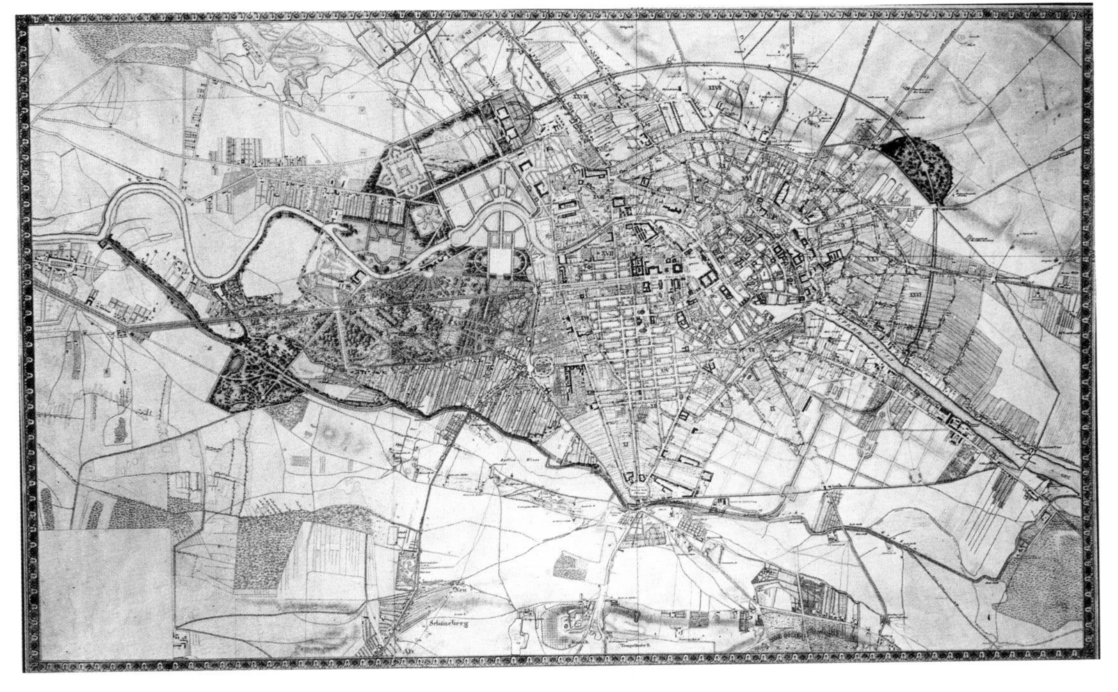

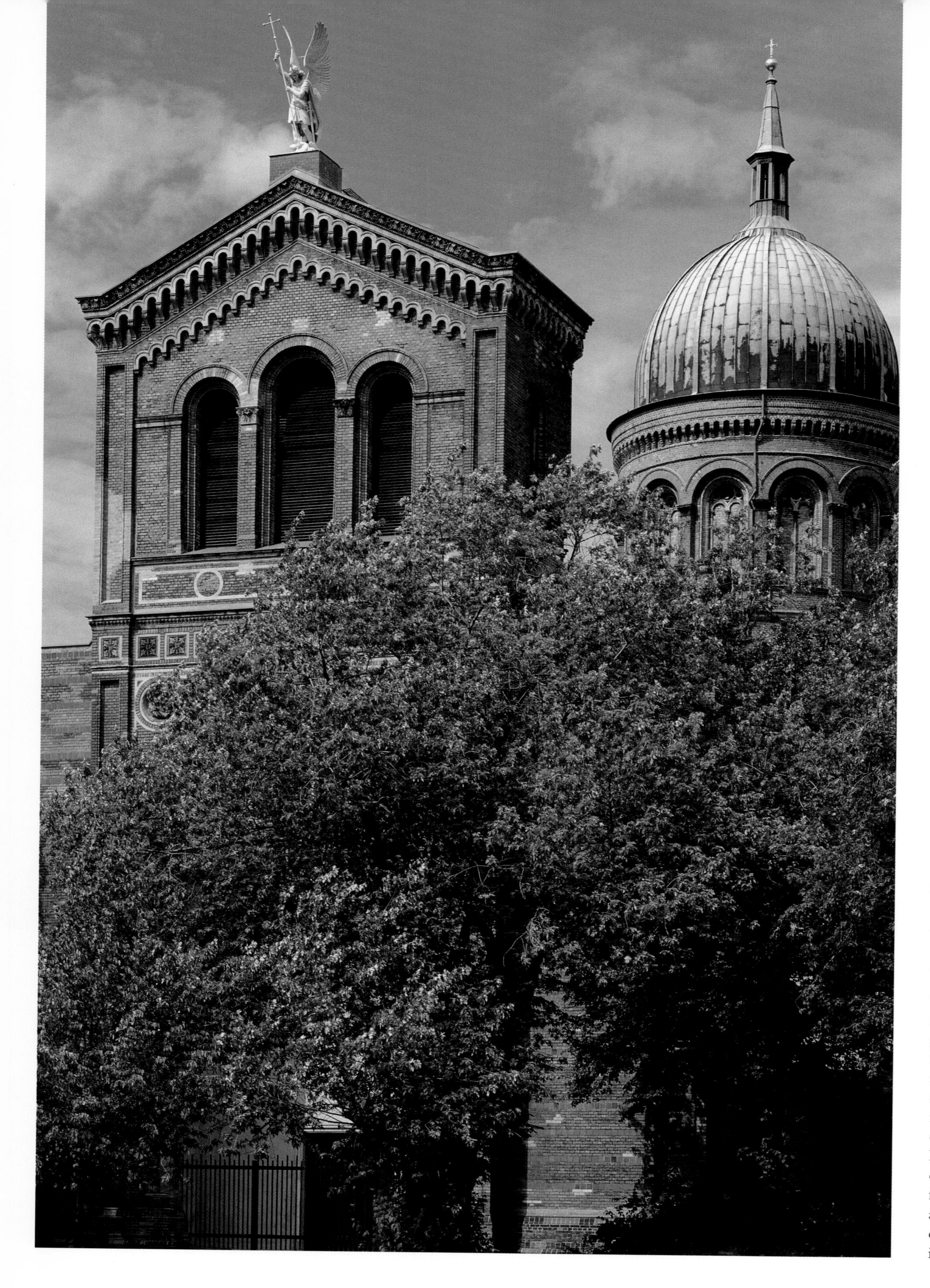

Opposite, above
Berlin, the Thomaskirche (1865–1869)
Friedrich Adler
(badly damaged in World War II; the exterior was restored in 1963)

This church, situated on the narrow side of the Mariannenplatz, contains elements of both a nave and a centrally designed type of church building. Behind the façade with its twin towers, the square nave leads to another rectangular area; the round dome rises above it, with side apses and an apsidal choir; and inside there are ambulatories resembling side aisles. In the cumulative plan of the building, formal features adapted from the Romantic architecture of the Rhine area are combined with a basic Neo-classical structure.

Berlin, Church of St. Michael (1851–1861)
August Soller
(ruined in World War II; parts of the transept and choir restored)

The façade has no tower, but high round-arched niches and a bell-tower gable end above them give the building the appearance of a basilica. The choir and transept are dominated by the dome, which rises on a tall drum above a rectangular base. The situation of the church by the Engel Basin of the Luisenstadt Canal accentuated the canal's change of direction here, a feature of importance for the architectural planning of the city, and one that the walls of the church were intended to echo.

towerless façade of the church of St. Michael beside the Engel Basin on the Luisenstadt Canal emphasized the canal's change of direction at this point, which had important implications for the planning of the city (see above). Churches like the Church of Matthäuskirche and the Thomaskirche emphasize the flowing outline of the built-up areas (see page 331). In a heightened format they assumed the purpose of Schinkel's suburban churches, plain buildings that had played their part in the social integration of early industrial settlements outside the city gates. Buildings known as "family houses," modeled on

the city. The project discussed by Lenné and Schinkel as early as 1840 for the development of Berlin north of the Brandenburg Gate fell victim to the Hamburg Rail Station and the extensive complex of lines around it (see page 334).

Similarly, when Lenné planned the Humboldt Harbor he was unable to prevent the heart of the city from being torn apart by traffic and industrial areas at that point.

Sadly, he had no opportunity to put his ideas on the integration of the railroads and their station complexes into the organism of the city as a whole into practice, though here again he displayed his creative imagination and wide-ranging abilities as a town planner – he really wanted to provide the city, now growing at such a rapid pace between the Landwehr Canal and Kreuzberg, with a green space running all the way from the Hasenheide to Charlottenburg, and consisting of boulevards interspersed by ornamental squares. His design looks like a variation on the axis of streets lined by stone buildings that had grown up in the course of history from the Frankfurt Gate to

Berlin, the Matthäuskirche (1844–1846)
August Stüler
(destroyed in World War II and rebuilt in 1956–1960, with changes to the interior)

This building, a Protestant church with three naves, originally stood on a small square still perceptible in outline today. Pilaster strips on the exterior mark the interior divisions, and red horizontal bands emphasize the structure of the yellow brickwork. Clarity and an airy, light form relieve the monumental size of this church, which can hold 1,500 people.

David Gilly's utilitarian buildings in the country, had gone up around the suburban churches. The development of grid patterns now led to block building in these areas: there were apartment buildings on several floors, often with a graduated series of several yards – the aim was still the social integration of tenants living on the upper and the lower floors or at the fronts and backs of these buildings.

The planners did not oppose the proliferation of housing, but sought to integrate the shapeless complexes of dwellings, factories, and smoking chimneys into a city with its skyline marked by church towers and cupolas, and set against the surrounding countryside. The synagogue built in Oranienburger Strasse 1859–1866, with its tall, richly gilded domes, made a handsome focal point (see page 332). Similarly, the Bethany Hospital in the Köpenicker Feld, built in 1846, was an attempt to give significant structure to this new part of the city (see page 333). With its complex of buildings, reminiscent of a monastery, and its linking of the concepts of church and hospital, it was intended to encourage the links between faith and charity, and so have a beneficial effect on society.

The impact of planning new traffic routes

In planning new traffic routes, Lenné gave obvious precedence to the traditional waterways between the Havel and the Spree, and tried to integrate them fully into the city. He thought them more important than roads as trade routes and for the siting of industry.

Lenné had to face the necessity of extending the railroad network (as a result of the development of the iron and steel and engineering industries, and also the use of steam power) only when the railroads began to impinge on the realization of his plans for

פתחו
צדיק שמר אמנים

the Brandenburg Gate north of the Spree. Lenné was anticipating the ideas of the garden city movement.

In addition, his plans included a Road of Honor and Remembrance – a memorial to the Wars of Liberation. However, its central point was to have been Wahlstatt Platz, which happened to be situated between the Potsdam and Anhalt railroad lines and freight reloading points advancing into the city from the south. There was nothing to be done about this situation, and Lenné solved the problem by planning to divide Wahlstatt Platz into a western and an eastern half, with shopping streets and harbor basins between them on a lower level and parallel to the railroads. Through traffic was to be interrupted at this point to preserve the visual axis, and would reach the traffic junction, which was surrounded by avenues, along access roads carried on ramps. It would have been possible to look down from both sides of the square, as if from a viewing platform, on the busy commercial traffic by road, rail, and water, on whistling locomotives puffing out steam, sails billowing in the wind, and vehicles of all kinds. Lenné showed that

Above
Eduard Biermann
The Bethany Hospital (1846)
Watercolor, 22.4 x 31.2 cm; Potsdam, Stiftung Preussische Schlösser und Gärten Berlin-Brandenburg, Plankammer

This complex of buildings, designed in 1845–1847 by Persius and Stüler, expresses the king's ideas of social and town planning. Greenery and expanses of water, like the Luisenstadt Canal in the foreground, were to provide facilities for both traffic and relaxation.

Opposite
Berlin, the synagogue in Oranienburger Strasse (1859–1866)
Eduard Knoblauch
(damaged in an air raid in 1943, rebuilt as the Zentrum Judaicum in 1988)

Between the towers, the wall containing the entrance stands back from the street; access is through arches. Behind them, a 12-sided drum rises above the entrance hall and carries the dome. Oriental and medieval forms are subordinated to the severe system of the Schinkel school.

Berlin, the Bethany Hospital (1845–1847)
Ludwig Persius and August Stüler

Two narrow octagonal towers at the center of the broad façade indicate the church situated behind the vestibule. It was intended to be the focal point of the building, adding a religious element to the social significance of the institution.

Berlin, Hamburg Rail Station (1845–1847)
Friedrich Neuhaus and Ferdinand Wilhelm Holz

The twin tower motif of Italian Renaissance villas, also used in buildings erected in Potsdam to provide views of the landscape, is here part of the gateway. After World War II, only the central part of the façade was left, and this was damaged; with the side wings, added later, it was rebuilt for use as a museum.

aesthetic solutions could be found even for the new kind of urban development affected by technology.

Berlin developed inexorably in size and in extent. One of the main reasons was the close connection of the country's capital with its provinces once the new railroad lines were built: the first stretch of line, to Potsdam, was opened in 1838, and had been extended to Magdeburg by 1846.

In the years following 1841, lines to Anhalt, Silesia, and Breslau were opened, and the line to Hamburg was completed in 1846. In the same year, work began on the Ostbahn, the first Prussian railroad to be built with state funds. It was to link the eastern parts of the country with Berlin. The extension of the railroads encouraged the technical and industrial development of Prussia to a crucial extent.

Frederick William IV, for instance, considered the building of the Ostbahn one of the major achievements of his reign. Stüler designed the architectural superstructures for the bridges over the rivers Vistula and Nogat, which were completed in 1859 (see page 335). Their portals imitated medieval city gates, and were intended to emphasize the fact that the bridges were works of national Prussian architecture. So was the sculptural ornamentation on them: the Nogat Bridge had statues of Prussian Grand Masters of the German Order of Chivalry; reliefs showing the conversion to Christianity of the Lithuanians by the Order; and a relief of the inauguration of the bridge itself by Frederick William IV. The same point was clearly made by the choice of location for the Nogat Bridge, crossing to the fortress and buildings of the

Eduard Biermann
Bridge over the Nogat
Lithograph, 69 x 86 cm; Potsdam, Stiftung Preussische Schlösser und Gärten Berlin-Brandenburg, Plankammer

The artistic design of this bridge, and the fact that it leads to the fortress complex of the Marienburg, were intended to make it both a symbol of technological progress and a historic memorial. Technically it is a fine achievement, and strongly influenced by British examples. The handsome architecture of the gates is by August Stüler.

Otto Hoppe
New bridge over the Rhine in Cologne
Lithograph, 23.6 x 34.4 cm; Cologne, Kölnisches Landesmuseum

The view of the Rhine Bridge, seen from the cathedral, shows the traffic links it provided, bringing together two railroad lines to form a network running from Minden to the Belgian border. The bridge over the Rhine symbolizes the integration of the provinces.

Marienburg on the eastern bank, and deliberately symbolizing the connection of modern traffic and transport with the historical building to the outer courtyard of which the bridge led. The bridge over the Rhine in Cologne, also opened in 1859, was directly influenced by the king's wishes and built on the cathedral's longitudinal axis, so that the choir of the cathedral on the west bank of the Rhine would meet the traveler's eyes (see below). These bridge links symbolized the inseparable unification of the provinces and their full integration with Prussia. The traffic routes thus represented the last examples of deliberately executed programmatic architecture, an approach that by now was falling into disuse. The fact was that the use of architectural forms to express symbolic meaning seemed to be increasingly less important as time went on. The idea that the appearance even of secular functional buildings should illustrate their purpose did linger for some time, but it increasingly conflicted with the pure utilitarianism of mass housing and industrial architecture, not only in remote areas but in the two Prussian residences, Berlin and Potsdam, and the larger towns of Prussia.

Potsdam, the New Garden, the kitchen building and Marble Palace on the bank of Lake Heiliger

The artistic exploitation of the river and lakeside landscape of the Havel at Potsdam began in 1787 with the building of the Marble Palace and the laying out of the New Garden on the bank of Lake Heiliger.

Landscape Gardening in the Potsdam Parks

A summer evening on the Glienicke Bridge – to the south is Babelsberg Palace, seen across gently rolling meadows, on one bank the pump house, the Little Palace reflected in the water; and on the other bank, the Glienicke side, the casino, the Norman tower of the engine house, and a northward view across the water to the Heilandskirche (the Church of the Redeemer) in Sacrow, over a kilometer away. It might seem the ideal point from which to enjoy the beauty of the landscape. But those familiar with Potsdam will be aware that no single ideal point exists; they will already be feeling the urge to go out on the river Havel, see the little castle on Peacock Island in the distance on the right, the Marble Palace on the banks of Lake Heiliger beyond a land bridge on the left, and then, only a little later, allow their gaze to move up and linger on the façade of the Belvedere on the Pfingstberg. The alluring landscape seems to move constantly from woods and hills to palaces, garden buildings, meadows, and stretches of water, combining them into unexpected and ever-changing scenes. It is an *intelligent* landscape in the sense that it is a landscape where the visitor can pick and choose. It was created over a period of two hundred years, at first slowly, and then with gathering momentum, out of a natural landscape that was not particularly fertile but very "picturesque," containing the lake-like expanses of the river Havel, marshes, and a variety of low hills.

The sporadic locating of palaces and gardens in the countryside around the Havel, a process begun by the Great Elector around 1660, slowed down to some extent under his successors. Frederick the Great had created a companion piece in the castle and gardens of Sanssouci, one equal in size to the city but greatly superior in artistic importance, and thereby made the name of Potsdam synonymous with landscape gardening. When the vineyard castle and its terraces were set among the natural beauties of the landscape of Potsdam, the hill on which it was built, with its wide variety of views, was transformed. In the following eight decades, between 1787 and 1867, the landscape was developed by a felicitous combination of artistic vision and royal power. UNESCO recognized its unique nature in 1990 by designating it part of the world's cultural heritage.

A crucial figure in this development, though less fortunate as a statesman, was Frederick William II. In planning his palace and park on the banks of the Havel, he drew his ideas of landscape gardening from the Wörlitz site. Deliberately distinguished from the gardens of Sanssouci even in name, the New Garden was laid out on the western bank of Lake Heiliger, with the Havel forming its northern boundary. Work on it began in 1787. The palace itself, known as the Marble Palace, projects slightly out into the lake (see opposite), and the garden goes down to the bank on both sides of the building. The towers of the Gothic Library and the Moorish Temple, no longer extant, stood at the two ends of the garden (see pages 280 and 281). The ridge of land opposite, between the lake and the Havel, with the Babelsberg hill rising to a height of 50 meters (164 feet) above water level, was covered with fields and windmills until well into the 19th century. As with Wörlitz, upon which it was modeled, the park here formed a unified whole with the farmland. Today, the fields have made way for the suburban villas and gardens of Berlin. The landscaping of the New Garden and the planting of trees there was the work of the landscape gardener Johann August Eyserbeck; he came from the estate at Wörlitz, his model, to take up the appointment. Later on, the New Garden was redesigned by Peter Joseph Lenné, who retained several characteristic features and integrated them into new structures.

But to return to the time of Frederick William II: on his return from the war against Revolutionary France in the later months of 1793, he had Peacock Island, which lay in an area of uncultivated land 4 kilometers (2.5 miles) to the east of the New Garden, made part of the garden design (see below). The prolongation of the river view into the distance, and Frederick William's decision not to alter the existing gardens to accommodate this new area, were crucial factors in the further development of the parkland. It took only a year to build the little palace with its white façade on the island, facing the Marble Palace (see page 292), and it was known as the "Roman Country House" because of its interior furnishings and the Roman arches of its windows. An important reason for making the island part of the overall design of the landscape, though not the only one, was its light forestation with oaks over four hundred years old. Another idea finds expression in the palace's Tahitian Cabinet (see page 293). The

Potsdam, view of the castle on Peacock Island from the New Garden

Berlin, Peacock Island, Nobleman's House, "guarded" by an ancient dead oak

The house, built 1803–1804 as a model farm and to accommodate a gardener, was rebuilt by Karl Friedrich Schinkel as the Nobleman's House (Kavalierhaus) in 1824–1825. The tower on the right is copied from the late Gothic façade of a patrician house in the Brodbänkengasse in Danzig.

interior decoration of this room, intended to imitate a bamboo hut, has murals between the windows showing painted views of Peacock Island and the New Garden, together with tropical flora and fauna. In the second half of the 18th century, the nostalgic yearnings of civilized Europe for a primitive paradise found subjects of absorbing interest in the contemporary voyages of discovery to the South Sea Islands, and the accounts of their journeys written by Louis Antoine de Bougainville, and Reinhold and Georg Forster. Influenced by the literary myth of island life, at Potsdam the dream of Tahiti merged with the bleaker and more northerly wilderness of Peacock Island. To the northeast of the large island, a walk through the carefully preserved oak woods led to a dairy theatrically designed in the form of a Gothic ruin, very much in the spirit of a return to nature.

The garden on the island had its finest hour in the time of Frederick William III, who used to visit it in the summer months. From 1816 onward, Lenné and the court gardener gave the island a design that was shaped by the dynamic of its paths and views, and the peaceful calm of the various separate garden areas. The buildings already present were placed in new settings, and the island theme was further developed with new variations. Tropical and exotic themes became tangible reality in the Palm House, built to Schinkel's plans (it was destroyed by fire in 1880), and in the groups of foliage plants growing in front of it. Schinkel's Nobleman's House (Kavalierhaus) continued the theme of Gothic architecture on another plane (see below). The tradition of fountains and irrigation devices in the Potsdam gardens began with the cascade built on the island in the form of a

Berlin, Peacock Island, fountain and view through the woods to the castle

In 1825, successful irrigation of the Potsdam gardens at last began with the installation of a steam engine on the British model. At the crown prince's suggestion, this cast-iron Roman fountain was erected in the reservoir at the highest point of the island. For a moment it turns the water, on its way to the gardens to supply other fountains and irrigate the plants, into a delicate veil of spray.

candelabrum in 1825. Lenné laid out the first rose garden in Prussia on the island in 1821. In 1840, after the death of Frederick William III, the island became a garden of remembrance and underwent no more major modifications.

Parallel to the development of Peacock Island, another garden was laid out on the island called Glienicker Werder, south of Peacock Island. Karl Heinrich August, Count von Lindenau, acquired the estate of Klein-Glienicke in 1796. It was situated on the first major highway in Prussia, which linked Berlin to Potsdam and had recently been completed. Besides building a large glasshouse, Lindenau's endeavors at Glienicke tended more towards "ornamented agriculture," in order to emphasize the theatrical effect of the picturesque views of Potsdam and the New Garden from the hills of Glienicke. At the end of the 18th century, the New Garden, Peacock Island, and the Glienicke complex formed a triangular landscape garden around the lake of Jungfernsee. Lenné recognized its importance when he arrived in Potsdam in 1816, and, with energy and enthusiasm, developed it further. In the spring of 1816, he was asked to submit proposals for improvements to the now antiquated Potsdam gardens; he stayed on at Potsdam until his death in 1866. His first private commission came from Prince Hardenberg, for the pleasure grounds of Glienicke. His draft plan (which has been preserved, though it was altered in the execution) already displays all the outstanding

Carl Daniel Freydanck
View over Glienicke to Potsdam (1838)
Oil on canvas, 28.9 x 35.9 cm; Berlin, KPM-Archiv, Schloss Charlottenburg

A view of the Glienicke castle complex seen from above, in the area of the park where the Roman Bench later stood. The Heiliggeistkirche (Church of the Holy Spirit) can be seen on the left, and on the right, framed by trees, stands the Garnison Kirche (Garrison Church). It is interesting to compare this view with the watercolor painted 13 years later (see opposite).

features of his genius as a garden designer: landscaping that makes the most of the natural beauties already present or artificially created, and which allows visitors walking in the gardens to come upon a fascinating series of vistas. Around the curves in the paths unexpected views come into sight, crossing and sometimes intersecting, and leading the eye on to the skyline of the city of Potsdam and the distant Kirchberg. In 1820, Lenné persuaded Chancellor Hardenberg to acquire a piece of meadowland lying on the other side of the road from Berlin to Potsdam, so that he could make sure his views remained unobstructed. One of the reasons why the Potsdam landscape gardens were so successful was Lenné's enthusiastic tendency to design features over and above the terms of his actual commission. Hardenberg died in 1822, and the king's son Prince Carl acquired Glienicke in 1824. Lenné and Schinkel had both been employed there by Hardenberg, and now immediately returned to their work. Schinkel converted the modest billiard house on the banks of the Havel into a casino (see page 298), and by mutual agreement between the two colleagues the building was integrated into the garden by the use of extensive pergolas. In the winter of 1824–1825, Lenné submitted a plan for converting the land around Glienicke into a park. The courtyard bordered by the castle and the Nobleman's Wing became a flower garden, and the series of buildings and courtyards beginning at the entrance and ending at the casino formed an unusual and striking line of demarcation between the pleasure ground and the park. The very varied terrain of the land at Glienicke, with the steep bank on the western side of the park, gave Lenné the opportunity to provide through his landscaping views of the New Garden, the city of Potsdam, and the open country (see opposite and below).

When guiding the royal princes in their choice of palaces and parks of their own, Lenné took great care to choose sites that had the potential to be developed into an integrated landscape. When the marshy, flat land of the farm of Charlottenhof, south of Sanssouci, came on the market in December 1826, Lenné was all in favor of its purchase. At Christmas 1825, the crown prince, later to be Frederick William IV, received a deed of gift of the property together with a first draft design by Lenné. The crown prince, his architects, and his landscape gardeners worked together on plans of an ever-increasing degree of maturity. The project concluded with the laying out of the rose garden (see page 342) in 1835, in between the pump house and the exedra; the hippodrome was built at the same time. Lenné had mastered the geometrical garden forms of which Schinkel had acquired a knowledge from his study of classical architecture and accounts of gardens in antiquity, a subject previously unfamiliar to Schinkel but easy enough to understand after his visit to France. A carriage drive from Sanssouci leads past the gardener's house and the Roman Baths to the palace, and then turns again as it makes its way toward the New Palace. The artificial hills created by the excavation of the pool for the pumping station are carefully and sparingly distributed. Interest is created by the way in which the drive rises gently towards the Roman Baths, still out of sight, and then, having reached the top of the hill, goes rapidly down again once the view is revealed. In a further variation, the drive now describes a wider arc and climbs a gentler slope as it leads on to the castle. The network of gently curving paths is scarcely visible as it winds its way over areas of ground at different levels divided by groups of trees. The direct east–west axis through the castle began in the east with the chimney of the engine house (no longer extant), which was then followed by the highly symbolic rose garden, the exedra, and the castle terrace (see pages 302 and 303). To the west of the castle the line continued through the dark "Poet's Grove" of chestnut trees, planted in a rectangular pattern, and led to a regularly shaped pool that reflected a statuary group representing Sleep and Death, set in a niche formed by a hedge. A dark copse rose behind the hedge, with narrow, curving paths leading through it and to a broad and surprisingly open hippodrome; this is recognizably the *stibadium* that the Roman writer Pliny describes in his account of his Tuscan villa, as reconstructed by Schinkel. Only the plan shows that the hippodrome actually lies on the same axis. From the palace terrace, the eye moves from the Roman Baths in the northeast over the Tyrolean vineyard and on to the dome of the New Palace in the northwest (see page 343).

Ferdinand von Arnim
View of Potsdam from the Roman Bench in Glienicke (1851)
Watercolor, 18.7 x 26.3 cm; Berlin, Stiftung Preussische Schlösser und Gärten Berlin-Brandenburg, Plankammer

By comparison with Freydanck's view (see opposite), the dominating tower of the Nikolaikirche now appears between the towers of the Heiliggeistkirche (Church of the Holy Spirit) and the Garnison Kirche (Garrison Church). Groups of trees, still young, are planted on the plain in front of the artificial lake on the hilltop. Babelsberg Palace is on the far left.

As early as 1824, Lenné saw that the Babelsberg, opposite the palace at Glienicke and unoccupied since Napoleonic times, was an ideal site for another princely palace and garden (see pages 344 and 345). But it was not until 1833 that the thrifty Frederick William III made up his mind to let Prince William, later emperor, build on the Babelsberg. It was well suited to provide many fine views of the city of Potsdam, the New Palace, and the sheep pastures of the Geltow hills, views quite different from those afforded by the heights of Glienicke. Lenné's plans indicate the location of these views as seen from the winding paths or other specially chosen vantage points. The prince's financial means were very limited, and consequently the laying out of a park on the sandy hills was a laborious task, with many setbacks. However, when the childless Frederick William IV came to the throne and his brother Prince William became crown prince, William had more money available. In 1843, Prince Pückler, who knew the prince's wife, took over the landscaping of the park and expressed severe criticism of what Lenné had done so far. The engine house had been built to Persius's plans on the bank of the Havel, and in 1845 the engine and pumps made it possible for the Babelsberg fountains to play. The garden, now well irrigated, grew vigorously (see pages 328 and 329). As at Glienicke, an artificial lake, the "Black Sea," was created on a hill top, with artificial waterfalls cascading down to the Havel; they are much more delicate in appearance than those in the park at Glienicke, largely because the terrain at Babelsberg was not suited to the creation of ravines like those at Glienicke. At the bottom of the sloping meadowland gently rolling down from the palace to the river, and known as the "Bowling Green," the great jet of the Geysir rises 40.5 meters (132 feet) into the air from the waters of the Havel, a clear allusion to the palace of Sanssouci, with its regular terraces and the fountain rising from the round basin in its parterre. Prince Pückler's departure from Lenné's landscaping principles is evident in the changes made to his network of paths, in his extensions to the park, and also in the design of the pleasure ground with its baskets of flowers. It must have been painful for Lenné to hand Babelsberg over to Prince Pückler, but the work the prince did on the landscape gardens of Potsdam enhanced them considerably. Moreover, when Frederick William IV came to the throne, he gave Lenné, of whom he was fond, a wide range of new commissions, and the celebrated landscape gardener could easily relinquish his involvement at Babelsberg.

The designing of the Potsdam landscape gardens was approaching its conclusion. Frederick the Great had set an ornamental series of Roman ruins on the hill visible from the colonnaded courtyard of Sanssouci; the water reservoir to supply the fountains that would never play regularly for him was also on this hill (see page 188). The arable land of its slopes came down to the point where the climb up from Sanssouci began, and so Frederick William IV, who on coming to the throne chose Sanssouci as his permanent residence, consulted with his landscape gardener on ways to enhance the beauty of the countryside here. The land itself was under

Potsdam, Sanssouci, the Charlottenhof park

The rose garden, first laid out in 1836 and restored in 1997

Concentric circles of rosebeds are grouped around an arbor in an octagonal pattern. A relatively new feature of garden design in Prussia, the rose garden introduced an intimate note to the landscaping of the Charlottenhof park.

Potsdam, Sanssouci, the Charlottenhof park, view of the dome of the New Palace from the castle terrace

cultivation, and, in order to have a free hand with redesigning them, the king, on Lenné's advice, acquired the estate of Bornstedt (see page 346). Lenné began drawing up plans at once, and work started in the winter of 1841–1842. He revealed the beauty of the landscape by moving the course of the main road and creating alternating views from paths leading up and around the hill (see page 346). In 1845, the Norman Tower was added to Frederick the Great's ruined wall to provide a panoramic view over the treetops of Sanssouci (see page 347) and the fields stretching away to the north, known as the Lenné Fields after his plantings of hedges and paths. The Ruinenberg now lay like a park linking the artificially created gardens of Sanssouci and an area of farmland remodeled on aesthetic principles. It was a landscape that revived the Virgilian literary tradition of the virtues of country life, an idea very much in tune with the endeavors of Lenné and the king to make the countryside around the royal castles and gardens an aesthetically pleasing and harmonious unity by including agricultural land in the general design. After almost a century, the water reservoir on the Ruinenberg could now fulfill its original purpose. On October 23, 1842, when the fountain below the terrace of Sanssouci began to play, the waterworks of the gardens finally came into their own.

A hundred years after building had begun on Sanssouci Palace, the devoutly Christian Frederick William II laid the foundation stone for a church, a feature that the atheist Frederick II had never see as forming any part of his park. It was to be built between the hop yard and the kitchen garden,

which Lenné was commissioned to redesign. This garden, lying between Lenné's own official quarters and the church and measuring 4 hectares (10 acres), became famous as a typical example of Lenné's landscaping of a site so as to bring out a range of symbolic meanings. It also formed a delightful contrast to the Friderician design of the adjoining pleasure garden to the east, which was restored largely in its original form at the king's wishes – an early example of a memorial garden motivated by family piety. At a very early date, Lenné had cast his eye over the Sacrow estate, which lay among the landscape gardens around the Jungfernsee. It is the keystone in the composition of the rectangle made up by Peacock Island, Glienicke, Babelsberg, and the New Garden, and has a wide-ranging view over the landscaping beside the water. In his plan of 1833 for the enhancement of the area, Lenné had already designed a generous park for Sacrow, reaching from the Havel to the bank of Sacrow Lake and covering an area larger than that any of the other four gardens. In 1840, a few months after coming to the throne, Frederick William IV bought the Sacrow property. The local parish church had been in a state of disrepair for years, and the king, as its new patron, now had the opportunity of building a church that would be reflected in the waters of the Havel, in accordance with ideas that he had long cherished. The Heilandskirche (Church of the Redeemer) on the Sacrow harbor basin, consecrated in 1844, was a focal point in the harmonious integration of architecture and the landscape (see page 347), in the same way as the landscaping of Glienicke had been in 1824. Lenné methodically opened up views to Glienicke, Babelsberg, Potsdam, and the New Garden from the remote and unassuming manor

Potsdam, the Babelsberg park, view from the Law Court Pavilion to the Flatow Tower

Potsdam, the Babelsberg park, view of the Flatow Tower from the east

A Dutch windmill, famous for the fine view it provided, once stood at the southern foot of the Babelsberg. Like its sister in Sanssouci, it was an ornament to the park until it was destroyed by fire in 1848. The Flatow Tower was built in the same prominent position to replace it in 1853, and was modeled on the Eschenheim Gate in Frankfurt am Main.

house of Sacrow, which was never in fact converted into a small palace as originally planned. These structural measures were followed by the landscaping of the park around the Jungfernsee to provide a variety of views from the 1,200-meter (4,000-ft) path along the bank. The gaze travels from the Heilandskirche uphill to the church of St. Peter and St. Paul, with its Russian-inspired onion dome, another church that, as well as serving a sacred purpose, greatly enhances the beauty of the landscape. It was consecrated in 1837.

The architecturally unfinished belvedere on the Pfingstberg, its surroundings landscaped by Lenné, is the culmination of the buildings constructed to offer views in the Potsdam park landscape, and provides a fine view in itself. In accordance with ideas sketched out by the king, it was to combine themes from two Italian Renaissance villas, the belvedere of the Villa d'Este, and the casino and terraces of the Villa Caprarola. From 1849 to 1852, work was in progress on the twin towers and the inner courtyard, between high walls, which contains the water tank for the New Garden. The building, which remained a shell, concluded 1860–1863 with a pillared hall of triple arches, but without the hanging garden and casino that were part of the original plan. In 1862, Lenné was commissioned to surround the king's architectural dream, which was never to be fully realized, with landscaping that would lend the whole building a historically interesting character. His life's work, and that of his royal patron, ended here.

The garden paths of the Pfingstberg provide fine long-distance views of Peacock Island, Glienicke, Babelsberg, and the city of Potsdam. The Belvedere is a landscape garden building pure and simple, since its sole purpose is to give (and indeed provide) a fine view. Towers, arcades, galleries, and stairways allow the visitor to make a complete circuit of the low-lying courtyard, and meanwhile the eye can linger, from different heights, on the landscape of the

Potsdam, the Babelsberg park, Law Court Pavilion on the Lenné Height

The 13th-century Law Court Pavilion (Gerichtslaube) of the old Berlin Rathaus (City Hall) was moved to the park at Babelsberg when the City Hall was demolished in 1871. It was also quite usual to move historic buildings to new sites in English landscape gardening of the 18th century.

Julius Hennicke
View of the Ruinenberg from the West, With the Village and Crown Estate of Bornstedt (c. 1850)
Watercolor, 22.8 x 33.9 cm; Potsdam, Stiftung Preussische Schlösser und Gärten Berlin-Brandenburg, Plankammer

The village church was rebuilt in Italianate style 1855–1856. Every feature of a landscape, natural, architectural, and agricultural, could be designed or redesigned so that it contributed to the general effect of a view.

Potsdam parks. Designed as its focal point, the two always-visible towers of the Belvedere enhance the park with their Romantic appearance.

In 1853, Peter Joseph Lenné, writing in the third person, stated: "The aim was to link the many ornamental buildings both old and new in the vicinity of Potsdam together in the landscape, and Lenné drew up such a plan as early as 1833 … The overriding idea was to surround the Havel, which here appears a lake, with a large park extending over almost two German miles from the Karlsberg at Baumgartenbrück to Peacock Island." Such was the task. As for its successful accomplishment, it may be said that the development of landscape gardening achieved its classic culmination with Lenné's dramatic designs. In 1825, he wrote of the design of his ornamental paths: "All the forms to be seen along the interesting lines of the paths are diverse and lively. Each step shows them from a different direction, in different outlines and combinations; and when one moves fast along the curving line they seem to circle around like living, dancing figures." On another occasion he wrote: "It is not sufficient for us to see some object or other in nature, though it may be attractive and ornamental of its kind. We feel a need to bring everything together into pleasing compositions, and not merely from one viewpoint or another, but in a constant process of evolution, in scenes that are ever new, sometimes expected and sometimes surprising, sometimes agreeably confined, then opening out to a wide expanse again." This intellectual linking of related elements from the ideal world of the garden both with the city and with the wider landscape by means of prospects was an idea deriving from the belief that landscape gardening, embracing many arts at once, could achieve the harmonious union of the natural and the manmade. The great gardens of Sanssouci – the New Garden, Sacrow, Peacock Island, Glienicke, and Babelsberg – surround the historic center of the city of Potsdam, covering 737 hectares (1,820 acres) in all. Not only do the gardens themselves deserve to be conserved and restored, but also so do the visual links that are the meaning of the landscape, connecting the gardens as

Julius Schlegel
The Crown Estate and Church of Bornstedt, a View from the East (1857)
Ink drawing, 28.6 x 45.3 cm; Potsdam, Stiftung Preussische Schlösser und Gärten Berlin-Brandenburg, Plankammer

An idea cherished by Peter Joseph Lenné was that of linking the gardens of Sanssouci with "ornamented" farmland. It was realized when the redesigning of the Ruinenberg and the fields on its slopes began in 1841. Later, the wide curves of the Bornstedt road brought the Italianate outline of the redesigned village of Bornstedt into view, as well as Sanssouci itself.

Carl Daniel Freydanck
Sanssouci from the Ruinenberg (1847)
Oil on canvas, 28.5 x 35.9 cm; Berlin, KPM-Archiv, Schloss Charlottenburg

As his standpoint, the painter chose the Norman tower built in 1845 to designs by Ludwig Persius and to complement Frederick the Great's ruins. The campanile of the Friedenskirche (Church of Peace) is to the left of the picture, where the minaret of the engine house is also visible as a smoking chimney. To the right of Sanssouci the picture shows the steam mill built in 1842 on the banks of the Havel for the royal lakeside trade – an industrial building harmoniously incorporated into the landscape. Lake Templiner stretches to Caputh beyond it. The Sanssouci mill is in the middle ground on the right of the picture.

Potsdam, the ambulatory of the Heilandskirche at Sacrow

The Heilandskirche (Church of the Redeemer), consecrated in 1844, continued the tradition of churches integrated into the design of the landscape that began in 1837 with the Church of St. Peter and St. Paul on the hill opposite Peacock Island.

seen from different viewpoints and as linked by pathways, and always relating them to the surrounding farm land, woods and lakes, and also to the domes and towers of the city. The recent development of the kind of modern art in which chance and nature play an important part allows us to see the landscape gardens of Lenné and Pückler in a way that their contemporaries could not – to understand, appreciate, and enjoy the value and significance of the transformations of the sites they found, the nature of the flora there, and the ever changing conditions of time, the seasons, and the weather.

Michael Seiler

SCULPTURE

Saskia Hüneke

Theory and Early Achievement: Johann Gottfried Schadow and His Circle of Pupils

After the drastic cuts in the financial budget made by his father Frederick William I, Frederick II tried to attract skilled sculptors to Berlin from the other German principalities, from Italy, and above all from France, giving them official appointments and attempting to create an encouraging artistic climate in the city. In the last decade of his reign (he died in 1786) the artistic life of Berlin had already begun to develop of its own accord, and no longer was exclusively dependent on royal commissions. The revival in 1786 of the Berlin Academy of Arts (Akademie der Künste), which had been efficient reorganized, laid the foundations for the emergence of a style native to Berlin. It derived first from the sculptural training provided in the French Studio directed until 1788 by Jean Pierre Tassaert, and then, increasingly, from the classes of the Academy and its exhibitions.

A process now started that would fashion the development of the Berlin school throughout the 19th century, involving the systematic training of artists and craftsmen in a wide range of artistic and technical skills. Meanwhile, a lively interest in art was felt by the public at all levels of society. Technical innovations such as various reproduction techniques were encouraged, and as a result many works acquired an enormous popularity that, reaching the most remote parts of the kingdom, was by no means confined to Berlin.

Johann Gottfried Schadow had studied with Tassaert, but like many others he then went to Italy and sought to strike out along a path of his own. When the news of Tassaert's death and the opportunity of succeeding him brought him back to Berlin in 1788, his style immediately began to develop its

Johann Gottfried Schadow
Tomb of Prince Alexander of the Mark (c. 1788–1789)
Marble, height 600 cm; Berlin, Staatliche Museen zu Berlin – Preussischer Kulturbesitz, Alte Nationalgalerie

The death of Friedrich Wilhelm Moritz Alexander, Count of the March of Brandenburg, the eight-year-old son of King Frederick William II and Wilhelmine Ritz, later Countess Lichtenau, was a shattering blow to his parents, who maintained a lifelong close relationship. The king expressed his grief by commissioning an expensive tomb in the Dorotheenstadt Church, and the tomb was designed by Schadow from ideas by the Berlin painter Johann Gottlieb Puhlmann. It was Schadow's first major work, and he showed his early maturing skills in the sensitive depiction of the child, apparently asleep, with the figures of the three mourning Fates in a niche above him.

own exceptional qualities. All his great masterpieces were created in a single decade: they include the reliefs of standard-bearers for the Parole Hall of the Berlin Palace, 1788; the tomb of Count Alexander of the March, 1788–1789 (see opposite); the monument to Frederick the Great in Stettin, 1791; the monument to General von Ziethen, 1794; his self-portrait, 1790–1794 (see below); the quadriga for the Brandenburg Gate, 1794; and the double statue of Princesses Louise and Frederica, 1794–1797 (see page 350). The statue of the two princesses, which combines a delight in detail with the emulation of classical antiquity, is an excellent illustration of early Neo-classicism in transition from the Rococo style. While Schadow's works retain some 18th-century features, they establish the Neo-classical ideal; each of them represents the origin of a new departure in the art of sculpture in Berlin.

Artistic development in sculpture was so rapid after this first decade that Schadow himself received very few major commissions. The exceptions were his monument to Leopold of Dessau for the Wilhelmsplatz in Berlin, created in 1800, and his monument of 1819 to Blücher in Rostock. The commission for the sarcophagus of Queen Louise, who died in 1810, went to Christian Daniel Rauch; Schadow commented ruefully that his own fame had gone up in smoke (German *Rauch*). However, his artistic influence extended well beyond his own works and his years as a teacher, and was felt far into the 19th century.

Schadow's portraits represent a world of their own. Close to the works of the painter Anton Graff in their realism, they brought the close depiction of a human likeness into the art of sculpture in Berlin, a quality perceptible even in 1783 in his early portrait of Henriette Herz, whose salon was an intellectual center of the city (see above). His many subjects included his self-portrait of around 1790, and his portraits in 1794 of Princess Frederica and Princess (later Queen) Louise. From the earliest of these likenesses, a precursor of the double statue, to a recently discovered posthumous portrait of 1811, they are among his very best portraits. He imparted the sensitive realism of his early Neo-classicism to his pupils, including the brothers Carl Friedrich and Ludwig Wilhelm Wichmann (see pages 350 and 351), who in turn influenced such young sculptors of the next generation as Julius Franz and Hugo Hagen (see page 351), and the court wood carver Jakob Alberty.

Schadow's portraits also illustrate his interest in a Neo-classicism more closely bound to the ideals of classical antiquity, as in his 1798 portrait of the young architect Friedrich Gilly, himself influential in establishing the early Neo-classical style; in the heroic portrait of the actor August Wilhelm Iffland, carved in 1803; and in the 1804 portrait of his son Ridolfo. Under the influence of Thorwaldsen in Rome, this approach found adherents in Schadow's pupils Friedrich Tieck, Emil Wolff, and Schadow's own son Ridolfo, who had been born in Rome.

Left
Johann Gottfried Schadow
Henriette Herz
(Cast of 1901, from the clay bust of 1783)
Plaster, height 60 cm; Berlin, Staatliche Museen zu Berlin – Preussischer Kulturbesitz, Alte Nationalgalerie

The salon of Henriette Herz was one of the centers of intellectual life in Berlin at the turn of the century 19th century, and Schadow himself belonged to its inner circle. This bust, his first independent work of sculpture, is extant only in the form of a plaster cast taken from the lost original. Schadow freed himself from the influence of his master Tassaert by expressing both individuality and the ideals of classical antiquity in his portrait of this greatly admired young woman.

Below
Johann Gottfried Schadow
Self-portrait (c. 1790–1794)
Fired clay, height 41 cm; Berlin, Staatliche Museen zu Berlin – Preussischer Kulturbesitz, Alte Nationalgalerie

This self-portrait typically combines realism with idealism. The meticulously observed features radiate the lively, youthful self-confidence of the artist facing his major tasks, while the bust also retains sensitivity.

Friedrich Tieck: an Individualist

In 1798 Tieck, who was born in 1776, began six years of studying sculpture with Heinrich Sigismund Bettkober; but he drew his real artistic ideas and inspiration from Schadow. During the first decade of the 19th century, he also educated himself in literature and art history. His artistic stance, somewhere between Neo-classicism and Romanticism, was influenced by his friendships with the Romantic poet Wilhelm Heinrich Wackenroder, with Caroline and Wilhelm von Humboldt, and later with the circle of early Romantic artists around August Wilhelm and Friedrich Schlegel in Jena, as well as by the time he spent in Paris in 1798 in the studio of the celebrated French painter Jacques-Louis David.

The reason, or perhaps the pretext, for Tieck's delay in returning to Berlin may be traced to the large works commissioned from him after 1805, such as the relief frieze and statues in both the stairway and White Hall of the palace at Weimar; his visit

Johann Gottfried Schadow
Princesses Louise and Frederica of Prussia (1794–1797)
Marble, height 172 cm; Berlin, Staatliche Museen zu Berlin – Preussischer Kulturbesitz, Alte Nationalgalerie

The society of Berlin in general had given an enthusiastic welcome to the young wives of the two Prussian princes, Crown Prince Frederick William and his brother Ludwig, when they arrived in the city in 1794. Even at this distance in time Schadow succeeds in conveying a sense of that enthusiasm in his personification of a human ideal. The work is a masterpiece of early Neo-classicism. The original group, in biscuit porcelain, enjoyed great success at the exhibition of the Berlin Academy of Arts in 1795, and a marble copy was commissioned and executed by Claude Goussaut of the French Studio in Berlin. King Frederick William III, however, did not like the masterpiece, and would not have it displayed until 1810, the year of Queen Louise's death, and then only in a remote location. In 1918 it was finally displayed in the place originally intended for it, the Parole Hall of the Berlin Palace.

Carl Wichmann
Seated statuette of Alexandra Feodorovna (after 1827)
Biscuit porcelain, height 43 cm; Berlin, Schloss Charlottenburg, on loan from the Freunde der Preussischen Schlösser und Gärten

Right
Ludwig Wilhelm Wichmann
Bust of Henriette Sontag (1829)
Marble, height 56 cm; Berlin, Stiftung Preussische Schlösser und Gärten Berlin-Brandenburg, Schloss Charlottenburg

Henriette Sontag was one of the most famous singers of her day. Born in Darmstadt in 1806, she was still very young when her outstanding talents made her name in Paris and London as well as Vienna, Leipzig, and Berlin, where she was enthusiastically admired on her appearance at the Königsstadt Theater in the Alexanderplatz in 1825. An unusually high salary and an appointment as singer in the Royal Court and Chamber Musical Ensemble were offered, in vain, to persuade her to stay in the city. She died of cholera while on tour in Mexico, and is buried in the convent of St. Marienthal near Görlitz.

Far right
Hugo Hagen
Bust of Augusta of Saxe-Weimar (1862)
Biscuit porcelain, height 53 cm; Potsdam, Stiftung Preussische Schlösser und Gärten Berlin-Brandenburg, Schloss Babelsberg

The daughter of the Grand Duke of Saxe-Weimar, a close friend of the poet Goethe, was a well-educated and self-confident princess when she married Prince William, later Emperor William I, in 1829. The couple lived in the palace built especially for them in 1834–1835, to plans by Schinkel, situated on the Babelsberg on the south bank of the Havel and set in a park magnificently landscaped by Lenné and Prince Pückler. A colored copy of Hugo Hagen's porcelain bust was among the losses suffered by the palace in World War II. It was replaced in 1995 by the purchase of this bust.

to Rome; and a long period working in Carrara from 1812 to 1819, where he spent most of his time executing commissions for other sculptors. When he did go back to Berlin, in 1819, he embarked upon his most artistically fruitful period as a sculptor, a period marked by his close collaboration with Rauch and Schinkel.

Tieck contributed several works to the joint project of creating the Kreuzberg monument on the Tempelhofer Feld. It was erected in 1817–1820 to designs by Schinkel, and was later ornamented with personifications illustrating the Wars of Liberation, works sculpted by Rauch, Tieck, and Ludwig Wichmann. The Royal Iron Foundry in Berlin was responsible for the fine technical execution of the project.

The most important of Tieck's sculptures for buildings were created in close collaboration with Schinkel: they were the gable relief on the Schauspielhaus (theater) of around 1820; the groups of horse-breakers, with August Kiss, for the Museum of Antiquity (Antikenmuseum), built in 1830 to plans by Schinkel in the Lustgarten in Berlin; and the statues on brackets for Queen Elisabeth's tea salon in the Berlin Palace (see page 352). The design of one of Tieck's most powerful works, the tomb for the army commander in the Wars of Liberation, Gerhard von Scharnhorst, was also influenced by Schinkel. It was created in 1832–1833 for the Veterans' Cemetery (Invalidenfriedhof) in Berlin (see page 505). A sleeping lion rests on the plinth, which is ornamented with animated reliefs of battles. One of Tieck's last great public commissions in Berlin was the design for a statue in memory of Karl Friedrich Schinkel, who died in 1841, commissioned by King Frederick William IV for the entrance hall of the Museum of Antiquity. Its execution in marble, by Tieck's pupil Hermann Wittig, was not completed until 1850.

After 1830, works of sculpture for specific buildings were increasingly entrusted to August Kiss, a pupil and colleague of Rauch and Tieck who had already worked on the groups of horse-breakers.

Meanwhile, Tieck himself turned to the restoration of classical works destined for the Museum of Antiquity; he had been appointed its first curator because of his great archaeological knowledge. Beside his works for various buildings, it was chiefly with portraits that Tieck made his mark in the history of sculpture in the 19th century. In his 115 busts and 20 medallion portraits he sought a middle way between idealism and realism. Every bust he created paid tribute, as if in a monument, to the qualities of the individual it portrayed (see page 352, top). His classical ideals led him to depict his subjects in classical robes, while Rauch and his school preferred to show their sitters in contemporary costumes.

Director of All Sculptures: Christian Daniel Rauch and His Pupils

Unlike Friedrich Tieck, Rauch did not sever his ties with Berlin during his years in Italy, and those links became much closer when he was commissioned, through the agency of Wilhelm von Humboldt, to work on the tomb of Queen Louise, one of his major achievements. In 1819 he moved into a studio in Berlin in the Lagerhaus on Klosterstrasse, where Tieck joined him in the same year.

This studio became the scene of extraordinarily varied activity, and exercised a great influence on the art of Germany as a whole. Like Schinkel and later Persius and Stüler in architecture, or like Lenné in landscape gardening, Rauch held what amounted to informal ministerial office as Director of All Sculptures. As well as his own work, he was involved on a broad basis with the training of the next generation of sculptors, both through his practical work with them in the studio, and through his teaching at the Academy and other training institutions he had co-founded. He advised the king, arranged the offer of commissions, encouraged hopeful talents, and also introduced technical innovations. His close and congenial collaboration with both Schinkel and his successors Ludwig Persius and August Stüler was of fundamental importance to developments all over

Friedrich Tieck
Karl Friedrich Schinkel (1819)
Marble, height 66 cm; Potsdam, Stiftung Preussische Schlösser und Gärten Berlin-Brandenburg, Schloss Charlottenhof

This portrait of the architect Karl Friedrich Schinkel is one of those in which the portrait sculpture of the Berlin school rose far above local artistic standards. Here Friedrich Tieck was able to express his own profound understanding of the sitter. The bust unites precise observation and perfect technical execution with a sure sense of the complex, talented, and idealistic Schinkel, a man who exerted unparalleled influence on his time as architect, architectural theoretician, interior designer, painter, draftsman, and theatrical set designer, an authority on the architecture of Prussia in general, and not least an inspiring teacher.

Christian Daniel Rauch
Equestrian monument to Frederick the Great (1839–1851)
Bronze, height 566 cm, plinth, height 784 cm; Berlin, Unter den Linden

Projects for a memorial to Frederick the Great were initially promoted by Frederick William II at the end of the 18th century, but the idea actually materialized only through the efforts of Schinkel (from 1822) with the collaboration of Rauch (from 1830). Various designs had been submitted; the one adopted showed Frederick II on horseback and in the costume of his time, raised on a plinth featuring portraits of contemporary figures (chosen by a committee set up especially for the purpose) and surrounded by the cardinal virtues of Sapientia (wisdom), Justitia (justice), Fortitudo (fortitude), and Temperantia (temperance). The unveiling of the memorial in Unter den Linden on May 31, 1851, was celebrated by the entire population of Berlin. The monument to Frederick the Great is both a portrait of an 18th-century ruler and his time, and an assured expression of the craft of the sculptors of Berlin, with their systematic training and their artistic and technical sophistication.

Opposite
Friedrich Tieck
Statues on brackets, the tea salon of Queen Elisabeth of Prussia, Stadtschloss, Berlin (1825; destroyed during World War II)
Plaster, height between 73 and 85 cm; photograph (c. 1910)

Friedrich Tieck made 15 statues of mythological subjects to stand on brackets in Queen Elisabeth's tea salon, designed by Schinkel from an idea by the crown prince. In March 1825, Tieck began work on the small statues of Odysseus, Iphigenia, Achilles, Omphale, Electra, Hippolytus, Heracles, Psyche, Amor, Demeter, Proserpina, Theseus, Ariadne, Bacchus, and Cassandra. They resemble genuine statues of classical antiquity. The expression of Tieck's ideal of sculpture as strictly in accordance with classical standards is here integrated with the whole concept of the room, which derives from the interplay of the furnishings, the mythological scenes on the wall and ceiling frescos, and the statues.

the country. Against this background some great public works of sculpture were created, including the Kreuzberg Memorial, the figures on the Schlossbrücke, the Column of Victory, the monument to Frederick the Great (see above), and the collaboration on Leo von Klenze's Valhalla in Regensburg (see page 355). Without the extensive work for the monument to Frederick in Unter den Linden done by Rauch's pupils Carl Wolgast, Hugo Hagen, Adolph Bräunlich, Bernhard Afinger, Julius Franz, and Rudolph Piehl, it would scarcely have been possible to carry out the project.

Among Rauch's pupils were sculptors who achieved great fame elsewhere, for instance Ernst Rietschel, who was appointed to the Dresden Academy of Arts in 1832, and Albert Wolff and Friedrich Drake, whose major works were distributed far beyond Berlin. Others, like Heinrich Berges and Karl Heinrich Möller, whose own works inclined to Romanticism, helped Friedrich Tieck to restore works of classical antiquity for the king and the new Museum of Antiquity in the Lustgarten. The Cauer family of sculptors, Friedrich Anton Schievelbein, August Wredow, Gustav Bläser (see page 354), and Julius Troschel all created their own bodies of work, although space does not allow us to do them justice here. Theodor Kalide, August Kiss, Wilhelm Wolff and Julius Franz were among the generation of sculptors bold enough to embark upon a spatially exciting and dynamic new style (see pages 356 and 357). Gradually, they rejected Neo-classicism and its austere ideals in favor of a more vivid and emotionally direct style; the way for it had already been paved by the development of the Neo-Baroque style by Carl and Reinhold Begas in Berlin. In Christian Daniel Rauch's portraits, his sources of inspiration – Schadow's realistic approach combined with the Neo-classical ideals of the followers of the celebrated Danish sculptor Bertel Thorwaldsen – seem to have united to influence a whole school of portraiture (see page 355).

While Tieck raised a monument to the mind, Rauch brought out the exemplary personal qualities of his subjects. His portraits convey an idea of the universal validity of a social ideal that was to impose itself in the next decade. Among such portraits are his busts of Princess Charlotte of Prussia (later to be Empress of Russia and known as Alexandrovna Fedorovna) and her brother Crown Prince Frederick William of Prussia. The bust of Charlotte conveys a sense of the 18-year-old princess's energy, intelligence and strength of mind, and the bust of the crown prince shows him in the prime of his optimistic ideas and ideals (see page 355). Rauch's pupils were not to attempt this heroic manner, and were to some extent content to depict surface idiosyncrasies.

Left
Gustav Bläser
Statue of King Frederick William IV of Prussia (1873)
Marble; Potsdam, Stiftung Preussische Schlösser und Gärten Berlin-Brandenburg, Orangerie, Park Sanssouci

The statue stands in front of the central building of the Orangery, a fine example of architecture to the north of the park, built by Schinkel's best pupils Ludwig Persius, August Schüler, and Ludwig Ferdinand Hesse 1851–1864. Its design, after Italian models, was much influenced by the wishes of Frederick William IV. The king died in 1861, and his wife Elisabeth commissioned the statue in homage to his merits as a patron of the arts; the reliefs on the plinth show allegorical figures of music, sculpture, poetry, and landscape gardening. Architecture, the art practiced by the king, is not represented, but it may be taken to be embodied in his own person, or in the Orangery itself.

Opposite, far right
Christian Daniel Rauch
Seated Victory Throwing a Garland (1844)
Marble, height 157 cm (without wings); Berlin, Staatliche Museen zu Berlin – Preussische Kulturbesitz, Alte Nationalgalerie

Rauch was commissioned to provide six statues of Victory for the Valhalla built at Regensburg by the architect Leo von Klenze for King Ludwig of Bavaria between 1830 and 1842. The *Seated Victory Throwing a Garland* is a replica of the design for the fourth Victory, executed in 1841 in marble for the Valhalla, and was commissioned by King Frederick William IV of Prussia. After going on display at the 1844 exhibition of the Berlin Academy of Arts, it was installed in the White Hall of the Berlin Palace, where it remained until the building was destroyed during World War II.

Christian Daniel Rauch
Bust of Princess Charlotte of Prussia (1816)
Marble, height 62 cm; Potsdam, Stiftung Preussische Schlösser und Gärten Berlin-Brandenburg

The bust is one of those portraits by Rauch that unite an expression of the sitter's essential characteristics and intellectual qualities with relatively realistic reproduction of the features.

Christian Daniel Rauch
Bust of Crown Prince Frederick William of Prussia (1823)
Marble, height 65 cm; Potsdam, Stiftung Preussische Schlösser und Gärten Berlin-Brandenburg

This bust was probably a gift from the crown prince to his wife, Princess Elisabeth of Bavaria.

The works of the Berlin school of sculpture in the late 18th century and the 19th century met a positive response from society seldom that was achieved by sculptors before or since. Their high artistic claims derived as much from the intellectual climates of Romanticism and Neo-classicism and a deeply felt sense of religion as from patriotic feeling after the Wars of Liberation and the confidence inspired by the revival of the economy (see page 358). Those claims were reflected in the founding of a Schinkel Museum in the Architectural Academy in 1832 and in the founding of a Rauch Museum in 1859; the sculptor Hugo Hagen became its curator in 1865.

Artistic Perfection and Technical Innovation

For a number of reasons it proved impossible to put into practice Tieck's project for creating a comprehensive collection of copies of celebrated marble busts. Such a series of copies would have been too time-consuming and therefore too expensive to make. However, other methods of reproduction were being perfected, and they helped to spread a knowledge of works of art to an increasingly wide circle. Papier mâché, which had seen a brief period of popularity at the end of the 18th century, was not a sufficiently durable material. However, it became usual in sculptors' studios, and especially Rauch's large workshop, to make and sell plaster casts of the portrait busts of prominent people: artists, generals, or members of the royal family. The process was taken up by Berlin firms specializing in plaster casts. The company founded in 1824 by Sigismondo Micheli was run by several generations of the family, and remained in existence until 1939; the founder of another firm, Georg Eichler, gradually extended his range to making copies in ivory, zinc alloy, and terracotta.

Following the 18th-century use of cast iron for everyday commodities, the art of iron-casting was developed further in many foundries, for instance in Lauchhammer at the end of the 18th century, and at Gleiwitz in Silesia from about 1804. The Royal Iron Foundry set up in Berlin in 1804 concentrated on artistic iron-casting, which increased in importance during the Wars of Liberation. It enabled craftsmen to manufacture and copy filigree jewelry and other items, and these works were of increasing artistic significance at a later date.

With recognition of the limitations of cast iron (which could not be used for large works and was unsuitable for outdoor items because it deteriorated under the influence of the elements), and with the generally felt wish to erect memorials to the heroes of the Wars of Liberation, the casting of large bronzes regained importance. Bronze-casting had largely fallen into disuse since Andreas Schlüter cast Andreas Jacobi's equestrian monument to the Great Elector in 1701. Now Schadow suggested bringing two Frenchmen experienced in bronze-casting and chasing, Louis François Coué and François Léquine, to Berlin to work on his monument to Blücher, a bronze erected in Rostock in 1819. They not only cast the statue to general satisfaction, but also taught their skills to others. Through Rauch, they began

Opposite
August Kiss
Amazon in Battle (1837–1842)
Bronze; Berlin, Staatliche Museen zu Berlin – Preussischer Kulturbesitz, Altes Museum

Karl Friedrich Schinkel had suggested the figure of a fighting Amazon for one of the stairways outside his museum building in the Lustgarten in Berlin. Various designs were made from 1834 onward. The model for the Amazon was made in 1837 and is preserved in a plaster *bozzetto* (small preliminary model) in Potsdam. The vigorously dramatic character of the group caused much controversy in the artistic world of Berlin. The king paid only for the model, and a committee was set up to find funds for its casting in bronze; Schinkel was one of the committee members. The cast was made in 1842 and set up in the place designed for it in 1843. Albert Wolff's figure of a man fighting a lion was added as a pendant in 1861.

Julius Franz
Shepherd Fighting a Panther (1851)
Zinc alloy cast, height 108 cm; Potsdam, Stiftung Preussische Schlösser und Gärten Berlin-Brandenburg

This extremely dramatic scene of conflict had become famous as a technical innovation at the Great Exhibition of 1851 in London. In 1852 it was displayed at the exhibition of the Berlin Academy of Arts. It was acquired by King Frederick William IV, and placed in the Sicilian Garden that Peter Joseph Lenné began to lay out in 1857. Today it has been replaced in the same location by a bronze cast of it.

Left
Christian Daniel Rauch, Albert Wolff
Moses Praying with Aaron and Hur (1848–1863)
Marble, height 265 cm; Potsdam, Stiftung Preussische Schlösser und Gärten Berlin-Brandenburg, Friedenskirche

In the battle of the Israelites against the Amalekites, the Israelites had the better of it only as long as Moses kept his arms raised in prayer. Since the battle went on for a long time, his sons Aaron and Hur supported him. The idea of the group of three figures derives from a sketch made by Frederick William IV in January 1848, and the king commissioned Rauch to execute it. The making of the model dragged on from 1851 to 1854, and the marble statue itself was made in 1857. Rauch's pupil Albert Wolff took over the work, which Rauch himself had felt as a burden weighing on him until his death on December 3, 1857. The king, who had commissioned the statue, did not live to see it installed in 1863.

training students at the Berlin Institute of Trade and Commerce in 1820. In 1824 an institution to teach bronze-casting and chasing was founded as part the Ministry of Trade, Commerce, and Public Works, but it closed again in 1827. These ventures led to a rise in the quality of bronze-casting and chasing of such craftsmen as the Krebs brothers, August Fischer (see page 360), Ferdinand August Fischer, and Wilhelm and Heinrich Hopfgarten. Sculptors like Wilhelm August Stilaski, August Kiss, and Theodor Kalide combined the demands of sculpture with technical skills. It is significant that Alexander Vollgold, who became head of the chasing workshop at the Royal Iron Foundry in 1830, and liked to adorn his works with artistic silver inlay, was recognized in 1834 by the Berlin Academy of Arts as an "academic artist" (see page 361).

However, bronze-casting remained a time-consuming and expensive process, and casting in zinc alloy soon became very popular. The foundries set up in Berlin by Moritz Geiss and Simeon Devaranne, and in Potsdam by Friedrich Kahle, advertised their products in books of patterns and models, and were very successful throughout the

Opposite, right
Karl Steinhäuser
Easter candleholder (1859)
Marble, height 236 cm; Potsdam, Stiftung Preussische Schlösser und Gärten Berlin-Brandenburg, Friedenskirche

Karl Steinhäuser trained with Christian Daniel Rauch and then, in 1835, settled in Rome, where he created this Easter candleholder in 1850, apparently not as a commission, but for his own satisfaction. Steinhäuser's religious ideas – he converted to Catholicism in 1858 – such as the overcoming of evil and the way to salvation through the life of Christ, were expressed in terms of medieval iconography. This work probably appealed to the piety of Frederick William IV and his wife Elisabeth, since the king acquired it when he visited Rome in 1859 and then made it part the iconographic program of the Friedenskirche (Church of Peace), which was consecrated to Christ.

Five Muses
Terracotta, height 132–138 cm; Potsdam, Stiftung Preussische Schlösser und Gärten Berlin-Brandenburg, millhouse in Sanssouci park

These statues stand by the mill house built to the north of the park of Sanssouci as a guesthouse for Frederick William IV. They are casts of marble statues from the Berlin Collection of Classical Antiquities, which came to the classical temple at Sanssouci with the Polignac collection bought by Frederick II. They belonged to a group of statues reconstructed and completed by the sculptor Lambert Sigisbert Adam as the *Family of Lycomedes*, a reference to a classical myth. Around 1800, it was recognized that they were figures of the Muses. They were restored and reconstructed again in Christian Daniel Rauch's studio between 1826 and 1829.

Friedrich Alexander Theodor Vollgold
Bowl with frieze of Alexander the Great's triumphal entry into Babylon (1843)
Iron with silver chasing, height 81 cm, width 101 cm; Potsdam, Stiftung Preussische Schlösser und Gärten Berlin-Brandenburg, Schloss Babelsberg

This magnificent shallow iron bowl is ornamented with a frieze showing a small version of Bertel Thorwaldsen's depiction of Alexander the Great's triumphal entry into Babylon. Thorwaldsen had executed his relief, 229 cm (7.5 feet) in length, for a hall in the Quirinal Palace in Rome that was refurbished for Napoleon's visit to the city in 1812. The relief around the bowl copies a different version, of 1822, now in the Thorwaldsen Museum in Copenhagen. It was impossible to retain the full vigor of the magnificent relief when it was reduced to this very small size, but the animated sequence of Greek chariots and horsemen is still effective in more than a merely decorative manner.

19th century. In particular, they made the distribution of large sculptures possible – secondary casts taken from the casts of either classical statues or modern works. Sections of buildings and figures were cast, and in the course of time there were experiments with various surface treatments, such as white oil paint and galvanic copper-plating or gilding. Figures cast as ornamentation for fountains, and works exploring the maximum possible size (such as the secondary cast of the classical group known as the *Farnese Bull*, in front of the Orangery in Sanssouci park), were not very durable, and nor were the secondary casts in galvanized metal set up later in outdoor surroundings; they included the copy of Thorwaldsen's statue of Christ, almost three meters (10 feet) high, in front of the Friedenskirche (Church of Peace) in Potsdam. The largest of the many foundries set up later was that of the firm of Gladenbeck, which began reproducing monuments, portrait busts, and free-standing statues in all sizes in 1888.

Terracotta and artificial stone were of less significance in the art of sculpture, and were used mainly for parts of buildings and for ornamental purposes. Exceptions are the Muses at the mill house in Sanssouci park (see page 359); a few works by Albert Wolff in Potsdam, Berlin, Neustrelitz, and Schwerin; and the triumphal gate on the boundary of Sanssouci park, which has reliefs by Bläser and Schievelbein. In Berlin and its surroundings, Tobias Feilner and later Ernst March were particularly successful with such products, and the name of the sculptor Wilhelm Koch of Potsdam may be added to the list.

Within the process of social and economic development, the unusually close relationship between the arts and the crafts was to a great extent the joint work of Schinkel, Rauch, and Wilhelm Beuth, director of the ministerial department of Trade, Commerce, and Public Works. The growing interest in artistic matters, promoted not least by the new technology, did the rest. Moreover, King Frederick William IV was a knowledgeable patron, and his commissions for works in the royal castles and gardens of Berlin and Potsdam took effect on new developments with remarkable rapidity.

François Léquine and August Fischer
The Apollo Belvedere (1827)
Bronze, height 235 cm; Potsdam, Stiftung Preussische Schlösser und Gärten Berlin-Brandenburg

A Roman marble copy (c. 340 BC) of an original Greek bronze has been one of the best known of classical statues ever since the Renaissance, when it was set up in the courtyard of the Belvedere in the Vatican at the beginning of the 16th century. Joachim Winckelmann's account of it in 1756 pointed the way to its adoption as the classical ideal by the intellectual world of the late 18th century and the 19th century. This bronze cast of 1827 is one of the works used to replace the statues of classical antiquity taken to Berlin from the park at Sanssouci. They also reflect a new view of classical art.

PAINTING

Christoph Martin Vogtherr

The Academy, Classical Antiquity, and the Fatherland (1786–1810)

The accession to the throne of Frederick William II in August 1786 marked a watershed for the arts in Prussia (although not at first to the same extent in all the arts). A new era of Prussian sculpture opened up with the return to Berlin of Johann Gottfried Schadow in 1787. The first major works of Neo-classical architecture were Erdmannsdorff's royal chambers in the Berlin Palace, and the Brandenburg Gate built by Langhans shortly afterwards. But there was no comparable development in the painting of the time. Under Frederick II, Prussia had fallen behind other leading centers of art in Europe, and it took longer to make up for lost time in painting than in the other arts.

Only after 1810, and ultimately not until the 1820s, was Prussia of any real importance in European painting. In this, the significance of the year 1786 derives less from developments in painting itself than from the reorganization of artistic education. In the last months of Frederick II's reign, a fundamental reform of the Berlin Academy of Arts and Mechanical Sciences (Akademie der Künst und mechanischen Wissenschaft) had started, and within a few years an institution that had recently existed only in name was transformed into both an efficient educational establishment as well as an influential public forum for the discussion of art. Over the following decades the Berlin Academy became the foundation for a flowering of art in Berlin, and indeed in Prussia as a whole.

The reorganisation of the Berlin Academy of Arts

Frederick II's lack of interest in painting had threatened the very existence of the Berlin Academy of Arts, which had declined into a mere school of draftsmanship. The Prussian Minister of State and mining expert Friedrich Anton von Heinitz began its internal reorganization in 1786.

As President of the Royal Porcelain Manufacturing Commission, he had direct experience of the grave shortage in Prussia of experts trained in modern skills. In February 1786, he therefore asked Frederick II (still on the throne) to appoint him Curator of the Academy of Arts. His initial concern was with the country's production of luxury goods, which could not stand up to international competition; but as a man of artistic interests, Heinitz also knew that the general standard of Prussian painting, graphic arts, and sculpture was alarmingly low. In the wake of the reform of the Academy, he tried tackling this problem from two directions at once. First, artistic education was placed on a solid foundation by the provision of more funds and the appointment of new teachers; second, collections were built up for teaching purposes, and members and pupils of the Academy were granted access to the royal art collections. At the same time, the Academy acquired a new function as a middle-class forum for the public discussion of art.

The exhibitions

The exhibitions held in the Academy building in Unter den Linden, first annually and then once

MONATS-SCHRIFT
DER
AKADEMIE DER KÜNSTE
UND
MECHANISCHEN WISSENSCHAFTEN ZU BERLIN.

Erster Band. 1788.

BERLIN
im Verlag der Königl. Preuss. Akademischen Kunst- und Buchhandlung.

Title page of the *Monats-Schrift der Akademie der Künste und mechanischen Wissenschaften zu Berlin*
(Monthly Journal of the Academy of Arts and Mechanical Sciences in Berlin) *Volume 1, 1788, engraving by Daniel Berger after Johann Christoph Frisch, allegory showing the arts of Berlin, Stiftung Archiv der Akademie der Künste*

The Genius of the Arts offers a brush to the figure of Painting, who is at work on a symbolic representation of Nature in the shape of the many-breasted Diana of Ephesus. To the left, the sister arts of Architecture and Sculpture stand next to a statue of Athene, the Greek goddess of wisdom and the arts. The torso of the Apollo Belvedere, in the foreground right, refers to Classical Antiquity as the other main source of the arts together with Nature.

every two years, provided an extremely comprehensive survey of modern art in Prussia for the first time. They also showed individual works by major foreign artists – including the likes of Angelika Kauffmann, Johann Christian Reinhardt, and Bertel Thorwaldsen.

The new exhibitions helped artists to compare their works with those of others. It also contributed a great deal to the rise of art criticism and the discussion of art, subsequently encouraging an improvement in the quality of the arts in Prussia, which soon became very noticeable.

The introduction of exhibitions was certainly one of the most useful steps taken during these years, and they reached unusually large sections of the educated population. The process can be traced both in Chodowiecki's letters and in Schadow's chronicle *Kunstwerke und Kunstansichten* (Works of Art and Views on Art).

Improvements in artistic education and its spread to Prussian provinces

Improved artistic education also spread to the Prussian provinces. Art schools were founded around this time in the provincial capitals of Magdeburg, Breslau, Königsberg, and Halle. These schools offered craftsmen a fundamental artistic training: the idea was for further artistic education to be concentrated in Berlin, while the basics were taught in the provinces, where the best students could also be identified.

This systematic and centralized structure of training – like the exhibitions and the provision of bursaries for students to visit Rome – was introduced in imitation of the customs of pre-Revolutionary France. (After the Revolution, the Academy in Paris was closed down as an "absolutist" institution.)

The key to the upturn in artistic developments in Prussia was the new and enlarged class of patrons prepared to commission works: the importance of the middle classes to the visual arts was constantly increasing. Nonetheless, the court and the state remained pre-eminent as patrons.

Under Frederick William II, more public commissions were given in an attempt to stimulate the arts and set artistic standards. Accounts of works too large to be moved and put on display were therefore included in the catalogs of the Academy exhibitions; these were state buildings like the Brandenburg Gate, or the interior design of castles, or church altarpieces. Royal commissions were seen as part of an active artistic policy, something that had long been the custom in other European states.

Under Frederick William I and Frederick II, Prussia had been content to go its own way (Frederick II in particular regarded painting as essentially a private matter); but under Frederick William II, the country belatedly associated itself with wider European developments.

Johann Gottlieb Puhlmann
Self-Portrait with Classical Statue (c. 1808)
Oil on oak panel, 38 x 28.5 cm;
Berlin, Stiftung Stadtmuseum Berlin

In this small picture Puhlmann paints himself in a relaxed attitude. The Greek statue *The Discus Thrower* in the background indicates Puhlmann's artistic ideals; at the same time it forms a striking contrast to the carefully realistic depiction of the painter himself. The painting was probably shown at the Berlin Academy exhibition of 1808.

The state of Prussian painting after the death of Frederick II

A survey of the state of Prussian painting after the death of Frederick II gives the impression that while the period was of central historical importance, paradoxically enough it had no really significant painters. A glance at the major works of the time makes it clear that Neo-classicism was the dominant style in Prussia, as elsewhere. There was a process comparable to that in other countries, whereby Neo-classicism acquired specifically Prussian significance through the equation of classical antiquity (Greek rather than Roman) with contemporary Prussia, politically as well as artistically.

Friedrich Georg Weitsch
Princesses Louise and Frederica Crowning the Bust of Frederick William II (1795)
Oil on canvas, 285 x 207 cm; Berlin, Stiftung Preussische Schlösser und Gärten Berlin-Brandenburg, Schloss Charlottenburg

This picture was painted in 1795 in reference to the Peace of Basel, concluded in April of that year. By its terms, Prussia recognized the French Republic and its territories on the left bank of the Rhine, in order to keep its own back free for the forthcoming Third Partition of Poland. The olive branch for the "peacemaker," and the "dark grove of Peace" in the background, refer directly to the Peace of Basel. The choice of the bust (a work of 1792 by Johann Gottfried Schadow) is the painter's tribute to his sculptor friend and colleague.

In direct recognition of Winckelmann's maxim that only the imitation of antiquity would make modern art inimitable, classical art was regarded as a suitable representation for the artistic expression of the country's newly won political importance. While this message was only very gradually translated into painting, it was part of the whole program of the reform of the Academy. In 1788, when the Academy began publishing the *Monats-Schrift der Akademie der Künste und mechanischen Wissenschaften zu Berlin* (Monthly Journal of the Academy of Arts and Mechanical Sciences in Berlin), to distribute and propagate its aims and record the progress it had made, the title page of the first issue bore an engraving by Daniel Berger (after Johann Christoph Frisch) that conveyed the artistic ideals of Neo-classicism in allegorical form (see page 362).

In the years after 1786, Berlin's painters increasingly looked to new models. France, meaning Paris, temporarily lost its importance as a place for study and artistic orientation. Rome, however, the center of Neo-classicism, retained its pre-eminence as the artistic center of Europe. Prussian artists were now able to see the advantages of studying in Rome and conducting artistic exchanges with the city, and opportunities to do so were introduced by the Academy of Arts.

Bursaries and prizes for artists

Regular bursaries and prizes for artists enabled a large number of students from the Berlin Academy to visit Rome for an extended visit. Friedrich Rehberg, from Hanover, supervised the students from Berlin in the city.

In 1787, Johann Gottlieb Puhlmann was appointed to a post in Prussia. Puhlmann, from Potsdam, came with a great reputation, reflecting the esteem in which Roman Neo-classicism was held (see page 363), for he had studied with the most important Italian painter in Rome, Girolamo Pompeo Batoni. His duties included painting works regularly for the king, although his pictures did not really come up to expectations.

Puhlmann painted in an agreeably Neo-classical style, but he was capable of little variety, and he soon lost touch with later developments in Neo-classicism. Frederick William II appointed him supervisor of the picture galleries of Berlin and Potsdam, which he reorganized and cataloged.

The importance of British painters in the 18th century

In the 18th century, British painters played a major part in developments in the international art world for the first time. Previously the British had featured mainly just as buyers of works of art, but their architects, and in particular their painters, now attracted increasing attention, largely through the systematic studies they had made of classical antiquity. It is not surprising, then, that British art began to feature prominently in Prussia at this period.

As in France, the interest of such examples lay not only in their artistic quality but also in the social and economic modernity they reflected, something with which Heinitz, Erdmannsdorff, Langhans, and others were well acquainted from their own experience. In 1795, a work by the Brunswick painter Friedrich Georg Weitsch was displayed near the entrance to the Academy exhibition. It showed the two Prussian princesses, Louise and Frederica, embellishing the marble bust of their father-in-law King Frederick William II with roses and a laurel branch (see opposite). In this work, Weitsch was trying to achieve the classic "Grand Manner" of English portraits, in particular those of Sir Joshua Reynolds, president of the Royal Academy in London.

The columnar porphyry plinth, the marble bust, the tripod, and the open architecture of the columns all create a classical atmosphere, which is an appropriate setting for the two princesses in their plain, flowing robes. In much the same way as Reynolds had painted Lady Sarah Bunbury in a scene of homage to the Graces, the two princesses are cast in a role that pays a compliment to the subjects of the painting on several levels, and is also an intellectual game for the observer. The two princesses personify the Grand Manner: they can also be seen as exemplary daughters-in-law performing an act of family piety, and as good subjects honoring their king.

The aim of the painting was to raise the Prussian style of portraiture, long known for its sobriety, above the level of a playful costumed charade (as for instance in the painter Pesne) and present it as significant in content, and evocative of classical antiquity in form. Weitsch does not achieve the artistic vigor of his great British examples, but this flatteringly ironic piece of role-play, with its many illusions of form, is directly descended from British portraiture. The work paved the way for the artist's appointment as court painter in 1797. The road to success in Prussia was found by following British examples.

The Scottish painter Edward Francis Cunningham deliberately exploited this phenomenon in his own career. After visits to Italy, Paris, and St. Petersburg, among other places, he came to Prussia in 1784. His pictures in the "English style," both portraits and historical paintings, were influential. They were of only modest artistic quality, but his manner in both genres was well adapted to the Prussian taste.

The decorative interior painting at this period oscillated for some time between the Rococo and Neo-classical styles, as indeed it had done in the last years of the reign of Frederick II. The stylistic mixture is evident in the decoration of the rooms in the Berlin Palace, now destroyed, and the still extant

Johann Christoph Frisch
The Three Graces Honoring the Hero Grown to Manhood (1790)
Oil on canvas, 101 x 156 cm; Potsdam, Stiftung Preussische Schlösser und Gärten Berlin-Brandenburg, Marmorpalais

The Yellow Study in the Marble Palace, as in part a private room, has decoration with ornamental themes referring to the business of government and the virtues required of a ruler. This painting, set above the door to the vestibule, shows the ruler as a warrior hero of classical antiquity after winning a battle (symbolized by the figure of Victory in the background) while the Three Graces, the arts, offer him a cornucopia. The ruler, whose interest in music is indicated by the lyre leaning against his throne, thus harvests the blessings of peace and the patronage of the arts. The figures, painted in gray in front of the red-tinged marble of the niche, are designed to give the impression that painting was carved in two kinds of stone.

interiors of the Marble Palace in Potsdam, the work of Rode, his pupil Johann Christoph Frisch, and the theatrical set designer and decorative painter Bartolommeo Verona.

Here the illusionist style of the late Baroque period allows views of a heaven inhabited by mythological figures (as in the Dressing Room) to exist side by side with scenes resembling panel painting on a ceiling (as in the Yellow Study).

Frisch's two paintings in the Yellow Study represent a maturer Neo-classicism, referring back to classical vase painting or classical reliefs – an effect that is emphasized here by painting in colors resembling stone (see below). At the same time Asmus Jakob Carstens was already working for Heinitz on the severe Neo-classical frescos in the minister's palace in Berlin (now destroyed).

How Enlightenment played its part in the reform of the Academy

The reform of the Academy derived from late Enlightenment ideals. Social and economic utilitarianism was regarded as an important aim, and one that also affected contemporary works of art. Such ideas already had a muted presence at the court of Berlin, for instance in the work of Chodowiecki, and now they came into their own. Their ideas could be expressed in practical ways (for instance, the reform of the Royal Porcelain Factory at this time), or directly through art itself.

The conduct held up for admiration by artists at this time did not consist in the noble sentiments of great men but in practical action: for instance, the Duke of Brunswick helping victims of the flood on the river Oder, or a Spanish countess giving money to charity (see opposite, above). Again, Chodowiecki's work had set out a strategy for propagating the new middle-class concept of morality by showing positive and negative examples in opposition.

This idea, originally expressed in graphic art, was imported into painting by Chodowiecki's daughter Suzette Henry and other artists. They presented exemplary conduct, in this case family life that was in accordance with the ideals of the Enlightenment and of sensibility, in contrast to bad conduct: on the one hand the careful mother and housewife, content with her small domestic circle; on the other hand the society lady, neglecting her family (see opposite, right). Henry's five cycles of paintings

Christian Bernhard Rode
The Spanish Mother (c. 1793)
Oil on canvas, 80 x 123.5 cm; Berlin, Stiftung Stadtmuseum Berlin

Rode depicts a story from the year 1786 that he had read in a newspaper: a Spanish countess weighs her children, who have just recovered from a dangerous illness, and gives their weight in gold to charity. Rode considered that the story set a good example of conduct for his own day and was thus a highly suitable subject for a painting.

Suzette Henry
A Game of Cards (c. 1802)
Oil on canvas, 62 x 52.5 cm; Celle, Bomann-Museum

Henry painted five cycles of pictures illustrating both the middle-class ideal of life and its opposite. This painting, from *The Consequences of Happy and Unhappy Marriage*, depicts the unhappy wife losing her money during a nocturnal game of cards.

Suzette Henry
Self-portrait (c. 1786)
Pastel, 33.1 x 28.8 cm; Berlin, Stiftung Stadtmuseum Berlin

were reproduced as prints, and the social influence of the ideas they put forward was increased by their wide distribution. The works of Rode and Henry are variations on genre painting, a form they attempted to raise from the sentimental to the moral plane by reference to its moral re-evaluation in Britain and above all in France.

Portraits made up a large proportion of the works of art of this period, in a wide range of styles between strict Neo-classicism and Realism. While Henry's self-portrait presents a very personal, informal image of herself (see page 367), Johann Carl Heinrich Kretschmar's portraits attempt to express the heroic Neo-classicism of the time, with the landscape and the weather being used to reflect emotions.

New art joins forces with old

An important phenomenon of the years around 1800 was the way in which new kinds of works of art joined the traditional genres. In 1788, Frederick William II had announced several prizes for artists, the highest to be awarded to a picture based on the history of Brandenburg and Prussia.

In 1799, Frederick William III urged artists to apply themselves to Prussian history and the Prussian landscape. As a result, the Academy exhibitions of 1800 and 1802 had a small separate section for scenes from Prussian history (though it was rather sparsely stocked). While Rode was stylistically conservative and remained an adherent of the Rococo, in content he is of central importance to this new trend in painting. His major project, however, was set back in the time of Frederick the Great: "With particular industry, and as a true patriot, he painted the most notable epochs in the history of Brandenburg, pictures that are still in his widow's house ... After the death of Frederick II he added seven more pieces portraying minor incidents in the life of that hero during the Seven Years' War." The series mentioned here by Ramler began in a conventional manner in 1787, with a scene of the king's death and two allegorical pictures relating to the Seven Years' War, largely in line with traditional Baroque iconography. However, the other pictures, depicting incidents from the now flourishing anecdotal literature about Frederick II, brought out a new, down-to-earth, human and even middle-class side of the hero's character. These paintings could be understood only by those who already knew the anecdote they depicted. *Frederick II Before the Battle of Torgau* is an early example in this series (see below). Rode emphasizes the historical proximity of the events by depicting characters in contemporary costume (rather than the Greek or Roman costume frequently used in history

Christian Bernhard Rode
Frederick II Before the Battle of Torgau (1791)
Oil on canvas, 118 x 151 cm; Berlin, Staatliche Museen zu Berlin – Preussischer Kulturbesitz, Gemäldegalerie

A contemporary anecdote presents Frederick II as a considerate and modest ruler: the king is said to have kept watch over the sleeping General Keith, and in doing so trod in the ashes of the camp fire over which a soldier's wife was cooking. Rode is here emphasizing the "human" side of Frederick II (in a manner that soon became quite common) in order to appeal to a middle-class public.

Edward Francis Cunningham
Frederick II at the Battle of Hochkirch (c. 1787)
Oil on canvas, 154 x 205 cm; Berlin, Stiftung Preussische Schlösser und Gärten Berlin-Brandenburg, Schloss Charlottenburg

Cunningham depicts Frederick II on the battlefield of Hochkirch saying farewell to General Ziethen, who has just fallen in the battle. Regal dignity and emotional reaction are effectively combined.

painting), and set the scenes in what is recognizably a view of the landscape of the March of Brandenburg. Under Frederick William II, and in his own old age, Christian Bernhard Rode received a number of further major commissions and participated in the great building projects of the time: the Berlin Palace, the Brandenburg Gate, the Marble Palace, and the Veterinary School. As director of the Academy, he occupied a key position (and was sharply attacked by Chodowiecki for his weak and undisciplined administration of his office). It is indicative of the transitional character of the epoch that a painter of the past generation, such as Rode, could be appointed to so important a position after 1786. His death in 1797, in the same year as that of Frederick William II, finally marked the end of the Friderician period in painting.

Influential in portraiture, as we have seen, Edward Francis Cunningham was of a similar significance in the early development of Prussian historical painting. According to Friedrich Schadow, he had "a good eye for Prussian military uniforms and bearing, and took the liberty of correcting our own masters, which was well received."

As a Scotsman, Cunningham had direct links with British painting, especially in the field of portraiture. British innovations in the field of contemporary historical painting reached Prussia mainly through prints. Edward Penny's *Death of General Wolfe*, of 1764, was influential in its consistent use of religious and classical formulae for the depiction of current events. Schadow himself referred directly to this work: "The same period saw the publication of that valuable print *General Wolfe's Death* after Benjamin West, and the battles after Trumbull, engraved by Clemens, old Müller, and Sharp. Cunningham and Clemens had come to Berlin to do the same for Prussian history" (see above).

Among the variety of patriotic themes that Frederick William III wanted artists to tackle in their work in 1799 was that of "the landscape of the

Daniel Berger, after Johann Christoph Frisch
The Death of Field Marshal Kurt Christoph Schwerin at the Battle of Prague (1790)
Engraving, 46.5 x 61 cm; Potsdam, Stiftung Preussische Schlösser und Gärten Berlin-Brandenburg, Plankammer

Daniel Berger's engraving is from a 1787 painting by Frisch that was shown at the same Berlin Academy exhibition as Cunningham's picture (see page 369). Frisch was directly following British examples, with particular reference to Edward Penny's 1764 painting, *Death of General Wolfe*. Like Penny, Frisch depicts the hero's death in the manner of a religious Lamentation of Christ.

Christian Bernhard Rode
The Zackenfall Cascade in Silesia (1794)
Etching, 30.4 x 18.6 cm; Berlin, Staatliche Museen zu Berlin – Preussischer Kulturbesitz, Kupferstichkabinett

Fatherland" – a considerable artistic challenge since there was no established artistic tradition of such pictures. Some landscapes of the March of Brandenburg had in fact been painted by artists in the circle around Pesne and Knobelsdorff, but to the contemporary mind the largely unspectacular countryside of Prussia did not seem a suitable subject.

Now, however, painters turned not only to the usual vedutas, but also to those two regions of Prussia that were most likely to convey an effect of the "sublime": the Harz Mountains and the Riesengebirge. Once again, Christian Bernhard Rode was of particular significance in the artistic discovery of these two mountain ranges (see left). His views of the area, sketched as private exercises on his journeys, were confined to the graphic arts, which were always more open to innovations than painting. Even more important for the discovery of the Harz Mountains as a subject for historical and landscape painting was the artistic Weitsch family of Brunswick. The patriarch of the family, Johann Friedrich Weitsch, had been painting views of the Harz before 1765. His son Friedrich Georg turned to the legends of the area; his *Feast of Sacrifice to Krodo* (see opposite), attempts to use its pre-Christian past as a historical subject, a procedure with parallels in many parts of Europe at the time.

This concern with the local landscape and its past history aroused quite a wide interest. It is worth noting that Frederick William III intended his call for the depiction of the history and landscapes of "the Fatherland" to promote public interest in the Academy exhibitions. The traditional idealized landscapes and depictions of the virtues of classical antiquity did not appeal to the general public, a phenomenon also observed at exhibitions both in Paris and London.

Graphic arts, and the importance of Friedrich Gilly

However, the most important work among these views of the Fatherland was created in the realm of the graphic arts, and by an architect rather than a painter. In 1794, the young Friedrich Gilly had accompanied his father David on a working trip to Marienburg in West Prussia. On this occasion, Gilly senior had suggested the demolition of the fortress so that its bricks could be re-used as building materials; his son, by contrast, was deeply moved by the partially ruined architecture of the citadel.

In 1795, Friedrich Gilly exhibited at the Academy his *Zeichnungen einiger merkwürdiger Partien aus dem alten Schlosse des teutschen Ritterordens zu Marienburg in Westpreussen* (Drawings of Some Remarkable Parts of the Old Castle of the German Order of Chivalry at Marienburg in West Prussia). From 1799 to 1803, a series of aquatints by Friedrich Frick from Gilly's drawings, partially revised and with additional figures added by Franz

Ludwig Catel, was published in several instalments (see page 372), together with some detailed views from pictures by Friedrich Rabe.

The aquatint series was also the beginning of a new and important genre in the development of painting and graphics in Prussia, the genre of architectural painting – although it was another decade before it really began to flourish. At the same time, Gilly's prints represented the first landmark in Prussia's historical and artistic involvement with the Gothic style. Gilly saw the Marienburg as a monument to the past glories of the Fatherland, and a place redolent of "the sublime." With these two ideas in mind, he produced prints going far beyond the traditional veduta.

Such graphic techniques as aquatint and mezzotint became well established in Prussia at this time, and were deliberately encouraged. Again, English masters like Charles Townley figured prominently, and so did Johan Frederik Clemens from Denmark. Friedrich Wilhelm Gubitz's revival of the woodcut also derived from the English example, while it was also seen as specifically German and in the tradition of the Dürer epoch (see page 373).

For the very reason that they had been so successful, the reforming ideals of the Academy of Art soon came up against the ideas of a new age. Before the utilitarian ideas of the Enlightenment promoted by the generation of Chodowiecki and Heinitz could be completely absorbed, there was a controversy within the Berlin Academy that signaled a new understanding of art throughout Europe. The two adversaries involved, one standing for the old,

Friedrich Georg Weitsch
Feast of Sacrifice to Krodo on the Harzburg (c. 1797–1798)
Oil on canvas, 127 x 162.5 cm;
Berlin, Stiftung Archiv der Akademie der Künste, Kunstsammlung

The explanatory note in the exhibition catalog of 1798 provides the key to this painting: the tribe's firstborn children and some Roman captives in the foreground are to be sacrificed to the Germanic god Krodo. Weitsch was drawing on the interpretation current in his time of the late medieval Altar of Krodo (now in the Goslar Museum), and uses it as the basis for a depiction of pre-Christian Germanic legends and culture.

Friedrich Frick, after Friedrich Gilly
Vaults Under the Great Refectory of the Marienburg
Aquatint

After its rediscovery by the architect Gilly and the publication of his drawings as aquatints, the Marienburg, a medieval fortress, was regarded as an important Prussian monument. The print above illustrates the overpowering impression made on Gilly by the huge and ruinous architecture of the fortress. The space of the vault dwarfs the human figures. His approach involves the idea of the "sublime" – the overwhelming, cathartic effect of awesome phenomena in nature and art – that was central to 18th-century aesthetics.

late 18th-century concept of art, the other for the new ideas of the 19th century, were Heinitz as director of the Academy, and the artist Asmus Jakob Carstens from Schleswig. Carstens had come to Berlin in 1788, after studying in Copenhagen, and was a protégé of Heinitz, who commissioned him to paint the interior decorations for a hall in his own town house in 1790. In the same year, Carstens was appointed to teach plaster casting at the Academy, a part of the students' training that more than any other expressed academic ideals: the study of a sublime and idealized nature was embodied by plaster casts and the sculptures of classical antiquity. In 1792, Carstens was given the coveted bursary for a visit to Rome. He never returned to Berlin, dying prematurely in Rome in 1795.

The fact that Carstens had stayed on in Rome beyond the two years for which the bursary was expected to run, and failed to send the specimen works required of him by the Academy back to Berlin on time, led to a violent argument with Heinitz, who had initially been very patient. While Heinitz insisted that Carstens must fulfill his obligations and demanded his return to his teaching post at the Berlin Academy, Carstens defied him in a famous statement to the effect that he was "... a member not of the Berlin Academy, but of mankind." He would not, he said, become "the slave of any academy." This was a significant conflict, illustrating the clash between two different views of the artist's role: on the one hand the socially integrated, institutionally trained artist who fulfills commissions and teaches others in his turn; and on the other, the independent artist of the 19th and 20th centuries, who in principle feels bound only to his own artistic ideals (see opposite, below). Carstens thus stands at the end (in terms of artistic concepts if not chronologically) of a brief but epoch-making period in the history of painting in Prussia.

Friedrich Wilhelm Gubitz
Albrecht Dürer (c. 1806)
Woodcut, enlarged copy, size of original: 7.3 x 6.3 cm (entire print), 5.2 x 4.2 cm (pictorial area); Berlin, Staatliche Museen zu Berlin – Preussischer Kulturbesitz, Kupferstichkabinett

Gubitz was the central figure in the revival of the woodcut, following a British fashion. Here he takes as his subject Albrecht Dürer, Germany's outstanding master of the technique. In 1806, when this portrait of Dürer was shown at the Academy exhibition, Gubitz presented Queen Louise with a colored woodcut after Cranach – another indication that the revival of the woodcut technique struck a patriotic note.

Asmus Jakob Carstens
The Voyage of Megapenthes (1795)
Tempera on canvas, 63.5 x 91 cm; Berlin, Stiftung Archiv der Akademie der Künste, Kunstsammlung

This picture by Carstens illustrates a scene from the Roman writer Lucian in which the tyrant Megapenthes is tied to the mast of a ship on his way to the Underworld. The cobbler Micyllus, whom he had persecuted during his lifetime, squats on his shoulders. The style of the figure painting derives from Michelangelo, whose work Carstens studied in Rome. The picture also makes a politically revolutionary statement. In 1795, Carstens sent this painting, which expresses a new, Romantic mood in art, to the director of the Berlin Academy, Heinitz, an obvious gesture of defiance.

New Ideals (1810–1840)

Painting from the years between 1810 and 1840 clearly reflects the hopes and crises of the period. While artistic and political landmarks did not always coincide exactly, they did occur close together in time. The introduction of Romanticism into Prussia, for instance, can be precisely dated to the year 1810, when, as a direct consequence of the Napoleonic Wars, the pace of political reforms was greatly increased. The accession to the throne of Frederick William IV in 1840 was a significant date in the arts, more particularly because Schinkel, Carl Blechen, and Caspar David Friedrich all died around then in the same 12-month period.

At the Congress of Vienna (1814–1815), Prussia acquired the Rhineland, an area with a rich artistic tradition of its own, and one far superior to that of Brandenburg-Prussia itself. While the other Prussian provinces never had much influence on the development of painting in Prussia, the Düsseldorf Academy became its second and for a long time its more important artistic center.

Art flourished in these three decades, reaching far wider sections of the population than ever before. The number of impoverished artists was also growing. Societies for the promotion of the fine arts were set up and thus formed a new link between artists and the public; they promoted the distribution of works of art by buying and selling them. The Society of Friends of Art founded in Prussia in 1825 was one of the first in Germany. At the same time, many collections of contemporary art, which sometimes included foreign works, were also being built up in Berlin.

Neo-classicism, Romanticism, and Realism

The artistic tendency of these years defies simple stylistic classification. Variants of Neo-classicism, Romanticism, and Realism coexisted. Romantic painting made its mark as soon as it was introduced at the Berlin Academy exhibition of 1810. It was at this time that the Brotherhood of St. Luke (usually known as the Nazarenes) moved from Vienna to Rome. The movement aimed to revive a specifically Christian form of German art, and Wilhelm Schadow's return to Berlin from Rome in 1819 established a link with this first modern group of artists.

From today's standpoint, landscape painting was the most important genre in the early 19th century. Its importance for the art of its time is based not only on the high quality of many of the works produced, but also on the diversity of its artistic concepts. Landscape painting in Prussia was not at first very highly esteemed; it was rescued from this shadowy existence first by Karl Friedrich Schinkel and then by Carl Blechen.

Schadow remarked on the importance of the Academy exhibition of 1810 at the time: "Historical painting was represented by the hands of true masters, and perhaps even more brilliant were the works in the landscape genre …"

However, he was not referring to what would have been regarded today as the most remarkable pictures in the exhibition, where Caspar David

Opposite
Karl Friedrich Schinkel
Medieval City on a River (1815)
Oil on canvas, 95 x 140.6 cm; Berlin, Staatliche Museen zu Berlin – Preussischer Kulturbesitz, Nationalgalerie

Schinkel's painting can be interpreted as an allegory of the Napoleonic Wars. The storm of the French occupation has moved away; the rainbow symbolizes hopes of a better future. A new Germany (like the cathedral in the picture) is still under construction as the emperor rides in. Similar symbolism was expressed later in the resumption of building on Cologne Cathedral, a project supported by Schinkel.

Karl Friedrich Schinkel
Landscape near Pichelswerder (1814)
Oil on canvas, 62.3 x 96.2 cm; Essen, Museum Folkwang

Schinkel painted this view of the town of Spandau from Pichelswerder. However, the painting is not primarily a veduta; rather, Schinkel has adopted Friedrich's idea of the Romantic "landscape of the soul." The two figures seen from behind in the foreground are part of its basic vocabulary.

Friedrich was represented by three major works: *Monk by the Sea*, *Abbey in the Oak Wood*, and a drawing. At the crown prince's urging, the king bought both paintings – a purchase that, together with the appointment of Peter von Cornelius to a post in Berlin, was the most important initiative in the field of painting ever taken by Crown Prince Frederick William, later King Frederick William IV.

The art critics paid a great deal of attention to Friedrich's paintings (Kleist's essay on the *Monk by the Sea* is the best known account) and their influence was soon perceptible. Most notably, Karl Friedrich Schinkel painted a series of Romantic landscapes directly deriving from Friedrich in the years that followed. In Schinkel's case, the impression made by Friedrich's works fell on fertile ground, for his *Gothic Church Behind Trees*, one of the first lithographs produced in Berlin and typical of Romantic ideas, was shown at the same 1810 Academy exhibition (see right). It was, as he said in the caption to his lithograph, "an attempt to express the pleasing, yearning melancholy that fills the heart at the sound of church bells ringing for divine service."

Left
Karl Friedrich Schinkel
Gothic Church Behind Trees (c. 1810)
Lithograph, 48.6 x 34.3 cm; Berlin, Staatliche Museen zu Berlin – Preussischer Kulturbesitz, Kupferstichkabinett

The Gothic church is shown here behind vigorous trees, a link frequently made at the time. However, the church is included to convey atmosphere rather than as an independent work of architecture. The lithograph was intended to express the deep emotions felt at the "sound of the church bells ringing for divine service."

Heinrich Anton Dähling
A Prince's Entry (1822)
Oil on canvas, 74 x 101 cm; Berlin, Staatliche Museen zu Berlin – Preussischer Kulturbesitz, Nationalgalerie

Only seven years after Schinkel painted a similar scene (see page 375, top), Dähling also painted the entry of a prince into a medieval city. In a manner typical of the social and political change that followed the end of the Napoleonic wars, Dähling transformed the theme of a political utopia into a genre scene.

Carl Blechen
The Camp of the Semnonii (1828)
Oil on canvas, 126 x 200 cm; now lost, formerly in Berlin, Nationalgalerie

This celebrated work united principles of classic landscape painting (the framing of a view, a clear division into foreground, background and middle ground, the addition of costumed figures) with an interest in prehistory and the local Prussian landscape, in this case the Müggelberge. *The Camp of the Semnonii* has been lost since World War II.

The depiction of an emotion rather than an object, and above all the attempt to find an equivalent to music in painting, are ideas central to Romanticism. Schinkel's *Landscape near Pichselswerder* of 1814 is a classic example of a Romantic "landscape of the soul" in which the transcendent shines through the visible (see page 374). Landscape becomes both the expression of such emotions as religious ecstasy and the screen on which they are projected. Schinkel also followed Friedrich in the use of color to convey such atmospheric effects as the morning light above a misty plain – effects specially designed to convey feelings of mystery and wonder.

Over the next few years Schinkel developed the "historical landscape" illustrating as many as possible of the social, political, and artistic aspects of a culture. Schinkel's concept of landscape painting is best summed up by his first biographer, the art historian Gustav Friedrich Waagen: "It is clearly distinct from all previously known kinds of landscape painting, in that it presents us with a complete and faithful image of the nature, art, and life of the various regions and periods of our globe, in beautiful and appropriate artistic forms." When he was painting in this genre, Schinkel drew on his experience of painting dioramas, and until 1811–1812 such works took precedence over his pure landscape painting.

His pictures of Gothic cathedrals were painted at the time when national feeling reached a peak during the Napoleonic Wars (see page 375, top).

Projecting his subject back into the Middle Ages, Schinkel portrays the utopian future of Prussia and Germany as a country of prosperous citizens united under imperial rule and the protection of the Church. Within quite a short time, however, the pictorial feeling in such images was entirely changed and drained of its political potential. Only seven years later, Heinrich Anton Dähling's painting of a similar subject transposed it into the middle-class Biedermeier style (see opposite). The community of the future became a community of the past, a stately architectural symbol turned into a cosy stage set. Political conflicts were glossed over.

Schinkel's outstanding contribution to landscape painting found few to emulate it in Berlin. At first, no school of landscape painting formed; even at the Academy exhibition of 1824 Schadow noted that the good landscapes were all by foreign artists – and this at a time when Carl Blechen, the greatest genius of Prussian landscape painting, was just embarking on his career.

In Blechen's work, the painting of Berlin in the 19th century reached its first high point. In many ways he was paradigmatic of the art of the period. He personified the new type of Romantic artist: he came from a poor background, he was extremely sensitive, emotionally unstable, and his works united apparently irreconcilable worlds. Artistically, he stood "between Romanticism and Realism." His early work was based on the Neo-classical landscape painting he had learned from his teacher, Peter Ludwig Lütke, at the Berlin Academy.

Blechen came to painting as a profession quite late. He trained as a banker and then took a course at the Berlin Academy of Arts while he worked in a bank. Through Schinkel's agency he became theatrical painter at the Berlin Königsstadt Theater in 1824, a position from which he resigned amidst some acrimony in 1827. The sale in 1828 of his *The Camp of the Semnonii* to the Society of Friends of Art of the State of Prussia enabled him to go to Italy. In this celebrated picture, Blechen depicted a scene

Carl Blechen
Trees in Sunlight in the Mill Valley at Amalfi (1829)
Pencil, pen and sepia on paper, 20.3 x 29.5 cm; Berlin, Stiftung Archiv der Academie der Künstler, Kunstsammlung

In his *Amalfi Sketchbook*, Blechen perfected the sepia technique in which he frequently chose to work. The sketches were made in an industrial landscape: a valley containing paper mills. This location gave Blechen the chance he needed to free himself from the overpowering classic tradition of Italy and devote himself entirely to capturing the effects of sunlight.

Carl Blechen
Interior View of the Palm House on Peacock Island From the West (1834)
Oil on canvas, 73.4 x 64.5 cm;
Berlin, Stiftung Preussische Schlösser und Gärten Berlin-Brandenburg, Schinkel-Pavillon

After accepting the contract given to him in 1832, Blechen produced five paintings in all, showing two different interior views of the Palm House. The building, which burned down in 1880, contained fragments of Indian palace architecture, visible on the left of the picture. The larger version shown here, which has only recently been rediscovered, was probably sent to the Russian Tsarist court, and is the one placing the greatest emphasis on the vegetation and the recumbent female figures, which are closer to the center of the picture than in preceding versions.

from the prehistory of the March of Brandenburg: the resistance offered to the Romans by the Semnonii, the legendary early inhabitants of the region; here there was a clear allusion to the Prussian resistance to Napoleon's armies. Blechen applied the laws of classical landscape composition to the landscape of the March, and created the first picture based on a prehistoric (if imaginary) episode set in the Berlin area.

Blechen made his artistic breakthrough while he was in Italy, even though his tour there in 1828–1829 was relatively short by comparison with the visits most German artists made to the country. This Italian journey represented his attempts to complete the classic form of artistic study upon which he had embarked late at the Berlin Academy. The results are all the more remarkable. Blechen took only a limited interest in the usual aims of a study tour. Instead he explored the landscape, the ordinary life and the light of Italy – a world very different from his home in Prussia. He produced a large number of drawings, watercolors, and sketches in oils while he was on his travels, and they formed the basis for his later works. The best of the drawings, which appear in what is known as the *Amalfi Sketchbook*, capture effects of light in a radical manner hardly ever achieved before (see page 377).

Blechen's Italian experiences determined the subsequent direction of his work. His colors were intensified to the utmost degree, and so was his sensitivity to light and its depiction. Blechen became neither a classic landscape painter nor a precursor of Impressionism, as he has often been described in the 20th century. His roots in the German Romantic tradition are always perceptible; even his more lighthearted works convey a sense of menace or instability. In his view of the Villa d'Este in Tivoli, for instance, the differences of scale between the architecture, the vegetation, and the figures are alarmingly unbalanced (see opposite). Blechen could not reconcile his own intense perceptions with the classic principles of composition.

His Italian sketches are among the best of that genre in the European art of his time, but something similar had been evident considerably earlier in the works of Achille-Etna Michallon and the young Jean Baptiste Camille Corot, in Christoffer Wilhelm Eckersberg and Johann Georg Dillis.

Later, these artists were able to integrate their Italian experiences into other works based on the classic principles, but Blechen never managed to achieve such a synthesis. It is the sense of a fracture running through his work that gives it its special quality of modernity.

Blechen was known almost exclusively as a painter in the landscape genre, and the part he played in the development of architectural painting has attracted far less notice from art historians. In 1834, Frederick William III, who liked views of Berlin and Potsdam, commissioned Blechen to paint the Palm House recently built on Peacock Island (see above). Once again, Schinkel had put forward Blechen's name, and his five paintings of two interior views of the Palm House were his first royal commission.

Schadow praised the "fine brushwork" in these pictures – a sign that Blechen had at least conformed to the demand for precision in architectural painting. At the same time, he transferred his experience of Italian light to the March of Brandenburg. Like the Palm House itself, his paintings are early Prussian masterpieces of a contemporary European phenomenon: a keen fascination with the exotic that was combined with a sense of superiority over it. The architectural painting of this period sprang from the depiction of medieval architecture, first near to home and then farther afield, that had begun with Friedrich Gilly's views of the Marienburg in 1794. The genre now turned more

Carl Blechen
The Villa d'Este in Tivoli (1831–1832)
Oil on canvas, 127.5 x 94 cm; Berlin, Staatliche Museen zu Berlin – Preussischer Kulturbesitz, Nationalgalerie

In the *Villa d'Este in Tivoli* Blechen draws on Schinkel's concept of a "cultural landscape." The villa is enlivened by figures in costume intended to suggest the Italian Renaissance. The painting is based on many sketches made at Tivoli by Blechen during his Italian journey.

towards the painting of southern works of architecture, or buildings seen as exotic.

Brücke's view of the church of Santa Maria in Aracoeli close to the Capitol in Rome may be taken as characteristic of this group (see page 380, left). Other features of such works are precision of detail and the population of the scenes with typical local figures. Brücke's painting, however, reflects a literally Prussian perspective: he painted it from a vantage point not far from the Palazzo Caffarelli, the residence of the Prussian Ambassador in Rome.

Our modern image of the Berlin of Schinkel's period has to a great extent been formed by the paintings of Eduard Gärtner, showing the Prussian

Below
Eduard Gärtner
Notre-Dame in Paris, From the South (1827)
Oil on canvas, 58 x 42 cm; Berlin, Stiftung Preussische Schlösser und Gärten Berlin-Brandenburg

In this major work of his Paris period, Gärtner painted an exact view of the cathedral in its everyday setting. Its main effect derives from the small figures in the foreground, which set off the dignity, huge size, and dark color of the cathedral.

Above left
Wilhelm Brücke
View of the Capitol in Rome (1831)
Oil on canvas, 72 x 62.5 cm;
Essen, Museum Folkwang

Brücke's painting shows a view from the Palazzo Caffarelli of the church of Santa Maria in Aracoeli. The artist skims over the Capitol itself, though the scene of everyday life is populated by figures added with particular care. There are several variant versions of this view.

capital at its most Neo-classical. The present interest in Gärtner himself is new, for his contemporaries did not think him a particularly important architectural painter. He modeled his pictures on Dutch townscapes of the 17th century: both periods felt pride in the community life of their cities, and that pride was reflected in their buildings.

Gärtner's picture of the cathedral of Notre Dame was painted at the end of his stay in Paris, from 1825 to 1827, and is one of his earliest works (see above, right). He had already learned to paint scenes in faithful detail during his training with the Royal Porcelain Manufactory; while he was in Paris he discovered how to treat color with more freedom, and he also took an increasing interest in the daily life of the city, a very typical aspect of his work. Gärtner's major painting was his six-part panorama of Berlin from the roof of the Friedrichwerdersche Kirche (see opposite). This work is in the tradition of large all-round views, but transfers it to the panel painting format. Each section of the picture is seen from the church, and the royal buildings are included as part of the city. Viewer and viewpoint are both middle class.

Two years after Gärtner had painted this panorama, Schadow expressed the opinion that architectural painting was "that branch of painting which has now grown to the greatest maturity."

Like Gärtner's views of Berlin, Franz Krüger's paintings of parades express a middle-class sense of pride. Krüger turned an existing pictorial genre, the depiction of military ceremonial, into a representation of community life. The setting for his first parade, painted between 1824 and 1830, is therefore what was then the most modern part of the Unter den Linden area, with architecture more reminiscent of the era of reform and the Napoleonic Wars than the traditions of the ruling house of Prussia (see page 382).

Members of Berlin society participated in the event, and they are shown in the foreground of the painting as a community of individuals. This is particularly remarkable because Krüger's picture was commissioned by the later Tsar Nicholas, and another version of it was one of the few belated purchases of works of art made by Frederick William III. Only when the cities and rural communities of Prussia commissioned a painting from the artist as a gift for Frederick William IV was tension apparent between the donors and the royal recipient, whose neo-absolutist ideal of kingship was the direct opposite of Krüger's concept of kingship.

The artistic currents as shown through portrait paintings

Many different artistic currents came together in the portrait painting of this particular time. The austere Neo-classicism of such painters as Kretschmar soon gave way to the influence of the Nazarene movement, which looked back to German, Dutch, and Italian art of the 15th century. The Nazarene style was introduced into Berlin by Johann Gottfried Schadow's son Wilhelm. Wilhelm Schadow had originally joined the Nazarene group during his stay in Italy from 1811 to 1819, and he converted to Catholicism in 1814. While in Rome, he took part in the painting of frescos for the Casa Bartoldi; they marked the beginning of a new kind of monumental art and an attempt on the part of German painters to revive the Italian Renaissance style. Schadow's self-portrait with his brother Ridolfo and Bertel Thorwaldsen is an outstanding example of the Romantic theme of friendship, a subject especially popular among the Nazarene painters (see page 383, above).

Eduard Gärtner
Panorama of Berlin from the Roof of the Friedrichwerdersche Kirche (1834)
(Section, view looking north)
Oil on canvas, 58 x 42 cm; Berlin, Stiftung Preussische Schlösser und Gärten Berlin-Brandenburg, Schinkel-Pavillon

The section of the circular panorama shown here is a view north over the city to the Architectural Academy. The building work in progress on both the church and the Academy illustrates the sense of vital change the city was undergoing as it expanded, a process that the citizens of Berlin could observe clearly from the church roof.

Franz Krüger
Parade on the Opernplatz (1824–1830)
Oil on canvas, 249 x 374 cm; Berlin, Staatliche Museen zu Berlin – Preussischer Kulturbesitz, Nationalgalerie

Krüger was commissioned by the later Tsar Nicholas to paint a Berlin regiment parading in front of the King of Prussia. It is typical of Krüger, however, that the general impression is middle class rather than regal. The foreground contains artists and intellectuals as well as members of the government, the court, and the army.

Johann Erdmann Hummel was in the same tradition, and together with Gärtner he is now the best known of the architectural painters of Berlin, though he had more real influence on artistic developments in the city as professor of perspective at the Academy. Questions of perspective are usually very evident in his own paintings, for instance *The Game of Chess* (see opposite, below). Among the men depicted here, who include Hummel himself and the archaeologist Aloys Ludwig Hirt, is Count Ingenheim, who was the son of Frederick William II and Julie von Voss, and who took a great interest in pre-1500 art, a subject much discussed at this time in Berlin. In his painting of the chess players, Hummel, who had just returned from a journey to the Netherlands, referred back to the rigid construction of perspective and the still, almost frozen attitudes of the figures in the old Flemish masters and early Italian Renaissance. He and the young Wilhelm Schadow were fervent Neoclassicists, but at the same time they owned allegiance to the ideals of the Nazarenes and their search for a more "primitive" kind of art.

Franz Krüger's portraits point in quite a different direction. At an early stage Krüger took as his model the contemporary French art he was able to study in the royal collections and some private collections in Berlin; he did not visit Paris himself until 1846. His early portrait of Prince Augustus immediately reveals its French models, since he places the prince in front of François Gérard's portrait of Augustus's mistress Madame Récamier (see page 384).

There were several works by Gérard in the Prussian royal collections at this time. In a similar way, Charles Vernet's *Dedication of the Prussian Banners on the Champ de Mars*, also owned by the king, had been the point of departure for Krüger's parades. Like the young Gärtner, Krüger combined the attempt to achieve lively immediacy with ideas of painting learned from France, a combination particularly evident in his smaller works.

In the years around 1800 there had been very few commissions of any note in the field of religious painting. That situation altered dramatically after 1815. The Nazarenes had placed themes based on religion at the center of their work, taking their guidelines from the Middle Ages and the early Italian Renaissance, which they interpreted as periods of naïve and sincere religious art. Major commissions responded to this new artistic interest.

In 1816, soon after his return from Paris, Frederick William III commissioned a series of paintings for the Garnisonkirche in Potsdam. The king's uncertainty of his own opinion in artistic matters is expressed in his instructions that the paintings should imitate those of the Old Masters; some in the series are in fact direct copies. Three of the paintings were replaced in 1824 and 1830 by works by Wilhelm Schadow, Karl Begas, and Peter Rittig, clearly illustrating the great improvement in the quality of the genre made during the intervening years.

Begas was first employed by Frederick William III as a copyist. The painter had gone to Paris in 1813, and there studied in the studio of Baron Antoine Jean Gros. The King of Prussia saw several of his copies of Raphael there, and then bought some of his own religious works. In 1820, Begas completed the altarpiece for Berlin Cathedral, recently restored by Schinkel.

Wilhelm Schadow
Self-Portrait with Ridolfo Schadow and Bertel Thorwaldsen (c. 1818)
Oil on canvas, 91 x 118 cm; Berlin, Staatliche Museen zu Berlin – Preussischer Kulturbesitz, Nationalgalerie

The Schadow brothers, sons of Johann Gottfried, had been working in Rome since 1811. Thorwaldsen, who commissioned the picture, is shown bringing together the brothers Ridolfo and Wilhelm Schadow, who represent sculpture and painting.

Johann Erdmann Hummel
The Game of Chess (c. 1818–1819)
Oil on canvas, 38.5 x 44 cm; Berlin, Staatliche Museen zu Berlin – Preussischer Kulturbesitz, Nationalgalerie

This picture shows, from the left, the architect Hans Christian Genelli, the archaeologist Aloys Ludwig Hirt, Count Ingenheim, Hummel himself, the painter Friedrich Bury, and Count Friedrich Wilhelm of Brandenburg, one of Frederick William II's many sons. In a manner typical of Hummel, the painting unites complex effects of perspective and reflections.

Franz Krüger
Prince Augustus of Prussia (c. 1817)
Oil on canvas, 63 x 47 cm; Berlin, Staatliche Museen zu Berlin – Preussischer Kulturbesitz, Nationalgalerie

Prince Augustus, with the attributes of a field marshal, stands in the reception room of his palace, just completed to Schinkel's plans, in front of the painting by François Gérard of his Parisian mistress Madame Récamier, a picture now in the Musée Carnavalet in Paris. Krüger's painting is therefore both a portrait and an illustration of the theme of friendship.

Begas himself thought highly of this painting, and included a depiction of his own family in a preliminary study or small copy of the picture. His painting *Pentecost* (see opposite, left) shows why (as he complained) he was considered too German in France and too French in Germany, for at that time there was nothing in Berlin to compare with his painting in its monumentality, which was derived from Raphael, and its strong, melting colors. Wilhelm Wach came back from studying in Paris with similar qualities of style.

Monumental painting: the pre-eminent genre

In the judgment of contemporaries, monumental painting was the pre-eminent genre. Prussia lagged far behind Munich in this field, but Prussian painters produced a number of large cycles. German monumental painting of the 19th century originated in the Nazarene frescos for the Casa Bartoldi in Rome, painted between 1815 and 1817.

As we have seen, one of the artists who had worked on them came later came to Berlin: Wilhelm Schadow. While commissions for monumental paintings had still been few and far between under Frederick William II, and were largely confined to allegorical interior decoration in the royal palaces, the genre now spread further afield and made claims of a more exalted nature. It addressed the general public, or at least educated circles, and helped to express and distribute new political messages.

One of the main themes was Prussian patriotism, taking up ideas from the patriotic pictures of around 1800; the stained-glass cycle for the summer refectory of the Marienburg may be regarded as a typical example. Commissioned as a gift from the royal family, this cycle was carried out from 1821 onward to designs by Karl Wilhelm Kolbe the Younger and Wilhelm Wach. The first window was shown at the Academy exhibition of 1822, and all ten windows were installed by 1828 (see opposite).

Arguments about the choice of scenes between the royal family and the official responsible – the Administrative District President, von Schön – show that, while the cycle gave visual expression to contemporary ideas of Prussian history, those most closely involved did not agree about the kind of link between the past and present of Prussia it was supposed to represent. Besides this strictly Prussian historical painting, pictures referring to more general human values found their way into churches and cultural institutions.

The first such large-scale project was the interior decoration of the Berlin Schauspielhaus (theater) between 1819 and 1821. The genre reached its peak in Schinkel's designs for the wall painting of the front hall and stairway in the Old Museum (Altes Museum). These works were allegories of civilization and art, and of the human and natural dangers confronting them. The frescos were not painted until after Schinkel's death, when they were executed under the direction of Peter Cornelius.

A similar if more optimistic message is conveyed by Schinkel's last great canvas, *Greece In Her Prime*, which the city of Berlin commissioned from him as a wedding present for Princess Louise (see page 386). Here, the ideal Greek city state is taken as the model for the cultural flowering of Berlin and Prussia.

The Düsseldorf school

In 1826, the year when he painted the *Genius of Poetry*, Wilhelm Schadow was appointed as director of the Düsseldorf Academy, founded in 1819, to succeed Peter Cornelius. Seven of Schadow's pupils left Berlin with him and rose to eminence in the next few years as leading painters of the Düsseldorf school. The new movement had its first triumph at the Berlin Academy exhibition of 1828, and what had begun as a Rhineland offshoot of the painting of the capital soon overtook the art of Berlin itself in the next few years.

For some time the Düsseldorf painters were the most highly esteemed of all the German schools of painting, and they made an international name for themselves. The Düsseldorf school initially became known for its historical paintings. Among the first great successes it celebrated was Eduard Bendemann's *The Mourning Jews in Exile*, painted in 1832 (see page 389). It is typical of a whole generation of Düsseldorf paintings that show their protagonists suffering profound emotions, and usually incapable of action. Bendemann derived the monumentality of his figures from the Nazarene tradition, together with his classical composition – modified in Düsseldorf by realism of detail and delicacy of color. Schroedter's *The Grieving Tanners* (see page 389), a gentle satire on Bendemann, shows that the successful thinking behind this first group of major works by the Düsseldorf School was already familiar and well understood.

The years 1835 and 1836 can be regarded as the first high point of the Düsseldorf school. Karl Friedrich Lessing's *Hussite Sermon* of 1836 was one

Karl Wilhelm Kolbe the Younger
Bishop Christian of Kulm asks Hermann of Salza for Aid Against the Heathen Prussians (c. 1826)
Oil on canvas, 51.7 x 39.4 cm; Berlin, Stiftung Preussische Schlösser und Gärten Berlin-Brandenburg, Schinkel-Pavillon

The windows and original designs for the stained-glass cycle in the summer refectory of the Marienburg have not been preserved, but most of the paintings in a series made for Prince Frederick from the same designs are extant. The scene here depicts the German Order as the defenders of Christianity.

Above
Karl Begas
Pentecost (1820)
Oil on canvas, 324 x 255 cm; Berlin Cathedral

Begas painted this picture in Paris. He employed the strong coloring and monumental composition of Italian Renaissance works such as Raphael's *Transfiguration*, which was on display in Paris until 1815. This altarpiece by Begas, much influenced by French art, was given a particularly prominent place in the recently restored Berlin Cathedral. The painting marked the beginning of the artist's career in Berlin.

Wilhelm Ahlborn, after Karl Friedrich Schinkel
Greece In Her Prime (1836 copy of the original of 1825)
Oil on canvas, 94 x 235 cm; Berlin, Staatliche Museen zu Berlin – Preussischer Kulturbesitz, Nationalgalerie

The eye travels from the building site of a temple to a Greek city, which Schinkel presents to contemporary Berlin as an exemplary model.

of its best known and most controversial works (see page 391). The choice of subject by the Protestant Lessing was seen, by Wilhelm Schadow himself, as provocative. There was certainly some political significance in the scene, which contains a message implying political liberty and independence from the Catholic Church. In this work, Lessing is typical of the Düsseldorf school in emphasizing the emotions of the congregation rather than the action itself. It was in line with the ideas of the first two directors of the Düsseldorf Academy, influenced by the Nazarenes, to see cycles of frescos as an important artistic task. Even before Schadow's appointment, Düsseldorf students were carrying out a number of projects for such works, the most important being scenes from the life of the Emperor Frederick Barbarossa painted in 1825 in the garden hall of Schloss Heltorf, for Imperial Count von Spee.

Landscape painting in Düsseldorf was initially influenced by historical painting, and its outstanding practitioner was Karl Friedrich Lessing, who united Schinkel's concept of "cultural landscapes" with

certain elements of Friedrich's "landscapes of the soul" in producing such atmospheric pictures as his *Monastery Courtyard under Snow* of 1830. This picture was sharply criticized by the poet Goethe for its life-negating message (see page 390). Lessing's landscapes typically and deliberately exercised control of atmosphere through the combination of elements that were sometimes banal.

After 1827, Lessing and Johann Wilhelm Schirmer ran a society of their own outside the Academy. Schirmer's many landscape sketches illustrate (far more clearly than Lessing's work) the close observation of nature that was a basic feature of the painting of the Düsseldorf school, though it never became an independent quality expressed in great works of art (see page 390).

The swift success that had been achieved by the Düsseldorf school led quite early to the first movements of reaction against it. In 1836, for example, Johann Peter Hasenclever's *Studio Scene* (see page 391) ironically questioned the ideas of Wilhelm Schadow and his circle from the viewpoint of his

Wilhelm Schadow
The Genius of Poetry (1826)
Oil on canvas, 101 x 101 cm; Berlin, Stiftung Preussische Schlösser und Gärten Berlin-Brandenburg, Schinkel-Pavillon

The painting pays tribute to the power of poetry, here implicitly recognized as the inspiration for the visual arts. The figure of Poetry (a portrait of the daughter of an art collector friend of the artist's) is adding the name of Ludwig Tieck, another friend of Schadow's, to a list of the names of great poets. In line with Schadow's thinking, the painting emphasizes the significance to the visual arts of imagination, emotion, and inspiration.

Rudolf Julius Benno Hübner
Triple Portrait of the Painters Karl Friedrich Lessing, Karl Sohn, and Theodor Hildebrandt (1839)
Oil on canvas, 38.6 x 58.4 cm; Berlin, Staatliche Museen zu Berlin – Preussischer Kulturbesitz, Nationalgalerie

The painting shows three of Schadow's pupils who accompanied him to Düsseldorf in 1826. Lessing, who did not teach at the Academy, is set clearly apart from Sohn and Hildebrandt. As an important early portrait of the Düsseldorf school, the painting shows development in the direction of immediacy and realism.

students: the large-scale historical painting is used as a room partition, the classical attitude of the Borghese swordsman's stance is mocked by the figures in the scene, as is the Romantic "robber" tradition so popular in Düsseldorf. Hasenclever's later work gave even stronger expression to the irony of this early painting, and not much later he adopted an unmistakably political position in promoting ideals of liberty.

Eduard Bendemann
The Mourning Jews in Exile (1832)
Oil on canvas, 183 x 280 cm; Cologne, Wallraf-Richartz-Museum

Bendemann, Johann Gottfried Schadow's son-in-law, was from a Jewish family. The painting – one of the first great public successes of the Düsseldorf school – intentionally elevates the experiences of the artist's family to the rank of international history. His contemporaries saw the picture as a plea for Jewish emancipation.

Adolf Schroedter
The Grieving Tanners (1832)
Oil on wood, 32.5 x 30.3 cm; Frankfurt am Main, Städtische Galerie in the Städelsche Kunstinstitut

In this genre painting, Schroedter gently satirizes the big historical paintings by Bendemann (such as *The Mourning Jews in Exile*, above) and Lessing (*The Mourning Royal Couple*), which were a great sensation at the time. Unlike the dignified historical figures in those works, the tanners are grieving for the loss of their skins, and thus of their income.

Johann Wilhelm Schirmer
Italian Landscape (1839)
Oil on paper on card, 48 x 76.6 cm;
Düsseldorf, Kunstmuseum (on permanent loan from the Staatliche Kunstakademie)

Unlike Schirmer's large-scale compositions, his landscape sketches demonstrate the importance of direct natural observation in the work of the Düsseldorf school. The sketch reproduced here catches the light and atmosphere of an Italian landscape.

Karl Friedrich Lessing
Monastery Courtyard under Snow (1830)
Oil on canvas, 61 x 75 cm;
Cologne, Wallraf-Richartz-Museum

Lessing's painting has links with Caspar David Friedrich's winter landscapes, but unlike them does not suggest religious certainty beyond the transience of this world. The poet Goethe saw this painting by Lessing as "the sheer negation of life."

Johann Peter Hasenclever
Studio Scene (1836)
Oil on canvas, 72 x 88 cm;
Düsseldorf, Kunstmuseum

Hasenclever depicts himself with five of his student colleagues at the Düsseldorf Academy. Many details suggest the cheerful if penurious life led by the students. More particularly, however, Hasenclever is making an ironic comment on the running of the Academy and the staid artistic preferences of his teachers in Düsseldorf.

Karl Friedrich Lessing
Hussite Sermon (1836)
Oil on canvas, 230 x 290 cm; Berlin, Staatliche Museen zu Berlin – Preussischer Kulturbesitz, Nationalgalerie (on permanent loan to the Kunstmuseum, Düsseldorf)

The painting shows the reactions of the various members of a congregation differing in age, character, and social rank, to the sermon preached by a Hussite, who is holding aloft the chalice of wine to be withheld from the Holy Communion service. The subject had personal significance for Lessing, who was himself descended from a Hussite family. As with other works by Lessing, the choice of theme was sharply criticized by his Catholic colleagues.

Stage Sets and Reality (1840–1871)

Prussian painting in the decades following 1840 was not uniform in character, and it proved impossible to maintain the levels of quantity and quality achieved during the reign of Frederick William III. Political stagnation, the shock of the 1848 Revolution, and the rapid social changes of the time found more direct forms of expression. From today's viewpoint, Adolph Menzel stands largely isolated as the outstanding artistic figure of his period, which he observed and recorded without being typical of it himself.

With the accession of Frederick William IV, an era of monumental painting began in Prussia, following the example of Munich under King Ludwig I. The genre was, in fact, imported to Berlin by leading masters from Munich: first Peter Cornelius in 1841, then Wilhelm von Kaulbach in 1847. After 1840, a number of extensive a major cycles were painted: the frescos designed by Schinkel for the Old Museum (Altes Museum) were executed by painters of Cornelius's school in 1841–1849, and chapel in the Berlin Palace was painted by leading artists of the Berlin school in 1846–1852. Further frescos were painted in the Marble Palace in Potsdam, and in the churches of Potsdam and Berlin. Other projects never got beyond the planning stage; the most important would have been the "Camposanto," designed for a new cathedral to be built in Berlin and ornamented with frescos by Cornelius.

The most significant and extensive frescos of Berlin during these years were those in the New Museum (Neues Museum), on which work began in 1847. When Frederick William IV came to the throne, immediate plans were put together for the museums of Berlin, culminating in the idea for what is now the Museum Island. In 1843, building began on the New Museum, as the first stage in plans for a large and comprehensive complex. Its center is the Great Stair, which rises through three floors. The frescos executed there by Wilhelm Kaulbach between 1847 and 1866 (destroyed during World War II) expressed the historical views of their time (very different from those presented by the Old Museum) and drew together the content of the museum's heterogeneous collections. The central element in the pictorial program consisted of six depictions of turning points in the history of the world. At the same time they told the story of the gradual selection of "superior races." This historical cycle, which could be described as heavily laden with allegory, concluded with a picture of the

Wilhelm von Kaulbach
The Battle of the Catalaunian Fields (1854)
Destroyed, formerly in the Neues Museum, Berlin

The scene shows a legendary battle in the next world between Romans and Huns, its theme being the clash between culture and barbarism. Kaulbach's first painting on this subject, of 1835–1837, remained unfinished. Count Raczynski acquired it for his Berlin gallery in 1837. In 1854 Kaulbach painted the large fresco in the stairwell of the New Museum from this design.

Alfred Rethel
Study for the fresco in the Rathaus of Aachen, Otto III to the Vault of Charlemagne (1847)
Oil on canvas, 52.5 x 82.7 cm;
Düsseldorf, Kunstmuseum

The picture aims to convey an idea of the continuity of the imperial tradition. According to Rethel's own account: "Otto III goes on pilgrimage to Aachen, has the vault opened, and in fervent prayer before the mighty corpse fortifies himself to emulate Charlemagne in thought and deed." In Rethel's typically dramatic manner, the chiaroscuro emphasizes the fact that the figure of Charlemagne is an apparition.

Reformation, and thus it deliberately avoided confronting any contemporary problems.

The fourth picture in the series, the *Battle of the Catalaunian Plains* (known in Germany as the *Hunnenschlacht*, the Battle with the Huns) was based on a large unfinished painting acquired in 1837 by Count Athanasius Raczynski (see opposite). This combination of allegory and dramatically realistic stage setting attracted a great deal of attention in Berlin, as Schadow's own account makes apparent: "In September, Kaulbach's great cartoon *Die Hunnenschlacht* was displayed in Count Raczynski's hall. It gave us our first inkling of the stature of this artist, and of the clarity of his imaginative power in facing this dream-like task. Our admiration verged on amazement."

Work also began on large frescos in the Rhineland in the years immediately following 1840, mainly by painters of the Düsseldorf school, and included the largest of the religious projects, the interior decoration of the Apollinariskirche at Remagen, which occurred between 1843 and 1853. Under the auspices of the Düsseldorf Society of Art for the Rhineland and Westphalia, preparations were made in 1839 to paint the hall of the City Hall in Aachen with scenes from the life of Charlemagne. Alfred Rethel, a student of the Düsseldorf Academy and of Philip Veit in Frankfurt am Main, and himself a native of Aachen, won the first competition to carry out the paintings. His cycle of pictures depicts the rise of the great Christian power of Germany through scenes from the life of Charlemagne. The first fresco to be executed, the *Visit of Otto III to the Vault of Charlemagne*, shows one of Charlemagne's medieval successors paying tribute to the founder of the Empire. Charlemagne appears as an overwhelming historical figure whose glory casts the present in a rather pessimistic light (see above). As in Kaulbach's designs for Berlin at the same period, Rethel rendered his chosen scenes in a highly dramatic manner, and they carry more psychological weight and relate more directly to the present day of the times than Kaulbach's frescos.

These paintings by Kaulbach and Rethel were in preparation when an event took place that brought radical change into the historical painting of the German school (though less so in Düsseldorf than in Berlin). In 1842, two large historical scenes painted in the previous year by the Belgian artists Louis Gallait and Edouard de Bièfve were exhibited in many artistic centers in Germany, including Cologne, and they came to Berlin at the end of the year. Both paintings (*The Nobles of the Netherlands Compromising to Repel the Inquisition* and *The Abdication of Charles V in Brussels*) were of scenes that would appeal to the middle classes. This was a life-like, immediate, carefully researched, and dramatic form of history painting. The persuasive force of the pictures rested essentially on strong, thickly painted color deriving from the Venetian tradition and from contemporary French painting. They were seen as a direct and welcome attack on the Romantic and Nazarene pictorial depiction of ideas, as represented in Berlin by the recently appointed Cornelius. The Düsseldorf school, on the other hand, had already developed a similar historical style of its own and was therefore less affected by the impact of the Belgian pictures, although comparisons were made with the historical paintings of Lessing, which now came under much critical fire.

The Belgians superseded the Düsseldorf painters as the models most followed by the painters of Berlin, for instance in such works as Becker's *Emperor Charles V Visiting Jakob Fugger* (see below), which were directly related to the paintings of Gallait and de Bièfve in their choice of subjects, their immediacy, and their treatment of color.

At the same time as Kaulbach and Rethel were painting their frescos, some very different works were being produced – the early graphic art and sketches in oils of Adolph Menzel. Menzel was the first great Prussian painter of the 19th century in whose training academic study played little part. Of dwarf-like stature, and already the family bread-winner at the age of 16, Menzel had been an outsider from youth, and his experiences made him an uncompromisingly ironic observer who none the less yearned to belong. He taught himself to become one of the most brilliant graphic artists of the century, and after the 1840s he was also an outstanding painter.

Menzel's rediscovery as a "modern" painter around the turn of the 20th century was largely related to the sketches in oils upon which he began in the 1840s. They were mistakenly seen as precursors of Impressionism, although they represent purely personal observations and experiments on his part, and he never intended them for exhibition. The sketches in oils are therefore from Menzel's immediate environment. Beside their highly picturesque quality, they cast a keen eye on what at first seem like commonplace themes, but also generally contain a somber element. As an observer, Menzel was a chronicler of his time; he painted construction

Carl Becker
Emperor Charles V Visiting Jakob Fugger (1866)
Oil on canvas, 101 x 127 cm; Berlin, Staatliche Museen zu Berlin – Preussischer Kulturbesitz, Nationalgalerie

The emperor's visit to the banker's house was a historical subject that could easily be associated with the contemporary social situation. The immediacy with which Becker sets the stage for his theme emulates Belgian painting of the period.

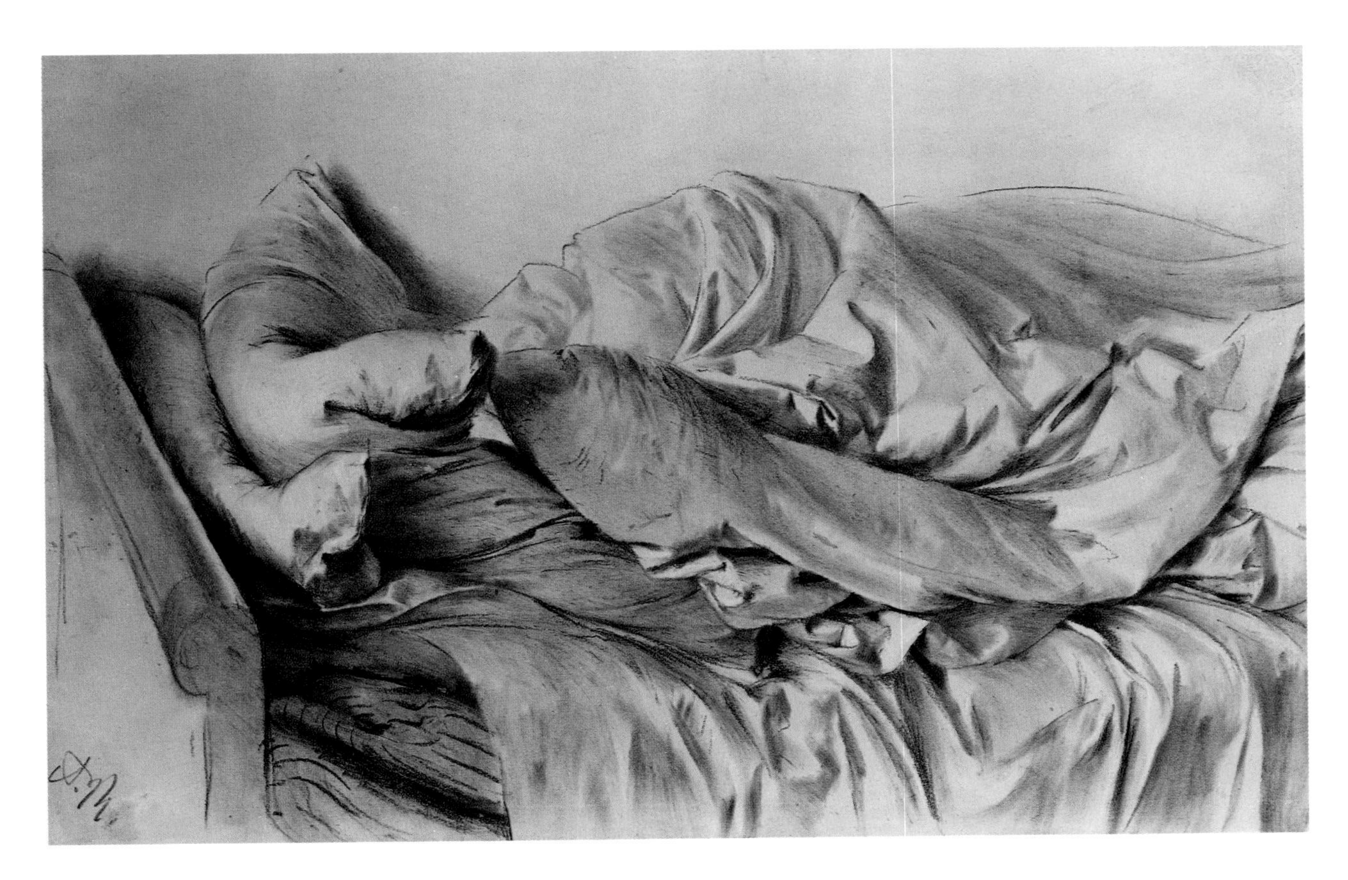

Adolph Menzel
Unmade Bed (c. 1845)
Brushed chalk on gray-green paper, 22.1 x 35.3 cm; Berlin, Staatliche Museen zu Berlin – Preussischer Kulturbesitz, Kupferstichkabinett

Menzel's very precise and detailed rendering of his subject results from a gift for keen observation that he turned on the everyday, and sometimes more disturbing, aspects of his environment. The *Unmade Bed* is typical of hundreds of graphic works by Menzel.

Adolph Menzel
The Berlin-Potsdam Railroad (1847)
Oil on canvas, 42 x 52 cm; Berlin, Staatliche Museen zu Berlin – Preussischer Kulturbesitz, Nationalgalerie

Here Menzel has painted the view of the recently built railroad line from Berlin to Potsdam from somewhere near today's Grossgörschenstrasse, though he was not in fact attempting to establish a precise location. Instead, the sketch records the inexorable spread of the city and of new technology in the artist's own environment. Menzel was living very close to this area when he painted the sketch.

Adolph Menzel
Funeral of the Fallen in the March Revolution (1848)
Oil on canvas, 45 x 63 cm; Hamburg, Kunsthalle

The fallen men had been shot by the army during the March Revolution. The black, red, and gold flags on the buildings in the background are just visible. Menzel remains clearly detached from the events shown, recording them as a state of unrest in the city.

Adolph Menzel
The Flute Concert (1850–1852)
Oil on canvas, 142 x 205 cm; Berlin, Staatliche Museen zu Berlin – Preussischer Kulturbesitz, Nationalgalerie

As a ruler who took an interest in music, Frederick the Great is shown here approximating to middle-class ideals. Menzel set this scene in the concert room of Sanssouci Palace, and tried to bring it to life, as he himself remarked later, by paying particular attention to the light from the chandeliers and candles.

Johann Peter Hasenclever
Workers Before the City Council (1848)
Oil on canvas, 154.5 x 224.5 cm;
Düsseldorf, Kunstmuseum

Hasenclever depicts a Düsseldorf scene from the time of the Revolution, in which he himself took an active part. Representatives of the Revolutionary People's Club came to demand employment from the city council. In his painting, Hasenclever points up the contrast between the dignified workers, confident but unpracticed in the exercise of power, and the shaken authority of the council.

work in progress and the still new railroads, as well as the funeral of those who had fallen in the 1848 Revolution, a picture giving a sympathetic if detached record of the event and its effects on the city (see opposite, top).

The Revolution was the subject of a great many works of art, reflecting the entire range of artistic and political attitudes of those years. For the first time, some of them showed open sympathy with the revolutionaries. Works of the 1830s had expressed political views through historical subjects, but now Johann Peter Hasenclever painted a delegation of workers appearing before the Düsseldorf city council that clearly expressed his own sympathy for the workers (see above). He employed the familiar pictorial language of genre painting, but then went beyond its conventions in the size of the picture and its clearly organized composition. There were no new stylistic methods immediately available to depict so new a subject. In his *Dance of Death*, on the other hand, Alfred Rethel presented the Revolution as a conspiracy compounded of cunning, lies, vanity, madness, and bloodlust. His condemnation went hand in hand with his reference to the woodcut technique of the Dürer period: woodcuts were both a means of distributing his message widely and detaching it from its real subject in time. By disregarding the political and social causes of the Revolution, Rethel interpreted it as human folly and the triumph of death.

Menzel's pictures of Frederick the Great (his best known paintings) can also be seen as a reaction to

Alfred Rethel
Death Rides to the City, from Another Dance of Death From the Year 1848 (1849)
Woodcut, 22.4 x 32.5 cm; Berlin, Staatliche Museen zu Berlin – Preussischer Kulturbesitz, Kupferstichkabinett

Death rides towards a modern city with a medieval church and smoking factory chimneys. The cigarette in Death's mouth is an allusion to the right, won in the Revolution, to smoke in public. In Rethel's series of woodcuts, this print comes at the start of Death's journey through a day, a day that ends with his victory on the barricades.

Adolph Menzel
Deserted Ruins of a City Laid Waste (vignette from the History of the Seven Years' War) *(1844)*
Woodcut engraving, 10 x 11.2 cm; Berlin, Staatliche Museen zu Berlin – Preussischer Kulturbesitz, Kupferstichkabinett

Menzel's woodcut illustrations presented the image of Frederick the Great and his times with great immediacy. This scene of war is from his illustrations of the king's achievements, and in its stark realism is typical of Menzel's unemotional view of history.

Adolph Menzel
Speech of Frederick the Great Before the Battle of Leuthen (1859–1861)
Oil on canvas, traces of white chalk outlines, 318 x 424 cm; Berlin, Staatliche Museen zu Berlin – Preussischer Kulturbesitz, Nationalgalerie

This last and unfinished painting in Menzel's Frederick series marks the artist's moment of failure. The scene depicts Frederick the Great making a speech to his generals and urging them on before the battle of Leuthen in the Seven Years' War, a battle in which the losses were very heavy. In tackling this subject, Menzel stood back from his view of Frederick as an ideal figure, and depicted him as all too human. But at the same time he failed, in depicting the other participants, to convey the tragedy of the events about to unfold.

the 1848 Revolution and as an expression of the artist's disillusionment with Frederick William IV. Menzel built on the studies and experiences he had accumulated since 1839 to produce about 400 woodcuts illustrating Kugler's book *Geschichte Friedrichs des Grossen* (History of Frederick the Great). The unemotional, direct style of the illustrations and Menzel's feeling for the Rococo brought Frederick to life, and the popular image of "old Fritz" still current is very much his creation (see page 396, bottom).

The 11 large-scale paintings in the series on Frederick represent Menzel's most ambitious works up to that date. It is remarkable, therefore, that they were not painted originally on commission but for his own satisfaction, and were directly inspired by the Revolution. Menzel's comment on Frederick William IV's deliberate reference to his greatly superior ancestor was to show Frederick as a king who could not be matched by the present king – a view emphatically middle class in character. Menzel himself identified to a high degree with Frederick the Great, personally as well as politically: he saw his own lonely life without a partner as parallel to the king's. It was not until much later that Menzel's paintings of Frederick came to be misunderstood as works of simple patriotism. The series concludes with an unfinished picture, the *Speech of Frederick the Great Before the Battle of Leuthen* (see above).

Quantitatively, the middle-class portrait in the grand style remained the major pictorial genre of the time, and for many painters it was their most important source of income. Like the historical and genre painting of the Düsseldorf School, portraits increasingly concentrated on mood and atmosphere rather than clearly defined personalities. The close connection between historical painting and portraiture is particularly clear in the work of Carl Ferdinand Sohn (see page 399, top right). The most successful portrait painter in Berlin at the time was Eduard Magnus. His

Eduard Magnus
Jenny Lind (1846)
Oil on canvas, 119 x 94.5 cm; Berlin, Staatliche Museen zu Berlin – Preussischer Kulturbesitz, Nationalgalerie

Magnus was the most successful portrait painter of Berlin in the mid-19th century. In his portrait of the celebrated Swedish singer, the style of the painting is fresh, but the singer is shown in a stereotyped role. Her glance, looking away with eyes slightly raised, is meant to suggest both innocence and musical inspiration.

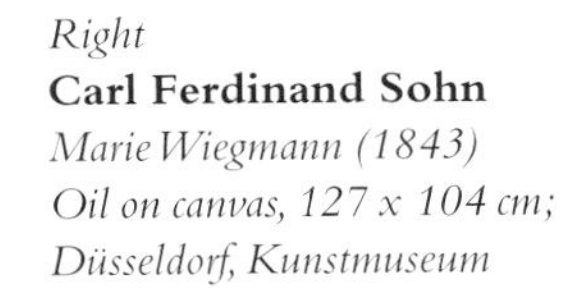

Right
Carl Ferdinand Sohn
Marie Wiegmann (1843)
Oil on canvas, 127 x 104 cm; Düsseldorf, Kunstmuseum

Sohn paints one of his own pupils, Marie Wiegmann, at the age of 17; she herself later became a painter of genre scenes and portraits. The lowered book and her thoughtful expression, with the extensive landscape in the background, make this picture the expression of a mood rather than a portrait.

Karl Begas
Washing the Black Woman (1841)
Oil on canvas, 66 x 86 cm; Heinsberg, Kreismuseum

The main emphasis is on the child's naïveté in attempting to wash the black woman's skin white, the picture relying heavily on generally accepted social prejudices. This composition was so popular that Begas had to paint several versions. This version is the earliest.

Carl Eduard Biermann
Borsig's Mechanical Engineering Factory in Berlin (1847)
Oil on canvas, 110 x 161.5 cm; Berlin, Stiftung Stadtmuseum Berlin (on permanent loan from the Borsig archives in Berlin)

Since Biermann's view was commissioned by the owner, the factory dominates the picture. The painter takes an artistic liberty with the topography of the site by including the terrace of an entrepreneurial villa in the foreground, complementing the factory, and he dwells on the clouds of smoke above its chimneys to add drama.

Below
Carl Graeb
Potsdam: The "Eight Corners" (1854)
Watercolor and pen in gray and brown ink on paper, 30.2 x 20.2 cm; Potsdam, Stiftung Preussische Schlösser und Gärten Berlin-Brandenburg, Aquarellsammlung

Graeb's watercolors present Potsdam as a picturesque residence with a proud past. Of the four corner buildings at this street junction close to the Neuer Markt, only one still stands today.

works, like Sohn's, are distinguished by the vivid use of color and a comparatively unaffected depiction of his subjects, although he often presented them in stereotyped roles (see page 399, left).

It is difficult to understand the interest shown during this period in genre painting, which, like portraiture, flourished. An example is one of the most successful works by Karl Begas: *Washing the Black Woman* (see page 399). Begas had to make several copies of this celebrated composition, an apparently humorous scene with an instantly accessible meaning, and executed with much artistic skill. It is typical of the sentimental genre painting so popular at the time in its reliance on established prejudices and accepted attitudes to achieve the desired effect – in this case, on the assumption that a white skin is the norm.

Landscape painting had reached a generally high standard in Berlin and Düsseldorf, to a great extent through Blechen's teaching at the Academy in Berlin, and in Düsseldorf through the landscape classes of Johann Wilhelm Schirmer, one of whose pupils was Andreas Achenbach. However, apart from Menzel's sketches, which constitute a phenomenon lying outside academic theory, landscape painting was no longer the dominant genre it had been in the previous generation. The line of demarcation between landscape and architectural painting was increasingly blurred.

Carl Eduard Biermann tried to respond to new circumstances and new requirements with his view of the Borsig factory (see above). While Blechen's factory building at Eberswalde and Menzel's *The Berlin-Potsdam Railroad* (see page 395) reflected the artists' distress at the changes to their own familiar surroundings, Biermann intended to produce a picture in the grand style for the owner of the firm, and in this his painting resembles Rethel's view of the Harkort factory, painted in 1834. Carl Graeb's picture linked architectural and landscape painting in a manner typical of his time (see left). His paintings and watercolors bore dramatic witness, through atmosphere and brilliant color effects, to a great and now overwhelming past. Meanwhile, the present of

the emerging imperial society had already announced its advent in art some time earlier. Portrait painting of the time, like Biermann's factory view, answered the requirements of the new property-owning class, requirements that can also be identified in the historical painting of the time. In his paintings, Menzel recorded this phenomenon with great precision. His increasingly isolated and sober examination of the heights reached by national euphoria in these years built a bridge back to the first half of the century. Menzel painted the departure of the future Emperor Wilhelm for the Franco-Prussian War as a Berlin street scene, emphasizing the very varied reactions of the bystanders and ironically reversing the importance of the main and subsidiary subjects (see above). His detached attitude was superseded in subsequent years by the art of Anton von Werner. The high esteem Menzel enjoyed during the imperial period as a painter of Hohenzollern history was based on a profound misunderstanding of his intentions.

Adolph Menzel
The Departure of King William I for the Army on July 31, 1870 (1871)
Oil on canvas, 63 x 78 cm; Berlin, Staatliche Museen zu Berlin – Preussischer Kulturbesitz, Nationalgalerie

The small figures of the imperial couple to the left, in the middle ground, can be picked out easily only because of the white upholstery of their carriage. Menzel shows a wide variety of scenes on the pavement of Unter den Linden, distracting attention from the state event taking place at the same time. The two men reading newspapers in the left foreground are missing the real action behind them altogether.

THE APPLIED ARTS

Burkhardt Göres

The Neuwied Cabinet, writing desk for Frederick William II (Neuwied, 1779)
David Roentgen
Two varieties of maple; marquetry in maple, hornbeam, applewood, mulberry wood, rosewood, Brazilian rosewood, walnut, pearwood, mahogany, gilded bronze, enamel, brass and steel; Berlin, Staatliche Museen zu Berlin – Preussischer Kulturbesitz, Kunstgewerbemuseum

Neo-classicism and the Applied Arts

The short and brilliant flowering of the applied arts of early Neo-classicism began in Berlin only after the death of Frederick the Great in 1786, much later than in the rest of Europe. Frederick's own orders for porcelain show that he himself preferred the Rococo style up to the last years of his life. In the private houses of the Prussian aristocracy, however, and to a modest extent in the homes of the middle classes, it is clear that transitional styles came in very much earlier. For instance, the oval banqueting hall in the palace of Minister von Görne (the Dutch Palace), designed by Carl Gotthard Langhans before 1779, is one of the earliest and most beautiful rooms in the mature early Neo-classical style in Berlin.

In the last 15 years of his reign, Frederick the Great had ordered the construction of about 300 apartment buildings of three or four floors (called "immediate buildings") to mitigate the housing shortage among the constantly growing population and enhance the appearance of the city itself. His successor continued this project. The aristocracy also built themselves modern houses in Berlin, and these houses needed furnishing. More than a decade later, looking back at the last years of Frederick the Great's reign, the Berlin historian Johann Anton König wrote: "Fine dwellings require fine furniture, and the furnishings of the great and wealthy were the models. Old, durable, solid items made to last for generations were thrown out because they no longer seemed pleasing. Novelties were devised without a thought for their worth and durability, and these innovations followed so fast upon each other that you had to change your furnishings every ten years if they were to remain in fashion, and no one wished to be outdone. Such purchases were made on credit, and the result was often bankruptcy after a man's death. We no longer see the simple citizen of the March of Brandenburg or Pomerania who would sit in his upholstered chair and scorn the glories of palaces, being content to live without pier glasses, chandeliers, divans, and fine wallpapers. Now he makes haste to Berlin to purchase these pretty follies, and cheerfully pays the price of his fields and flocks in return."

Chest of drawers (c. 1785)
Johann Gottlob Fiedler
Mahogany and macoree on oak, marquetry figures in maple, gilded bronzes, inlaid marble top; Potsdam, Stiftung Preussische Schlösser und Gärten Berlin-Brandenburg, Marble Palace

Frederick's successor, King Frederick William II, certainly appreciated the modern decorative crafts of around 1780, for the Neuwied Cabinet was delivered to him in 1779 (see opposite), and he acquired a cylinder writing desk in 1783, both from the famous Neuwied firm of David Roentgen. These items, and other furniture supplied to the king in and after 1787, set standards for the craft of cabinet making in Berlin.

Towards the end of the century, the joiners' guild of Berlin had several hundred master joiners, and was the largest in Germany. The art of cabinet making took its principal models from the workshops of Johann Gottlob Fiedler (see left), Franz Ephraim and Johann Ephraim Eben, and after 1791 from David Hacker (see page 404, top), a pupil of David Roentgen. Their furniture is among the finest produced by German craftsmen working in marquetry at the end of the 18th century.

When King Frederick William II of Prussia came to the throne late in the summer of 1786, all the conditions favorable to the rapid further development of a specific Berlin style of early Neo-classicism were already present. The appointment of men with outstanding artistic gifts – such as Friedrich Wilhelm von Erdmannsdorff, appointed from Dessau in 1786, Carl Gotthard Langhans, appointed from Breslau in 1788, David Gilly, appointed from Stettin in 1788, and Gottfried Schadow, appointed from Rome in 1788 – inspired the art of Berlin in general and with it, of course, the applied arts and crafts. Works of the highest quality were now made. After 1786, when Berlin had once again become the main royal residence, new court commissions for buildings and furniture contributed to the upturn in the luxury trade in arts and crafts.

The design of interiors and furniture in the early Neo-classical style

Erdmannsdorff's first commission in Berlin pointed the way: it was for the redesigning of the study and bedroom in Sanssouci Palace, on which he began work in 1786, the year of Frederick II's death (see pages 272–275). The style of Erdmannsdorff, who had trained in England and Rome, united the plain, sober forms of British Neo-classicism and features from the art of ancient Rome. He drew many ideas, particularly for furniture, from French engravings, and the pictures of patterns and models that were published in England by Thomas Sheraton and George Hepplewhite.

The design of interiors and movable furniture in the early Neo-classical style in Berlin reached its peak in the royal chambers of the Berlin Palace, the king's new apartments decorated and furnished in 1787–1789 to designs by Erdmannsdorff, Carl von Gontard, and the castellan Carl Ludwig Bauer. The furniture, which apart from a few pieces taken to the Soviet Union in 1945, was among the major achievements of its kind in Germany.

The marquetry floors in many of the rooms, the work of Johann Gottlieb Fiedler, were particularly fine features (see page 291). In 1791 Fiedler also supplied a magnificent longcase chiming clock with an astronomical action by Möllinger (see page 404, bottom). From 1788 to 1791, Langhans furnished a large new apartment in the Berlin Palace for Queen Frederica Louise (see pages 287 and 288). Fiedler again designed the floors.

During his short reign, Frederick William II did very little new building of castles, and concentrated more on interior decoration. The exceptions were the Marble Palace in the New Garden in Potsdam, built by Gontard and Langhans in 1787–1793, and the castle built on Peacock Island in 1794–1795. These were buildings for his personal use. The orders placed for furniture for the Marble Palace, probably in 1791, show that two master cabinet makers in particular were entrusted with the commissions for large pieces. We may assume that Langhans provided designs or sketches for most of the chairs and suites.

Chest of drawers from the Marble Palace (after 1791)
David Hacker
Mahogany, gilded bronze decoration, plaque with Wedgwood relief, marble surface verde antico surrounded by giallo di Siena (reconstructed); Potsdam, Stiftung Preussische Schlösser und Gärten Berlin-Brandenburg, Marble Palace

They are among the finest early examples of Neoclassical furniture in Prussia, and in some cases there is definite proof that Langhans was responsible.

The order for chests of drawers and cupboards for the lower floor of the palace went to David Hacker, who in 1791, at the suggestion of his teacher David Roentgen, had settled in Berlin, bringing with him materials and bronzes from the large Neuwied firm. A similar commission for furniture for the upper floor obviously went to the Berlin master cabinet maker Johann Ephraim Eben. We can only speculate on whether he also supplied the large number of massive mahogany firescreens on both floors. At present, only the bedroom in the Marble Palace can be definitely ascribed to the most important of the court craftsmen in wooden inlay work, Johann Gottlob Fiedler.

It was Eben again who supplied furniture for the castle on Peacock Island in 1795, and it has been preserved almost intact. He also provided most of the furniture for the last apartments fitted out for the king, the Winter Chambers in Schloss Charlottenburg, designed by G. F. Boumann in 1796–1797 with the active participation of Countess Lichtenau. Some of the Roentgen's style furniture for these rooms was bought from David Hacker.

Because of the heavy losses suffered during World War II, the quality and unique design of the Berlin chandeliers of this period can now be seen only in the Winter Chambers of Charlottenburg Palace. The chandeliers here were supplied in 1797 by the bronze factory of Werner & Mieth, founded in 1791.

Hardly any of the goldsmith's work once in the castles of Prussia and dating from the time of Frederick the Great has been preserved; it was melted down in 1809 as part of the war contribution to fight Napoleon, although obviously there had been a wealth of it when all the castle furnishings were still extant.

The Royal Porcelain Factory developed along new and productive lines in the 11 years of Frederick William II's rule (beginning in 1787), under the circumspect direction and encouragement of the Minister of State Friedrich Anton von Heinitz, President of the Royal Porcelain Manufacturing Commission and Curator of the Academy of Arts.

As a minister of state, and President of the Inspectorate of Mines since 1777, Heinitz had already headed the Department of Mines and Ironworks, and he was one of the greatest experts of his time on the iron and steel industry. He thoroughly reformed the Academy of Arts, and in particular ensured that the Royal Porcelain Factory was brought up to date with modern techniques. As Curator of the Academy, he also took a natural interest in raising its artistic standards, which he intended to improve through the influence of the Academy.

After 1788, the Manufactory began displaying its products at the Academy exhibitions. The recruitment of Gottfried Schadow to work for the Royal Porcelain Factory also led to improvements in quality. Many new forms of tableware were made, as well as models for large epergnes such as the *Natural Kingdom* of 1791, completed for the double wedding of the king's daughters, *Mount Olympus* (1800), and *Flora* (1801), with china services for the dowries of the daughters of Frederick William II, miniature

Longcase clock from the King's Chambers in the Berlin Palace
Design: C. L. Bauer (?); Johann Gottlob Fiedler (case), carving by Bartels, Johann Christian Möllinger (clockwork and actions)
Mahogany on oak, gilded carving, gilded bronze, iron, steel, painting, enamel; Potsdam, Stiftung Preussische Schlösser und Gärten Berlin-Brandenburg, Marble Palace

busts in biscuit porcelain, small statues, and sundry other items.

In 1801, the new royal couple gave an epergne entitled *Psyche Abducted by Zephyr* to their friend the Hereditary Grand Duchess of Mecklenburg-Schwerin (see below).

The death of Frederick William II in 1797 concluded a period whose brief late flowering had given Berlin many important contemporary works in a number of fields, including the applied arts and crafts. The young royal couple, Frederick William III and Queen Louise, set new standards with the deliberately plain furnishing of their summer residence of Schloss Paretz, built in 1797–1799. The change of approach extended to the wall coverings, though some of them were still in lavishly painted wallpaper, and to the very plain furniture. Even after his accession, Frederick William III and his wife still lived in the palace he had occupied as crown prince, although it was now known as the royal palace. The new post-1800 furnishings of some of the rooms there have not been preserved.

The state chambers of the palace in Potsdam, which were destroyed in 1945 but recorded in photographs, were redesigned between 1799 and 1804 by Friedrich Gottlieb Schadow, and represented an attractive Prussian variant on the French Empire style, but it developed no further after the defeat of Prussia by Napoleon in 1806. The Etruscan Cabinet at Potsdam was a singular work, with its wood paneling in intarsia and areas of stucco ornamented with figures in the "Etrurian" style, made by the manufacturing firm of Catel (see page 406).

Karl Friedrich Schinkel and the Applied Arts and Crafts

Scarcely any other architect whose activities were as extensive as those of Karl Friedrich Schinkel devoted as much time as he did to the applied arts. They must at first have been partly a way for the young architect to earn a living as he set out on his career, but in his later work craft designs specifically connected with his buildings occur with increasing prominence. He planned the palaces he built with their entire fittings and furnishings, down to many small details. A wealth of drawings provides information about Schinkel's later designs in this field, and up to the time of World War II a great many items made from them were still extant. Of the works from his early period, however, only sporadic mentions in contemporary sources and a few designs have come down to us.

In 1798–1799, while Schinkel was still training, he supplied designs to the stoneware factory of Baron von Eckardtstein in Berlin, for which his teacher David Gilly also provided designs. The first mention of his designs for furniture and porcelain dates from 1800, and Schinkel's interest in interior design is confirmed by the plans he drew up for the palaces of Köstritz and Elley in the Baltic duchy of Courland, although they were never carried out.

When Schinkel came back from his first journey to Italy in 1805, and subsequently took rooms in the house of the silk manufacturer Gabain (where he stayed until 1809), it was natural enough in the circumstances, considering the shortage of

Chandelier from the Winter Chambers of the Charlottenburg Palace (Berlin, 1797)
Werner & Mieth
Gilded bronze, glass drops; Berlin, Stiftung Preussische Schlösser und Gärten Berlin-Brandenburg, Schloss Charlottenburg

Epergne *Psyche Abducted by Zephyr* (1799–1800)
Design: Hans Christian Genelli; models: Johann Carl Friedrich Riese, Royal Porcelain Factory, Berlin
Biscuit porcelain: Schwerin, Staatliches Museum, Kunstsammlungen, Schlösser und Gärten

Etruscan Cabinet in the Potsdam Palace (before 1803–1804)
F. W. Klose
Watercolor: Potsdam, Stiftung Preussische Schlösser und Gärten Berlin-Brandenburg, Plankammer

A corner room in the Parade Chambers of the Potsdam Palace was redecorated in 1803–1804 to designs by the architect Franz Ludwig Catel. With its valuable inlaid wood paneling of walnut, chestnut, acacia, mahogany, black poplar, and ebony, it is a fine example of Berlin room decoration in the early Neo-classical style. Colored marble areas containing ornamentation reminiscent of classical vase painting lend the room its individual character. The decorative items were from the factory set up by the elder Catel, Ludwig Friedrich, to make mosaics.

architectural commissions, for him to provide his landlord with designs for silk working. In the Academy of Arts exhibitions of 1806 and 1808 respectively, the manufactory of Georg Gabain exhibited a stove screen worked in silk and a silk fire-screen, both from designs by Schinkel. In 1807, he designed a candelabrum for Gottfried Schadow's sculpture studio. His later very fruitful work for Tobias Feilner's earthenware factory was foreshadowed by a design (still extant) for a stove, made for Höhler & Feilner and dating from 1808. In the Academy exhibition of 1814, Feilner showed a drawing of a stove by Schinkel, with parts of the stove made from it. Until his death, Schinkel was constantly involved in the design of stoves and fireplaces, but furniture and many other details of interiors are the focal point in his designs for private and public buildings, royal and princely palaces, Neo-classical villas and buildings resembling medieval castles.

It is not known who recommended the young architect to redesign the Chamois Room in the royal palace in the later months of 1808. The occasion was obviously the royal family's imminent return from Königsberg in East Prussia. It may have been through Wilhelm von Humboldt, who came back to Berlin from Rome in 1808, that Schinkel obtained this first commission for the Prussian court. Details of the work are extant in designs for the wall and ceiling decoration and the suites of furniture. An inventory entry of October 1808, a contemporary picture of an interior, and pre-war photographs prove that the young architect's designs were indeed carried out. He was inspired by Charles Percier and Pierre-François-Léonard Fontaine, and he probably also drew on his memories of his time in Italy.

When Schinkel had completed his studies and began designing furniture, he was at first entirely under the influence of his friend and teacher Friedrich Gilly. A study tour of Italy and Paris from 1803 to 1805 must have made a lasting impression on him, more particularly Paris, where Percier and Fontaine worked and had already, in 1801, published their *Recueil de décorations intérieures* ... (Collection of Interior Decorations ...), a work of fundamental importance for the Empire style. Sketches made by the young Schinkel in Paris show that furniture was already at the center of his interest in interior decoration.

Until now, Schinkel's appointment in 1810 (through the agency of Humboldt) as Privy Buildings Assessor in the Supreme Planning and Building Department, where he was responsible for "state public buildings" and the buildings of the court, has always been seen solely in connection with the production for the royal family of his diorama *Landscape with Themes From the Coast Near Genoa.*

Upholstered chair from the Yellow Study of the Marble Palace (Berlin, around 1790)
Design: Carl Gotthard Langhans
Solid mahogany, gilded bronze; Potsdam, Stiftung Preussische Schlösser und Gärten Berlin-Brandenburg, Marble Palace

However, the redesigning of the Chamois Room (now dated to 1808) provides good reasons to show that the royal couple were already sufficiently satisfied to give Schinkel his next commission for new decorations to Queen Louise's bedrooms in the castles of Potsdam and Charlottenburg (see above). These decoration schemes followed the Paris fashion in the gossamer-like effect of white voile hangings against a pink background, but in Schinkel's Prussian variant the effect was more restrained and attractive. The furniture at Charlottenburg, inspired by Empire furniture in France, is also more sober in style than its French models.

When Queen Louise died suddenly in the summer of 1810, Schinkel was asked to design her mausoleum, and for this he drew on both Gothic and Neo-classical features. The hall of the building, built by Heinrich Gentz, contained a chandelier that Schinkel had already designed for the queen herself. Queen Louise had also probably suggested that when he was designing the kneeling female figures carrying the lamps he might refer to the similar figures on her monumental dressing mirror, a gift from Tsar Alexander I, and made in St. Petersburg in 1803 to designs by Andrei Voronikhin. Before the chandelier was installed in its new position it was shown at the Academy exhibition of 1810. This event obviously marked the beginning of Schinkel's fruitful collaboration with the bronze factory of Werner & Mieth, which made the piece; the firm, founded in Berlin in 1791, had been the leading company in its field in the city for decades.

Over the next few years the events of the war kept Schinkel increasingly busy with the design of monuments and tombs (see pages 496, 497 and 505). His collaboration with the Royal Iron Foundry set up in Berlin in 1804 was particularly productive: he created a wide variety of designs for the foundry, from monuments to jewelry. Works made of iron, a "patriotic" material occurring naturally in Prussia, became very popular, and constant improvements were made in the casting technique. Iron remained a major material for artistic expression even when the economic situation gradually began to recover. Schinkel used iron in many different ways in his later architectural works.

His series of designs for memorials begins in 1811 with those for the Queen Louise Gate (Luisenpforte)

Bed and two flower tables for Queen Louise's bedroom in the Charlottenburg Palace (Berlin, 1810)
Design: Karl Friedrich Schinkel
Pearwood; Berlin, Stiftung Preussische Schlösser und Gärten Berlin-Brandenburg, Schloss Charlottenburg

Bronze dressing table with mirror surface for the great gilded toilette set of Princess Alexandrina of Prussia (Berlin, 1822)
Design: Karl Friedrich Schinkel; sculptural ornamentation probably from models by Ludwig Wichmann, 1817; manufactured by Werner & Neffen, gilded bronze, mirror glass, surmounted by parts of the gilded toilette set by Jean George Humbert, also to designs by Schinkel
Dressing table: Staatliches Museum, Schlösser und Gärten Schwerin, Schloss Ludwigslust
Toilette set: Museum für Kunst und Gewerbe Hamburg

in Paretz, and the monument to Queen Louise in Gransee (see page 296). The New Year plaques issued by the Royal Iron Foundry record its major artistic achievements in cast iron, and items that were made to Schinkel's designs feature repeatedly: there are memorials for tombs, usually in the form of stelae or obelisks, monuments such as the memorial on the Kreuzberg and the monument to Prince Kutusov in Bunzlau, railings for bridges, balconies and ramps, gateways and portals, street lamps (including the first public gas lamp in the Schlossplatz), vases and garden furniture. The foundry supplied fountains for Glienicke and Charlottenhof. The magnificent iron stairways in the palaces of Prince Carl and Prince Albrecht incorporated modern techniques into interior decoration in the grand style.

A whole series of designs by Schinkel were cast in iron and bronze. After the consolidation of the economic situation in particular, bronze casting once again assumed importance in the applied arts. There had been good bronze-casting workshops in Berlin and Potsdam since the middle of the 18th century, and it depended on the economic situation of the state whether they flourished or declined. One of the earliest designs for a work in bronze by Schinkel, with his chandelier for Queen Louise, is a print showing a bronze table made in 1817 for the dowry of Princess Charlotte of Prussia, the king's eldest daughter. It subsequently served as the model for similar items made for all the king's daughters (see above). It must have been made in the factory of Werner & Neffen, which had survived the decline in the luxury goods trade to become the most important institution of its kind, receiving state support in the form of commissions and credit. The firm is singled out for mention by Zedlitz in his *Neuesten Conversations-Handbuch für Berlin und Potsdam* (Latest Conversational Manual for Berlin and Potsdam), published in 1834: "The works produced by the said factory in gilded bronze are comparable to the best French items of the kind, in view of their fine craftsmanship and handsome gilding. It is interesting to see the firm's collection of excellent drawings of magnificent epergnes, candelabra, chandeliers and so forth, and the fine models that are in the possession of this factory. The former are largely designed by the masterly hand of Supreme Building Director Schinkel, and the

Opposite, left
Set of vases, known as the Lalla Rookh Vases
Design: Karl Friedrich Schinkel (1823)
Made by: the Royal Porcelain Factory, Berlin (1824)
St Petersburg, the State Hermitage Museum

The "Lalla Rookh" court festivities in honor of Grand Duchess Alexandra Feodorovna (née Princess Charlotte of Prussia) and Grand Duke Nicholas were held in the Berlin Palace in 1821. The poem "Lalla Rookh," by the Irish poet Thomas Moore, was performed on this occasion by the entire court and its guests, with the assistance of women singers from the Berlin Opera. The design of the decorations and the arrangement of the groups were in the hands of Schinkel.

Right
Chandelier from the General Command building (Palace of Prince William, later Emperor William I)
Design: Karl Friedrich Schinkel; supplied in 1829 by the firm of Werner & Neffen for the sum of 432 talers
Circular crowns of bronze with eight eagles and glass drops

latter were made in the workshops of Professors Rauch, Tieck and Wichmann ..." Among the major creations of the firm was the bronze grille for Berlin Cathedral in the 1820s, designed by Schinkel when the building was being restored.

The majority of bronze chandeliers from designs by Schinkel must also have been made by Werner & Neffen, since Werner & Mieth had already concentrated on that area in the 1790s (see right).

In 1815, the bronze caster Léquine and the engraver Coué were summoned to Berlin to cast the metal for a memorial, and a bronze-casting workshop was set up for them in the Royal Iron Foundry. The workshop for bronze casting in the Institute of Trade and Commerce was already able to make small sculptures and other items by the mid-1820s. Its major work, designed by Schinkel in 1829, was a fountain for the courtyard of the Institute of Trade, executed in 1831 with the participation of Rauch, Tieck, and Wichmann.

Soon after the Second Peace of Paris, the Royal Porcelain Factory, which had received no commissions from the king worth mentioning during the Napoleonic occupation and the war years of 1813–1815, was given the honor of making large new services for the Allied army commanders. The most famous was for the Duke of Wellington, and was not completed until 1818. Schinkel now turned his attention once again to designs for porcelain, though they are not all extant. Certainly some by him were for table tops, candelabra and candlesticks, but most were for vases and bowls.

A series of works made for the court to mark particular occasions is outstanding: the first monumental vase made by the Royal Porcelain Factory, with rich bronze ornamentation and a bronze pedestal, designed by the architect for King Frederick William III, was shown at the Academy of Arts exhibition in 1824.

In 1823, Schinkel was commissioned to design a "Persian" vase to commemorate the "Lalla Rookh" festivities at court, an occasion on which he himself had created the scenery for the "living tableaux." The vase was delivered in 1824, together with two smaller companion pieces modeled on the so-called Alhambra Vases. The smaller vases show the "living tableaux" from drawings by Wilhelm Hensel, and the large central vase depicts the festive procession, from a design by August Kloeber (see left).

Since almost all the king's silverware had been melted down in 1808–1809, along with that of citizens who were much more extravagant than their king, the silversmiths found themselves in demand again soon after 1815. Not surprisingly, Schinkel again had a hand in designing their products.

The king needed new silverware himself, he had to provide for his daughters' dowries, and there were silver services to be made for his sons' weddings as well. Outstanding among Schinkel's extant designs

are several for memorial cups and epergnes. At first they were made by various court goldsmiths such as G. L. Howaldt and J. G. Humbert; at a later date the goldsmith J. G. Hossauer received most of the court commissions. He worked very closely with Schinkel, whose designs he collected, making items from them even after Schinkel's death in 1841. To the annoyance of the older goldsmiths, Hossauer used the modern technical methods he had learned in Paris, and the state approved of this approach (see page 410).

The encouragement of arts and crafts was seen as a prime concern in the efforts made to consolidate the state after the Wars of Liberation. A leading figure in this was Peter Christian Beuth, director of the Technical Deputation for Trade and Commerce, working in close collaboration with Schinkel. The major method employed was distribution of the *Vorbilder für Fabrikanten und Handwerker* (Models for Manufacturers and Craftsmen), a work divided into three sections. The first covered "Architectonic and Other Ornaments," the second "Vessels and Utensils," and the third provided "Models for the Ornamentation of Textiles and the Working of Fabrics." The models reproduced were chosen from classical antiquity and the Renaissance, and patterns for textiles also came from the Islamic east. Contemporary designs were represented only by Schinkel himself, with 40 prints showing examples of his work. The separate sheets of the "models" were printed and distributed free of charge to public libraries, the Prussian state authorities in the fields concerned, schools of draftsmanship, and "meritorious" artists and craftsmen. They were collected into a volume of 94 plates in 1830. A second volume containing 54 plates was published in 1837, and an

Commemorative tankard for the "Magic of the White Rose" festivities
Design: Karl Friedrich Schinkel; made by J. G. Hossauer
Silver, partially gilded, enamel; Berlin, Stiftung Preussische Schlösser und Gärten Berlin-Brandenburg, Silberkammere, Schloss Charlottenburg

The tankard was made for a tournament held in the Court of Honor, the castle theater and the halls of the New Palace at Sanssouci to celebrate the birthday of Empress Alexandra Feodorovna of Russia (née Princess Charlotte of Prussia) on July 13, 1829.

unrevised reprint came out in 1863. In the *Magazin von Abbildungen der Gusswaren aus der königlichen Eisengiesserei zu Berlin* (Magazine of Copies of Cast Ware from the Royal Iron Foundry in Berlin), which appeared in eight numbers (each with eight plates) between 1815 and 1833, about half the designs are once again by Schinkel.

A work entitled *Schinkels Möbelentwürfe, welche bei der Einrichtung prinzlicher Wohnungen in den letzten zehn Jahren ausgeführt wurden* (Schinkel's Designs for Furniture Executed in the Last Ten Years for the Furnishing of Princely Dwellings) was published by Ludwig Lohde from 1835 to 1837, and comprised five issues.

In 1837 George Gropius published his *Musterblätter für Gold- und Silberarbeiten* (Patterns for Gold and Silver Work), again with designs by Schinkel, and the designs published by Moritz Geiss between 1841 and 1849 for his works in cast zinc alloy were also partly influenced by Schinkel. Through these publications Schinkel's influence in the field of craft and design extended to every corner of Prussia, entirely in line with his duties as Supreme Director of the Prussian authority responsible for all public buildings.

Schinkel also turned his attention to other fields of applied art, whether in glass, fabric, terracotta and stoneware, picture frames, medals or even smaller items. His stage sets for the Royal Theater (Königlichen Theater) in Berlin were particularly famous. Only a few of his designs for items in the materials mentioned above are extant, but many drawings for furniture designs have been preserved and are now in the Cabinet of Engravings of the Berlin State Museums.

The records show that Schinkel became really active in design only after 1815, when the Napoleonic era was over and Prussia could afford new designs on a larger scale. At first he was chiefly involved in the redecoration of interiors: in 1815–1817 the victorious army commander Prince Augustus of Prussia had the interior of his palace in Wilhelmstrasse redecorated by Schinkel (see p. 384), and the king's nephew Prince Friedrich had his apartments in the building diagonally opposite furnished in 1817 at more modest expense. In 1818–1821, the designs for the furnishing of the new Schauspielhaus (theater) were drawn up.

In 1820–1823, work was in progress on the conversion of Neuhardenberg Palace for the state chancellor, at almost the same time as work was being done on Tegel Palace for Schinkel's old patron, Wilhelm von Humboldt; it was finished in 1824. The years 1822–1824 saw the building of the Antonin hunting lodge for the Radziwills. The designs for the reconstruction of the crown prince's apartments in the Berlin Palace in 1824 to 1827, for the New Pavilion in Charlottenburg for the king (1824–1825), and for Glienicke Palace and the casino (finished in 1827; see pages 298 and 300) were the first of a wide and diverse range of work on the royal family's palaces, going on into the 1830s and leading to a vast number of designs for furniture.

Charlottenhof Palace was built for the crown prince between 1826 and 1828, and the extensive

The Tea Salon of the apartments of the crown prince and princess in the Berlin Palace
Artist unknown
Watercolor (before 1834); Potsdam, Stiftung Preussische Schlösser und Gärten Berlin-Brandenburg, Plankammer

The Tea Salon was among the finest of Schinkel's interior designs for the decoration of the apartments of the crown prince and his wife. It was intended for a small circle of guests who would gather around the great curved seat in the evening. The tall paneled plinth contained cases to hold and display collections. The high stucco surfaces above it were enlivened by sculptures by C. F. Tieck and paintings by C. W. Kolbe, J. Schoppe, and H. Stilke. The exedra is one of the finest designed by Schinkel, and was modeled on examples from classical antiquity. The chandelier and furniture were also made to the architect's designs.

Armchair from a suite for the crown prince's apartments in the Berlin Palace (c. 1825)
Design: Karl Friedrich Schinkel, Berlin
Wood, carved and gilded, silk upholstery; Berlin, Stiftung Preussische Schlösser und Gärten Berlin-Brandenburg, Schloss Charlottenburg

The furniture was for the Tea Salon (see opposite) and the Star Hall, both of them handsome rooms designed in the style of classical antiquity. Schinkel was influenced by Percier and Fontaine in designing this armchair.

reconstruction and extension of Prince Karl's palace in Wilhelmplatz, where Schinkel decorated and furnished a large number of rooms in styles of endless variety, was carried out in 1827–1828. The impressions Schinkel had absorbed on his visit to England in 1826 are to some extent reflected in the interiors of these rooms (see below). In 1828, on the occasion of the forthcoming wedding of Prince William, work began on the conversion of the General Command building to designs by Schinkel, and it was completed in 1829.

Prince Karl's palace and the reconstruction in 1830–1833 of the interior of Prince Albrecht's palace (a Baroque building of the 1730s) are the principal examples of Schinkel's later, and here often particularly magnificent style of Neo-classical decoration.

In 1833, Schinkel planned Babelsberg Palace, at Princess Augusta's request, as a "Gothic" cottage, after a Lugar engraving (on which the larger palace eventually designed by Schinkel was also based). Construction work was at first confined to the left side, and was completed in 1835. When building resumed in 1844–1849, supervised by Persius and Strack, Schinkel's plans were altered. Unfortunately, only a few fragments of his original designs for the furnishing of the castle survive today, but they included a set of graceful Brazilian rosewood chairs.

The huge project for a classical villa as a summer residence for the Tsar at Orianda in the Crimea did not include designs for furniture, but a museum of the Crimea's classical antiquities was envisaged in the plans. Like so much else, this remained a dream – the

Empress of Russia preferred the idea of a small country house in the style of classical antiquity.

Towards the end of his life, a life of unflagging creativity, Schinkel saw some of his schemes of interior decoration sacrificed to the fashion for the Second Rococo style. But with the distribution of his own designs, and through the great number of his pupils, his severe Neo-classicism remained very influential in Berlin in many fields, including those of the applied arts, at least until the 1850s.

Chair from a suite for the living room of Princess Marie, wife of Prince Carl, in the Wilhelmplatz Palace (Berlin, 1828)
Design: Karl Friedrich Schinkel
Hornbeam, black lacquer, gilded inlay, gilded lead ornaments, silk upholstery; Berlin, Stiftung Preussische Schlösser und Gärten Berlin-Brandenburg, Schloss Glienicke

Though French design was a particularly important influence on Prussian applied arts and crafts at this time, British influence, noticeable also in architecture and painting, was also significant. This chair was designed to contemporary English models.

Prussia and the German Empire
1871–1918

1871 Founding of the German Empire: the Prussian king, William I, is declared German Emperor on January 18 in the Hall of Mirrors at Versailles near Paris. The Empire is a federal state under Prussian hegemony in which the Emperor is military commander-in-chief. The Prussian Premier, Otto von Bismarck, is also the Imperial Chancellor.
Some 62.8% of the Prussian population live in communities of 2,000 people; in the Rhineland the figure is only 42.7%. The population of Berlin is 1.93 million.

1872 Bismarck embarks on his *Kulturkampf* (cultural struggle) against the Catholic Centrist Party in the rivalry for political supremacy. The Prussian state assumes responsibility for all schools in its jurisdiction.
A reorganization of local government in Prussia's five eastern provinces abolishes the rights of the estates to police their own territory.
Rudolf Mosse founds the *Berliner Tageblatt* newspaper.

1873 The strong economic upturn of the founding years of the Empire (years known as the Gründerjahre) ends in the crash of a global economic crisis.
In the Polish parts of Prussia, German becomes the compulsory language of instruction.
In the center of the Prussian coal mining industry, the Lower Lausitz, 1,559 miners produce 701,578 tonnes of soft coal in 61 pits.

1876 The National Gallery (Nationalgalerie), by Johann Heinrich Strack from designs by Friedrich August Stüler, is opened in Berlin.
By discovering the anthrax bacillus, Robert Koch proves for the first time that an infectious disease is caused by a living micro-organism.

1877 Bismarck issues the "Socialist Laws" in order to suppress the workers' movement. A minor state of siege is declared in Berlin.

Emperor William I, painting by Paul Bülow, 1880

1879 Werner von Siemens is responsible for building the first electric locomotive.
The first electric arc lamps are erected in the Leipziger Strasse in Berlin.

1880 Konrad Duden publishes his *Orthographisches Wörterbuch der deutschen Sprache* (Orthographic Dictionary of the German Language).

1882 Robert Koch discovers the tubercle bacillus.

1883 Otto von Bismarck begins a program of social welfare legislation.
The Reichstag passes health insurance laws.
In Berlin, the first exhibition of French Impressionists in Germany is held.
August Bebel publishes *Die Frau und der Sozialismus* (Women and Socialism), and the German philosopher Friedrich Nietzsche publishes *Also sprach Zarathustra* (Thus spake Zarathrustra).
Robert Koch discovers the cholera bacillus.

Empress Augusta, painting by Minna Pfüller after Franz Xaver Winterhalter

1884 As part of a social welfare legislation program, the Reichstag passes a law relating to accident insurance.

1885 Some 3,000 Poles with Russian and Austrian citizenship are expelled from Prussia's eastern provinces. In the Reichstag and the Prussian Assembly there are fierce debates on the "Polish Question."

1888 Frederick III (1831–1888) crowned Emperor and King. Frederick, who suffered from cancer of the larynx, was already a very sick man when he ascends to the throne and dies after reigning for only 99 days.

Picture commemorating active service (c. 1900)

1888–1918 The reign of Emperor and King William II (1859–1941).

1889 Large-scale strikes led by miners in the Ruhr.
Pension and disability insurance introduced.
Gerhart Hauptmann's play *Vor Sonnenaufgang* (Before Sunrise) is performed.

1890 William II dismisses Bismarck.
The "Socialist Laws" are abolished.
51.6% of the Prussian population live in communities of less than 2,000 people.
The Free People's Stage (Freie Volksbühne) in Berlin is founded as the first workers' theater.

1891 The maximum working day for female factory workers over the age of 16 is set by law at 11 hours. Children under the age of 14 may not work in factories.
Tax reforms of the Prussian Minister of Finance, Johannes von Miquel: a graduated tax scheme on the basis of self-assessment is introduced.
A reorganization of rural communities in the eastern provinces broadens suffrage criteria for local elections, but affirms the independence of those districts attached to large estates.
Friedrich Engels publishes *Die Entwicklung des Sozialismus von der Utopie zur Wissenschaft* (The Development of Socialism from Utopia to Science).
Frank Wedekind publishes his play *Frühlings Erwachen* (Spring Awakening).

1892 Gerhart Hauptmann publishes his controversial play *Die Weber* (The Weavers).

1893 Economic crisis in Germany: one-third of all workers are either unemployed or underemployed.
The Meteorological Observatory in Potsdam, Germany's first, is opened.

Crown Prince Frederick William (Frederick III) with his wife, Princess Victoria of England, photograph (c. 1870)

Demonstration in Berlin against discriminatory electoral laws, photograph (c. 1910)

The artist Käthe Kollwitz begins work on her cycle of graphic works *Rebellion of the Weavers*, inspired by Hauptmann's *Die Weber*.

1894 Following the premiere of Gerhart Hauptmann's controversial play *Die Weber* in the Deutsches Theater in Berlin, Emperor William II relinquishes the royal box.

1895 The police commissioner of Berlin decrees the temporary disbanding of 11 Social Democratic organizations, including the executive committee of the Social Democratic Party of Germany.

1897 Alfred von Tirpitz becomes State Secretary of the Imperial Admiralty and at the instigation of William II applies himself to the task of building up the existing German fleet.
Adolph Slaby and Georg Graf begin the first experiments in wireless telegraphy near Potsdam.

Locomotive plant of the Berlin firm, Borsig; photograph (c. 1910)

1898 The artist Max Liebermann becomes the founder of the Berlin Secession.
Alfred Messel begins work on the Wertheim department store in Berlin (completed in 1904).
Theodor Fontane publishes his novel *Der Stechlin*.

1901 Celebrations are held to mark the 200th anniversary of the Prussian kingdom.
Käthe Kollwitz begins work on her cycle entitled *The Peasants' War*.

1902 The first stretch of the Berlin elevated and underground railway is opened.
The historian Theodor Mommsen is awarded the Nobel Prize for Literature.

1903 The first motorized buses appear in Berlin.

1904 The first provincial "conservator" is appointed in Brandenburg, and begins a survey of the architectural and artistic monuments of the region.
Ernst Eberhard von Ihne completes the building of the Emperor-Frederick-Museum in Berlin (today known as the Bode-Museum).

1905 William II causes the first Morocco Crisis.
Max Reinhardt takes over the Deutsches Theater located in Berlin.
The new Berlin Cathedral is completed by Julius Raschdorff.
Hermann Hesse publishes his novel *Unterm Rad* (Under the Wheel).

1906 Legislation is passed which states that the working day in railway workshops in Prussia and Hesse may not exceed nine hours.
So-called "Polish School Strike" takes place in Posen (Poznán) and West Prussia in protest at German language religious instruction.
The Imperial Cabinet forbids public institutions to purchase or display work by Naturalists or Impressionists.
Wilhelm von Bode is named as the General Director of Berlin's museums.
A large transmitter is built in Nauen, which is located northeast of Berlin.

1908 In elections to the Reichstag, the Social Democrats achieve their best result since 1890; they send seven deputies to the Prussian Assembly.
William II gives the British newspaper the *Daily Telegraph* an interview, and is subsequently heavily criticized both at home and abroad.
The Expropriation Law allows the government to purchase compulsorily up to a total of 70,000 hectares (173,000 acres) of land in Polish ownership and sell it to German settlers.

1909 Ludwig Justi becomes Director of the Berlin National Gallery (Nationalgalerie). Peter Behrens builds the AEG Turbine Assembly Plant in Berlin.

1909–1910 At the Prussian party conference of the Social Democrats, Karl Liebknecht gives an address entitled *Erringung der Demokratie in Prussen* (The Establishment of Democracy in Prussia).

Empress Auguste Victoria, painting by Heinrich von Angeli, 1880

38.4% of the Prussian population live in communities of fewer than 2000 people (in the Rhineland the figure is 20.7%).
Technical University of Breslau is founded.
August Bebel publishes *Aus meinem Leben* (From my Life).

1911 The mission of the German gunboat *Panther* leads to the second Morocco Crisis. At 671 gold marks, the per capita income of the Prussian population is twice what it was in 1871.
A landing area for air ships, a hangar and a branch of the Friedrichshafen Airship Company are built on the banks of the Havel at Potsdam.
Together with Staaken, it is the intention that Potsdam will become Berlin's port for airships. The hangar is torn down in 1920.
The first silent movie is made in Potsdam-Babelsberg.

1912 The Social Democrats become the strongest party in the Reichstag.
There are approximately 30,000 millionaires in the German Empire; the richest of them are William II and the industrialist Herta Krupp.
At a demonstration organized by the Social Democrats, a quarter of a million people protest against the Balkan War being fought between Bulgaria, Serbia, Montenegro, and Turkey.
There is a vote of no confidence in the Reichstag on Prussia's Polish policies.
Herwarth Walden opens the art gallery Der Sturm (The Storm) in Berlin with an exhibition by Der Blaue Reiter (The Blue Rider) group of Expressionist artists.
Kurt Tucholsky's novella, which is entitled *Rheinsberg: ein Bilderbuch für Verliebte* (Rheinsberg: A Picture Book for Lovers), is published.

1913 The Reichstag approves the largest expansion of the army since 1871: an extra 136,000 men brings the peace time strength up to 780,000.
Albert Einstein is called to the Prussian Academy of Sciences and the directorship of the Emperor William Institute for Physics in Berlin.

1914 Political tensions in Europe lead to the outbreak of the First World War.
The Social Democrat Karl Liebknecht is the only deputy in the Reichstag to vote against the second war credit.
The International Conference for Women is held in Berlin. Meetings in Berlin and in the provinces call for women's suffrage.

1915 Celebrations of the 500th anniversary of the reign of the Hohenzollerns takes place in the province Brandenburg.
Ration cards for bread are introduced for the first time.

1916 In the second winter of the war, every Berliner receives a weekly ration of 1,900 grams of bread, 2,500 grams of potatoes, 80 grams of butter, 250 grams of meat, 180 grams of sugar, and two eggs per month.
The law requires all men between 17 and 60 to undertake some form of work.
Max Planck publishes the first volume of his five-volume *Einführung in die theoretische Physik* (Introduction to Theoretical Physics). The last volume appears in 1932.

1917 William II promises the implementation of direct secret elections in Prussia.
Catastrophic supply problems lead to unrest and strikes for bread and higher wages.
The Swedish turnip becomes the main staple of the German diet.
Georg Grosz publishes his graphic series *The Face of the Ruling Class*.
The Universum-Film-AG (UFA) company is established in Potsdam.

1918 End of the First World War. William II's abdication and his exile to Holland brings the reign of the Hohenzollerns to an end in Brandenburg-Prussia. Prussia becomes a republic.
The founding party conference of the Communist Party of Germany (KPD) is held in the Prussian Assembly in Berlin.

Emperor William II and his six sons on their way across the Palace Bridge for the changing of the guard at the Arsenal, New Year's morning 1913, photograph

ARCHITECTURE AND URBAN DEVELOPMENT

Bernd Nicolai

The reader who today delves into that early 20th-century German classic, Georg Dehio's *Geschichte der Deutschen Kunst* (History of German Art) can expect very little information about the then unfashionable architecture of the previous century. With hindsight we can see that the last years of the 19th century did not give rise to a genuinely Prussian architecture. The only exception is the Reichstag (legislative) building by the Frankfurt architect Paul Wallot, a programmatic and most un-Prussian prelude to the style of modified historicism.

This impression is little altered if we consult Wolfgang Herrmann's important 19th century anthology of architecture: he includes the Martin-Gropius Building and the Anhalter Railroad Station. Finally, that incorruptible chronicler of 19th-century architecture, Cornelius Gurlitt, completes the list merely by adding Protestant church architecture and the apartment blocks in Berlin as belonging to Brandenburg's cultural achievements!

There are sound reasons for this point of view: there were no great successes in Berlin and Prussia between 1861 and 1900. The later reformist architecture that developed under the aegis of the Deutscher Werkbund, an association founded in Munich in 1907 by artists, architects, craftsmen, and industrialists in order to raise the standards of industrial and architectural design, is linked to broader national and international debates. In the second half of the 19th century, the centers of German art initially lay outside Prussia. Dresden took the lead after 1838 with Gottfried Semper and the establishment of the Neo-Renaissance as a counter-movement to Neo-classicism and the Neo-Gothic style.

Berlin, Schöneberg District, Wittenbergplatz
Photograph, 1905

The square on the city's southern boulevard (today's Tauentzienstrasse) called for in the Hobrecht Plan was not built until after 1890, and was oriented towards the Emperor William Gedächtniskirche (Memorial Church).

Munich under Maximilian II attempted the creation of a unified style with a competition for the Maximilianstrasse in 1852. The Viennese Ringstrasse (Ring Road) competition of 1857 and its construction – which continued to the end of the century – created a theoretically grounded, strictly historical architecture that sanctioned a plurality of styles and "genres." The quotations of different historical styles became important as bearers of meaning: the Neo-Gothic city hall embodied city liberties; the Renaissance forms of the university expressed a claim for humanist education; the Roman High Renaissance forms of the museums and the New Court (Neue Hofburg) were to convey, for one last time, the majesty of the Habsburg Empire. But the gigantic urban redevelopment of Bonapartist Paris (1852–1870) under Georges Haussmann overshadowed all the schemes already mentioned. It was the beginning of a modern, capitalist real estate economy, the introduction of new forms of urban services and hygiene, such as sewers, as well as an economic and social infrastructure. Paris was celebrated not only as the very embodiment of the new urban architecture, but also as the home of epoch-making architects such as Jacques-Ingnaz Hittorf, Henri Labrouste, Victor Baltard, Eugène-Emmanuel Viollet-le-Duc, and Charles Garnier.

It was not until Bismarck's appointment to the Prussian premiereship in 1861 that Prussia's hegemony within the German League started to make itself felt. In 1866, in the wake of Austria's defeat in the "War of Brothers," it led to the territories of the Prussian state finally being incorporated with one border, when the provinces of Hesse-Kassel, Hesse-Nassau, and Hanover were annexed. The result was the founding of the German Empire without Austria and, in 1867, the founding of the North German League.

Berlin, Schöneberg District, Wittenbergplatz
Photograph, 1927

In 1905, just eight years after being constructed, the buildings on the southern side of the square had to make way for Emil von Schaudt's KDW (Department Store of the New West) (left). Alfred Grenander's underground station (in the foreground), which marked the intersection of three train lines, was modeled on the tomb of Galla Placidia in Ravenna and added in 1911–1913.

Berlin, Tiergarten District, Reichstag (1884–1894)
Paul Wallot
Photograph, 1899

This innovative building for the Reichstag (legislative) building by Paul Wallot freed architecture from the chains of a "rigid historicism." Wallot used an iron and glass construction for the dome. The conversion of the building into the seat of the Bundestag (lower house of the German Parliament) by the English architect Norman Foster (1995–1999) will preserve only the façade.

Otto von Bismarck's domestic policies and the constitutional conflicts they aroused during the years 1862–1865 delivered a third defeat to parliamentary liberalism after those of 1819 and 1848. In the light of their growing economic strength, but continuing political impotence, the anxious middle classes looked to national symbols and the aristocracy for their models after the Empire was established in 1871. In architecture, the Schinkel School was astonishingly tenacious and new forums for debate opened up only around 1870.

The political forces at work

Three political forces were active in the new imperial capital of Berlin and left their mark on the public architecture: the German Empire, the state of Prussia, and the city of Berlin. This begs the question as to what extent we can talk at all about a genuinely "Prussian" architecture after 1871. In contrast to Moeller van den Bruck's ideologically motivated worship of the Prussian style at the time of World War I, in the years around 1870 influential architectural critics like KEO Fritsch, editor of the *Deutsche Bauzeitung* (German Building Gazette), emphasized change through continuity. Schinkel and the Berlin School were to be the yardstick with their tenets of economy, uniformity, and restraint. An understated architecture was considered characteristic of the city: "The uniqueness of Berlin's architecture," according to Fritsch "always had less to do with brilliant showpieces than with the care and diligence applied to all structural tasks." One might almost believe then that Berlin's architectural culture would produce buildings devoid of character; in practice, however, this was not the case.

Berlin, Central District, Kaiser-Wilhelm-Strasse, entry buildings (1885–1887; destroyed during World War II)
August Orth
Photograph, 1938

The opening to the east of Berlin created by August Orth was part of a larger reconstruction program for the inner city, a program never realized. This street separated the palace from the Lustgarten and surrounded it with roads on three sides.

Berlin's development from "a capital city into an industrial metropolis" changed its architecture as radically as it did its society. The critical view of the Wilhelminian Era, the imperialist phase of the German Empire between 1890 and 1918, often leads one to forget that developments in art and architecture were very diverse during this period. There was, to a large extent, a plurality of styles; the modern coexisted alongside the traditional, with court, state, city, industry and private clients having diverging interests. An appeal to a Prussian identity might have a retarding effect for some of these sectors, yet for others be turned to avant-garde purposes.

Modern Town Planning: The Example of Berlin

The city's architectural appearance was based on the much-derided plan by James Hobrecht, approved in 1862 and in force as a binding document until 1925. The Hobrecht plan introduced Berlin to a modern urban infrastructure on the model of both London and Paris.

In spite of the criticism it attracted, the plan remained the greatest achievement of Prussian Berlin, and would have provided for a measured growth of over one million inhabitants had not municipal and private interests acted to prevent this. After the Haussmann Plan for Paris and the Cerdà Plan for Barcelona, it was the most comprehensive plan of its day for regulating urban growth, and served as the model for a number of expansion projects elsewhere in Germany, such as the Stübben Plan in Cologne. When, in 1910, Scheffler bitingly criticized this "New Berlin" as the "most monumental example of modern dilettantism in urban planning," he had lost sight of the connection between the cause and the effect of the plan on the contemporary cityscape. The Hobrecht Plan broke with the techniques of traditional urban planning, such as Peter Josef Lenné's *Schmuck- und Bauanlagen der Residenz Berlin* (Decorative and Structural Designs for the Capital, Berlin) of 1843, and the design of the Luisenstadt which followed.

A decisive step was taken with the building regulations of 1853, when planning authority was transferred to the police headquarters. The new development plan was revealed as nothing more than an alignment plan or a prescription for the arrangement of buildings. According to Geist and Kürvers, urban planning degenerated into "negotiations between competing interest groups; the social considerations which should have found their way into the urban plan were therefore ignored."

The Hobrecht Plan provided for both an internal and an external ring road that were to extend far beyond the city limits. By using alternating square, circular and star-shaped open spaces and incorporating large boulevards, he followed the Parisian model, but he also remained faithful to the Lenné Plan. A new element was the extraordinarily large size of the city blocks, which would have required access through private roads.

As the implementation plan did not fall into the jurisdiction of the Prussian state, nothing came of this. The landlords, who formed the majority on the Berlin city council, insisted on a maximum utilization of their property. Encouraged by the artificial restriction of Berlin to what is today the inner city, by 1910 the "largest tenement city in the world" had arisen with densely built backyards and a mixed use of homes and workplaces – a development that had neither been intended nor predicted in 1862.

In their first criticisms of the plan, representatives of the Berlin Architectural Academy such as Richard Lucae in 1870–1871 overlooked the fact that the plan had been modeled on Vienna. Hobrecht pointed to the regulatory nature of the zoning plan, which only stated where building could not take place. The city's design and aesthetic was left in private hands. All the same, Hobrecht had developed a sensibility for social concerns in housing on the basis of his observations of London and Paris. The result was the "Berlin Mixture," which was to prevent the separation of social groups and the formation of slums. The ideal was for a balance of social classes in one housing unit: "For ethical, and therefore for State reasons, it is not 'isolation' but 'mixing' which seems to me to be what is required."

However, after both this plan and the indicative floor plans of the residential blocks were published by Gustav Assmann in 1862, "over speculation" led

not only to a shortage of housing, which peaked in the slum developments of 1872–1873, but to the long-term crowding of individual apartments and even to the use of cellars and attics. It was these impossible social conditions and not the architecture itself that caused the Berlin tenement building to be so emphatically rejected. In fact, today's much lower residential densities have shown the value of the tenement as a flexible and comfortable residential building. In its purest form the plan was only put into effect in Charlottenburg and Schöneberg – evidenced by the example of the Wittenbergplatz as part of the general block plan (see page 416).

Construction of this square did not begin until the mid 1890s. But even in this relatively prosperous area of the then city of Schöneberg there was pressure to exploit property. This meant that from 1905 to 1907 the new buildings on the southwestern side of the square had to make way for the first department store in the "new West," the KDW (see page 417).

The architectural reconstruction of the city, and the Schinkel School

These planning measures did not affect the old city center. Hobrecht left the building of the inner areas to the future and described them as "untenable given current conditions ... already, small steps in this direction have led to endless difficulties."

A thorough reconstruction of the center and an opening up to the east did not succeed in the Weimar Republic either under the City Surveyor, Martin Wagner; it was only finally achieved with the mania for demolition which reigned in the post-war era. Structurally, these failures were rooted in the fragmentation of the planning authorities, which continues to this day. As early as 1877 Fritsch had noted critically: "Until now there has been a complete lack of the necessary authoritative body with the remit to assess all questions pertinent to the development of Berlin and to decide the issues in the case of individual decisions."

The desire for a modern inner city in what had been medieval Berlin was only realized in piecemeal fashion after 1871. The large number of opposing interest groups actually prevented any unified solution from being reached. Between 1885 and 1887, August Orth, one of the most important city planners of the imperial era, was able to realize his planned project of 1871 in opening up the city east of the Palace and Lustgarten by means of the Kaiser-Wilhelm-Strasse, today the Karl-Liebknecht-Strasse (see page 419).

In line with its representative surroundings, Orth accentuated the entrance to the new street as a gateway using Neo-Baroque structures that were topped with cupolas. The new imperial center with its banks, businesses, and newspaper offices in assertive Neo-Renaissance and Neo-Baroque styles, however, developed in the more extensive district of Friedrichstadt.

The history of urban planning in Berlin took another turn with the successful election of Hermann Blankenstein to the office of City Surveyor in 1872. During his 24 years in office Blankenstein, together with his staff, erected countless city buildings that markedly improved the city's infrastructure. Foremost among these were schools, which were built at a breath-taking pace: in 1861 there were 20 district schools; by 1895 the figure was already 211. As one of the second generation of the Schinkel School, until 1896 Blankenstein perpetuated the idea of a functional aesthetic and, in emulation of Schinkel's Architectural Academy, made characteristic use of brick as a building material.

The construction of markets and hospitals was to follow closely behind that of schools. The Central Markets built on the Alexanderplatz between 1883 and 1886 were based on patterns of their Parisian counterparts but instead combined iron construction techniques with a brick envelope. Market Hall IX, built in 1890–1891 in the southeast

Left
Berlin, Tiergarten District, Packhofanlage on the Lower Spree (1883–1886; demolished 1957)
Fritz Wolff
Photograph (c. 1900)

This goods depot was modeled on Schinkel's Architectural Academy in Berlin. These functional brick buildings were both remarkably practical and displayed a high aesthetic standard.

Berlin, Kreuzberg District, "Am Urban" Hospital (1887–1890)
Hermann Blankenstein

Large hospitals and clinics were required as the city grew. Blankenstein built the first of these while still City Surveyor. The pavilion method of construction was borrowed from Paris.

Berlin, Kreuzberg District, Martin Gropius Building, formerly the Museum of Applied Arts (1877–1881)
Martin Gropius and Heino Schmieden

The diversity of the façade's material has its origins in the building's former function as the Museum of Applied Arts (Kunstgewerbemuseum): the exterior was designed to reflect the museum's function. The particular importance of this building is derived from its synthesis of structural elements taken from Schinkel and Semper.

Berlin, Central District, Imperial Bank (1869–1873, destroyed during World War II)
Friedrich Hitzig
Photograph (c. 1900)

The Imperial Bank was a response to the new buildings by Heinrich von Ferstel on the Ringstrasse in Vienna. Around the turn of the century, the huge Imperial Bank already occupied its own quarter in the Friedrichswerder district.

of Kreuzberg, which is still well preserved, once belonged to a system of 14 markets that existed throughout the city.

To its main façade on Eisenbahnstrasse were added sandstone pillars and an architrave, and so also, in accordance with Carl Boetticher's theory of structural and artistic form, an iron framework.

As a pendant to Blankenstein's Central Stockyards on the Ringbahn (1878–1881), the Packhofanlage by Fritz Wolff was built on the Spree (see page 420) opposite the gracious Alsenviertel and close to the Humboldt Harbor and the Lehrter Railroad Station. Its style was a reference to Schinkel's Architectural Academy. The monumental structure, however, placed Schinkel's innovations in the context of a purely utilitarian building, a tendency that is also expressed in numerous water towers and gasometers. These designs by Schinkel had been intended in their day for churches, villas, and apartment houses.

Hermann Blankenstein's most significant building in the city center was without doubt the Police Headquarters on the Alexanderplatz (1886–1890), which was destroyed during the war. Its massive extent of almost 200 meters (656 feet) gave him the punning nickname "Steineblank" (Stone Blank). The controversies after 1890 surrounding his aesthetics failed to take into account that Blankenstein had adopted some of the most modern building types; his "Am Urban" hospital (see page 420) (1887–1890) consisted of discrete two-storied pavilions and was built on the Parisian model. The first hospital of this type to use the brick building methods and detailed decoration of the Schinkel School was built by the architectural firm of Gropius & Schmieden in Friedrichshain.

The views of the architects

These architects played an important role in transforming brick architecture in Berlin. Their contribution to contemporary debates on style and function was to combine Schinkel's position with both Semper's and Boetticher's theories – as indeed Blankenstein had done also. Between the years 1877 and 1881 they synthesized these concepts in exemplary fashion with the construction of the Museum of Applied Arts (see page 421). This is the most important building from the founding years of the Empire in Berlin. It is the last manifestation of the Schinkel School in Prussian architecture but transcends the style by applying Semper's theories on color and façades.

The palazzo-like cube form is an obvious reference to the Architectural Academy, but is in general more richly detailed, its complex ornamentation indicating the variety and material diversity of the applied arts. The spacious design of the interior, in addition to the iron construction used in the atrium, are indications that Gropius & Schmieden had been stimulated by Stüler's New Museum (Neues Museum) in the interplay of constructive form and ornamentation. The central spatial alignment is taken from the Viennese Museum for Art and Industry (1868–1871) by Heinrich von Ferstel, whose work on the Viennese Ringstrasse was also in brick. The use of polychrome as well as ceiling and wall claddings to match the displays should be understood as a didactic underpinning of the exhibition departments.

These principles had already been articulated in Stüler's work and did themselves refer back to Semper's writings. The museum itself became a "total work of art" that, in Neo-Renaissance fashion, allowed architecture to employ materials in such a way as to locate the plastic arts either in a position subservient to the building or alternatively to allow them equal importance, depending on the type of museum.

Friedrich Hitzig's late classicist Imperial Bank in brick (1869–1873) represented a completely different approach (above, left). Hitzig also attempted to transpose the principles of Viennese Ringstrasse architecture to Berlin. Along with Ferstel's work, the design of the Vienna Stock Exchange (1868) by Theophil von Hansen served as a model (built between 1873 and 1877 in brick linked by freestone columns); Stüler's War Ministry in the Leipziger Strasse was yet another. This building marked the end of a style; the classicist metaphors of the Schinkel School were, in the strictest sense, no longer capable of being developed.

Apart from urban construction projects, the Schinkel School was both successful and innovative when it came to new building types, especially in the area of functional buildings serving a symbolic or representational purpose.

The former Postal Depot in the Oranienburger Strasse by Carl Schwatlo was a particular showpiece. Schwatlo, together with Wilhelm Tuckermann, constructed the depot on a difficult corner site from 1877 to 1881 (see below). With its triumphant entry arch that lead in to the post office counters, the quality of the molded brickwork (which was influenced by the Architectural Academy), the high entrance hall, and the octagonal dome with two smaller flanking cupolas as a focus, the Imperial Postal Service deliberately located itself in an inner city area that was defined by the orientalizing dome of the nearby Synagogue (see page 332). This latter building had already seen the synthesis of a detailed brick frontage and modern cupola construction from 1857–1866. Schwatlo, who rose to become the post office architect for Berlin, quoted various historical styles for his buildings, depending on the nature of the location.

Further attempts to develop brick architecture into a form suitable for public buildings failed. A telling example of this was Friedrich Waesemann's Rotes Rathaus (Red City Hall) in Berlin, of which it was maintained that it was "neither Romanesque, Gothic, Renaissance, Rococo, nor Classical"; a building altogether devoid of style. The Rotes Rathaus was not popular because it was a synthesis of the most diverse elements and lacked any sort of unity.

Berlin, Central District, former postal depot (1877–1881)
Carl Schwatlo and Wilhelm Tuckermann

The wagons of the Imperial Post, which was run by Heinrich von Stephan, were once parked at this location. The brick of the building, as well as its dome, harmonized with the Berlin Synagogue, which had been built shortly before on the Oranienburger Strasse.

Above
Berlin, Kreuzberg District, Anhalter Railroad Station (1871–1880; demolished 1961)
Franz Schwechten and Heinrich Seidel, view of Askanischer Platz, 1901

The "railroad's mother cave" was how the cultural critic Walter Benjamin described the station in his essay "Berliner Kindheit um 1900" (A Berlin Childhood, Circa 1900). This startling new building marked a renew of architectural forms in Berlin.

Railroad stations

The innovative strength of the Schinkel School was demonstrated in a new building type that only gradually began to take shape with Prussia's industrialization from the middle of the 19th century: the railroad station. Prussia set the pace, and between 1866 and 1880 Berlin established the benchmark for station buildings. There then followed between 1875 and 1895 stations in Hanover, Frankfurt am Main, and Cologne, all of which were on Prussian territory. But Germany still lagged behind in this field: both Paris (Gare de l'Est, Gare du Nord) and London (King's Cross, St. Pancras) had already set the standard for railroad stations in the 1850s and 1860s.

The most striking example in Berlin was the former Anhalter Railroad Station (below), which was built between 1871 and 1880 by Franz Schwechten, together with the engineer and novelist Heinrich Seidel. The Anhalter project was built entirely of brick and represented a new type of station. The entrance hall, the vestibule, and a new type of transverse platform from which the enormous building could be accessed were now delineated; the platforms themselves were elevated so that the trains could cross the city unimpeded. A new form of monumental architecture developed that was determined by the purpose of the building: the structure was not only utterly functional "but it will, as a distinct and unified organism, embody its purpose with dignity and character and, on the strength of its absolute artistic value, assume an honorable place among the monumental structures of the new German capital." What is more, added Fritsch, "it is to be expected that it will assert a useful influence on the design of later railroad buildings, both as an example of a sound solution and as the method for arriving at that solution."

This last comment referred to the good working relationship between the architect and the engineer. At a time when the sharp distinction between architecture and engineering was being challenged, it seemed important to combine the two functions

more closely. Railroad stations were particularly well suited to achieve this, because through them the traveler experienced the transition from a high-speed transport system into the static structure of the city. In 1869, Richard Lucae, arguing that they lacked art and had no clear spatial boundaries, referred to the iron and glass sheds of railroad stations as "non-architecture." In the Anhalter Station, Schwechten countered this criticism with his subtle fusion of engineering and architecture. The characteristic design element of the building is its front façade, which is modeled after classical thermal baths. This was an evocation of Philbert de l'Ormes famous design for a basilica (1648) that had entered the architectural discourse in Berlin in 1798 via monumentalized copies by David Gilly and Karl Friedrich Schinkel. In contrast to the Gare de l'Est in Paris (1847–1850) by François-Alexandre Duquesney, the Anhalter Station was not given an historical frontage. Instead, the comparatively sober material of brick was used to emphasize its characteristic "solidity." A similar type had already been built in London; the façade for the twin halls of King's Cross Station (1851–1852) by Lewis Cubitt had been defined by two segmented gables with classical thermae windows. In the construction of the Anhalter's halls, which were supported by brick walls, Seidel and Schwechten repeated the famous station designs that Schwedler and Orth had carried out in the 1860s for the Görlitz and Ostbahnhof stations. Their design was also patterned on the largest iron hall constructed anywhere in the world: St. Pancras Station in London, built from 1863 to 1870 by engineers William Henry Barlow and Rowland Mawson Ordish. At 66 meters (216 feet), the span of St. Pancras was still 4 meters (13 feet) wider than the Anhalter Station; but the huge hall of St. Pancras station is concealed behind Gilbert Scott's Neo-Gothic hotel. Just how innovative the Anhalter Station was in its large, clearly defined form can be seen in a comparison with the Lehrter Bahnhof, built 1869–1871 as a royal railroad station by Lent, Scholz, and La Pierre. The traditional motif of the Lehrter station's triumphal arch was borrowed from the Budapest East Station and its frontage served purely as a façade.

There was a limit to how the design of Berlin's terminal stations could be applied to Germany's through stations. The most interesting example of the use of the Berlin brick-build method was the Hanover Railroad Station by Hubert von Stier (1875–1880); this project reflected the controversial nature of public architecture in a province that had been annexed in 1866.

The Neo-Renaissance project begun by Hitzig was halted in 1873 after protests that pointed to an architectural tradition native to Hanover and based on the classicism of Laves as well as the Neo-Gothic style of Wilhelm Hase. Only the office building to

Top
Hanover, Main Railroad Station (1875–1880)
Hubert Stier

Stier created a synthesis of the Berlin round arched style and traditional Hanoverian architecture. Following protests against the imposition of "Prussian" architecture, he was able to take over construction in 1873; Hanover's new Prussian masters had first favored another architect.

Frankfurt am Main, Main Railroad Station (1883–1888, outer halls 1923–1925)
Hermann Eggert

Eggert created one of the first modern metropolitan railroad stations and on a scale previously unknown in Germany. The play between the façade and the architecture of the great halls emphasize the station's function as a new city gate.

Cologne, Main Railroad Station, Platform Hall (1891–1894)
Georg Frentzen

The massive trusses of the arches were modeled on the those of the Galerie des machines at the Paris World Exposition of 1889. The single span of the hall was not superseded until the hall of the Hamburg Main Station was built in the early years of the 20th century.

the south was eventually completed by Hitzig. The importing of the "Berlin Renaissance" style was felt to be an imposition. The Prussian Ministry of Commerce finally relented and commissioned Hubert Stier, who had strongly criticized the 1869 competition and was still considered an opponent of the Neo-Renaissance. Stier not only absorbed the functional achievements of the Berlin stations but, in the tradition of the Berlin round arch style, in 1875 he developed a detailed design whose elements showed a number of characteristics related to Berlin's Rotes Rathaus. The palatial appearance was intensified by defining the station as the focus of a large axis running from the Altstadt (Old Town), but the spare fomal language of the Hanover station does not attain the monumentality of the Anhalter Station. Stier was not to achieve that feat until the building of his Bremen Station (from 1885). The Hanoverian type, however, became the model for the Strassbourg Station by Eduard Jacobsthal (1879–1883). Jacobsthal was the architect responsible for the stations built from 1878–1882 on the new Berlin metropolitan railroad, one of the first state railroad lines. He applied the innovations of the Anhalter Station to those on the Alexanderplatz (later remodeled several times) and at Bellevue. The Hackescher Markt Station (formerly the Stock Exchange Station), which still exists, was built according to the same concepts between 1878 and 1882 by Johannes Vollmer.

The rejection of brick and the increase of the Anhalter Station's influence can be seen in the Frankfurt Central Station (see page 425, bottom). It was here that the largest passenger terminus in Germany was built from 1883 to 1888 to a Neo-Renaissance design by Herman Eggert.

It had been preceded by an international competition in 1880 in which the new Academy of Architecture in Berlin had functioned as jury; it was to judge all public competitions until 1900. Eggert's final design had to incorporate essential elements of the façade layout by the second prizewinner, Georg

Frentzen, who was to erect the Cologne Central Station between 1891 and 1894. Schwechten, Wallot, Thiersch and others were unsuccessful in Frankfurt. The three large railroad halls with their glazed gables and separate office block borrowed from certain aspects of the preliminary designs for the Anhalter Station. The entry building, extending out from the station itself, borrowed from Frentzen's ideas. It dominated still further in the detailed design, so that it appeared as a slightly smaller continuation of the central shed in the basilica scheme of de l'Ormes mentioned above. The great vestibule façade with its highly visible station clock and group of figures around Atlas – who, with the aid of the personification Steam and Electricity, bore up a globe – articulated the idea of a new entrance to the city in a newly designed station district. The building itself was in a freely interpreted Roman Renaissance style and built of earthy-brown sandstone. It displaced the frequently used brick station buildings, which had connotations of mere functionalism, and served to lift the lowly railroad station into the category of monumental public architecture. A technologically significant feature of Schwedler's hall construction was the introduction of the triple jointed truss construction, which was later to play an especially important role in Cologne and Hamburg. The Cologne station's mighty 63-meter (207-feet) span (see page 426), executed with only double jointed trusses, was in fact modeled on the very much larger Galerie des machines at the Paris World Exposition (1889) by Dutert, Contamin, Pierron, and Charton. Frentzen, however, was unable to unite this structure with the station entrance hall that, in clumsy Renaissance style, looked ill at ease in the proximity of the cathedral.

The search for a national style: the debate on the Neo-Renaissance style

In the last quarter of the 19th century, all the attempts of one faction of the Berlin School to establish Neo-Gothic as a universal style (which Johannes Otzen had called for 1878 and 1900) had failed. Instead, the Neo-Renaissance was established as the predominant style under the strong influence of Gottfried Semper, with his early epoch making theaters and museums, as well as his Zurich Polytechnic (1858–1864). But from the time of the "Schinkel Address" in 1862, in which Friedrich Adler praised the Baroque architecture of Andreas Schlüter, the idea of a more flexible concept of the Renaissance had begun to be discussed. In 1872, Joseph Durm saw the use of free-standing columns in the newly constructed Dresden Opera House as related to the forms of the High Baroque. Semper himself in his Imperial Forum in Vienna completed the transition to the Neo-Baroque. By 1880 it was evident that no one single style could dominate the national stage. Under such circumstances it is no wonder that Paul Wallot's Reichstag building in Berlin (1884–1894) was heralded as the birth of a new architecture. Its newness was apparent in the distribution of ornamentation as well as the form of the broad glass dome that, as a successor to the New Synagogue, completed the dome's transition from sacral to profane architecture in Germany. It is worth bearing in mind that the Reichstag's dome was a makeshift measure; the detailed design had called for it to be positioned over the entrance hall, but the Emperor had objected to this. Wallot then shifted it back on to the assembly hall, but because construction was at an advanced stage it was no longer possible to introduce new columns for a solid cupola. Wallot made do with one of iron and glass that the architectural historian Julian Posener has described as representing a "shift to Modernism." Posener's opinion harmonized with that of a co-founder of the Deutscher Werkbund, Hermann Muthesius, who called the Reichstag a "creation": "It marks the beginning of a new episode in German architecture. ... The liberation from the shackles of stylistic mimicry – that is the greatest service Wallot has achieved for German architecture." In the light of the 20th century's classical Modernism, the Reichstag has always been seen as standing for stagnation and a stylistic dead end. In reality, however, it forms the transition to a modified historicist style in which, rather than employing a close stylistic system, the architect draws upon a range of different styles, for example by using classical porticos and columns. This approach was first put into effect by Joseph Poelaert in his Palace of Justice in Brussels (1866–1883). The interior space of the Reichstag was staged so that it became a space with intriguing spatial effects; it was meant to have a dramatic impact on visitors. This principle was raised to bizarre proportions in the magnificent staircases of the Berlin law courts, such as the Central Law Court (1896–1904 by Paul Thoemer and Rudolf Mönnich, completed by Otto Schmalz) (see above) and the Criminal Court at Moabit (1902–1906 by Mönnich and Carl Vohl). Such structures contradicted the demands made for objectivity at the start of the 20th century and formulated by the Deutscher Werkbund in 1907. The Imperial Law Court in Leipzig (1887–1895) by Ludwig Hoffmann (appointed City Surveyor of Berlin in 1896 on the basis of these buildings) and the Palace of Justice in Munich by Friedrich von Thiersch (1889–1897) are direct successors to these buildings.

Influenced by the circle around Heinrich Burnitz, Thiersch, like Wallot in Frankfurt, had adopted a freer style. He was Wallot's main rival in the second Reichstag competition of 1882 and was awarded a joint first prize. The Reichstag marked the real beginning of Wilhelminian public architecture, which rooted in non-aristocratic tastes, did not appeal to the Emperor; William II described the

Berlin, Central District, Central Law Court (1896–1904)
Paul Thoemer, Rudolf Mönnich, Otto Schmalz

At the time of their construction, the Law Court was the second largest building in the city after the Palace. The façade fuses Baroque influences with Art Nouveau forms.

Berlin, Central District, Central Law Court (1896–1904)
Paul Thoemer, Rudolf Mönnich, Otto Schmalz

The models for Schmalz's superb creation were Baroque palace staircases and the playfulness of late Gothic church interiors of around 1500. When opened, the building attracted both praise and outright condemnation.

Reichstag as "the very pinnacle of bad taste." The leader of the Social Democrats on the other hand, August Bebel, demanded an opulent style for the new German parliament in order to emphasis its significance as the country's constitutive authority. All in all, the Reichstag building remained a difficult undertaking; it was a symbol of German society in general which now, after the founding of the Empire in 1871, extended far beyond Prussia's boundaries. A competition had already been held in 1872, which was won by Ludwig Bohnstedt, a brilliant polyglot from Gotha. The concept design of this "superbly superficial" architect who, together with Semper, had popularized the Neo-Renaissance, was not entirely uncontroversial. Bohnstedt's design anticipated many of Wallot's ideas but ultimately could not achieve either a political or aesthetic consensus. In his colonnades and triumphal arches, Bohnstedt employed forms that had been developed by the Schinkel School, particularly in Friedrich Hitzig's Berlin Stock Exchange, which is now destroyed (see opposite, top). Hitzig's most important public work in Berlin remains the new central building for the Charlottenburg Technical University (today's Berlin Technical University). This building was comprehensively planned by Richard Lucae (1876–1877) and Hitzig took over the work after Lucae's death in 1877. The arrangement of the main wing into round arches was contrasted in the central projection of the facade by the further development of a row of columns (see opposite, bottom) as had already been used in the Stock Exchange. Originally, double columns were to have flanked the central projection as an echo of the Portals I and II of the Berlin Palace. Julius Raschdorff, who took over construction following Hitzig's sudden death in 1881, changed several details and completed the university in 1884. Hitzig's original concept is today visible only in the façade facing the garden. The Technical University was an exceptional case. On the one hand, its three-winged construction was a response to the palace of Prince Henry on Unter den Linden (which had become Frederick-William University) at the opposite end of the city's east-west axis. The Charlottenburg Technical University therefore placed itself in direct competition with the distinguished Frederick-William University (which later became the Humboldt University), and so establish a leading role for polytechnics in Prussia. The main building consisted of an expanded four-winged complex with a central atrium and two inner courtyards. Hitzig's design therefore monumentalized the most modern type of technical educational institution, the Zurich Polytechnic, which had been built by none other than Gottfried Semper between 1858 and 1864. The Zurich Polytechnic was to serve as a model for this building type in the second half of the 19th century. This composite design was followed by August Thiede's Museum of Natural Science (1883–1889) (see page 430), an enormous complex flanked by the slightly lower buildings of the State Geological Institute and the School of Mines.

The façade projection was articulated by means of double columns and the spare Renaissance forms refer directly to the Zurich Polytechnic. In the context of a Berlin building, the huge and impressive atrium was a clear allusion to the Applied Arts Museum, as was the frequent use of decorative cast iron – the free-standing stair wells being the most

Berlin, Central District, Stock Exchange (1855–1858; ruins removed in 1958)
Friedrich Hitzig
Photograph (c. 1880)

The Stock Exchange was the most important private building from before 1860 to signal a turning away from the style of the Schinkel School. The Baroque formalism, which borrows from the style of a royal palace, did not, however, have any impact on Berlin architecture until after 1880.

spectacular examples of this. The palatial three-winged genre was used again in Berlin for the Prussian Assembly and House of Peers. Friedrich Schulze then erected the actual State Parliament (Landtag) – today Berlin's House of Deputies (1892–1897) (see page 430) – opposite the Applied Arts Museum as a palazzo-like cube, while the three-winged complex facing Leizpig Strasse (to be the future seat of the Bundesrat, the upper house of the German Parliament) was completed in 1904 in the Baroque style of Frederick the Great. Between 1877 and 1900, the extensive development west of the Wilhelmstrasse, which had previously been characterized by Baroque palaces and large gardens, was utterly transformed. The tension between the traditionalism of the Berlin School and the emergence of new forms was shown in the period between 1870 and 1890 in the work of Richard Lucae and Johann Heinrich Strack. Lucae built the Neo-Renaissance Borsig Palace on the Wilhelmplatz, which was incorporated into the new Reich Chancellery (Reichskanzlei) by Albert Speer, 1936–1939. Just prior to this, between 1872–1873, the architectural partnership of Ebe & Benda had built the nearby Pringsheim Palace, which featured a richly decorated Italiante façade. One of the few Neo-Renaissance buildings with stone facades still surviving is the Studio Building of the Office Association (Bürogemeinschaft) by Ende & Böckmann (1884–1886) in the Vossstrasse.

Lucae's greatest project, however, was not carried out in the Prussian capital but in Frankfurt, which had been Prussian since 1866, where he built the Alte Oper (1873–1880) (see page 431, top). The opera building was typical of the period in combining the basic plan of Schinkel's Schauspielhaus on the Gendarmenmarkt in Berlin (see page 306) with a modeled façade in Roman Renaissance style that

Berlin, Charlottenburg District, Royal Technical University Charlottenburg (TU Berlin), Main Building (1877–1884; front building destroyed during World War II)
Friedrich Hitzig, Julius Raschdorff
Photograph, 1895

This complex composed of three wings echoed the Frederick William University (today's Humboldt University) on Unter den Linden: the new polytechnic was determined to assert its role as Prussia's second university.

emulated the Vienna Opera House by Siccards von Siccardsburg and Felix van der Nüll. Cornelius Gurlitt saw a freedom to maneuver in Frankfurt that Berlin was not able to provide. Through the influence of Heinrich Burnitz and his pupils Oskar Sommer, Mylius & Bluntschi, as well as Lucae, Wallot, and Eggert the way was paved for the changes that had been signaled by the Reichstag. At the beginning of this evolution came the Frankfurt Stock Exchange by Burnitz and Sommer. After a competition held in 1873, the building was completed in 1877 in the manner of the Biblioteca Vecchia by Jacopo Sansovino and Vincenzo Scamozzi in Venice. There were echoes of Hitzig's architecture in Berlin, but the forms were given greater sophistication by the inclusion of double columns on the ground floor. The skylights of the Stock Exchange rooms were hidden behind the façade befitting the building's character, which can be described as "monumental".

In Berlin, architecture was dominated by Johann August Strack after Friedrich August Stüler's death in 1866. Strack's National Gallery (Nationalgalerie; 1866–1876) (see opposite, below) followed Stüler's design from the years 1862–1865, in which it was seen as a new Valhalla – the Pantheon by Leo von Klenze built near Regensburg with busts of German notables. Strack belonged to the first generation of Schinkel's pupils. In his Borsig Villa in Moabit (now destroyed) from the years 1849 and 1868–1870, he reinterpreted Italian architecture using brick in the fashion of his mentor. The former facades of the Rondell on the Belle-Alliance-Platz (today's Mehring Platz), built in 1877 but destroyed in the last war, were good examples of his terse Renaissance style. The final emancipation from the classicist and strictly Renaissance canons is evident in Strack's last work, the Joachimsthal Grammar School, which was built in 1875–1880 by Jacobsthal and Giersberg from Strack's preliminary design. Shortly before, Jacobsthal had built one of the most famous villas of his day (1870–1872), the Villa Hügel Baldeney near Essen for the "King of Cannons," the arms manufacturer Alfred Krupp (directly above). It is the adapted villa of a Renaissance prince equipped with the most up-to-date technology, as befitted the seat of an industrial magnate, and it was intended to assert the identity of a new industrial middle class.

The evolution of the Neo-Renaissance led to the same sort of schematism as the late classicism of the Schinkel School.

The influence of the Vienna Ringstrasse and the overwhelming impression gained by the astonished German troops who occupied Paris in 1871, meant that the Neo-Renaissance style became increasingly penetrated by elements of the Baroque. Finally, Wallot's Reichstag had the effect of showing that any style at all could be used in any format. This led to a distancing from historical sources and to an abstracting of formal details. It also led to the

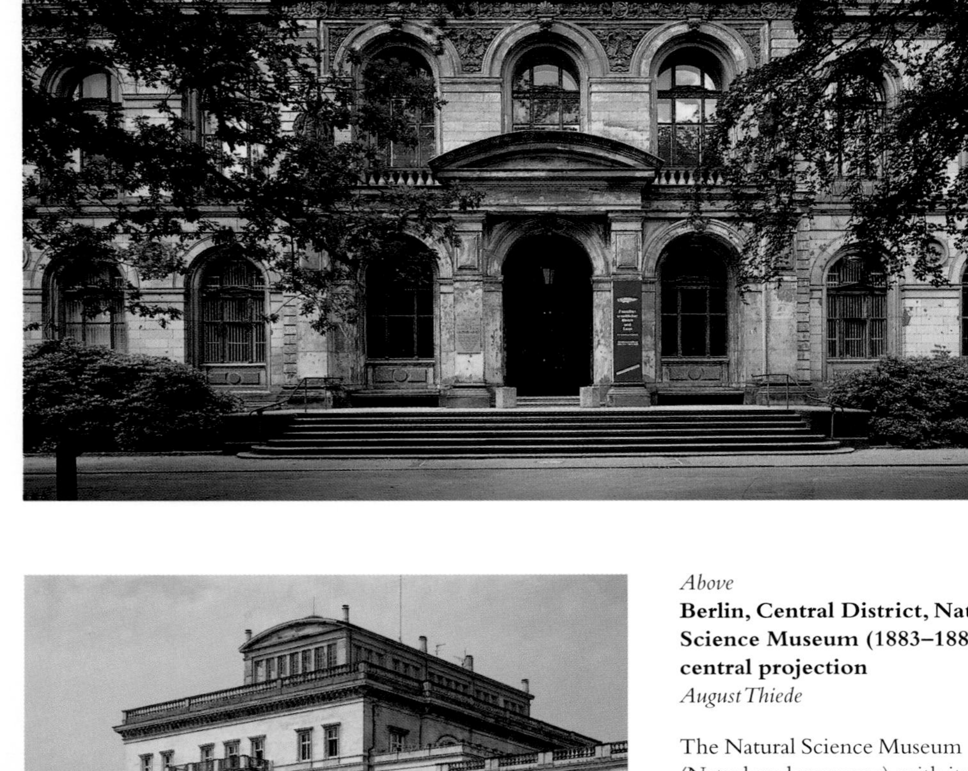

Above
Berlin, Central District, Natural Science Museum (1883–1889), central projection
August Thiede

The Natural Science Museum (Naturkundemuseum), with its outstanding collection, was built in the grounds of the abandoned iron foundry, alongside the School of Mines and the Geological Institute. Like the Martin Gropius Building, the museum housed a double-story atrium and fine cast-iron staircases.

Far left
Berlin, Central District, Berlin House of Deputies, former Prussian Assembly (1892–1897)
Friedrich Schulze

The buildings on the Wilhelmstrasse were the structural model for the Prussian Assembly. It was erected when the area was being transformed into a government quarter. The building will become the seat of the Bundesrat (upper house of the German Parliament).

Left
Essen-Baldeney, Villa Hügel (1870–1872)
Eduard Jacobsthal

A new type of industrialist's villa was developed for Alfred Krupp, which took as its model the villas of the Renaissance.

Frankfurt am Main, Alte Oper (1873–1880; reconstruction as concert hall, 1977–1981)
Richard Lucae

Lucae's models for this opera house were Schinkel's Berlin Schauspielhaus, Gottfried and Manfred Semper's second Dresden Court Theater, and the Braunschweig State Theater by C. Wolf and H. Ahlberg, all of which had already made use of spare Renaissance styles in the period between 1862–1868.

Berlin, Central District, The Old National Gallery (Alte Nationalgalerie), (1862–1876)
Friedrich August Stüler, Johann Heinrich Strack

The Old National Gallery (Nationalgalerie) was founded in 1861. Its style combines Leo von Klenze's Valhalla and Friederich Gilly's famous design (see page 294) for a monument to Frederick the Great, a Pantheon which, on the orders of William I, was to bear the inscription "To the German People."

Berlin, Central District, Faber Building (1882–1883, destroyed during World War II)
Hans Grisebach
Woodcut in Deutsche Bauzeitung (German Building Gazette), 1883

Some commercial buildings in the period between 1880 and 1900 were modeled after the German Renaissance of the 16th century. The stated aim was to create a picturesque cityscape in a style that had German roots.

Opposite
Berlin, Central District, Commercial Buildings on the Friedrichstrasse
Ferdinand Wendelstedt, Bruno Schmitz

This Neo-Gothic commercial property was oriented to Grisebach's Faber Building (see top left), which lay diagonally opposite. The Automat Restaurant by Bruno Schmitz (left), could not offer a more telling contrast to Wendelstedt's design.

rejection of "genre styles" (which are based on the assumption that there is a necessary relationship between a particular style and a specific building type). In view of the emergence of Art Nouveau towards the end of the century, calls for a new normative style with its own distinctive standards became louder. Opponents feared uniformity; protagonists like the Viennese Otto Wagner in his epoch making book *Moderne Architektur* (Modern Architecture) (1896) perceived in this a logical outcome and expression of democracy – and, indeed, of the modern age. Prussia, however, was not affected by the modern movement until the first decade of this century, when the Deutscher Werkbund was founded in 1907 as a pan-German project; at first, the debates about conflicting styles were to run a different course.

In the 1870s, a new urban model for residential and commercial buildings appeared: the German Renaissance. This paralleled the development of a new commercial building typical of Berlin that was to evolve into its own genre shortly before the turn of the century: the department store. The first building of this type in Berlin, the Kaisergalerie, caused a sensation; it was a new fashionable type of arcade on the French model (below). In 1870, and "on the highest orders," the architectural firm of Kyllman & Heyden built a passage connecting Unter den Linden with the corner of Friedrichstrasse and Behrenstrasse that was dedicated in 1883 in the presence of William I. A coffee house in the Viennese Style and the "Emperor's Panorama," which was the first device in the city to show stereoscopic photographs, brought a touch of the wider world to Berlin. The basic design was patterned on the Central Arcade by Heinrich von Ferstel in Vienna.

Central District, Kaisergalerie (1870–1873; destroyed)
Kyllman & Heyden
Interior view (c. 1900)

Berlin's first arcade was to bring a Parisian flair to the new capital city. This new type of German Neo-Renaissance was a mixture of Frenche château and "ye olde Nuremberg."

The retail area in the extended first floor and the continuous upper floors, which housed exclusive restaurants, were modeled on the façades of Parisian boulevards. Its great triumphal portal arch facing Friedrichstrasse and the corner of Behrenstrasse, as well as the flanking towers, were taken from the Renaissance vocabulary of palace architecture. The result was a mixture of the French Renaissance château of Chambord and the German Renaissance, a "colossal Nuremberg." But the arcade did not live up to the high expectations held for it. Around 1900, when the well-to-do areas of Berlin had migrated further west to reach the Kurfürstendamm, the Friedrichstrasse had become an amusement and tourist area. In the 1920s, Franz Hessel described the decline of the Kaisergalerie as follows: "One can feel the beer-hall Renaissance of these high vaults aging more and more; the dust of ages obscures the gallery windows and can no longer be cleaned off. The displays are the same as they were 20 years ago." Following the grandiloquence of the Kaisergalerie, the beginnings of a picturesque re-shaping of the cityscape on an "olde German" or "Nuremberg" model had been established. Already in 1869, Jabobsthal had called for buildings with bay windows to enliven the city. Hase built the shops of the Karmarschstrasse in Hanover in a picturesque "burgher's house" style that had its origins (in motivation rather than style) in England. Gottfried Semper and Hubert Stier saw the German Renaissance as imbued with classical and Gothic principles, but demanded that the Northern Renaissance be restricted to private buildings. Stier himself had constructed the palace-like river fountain on the Leine with a tower and ornate gables. Together with the Palais Pless (1884–1886) in Berlin's Wilhelmstrasse, a Parisian import by the architect Destailleur in the form of a French nobleman's palace, it remained the exception. The breakthrough for the urban building did not come until the Berlin Building Regulations of 1878. In 1882–1883, Hans Grisebach built a commercial property for Johann von Faber in the Französische Strasse in the style of von Faber's hometown of Nuremberg; it had ornate oriel windows, as well as distinct retail and residential areas (see top left). Diagonally opposite on the Friedrichstrasse Ferdinand, Wendelstedt followed the Grisebach pattern in 1898–1899 with a more pronounced Gothic design (see opposite). This structure contrasted sharply with the Automat Restaurant building by Bruno Schmitz of 1905–1906, which showed the transition to exclusively commercial buildings and offices after the turn of the century.

Hans Griesebach built numerous city houses and villas, among them his own house in the Fasanenstrasse (1891–1892) as well as the Kronprinzenzelt beerhall in the Tiergarten in 1887–1888. The idiosyncratic high point of his

City TANZSCHULE
Metzler-Hadrich
Modernes Antiquariat
& Tonträger/ CD's
BÜRGEL
Bar

Berlin, Central District, Berlin Cathedral (1893–1905), Spree side
Julius Raschdorff

The Berlin Cathedral was considered the very embodiment of Wilhelminian megalomania. Situated opposite the Old Museum and the Lustgarten and its palace, the cathedral completely disrupted the city's proportions. After 1918, there were continual calls for its demolition. The cupolas were rebuilt in a simpler fashion after severe damage during World War II. The reconstruction of the entire building is due for completion in the year 2002.

career was achieved in 1898–1902 with the construction of the Kreuzberg elevated railroad station, Silesian Gate, in a picturesque old German style which masked the new, ultra-modern electric railroad. This eclectic and unsystematic application of styles, the discrepancy between the façade and the inner structure of the building were increasingly seen as anachronistic, or even vilified as a "vain addiction to bombast" which had displaced "the noble simplicity and spirituality" of the Schinkel School. In the journal *Kunst und Handwerk* (Art and Craft) in 1897 Wilhelm Rolfs asserted that the Baroque, Rococo, and the German Renaissance – indeed, historicism in general – were over. This was an opinion shared by much of the public: but not, however, in the building commissions that had been influenced by William II.

The new supreme style: Neo-Baroque and Neo-Romanticism as political instruments

"In Prussia," claimed Georg Malkowsky in 1912, "that unity of judiciously exercised sovereign authority and emerging national consciousness has been produced that places artistic creation at the service of the State without binding it fast, or allowing it to ossify into conventional forms."

The artistic politics of the Hohenzollerns reached their zenith under the last ruler of the dynasty, William II – less in the quality of what was built than in the degree of influence that he had on artistic and architectural projects of all kinds. The Hohenzollerns had been architectural dilettantes since Frederick the Great, though of all the dynastic heads, Frederick William IV could be considered an artist in his own right. It was his designs from the 1830s for a new cathedral with a Protestant "camposanto" (modeled on the cemetery quarter of Pisa) that resulted in the first "expression of power" in Wilhelminian architectural politics: the Berlin Cathedral, built from 1893–1905 by Julius Raschdorff (see opposite). It was, in fact, a project of the Crown Prince (later Emperor) Frederick III who, overriding the relevant authorities and circumventing a competition, awarded the commission to Raschdorff in 1882–1883. Raschdorff's design for Prussia's main Protestant church was modeled on St. Peter's in Rome, with a centrally planned building and its own church in the crypt. As well as Michelangelo's architecture for St. Peter's, Raschdorff also made use of Andreas Schlüter's Baroque forms, which ultimately peaked in the failed Mint Tower project of 1706 (see page 100). The central church in the Lustgarten, which had been in the process of construction since 1894, did not conform to any preconceived standards and was bitterly criticized. In 1893, Baron Friedrich von Khaynach described the cathedral as nothing more than a "citadel of self-advertising for the Hohenzollern dynasty and the supremacy of the capital city." The new building had become the incarnation of the German nouveaux riches and all that was "un-Prussian." In retrospect, it is surprising that the Reichstag was seen as a positive example in comparison: "Then there is the famous new cathedral, which I didn't think would be quite so bad as it is. The four corner towers are quite out of place, without any organic connection with the structure. And the dome! … And everywhere there is the same superfluousness, not at all the fine and intimate distribution of ornamentation as in the Reichstag," wrote Bruno Taut in 1902.

The Neo-Baroque style had been formed in Paris. The Napoleonic Grand Opéra by Charles Garnier (1861–1875) was able to be completed without alteration even after the fall of Napoleon III in 1870. The middle classes had adopted the feudal formulas of architecture as an expression of their own identity. This phase, however, came to an irrevocable end toward 1900. A style defined by the court

Berlin, Central District, Bode Museum, formerly the Kaiser-Friedrich-Museum (1894–1904)
Ernst von Ihne

With his Kaiser-Friedrich-Museum, the royal court architect created a work central to the Neo-Baroque. The equestrian statue of Frederick III by Rudolf Maison from 1904 once stood at the head of Berlin's "museum island," which, like the Île de la Cité in Paris, is reached by a fine bridge.

Berlin, Central District, Bode Museum, formerly the Kaiser-Friedrich-Museum (1894–1904), domed hall
Ernst von Ihne

A Hohenzollern Pantheon was created on the model of the Hôtel des Invalides in Paris (1675–1706) by Hardouin-Mansart, and the Viennese Art Historical Museum (1872–1881) by Hasenauer and Semper. A copy of the statue of the Great Elector by Andreas Schlüter forms the focus of the hall.

could no longer rely on a consensus. This did not prevent William II from attempting to follow the Parisian model, but he imposed the Neo-Baroque style according to his own understanding of it, namely as the expression of a supreme "personal rule." The Neo-Baroque style represented the "neo-absolutist" claim to power of the emperor himself. In this he displayed the same lack of understanding as Napoleon III and Ludwig II of Bavaria before him. In the course of the 19th century the expressive formulas of absolutism in painting and architecture revealed ever more clearly the fiction at the heart of such claims to power, a fiction that could not be integrated into the realities of a monarchy constituted and determined by the common people.

The foremost German architect of the Neo-Baroque was Ernst von Ihne, who was educated first in Karlsruhe and Berlin from 1870–1876, and later completed his studies at the École des Beaux-Arts in Paris. Family connections meant that he was also familiar with developments in Britain, so that around 1900 he had one of the broadest educations among German architects. In Ihne, William II found an obliging court architect who perfected the illusion of "personal rule." In 1896, the Emperor approved the construction of a new Renaissance-style museum at the top of Museum Island (Museuminsel), the preliminary designs for which Ihne had worked on since 1889 (see page 435). Competitions held by the Academy in 1882 and 1884 had already earmarked Museum Island for completion. Planning was made difficult by the metropolitan railroad that cut through the island from 1878. A design by Alfred Messel in 1884 saw the complete construction of the top end of the island, the demolition of the Packhofanlage, and the rounding off of the island with a domed building to serve as a new entrance. Ihne, who only planned the area north of the metropolitan railroad, took up this concept and expanded the entry building into a Pantheon for the Hohenzollerns (left); dynastic monument and museum were therefore combined in one. In its monumental forms, Ihne applied various elements from the Reichstag and quoted several Baroque motifs from the city Arsenal.

In the Royal Library on Unter den Linden (opposite), which Ihne built from 1902 on the site of the Old Academy (Alten Akademie), both form and content became more generalized. When the library was dedicated in 1914, critics could offer only superlatives. It was celebrated as the most significant monuments to German scholarship, as one of the greatest libraries in the world – greater still than the national libraries of London and Paris – and as a symbol of "Germany's bid for world power." The library's director, von Harnack, saw in its economical architectural forms "the hallmark of rigorous scholarship." Its links with Reichstag and the Prussian Assembly were emphasized. Ihne's original design using "elegant Baroque forms" as an extended copy of the Potsdam Palace were increasingly simplified during construction so that at the time of its opening there was hardly any discernible difference from Ludwig Hoffman's work – an indication of the changes in architectural form taking place around 1910. The building's "powerful fortissimo" was encapsulated in the central domed reading room (destroyed) whose proportions (diameter of 37 meters; 121 feet) rivaled those of the Pantheon in Rome, and which consisted of a remarkable ribbed cupola of reinforced concrete (opposite).

Another example of what was then considered up-to-date can be seen in the house Ihne built between 1889–1893 for Victoria, the widow of Frederick III, who had ruled for a mere 99 days (and for which reason she was also known as "Queen Frederick"). The building, the Friedrichshof Palace in Kronberg in the Taunus hills near Frankfurt, borrowed from the English Tudor house tradition.

Twenty-five years later, this recourse to the style of English country houses seen in Paul Schultze-Naumburg's Cecilienhof Palace (1912–1916) (see

page 438) was criticized by contemporaries because of the world war then being fought: "Mr Paul Schultze-Naumburg has successfully designed a medieval travesty, which we might have admired 20 or 30 years ago, but this concept is crude and ineffective in comparison with the house built for the royal widow, Victoria." Schultze-Naumburg had to bow to the wishes of Crown Prince William; the result was a curious mixture of historicist forms and a clearly conceived functional complex. In contrast to the free interpretation of English models from the same era, such as Frank Lloyd Wright's "prairie house style," Schultze-Naumburg was unable to escape the tight parameters he was set. For critics, the Cecilienhof would always remain "a mere copy," even if the interiors by Paul Ludwig Troost and Joseph Wackerle were in a more contemporary style.

The Neo-Romanesqe style also enjoyed great popularity under William II. It could more effectively be declared a national style, for Gothic architecture had had its origins in France and was therefore obviously unsuitable. Even Fritsch referred to the historical importance of the German "transitional style" from the mid-13th century that corresponded to the glory of the Holy Roman Empire; he surmised that it could not be fully explored because of intrusions made into it by the Gothic style. One of the most ardent supporters of the Romanesque style at the Prussian court was the Chief Steward, Ernst von Mirbach. The "evocative power of the old Hohenstaufen art forms" was to assert the Hohenzollern monarchy and convey to the people an impression of the strength of their emperor. Max Spitta's Gnadenkirche (Church of Mercy), built between 1891–1895 for Empress Augusta in the Veterans' Park in Berlin, refereed for the first time to the architecture of the Marienkirche in Gelnhausen, built in the first half of the 13th century at one of the most important court sites of the Staufer kings. The Erlöserkirche (Church of the Redeemer) in Homburg vor der Höhe (page 438, right) was built from 1902–1908 from a design by Franz Schwechten in the tradition of Rhineland churches, especially that of Maria Laach and the Limburg Cathedral. The best example found of this style was the Emperor William Gedächtniskirche (Memorial Church) by Franz Schwechten (1890–1897) (page 439) on the Empress-Augusta-Platz (now the Breitscheidplatz) which, with the neighboring Romanesque House and the celebrated "Romanesque Café," formed an entire Romanesque ensemble in the new western part of Berlin. The Gedächtniskirche became a national monument that symbolized the imperial rule and kingship of William II. The continuity of the Empire from the Staufer dynasty through to the Wilhelminian Era – from Emperor Barbarossa to "Barbablanca," from "Redbeard to Whitebeard" – became programmatic and was given its first tangible form with restoration of the Imperial Court in Goslar in 1879.

In order to reinforce this continuity, clearly recognizable architectural quotes were used. The Gedächtniskirche combined the choir of the Marienkirche in Gelnhausen with the single tower and transept-like western part of the St. Aposteln

Berlin, Central District, City Library on Unter den Linden (1902–1912)
Ernst von Ihne
Photograph, 1914

Ihne's building replaced the venerable academy from the days of Frederick the Great. The new library, which adjoined the Potsdam Palace, was to become a national library on the British and French models.

Berlin, Central District, City Library on Unter den Linden (1902–1912), Reading Room (destroyed)
Ernst von Ihne
Photograph, 1914

The British Library had endowed the concept of a library with monumental status. Ihne transformed the British model into a modern ribbed dome of concrete and created one of the largest reading rooms in the world.

Left
Potsdam, Cecilienhof Palace (1912–1916)
Paul Schulze-Naumburg

Named after the Crown Princess, this building in the New Garden on the Jungfernsee lake was a clearly conceived, functional complex modeled on an English stately home. The half-timbered façade, prominent bay windows, and variously shaped chimneys resulted in the overall impression of a building effectively integrated into the surrounding garden.

church in Cologne. These buildings were to become stylized symbols of a historical evolution that had necessarily resulted in the "Empire of the German Nation" under the leadership of the Hohenzollerns. The symbolism was less about re-creating past ages than in staking a very real and present imperialist claim to power based on the territorial expansion of the Empire in the Middle Ages.

The Imperial Palace in Posen, built between 1905–1910 as a second Marienburg (a medieval fortress that once marked Germany's easternmost limit) in a Neo-Romanesque style by Schwechten, represented the pinnacle of this development (see opposite, middle). The style was inflected in a new way by means of the high tower (now destroyed). The overall impression calls to mind the first design for the Prussian Government Offices in Koblenz (1904–1906), which had been personally modified by the Emperor. What was the reason for situating this sort of building in Posen (now Pozna in Poland) so far to Prussia's east? Contemporary criticism provides the answer: "Reasons of a political nature required Prussian monarchical rule to be stressed in Posen Province." Polish "desires for secession" were to be challenged: "The heavy Romanesque forms of the new palace were placed in front of the entrance to the Altstadt, and its lofty corner towers seemed to cry out into the surrounding country: 'Here I stand, and here I stay'." The reconstruction of ruined castles in the western "border territories," like that of Hochkönigsburg by Bodo Ebhardt (1908–1914), can also be interpreted in this light. What the Habsburgs had lost, the Hohenzollerns would win back by referring to the imperial domains of the Staufer kings. Architecture as a guarantor of power is also expressed in the ensemble surrounding the railroad station in Metz (1904–1908) by Jürgen Kröger, who built a type of "imperial court" in the heart of a largely French city at the same time as work was underway in Posen. The main railroad station at Aachen (1900–1904) also belongs to this group. Comparatively low profile buildings such as the Rhine Bridge at Cologne (1906–1912), which was rebuilt in the Staufer style by Schwechten, linked dynastic identity (in the shape of equestrian statues of the four Prussian rulers of the city since 1840) with an appeal to the greatness of the city under the Staufer, who were stylized as a bulwark against the French to the west. All these projects, however, were heavily criticized and in themselves were unsuited to represent a nation that saw itself as an aspiring global power.

Neo-classicism: the way to a new architecture

Since 1900, Germany had found itself in a contradictory situation not only politically but also artistically. Reform movements, like the fashionable Art Nouveau, stood in sharp contrast to academic art, which was defined by the long-serving Academy president Anton von Werner.

A sea-change was about to occur in architecture, too. In spite of the bravado in architectural circles, Fritsch in his lecture of 1890, "Stilfragen" (Questions of Style), expressed a touch of resignation in the face of the huge momentum built up by the "resolute ship" of architecture: "We ply the ocean with rudder and sail towards an unknown goal ... Our destination

Bad Homburg vor der Höhe, Erlöserkirche (Church of the Redeemer) (1902–1908)
Franz Schwechten

In this fashionable Hohenzollern spa resort a symbol of "the Empire's greatness" was built in the late Romanesque style of the Rhineland. The town had once been an important center of the medieval Staufer dynasty.

Berlin, Charlottenburg District, Emperor William Gedächtniskirche (Memorial Church) (1890–1897; partly destroyed)
Franz Schwechten
Photograph (c. 1905)

This most important of Neo-Romanesque buildings was also a piece of political architecture. By deliberately playing on the Marienkirche in Gelnhausen, the Memorial Church referred to one of the most prominent buildings of the itinerant Staufer court. William I, as "Barbablanca" (Whitebeard), therefore assumed the mantle of founder of the Empire and became a new Barbarossa. As a building, the church was intended to manifest the power of his grandson, William II.

Posen, Imperial Palace (1905–1910; tower destroyed)
Franz Schwechten
Photograph, 1912

"Here I stand, and here I stay." The Emperor wanted a new Marienburg in Neo-Romanesque style. As a temporary home to the court, the interior was richly decorated. Like the Metz railroad station by Jürgen Kröger (1905–1908), it was to "secure the German-ness" of a so-called border region and thus cement territorial claims.

is far off and no one knows whether we ourselves … will reach it."

In spite of the prevailing stylistic imitations, Fritsch saw "turbulence and movement" everywhere and reassured his fellows: "We have absolutely no need to be ashamed of the position we occupy in the cultural work of this century with our stylistic aspirations."

Fifteen years later, a turning point was reached at which it became obvious that the architectural forms of the aristocracy and the Staufer Empire, as well as references to a medieval German burgher culture, were no longer adequate. A new collective German society had to be represented in more appropriate and more economical forms. Its expression was a simplified and standardized architecture like that demanded by Otto Wagner in 1896 and given tangible form in his celebrated pamphlet, entitled *Grossstadtarchitektur* (Metropolitan Architecture), of 1911.

The architect and urban planner Karl Heinrici, who had fought against this feared "tyranny of the T-square," still advocated an architecture of varied styles. The debate concerning the "type" and the "individual" in architectural expression then continued to smolder away only to burst into life once again in 1914 in the Deutscher Werkbund controversies between Hermann Muthesius and Henry van der Velde. What finally took shape in 1905 has been called "the Empire style of the industrial middle classes" by the art historian Tillmann Buddensieg. These changes were underpinned by a political re-orientation whose problems were outlined in 1908 by the politician and writer Walter Rathenau: "In the meantime, unparalleled economic growth has intellectualized the country and created a respect for the power of the middle classes … Given the backwardness of party organizations, though, this evolution has not yet found its political expression."

Because political participation for the upper middle classes was severely restricted until the time of World War I, a movement developed from outside which competed with the old aristocratic elite and ultimately created its own aesthetic paradigm. The institutional basis was created in 1907 with the founding of the Deutscher Werkbund, which was intended to raise the cultural standards of production in commerce, industry, and the art and crafts sector.

What was so "Prussian" about this movement? It harked back to the Prussian classicism of 1800, which was seen as the repository of such virtues as citizenship, thrift, succinctness and expressiveness. The rallying cry "around 1800" (the title of a famous book by the architect Paul Mebes that appeared in 1907) expressed this reformist spirit, which sought a break with the immediate past and a return to the values of Prussian architecture in the period between 1780 and 1810.

Neo-classicism as a new style that spanned all periods, and which embraced both tradition and modernity, was only one, albeit effective, facet of this development. When Alfred Messel's AEG office building (below), a city palace on the new "Grand Canal" (the Spree) was opened in 1905, the emperor is said to have commented: "I didn't realize that business premises could be built so poetically."

That a new style was presented to the emperor here was something entirely novel. Up to this point the middle classes had modeled themselves on the Prussian court. The strict composition of the façade, with its lisières and rusticated stonework, as well as the emphasis on the central façade projection, conveyed a heavy monumentality and physicality whose abstraction appeared more contemporary than historical, and was more appropriate to the nature of the owners' power and status. The interior

Berlin, Central District, AEG Office Building (1904–1905; destroyed during World War II)
Alfred Messel
Frontal view in Berliner Bauwelt *(Berlin Architecture), Special issue 5, 1905*

A palace on the "Grand Canal" of the Spree: even the Emperor was impressed by this "poetic" building. Messel succeeded in breaking through to the new, self-confident architectural language of the industrial middle classes.

followed classical forms, while the exterior was modeled on a Renaissance palace.

Peter Behrens took the abstract and monumental aspects of this design to their logical conclusion in an office building for the Mannesmann Works in Düsseldorf in 1911–1912 (below). The only traditional element in Behrens' otherwise monumentally articulated façade was the portal niche. At the new building's dedication in 1912, he said: "The development of monumental art has always been the expression of contemporary power structures. If one can speak therefore of ecclesiastical art in the Middle Ages, royal art in the Baroque era, and bourgeois art in the forms around 1800 ... then I think today's flourishing industry forms a power structure which cannot be without an influence on culture."

Messel's design for the Pergamon Museum from 1907 blazed a trail on the path to a new forms of public architecture (opposite). Encouraged by the patron Hugo Simon, the General Director of Museums, Wilhelm von Bode, approached Messel for a design. "I could not have hoped for anything more ardently!" Messel wrote to Simon. "It is too wonderful to be true: a monumental building for art under Bode's directorship! ... Truly a thing worth living for."

The building composed of three wings is a prelude to Neo-classicism and constitutes the new center of Museum Island. A new opening through to the Kupfergraben was to create a connection to the University quarter on the Dorotheenstrasse. The overall design was developed with particular attention to the Pergamon Altar, which had been partially reconstructed in the center of the building; the Pergamon Museum was therefore one of the first architectural museums anywhere in the world.

The central building is crowned by two quadrigas set in the center of a flight of stairs, a clear reference to the Brandenburg Gate. The massive Doric frontages facing the Kupfergraben celebrate the style of 1800, with Friedrich Gilly and Heinrich Gentz's use of the Doric as a particular model. Impressed by Messel's AEG building, the emperor approved the construction of the museum and in so doing indirectly caused a shift across the entire area of state architecture.

In spite of Karl Scheffler's (and later Adolf Behne's) criticism that the project was a retrograde step in comparison with the directness of Messel's Wertheim department store of 1896–1898 in the Leipzig Strasse (see page 443), contemporaries like the famous art historian Heinrich Wölflinn in 1911 saw Messel's architecture as a step forward: "Old forms have been used successfully here ... We stand on the threshold of great things."

The programmatic importance of the project was obvious: Messel had transformed a Prussian model into the architecture of a great city. The Pergamon

Düsseldorf, main administrative building of the Mannesmann Pipe Works (1911–1912)
Peter Behrens

Behrens, the founder of the Neo-classical movement around 1910, was influenced by the Prussian classicism of Friedrich Gilly and Karl Friedrich Schinkel. Industrial buildings, embassies, and offices were all articulated in a unified architectural language that also had a clear symbolic function.

Berlin, Central District, Pergamon Museum (1907–1930), view from the Kupfergraben
Alfred Messel, Ludwig Hoffmann

Messel's Pergamon Museum created a new center for Museum Island and a new type of museum – the very first architecture museum in which entire reconstructed façades could be seen. In the local architectural context, a connection with the Humboldt University (formerly the palace of Prince Henry) was established. A few technical problems and a period of economic inflation meant that completion took until 1930.

Museum was to be "an overture for the architectural work for a Greater Berlin."

The direction that Messel had taken with his AEG offices had its direct parallel in 1902–1911 in the Berlin City Hall built by his friend and "artistic companion" Ludwig Hoffmann, who had succeeded Blankenstein in 1896 as City Surveyor. Wanting to complement the Rote Rathaus, Hoffmann combined the typology of the urban palace with that of a large towered structure to echo the Palladian towers of the churches on the Gendarmenmarkt (see page 220). This was intended not only to recall Berlin's architectural tradition, but also to embody calmly "the strength and tranquility of an aspiring city of two million."

Hoffman's modified historicist approach was described as unoriginal and inferior when compared with a style such as Messel's. But this view disregards the new qualities which Hoffmann, together with Messel, had created in reformulating public building works. While one of his first large projects, the Märkisches Museum (1896–1901) (page 442, left) was conceived in a picturesque style in which every component was to embody an historical epoch by means of an architectural quote, his clinics in Buch, built in four phases from 1896 to 1912, represent an achievement equal to that of Messel. This consisted in functionality and technical innovation being combined with a modified historical vocabulary that made selective use of Renaissance, Baroque, or

Right
Berlin, Central District, Märkisches Museum (1896–1901)
Ludwig Hoffmann

Like Gabriel von Seidl's Bavarian National Museum in Munich, the exterior was conceived as a reflection of the collections inside. The architectural references are those of the Renaissance and Brandenburg's most important medieval buildings, such as the tower of the Bischofsburg in Wittstock and the Katharinenkirche in Brandenburg.

Far right
Entrance courtyard, Virchow Hospital (1896–1901), Wedding District, Berlin
Ludwig Hoffmann

Hoffmann designed buildings that were both functional and artistically satisfying, following the layout of Baroque palaces. They were intended as a signal departure from the utilitarian architecture of his predecessor Hermann Blankenstein.

Berlin, Pankow District, Hufeland Clinic in Buch (1899–1906)
Infirmary Pavilion
Ludwig Hoffmann

The hospitals and convalescent homes of Buch were largely influenced by the architecture of British university colleges. Working to very high medical standards, and built in a style that combined the best in functional, artistic, and urban design, they belonged to the most advanced buildings of their type in Europe.

classical forms (below). This process may also be seen in the main building of the Virchow Hospital (part of a complex which has largely been built over) that Hoffmann constructed in the style of a Baroque palace (above right). His "Florentine ensemble" in the Baerwaldstrasse (1896–1912) is also remarkable; at this location two sections of the Municipal Baths as well as a school and the domed Catholic-Apostolic church (1898–1901 by C. Schröder) were to form the center of the extended southern city in the Hobrecht Plan.

Borrowing from the Renaissance style was not considered to be an end in itself, but as "a means to a greater design." But neither Hoffman, Messel, nor Behrens attained such a radical simplification of Gottfried Semper's paradigm of the Neo-Renaissance as Otto Wagner had in Vienna. This can be shown by comparing the counter halls in Messel's National Bank and the Post Office Savings Bank in Vienna, both built from 1904–1906; Wagner transforms Messel's "additive" system into a synthesis of architecture and engineering work. In Germany, radical reappraisals in how to create unified systems of architecture and design remained the preserve of the so-called Art Nouveau artists, Joseph Maria Olbrich, Henry van de Velde, and August Endell.

In 1906, the almost 40-year-old Hans Poelzig from Breslau characterized the turmoil of his profession in his essay "Architektur" (Architecture): "We *cannot* dispense with the past in solving the problems of building in our own age. All that goes on in the exterior of a building may be ignored, but not the work which has gone into overcoming its structural challenges." The way was now clear for an abstraction of built forms that at the same time emphasized cubic volumes and the application of materials instead of ornamentation.

Reformulations of Prussian architectural principles

Between 1896 and 1912, Messels, Poelzig, and Behrens were able to achieve reformulations of Prussian architectural principles. They all had a different theoretical basis and in retrospect they can all be seen to have had a decisive influence on the direction of Modernism after 1918.

Messel's Wertheim department store on Berlin's Leipzig Strasse (1896–1898; destroyed during World War II) marked the beginning (see right). The size of the building was doubled, ultimately reaching the Leipzig Platz in 1904 with its severe Gothic façade (below). It was heralded as both a sensation and as a pioneering achievement.

Walter Curt Behrendt equated it in 1911 with the very founding building of Gothic architecture, the Abbey Church of St. Denis by Abbot Suger. The frontage of the department store on the Leipzig Strasse, which featured independent columns only slightly emphasized by the Baroque façade projection, was an early form of the pure skeleton construction being practiced by the Chicago School at the same time.

In Chicago, Adler & Sullivan as well as William Le Baron Jenny had built high rise commercial buildings influenced by Schinkel's public buildings. Messel stressed the relationship with Schinkel's Architectural Academy in the isolated position of the columns; Schinkel had first built the columns up in brick and then braced them against each other with horizontal supports. In contrast, Messel used steel girders which were later sheathed. This technique, impossible in Schinkel's day, produced a glazed façade with a strong emphasis on vertical lines.

The Wertheim department store had an enormous impact in Berlin and the competition reacted immediately. In 1899–1900, Bernhard Sehring and Ludwig Lachmann built the Hermann Tietz department store in record time on the Leipzig Strasse and the corner of Krausenstrasse; they were the first in Berlin to use a "curtain wall" façade (see page 444).

In 1901, the architectural historian Hans Schliepmann pointed out the essential difference between the two buildings. Sehring linked the "curtain wall" to elements of historicism: the three Neo-Baroque projections that articulated the façade. "While in Messel's building we see a frame which pleases the eye with its vertical stone pillars connected horizontally by stone and metal, the Tietz architects have sacrificed all aesthetic considerations in their building to self-advertising."

The Tietz department store had been transformed into an "advertisement" – or what would today be called "event architecture." The principles of the *Gesamtkunstwerk* (the total art work) that Schering had investigated in a traditional form – the Theater des Westens in Berlin (1895–1897) and his Art Nouveau theater in Cottbus (1908) – were now transferred to the department store. The fate of genre styles was finally sealed; new methods and techniques were about to ennoble functional architecture.

Messel, in the meantime, had made a valuable contribution to the architectural debate. His structural

Top
Berlin, Wertheim Department Store (1896–1898; destroyed during World War II), main building on the Leipzig Strasse
Alfred Messel
Photograph, 1905

The innovative clarity and boldness of its design makes Berlin's first department store was also one of the city's first harbinger of Modernism.

Above
Berlin, Wertheim Department Store (1903–1904; demolished 1955), façade on the Leipzig Platz
Alfred Messel
Photograph (c. 1910)

The square on which Messel built this façade soon became one of the great open spaces of the city. As the store was a "cathedral to consumption," the façade was fitted with pseudo-Gothic windows.

system was not able to be pursued on the Leipzig Platz as the site had been designated for a different type of architecture.

Messel turned to a narrow façade arrangement; this can still be seen today in the one remaining side building of the Rosenthaler Strasse branch of Wertheim's which, at the time of its construction, was compared with a glazed Gothic façade (opposite, below).

This form was widely copied in commercial buildings. At the same time the movement towards framework construction can be observed in those commercial premises in Berlin that were grouped around a courtyard and which now began to present street frontages.

Kurt Berndt and AFM Lange's Ritterhof as well as their Pelikanhaus in Kreuzberg (1906–1907) had façades derived from the buildings' structure, but which also announced their own architectural goals. At much the same time, Berndt designed the Hackesche Höfe, whose interior façades and festival halls by August Endell are the last surviving examples of Art Nouveau in Berlin.

That both of Messel's façade types found no successors among Berlin's department stores was due to the city's building regulations, which in 1904, for fire safety reasons, required that there be 1.2-meter (4-feet) high parapets between floors. The KDW (Department Store of the New West), designed by Emil Schaudt and built 1905–1907, was once again a conventional stack building. Furthermore, it was the beginning of a move towards the commercial buildings of the 1920s, with its horizontal format and bands of windows as they had first appeared in Poelzig's building on the Junckernstrasse in Breslau in 1910–1911 (opposite, above).

Outside Berlin, the monumental Tietz department store in Düsseldorf (1907–1909) followed the façade scheme of the Leipzig Platz; this was the last work by Joseph Maria Olbrich, an architect who died while still young (page 446).

Messel himself employed the column structures of Schinkel's Architectural Academy again in 1903–1904 in one of his finest surviving buildings, the former State Insurance Office (page 447), which was designed to contrast with the neighboring Märkisches Museum by Hoffmann. Apart from its emphasis on clarity and directness, the style and materials – a Baroque brick palace – is reminiscent of the New Palace in Potsdam.

While Messel "had his origins in Palladio" and instinctively arrived at a honed style appropriate to

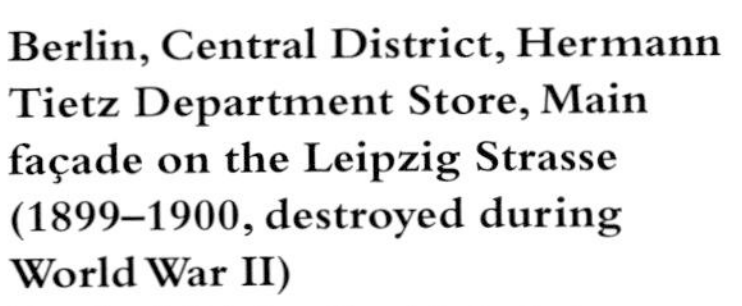

Berlin, Central District, Hermann Tietz Department Store, Main façade on the Leipzig Strasse (1899–1900, destroyed during World War II)
Bernhard Sehring (façade), Ludwig Lachmann (photograph, 1900)

Essentially a designer of theaters, Bernhard Sehring here designed a building that can be described as "window-display architecture." The contrast between the Neo-Baroque projections and the glass curtain façade was widely criticized. However, this was the first large "curtain wall" to be erected in Berlin.

Cottbus, City Theater (1908)
Bernhard Sehring

The Lower Lausitz Theater is a well-preserved example of a Gesamtkunstwerk, a total work of art, in the Art Nouveau style. In this building Sehring transformed his sensational Theater des Westens in Berlin into the architecture of Art Nouveau.

Breslau, Commercial property on the Junckernstrasse (1911–1912)
Hans Poelzig

Poelzig created one of the first department stores in so-called "fair-faced" concrete. His innovative horizontal structure was to serve as a model for the department stores of the 1920s.

Berlin, Central District, Wertheim Department Store, Rosenthaler Strasse branch (1900–1902; remodeled)
Alfred Messel

Only the side wing on the Sophienstrasse shows traces of the design Messel created for the Leipzig Platz. The Wertheim Department Store is the only department store by Messel still standing in Berlin.

the age that combined an assured expression with a sensitivity to place, Peter Behrens was an autodidact who proceeded on the basis of a program dominated, as his contemporary Scheffler put it, "by a somewhat speculative universal idea."

Following on from the Art Nouveau style of his design for a house in Darmstadt in 1901 were buildings from 1905 in "Tuscan style," of which the Hagen crematorium (1906–1908), won widespread admiration and marked the first step from an art of surfaces to an art of clarity. A "consultant in artistic design" at AEG from 1907, Behrens created a "corporate identity" for the concern that covered everything from letterheads to factory architecture.

Art was regarded as something educational and ennobling. Behrens considered Neo-classicism to be the new unified style capable of combining industry and aristocracy on the social level, Modernism and tradition on the intellectual level, and functional and symbolic elements at the level of architectural style: "The proper artistic expression of our age has still not been found," he wrote in 1911, "and when universal, classical education unites with the spirit of the age, our wish will be fulfilled. Art and technology belong together. The latter alone can never provide beauty, and the former is unthinkable without the principle of usefulness provided by technology. Our whole art is rooted in the rhythm and laws of antiquity, in tradition, and for that reason we can never give it up without denying our entire life."

Behrens formulated afresh in Neo-classical terms what Otto Wagner had called for in 1896 in *Moderne Architektur* (Modern Architecture): an architecture appropriate to the age under whose leadership art and science would be combined. At the same time, Behrens referred to Schinkel as the model of "today's functional artist," as Scheffler expressed it.

The AEG's principles, Emil and Walter Rathenau, were the very models of assimilated German Jews, and for them classicism was still essentially a pre-industrial style which reflected simplicity and Prussian virtues. In their private apartments (1905 by Johannes Kraatz) Neo-classicism served to separate the private sphere from the world of business. Behrens, however, convinced Walter Rathenau of the connection between "the serial possibilities of the classical formal vocabulary and industrial demands for standardization."

The principle of creating a strict order by means of an arrangement on a colossal scale is seen most clearly in the frontage of the Small Engine Factory on the Voltastrasse, where the columned façade of Schinkel's Old Museum (Altes Museum) was repeated in four sections (see page 447; compare with pages 309 and 310). Encased steel girders formed the framework of the building. This technique was taken up in Alfred Grenander's industrial office buildings (1914–1917), notably the Loewe armaments factory in Moabit and the Knorr Brake Works in Friedrichshain (see page 448). Behrens's tacit goal of translating Rathenau's politically and socially reforming ideas into a binding and comprehensible architectural language led to the building of the German embassy in St. Petersburg in 1911–1912, for which Mies van der Rohe was the building foreman.

The principles that had been developed for the Small Engine Factory were now expressed in a public building which, in spite of the emperor's approval, was ultimately rejected by court circles who spoke of "the confusion in the Foreign Office" and "the influence of revolutionary forces." Behrens made clear that his was not a unique position but that of "a general orientation in taste represented by the Deutscher Werkbund ... which is palpably

Düsseldorf, Königsallee, Hermann Tietz Department Store (1907–1909)
Joseph Maria Olbrich

The last building by the Viennese Art Nouveau architect Joseph Maria Olbrich – who in 1901 had built the artists' colony of Mathildenhöhe in Darmstadt – was closely modeled on Messel's department store system. Along with van de Velde, Olbrich was celebrated as one of the pioneers of Modernism.

beginning to conquer the world market for Germany's art industry."

Behrens can be described as the most important proponent of an "Empire style of the industrial middle classes" that was gradually absorbed into official architecture. The Imperial Naval Office by Reinhardt & Süssenguth (1911–1914) on the Reichpietschufer – later to achieve tragic fame as the headquarters of the Wehrmacht – is one expression of this tendency.

So too was the competition of 1913 for the Berlin Opera House in the Tiergarten, whose winning Neo-classical design by Hoffmann could not be completed because of World War I. The work of Messel and Behrens was a model for A. O. Pauly's Emperor Frederick Spa in Wiesbaden (1912–1914).

Behrens's most impressive project was ultimately the house for the archaeologist Theodor Wiegand's, built 1911–1912. Wiegand was the son-in-law of Georg von Siemens who, as a member of AEG's supervisory board, had recommended Behrens as architect. The Wiegand Villa, today the German Archaeological Institute in Berlin-Dahlem, is also impressive for its luxurious décor, additionally designed by Behrens. In essence, it attempts to translate the concepts behind Schinkel's country houses, in particular the Charlottenhof Palace, into the formal language of modern Neo-classicism. The two features that in particular marked the Wiegand Villa as a thoroughly modern building were the "asymmetrical symmetry" of the floor plan, and the execution of the façade entirely in shell-lime, which was a new element.

The highpoint of industrial building was the AEG Turbine Plant (see page 449), created by Behrens and the technical designer Karl Bernhard in 1909. Critics praised not only its force and monumentality, but also the modernity of this new "temple to science." The side façade refers to a classical temple by means of its prominent steel-girder construction. The main frontage exhibits sturdy corner pylons and a hexagonal gable seemingly at rest on the glazed façade and featuring the firm's logo in pseudo-Egyptian fashion.

Berlin, Wedding District, AEG Small Engine Factory (1910–1913)
Peter Behrens

The discipline of this colossal façade was inspired by Schinkel's Old Museum.

Berlin, Central District, State Insurance Office (1903–1904)
Alfred Messel

The severe frontage with its outsized pilasters extending through four stories is reminiscent of Schinkel's Architectural Academy. Messel's modified historical style was continued by his friend Ludwig Hoffmann.

In spite of this overwhelming impression, Behrens leaves the viewer in no doubt as to the construction techniques involved. All the surfaces, even those of the pre-formed concrete corners, are not load-bearing; the clearly visible steel construction forms the structural frame. For the first time, the corners of a building are "relieved" (not bearing the weight of the structure), a principle which Behrens's pupils Walter Gropius and Adolf Meyer were to translate into an entire glass-and-steel construction with glazed corners in their famous Fagus Plant building in Alfeld an der Leine in 1910–1912 (see page 450). Behrens' Turbine Plant was, then, a direct predecessor of Modernism.

The breadth of Neo-classicism itself is apparent in Behrens's work. The stimulus he provided to younger architects – who, like Gropius, van der Rohe, Le Corbusier, and even Adolf Meyer and Jean Krämer, were themselves to become models of Modernism – cannot be denied.

But for Behrens himself there was to be no logical development of his architectural ideas after 1918. The years before 1914 had aroused expectations that the war seemed to destroy. Moeller van den Bruch, a supporter of a Neo-Prussian style, raised the following lament after Germany's defeat and the Berlin revolution of 1918–1919: "We ought not to overestimate these expectations. The situation in which we found ourselves was burdened with a degree of egotism ... but there was power behind it; behind this development stood the Empire and the possibility that an imperialist and capitalist age would finally discover a superb architectural expression for itself." This remark reveals the problematic nature of that contrived and artificial "will to style" that dominated the final years of the German Empire. Adolf Behne's words "Not built form, but formed reality" were to be the rallying cry of the 1920s.

Opposite
Berlin, Lichtenberg District, Knorr Brake Works (1913–1917)
Alfred Grenander

After Behrens's Small Engine Factory, Grenander's building for Knorr continued the series of monumental industrial buildings. Industrial architecture, in which form and function are closely linked, played a leading role in the development of Modernism.

Berlin, Tiergarten District, Moabit, AEG Turbine Plant (1909)
View of the main façade
Peter Behrens, Karl Bernhard

Behrens created a "temple to technology" with what is probably his most spectacular industrial building. Despite the massiveness of the corner piers, they were in fact relieved of any load-bearing function; this can be seen in the tapering wall supports at the side, against which the central window projects out in order to carry the gable. This building was one of the key works in the development of Modernism.

Berlin, Tiergarten District, Moabit, AEG Turbine Plant (1909)
Peter Behrens, Karl Bernhard

Working in harmony with Behrens, the engineer Bernhard created an open hall with a single span which, with its triple jointed truss construction, was reminiscent of the great railroad stations. Enormous loads had to be carried along an internal street by cranes – an example of perfect cooperation between architect and engineer.

Alfeld an der Leine, Fagus Works (1910–1912)
Walter Gropius, Adolf Meyer

Gropius and Meyer dematerialized the corner pier that Behrens had emphasized in his turbine plant. Their confident use of steel and glass, taken from methods of American industrial construction, laid the foundation for the Modernism of the 1920s.

Towards Modernism

The city of Hagen, where the groundwork for Modernism had been intensively prepared, was an almost forgotten oasis among Prussia's territories. Hagen's patron, the banker's son Karl Ernst Osthaus, was one of the most important champions of a new beginning in the Deutscher Werkbund. It is to Osthaus that we are indebted for placing the debate in a broad international context, after his enthusiastic espousal of the designs of the Belgian architect Henry van de Velde's. Osthaus did not promote any pre-established notions of style. Along with Count Harry Kessler's Weimar, Hagen became a "sort of suburb of modern German architecture" in which "only the most brilliant German architects of their age were to build." In 1919, Scheffler castigated the "cultural hunger" of Prussia's western provinces and dismissed Osthaus's aspirations peremptorily: "If one considers the museum in Hagen and the colony outside the city, one feels compelled to speak of the man who has created all this on his own, and against the wishes of the majority, in language of the utmost respect; but one pinches oneself, unable to believe that we are living in such foolish times." Osthaus defended his pedagogic vision against what he saw as the centralism of the Prussian state: "The desolate state of our cities ... is not only the fruit of the system in general but also of a quite conscious repression of the provinces by the capital city."

The prelude to Osthaus's activities was the Folkwang Museum (1900–1902), whose interior design was taken on by the Belgian architect, Henry van de Velde, after intensive discussions (opposite). At the same time as the Darmstadt artists' colony was being built, therefore, the museum marked a willingness to reform. For Osthaus, van de Velde, who had been building the new Weimar School of Art (Kunstschule) as a sort of forerunner of the new style in architecture, known as Neues Bauen (New Building), was the "greatest living designer." Outside the city, the villa suburb of Hohenhagen was begun in 1907 when Peter Behrens constructed the Cuno and Schröder houses which, together with his Hagen crematorium, were to establish his reputation. Van de Velde crowned the city, so to speak, with the Hohenhof (see page 453), a villa for Osthaus in the style of a country house to contrast with Behrens's style. Below the Hohenhof, Jan Ludovicus Mathieu Lauweriks, whom Osthaus had also brought to Hagen, built the richly varied but rigorously proportioned houses of the Stirnband district. Hagen therefore adopted a position halfway between Art Nouveau and New Building.

Behrens's villas were highly influential models for Gropius and van der Rohe. Even Le Corbusier's early works, the Jeanneret and Schwob villas in his birthplace of La-Chaux-de-Fonds (1912–1915) in Switzerland, are inconceivable without these houses which he personally visited.

Hagen, Karl-Ernst-Osthaus-Museum, (1900–1902), entrance hall
Henry van de Velde; well by Georg Minne

By employing the Belgian architect Henry van de Velde, the patron Karl Ernst Osthaus sought to initiate reforms in design. This entailed the conscious rejection of ornament and the acceptance of a new style based on that of Belgian Art Nouveau. Osthaus' projects were thus comparable to Olbrich's design for the artists' colony of Mathildenhöhe in Darmstadt.

Hagen, Hohenhagen Villa Colony, Cuno House (1910–1911)
Peter Behrens

Behrens created this Neo-classical villa as a model for middle-class domestic architecture. It marked a new development in domestic architecture and influenced Le Corbusier's early work, the Schwob Villa in La-Chaux-de-Fonds. The clear cubic forms interrupted by the unornamented cylindrical structure in the middle embody a new concept of stylistic purity.

Moreover, the proportions of the Thorn-Prikker house in Hagen by Lauweriks provided the inspiration for Le Corbusier's famous Modulor, a system of proportions developed from the Golden Section and based on the human body. Close by, at Harkort an der Wetter, Bruno Taut built his first independent piece of architecture in 1907, the hydroelectric works, in a commission arranged for him by Osthaus. Taut's utopian designs of 1919–1920 for the Folkwang School were Osthaus's last attempts to pursue the aestheticization of culture under greatly altered political and social conditions. His disillusionment ultimately led to his sudden death in 1921.

Besides Hagen, the larger city of Breslau became an important "laboratory of Modernism" after 1903. While van de Velde was a champion of the revival of the crafts and building trades, the rise of his Breslau counterparts, the City Surveyor, Max Berg, and the Director of the Academies of Fine and Applied Arts, Hans Poelzig, was associated with the new material of reinforced concrete. In 1911, and under the motto "What constitutes the new style?" Osthaus prophesied that the use of concrete would lead to a new formal language. "That they [the new materials] will provide the impetus for modern forms is already clear today ... Concrete will lead to a much more compact design of the built form." Similarly, Poelzig saw the new (concrete) architecture as "that which has become nature." He set out in the opposite direction to Gropius: construction should not follow the principle of dematerialization, but rather that of becoming "solid." This approach can even be seen in the frame construction of the Junckernstrasse building, where the building's structural elements are visible in the projections of the columns, and in the steel skeleton construction for two buildings in Posen – the tower at the exhibition grounds, and the Luban Chemicals Factory, both from 1911. In contrast to Behrens and Gropius, architectural variety achieved programmatic status in the 1912 yearbook of the Deutscher Werkbund: "The style of the future lies on this route: by dispensing with the schematic use of traditional symbolic forms and by developing various typical arrangements which owe their forms precisely to a consistent improvement of new structural possibilities." The exhibition buildings in Breslau, erected in 1911–1913, together with Max Berg's famous Hall of the Century (Jahrhunderhalle), showed Poelzig's most obviously Prussian architecture in a new style, that of "fair-faced" concrete (see pages 454 and 455).

The "molded form" of Neo-classicism combined echoes of Schinkel's New Guard House in Unter den Linden and the towers of the Potsdam Commune. But Gilly's 1796 proposal to reduce the

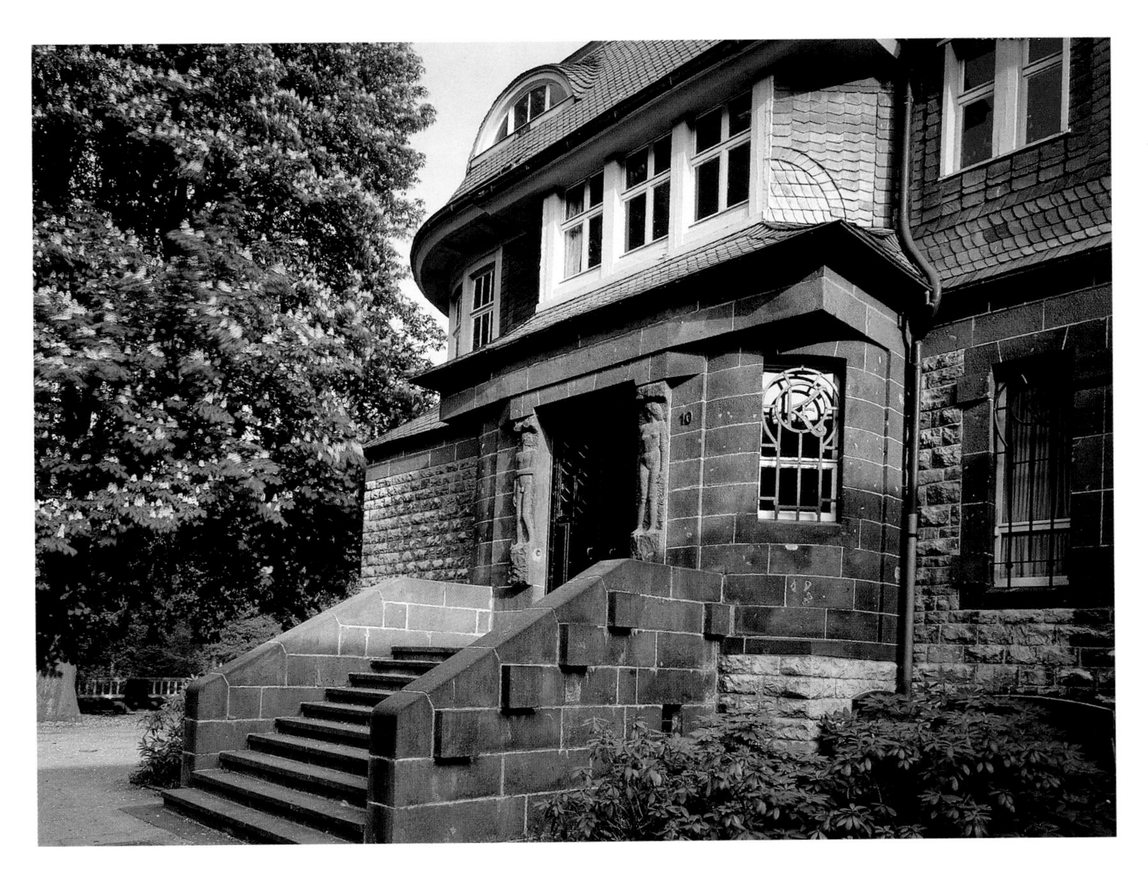

Left and below
Hagen, Hohenhagen Villa Colony, Hohenhof (1908)
Henry van de Velde

In this villa, van de Velde clearly drew on the tradition of British country houses. Here he created for Osthaus, his patron, one of his first "organic buildings," its rich style contrasting sharply with the Cuno House designed by Behrens (see opposite) in the same colony.

Breslau, Hall of the Century (1911–1913)
Max Berg

By further developing the construction principles employed in Friedrich von Thiersch's Exhibition Hall in Frankfurt, Berg created a steel and concrete construction whose 67-meter (220-feet) span made it the first building to have an arch greater than that of the dome of the Pantheon in Rome. Berg's centralized building stood for Germany's technological progressiveness and innovative strength in the years before World War I.

towers on the Gendarmenmarkt with "organic elements," such as basic ellipsoids, also found favor, and this was a technique that Poelzig was later to employ at the Berlin trade fair. Walter Curt Behrendt saw the exhibition as an important step: "The effects of a future reinforced concrete style have clearly been anticipated in this building, and it is with some surprise that one sees how strong the influences of a national art tradition, such as that of the buildings of Potsdam, can be detected in this architecture. One may be forgiven for seeing in this fact more than mere coincidence if one remembers that Poelzig is a Brandenburger by birth."

Poelzig's approach was closer to that of Theodor Fischer, who built the garrison church in Ulm (1906–1910) with fair-faced concrete supports, than it was to that of Wilhelm Fischer. At the Construction Industry Trade Fair at Leipzig in 1913, Kreis translated the pavilion dedicated to the steel construction industry back into the stone aesthetic of classical centralized buildings. Fischer on the other hand saw qualities in concrete that were "in the broadest sense, spatial." Fischer's pupil, Erich Mendelsohn, whose Einstein Tower at Potsdam (1918–1921) was a "molded sketch," explicitly made reference to van de Velde's fair-faced concrete work at the 1914 Work Federation exhibition in Cologne: "Only van de Velde with his theater [in Cologne] sought form. Concrete in the Art Nouveau style – and yet strong in thought and formal expression." The sculptural qualities of concrete were not recognized again until after 1945 in the *béton brut* of Louis Kahn and Le Corbuiser. Poelzig was to remain a gifted outsider.

Max Berg's Hall of the Century of 1913 in Breslau (see above, and opposite) attracted a great deal of attention; the architect Richard Konwiarz called it "a monument of the German people." It was certainly a very different "monument to the German people" from those created at about the same time by Bruno Schmitz: his Battle of the Nations (1896–1913) and his Kyffhäuser Monuments (1890–1897) (see page 460) combined the most modern means of construction with moribund formulae of pathos in a vain attempt to establish the identity of a "Greater Prussian" German Empire on the eve of World War I. The Hall of the Century was a brilliant structural achievement by the firm of Dyckerhoff & Widmann. It was a 45-meter (148-feet) high dome measuring 67 meters (220 feet) across. Apses joining the main arches, which rested on four columns and were bent backwards, extended the interior diameter to 95 meters (312 feet). This was greater than the dimensions of Hadrian's Pantheon in Rome (AD 118 and 125–128), which has a diameter of about 43 meters (141 feet). The entire building, including the ribbed dome, was built in 1911–1912 and left as fair-faced concrete. It was not, however, without precedent. Max Berg – who like Poelzig was a pupil of the Neo-Gothic stylist Carl Schäfer at the Technical University of Berlin-Charlottenburg – completed his studies with Theodor Fischer in Munich. During his time as a building inspector in Frankfurt, another significant figure of this period, Friedrich von Thiersch, had designed the spectacular Trade Fair Buildings (1906–1909), where he constructed a dome in iron, a structure that was to form the Hall of the Century's essential feature, the central dome.

The unfocused space and heterogeneous structure of the Frankfurt building was transformed in Berg's hands into a harmonious centralized building with the dome as a powerful climax. The almost expressionist qualities of the Hall of the Century derive from the sheer monumentality of its construction. It was not only the expression of a new aesthetic, it was also a symbol of the advanced technology – and therefore the dynamic power – of the German Empire. Breslau's wealth and its exceptional architects meant that it could appear more modern than Berlin. It is not surprising, then, that from 1919 to 1921 Breslau considered a range of innovative schemes, including the planning of a modern inner city (Max Berg and Ludwig Moshamer), the concept of satellite towns (Ernst May), and the prospect of the first high-rise city.

But the crisis caused by the search for a different architectural route was already in evidence before the outbreak of World War I. At the Deutscher Werkbund exhibition at Cologne in 1914, individualist artist-architects like van de Velde had to face designers like Hermann Muthesius, who argued in favor of a uniform style. The industrial concept was still full of ambiguities in this first phase of Modernism. Industry stood for progress, but also for those tendencies that led to war. In the Deutscher Werkbund, Friedrich Naumann dreamt of a greater Central European Empire under German tutelage. Bruno Taut answered this in his pavilion for the glass industry with the utopian and anarchic world of the writer Paul Scheerbart: Glasarchitektur (Glass Architecture). "A love of glass destroys hate," ran one of Scheerbart's aphoristic inscriptions. Between 1890 and 1918, it was not only the old Prussia and its culture that disappeared, it was also the system of values that artists and architects alike had helped to embody.

The changes of 1918 were radical: the war left bewilderment and insecurity in its wake. Artists had become seekers, as Taut put it. Gropius announced his return to the crafts in the first Bauhaus manifesto. After 1917, Mendelsohn broke radically with the Deutscher Werkbund and sought his models in the artistic avant-garde movements of Expressionism and Futurism.

The first state building of 1919 by German Bestelmayer – the Imperial Debt Administration – was couched in forms borrowed from Messel. For the Modernist movement, vision, abstraction, and the definitive rejection of history were the new principles. But the dream of an exemplary *Gesamtkunstwerk*, a "total work of art" reconciling art and science dreamt of since the 19th century, defined the entire Modern movement known as New Building, although now with a social orientation. After 1933, it would fail in a renewed attempt to achieve a total art work now dictatorially imposed by the State: an undertaking that would, dishonestly, claim its heritage from Prussia. The 20th century had finally fallen into fragments.

Breslau, Exhibition buildings for the Hall of the Century (1911–1913)
Hans Poelzig

Poelzig attempted to do justice to concrete as a building material and created a "molded form." Behrendt saw this process as the last expression of a Prussian building tradition.

SCULPTURE AND PAINTING

Annette Dorgerloh

Towards a New Conception of the Self: Images of the Unification of Empire

On the January 15, 1871, the painter Anton von Werner received a telegram from Versailles in which Count Eulenburg, the Court Steward, relayed a message from the crown prince: von Werner would witness something worthy of his brush, providing he arrived within three days. Despite a journey made more arduous by the chaos of the Franco-Prussian War, von Werner reached his destination at daybreak on the January 18, still unsure as to the nature of the promised event. He had assumed (as he recorded in his diary) that perhaps the assault on Paris was being alluded to … he could not have imagined that the fateful event he was to witness, in the Hall of Mirrors in the palace at Versailles, was the making of an emperor. He noted: "And then the prize of the war, the great historical event, so exceptional in its brevity and devoid of all pageantry continued to unfold … The spectacle was surely worthy of its historical importance and I turned to it with rapt attentiveness … saw that King William said something and that Count Bismarck read aloud with a wooden voice from something lengthy, but couldn't distinguish what it meant, and only awoke from my trance-like state when the Grand Duke of Baden stepped up to King William and bellowed into the hall: 'Three cheers for Emperor William the victorious!' A thunderous roar erupted in answer. Three shouts in all, accompanied by the clatter of swords. I, too, shouted aloud, and was quite unable to draw as I did so. From down below, the hurrah of the assembled troops replied in turn like a self-propagating echo. The historic ceremony was at an end, there was once again a German Empire and a German Emperor!"

A short while later the suggestion was mooted in the crown prince's circle that the German princes should present the emperor with a painting depicting the proclamation. Anton von Werner was entrusted with this task of creating a work that would be appropriate to the place where it would later be hung, the Berlin Palace. This vast historical painting, completed in 1877, was to shape the collective memory of the event like no other. In order to heighten the painting's impact, the artist devised a composition that altered the real event into a symbolic one and intensified its expressiveness. The art-loving public, however, like art historians, wanted to see a "historic document of diplomatic fidelity" (Rosenberg, 1877).

The emperor received the first version on his 80th birthday in 1877. The second version, painted in 1882, was destined for the newly erected Pantheon in the Arsenal in Berlin (see opposite). This complex, built from 1877–1891 by the architect Frederick Hitzig with the collaboration of a large number of painters and sculptors, aimed at a monumental representation of Prussian military success which, so depicted, could be seen to culminate inexorably in the unification of the Empire. Hence the representation of the Emperor's proclamation took up a central position on the north wall of the Hall of the Sovereign, together with a companion piece on the coronation of Frederick I in Königsburg in 1701; the paintings' relative positions thus became clear expressions of a political as well as an artistic agenda.

Pantheon in the Arsenal northeast wall
Friedrich Hitzig and others
Historical photograph

The Pantheon constructed in the Arsenal in Berlin from 1877–1880 was to be dedicated to the celebration of Hohenzollern military successes. Although an image of the goddess Victory had been positioned next to the large historical paintings in the Hall Of Rulers (1881), the courtyard was dominated by an enormous statue of Borussia by Reinhold Begas. The ensemble made Prussia's hegemony abundantly clear.

Anton von Werner
The Emperor's Proclamation in Versailles (1885)
Oil on Canvas, 270 x 270 cm;
Friedrichsruh, Bismarck-Museum

The imagery of this painting, commissioned as a record of the creation, at Versailles Palace, of a new German empire under William I, determined the public's enduring perception of the event. An event that eyewitnesses described as brief and sober becomes a dignified ceremony in von Werner's painting. Of the three versions of the painting, only this one, belonging to Prince Bismarck, has survived.

Anton von Werner
Allegory of the Origin of German Unity (1872)
Oil on Canvas, 138 x 282 cm; Berlin, Akademie der Künste

This study for the mosaic frieze of the Victory Column on the Grosser Stern in Berlin is an allegorical depiction of the part played by the German states in the unification of the empire. Located in the center is Borussia, the symbol of Prussian supremacy.

Anton von Werner
The Christening of Prince William of Prussia on June 11, 1882, in the Marble Gallery of the New Palace
Watercolor; Potsdam, Stiftung Preussische Schlösser und Gärten, Berlin-Brandenburg, Plankammer

Von Werner was greatly admired by the Emperor and often employed to record important events at court. Three years before the proclamation he had established his reputation with the painting *Baptism in My House*, which showed the crown prince at the center of those present. The painting of the baptism of the emperor's great grandson (left), formerly in the Hohenzollern Museum at the Monbijou Palace in Berlin, was lost during World War II.

Hermann Wislicenus
Germania Vigilant on the Rhine (1874)
Oil on Canvas, 104 x 77 cm;
Goslar Museum

Earlier, more gentle images of Germania, such as Phillip Veit's from 1848 in the Paulskirche in Frankfurt, were followed by a more combative type of woman. The figure of Joan of Arc, so loved by the French during the 19th century, has been transformed into a German and turned against the "traditional enemy."

This pairing of images was intended to imply that it was only through a promotion in rank of the Brandenburg-Prussian monarchy that the Hohenzollern Empire could be brought into being. Of the four versions of the painting that appeared in the following years, only the reworked modello, which owed its existence to the design for the new Pantheon in the Berlin Arsenal, has been preserved (see page 457). Bismarck received the smaller, so-called Friedrichsruher version for his birthday in 1885.

In the years that followed, Anton von Werner became the most noted chronicler of the Imperial epoch. He held important offices such as that of Director of the newly established Royal College of Art and was in charge of the Artist's Association of Berlin from 1887 till 1895. Buoyed by the high esteem in which Emperor William I held him, von Werner was entrusted with further public duties. He captured important events for posterity. Such events included the christening of Prince William of Prussia on June 11, 1882, in the Marble Gallery of the New Palace, entirely in the manner of a Court Artist (see opposite, bottom).

Shortly after the end of the war he designed the mosaic for the plinth of the Victory Column (Siegessäule), an allegory of the Franco-German War in the center of which stands the personification of Borussia (see opposite, top). Berlin, the old capital of Prussia and the new imperial capital, sought to show its superiority through the figure of a triumphant Borussia, while in other parts of the country many monuments of the early 1870s featured allegories of Germania (see left). In 1860, Lorenz Clasen had already created a new type of Germania with his monumental painting *Germania Vigilant on the Rhine*, which was vastly different from Phillip Veit's older depiction of Germania in the Paulskirche in Frankfurt (1848). The static, heraldic allegory in Veit's version gave way to a Valkyrie with a drawn sword and a fiery gaze standing high above the Rhine – "Germany's river not Germany's border" (E. M. Arndt) – her face towards France. Behind her cloak the viewer can see the imperial insignia. Her shield is embellished with the motto: "The German sword protects the German Rhine," and a double-headed eagle symbolizing hopes for a greater German Empire, which would have included Austria.

With the Prussian-Austrian War of 1866 establishing Prussian preeminence, the eventual form of unification was dictated "from on high" and finally sealed with the proclamation of the Empire after victory over the French in 1871. But the Empire so recently elevated to the exclusive society of great powers found it difficult to demonstrate its new self-confidence in an art that was both effective and artistically accomplished. As one contemporary critic remarked, it was a golden age for artists, whose commissions increased dramatically, and a barren time for Art. Various large-scale monuments were meant to embody visibly Germany's new standing and rank.

The practice of erecting monuments to middle-class achievements, observable since the beginning of the 19th century and constantly on the rise, now became channeled into expressions of nationalism as well as monarchism. Particular prestige came to be attached to the Niederwald Monument at

Friedrich August von Kaulbach
Germania (1914)
Distemper on nettle-cloth, 192 x 149 cm;
Berlin, Deutsches Historisches Museum

At the start of the World War I, an allegory was once again used to depict an aggressive defence and was elevated from the personal to the national; as a result, the work has a strongly retrospective feel.

Johannes Schilling
Niederwald Monument at Rüdesheim (1883)
Bronze, height 11.8 m

High above the Rhine the personification of the formidable figure of Germania rises up from her throne. Her fluttering hair points to a classical tradition in painting, that of the woman unleashed, an enraged maenad. This monumental sculpture erected on a plinth was an unambiguous triumphalist gesture towards France.

Rüdesheim, high above the Rhine (see left). In 1873, after several competitions, the monument committee awarded the commission to Johannes Schilling, a sculptor from Dresden. He fashioned a combative Germania along much the same lines as Clasen's images. The massive foundation was created by the architect Karl Weisbach. Schilling's prize-winning design was exhibited in a number of German cities and reproduced as a print, largely in an effort to encourage people to make donations to the cost of the monument. And in fact after the monumental work was unveiled in 1883, the organizing committee sought to claim that it had been financed "by the people." In fact the Emperor had contributed a substantial proportion of the total cost of 1.2 million marks from his own purse. A further substantial share came from the state coffers, with the approval of the Reichstag. Even during the Weimar Republic, this popular and commanding monument appeared on postage stamps, though by then more as a nostalgic memory of a more glorious past.

Yet as the German Empire consolidated, the design of monuments began to change. The female allegories of Germania and Borrusia were clearly no longer capable of embodying the differing concepts of the German Empire in an appropriate manner. Rudolf Siemering's Bismarck Memorial shows a Germania on horseback, being led by the reins by Bismarck. He guides her over and past a slain dragon, the symbol of discord. The starting point for this composition was a quote from Bismarck: "Only place Germany in the saddle, and she will ride." Germania allows herself to be directed by the heroic Bismarck and, as the critic Bruno Garlipp remarked in 1913, she has only to "look, as it were, with eyes full of longing into the future." In this rendering she is also the secular version of Ecclesia (the Church) in the tradition of the heavenly bride being led homewards by her manful bridegroom, Bismarck. The allegory of Germania is undoubtedly the female counterpart to the apotheosis of the heroic (German) male. She was now to represent the national virtues of intelligence, steadfastness, and self-defense.

A similarly terse but often impossibly symbolic triumphalism are characteristic of the monuments created during this period. Profits from the Franco-Prussian war enabled many local authorities to implement their own representational projects. The female allegory, as shown in the Frankfurt example, once again became subordinate to the figure of the heroic male. Before even Bismarck, it was the old Emperor William I himself who was to represent the new Great Power in symbolic fashion. Reinterpreted

Bruno Schmitz
Emperor William National Monument (1890–1896/97), Kyffhäuser

A conscious decision was made to site this monument in a location steeped in history, the mountain ridge of Kyffhäuser. According to legend, Frederick II, known as Barbarossa because of his red beard, would sleep here for a thousand years until the day of his triumphant return. Emperor William II – now called Barbablanca (White Beard) in reference to his illustrious forebear – was celebrated as his legitimate heir.

Reinhold Begas
Emperor William National Monument (dedicated 1897)
Bronze, Historical Photograph, Berlin Palace grounds

The monument, which has not survived, was preceded by a competition that produced 147 different designs, including the idea of building an enormous Triumphal Arch over the Brandenburg Gate. Begas's design was scorned by the competition judges but enjoyed the approval of the emperor. Without the Reichstag being consulted, a second round was declared in which, finally, Begas's design was approved. The architecture framing the equestrian statue was made by Gustav Halmhuber.

as Barbablanca (White Beard) he became a mythical figure, a modern version of the medieval emperor Barbarossa (Red Beard) brought back to life, as he was invoked by the Kyffhäuser Monument (see opposite, bottom).

In addition to these large projects, the Emperor William National Monument in Berlin (above), was to become an outstanding example of the ways in which national and dynastic elements were linked. By the time the 91-year-old monarch died in 1888, he had already become a monument to himself. The fate of the terminally ill crown prince and his 99-day reign as Emperor Frederick III almost certainly contributed to the need to underscore still further the importance of the monarchy. Whereas the other great monuments were erected in places of historical or geographical importance, the new monument was to define the capital's center and so guarantee the enduring presence of "William the Victorious" at the heart of power, even after his death.

The Reichstag approved the project on March 22. The planned 12–15 million marks were to be raised not through private donations but be taken directly from the Treasury: as the Treasury received its funds from the public at large, it was claimed that every German had contributed to the monument. Sculptor Rheinhold Begas's preferred location for the monument, the western section of the Palace

Emperor William Monument
Plinth: Bruno Schmitz, height 22 m
Bronze Sculpture: Emil Hundrieser
height 14 m; (Unveiled 1897)
Koblenz, Deutsches Eck

This work was constructed at a place of outstanding historical and geographical importance, the confluence of the Rhine and Mosel rivers. The monument, whose huge equestrian statue rises from a foundation of colossal proportions, echoes the National Monument in Berlin.

park, was eventually chosen and altered specifically for the purpose.

The design by Begas and the architect Gustav Frederick Halmhuber – "Gigantic in its bulk and its proportions" (Alfred Lichtwark, 1877) – was a reference to the Palace's portal by Eosander von Göthe. However, the colonnaded architecture of the National Monument here supplied a supporting framework for the mainly figurative equestrian group that dominated the area. For this long-term project Begas enlisted the aid of other sculptors, including Ludwig Cauer, Carl Begas, Peter Breuer, and August Gaul.

The lower area around the plinth was dominated by four exceptionally large, majestic lions that rested on trophies designed by Gaul. The sides of the plinth were embellished with reliefs depicting the themes of war and peace, while at the front the Emperor's insignia were prominently displayed. The corners were occupied by dynamic figures of Victory. Allegorical seated figures of War and Peace, arranged in profile, mediated between the base and the pedestal. Emperor William I was depicted in uniform seated on a horse being led by a winged female spirit; he was therefore not depicted in traditional Baroque fashion as an instrument of divine will, but as one of the Elect and an equal of the gods.

The colonnades were also provided with ornamental devices. These included the coats of arms of the four German kingdoms; allegories of Shipping, Trade, Science, and Art, as well as a quadriga with personifications of North and South Germany complemented by masks and cartouches.

William II admired this mélange of emotive naturalism and the Neo-Baroque, corresponding as it did to his idea of a triumphant and imperious form of representation that left no room for misinterpretation. This had been seen in the reaction to the Neo-Baroque portrait of William II completed in 1890 by the artist Max Koner for the German embassy in Paris. This painting, which was closely modeled on Hyacinth Rigaud's portraits of French kings, provoked in Paris the following sharp reply: "Ce tableau là – c'est la guerre!" (This painting means war!)

Another project on a grand scale was the Emperor William Monument at the Deutsches Eck in Koblenz (see above). It was unveiled in 1897 in direct competition with the National Monument in Berlin. The patron of the project, which had already been proposed in the year the Emperor died, was the parliament of the Prussian Rhineland province. After long and bitter debates over the question of its location, the Emperor decided upon the Deutsches Eck, an area steeped in history where the Rhine and Mosel rivers meet. This was where Teutonic Knights, whose last "German Master" was a Hohenzollern, had had its headquarters in the Middle Ages. The extraordinary importance of the church at Castor, located directly behind the Deutsches Eck, was another deciding factor. This was where the Contract of Verdun was drawn up in the year 842 and where, on June 1, 860, and with great solemnity, Charlemagne's empire was divided up between his sons Louis and Charles. This act was seen as marking the beginning of the German and French nation states. The monument's inscription celebrating "William the Great" makes explicit this link with Charlemagne's (Charles the Great's) empire.

The Avenue of Victory seen from Lennéstrasse
Historic photograph (c. 1903)

Emperor William II decided on the occasion of his 36th birthday in 1895 to present his capital city with a 750-meter (2,460-feet) long avenue lined with sculptures. The citizens of Berlin would be presented with a row of former rulers as well as the busts of important contemporaries, though the latter were to be placed in a much lower position. Locals aptly dubbed it "Puppet Lane."

An equestrian statue of William II stands on a huge 22-meter (72-feet) high plinth designed by Bruno Schmitz. In its day, the sculpture by Emil Hundrieser, who had studied under Siemerings, was the tallest in the world, being 14 meters (46 feet) high. The figurative group of the mounted Emperor being led by a guardian spirit seems like an enlarged replica of Begas's National Monument in Berlin. A bold inscription by Max von Schenkendorf emphasizes the idea of imperial unification: "If you remain faithful and united, the Empire shall never fall." The extravagant construction of a great parade ground at the foot of the monument shows that large national festivals were planned here, though they never materialized.

The combination of architecture and sculpture became characteristic of the new monuments. Architect Bruno Schmitz therefore became involved with other high ranking national monument projects such as the massive Kyffhäuser monument (see page 460) (1890–1896/97), the Emperor William Monument at the Westphalian Gate (dedicated 1896), and the Hohensyburg project (1893–1902).

Another large-scale sculptural project got underway in Berlin with the Avenue of Victory (Siegesallee) (see opposite, bottom). It played no small part in popularizing the idea of a Germany being afflicted with a "plague of monuments" (Richard Muther, 1902). A contemporary study of patriotic monuments discovered that 372 monuments had been erected to William I alone in the years up to 1904, the majority of them being in the Prussian provinces. An earlier poll in 1902 counted over 330 patriotic monuments, most of which had been proposed and carried out by local "monument committees." Since 1890 there had also been a steadily rising number of monuments and towers dedicated to Bismarck. These were a special case, however, as they could easily be interpreted as expressing opposition to the policies of William II. Ultimately these elaborate structures served to celebrate an Empire that had been founded from the top down. This earnest and somber monumentality was deflated by Thomas Theodore Heine's allegorical design for a ceiling painting for the chamber of the Reichstag (see top right). Published in the satirical journal *Simplicissimus* in 1896, Heine's design shows a group of unappealing figures crowded together beneath an outsized Prussian helmet in such a way that only their legs may be seen. Their trousers, derived from regional costume, show them to be representatives of the various German states.

The Avenue of Victory (see page 462), which was opened in 1901, marked a historic – though not artistic – watershed in German monumental art. Concepts of the Empire no longer played a part; the focus was now on emphasizing the importance of the family history of the Hohenzollerns for Brandenburg-Prussia. The emperor presented the Avenue of Victory to his capital city and imperial residence on the occasion of his 36th birthday in 1895. Patriotic history was to be portrayed through princely figures flanked on either side by busts of illustrious men of their age. The differences in importance ascribed to the various figures were made apparent through their position and size. Thus the fully rounded figures of the princes were place high on a plinth, while attendant figures were far below them on the backrest of a round bench that framed the ensemble. This extensive project, which dealt with an entire ancestral line, comprised 32 groups of sculpted monuments of varying quality. In his desire to complete the project as quickly as

Above
Thomas Theodore Heine
Design for a ceiling painting for the Reichstag Chamber (1896, designed for Simplicissimus)
Watercolor, Opaque White, Munich, Städtische Galerie im Lenbachhaus

This caricature depicts national unity brought about "from on high" in an ironic image that ridicules the usual earnest piety of national monuments. The traditional allegorical figures are here replaced by the representatives of the German states, recognizable from their various types of trousers, who crowd together under a celebrated symbol of Prussia, a spiked helmet known as a Pickelhaube.

Thomas Theodore Heine after G. Hörning
Childish Game, cartoon in Simplicissimus
Volume 6, No 30, 1902

"Little Willy plays with Berlin" is the caption beneath this caricature. The creation of the Avenue OfVictory (see opposite) is characterized as a chldish game. The use of tin soldiers reveals the poverty of the artistic concept of Avenue, which had no hint of distinction or grandeur.

Thomas Theodore Heine
A Vision of the Future, cartoon from Simplicissimus
Volume 6, No 52, 1902

Caption reads: "In order to impress the Egyptians even more, a manufacturer of monuments from Berlin has been commissioned to transform the Sphinx into a German National Monument." The cartoon lambasts the megalomania revealed by the ever-grander heroic monuments that seemed to appear on every street corner of Berlin at the turn of the century.

Ludwig Knaus
Discontented Man (1877)
Oil on Canvas 82 x 62 cm; Berlin
Deutsches Historisches Museum

The tavern scene is a commentary on contemporary events in the imperial capital, Berlin. The newspapers reveal the furious looking, bearded man to be a Social Democrat. His grim look is a reference to the repressive measures that were in place even before Bismarck's "Socialist laws" had been passed.

possible, the emperor had recruited second- and third-rate sculptors, and their efforts were criticized and ridiculed as soon as they went on display. William II, however, was utterly convinced of his artistic vision, and even of his cultural and political mission. In a speech given at the opening ceremony of 1901, he stressed the need for art to educate the masses: "Even after their great toil and effort, art must give the lower classes the opportunity to improve themselves through its ideals. For us, the German people, these great ideals have become constants, while other nations have, to a greater or lesser degree, lost sight of them."

For the artistically minded emperor, the cultivation of these ideals, so far removed from daily reality, was an important matter. His concern was to enforce the "laws of beauty" through a well-directed patronage of the arts. The Avenue of Victory was intended as part of this enterprise, an enterprise through which the products of the Berlin School of Sculpture would attain a standing equal to those of the Italian Renaissance.

But it was not only individual sculptures which bore the brunt of criticism; the Avenue of Victory as a whole was greeted with scorn from all sides for its empty clichés. It was referred to locally as "Puppet Lane." Contemporary caricatures constantly targeted the inappropriate conception of history in the project. In a caricature published in the Munich satirical journal *Simplicissimus* in 1902 Thomas Theodore Heine irreverently portrayed the Emperor, engaged in a *Childish Game* (see page 463, center) with his Avenue of Victory. His caption delivers the mortal blow; it reads: "Little Willy plays with Berlin."

After its partial destruction in World War II, the remains of the unpopular Avenue of Victory were removed. As with the Emperor William National Monument, only a few sculptures were marked for storage; the remainder were destroyed.

William the II's historicist conception of monuments and the hordes of like-minded local associations throughout the country were practically an open invitation to the satirists of the day. Another caricature by Thomas Theodore Heine printed in *Simplicissimus* in 1902 shows a *Vision of the Future* (see page 463, bottom): an Egyptian pyramid, refashioned with a Gothic spire, has become the National Monument – "At the German taxpayer's expense!" The Sphinx situated in front of the pyramid has been given Bismarck's head and a Prussian spiked helmet. According to the caption underneath: "In order to impress the Egyptians even more, a manufacturer of monuments from Berlin has been commissioned to transform the Sphinx into a German National Monument." The thrust of the caricature is aimed both at the exaggerated demand for commemorating the nation, and also at the "mass production" of contemporary monuments. Christian Morgenstern described his impression of the conflicting trends shaping the culture and art of Berlin in an ironic verse from 1902:

What victorious avenues of art!
What new lands to walk in!
It's a phenomenon quite apart,
This arty muddle in Berlin!

But a commercial for mouth wash that appeared in the magazine *Jugend* (Youth) in 1903, two years after the opening of the Avenue of Victory, remains unsurpassed. Instead of a group of princes, we now see a series of enormous bottles of Odol arranged on vast plinths. Passers-by, respectable middle-class men and women, and even army officers, are seen studying them. This depiction manages like no other to convey the sense of upheaval that brought about the modern age. The sudden intrusion of the world of commerce into the thoroughly traditional world of Wilhelminian monuments is a witty illustration of the changes the Emperor had attempted to keep at bay with his grandiose conception of art. Nevertheless, beyond the clearly different forms there is a surprising sense of convergence: it is the principle of series and endless repetitions that enable the gap to be bridged between the 19th century's "frenzy for monuments" and the images and symbols of the new industrial age.

Arrival and Departure: Painting of the Early Empire

In the years after the founding of the Empire, the question of Germany's achievements in painting began to be posed. Although not so public an art form as large-scale sculpture, critics and art-loving public alike expected it to provide answers to the pressing problems of the time. The search for an appropriate, all-embracing and above all unifying style was set against the gradual realization that styles and trends were moving ever further apart.

The status of young painters

The fame which artists of the mid 19th century, such as Peter Cornelius and Wilhelm von Kaulbach, had attained meant an immense boost in the status of younger painters, who were now highly conscious of their role in society. The phenomenon of the independent "artist prince" typifies one extreme of the spectrum of opportunities and possibilities open to artists of the late 19th century who were largely free of any personal ties to employers at court.

The Viennese artist Hans Makart and Franz von Lenbach, a portraitist from Munich, both came from modest backgrounds but were able, through the high prices their work commanded, to cultivate an exclusive lifestyle. Recognized as equals by crowned heads of state, not least because of their ostentatious lifestyle, their social ascent was an attractive model for younger artists to emulate. Towards the end of the 19th century, though, these few "artist princes" were far outnumbered by others who were barely subsisting. Victory over France and the founding of a German national state provided modestly talented artists with a great opportunity.

The Empire may have been fashioned "from blood and iron" (in Bismarck's words) but it still looked to art to legitimize its role, and to express the state's still emerging sense of identity and its

Robert Warthmüller
Everywhere, the King (1886)
Oil on canvas, dimensions and location unknown

As the title indicates, this historical painting depicts the omnipresent Frederick the Great dispensing comfort and aid, here to villagers after their village has burned down. The painting is a nostalgic and vivid evocation of the supposedly benign reign of the Hohenzollerns.

Adolph Menzel
Iron Rolling Mill (1875)
Oil on canvas, 158 x 254 cm
Berlin, Staatliche Museen zu Berlin – Preussischer Kulturbesitz, Alte Nationalgalerie

This painting is one of the high points in the artistic depiction of industrial developments in Germany. It is the result of Menzel's intense studies of the upper Silesian iron mill of Königshuette. The social tensions of the time did not escape his notice. The complex structure of the painting allowed the artist to unify a multitude of perspectives.

newly established power. The nation's wealth, which grew by leaps and bounds during the empire's founding years, also increased private spending power; now whole strata of society who hitherto had been excluded from the role of client, patron or collector wanted to see themselves represented in art. In addition, there was a whole wave of new museum projects whose substantial requirements for ornamentation were another source of work. These projects, which were highly regarded in middle-class society, were matched by smaller pictorial and decorative contracts, which led to a reappraisal of the status of the applied arts.

As late as 1869, the French artist Gustave Courbet, visiting Munich, observed that good painting was virtually unheard of in Germany. The Germans, he thought, were trapped in the negation of real art and had "come close to the simply anecdotal." They seemed concerned only with technical questions of perspective and the exact reproduction of costumes.

Certainly, a devoted study of the Old Masters had led to a positive revaluation of painting, after a long period in which the focus had been on the narrative quality of pictures. Yet the present could no longer be adequately captured with the styles of bygone age. So in the 1880s the question of "truth" in art was being increasingly pushed to the forefront of art debate. According to the slogan "true to nature," art was now required to be true to life.

"Essentially, the truth of art is nothing other than the revelation of the soul," wrote Hans Thoma in

Art Exhibition of 1879 was a turning point. Modern French artists were exhibited in a substantial part of the exhibition, which highlighted developments from Courbet to Millet, Bastien-Lepage, and Manet. There were also important works from the regional art scene, especially young artists from the "Allotria" group, an art society founded in 1873 by Karl Piloty and Franz von Lenbach, whose reputation later came to be associated mainly with the sociability of its members.

Among the exhibits were works by Hans Thoma, criticized for being "odd" and "incomprehensible," as well as Max Liebermann's controversial painting *Christ In The Temple*. Many observers were able to see in this only "the glorification of the unsightly through art," a criticism that has run like a continuous thread through the history of modern art.

As the most influential center of German art, Munich was the place where many of the main representatives of the later so-called German Impressionism began. Painters such as Rheinhold Lepsius, Louis Corinth, Emil Heilbut (the future Berlin art critic), Maria Slavona, and Käthe Kollwitz studied here. Max Liebermann and Max Slevogt, who only a few years later were to be among the champions of the Secessionist movement, were also active.

The International Exhibition of 1879 also served to stimulate the young Rheinhold Lepsius. In a letter to his father, he wrote that his aesthetic beliefs had undergone a fundamental change. "As a result of the undeniable progress in modern painting, the art of figure composition which I came to know through the drawings of the old school, and which I took to 1880. Artists must not exhaust their creativity merely depicting outward appearances, the accident of the moment, but rather render visible the inner life. These views were held above all by a circle of younger artists around the painter Wilhelm Leibl. According to Gustav Courbet, only this youthful group of Munich artists gave any cause for optimism. "They are determined," he wrote, "to throw away all that is outmoded. I have watched as young artists spat when the talk was of the uncrowned kings of German art."

The renewal of German art

In the art capital of Munich, the way was gradually paved for a renewal of German art. The International

Paul Friedrich Meyerheim
Machine Factory, from the 7-part mural cycle History of the Locomotive (1872–1876)
Oil on copper, 315 x 230 cm, Berlin, Stiftung Stadtmuseum, Berlin

Appropriately, the artist created this mural cycle for the Berlin villa of a leading industrialist, August Borsig.

Reinhold Lepsius
Portrait of the Bride Sabine Graef (1889–1895)
Oil on canvas, 37 x 33.5 cm; Berlin
Berlin, Staatliche Museen zu Berlin – Preussischer Kulturbesitz, Alte Nationalgalerie

The sitter is Sabine Graef (1864–1941), the future wife of the painter, who came from a family of artists. She was one of the founding members of the Berlin Secessionists, an adept painter of women and children; she was also an author and the center of a noted literary salon. In its subtle use of color, this portrait is a good example of the Impressionistic "art of nuance" from the turn of the century, which had been practiced by artists such as James McNeill Whistler.

Reinhold Lespius
Portait of Ernst Ludwig Curtius (1891)
Oil on canvas, 88 x 70 cm, Berlin
Berlin, Staatliche Museen zu Berlin – Preussischer Kulturbesitz, Alte Nationalgalerie

Lepsius already knew the classically trained archaeologist and philologist Ernst Ludwig Curtius from his parents' home. Curtius had excavated at Olympia (from 1875) and was a friend of Reinhold's father, Richard Lepsius, an important figure in the development of Egyptology. This portrait, which was awarded a gold medal in 1897 in Florence, cemented the reputation of the artist as a sensitive portraitist of intellectuals. Another version was sold to Harvard University.

be exemplary, has now, in my opinion, become totally invalid."

What was now to become important to him was the "composition of personality" (see left and below). He was no longer concerned, as he had been in the beginning, with representing his sitters as a social type, but rather with capturing what was unique to an individual.

The painters who influenced modern portraiture at the time were Wilhelm Leibl, Wilhelm Teübner Albert von Keller, Hugo Habermann and, above all, Franz von Lenbach. By 1873, Leibl had left Munich for the countryside but his work, which clearly showed his close study of Courbet, exerted a profound influence.

Contemporaries perceived their age as one of transition towards greater subjectivity. Apart from new pictorial concepts, painters now also developed new themes and forms inspired by urban life. Young artists aligned themselves chiefly with modern French painting and journeyed to Paris to pursue their studies, despite a prevailing bias there against Germans as a result of the Franco-Prussian War. Renowned private schools such as the Académie Julian, where Lovis Corinth and Sabine Lepsius completed their training in the 1880s, attracted many students and acted as a channel for international trends in art.

The Anniversary Exhibition: its significance

In the meantime, an attempt was made to take stock of what had happened in Germany. Reviewers and organizers of shows alike recognized the importance of the Anniversary Exhibition of 1886 in

Lovis Corinth
Woman Dressing (1911)
Oil on canvas, 10 x 90 cm;
Hamburg, Kunsthalle

This scene, flooded in light, shows a woman involved in her morning toilet. The subject and its treatment are derived from the paintings of the French Impressionists, who had turned their attentions to modern urban life.

Berlin, occasioned by the celebrations by the Berlin Royal Academy of Art (Königlichen Akademie) of a century of exhibitions. The art critic Friedrich Pecht, writing in the popular magazine *Die Kunst für Alle* (Art For Everyone), declared that everyone, whether consciously or unconsciously, was eager for answers to fundamental questions from the "revelations of the creative spirit of our people." He spoke for an art-loving public "which knows and feels that art is, or should be, the supreme expression of our national life; that it never fails to show us what is about to come and what is passing away in that very same life. Who, therefore, is not aware that this first great exhibition in the heart of the new German Empire had a significance that went far beyond the conventional?"

With reference to Germany's hitherto unsatisfactory results at world exhibitions (those "bloodless battles of the modern era"), Pecht now expected an answer from the arts as to the symbolic standing of the German Empire. He was of the opinion that "the whole advantage that the French and British still have over us rests on the strength of their national spirit, which immediately leaves its stamp on all their products; while we are only just aspiring to this." What therefore seemed especially commendable to Pecht was the tendency either to concentrate exclusively on the history of the Fatherland, or to locate the scene of "myths, religious or otherwise, directly in the lap of one's own nation, the soil of one's homeland; indeed, to transpose them into the immediate present."

This exhibition, like most others of the time, also displayed paintings that portrayed rural life in a sentimental manner. Ludwig Knaus's *The Forester* is representative of this kind of nostalgia. The forester, pipe in hand, enjoys his leisure time while the young woman to his right tends to his comforts. An ideal, patriarchal world is depicted here; but it was painted for an urban audience, and was intended to counter images of city life.

That Knaus was not only aware of the conflicts of his age but also expressed them on canvas is shown by his painting of 1877 *Discontented Man* (see page 464) which, significantly, was not included in the exhibition. A pub scene is shown in a narrow compositional frame. A bearded worker, his head resting on his hand – a posture reminiscent of Albrecht Dürer's famous woodcut *Melancholia I* – sits with a glass of beer and a newspaper. The newspaper holders on the wall show that the paper in question is the *Berliner Freie Presse* (Berlin Free Press), the organ of Social Democrat opinion in Berlin. The merry forest warden is contrasted with the dissatisfied Social Democrat, a figure who tells us a great deal about the repressive measures that free thinkers were subjected to, even in the days before Bismarck's "Socialist Laws."

However, such pictures were excluded from the selective exhibition in favor of depictions of a national self-image in which all conflicts had been resolved. Such a type is exemplified by Robert Warthmüller's *Everywhere, the King* (page 465). Frederick the Great is shown comforting the victims

Max Liebermann
The Artist's Studio (1902)
Oil on canvas, 68.5 x 82 cm
St. Gallen, Kunstmuseum

The picture shows Liebermann's spacious studio in the attic of his house on the Paris Platz in Berlin. The paintings on the walls are by artists whom the painter admired, including Velázquez and Manet. In the foreground to the right are his wife and daughter; we can see the artist himself in the mirror in the background.

Adolph Menzel
Travel Plans (1875)
Gouache, 15 x 31 cm;
Essen Folkwang Museum

This watercolor depicts the summer holidays of Berliners in a manner that lends the scene a Parisian air. It is bright and summery, couples are talking, and another woman carrying a red parasol arrives. At once crowded and expansive, relaxed and expectant, they awaken in the viewer vague memories of novels such as Fontane's *Cecile*.

of a village fire, while they reverently gather round him as if he were a saint. According to the critic Ludwig Pietsch, the painting was "aimed at the portrayal and glorification of the heroic monarch as a true provider, father and leader of his people, on whose behalf he intervenes everywhere, even in times of peace."

Even before the unification of the empire, Adolph Menzel's illustrations of the monarch's life had popularized the figure of Frederick the Great; and through works of this sort he came to be stylized as the Father of the Nation. The idealized image of a monarch worshipped by the people, and admired for his efforts to address personally the needs of his subjects, was intended to strengthen the notion of a tradition of beneficial Hohenzollern rule. In this picture, observed Pietsch, a line was being drawn that linked three figures, the Great Elector, Frederick the Great, and Emperor William I, a connection he celebrated as the "most luminous example of a complete unity and fusion of the two great virtues of rulers: the bestowal of good fortune on their own land, while defeating the nation's enemies; and the efficient organization of their states and armies."

Even in the early stages, there was opposition to this strictly subject-based art, both in terms of how its was conceived and also how it was received. The painter Anselm Feurbach poured scorn on the art business in Germany from his adopted homeland of Italy. "And then those little genre paintings! How delightfully patriotic feelings dance their way into German family life. And why should this sham bother us – we fail to notice it anyway, as long as spirit and soul are in evidence. And there is only one German soul!"

What Friederich Pecht had praised as an art that had striven to become universal – "genre painting rooted in the authentic national soil" – was increasingly called into question, even if the public as a whole treasured these idealistic works, so full of "real feeling."

A decade later, the art historian Richard Muther summed up the situation by saying that historical and genre painting had in fact been dealt a death blow by the Franco-Prussian and German reunification. The inoffensive, comforting genre paintings of those documenters of village life had been the product of an era in which Germany had stood in the wings of the global stage.

The age of the post chaise and the spinning wheel was now followed by the age of the locomotive, the telegraph, and world trade. "We no longer had a feeling for the art of the summerhouse, for the sweet and the sunny. We had become too serious to greet paintings such as *Teacher's Coming, Barber's Day in the Monastery, Sleep Child Sleep, The Broken Doll* with anything but laughter ... The earnest, objectively modern painting of the age had to be the historical painting of young Germany.

Adolph Menzel
The Dinner Dance (1878)
Oil on canvas, 71 x 90 cm;
Berlin, Staatliche Museen zu Berlin – Preussischer Kulturbesitz, Alte Nationalgalerie

Menzel invests the radiant atmosphere of this late-19th-century ball with a multitude of individual observations, each of which offers a different comment on the whole. With his careful layering of space, the artist creates a labyrinth of reality whose disruptions and depths are themselves a celebration of the painter's art.

Adolph Menzel
Corpus Christi Procession in Hofgastein (1880)
Oil on canvas, 51.3 x 70.2 cm
Munich, Bavarian State Collection, Neue Pinakothek (on loan from the Federal Republic of Germany)

While a colorful procession takes place in the background, the knowing gaze of the young city dweller in the foreground has the effect of keeping the viewer at a distance. He becomes our point of reference, for he provides the picture with an explicitly urban perspective.

"The Earnest, Objective Modern Painting of The Age"

With his acute and unsentimental powers of observation, Adolph Menzel managed, like no other, to live up to this demand. His art had contributed to new standards in criticism. Paintings like his *Iron Rolling Mill*, later known as *Modern Cyclops*, from 1875 show a multifaceted picture of society, viewed in a specific place and situation (see page 466). Extensive studies undertaken in the iron works of Upper Silesia completed Menzel's close study of the subject. In a quite radical way, his painting takes social issues as its theme, and embeds them in a vast and meaningful panorama.

At approximately the same time, Paul Meyerheim was painting his seven-part *History Of The Locomotive*. This was a mural cycle painted on copper for the loggia of the villa constructed by Heinrich Strack for the industrialist August Borsig in Berlin-Moabit (page 467). In such depictions, art expresses and celebrates the feelings that the developments in technology had managed to arouse in the empire's founding years. Meyerheim, in all probability influenced by Menzel's *Iron Rolling Mill*, abandoned allegory in favor of a realism close to that demanded by Muther. Menzel, an acute observer, had an astonishingly sober eye for a variety of phenomena, which he treated equally and without preference, so that his work displays an astonishing breadth of subject matter and artistic solutions. In the same year in which he painted *Iron Rolling Mill*, he also produced the small gouache picture *Travel Plans* (see page 470), which in its brightness and confident technique seems like an affectionate memory of the artist's stays in Paris. The setting is a garden terrace in early summer; two men bent over a map, while in the background women are chatting and enjoying their surroundings; another woman is about to climb a flight of stairs. The pleasures of upper middle-class life are captured in such a charming and informal way as to cast a lasting spell.

Menzel's *The Dinner Dance* (see page 471) and his *Corpus Christi Procession in Hofgastein* (above) treat metropolitan life and its rural counterpart in a different manner. The central position occupied by the city dweller, whose aloof position acts as a disrupting factor, shows that the narrative perspective on the festival is an exclusively urban one.

Even in *The Dinner Dance*, and in spite of the scene's great wave of color, the viewer is kept at a distance from the event. A closer look causes the picture to dissolve into a kaleidoscope of individual moments, of all-too-human situations. Menzels seemingly objective viewpoint remains an eminently critical and subjective one, even if depicted passionately and in opulent colors. An understanding of role-playing, of appearances and

Ludwig Cauer
Thirst (1892)
Bronze, height 2.10 m, width 1.45 m, depth 1 m;
Bad Kreuznach, Roseninsel

The sculpture, bought by Emperor William II, depicts a a fight for life. Colonial troops (probably British) bitterly fight for their last drop of water. The theme of victory and the survival of the fittest imply that Darwin's writings influenced the piece.

Reinhold Begas
The Tomb of Arthur Strousberg (from a model of 1874, cast 1900)
Bronze, height 1.60 m, width 2.72 m, depth 1.29 m;
Berlin, Reinickendorf town cemetery

Railway owner Bethel Henry Strousberg, who was an important collector and patron of the arts, had a high opinion of the sculptor Reinhold Begas. He already owned some of Begas's sculptures when his son died at a young age, and he commissioned Begas to design his son's memorial. Begas created a scene with a grieving widow and two cherubs, who can be understood as the dead man's children. After his spectacular bankruptcy, Strousberg was unable to pay for the work and Begas eventually had the piece cast at his own expense.

reality, runs throughout his art: illusions are always knowingly disrupted.

This disruption can also be seen in life itself in the early empire, an example being the career of the railway magnate Bethel Henry Strousberg, whose meteoric rise was brought to an end by bad investments. Collecting and commissioning art played an important role in boosting one's social standing; art became a vital means of creating an image of how the successful wanted to be seen by society, and this in turn influenced how they actually saw themselves. After the death of his son in 1873, Strousberg hired the highly regarded Reinhold Begas to design a lavish tomb, which was almost certainly intended convey his own importance (see below). It shows the death bed of the young man, who is being mourned by his wife and his two cherubic sons. Strousberg was unable to pay for the work, so the tomb could no longer serve its original purpose. Nevertheless, the composition was awarded a Grand Prize at the World Exhibition of 1900.

The often bitter experiences of the early empire, with its many opportunities for upward mobility matched by the rapid decline of seemingly prosperous areas of activity, increasingly led to the depiction of themes of conflict. A characteristic example of the theme of "the struggle for survival" is Ludwig Cauer's *Thirst*, made in 1892 in England (see above). Two soldiers in tropical uniforms are locked together in a bitter struggle for their last drop of water. Darwin's doctrine of the survival of the fittest

dictates that only the stronger will survive; in this instance, the stronger figure is also the more negative one, and so the work runs counter to the usual values of monumental sculptures. The sculpture, conceived in the round, was bought by Emperor William II during an exhibition at the Royal Academy in London (where, out of respect for British feelings, it was not actually on public display). The accurate rendering of the clothing would have left no doubt as to the nationality of the figures. Ludwig Cauer was held in high esteem by the emperor, and he also worked on the Emperor William National Monument as well as the Avenue of Victory. In later years, his attention to realistic detail and his penchant for heightened drama would become less popular. It was then that work such as Louis Tuaillon's Classical *Amazon on Horseback* (see page 475) was to come to the fore. The judgment of the Modernist style was soon to overtake both Neo-Baroque exuberance and detailed naturalism.

Lesser Ury
Berlin Street Scene (Leipzig Platz) (1898)
Oil on canvas, 107 x 68 cm;
Berlin Berlinische Galerie

This night scene, illuminated by artificial light, is a careful rendering of the poetry of the modern metropolis's character, its traffic and sense of increasing speed.

"Gutter Art": Secessionism and the Path to Modernism

Modernism's judgment was soon also to touch on the question of quantity. An increasingly fundamental criticism of the traditional trade in art was directed against conventional practices of exhibiting work. It was still customary to expect the public to view thousands of pieces that differed greatly in quality and were only categorized according to subject matter.

The Anniversary Exhibition of 1886, in which over 3,000 paintings and sculptures were on display, was a prime example of this approach. The old academic hierarchy of genres still influenced the planning of exhibitions: the highest category was that of historical painting, and the scale continued down to portraiture, where lifelikeness was the unquestioned standard.

This approach to the practice of art, which negated quality and individuality, was opposed by the Secessionist Movement established in Germany in 1890s. It was part of a process that gradually spread to all the centers of European culture, and was mainly targeted at the academies and their restrictive exhibiting practices. Artists united under the banner of Secessionism were impassioned in their demands for artistic freedom.

The Secessionists

The expression "Secessionist Art" does not describe a single style but rather a whole assortment of styles and movements that had in common their rejection of traditional academicism. In contrast to the artistic movements of the early 19th century, they did not propose specific programs as much as a general thrust towards an international Modernism. The way forward was led by Paris. The Société des Indépendants, in which the Impressionists broke radically with the French Salon, had already been established in 1884.

A Secession group was founded in Munich in 1892, in Vienna in 1897 and, a year after that, in Berlin. Through the energetic leadership of Max Liebermann and Walter Leistikow, the Secession group in the imperial capital was able to build on the work of its two predecessors, Vereinigung der XI (The Club of Eleven), founded in 1892, and the Freie Künstlervereinigung (Society of Free Artists). The latter organization had been founded in 1893 as a protest against the closure of an exhibition featuring the works of the Norwegian painter Edvard Munch by the conservative Artist's Society of Berlin, led by Anton von Werner.

Other Secessionist groups soon followed, such as those in Freie Vereinigung Dresdener Künstler (Free Artist Society of Dresden) in 1896 and the Karlsruher Künstlerbund (Artist's Association of Karlsruhe). The Secessionists were united by their vow not to exhibit in the official Salon. Their own exhibition buildings were purpose built in accordance with their principle of focusing on quality rather than quantity. And in an unprecedented move, the Secessionists also extended membership to female artists.

As a rule, the Secessions groups, who at first were only active in their own regions, had "corresponding members" abroad who also took part in the annual exhibitions. Art dealers, for example Paul Cassirer in Berlin, were of crucial importance to the Secessionists. These dealers were extremely successful at marketing the works of Secessionist artists both nationally and internationally. The Secessionists, who were usually privately organized, were able to react flexibly to the changing needs of a new upper middle class. These clients in turn often acted as patrons by generously contributing to the building as well as extending of museums, above all in their support of the relatively new National Gallery (Nationalgalerie). Although all official purchases required the approval of the emperor and the State Art Commission, progressive museum curators such as Hugo von Tschudi and his successor as Director of the National Gallery, Ludwig Justi, were able to acquire some of the best work of the modern era with the aid of patrons. These generous benefactors were often from the Jewish upper-middle class, who played an extremely important role in commissioning Secessionist work. The industrialist and writer Walther Rathenau, purchased the work of up-and-coming artists early in the history of the Secessionist movement and in 1907 he had his portrait painted by Edvard Munch; he also commissioned portraits from Max Liebermann, Lesser Ury, and various others. Other patrons, such as the banker Eduard Arnhold, were also active as collectors. Private collections, such as the early French Impressionists of Carl and Felicie Bernstein shown in the early 1880s, opened many artists' eyes to completely new ways of seeing.

Publications such as the exclusive journal *Pan* (established in 1895) or Karl Scheffler's *Kunst und Künstler* (Art and Artists) (from 1903), which had committed themselves to promoting the so-called German Impressionists, contributed significantly to the dissemination and recognition of the new art. The Secessions provoked a split in the art-loving public between the supporters of Modernism and the conservative guardians of traditional forms and values.

Artistic rivalry: two large exhibitions in Berlin at the same time – something will have to be done for the publicity
In *Lustige Blätter* (Whimsical Papers), *Vol 14, No 18, 1899*

With the first successful exhibition of the Berlin Secessionists in 1899, two organizations were mounting exhibitions in direct competition for the first time. The figure advertising the Great Berlin Art Exhibition is dressed in historical, folkloric manner, while the Secession is depicted in fashionable top-hat and tails.

Louis Tuaillon
Amazon on Horseback (1890–1895)
Bronze, Berlin, Tiergarten

Tuaillon broke free from the Neo-Baroque of his teacher Reinhold Begas and turned to a style that combined echoes of classicism with a nervous diagnosis of his own time. The artist also belonged to the Secession and this sculpture is considered his most important work. The Amazon shows uncharacteristic calm as she sits on a perfectly still horse.

Professor von Lenbach in his studio: serial production of a successful design
In Kladderadatsch, 26.2.1893

The wealthy aristocratic artist Franz von Lenbach had painted a "gallery of potentates" and was in great demand among the European elite. The caricature refers to his habit of repeating a pictorial formula if it proved successful. The uniqueness of the portrayed figures, at least as depicted by Lenbach, is therefore questioned.

A caricature in the *Lustige Blätter* (Whimsical Papers) from 1899 takes as its theme artistic competition: *Artistic rivalry: Two large exhibitions in Berlin at the same time – something will have to be done for the publicity* (see page 475). Two figures are shown with their backs to the viewer and each has a sign with directions on it. To the left is the Secessionist exhibition and to the right the Great Exhibition of Berlin.

Just as the exhibitions differ sharply, so do the figures promoting them. The individual pointing towards the Secessionist exhibition is a slim city-dweller complete with top-hat and tails. The character on the right seems to have sprung from a world of fairy tales and myth: a portly, bow-legged gnome whose hat is bedecked with little bells and braids, he refers to the popular images of old Germany which, it appears, are better value for money: the entrance fee to the Secession is one mark, while the visitor to the Great Art Exhibition of Berlin can see a far larger number of pictures for half the price.

After only a few years, the art of the Secessionists had succeeded in establishing itself within the educated middle classes, not least due to the impassioned commitment of progressive art critics in the influential liberal press. Nevertheless, fierce debates continued in Berlin. The political dimension of the dispute arose from the open opposition of the Court to the Secessionists, particularly from the emperor himself. He not only took a great deal of interest in questions of art, he had clear views of his own about the role art had to play in edifying of the populace – as witnessed by the Avenue of Victory. He believed that artistic standards should be set by his own aesthetic sense and for the benefit of all his subjects. He was supported in this view by Director of the Academy, Anton von Werner.

A caricature from 1901 by F. von Reznicek for the New Year edition of the satirical magazine *Simplicissimus* shows the La Serenissima, the Empress, at the Secessionist exhibition with Max Liebermann as *spiritus rector* looking on respectfully. "This modern art is dreadful," she tells him, "And my husband has told these people so often how to paint!"

The absurdity of this imperial presumption was obvious. Directly behind the figure of the empress is a painting reminiscent of one of Walter Leistikow's scenes at Lake Grunewald (see bottom). Prior to the

Walter Leistikow
Lake Grunewald (1898)
Oil on canvas, 75 x 100 cm;
Kiel, Kunsthalle

Leistikow combined a decorative form influenced by Art Nouveau with a precise, atmospheric depiction of nature. Landscape painting became extremely popular in the late 19th century, and artists painted and drew directly from nature. Until his death at a relatively early age in 1908, Leistikow, together with Max Liebermann, managed the affairs of the Berlin Secession.

Karl Hagemeister
The Forest Pond (1908)
Oil on canvas, 125 x 210 cm;
Berlin, Staatliche Museen zu Berlin – Preussischer Kulturbesitz, Alte Nationalgalerie

Hagemeister was consistently able to capture the atmospheric effects of the Brandenburg landscape. His decorative skills can be seen in an increasingly generous palette, which is integrated into a compact, dynamic style.

founding of the Secessionist movement, one of these paintings had incurred the displeasure of the emperor, who expressed his disapproval by saying that he was not able to discern the landscape described in the title, even though he, as a huntsman, knew the Grunewald well!

From the very beginning, artists and the public were forced into taking opposite sides. They had to choose between modern art, in other words the art of the Secessionists and the newly established artists' colonies, and the "art of the court." The criteria for distinguishing between the two were summarized by the art historian Alfred Koeppen in 1902: modern art stands out by virtue of its eminently personal quality; moreover, its technique distinguishes it noticeably from older styles in that "the tenets of local color, light and shade have all been abandoned, and another aspect, which reveals the life of the modern mind and its emotions" has come to the fore.

The old hierarchies seemed finally to have been repealed. For Max Liebermann, a well-drawn turnip was the equal of a Madonna – as a purely artistic problem. Lovis Corinth was unconcerned whether he drew a dog or a spiritual hero. The life of the big city, which had previously received scant attention, now began to be more widely depicted. Franz Skarbina and Lesser Ury, for example, painted quite striking street scenes (see page 474). Other artists, such as the artist couple Reinhold and Sabine Lepsius from Berlin, rejected the "gray and wretched painting" of Naturalism and attempted to render the nervousness of urban life in their portraits of intellectuals.

In his attempts to depict modern, complex states of mind, Reinhold Lepsius found it increasingly difficult to capture the contradictory aspects of a personality in a painting. His work points to future solutions, such as those adopted by Cubism, in its development of its simultaneous multiple perspectives.

Around the turn of the century, the emphasis was still on the celebration of the object (in the still-life) or the "interesting" personality. Both the Lepsiuses set out to depict "the faces of humanity," not the "faces of pipe bowls." The sensitive portrait of the Greek classicist Ernst Ludwig Curtius, from 1891 (see page 468), and the bridal painting of his wife Sabine, née Graef, completed some years later (see page 468), are typical for adopting a position halfway between traditionalism and Modernism; these paintings are representative of a style that subtly builds up figures through nuances of color.

In contrast to the Berlin cult of vitality, such as that of Lovis Corinth, Lepsius preferred to work more with mood and gesture. And contrary also to his Munich teacher, Franz Lenbach, he was not concerned with the serial production of a successful motif, a practice lampooned by the journal *Kladderedetsch* in February 1893 (opposite).

The increasing importance of landscape painting

Studies of developments in recent French art also lent landscape painting a new and greater importance. Artists painted *plein air* to capture the effects of light, air, and particular moods. As part of this process, artists began to pay special attention to certain regions of the country. Individual artists and, increasingly, colonies of artists settled in the countryside, to develop a regional art whose focus was the

Far right
Fritz Klimsch
Bronze, height 47 cm; Berlin
Berlin, Staatliche Museen zu Berlin – Preussischer Kulturbesitz, Alte Nationalgalerie

At the turn of the century, sculpture too increasingly devoted itself to the problems of dance and movement. The self-absorption of the girl in her dance derives from a formal balance created by her ecstatic movement. The model for this piece was the celebrated dancer Valentine Petit.

Right
Walter Schott
Bowls player (first version, c. 1900)
Bronze, height 46 cm; original 1898
Düsseldorf, city park, on permanent loan from the Düsseldorf Kunstmuseum

Around 1900, the female bowls player was a popular motif; Schott expresses it in a concentrated movement formed by gracious lines. A finely balanced tension is created by the contrast between this flowing movement of the material and the girl's hair, and her poise as she prepares to throw the ball.

natural world. Its twin poles were what may be described as the "German inner life" and a parochial type of nationalism. The peasants' life was often depicted in Neo-Romantic terms as being set in a fatalistic yet still intact, patriarchal world.

Among the most important artists' colonies at the turn of the century were Worpswede near Bremen (where Otto Modersohn, Paula Modersohn-Becker, and Heinrich Vogeler were active); Dachau, near Munich; and the so-called Goppeln Circle around Carl Bantzer, in Hesse. The influence of stylistic art, of Impressionism and the more decorative movements led to notable artistic achievements. The same was true of the artists who worked in the area around Berlin, such as Walter Leistikow and Karl Hagemeister, who frequently took the Brandenburg landscape as their theme. The typical features of this landscape are stretches of water and dense growth on river banks or lake shores; Leistikow's painting *Lake Grunewald* of 1898 (see page 476) and Karl Hagemeister's *The Forest Pond* of 1908 (see page 477) are characteristic examples.

Later in life, Max Liebermann also turned increasingly towards nature, though he was more interested in inhabited or publicly used spaces such as the Garden Tavern at the Havel-Nikolskoe (see opposite). The sometimes somber motifs of his earlier paintings, including the *Geese Pluckers* of 1871–1872 (see page 480), later underwent a transformation and became jollier, more urban, the light brighter and more colorful.

Themes used by painters and sculptors

Painters and sculptors also took up themes of theater and dance. Fritz Klimsch had already created the figure of a dancer in 1898 (see above, right). These graceful figures have much in common with Walter Schott's bowls players of the same period (see above, left). Guest performances in Berlin by the Ballets Russes with Anna Pavlova in 1908 gave renewed impetus to the artistic reworking of the dance motif. Max Slevogt completed his painting of her in 1909 (see page 481). Another female type was pained by Corinth with his Salomé – the theme of the *femme fatale* was to feature strongly around the turn of the century.

Edvard Munch had earlier painted images of evil and dangerous women, a theme that he approached yet again in his woodcut *Jealousy* of 1896 (see page 483, top).

The artists of the early Secessionist years were united by their absolute certainty that they were creating something new. Titles of pictures such as Ludwig von Hoffmann's *Spring Storm* and the programmatic names given to journals such as the

Max Liebermann
Garden Tavern on the Havel-Nikolskoe (1916)
Oil on canvas, 71.5 x 86.5 cm; Berlin, Staatliche Museen zu Berlin – Preussischer Kulturbesitz, Alte Nationalgalerie

After 1900, Liebermann turned increasingly to subjects in the immediate vicinity of his villa on Lake Wannsee. Here he shows people relaxing and enjoying themselves on a Sunday afternoon in the Garden Tavern in Nikolskoe.

Thomas Theodor Heine
Poster for the exhibition of the German Association of Artists (1905)
Lithograph, 67 x 45 cm

On the occasion of the opening of the Avenue of Victory, William II had dismissed Secessionist art as "the art of the gutter." This picture takes up the expression and shows the simply dressed personification of Secessionist art plucking roses from the gutter while traditional art, elaborately dressed, carries a golden pot of withered plants.

Viennese art magazine *Ver Sacrum* (Temple of Spring) and the Munich periodical *Jugend* (Youth) proclaimed a spirit of awakening, which oscillated between the sober and the celebratory.

Emperor William II, however, was able only to see the "art of the gutter" in the new movement. The Deutsche Künstlerbund (German Association of Artists), an umbrella organization for the Secessionists founded in 1904 by Count Harry Kessler in Weimar, used this remark in an advertising poster for its first exhibition in Berlin in 1905 (see left). A woman simply dressed in plain black is plucking the finest of roses from the gutter, while in the background a snobbish Neo-Renaissance woman carries a golden vase with a withered stem. The rose had already appeared in a caricature by Thomas Theodore Heine in an issue of *Simplicissimus* in 1902. It shows German art in a black and white coffin being carried to its grave by two policemen with spiked helmets; the coffins bears the inscription: Rest in Peace.

A protruding foot and a hand holding a rose prove, however, that art is by no means dead. "August, shut the lid, she's still alive," one policeman says to the other. As many other caricatures of the imperial era show, the policeman and Prussian soldier had become the symbolic enemies of modern art. Nevertheless, official policy on art proved to be powerless in the face of the successful institutionalization of modern art.

The dispute over Germany's artistic contribution to the 1904 World's Fair in St. Louis sparked yet another power struggle between the two rival factions. The decision to build the German pavilion as a small scale replica of the Charlottenburg Palace was a comment on how the new empire perceived itself, preferring to look to the past of Prussian history for an image.

The German government had shown only tentative interest in participating in an international art show during the World's Fair. The emperor, however, insisted on German involvement in precisely this field. Initially, all artistic movements were to receive appropriate representation – but the conservative art establishment was firmly opposed to the idea, as were the emperor and Anton von Werner. The Secessionists in Berlin and Munich demanded their right to participate and threatened a boycott. Anton von Werner, however, succeeded in forcing another debate on the resolutions. The planned exhibition of German art in St. Louis prompted a flood of caricatures. Wilhelm Schulz's cartoon *From The Great Art Exhibition Of Berlin 1904* in *Simplicissimus*, May 1904 (see page 483, bottom left) pokes fun at the leveling

Max Liebermann
Geese Pluckers (1871–1872)
Oil on canvas, 119.5 x 170.5 cm;
Berlin, Staatliche Museen zu Berlin – Preussischer Kulturbesitz, Nationalgalerie

Liebermann painted this work while still a student in Weimar; the theme was inspired by Mihaly Munkácsy. It is the first picture publicly exhibited by the artist. In spite of criticism of its subject, lower-class life, and its dark colors it was bought by the railroad millionaire Bethel Henry Strousberg. Its sale enabled Liebermann to travel to Paris where he studied the work of Courbet and Millet.

Opposite
Max Slevogt
The Dancer (1909)
Oil on canvas, 173 x 128 cm;
Dresden, Galerie Neue Meister

The triumphant guest performances of the Ballets Russes with the prima ballerina Anna Pavlova in 1908 increased the tendency of artists to treat dance as a theme in their paintings. Capturing and depicting movement proved a stimulating challenge for many artists.

formalism of Anton von Werner. Dressed in an officer's uniform, Anton von Werner stands in front of a row of pictures of equal size lined up as though standing to attention. As the caption makes clear, the caricature's comic effect is produced by the contrast between the freedom of art and military principles of order: "Your subordinate, Anton von Werner, wishes to report: the exhibition will find praise at the highest levels, and the pictures are all present and correct!"

The pressure on independent artists

During this period, when enormous pressure was being brought to bear on independent artists, the Deutsche Künstlerbund was formed as an umbrella organization for the Secessionists. The Association was to be a forum for all those modern artists who no longer felt that they had a spiritual home in the regional organizations of the Allgemeine Deutsche Kunstgenossenschaft (General Cooperative of German Artists). They had the same aim as the Cooperative, namely to promote Germany's contribution to world art, but their cultural patriotism was more restrained.

In order to lend weight to the concerns of its members, Count Leopold of Kalckreuth, an artist descended from a long line of nobility, was elected as President of the Association. Yet even his efforts were without success. The issue of a budget sparked a debate in the Reichstag on the character of modern art in general and, in particular, Germany's contribution to the World's Fair in St. Louis, In an astonishing show of unanimity, widely differing political groups defended the freedom of art. Although the Emperor was unable to assert his position fully, it proved too late for the exhibition in St. Louis to be changed to accommodate a greater diversity.

This situation provided a field day for caricaturists. Once again art was contrasted with a military cliché. The cartoon *At Gustav Kühn's in Neu-Ruppin ... The Americans can't do that!* (see page 482) takes a wry look at the German contribution seen as the clumsy paintings of soldiers in the style of the *Neuruppiner Illustrated Broadsheet.*

Lovis Corinth
Salomé (1900)
Oil on canvas, 127 x 147 cm;
Leipzig, Museum der Bildenden Künste

Along with the Old Testament figure of Judith, depictions of Salomé, who had demanded the head of John the Baptist as a reward for her dance, were a popular theme in art around 1900. The *femme fatale* as an image of a sensual, lascivious but dangerous woman formed the opposite pole to the code of behavior demanded from middle-class women at the turn of the century. Oscar Wilde's play *Salomé* of 1893 lent the theme further popularity.

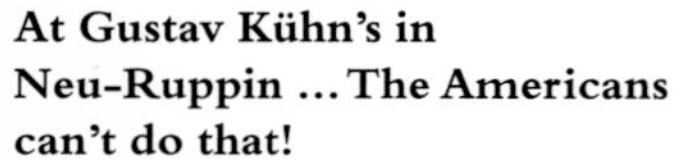

At Gustav Kühn's in Neu-Ruppin ... The Americans can't do that!
In Whimsical Papers, *Vol 19, No 8, 1904*

The military is once again taken as a synonym for Prussia in order to lampoon the emperor's failed arts policy at the World's Fair in St. Louis in the USA. Instead of being represented by the most modern art, the German contribution was formed from older pictures, some of which had been loaned from museums.

Bruno Paul was even more direct in *Simplicissimus*. He characterized the transport of official art from Berlin to St. Louis as a scene from an opera (see opposite, bottom right). A white swan wearing a crown pulls a gondola with two passengers: a young woman dressed as a medieval German Gretchen figure with pigtails and a plain dress, and William II as a fanfare-blowing herald dressed in Renaissance finery. An unmistakably hostile and bitter verse comments on the scene:

Oh, sail west, German Art so syrupy sweet,
Go west and to find those who don't spit at your feet,
Embrace all those who love you, you gentlemen so fine,
and ... don't come back; we won't pine.
A safe journey – and good riddance!

"Style is Dead: Long Live Styles!"

Increasingly, the Secessionist movement began to pull in different directions in the years after the turn of the century and so gradually lost the basis of its support. Karl Scheffler characterized developments at this time in the phrase: "Style is dead: long live styles!"

The founding generation of artists, who had by now established themselves, attempted, for their part, to exclude newer movements and groups. Splinter groups emerged. In 1910, the New Secession was formed in Berlin from artists of the Expressionist Die Brücke (The Bridge) Group and rejected Secessionists. In 1914 Liebermann, Slevogt, Cassirer and the majority of the old Secession left to form the Freie Secession (Free Secession). In the same year Herwarth Walden held his celebrated First German Autumn Salon, in which young Expressionist artists held center stage. The Secessionist artists still had a strong public profile, particularly in the field of sculpted monuments. Fritz Klimsch in particular stands out; his monument to the pathologist and public hygienist Rudolf Virchow, made from 1906 to 1910 for city of Berlin, represents a break with older traditions of scholarly monuments (see page 485, top). An allegorical battle between medicine and disease is depicted on a high square plinth with Doric corner pillars: Titan defeating the Sphinx. The plinth is embellished with a portrait medallion and a relief on the theme of the physician's vocation.

With his monument to Theodor Mommsen, created for the Courtyard of Honor at the

University of Berlin in 1909 (see page 484), Adolf Brütt modernized the monument type depicting a seated scholar, which had been established by Reinhold Begas's and Martin Paul Otto's Alexander and Wilhelm von Humboldt memorial of 1882–1883. The white marble sculpture shows a moment of spontaneous attentiveness by Mommsen as he turns in his block-like chair. Nervous movement and not a somber immobility define the expressiveness of this work.

A comparable dynamism is evident in the work of the animal sculptor August Gaul, who was one of the founders of the Berlin Secession (see page 485, bottom). He had already established his reputation with the lions for the Emperor William National Monument, and this was reinforced by his psychologically sensitive sculptures of animals. Like most of his Secessionist colleagues, he too became successful.

The Secessonists' task was completed shortly after the turn of the century. They had built the institutional framework for Modernist art and therefore helped to bring it into the world.

At the same time, they had managed, after years of artistic isolation, to engage with international movements and debates, and even to enrich them with their own distinctive contributions.

In this phase of Modernism, which was developing internationally, it is difficult to isolate elements that are specifically Prussian. Emperor William's decisive rejection of Modernism and his frequent interventions provided the Secessionists over many years with a common enemy to unite against; to acknowledge this meant to acknowledge the political nature of art. As the Reichstag debates over the St. Louis exhibition in 1904 had already demonstrated, a broad cross-party consensus already existed in favor of a new developments in art. The importance of

Above
Edvard Munch
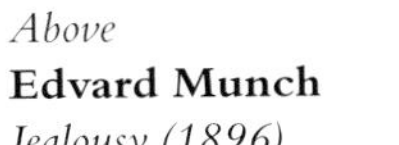
Jealousy (1896)
Colored woodcut, 33 x 45 cm

The origins of this tense image were real conflicts surrounding Munch, the dramatist Strindberg, the Polish poet Przybyszewski, and Przybyszewski's wife, the temperamental but attractive Dagny, née Juel. Munch developed an expressive artistic form for this painful network of relationships.

Below, left
Wilhelm Schulz
"Your subordinate, Anton von Werner, wishes to report: The exhibition will find praise at the highest levels, and the pictures are all present and correct!"
In Simplicissimus, *May 17, 1904*

The caricature shows a von Werner who, in ignorance of real artistic criteria, has ordered the paintings according to size. This military principle, when applied to art, appears grossly out of place.

Bruno Paul
Official German Art in St. Louis.
Oh, sail west, German Art ...
In Simplicissimus, *1904*

The transport of German art to the World's Fair in St. Louis is depicted as an operetta-like farce. Traditional art, praised by her herald, the grandly dressed William II, is a demure German maiden in historical costume.

these developments was now beyond dispute, because they had to a large degree become part of the art establishment; even the emperor had to accept this.

If the caricatures of the period liked to ridicule the clash between modern art and the Prussian military order, pitting artistic subjectivity against unthinking conformity, it does not follow that this character can be directly attributed to the legacy of Prussian policy on art.

A look at William II's predecessors – like the similarly artistic "Soldier King," Frederick William I – does indeed reveal certain continuing themes in the Prussian temperament and the art it produces. Prussian traditions always provided fertile ground for debates, even if only as something to react against. It may be that the tendency to a sober, if slightly Impressionist Realism, which so obviously left its mark on the art of the Berlin Secessionists, can be explained by certain Prussian traditions. Symbolist art, for example, was only ever of peripheral interest in Prussia.

The question must be asked whether, by focusing on Berlin, we are not in danger of distorting and narrowing the real picture. The historical situation, however, was such that developments were taking place like a film in fast forward. The tremendous rate at which the city was growing accelerated processes in art which would have taken a much longer period of time elsewhere.

Contemporaries were aware of this rupture; in 1916, for example, the artist Sabine Lepsius published a book on changes in lifestyles. That Georg Galland, a renowned writer on art, would mainly examine the representatives and phenomena of the Berlin art scene in a collection of essays *Nationale Kunst* (National Art) in 1910, now seems entirely symptomatic. In spite of all the criticisms leveled at Berlin in the first decades of the century (coexisting with a euphoric attitude to the big city and its role in Germany) the imperial capital developed into the most important national center for art, forcing Munich into second place. Berlin, said Nietzsche, was the place "where a person comes into the world drained and jaded."

Friedrich Walser, on the other hand, saw the city as a "naughty, cheeky, intelligent rascal," taking what he pleases, and throwing away what he has grown tired of. He especially valued the "intellectual waves" of the city, which both refreshed and then flowed on. Fascination and disgust, attraction and repulsion, intimacy and distance all belonged to the nature of the metropolis. One of the most sensitive philosophers of his age, George Simmel, dedicated a highly important study to the theme of "great cities and the life of the mind." For the up-and-coming Expressionists, city life was second nature. According to Joachim Schloer, the city was "the site of Modernism, its stage, its place; the symbol for modernity is ... the street." The city as a collection of challenges demanded the adoption of "modern," contemporary patterns of behavior, while at the same time it offered ways and means of coping with these challenges.

Adolf Brütt
Mommsen Monument (1909)
Marble, Berlin, courtyard of the Humboldt University

The white marble sculpture shows the scholar in a modernized version of the seated pose traditional in such portraits. The movement of the figure in the frame formed by the chair lends the block-like monument a spontaneous quality that indicates Mommsen's intellectual agility.

Fritz Klimsch
Monument to Rudolf Virchnow (1906–1910)
Limestone; Berlin; Karlsplatz

This monument in shell-lime was made by Klimsch for the city of Berlin. The subject is not depicted seated, as is usual. Instead, a medallion portrait of Virchnow is dominated by an allegory that symbolizes the struggle between medicine and disease: Titan vanquishing the Sphinx.

Arcadias and the Apocalypse: The Eve of the World War

The beauty of the city so enthusiastically praised by August Endell, and pursued with radically new techniques by artists like Ernst Ludwig Kirchner, had its counterpoint in the depictions of conflict by socially critical artists such as Käthe Kollwitz and Hans Baluschek. Kollwitz's examination of misery and death and the portrayals of the hard-working life, as pictured in Baluschek's *Noon Break* (1911–1912) (see page 486) form a marginal area in Secessionist art. Nonetheless, these were themes that were meticulously observed; Käthe Kollwitz's magnificent graphic series entitled *The Revolt of the Weavers* from 1897 is almost without equal in its expressive intensity and haunting power (see page 487, top). She had been inspired by Gerhart Hauptmann's drama *Die schlesischen Weber* (The Weavers), which had already received as many brickbats as it had bouquets. In response to a performance, the emperor intended canceling his private box at the Deutsches Theater.

The increasing celebration of "the Beautiful" in established middle-class art was opposed by the work of younger artists such as the members of Die Brücke, who had moved from Dresden to Berlin, and Ludwig Meidner who reacted with gaudy, neurasthenic visions of the city. Meidner especially painted apocalyptic visions in the years leading up to the war which, in hindsight, seem like a clairvoyant anticipation of the devastating events of the war. His *Day of Judgement* from 1916 reveals the deep cracks in an old imperial world doomed to destruction (see page 488).

Friedrich August von Kaulbach's *Germania* of 1914 shows clearly that the older generation of artists once more attempted to invoke traditional symbols and allegories (see page 459, bottom). However, in view of the rise of the avant-garde, with its shattering of forms and its keenness to put the boundaries of art forward, this armored figure of Germania seems like nothing so much as a reflex response from a bygone age. The enthusiasm for war, which young and old artists alike shared, gradually subsided when faced with the reality of pointless battles of attrition and needless slaughter. Heinrich Zille's lithograph *The Iron Cross* from 1916 has these aspects of war, repressed by society at large, as its theme (see page 487, bottom). The death of hopeful young artists such as August Macke and Franz Marck, as well as as the bitter memories of war brought back from the front, led to a decisive change in direction for artists like Otto Dix.

A retreat into pathos or into idylls was not a fitting response to this era of catastrophic change. The young sculptor Wilhelm Lehmbruck opened up new paths with his sensitive, deeply felt work. His sculptures *The Fallen Man* (1915–1916) (see page 489, top) and *Head of a Thinker* (1918) (see page 489, bottom) represent the difficult transitional phase from the German Empire to the Weimar Republic. The experience of existential danger conveyed by the body of *The Fallen Man* and the pain of raising oneself up evident in the configuration of the *Head of a Thinker*, a scarred figure, allow us to recognize the possibilities for German art that went go beyond triumphalist pathos and its Arcadian opposite.

The connections with Prussia as such are limited here, but an understanding of the post-war situation in Germany can be formed from the intersection of a multiplicity of views, Prussia's included. The conclusion of World War I brought about the eclipse of the Hohenzollerns and the Prussian dominated Empire; it also raises questions about developments

August Gaul
Eagle at Rest (1908)
Bronze, height 117 cm; Berlin; Nationalgalerie, Staatliche Museen zu Berlin – Preussischer Kulturbesitz

August Gaul, who made his name as a sculptor of animals, rejected superfluous naturalistic detail in order to give form to the essence of these creatures. His *Eagle at Rest*, which was exhibited in World's Fair in St. Louis, is the very embodiment of this genre; the artist's sensitive modeling even endows the animal with individuality.

H.BALUSCHEK.

Opposite
Hans Baluschek
Noon Break, (around 1911)
Oil on canvas, 180 x 130 cm;
Berlin, Kunstamt Kreuzberg

The painting shows a typical lunch break at a factory. Women, some accompanied by small children, are bringing lunch to their hard-working men. Influenced at an early stage by the novels of Émile Zola, the artist was concerned to show the plight of the proletariat and lower classes.

Left
Käthe Kollwitz
Explosion,
Image 5 from the cycle
The Revolt of the Weavers (1897)
Etching, 50.7 x 59.2 cm

Gerhart Hauptmann had already dramatized the fate of the Silesian weavers. Käthe Kollwitz attended the premiere of his play in 1893 in the New Theater under Otto Brahm, and used the story for this graphic series. The following year, the Deutsches Theater in Berlin was to achieve enormous success with the play. Max Liebermann's recommendation that Käthe Kollwitz be awarded a Gold Medal for this cycle was personally vetoed by the emperor.

in both the history and art history of the past few centuries. The viewing of history from outcome has a way of obscuring its beginnings. In this respect, Lehmbruck's sculptures are the expression of a painful transition.

Much must remain unresolved. The line drawn here may seem arbitrary, if one considers that Prussia continued to exist within the Weimar Republic. In any case, the development of art was no longer associated with the country's rulers. In the decades of William II's reign, the story of art unfolded in opposition to sources of authority. Ultimately, this had the consequence that the tools necessary for the promotion of Modernism were even further refined.

Heinrich Zille
The Iron Cross (1916)
Lithograph on Japanese paper,
43.5 x 32 cm

The general enthusiasm that greeted the start of World War I gave way only gradually to a more skeptical view of it, largely because of the growing number of casualties. The Iron Cross as an acknowledgement of heroism appears like a cruel joke in view of the family whose provider has been sacrificed as canon fodder. Zille captures the real situation precisely, extending the theme of a "hero's death" *ad absurdum*.

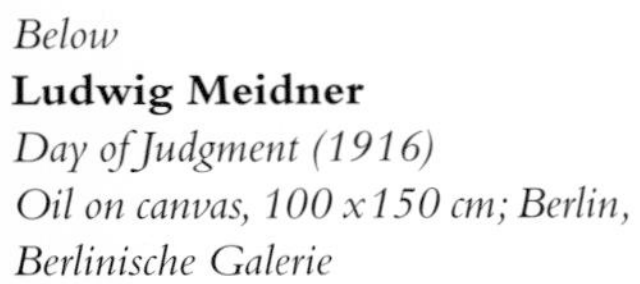

Below
Ludwig Meidner
Day of Judgment (1916)
Oil on canvas, 100 x 150 cm; Berlin, Berlinische Galerie

Ludwig Meidner's powerful visions of the Day of Judgment and the end of the world are darkly prophetic. Meidner, a member of the leftwing Expressionist periodical *Die Aktion* (Action), had been developing his apocalyptic landscapes before war even broke out. Their trademarks are distorted perspectives, stark colors, and tempestuous brushwork.

Ernst Ludwig Kirchner
Street Scene (Friedrichstrasse, Berlin) (1914)
Oil on canvas, 121 x 91 cm;
Stuttgart, Staatsgalerie

In 1911, artists from the Dresden Expressionist Die Brücke group moved to Berlin. Their clashes with life in the big city resulted in highly original works. Kirchner's Expressionistic street pictures employ shifting perspectives and strong colors. In the center of this picture are strolling prostitutes and male passers-by. The principle of showing figures in series as a symbol of modern urban life is often used by Kirchner to heighten the impact of his street scenes.

Wilhelm Lehmbruck
The Fallen Man (1915–1916)
Plaster; Duisburg, Wilhelm-Lehmbruck-Museum, Duisburg

Lehmbruck, one of the chief representatives of Expressionist sculpture in Germany, experienced the battles in France as an official war artist. Before emigrating to neutral Switzerland in 1916, he produced this sculpture, which is concerned with death in war. He transformed his experience of war into an existential gesture, the work being an expression of suffering and death that transcends national boundaries.

Wilhelm Lehmbruck
Head of a Thinker (1918)
Plaster, 64 cm high; Berlin, Stiftung Stadtmuseum Berlin

This fragmentary sculpture is to be read as a disguised self-portrait of Lehmbruck. The dominant expression of sorrow and pain corresponds with apersonal crisis that in 1919 drove the sculptor to suicide. Sculptures like this raise personal experience to a general level and present the existential condition in a spare style that points the way to abstraction.

Urban Planning and Berlin's "Green Lungs"

Between 1861 and 1914, Berlin went through a dramatic transformation, the population of the inner city growing from 521,000 to 2.1 million. The city acquired its importance by virtue of its central location in the Prussian state: midway between the coal and steel producing areas of the Ruhr and Upper Silesia, it became the largest industrial city in German-speaking Europe. The railroads, which spread out from Berlin like the rays of a star, not only encouraged urban immigration, they also satisfied strategic goals.

Mounting criticism of the 1862 Hobrecht Plan for the development of Berlin quickly led to the demand for the city's orderly expansion, an expansion that was to include open space. In 1874, under the pseudonym Arminius, the Countess Dohna-Poinski had published a pamphlet entitled *Grosstädte in ihrer Wohnungsnot und die Grundlagen einer durchgreifenden Abhilfe* (The Housing Plight of Large Cities and the Foundations of its Comprehensive Remedy), which provided for dividing up the city and its suburbs with green strips and belts. The basis of modern urban planning in Berlin had been established in 1905 in the privately organized Greater Berlin Committee, from which emerged the Administration Union of Greater Berlin. The intention was to work out a basic plan for the construction of Greater Berlin, which was then displayed in the spectacular General Urban Planning Exhibition of 1909–1910. The city had been kept artificially small. The Union declared an area of strategic interest that went beyond both the city limits of 1920 with its 4.3 million inhabitants and today's metropolitan area. Plans were made for a metropolis of five million. Apart from redesigning the center of the city, the reform of infrastructure and social conditions were emphasized in order to alleviate squalid tenements and improve the flow of traffic. A modern division of the city into various zones was also introduced: "The distinction between industrial, business and residential districts has been accomplished by all the planners. It counts among the most important social and economic achievements of modern urban architecture," Brinckmann concluded in his report on the exhibition. In parallel with the exhibition, urban planning established itself as an independent discipline and was taught at the Technical University of Berlin-Charlottenburg by Genzmer, Brix, and Jansen, and promoted by Eberstadt, Goecke, Behrendt, and Hegemann. In view of the political circumstances and a liberal rent law, a reform of the tenements in the inner city was out of the question. The planners' proposals made reference to the outskirts, such as the Tempelhofer Feld, where the new concept of building housing developments on the outskirts of the city were being advanced (see left). Few impulses for reform came from the cooperative house building sector in which Alfred Messel had already been active with schemes for the Savings and Building Society in Sickingerstrasse (1893–1895), Stargarderstrasse (1897–1898), and Proskauerstrasse (1899–1900) in the suburbs of Moabit, Prenzlauer Berg, and Friedrichshain; Messel's houses in these districts were created as residential courtyards, the buildings having no side-wings. One of the most important reforming architects after 1905 apart from Paul Mebes, architect of the Civil Service Housing Society, was the surveyor for Charlottenburg, Albert Gessner, who published a detailed survey on the German apartment building in 1909, which transformed the traditional block shape (opposite). The distinction between houses facing the street and those to the rear was, as with Riemer's Hofgarten, abandoned from 1882 in favor of large residential courtyards. However, his houses in Charlottenburg built between 1906 and 1911 are examples of an upper-middle-class style. In 1910, these differing notions of housing reform were absorbed into the Greater Berlin competition, but it was not until the new building regulations of 1925 that building behind existing houses and overcrowding were made illegal.

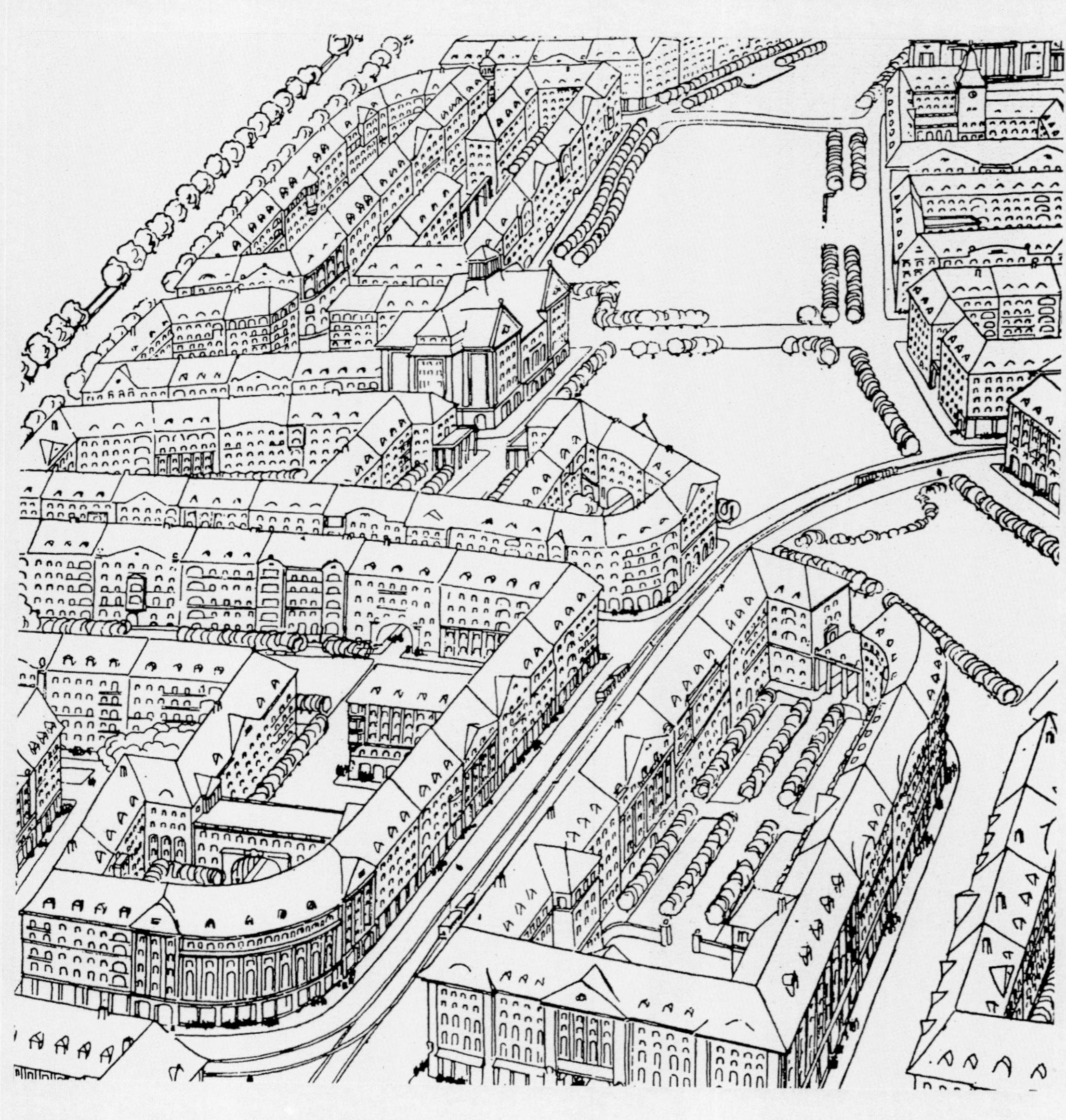

Tempelhofer Field District, Berlin, Competition for Greater Berlin (1910)
Hermann Jansen
Perspective drawing, not executed

In one of the projects awarded first prize in the Greater Berlin competition of 1910, Jansen produced a differentiated urban and infrastructure plan for the city. The planned population of five million meant that new suburbs were necessary. Jansen's proposals contained his own conclusions from the debate on reforming tenement houses. Individual backyards and side wings disappeared in favor of large planted courtyards.

Left and below
Berlin, Charlottenburg, apartments on Mommsenstrasse (1906–1907)
Albert Gessner

Gessner was an important proponent of a new and more elegant style of apartment block, and his houses were mostly reserved for a wealthy clientele. The detail left shows the entrance of the apartments below.

Berlin, Charlottenburg, apartments on Mommsenstrasse (1906–1907)
Albert Gessner
Entrance of the house shown on the right

In the then independent city of Charlottenburg, Gessner built a new type of house that broke with the rigid block plan, and avoided the poorly lit rooms typical of Berlin.

The leap from mere growth of cities to urban planning, with urban greenery and open spaces, was accomplished by Martin Wagner in his dissertation *Das sanitäre Grün der Städte. Ein Beitrag zur Flächentheorie* (The Hygienic Greenery of Cities. Contributions to a Theory of Space Planning), which was published in 1915. As Berlin's City Surveyor from 1926 onwards, he was to make the transformation from architect to engineer and, together with Ernst Reuter, found modern urban studies. The title of Wagner's publication is patterned on that of Wille Sitte's influential work *Der Städtebau nach seinen künstlerischen Grundsätzen* (Urban Planning According to its Artistic Principles), whose fourth edition of 1904 distinguished for the first time between the beneficial and merely decorative properties of urban greenery. Sitte's treatise was less a contribution to urban beautification than a fundamental work on the phenomenon of the metropolis in the final years of the 19th century. "Decorative greenery" was a term used to describe those places which had been planted primarily to beautify the

Berlin, Friedrichshain, Friedrichshain public park, Fairy Tale Fountain (1902–1914)
Ludwig Hoffmann, built by Albert Brodersen

The public park in Friedrichshain was a designated "green area" planted both for ornamentation and public health. This first purely public park by Gustav Meyer, a pupil of Lenné, was provided with a fountain by Ludwig Hoffmann, which today still serves as a decorative and recreational area.

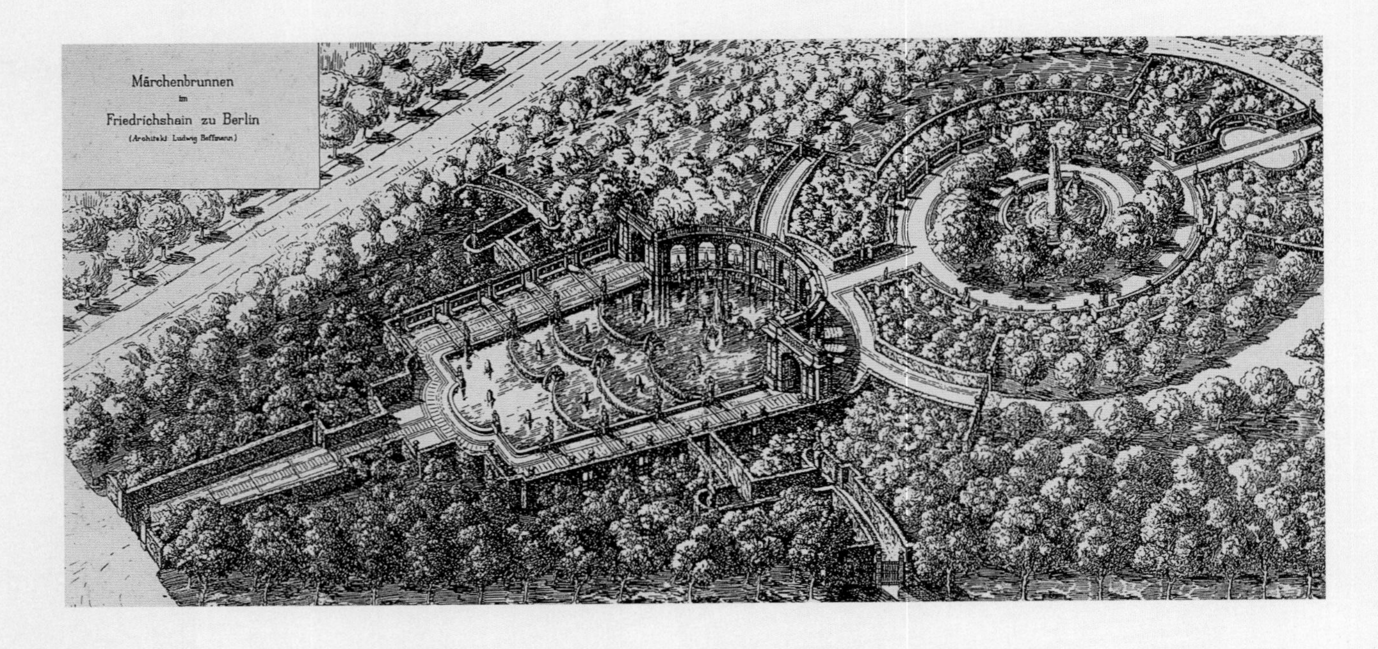

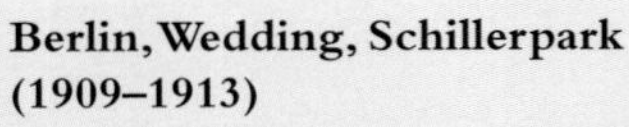

Berlin, Wedding, Schillerpark (1909–1913)
Friedrich Bauer; photograph before 1933

After an interminable planning phase, the Schillerpark was one of the first modern parks in the city to anticipate Wagner's idea of "green areas for public health." Playing areas and wide open lawns – in other words, space in which people could exercise in natural surroundings – were reforming ideas at the time.

city, a tradition established in Berlin by Peter Josef Lenné. At the same time as the development of the Tiergarten, Friedrichshain, and the Treptower Park (by Lenné's successor Gustav Meyer and Hermann Mächtig), there arose the modern movement for public parks (see above, top). Examples of the decorative areas from around 1900 are the Viktoria-Luise-Platz by Fritz Encke (1899) and the Wittenberg-Platz of 1913 by Erwin Barth. A transition to a new style of directness can be seen in a comparison of the city's various parks. Wagner's work, which despite its innovative approach was firmly rooted "in the soil of Wilhelminian reform" (Julius Posener), see things differently: "The importance of 'hygienic greenery' for the people of a great city has less to do with its merely being there, than with its usefulness." Statements of this kind addressed themselves to planning issues based on people's needs, as well as the idea that green areas existed primarily to minister to the physical requirements of the "interned city population." The first amusement and recreation park on the American model was built by Friedrich Bauer in his Schiller Park in Wedding (1909–1913) (see above). Wagner underscored the importance of easily accessible and well-proportioned parks for densely populated areas. He therefore criticized the relatively generous public park in Friedrichshain for being too small: the park

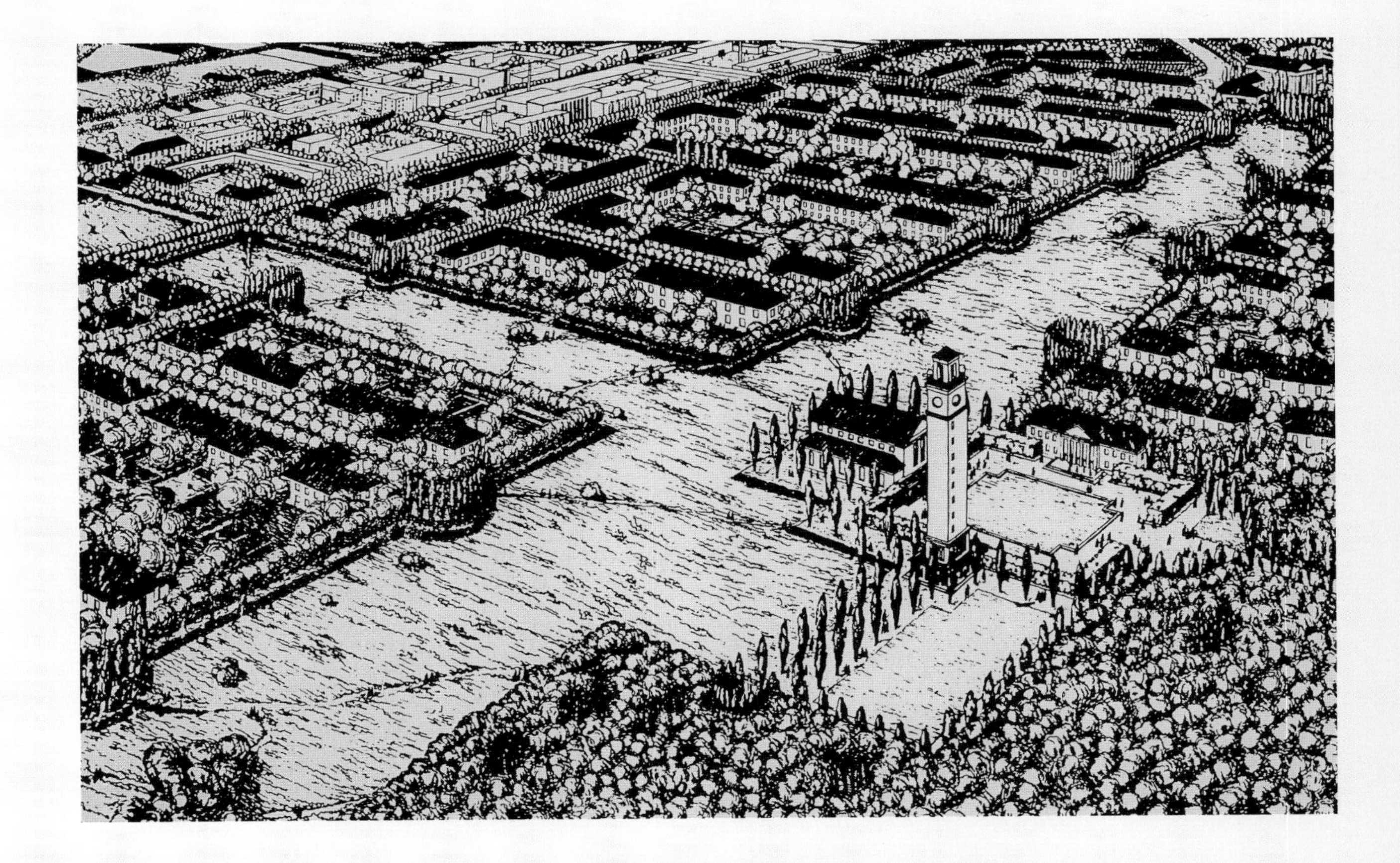

Suburban project, green belt, diagram, not constructed (1915)
Martin Wagner

In his dissertation of 1915, Wagner combined previous approaches to the planning of municipal open space. His proposals were still influential as late as the 1970s. In the project illustrated here, he once again took up the tradition of the garden city; this was, however, an approach essentially at odds with the concept of the modern city.

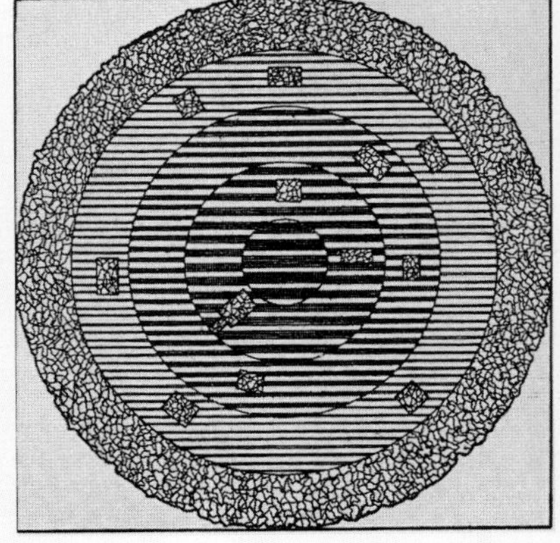

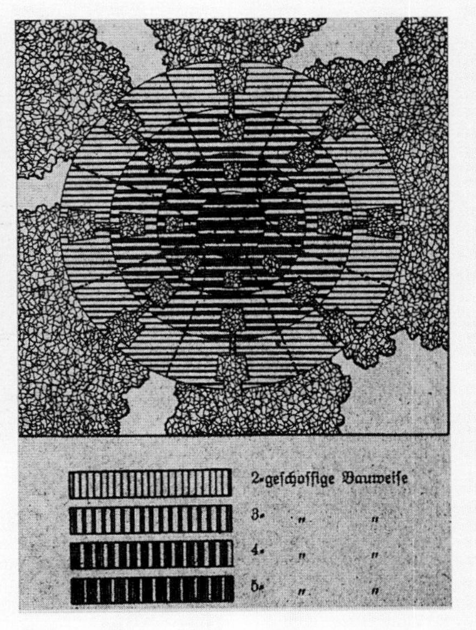

Sketches for the Greening of the Metropolis
Martin Wagner

Wagner's schematic diagrams combine the approach of Joseph Brix and Felix Genzmer, with their wedge-shaped green areas (near right), and Jansen's proposal, which was based on the concept of concentric rings (center). Both were joint first prize winners in the Greater Berlin competition of 1910. Wagner replied to these schemes with one oriented to the needs of the population (far right).

had a capacity for 85,000 people, though the population of the park's catchment area was 630,000.

Wagner's scheme of 1915 rejected both Jansen's concentric system and the radial plan of the Eberstadt Group (see above). Both were prize winners in the Greater Berlin competition. Wagner's mixed type was oriented towards the users' requirements. The Körner Park by Killenberg and Gutzeit from 1912–1916, the Rüdesheimer Platz by Paul Jatzow, the Schöneberg city park, and the Lietzensee Park constructed in 1912–1914 by Erwin Barth, were attempts to put these reforming ideas into reality. Wagner himself, head of the Administration Union of Greater Berlin from 1914, ensured that large wooded areas around Berlin were acquired and taken out of speculative circulation (see above, top). His reform proposals were always associated with the concept of a social utopia. In his capacity as City Surveyor of Schöneberg, and working with Bruno Taut, he put the final touches to designs for the Lindenhof Estate in the last days of the war. From there it was a small step to the famous Britzer Hufeisen Estate. Political circumstances meant that the central city remained unaffected by these measures. It was therefore understandable that Wagner would continue to dream of the "gradual dissolution of the city" as a consequence of his ideas for garden cities.

Bernd Nicolai

Cemeteries and Tombs in Berlin and Brandenburg

From churchyard to graveyard

There is scarcely a churchyard or cemetery in Brandenburg today that looks as it did in earlier times. The cantor or sexton no longer planted out those areas without graves in fruit trees or vegetables in order to feed their large families, as they once did. The wooden crosses and earthen grave mounds of the poor have also passed into another age, as have the many infant graves. Only the expensive and, therefore, durable family burial plots of the wealthy have been preserved. Tombs from the Middle Ages and the Renaissance have survived in churches. In the old churchyards of Brandenburg, on the other hand, Baroque gravestones are often the oldest monuments (see below).

The cultic character of the churchyard died out with the establishment of the Reformation. Previously, as a consecrated space, it had served similar functions to the church. These functions were a consequence of the belief that one was obliged to attend to the salvation of the deceased and to help the soul purify itself in purgatory. According to Martin Luther, man attains grace only through faith and for this reason one has to die in a state of salvation. Death was final: nothing could be done afterwards. For this reason, the more radical Calvinists rejected even burial rites and refused to mark their graves.

After the Reformation, then, there were no ideological objections to turning the churchyard into a profane place. Churchyards became storage depots, grazing areas, and open-air laundries. In 1527, Luther had written in "On Whether One Should Flee From Death": "Therefore, proceeding from such examples, my advice is to make provision for the deceased outside the city." Luther appealed for a pious attitude to graveyards and for field burials for the inhabitants of cities.

The first field burials were a matter of necessity: "plague pits" were established outside the city for reasons of hygiene, and in several places they formed the core of normal cemeteries. The practice of field burial was legally anchored in the General Code of Law for the Prussian States of 1794, which stated: "No corpses are to be buried in churches or populated areas of the city." In practice, however these regulations were not strictly adhered to.

The General Code of Law prepared the way for the legal separation of cemeteries from the Church. In Prussia, both military cemeteries and the abbey cemeteries taken over after the Reformation had already been secularized. Now, local district cemeteries were also to fall into the purview of the state. Church congregations, of course, had a considerable economic interest in the burial of their parishioners and tried to prevent the establishment of competing local cemeteries – something that was successfully done in Berlin, for example.

The "God's acre" of the Herrnhut Brethren, consecrated in November 1730, was a renowned example of the type of cemetery that lay outside town limits. In 1735, Samuel Benjamin Walther wrote of the Herrnhut Brethren: "Their graveyard, lying on a hill called Herrnhut, is perfectly laid out in

Right
Grave for Frau J. C. C. Schneider (died 1799)
Altgolssen churchyard (Dahme Spreewald)

Freestanding Baroque graves like this are now rare in the churchyards of Brandenburg. The Schneider grave consists of an inscribed tablet (broken off) on a plinth, with allegorical figures (Faith, Hope, and Time).

Far right
Grave for the chaplain, Andreas Kelner (1754–1788)
Potsdam, Old Cemetery (Alter Friedhof) (Heinrich-Mann-Allee)

Potsdam citizens erected this elaborate gravestone of sandstone to a Catholic priest in gratitude for his pastoral services. Its design anticipates the "altar style" that classicism was later to make popular.

Grave of the mayor, Georg Tismar (1710–1789)
Brandenburg/Havel, Neustädtischer cemetery (Kirchhofstrasse)

Death (Thanatos) stands in a niche with a round arch. The depiction of death as a brother of sleep was of classical origin and was popularized by Gotthold Ephraim Lessing's essay from 1769 *Wie die Alten den Tod gebildet* (How the Ancients Shaped Death). Classical gravestone designs provided this motif with a number of variations until around 1850.

a square and, as it were, divided into six rows of cultivated beds and has a most pleasing appearance and attractive view." The six rows were a reference to the "choirs" in which the sexes were buried separately: children, single people, and married couples. The Brethren's synod of 1764 reasserted the basic ideas behind the unified design: "We require that, apart from name, place and date of birth and death, the gravestones bear no further inscription and that, in our cemetery, only gravestones of the same size may be erected."

The cemetery of the Herrnhut community was not a direct model for those of the 19th century as it had a deep religious significance. Its structure reflected that of the community. In contrast to the temporary resting places in church and district cemeteries, the gravesites were not allowed to be re-used. Even the system of paths in the Herrnhut scheme did not impose a hierarchy.

The Dessau cemetery designed by Friedrich Wilhelm von Erdmannsdorf, opened in 1787, ultimately set the standard for the design of cemeteries. While the graveyard of the Herrnhut Brethren was reserved for members of that community, the Dessau cemetery was to be open to all religious denominations. Its basic structure was that of a square area divided into four quarters by paths. Grave mounds were to be used instead of gravestones, something that Joseph Furttenbach the Elder had already suggested in 1628 in a design proposal. The cemetery was surrounded by a 2-meter (6-feet) high wall with family vaults; these were to be marked with uniform plaques and to have their roofs planted in grass.

Around the turn of the 19th century, plants began to assume a greater importance in the design of cemeteries and graves. Graves had been planted out in the Middle Ages, though mostly with plants that had either a symbolic value (for example ivy and evergreen for eternity, and the Madonna lily for purity) or the power to ward off evil powers. These practices had fallen into disuse by the end of the 18th century at the latest.

When the literary movement of "sensibility" became widespread and the fascination with nature reached its peak, there was a far-reaching change in garden design that has left its mark on cemeteries until the present day. The Enlightenment's emphasis on the rational was now challenged by the concept of the "sentimental." Christian Cajus Hirschfeld, in his *Theorie der Gartenkunst* (Theory of the Art of Gardens) 1775–1778, numbered cemeteries among the "melancholy type of gardens." Death had become aestheticized. Theatrical Baroque graves, with their pretentious inscriptions, death's heads, and skeletons disappeared and made way for simple memorials with classical symbolism.

In 1811, the "Royal Kurland Government" published design regulations that recommended locating churchyards "at least 500 paces from the settlement and preferably downwind from prevailing winds." The basic elements of the cemetery were to be right-angled or diagonally intersecting paths to divide the area into four, a round space in the middle where the bereaved could gather, and a perimeter path. Between this path and the cemetery wall, black poplars or silver birch trees were to be planted, beneath which

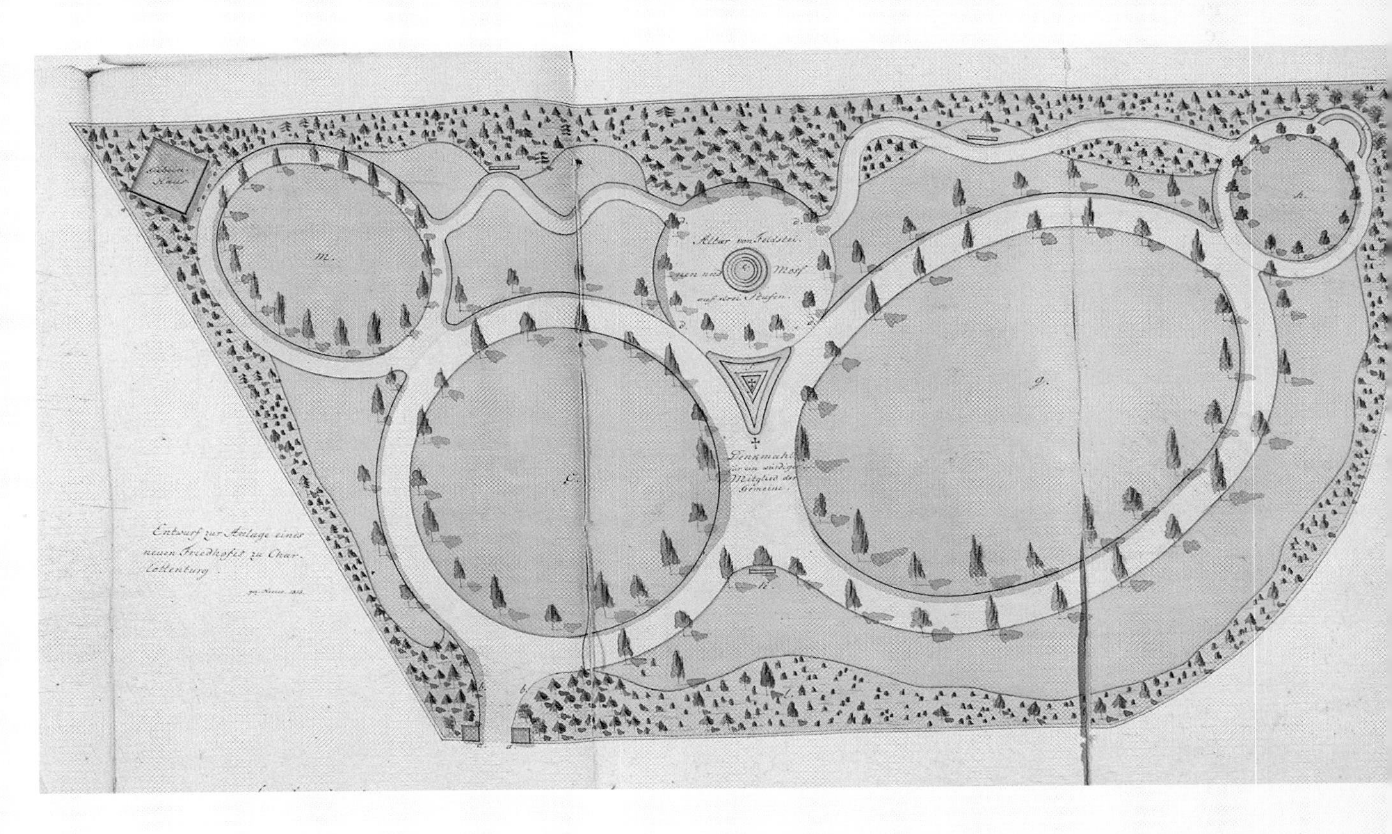

Design for a new cemetery for Charlottenburg, by the Court Gardener George Steiner (March 3, 1815)
Potsdam, Brandenburg Archives

Steiner's design already displays elements of the later park cemetery, but uses geometric forms. The central area was to be planted out with six oak and six linden trees at the edges, and features an altar of field-stones around which mourners could gather. A circular area with viburnum shrubs and white roses was intended for infants' graves. The cemetery (at 1. Luisenfriedhof, Guerickestrasse) today no longer has this design.

Grave of the architect David Gilly (1748–1808)
Berlin, II cemetery of the Jerusalem and New Church Congregation outside the Hallesches Gate (Zossener Strasse)

Gilly was the most important early Neo-classical architect in Berlin and Brandenburg. This very simple wall tomb from 1805 with its receding half arch was probably designed by Gilly himself.

Grave of Karl Friedrich Schinkel (1781–1841)
Berlin, Dorotheenstädtischer cemetery (Chausseestrasse)

Schinkel is considered the most significant German architect, designer and artist of the 19th century. His grave, with its palmette acroterion set on a classical stele, is designed on the classical model. It belongs to a group of five types of monument that Schinkel designed in 1821 and which became very popular. The portrait medallion was made by August Kiss after a model by his teacher Christian David Rauch.

graves could be placed. The four quarters of the cemetery with their thick carpets of neat, well-tended grass, were to be planted out in trees (poplars, lindens, white birch, or fruit trees) and flowering shrubs, which were thought to "disperse and suppress the emanations of mephitic vapors." Only roses or other easily transplantable varieties were permitted. The recommendations of the Kurland Government clearly show the influence of the Dessau cemetery. They were adopted, with minor variations, by the court gardener, George Steiner, in 1815 and used in the design of the new Charlottenburg cemetery (see page 495). The older section of the Trinity Congregation cemetery on the Bergmannstrasse in Berlin still bears traces of the government's intentions. It was generally easier to keep to the guidelines in new rather than in older cemeteries. The idea of closing the churchyards was opposed by those who argued that relocating the cemeteries away from the towns would destroy the communal bonds between the living worshippers in the church and the dead outside it. Apart from walls and gates, the new cemeteries had no other structures. The dead were laid out and rituals held in the ceremonial hall. Not until 1835 was a mortuary built in Berlin, in the French cemetery outside the Oranienburg Gate. Potsdam did not have such a building until 1851; it was equipped with the latest alarm device for those who may have been declared dead by mistake. Mortuaries developed into the ceremonial halls, or chapels of rest, of today's cemeteries.

From 1840 on, the recommended design principles began to be accepted, mainly in Brandenburg's cities. Peter Joseph Lenné in his redesign of the Potsdam cemetery (today's Alter Friedhof) did not therefore employ a landscape garden design, but rather opted for set geometric forms. Lenné recognized that parks and cemeteries had different functions and respected the official standards that the State had set for the design of graveyards.

The mid-19th century saw the first beginnings of historic conservation in cemeteries. In 1815, Karl Friedrich Schinkel had already lamented the loss of grave monuments. Forty years later the public body responsible for graveyards, the Prussian Ministry for Religious Education and Medicine, banned the removal of gravestones that had either a documentary value on the basis of their inscriptions, or whose design gave them an artistic value. Berlin's Neo-classical sculptors and architects were responsible for some superb pieces in the cemeteries of the capital and in Brandenburg (see page 497 bottom left, and above). Also protected were monuments that had been designed by well-known artists and which were made in the Royal Foundries of Berlin (see page 497, bottom right, and page 505); the often magnificent wrought-iron or cast-iron grave gates (see page 498, top left); and the unique and sometimes enormous mausoleums of those who had achieved great wealth (see pages 498 and 499). Until World War I, high quality work had been created for Berlin's graveyards by the city's School of Sculptors (see pages 498–500).

The nature of cemeteries continued to change in the second half of the 19th century: the ideals of equality in death and the modest cemetery designs that this implied were no longer in the ascendant. The need of individuals to display their identities, together with the varied products of the cemetery industry, created a heterogeneous image that owed nothing to an overall landscape concept. Instead, cemeteries became functional places that were designed as gardens only in those places where they needed to be "beautified." Not until after 1900 was there a series of proposals designed to moderate the massing of gravestones in urban cemeteries by ordering them through architectural elements. Adolf von Hildebrand suggested creating "family plots" in which individual tombs could be placed (see page 500). In general, graveyards turned away from the gated quarters typical of the 19th century and became divided into areas enclosed by small hedges. These are still typical for the cemeteries of Berlin and Brandenburg today.

A quite new design challenge for both cemeteries and their buildings was posed by the appearance of cremations in the last quarter of the 19th century. The first burial of "cremated remains" took place in Berlin in September 1887 in the city cemetery of Friedrichsfelde, where Prussia's first columbarium was built three years later. In 1911, the Prussian Church finally dropped its opposition to cremation and thus opened the way for Berlin's first crematorium to be put into operation in 1912 in Wedding (Gerichtstrasse). Until that time, cremations had had to be carried out in Gotha. The first crematoria provided for the burial of ashes in a columbarium, which in general was included in a complex containing waiting rooms, a chapel of rest, and the crematorium's furnace, which was usually hidden from view. Later, cemeteries were equipped with their own columbaria, for which particular design solutions (for example in Potsdam) had to be found.

Cemetery design received new impulses from the back to nature movements that had developed in the first third of the 19th century as a reaction against industrialization and the increasing alienation of people from their natural environment. The movements found practical expression in the advocacy of public parks and for the reform of cemeteries. From 1877, Wilhelm Cordes created his famous park cemetery in Hamburg-Ohlsdorf, which combined the functions of burial place and recreation ground. Director of Gardens, Hermann Mächtig, began Berlin's first district cemetery, the central cemetery of Friedrichsfelde, along these lines in 1881.

Around 1900, the forest cemetery became more popular than idyllic park cemeteries with their concealed graves. By regarding burial as the dedication of the body to the natural world of the forest, and therefore to the ceaseless cycle of the elements, the forest cemetery merged with the romanticism of the contemporary outdoors

Grave of Friedrich Ludwig Persius (1803–1845) in the Sello family plot
Potsdam-Bornstedt churchyard

The stele by Stüler bears a relief showing an authentic portrait of the architect in classical clothing bidding farewell to life.

Left
Grave of Lieutenant General Friedrich Otto von Diericke (died 1819)
Berlin, Alt-Schöneberg cemetery (Hauptstrasse)

A classical altar with a fluted urn, this monument is of cast iron and was made at the Royal Foundry in Berlin from a design by Karl Friedrich Schinkel.

Far left
Grave of Helene Charlotte von Lestwitz (died 1803), known as "Frau von Friedland," in the family plot of the Lestwitz and von Itzenplitz families
Kunersdorf (Märkisch-Oderland)

Helene Charlotte von Lestwitz was an agrarian reformer and one of the most important Prussian women of the late 18th century. Her grave, by Keller, shows an urn with allegorical depictions of agriculture.

Left
Tomb of Franz Anton Egells (1788–1854)
Berlin, Old Cathedral Cemetery (Alter Domfriedhof), St. Hedwig's Cathedral (Liesenstrasse)

Egells founded the first private iron foundry in Berlin in 1821, so it is appropriate that his tomb is noted in particular for its beautiful Neo-classic railings. Wrought-iron or cast-iron railings around family tombs were characteristic of cemeteries in the 19th century; to some extent they were required by cemetery regulations.

Right
Oppenfeld family vault (1828)
Berlin, churchyard of the Dreifaltigkeitskirche (Bergmannstrasse)

The von Oppenfelds, descendants of the Jewish banking family, the Oppenheims, were merchants and owners of a manorial estate. The name Oppenfeld was adopted in 1827 when they converted to Christianity. This unique mausoleum in the Egyptian Revival style of the early 19th century was erected by the Oppenfelds in 1828. The structure resembles the stump of a pyramid; it supports a broad splayed platform of cast iron on which is set the shallow conical roof.

Grave of Olga Malcomess (1852–1904)
Berlin, Old Garrison Cemetery (Alte Garnisonfriedhof) (Kleine Rosenthaler Strasse)

Olga Malcomess was the daughter of the von Ziethens, an aristocratic Brandenburg family. Adolf Jahn created the praying figure (which is not a portrait of the deceased) in marble in 1908; its flowing forms show the influence of both Neo-classicism and Art Nouveau, and demonstrates a turning away from the dramatic pathos of Neo-Baroque designs.

Hansemann family vault and plot (1790–1864)
Berlin, churchyard of the Alter St. Matthäus church (Grossgöschenstrasse)

Adolf von Hansemann, the son and successor to the banker David Hansemann, had this plot, which covers 220 square meters (2,370 square feet), designed by the architects Friedrich Hitzig and Hermann Ende. Heinz Hoffmann and Adolf Itzenplitz were the sculptors.

Opposite, above right
Grave of Adolf Menzel (1815–1905)
Berlin, churchyard of the Dreifaltigkeitskirche (Bergmannstrasse)

The painter and graphic artist Adolf Menzel was famous for his historical drawings and pictures. This naturalistic sculpted portrait is the bronze cast of a marble bust that Reinhold Begas had made for the National Gallery (Nationalgalerie) in 1877, while Menzel was still alive.

Grave Nobel laureate Emil Fischer (1852–1919)
Berlin, New Cemetery (Neuer Friedhof), Wannsee (Lindenstrasse)

The relief depicts a young couple holding a chalice containing the Waters of Eternal Life. Carved by Fritz Klimsch, it contains both Art Nouveau and Symbolist motifs.

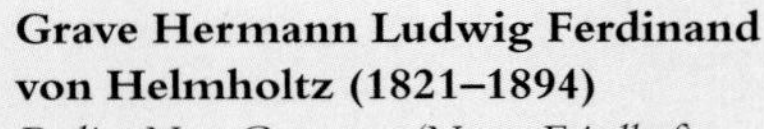

movement, known as Wanderbewegung. From 1905 to 1907, Hans Grässel in Munich created the paradigm of forest cemeteries. The site was a 40 to 50-year-old cultivated fir forest into which the graves were blended in such a way that the character of the forest was largely untouched.

In Berlin, the concept of the forest cemetery was put into effect by the city's synod in the Ahrensfelde Eastern Cemetery (1908) and Stahnsdorf Southwestern Cemetery (1909).

Louis Meyer designed the latter with elements of the parkland cemetery and created one of the largest and finest forest cemeteries in Germany. Stahnsdorf is one of the most important cemeteries in Berlin and Brandenburg because of the quality of its gardens as well as the numerous excellent graves that mark the last resting place of a number of famous people.

Building on this tradition, the architect Richard Neutra created a forest cemetery in the industrial city of Luckenwalde in 1921–1922, the focus of his design being a complex of terraces. The artist used a symbolic style in his essentially Expressionist design, borrowing ancient Egyptian and classical motifs, and using plants according to their symbolic meaning. Although this cemetery has been greatly changed over the years, the original plan can still be seen very clearly; a restoration would be very successful.

Military cemeteries

As a rule, Brandenburg's military towns did not have their own burial sites. The garrison's soldiers were buried in local cemeteries, where one often finds areas or even groves dedicated to the fallen.

The oldest military cemetery in Berlin and Brandenburg is the Old Garrison Cemetery (Alter Garnisonfriedhof) in Kleine Rosenthaler Strasse, built after 1701. Today, only the officers' cemetery survives; the rest was converted into a park in 1978. Of special interest is the grave for General von Holtzendorff and the Neo-Gothic, cast-iron memorial to the Teichert family, both designed by Karl Friedrich Schinkel (see page 505).

The Veterans' Cemetery (Invalidenfriedhof) from 1748 in the Scharnhorststrasse has, since the start of the 19th century, been the burial ground of Germany's top-ranking military officials and is Berlin's best-known military cemetery. Here too the most striking memorial, the grave of General Gerhard von Scharnhorst, is by Karl Friedrich Schinkel (see page 505).

Cemeteries for the prisoners of war

In Brandenburg there are several cemeteries for prisoners of war who have died in Germany. The locations of these graves have often been forgotten or only parts of the original cemeteries are known. Among those still tended are the British and Italian military cemeteries in the Stahnsdorf Southwest Cemetery near Berlin.

The layout of the British cemetery corresponds to a law passed by Parliament in 1918 that provided for the design of military graveyards; the sarcophagus-like memorial stone is typical, as is the high cross with a bronze sword. There was a large international military cemetery from World War I near Zehrendorf on the parade grounds near Wünsdorf, south of Berlin. The cemetery has today been completely destroyed.

Grave Hermann Ludwig Ferdinand von Helmholtz (1821–1894)
Berlin, New Cemetery (Neuer Friedhof), Wannsee (Lindenstrasse)

Hermann von Helmholtz was president of the Imperial Physical Technical Institute and did fundamental work in various areas of physics. Due to family connections, he is buried in the Siemens family plot. Adolf von Hildebrand, sculptor and art theoretician, created the "memorial garden" in 1910 and contributed a number of sculptures to it.

Wissinger family plot
Berlin, Southwest churchyard of the City Synod, Berlin (Stahnsdorf, Bahnhofstrasse)

The family grave of businessman Otto Julius Wissinger (1848–1920) is an Expressionist baldachino tomb of concrete, built in 1922–1923 from a design by the architect Max Taut, brother of Bruno Taut. The structure aroused protests and the church especially demanded its removal. A grave sculpture by Otto Freundlich, with mystical and Jewish symbols, was destroyed shortly after being erected.

Medallion on the grave of Frédéric Ançillon (1767–1837)
Berlin, French Cemetery (Französischer Friedhof) (Chausseestrasse)

Emperor Frederick William IV donated this grave, a large Roman marble sarcophagus, to his tutor, Frédéric Ançillon, who was a noted theologian, historian and statesman. It was designed by Karl Friedrich Schinkel.

The cemeteries of religious communities

In Brandenburg only a few cemeteries belonging to different ethnic groups and religious communities have been preserved. Exceptions are the historical burial sites of the West Slavic Sorbs in their villages in the Lower Lausitz. Even the Dutch and Swiss immigrants of the 17th and 18th centuries once had their own cemeteries, but these have since been absorbed into local graveyards. Another exception were the Jews for whom, for religious reasons, the building of a cemetery was more compelling and important than the construction of a synagogue. Normally there was no separate cemetery for the various Christian denominations.

In the teeming city of Berlin, however, religious denominations were able to operate their own cemeteries. From 1834, the Catholics buried their dead in the St. Hedwig's Cemetery in the Liesenstrasse; the graveyard still exists today. Of the graveyards built in Berlin by the French Reformed community (Huguenots) since 1687, the cemeteries on the Chausseestrasse and the Liesenstrasse still remain. Apart from French inscriptions and names on several gravestones, it is difficult to make out specific design features (above). At the beginning of the 18th century, Bohemian religious refugees were settled in and around Berlin (Rixdorf) who belonged either to various communities of the Brethren, and the Bohemian Lutheran the Bohemian Reformed Churches. The "God's acre" of the Brethren beyond the Hallesches Gate was largely removed in 1971. But in the cemetery of Böhmisch-Rixdorf (today in Berlin-Neukölln, Karl-Marx-Platz) there are still gravestones with Czech inscriptions from the 18th century. The Russian Orthodox community in Berlin established a cemetery in 1893–1894 in Tegel (Wittestrasse). The gravestones with their almost exclusively Cyrillic inscriptions display typically Russian Orthodox symbolism, notably the Cross of St. Andrew. Today's Moslem cemetery (on the Columbiadamm) was presented by William I to the Turkish government in 1866. The gravestones either bear Arabic inscriptions and a half-moon motif, or imitate European designs.

Pogroms and expulsions scattered the Jewish communities and led to the disappearance of many of their medieval cemeteries, from which only a few gravestones remain. In the 18th century, as a rule, cemeteries were only established by larger communities, in which the deceased from smaller communities might be buried. After a government regulation from 1814 imposed restrictions on the transport of corpses, this was no longer possible; new cemeteries had to be built.

Not until after synagogue districts were formed in the middle of the 19th century and, reinforced by the economic flight of Jewish families from the countryside, were the cemeteries of larger communities again preferred. Larger graveyards were better able to provide for the observance of

Jewish graves of the 18th century
Potsdam, Jewish Cemetery (Jüdischer Friedhof) on the Pfingstberg

Potsdam already had a large Jewish community in the 18th century and they established this cemetery in 1743. Despite the depredations of the Nazi era, a large number of typically unsupported gravestones with Hebraic inscriptions have been preserved.

prescribed rituals. Local cemeteries assumed a lesser importance. The destruction wrought by the Nazis meant that they became even fewer. In spite of this, Jewish cemeteries or their former sites are today a stronger reminder of Jewish life in Brandenburg than synagogues. There are still significant numbers of graves from the 18th century in the cemeteries of Wriezen (built in 1730), Potsdam (1743) (see above), Beelitz (before 1743), and Müncheberg (1756). The gravestones are stone slabs without foundations and have a purely Hebraic script. They are sparingly ornamented: they may feature, for example, the blessing hands of the *kohanin* (priests), which point to the name of the deceased; the bowl and jug of the Levites; depictions of animals; or the crown as the sign of a good name.

After the Emancipation Edict of 1812, which declared that Jews in Brandenburg were entitled to have full rights, the use of the German language was made obligatory. Gravestones were now inscribed in both languages, although the German inscription is generally not a direct translation of the original Hebraic text.

With the ongoing assimilation of the German Jews, Jewish cemeteries gradually lost their specific character. Even the use of Hebraic script became increasingly less common. The oldest Jewish cemetery founded in Berlin (1672) is in the Grosser Hamburger

BEI GR. GOERSCHEN VERWUNDET
AN DIESER WUNDE GESTORBEN
ZU PRAG. D. 28 JUNIUS 1813.
BEWAFFNUNG ZUM KAMPFE VON 1813.

Right
Cast-iron tomb of the Teichert family (1853)
Berlin, Old Garrison Cemetery (Alte Garnisonfriedhof) (Kleine Rosenthaler Strasse)

This small cast iron baldachino was designed by Schinkel for the Teicherts, an old military family. Originally it featured a figure of Death (Thanatos) on a plinth decorated with a coat of arms. It was made by the Royal Foundry established in 1803.

Opposite and above
Grave of General Gerhard von Scharnhorst (1755–1813)
Berlin, Veterans' Cemetery (Invalidenfriedhof) (Scharnhorststrasse)

This monument, a raised sarcophagus on two pillars, was erected after Scharnhorst's remains were transferred from Prague to Berlin in 1826 and designed by Karl Friedrich Schinkel. Tieck carved the reliefs (see opposite) depicting scenes from the general's life. On the massive sarcophagus lid rests a lion, naturalistically modeled by Christian Daniel Rauch.

Strasse. In 1827, a new burial ground for a now much larger community was consecrated in what is today the Schönhauser Allee. Both the grave markers and tombs demonstrate all the stylistic variety of the 19th century, from pure classicism through to historicist styles and the occasional use of oriental motifs.

Towards the end of the 19th century, yet another cemetery had become necessary. In 1880, the largest Jewish cemetery in Berlin, in Weissensee (now Herbert-Baum-Strasse), was consecrated in which, apart from numerous historicist graves, there were also examples of modern architectural deign. Also in Weissensee (in the Wittlicher Strasse) is the cemetery of the Orthodox Jewish community, Adass Jisroel, which was dedicated in 1880.

Klaus Arlt

Glossary

acroterion An architectural feature, such as a small statue of decorative device, that stands on the ridge of a building, usually the pediment of a classical building.

aedicule An opening (usually shrine or a niche for sculpture) framed by a pair of classical columns or *pilasters* and surmounted by an *entablature*, possibly also a *pediment*.

aisle The narrower side parts of a church flanking the nave or choir, between the inner arcade and the outer walls.

ajour Of carved decoration, standing free of its background, pierced.

ambulatory A continuation of the *aisles* round the back of the high altar of a church. Used in processions.

apse Semi-circular annex to the east end of a church or east wall of a *transept*, usually forming a chapel.

architrave Lintel forming the lowest part of an *entablature*.

Ascanian The German dynasty that ruled Brandenburg from its capture from the Slavs in 1134 to the death of Albrecht III in 1320.

atrium Courtyard surrounded by columns, open to the sky.

Augustinian canons Communities of clerics who, living according to the Rule of St. Augustine, renounce private property. The communities emerged in the 12th century.

baldacchino A canopy or roof-like structure over a throne, altar, tomb etc.

Baroque The dominant European style of art and architecture from c.1600 to c.1750. Its characteristic emphasis on heroic themes and grandiose, often theatrical, effects made it the perfect vehicle for the absolutist courts of Europe. It gradually gave way to the more decorative *Rococo*.

basilica Originally, a Roman market-hall or meeting hall; in Christian architecture, a church consisting of a *nave* in the center and narrower columned *aisles* on each side. The nave is higher than the aisles, and is lit by a *clerestory*.

bay 1) A unit of a *vault*, from one supporting *pier* to the next: the length of a church is counted in such bays. 2) A structural division of a building, usually marked by buttresses or pilasters. 3) A projecting part of a building (usually round), as in a bay window.

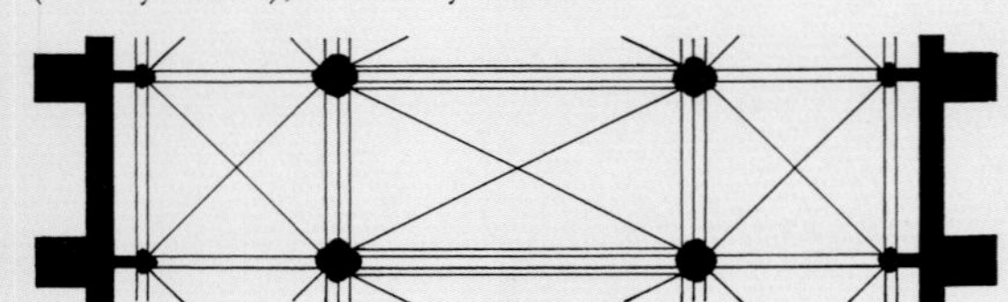

berceaux de treillage (French) A walkway covered with latticework over which plants have been trained.

béton brut (French) Concrete left in its natural state, e.g. with the marks left by the boards of its mold clearly visible.

Biedermeier style A style in German art, furnishing, and decorative crafts during the 19th century.

blind gable A form of ornamented *gable* which has no openings (such as windows).

boscage A grove; a mass of trees or shrubs.

boss An ornamental block at the apex of intersecting vault ribs.

boulle work Furniture decoration consisting of inlays of ivory, tortoiseshell, metals etc.

bozzetto pl. *bozzetti* (Italian) A small preliminary model, usually of a sculpture; a small oil sketch.

buttress A masonry support, usually on the outside of a building, designed to counteract the outward thrust of the walls caused by the weight of the roof.

cartouche Architectural ornament comprising a scroll-like tablet bearing an inscription or decorative motif.

casino Ornamental pavilion in the grounds of a grand house, used for various entertainments.

chancel The *choir* and *sanctuary* of a church, at the east end. Runs from the *crossing* to the altar.

choir Part of a church at the east end used by the canons and monks for prayer and singing. Usually separated from the lay part of the church by a *choir screen* or stalls.

choir screen Wood or stone structure separating the *choir* from the secular part of the church.

church The main parts of a church are the *nave*, the *transept*, the *crossing*, and the *choir* (or chancel). See also *aisle*.

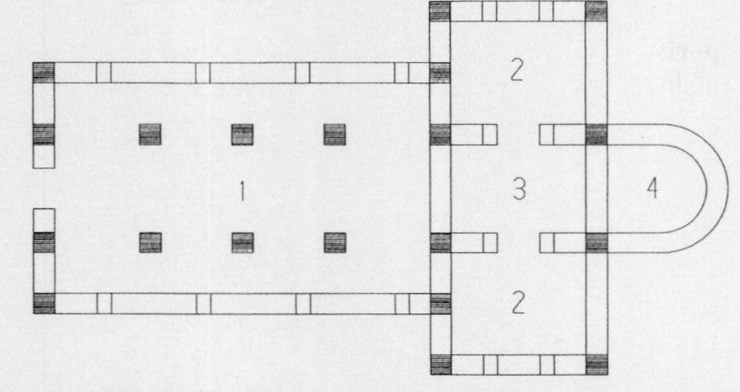

Cistercians A breakaway order of Benedictines who established themselves at Citeaux in France in 1098. The order was characterized by hard agricultural labor combined with practical enterprise. They built monasteries according to the same straightforward architectural pattern all over Europe.

classicism The styles of art and design of Greek and Roman antiquity; any later style based on these.

clerestory The window story above the roofs of the *aisles*, i.e. the highest part of the *nave* of a *basilica*.

cloister Rectangular covered (colonnaded) walkway around an open square on the south or north side of a monastic church.

columbarium A vault with niches for holding the ashes of the dead.

communs (French) The outbuildings of a French noble residence, used as administration offices and as accommodation for staff.

cornice The top part of an *entablature*.

corps de logis (French) The main building of a palace or complex, as distinct from the wings, service buildings etc.

cour d'honneur (French) Front or main courtyard of a palace or grand house, where guests were welcomed.

crossing The rectangular area where the *nave* and *transept* of a church intersect.

crosswork A massive tower-like structure extending across the whole width of a church at the west end, and used for defensive purposes in times of danger.

cruciform Cross-shaped: said of a ground plan containing (for example) a *nave* and *transept*.

crypt A chamber under a church, usually under the *choir*, often used for storage.

cupola A small dome on a roof or turret.

curtain wall A non-load bearing wall, attached to the framework of a building.

Deposition The removal of Christ's body from the Cross.

Dominican A preaching order established by St. Dominic in 1220. Also known as a *mendicant order* and (in German) as the Preaching Order.

dormer Small vertical window in a roof with its own roof and sides, usually set back from the plane of the façade.

Ecce Homo The scene in the Passion when Pilate presents the scourged Christ to the Jews, saying "Behold, the Man!"; an image of Christ being tormented.

enfilade An alignment of door openings on a single axis through a series of rooms.

English garden A relaxed, "naturally" arranged garden or landscape, in contrast to the strict geometrical gardens (especially French gardens) of the *Baroque*.

entablature The complex crosspiece supported on the columns, e.g. in a classical arch, or above a window or doorway. Consists of *architrave*, *frieze*, and *cornice*.

evangelistary A medieval book of gospel readings ordered according to the dates used in church services.

exedra 1) Semi-circular extension of a building. 2) a semi-circular seat in a garden.

fêtes galantes (French) Scenes of elegant dalliance in a garden or rural setting.

float stone Stone used to rub down other stones and bricks to give a smooth finish.

Franconia Province of the Holy Roman Empire, now part of Bavaria between the Main and Danube.

Franco-Prussian War War fought July 1870 to May 1871 between France and Prussia, which was attempting to secure its western border. France was defeated and lost the region of Alsace-Lorraine to Prussia.

fresco A wall painting technique in which pigments are applied to wet plaster. The pigments bind with the drying plaster to form a very durable image. Small amounts of retouching and detail work could be carried out on the dry plaster, a technique known as *a secco* (dry) fresco.

frieze An ornamental strip decorating a wall or on an *entablature*. On external walls it is usually sculpted, on internal walls lightly sculpted and perhaps painted.

gable Vertical end wall of a saddle roof, either on a building or a window. It can be shaped with scrolls or curves, stepped or angled. In classical architecture, a gable is called a *pediment* and is mostly triangular or segmental.

gallery 1) In a church, the space above the aisles or above the west entrance; 2) a covered walkway above ground level inside a courtyard, with open arcading; 3) a very long upper room in a great house, used for walking; 4) since the 19th century, a covered shopping arcade.

genre painting The depiction of scenes from everyday life. Elements of everyday life had long had a role in religious and other works, but it was in Holland in the 17th century that it became an independent form.

giallo di Siena A yellowish ornamental marble.

Golden Bull The name given to several important medieval decrees or enactments. The Golden Bull of Rimini (1226) granted the Teutonic Knights authority over the Lithuanian Prus. The Golden Bull of the Emperor Charles IV (1356) confirmed the rulers of Brandenburg as one of the seven imperial electors.

Gothic The style of European art and architecture during the Middle Ages, following Romanesque and preceding the Renaissance. It originated in northern France about 1150; in Italy, it came to an end as early as 1400, while elsewhere it continued until the 16th century.

hall church A non-basilican church, i.e. one in which nave and aisles are all the same height.

herm Pillar-shaped shaft on which sits a bust.

historicism The systematic use of architectural styles of the past: 19th-century Gothic Revival, which draws upon medieval forms, is an example of historicism.

hortus conclusus A walled garden; a place of safety or refuge.

lambrequin Tongued-shaped, zigzag or looped carved ornament with tassles made of material, metal, wood or stone. It occurs in sculpture, architecture and craft work alike. Lambrequin motifs often appear in faience and porcelain.

lantern A small turret on top of a dome through which light or air enters an interior.

lesene A flat strip decorating a wall like a pilaster, but with no decorative capital or base.

light The area of window between the mullions; a panel of a stained-glass window.

loggia A gallery or room open on one or both sides, its roof supported by columns. When a part of a house or palace, loggias were generally on the upper levels. They are also separate structures.

lost wax method A metal-casting technique in which a model made of wax is coated in plaster to form a mold; when the molten metal is poured into the mold the wax melts and is replaced by the metal.

lucarne A window which is flush with the front wall or façade; a small opening in an attic or spire.

maison de plaisance (French) A country mansion used for entertainment, a house occupied during the summer.

mansard roof Pitched roof with a shoulder halfway, i.e. the bottom part is steeper than the top part, allowing more space inside. The room inside is therefore usually inhabitable. Named for French architect J. K. Mansart.

march (German Mark) A medieval border or frontier territory; the term often became part of a name, e.g. Altmark, the March of Brandenburg.

mendicant orders From the 13th century, religious orders whose members earn their living from work and begging (rather than through the possession of land). The Franciscans, Dominicans, and Carmelites were mendicant orders.

misericord A hinged seat in a choir stall with a carved ledge on the underside which could be used by canons for support when standing during divine office .

monopteros A circular temple whose roof is supported by columns rather than walls.

nave The long central area of a church, stretching from the *crossing* to the west end.

Neo-classicism A style in art, architecture and crafts c.1750–c.1850 characterized by a return to the aesthetic principles and motifs of classical antiquity. It marked a rejection of the flamboyance of the Baroque and Rococo styles.

obelisk Monolith rising to a pyramidal point erected on a square base. Form of monument from ancient Egyptian architecture that remained popular until the 19th century.

Order of capitals

orangery During the Baroque and Rococo periods, a single-story building with tall windows and usually glass doors, used for growing exotic trees.

Palladianism Dominant classical style of architecture in 17th century based on the villas and publications of the Italian architect Andrea Palladio (1508–1580), whose designs were influenced by the architecture of ancient Rome. Revived in the 18th century as Neo-Palladianism.

Passion The suffering of Christ, from his arrest in the Garden of Gethsemane to his Crucifixion and Death. The iconography is divided into the Stations of the Cross.

pavilion 1) Small, free-standing building close to a great house. 2) An end block of a Baroque great house or palace, emphasized by having a separate roof.

pediment A triangular or segmental gable over a classical *entablature*. Often contains sculpture.

pergola Columns and trellises to carry climbing plants; an open walkway of a similar nature.

peristyle A line of columns surrounding a classical building or courtyard; a building surrounded by columns.

piano nobile (Italian) The main floor of a large house.

pier A massive support of an arch in an arcade; the profile can round, square, or composite.

pilaster A rectangular column set into a wall, usually as a decorative feature, and often fluted.

pilier cantonné A Gothic – *pier* consisting of a large column surrounded by smaller columns.

polygon In mathematics, a many-sided figure, e.g. an octagon. The polygon at the east end of a church is generally half of such a figure attached to a straight-sided choir.

portal A grand doorway with a complex frame.

portico A porch in front of a door and open on all three sides. A classical portico consists of a *pediment* and *entablature* carried on free-standing columns. Must have its own roof.

predella The bottom part of an altar, sometimes decorated with paintings.

Premonstratensian An order of Augustinian canons founded by St. Norbert at Prémontré in 1120. Important for the early history of Brandenburg under the Ascanians.

quadriga A sculpture group consisting of a chariot drawn by four horses, and usually capping a monument.

querriegel A transverse fortified structure at the west end of a church; a – *crosswork*.

Rathaus A city hall, a building possessed by every German town or city, where the *Rat* (council) has its meetings.

recess chapel A chapel built between the buttresses of a *hall church*.

refectory The dining hall or (*frater*) of a monastery.

retable Carved or painted altarpiece containing no hinged panels.

rocaille Shell-shaped, asymmetrical decorative motif of the *Rococo* style.

Rococo A style of decorative art that emerged in early 18th century, characterized by profuse and graceful decoration, often based on such natural forms as leaves, tendrils, and shells.

Romanesque Building style of Western architecture from the 10th to late 12th centuries. Main features: round arches, heavy walls, round piers, and barrel vaults. Romanesque gave way to Gothic.

rotunda In classical architecture, a circular building (or part of a building), usually domed.

roundel A garden feature consisting of a circle or semicircle formed by statues and bushes, often situated where several paths meet; they are usually named after the statues.

rubble Broken stone of different sizes, used for building. *Coursed* rubble uses small pieces to make regular courses of masonry. *Random* rubble does not have courses.

Sacred Monogram IHS, supposedly an abbreviation for the name of Jesus in Greek.

sacristy A room attached to the choir of a church for keeping church plate, robes, and other articles used in divine office.

saddle roof A tall pitched roof with two steep slopes.

sanctuary The part of the church around the high altar in the choir.

Schloss The German word for a residential castle, mansion, or palace. Broadly equivalent to French *château*.

soffit The underside of an arch, vault, or cornice.

sopraporta (Italian) A painting or relief placed over a door, usually framed in harmony with the doorframe.

Staufen (or Hohenstaufen) Medieval dynasty that ruled Germany and the Holy Roman Empire in the 12th and 13th centuries. Their concept of a strongly centralized empire strongly influenced later German rulers.

tabernacle Receptacle for sacraments near the altar.

tetraconch A building or part of a building formed by four half domes.

Teutonic Knights A religious order of knights formed in the 12th century during the Crusades that later set up an independent state in East Prussia. Defeated by Polish forces at the battle of Tannenberg in 1410.

thermae window A semi-circular window divided vertically by two mullions.

tracery The internal stone supports and decorative pieces of Gothic windows. Early windows contained plate tracery, i.e. the window was cut into a thin wall of stone. Later windows used bar tracery, building patterns with slender shafts of stone.

transept "Arms" of a cross-shaped church; the shorter transverse section intersecting with the *nave* at the *crossing*.

triptych A painting in three sections, usually an altarpiece, consisting of a central panel and two outer panels, or wings. In many medieval triptychs the two outer wings were hinged so that could be closed over the center panel. Early triptychs were often portable.

tromp l'oeil (French) Of a painting, illusionistic, creating the impression that objects depicted are actually present.

typology In Christian thought, the drawing of parallels between the Old Testament and the New. Typological studies were based on the assumption that Old Testament figures and events prefigured those in the New, e.g. the story of Jonah and the whale were seen as prefiguring Christ's death and resurrection.

vault A roof or ceiling whose structure is based on the arch. There are a wide range of forms, including: the barrel (or tunnel) vault, formed by a continuous semi-circular arch; the groin vault, formed when two barrel vaults intersect; and the rib vault, consisting of a framework of diagonal ribs supporting interlocking arches.

veduta pl. vedute A painting or drawing of a city or landscape which is topographically correct; a "view."

velarium An awning hung over an open space or ceiling.

verde antico A greenish ornamental marble.

villa Originally an ordinary residence in the country, but after the Renaissance acquired palatial features.

westwork The west end of a Carolingian or Romanesque church, usually consisting of a small room above the main portal, galleries, stair turrets, and a tower.

winged altar A Gothic altarpiece consisting of a center section (the shrine) with hinged side panels, which contain carvings or paintings.

Artist Biographies

Corina Pertschi

Adam, François Gaspard
23.5.1710 Nancy – 18.8.1761 Paris Sculptor. Member of the Adam family of sculptors: youngest son of Jacob Sigisbert Adam, brother of Lambert Sigisbert Adam and Nicolas Sébastien Adam, uncle of Sigisbert and Claude (Clodion) Michel. Trained in his father's workshop until 1729; 1730 followed his brothers to Rome to study and work on restoring classical antiquities there; 1733 returned to France with Sigisbert Adam and settled in Paris; 1741 awarded first prize for sculpture and a scholarship to Rome by Académie Royale; 1746 returned to Paris via Florence, where the title of Professor of the Academy for Painting and Sculpture was conferred on him; 1747–1759 principal court sculptor of Frederick II; 1759 settled in Paris.
Representative of French Rococo whose work shows influence of French Baroque; did numerous works for Sanssouci Park in Potsdam.
Selected works: Sanssouci Park: figures round large fountain: *Apollo with Slain Python*, 1752. *Diana Bathing*, 1753. *Fire*, 1756. *Juno with a Peacock*, 1753, *Jupiter and Io*, *Earth*. 1758, *Minerva*, 1760, SPSG, Potsdam.

Adam, Lambert Sigisbert
10.10.1700 Nancy – 13.5.1759 Paris Sculptor. Most important member of the Adam family of sculptors. Eldest son of Jacob Sigisbert Adam, brother of François Gaspard and Nicolas Sébastien Adam, uncle of Sigisbert and Claude (Clodion) Michel. Pupil of his father; trained in Metz, worked in Paris from 1719; 1723 scholarship to Rome, where he restored Cardinal Melchior de Polignac's collection of antiquities; 1733 invited to Paris by the Duc d'Antin; 1737 member and 1744 professor of the Académie Royale in Paris.
His mythological and allegorical figures reveal a Rococo style tinged with classicism. Restored numerous ancient works in Rome that later passed into Frederick II's possession.
Selected works: Busts: *Eldest Daughter of Lycomedes*, *Odysseus*, *Leaning Daughter*, *Deidamia*, all after 1729, SPSG, Potsdam. *Air (Return from the Hunt)*, 1749, SPSG, Potsdam.

Arnim, Heinrich Ludwig Ferdinand von
15.9.1814 Treptow an der Rega – 25.3.1866 Potsdam. Architect and watercolorist. 1833 studied land surveying in Berlin; 1833–1838 student at the Architectural Academy under K. F. Schinkel and J. G. K. Hampel; 1844 Royal Inspector of Works; 1845 court architect for immediate works at the Court Building Commission; 1849 court architect to Prince Frederick Charles of Prussia as successor to Persius; 1846 teacher at Architectural Academy; from c. 1857 Professor of Design; 1861 head of Court Planning and Control Office.
Representative of the Schinkel School. His watercolors depict landscapes and especially buildings of Potsdam, the Rhine valley, and Italy.
Selected works: buildings in Glienicke: *Cloister*, 1850. *Gatekeepers' lodges*, 1842, 1849; *Hunting lodge*, 1859–1862; *Swiss Houses*, c. 1865. Buildings in Potsdam: *Mortuary Chapel*, 1846; *Villa Arnim*, 1847. As site architect: *Friedenskirche*, 1845-1848; *Pfingstberg Palace*, 1849-1862; *Lindstedt Palace*, c. 1858.
Watercolors: *Nikoliakirche in the Old Market Place*, c. 1850, Plankammer, SPSG Potsdam. *The Friedenskirche in Sanssouci*, c. 1850, Plankammer, SPSG Potsdam.

Begas, Reinhold
15.7.1831 Berlin – 3.8.1911 Berlin. Sculptor. Son of the court painter Karl Begas senior and brother of Karl Begas junior; pupil of J. G. Schadow at the Berlin Academy; 1848 joined the studio of C. D. Rauch; 1855–1858 in Rome; 1860–1863 taught at the Grand Ducal School of Art in Weimar; 1863–1864 in Rome; from 1865 in Berlin; 1876 head of a master studio at the Academy of Arts.
Main representative of Neo-Baroque and representative of the "state style" of the Emperor William II. His sensuous, painterly style displays features of both the Baroque and Neo-classicism.
Selected works: *Amor and Psyche*, 1857, sculpture collection, SMBPK Berlin. *Venus and Amor*, 1864, Neue Pinakothek, Munich. *Tomb of Frederick III*, mausoleum in Sanssouci Park, SPSG Potsdam. *Neptune Fountain*, 1886–1891, Alexanderplatz, Berlin. *Emperor William National Monument*, 1892–1897, formerly in front of the Berlin Palace, demolished with it in 1950. *Bismarck Monument*, 1897–1901, formerly in front of Reichstag, since 1938 at the Grosser Stern.

Behrens, Peter
14.4.1868 Hamburg – 27.2.1940 Berlin. Painter, designer and architect. 1885 student of painting at Karlsruhe School of Art; 1888–1889 private pupil of the painter Ferdinand Brütt in Düsseldorf; 1889 moved to Munich; private pupil of the painter H. Kotschenreiter; became independent painter; 1893 co-founder of the Freie Vereinigung Münchner Künstler (Free Union of Munich Artists); 1897 abandons painting; does designs for the Vereinigte Werkstätten für Kunst im Handwerk (United Workshops for Art in Craft), founded 1898; correspondent of the art periodical *Pan*; 1899; invited by Grand Duke Ernst Ludwig of Hesse-Nassau to join the newly established art colony in Darmstadt (Darmstadter Künstlerkolonie); 1903–1907 director of Düsseldorf School of Arts and Crafts, where he reorganized the teaching; from 1907 artistic adviser to AEG manufacturers in Berlin; 1922 succeeded Otto Wagner as head of the master architects' school at the Academy in Vienna; from 1936 head of the masters' studio at the Academy of Arts in Berlin.
His AEG turbine shop (1908–1909) was the first artistic design for an industrial building of steel and glass.
Selected works: buildings in Berlin: *AEG turbine factory*, 1908–1909. *Berolina Building*, 1929. Buildings in Frankfurt: *Hoechst Administrative*, 1920–1924.

Benckert, Johann Peter
11.9.1709 Neustadt an der Saale – 14.12.1769, Potsdam. Sculptor. Pupil of Kaspar Eygens in Eichstätt, then self-educated in Munich; apprenticed to F. A. Schlott, whose workshop he took over in 1739; from 1740, joint workshop with Gottlieb Heymüller; appointed to Bamberg by Prince-Bishop Frederick Carl, Count Schönborn; after 1746, appointed to Potsdam.
A leading sculptor under Frederick II, he worked in sandstone, marble, and wood, and also designed sculptures for casting in lead and bronze.
Selected works: Potsdam Palace: *Corps de Logis*, central block, groups of figures left and right of entrance: *Apollo and Minerva*, 1750; banisters and herms in stairwell. Lustgarten: *Triumph of Neptune*, group of figures cast in lead 1748 (collaboration, design by J. A. Nahl, 1746). Sanssouci Park: statues in front of art gallery; *Neptune and Two Nymphs* in the grotto. Chinese House: *Group of Chinese Drinking Coffee; Group with Falconer; Bombardon Player; Harpist and Castagnet Dancer; Melon-eating Group; Female Bell-ringer; Lute-player*, all 1754–1757. Façade sculptures of art gallery: *Sculpture; Painting; Geography; Optics; Engraving; Geometry; Patronage*, all 1758–1760. Façade sculptures of New Palace (Neues Palais): *Two Nymphs; Female jamb figure; Youth; Diana; Clytemnestra or Penelope; Agamemnon or Odysseus; Pyrrha; Deucalion; Hunter*. City of Potsdam: obelisk in the Old Market Place: *Sphinxes on the Cornice, and Medallions with the Prussian Rulers*, 1758–1760.

Blechen, Carl
29.7.1798 Cottbus – 23.7.1840 Berlin. Painter. 1822–1823 studied at the Berlin Academy of Arts under landscape painter P. L. Lütke; 1823 study tour of Saxony and Dresden, where he visited the painter J. C. C. Dahl and presumably encountered Caspar David Friedrich as well; 1824–1827 scenery painter at the Königstädtisch Theater in Berlin; 1826 admitted to Berlin's Künstlerverein (Society of Artists); 1828–1829 Italian tour; from 1831 Professor of Landscape Painting at the Berlin Academy; from 1835 Member of the Academy; 1835 trip to Paris; 1836 excused teaching work at the Academy because of mental illness.
One of the most important landscape painters of the Romantic era and forerunner of Realism in Germany.
Selected works: *The Villa d'Este in Tivoli*, 1831–1832, National Gallery, SMBPK Berlin. *Terni Park with Girl Bathing*, 1835, National Gallery, SMBPK Berlin. *Palm House Interior* (series) 1832–1834, SPSG Potsdam. *Rolling Mill near Eberswalde*, 1834, National Gallery, SMBPK Berlin.

Bodt, Jean de
6.5.1670 Hoquoncourt/France – 3.1.1745 Dresden. Architect and engineer. Studied in Paris under N. F. Blondel and in London; visits to Holland and England; 1698 appointed to Berlin as inspector of all civil and military buildings; 1700 took over construction work on the palace in Potsdam, 1728 invited to Dresden; from 1738 director of civil architecture there.
Representative of quasi-classicist Dutch-French Baroque. Exercised great influence on Saxon architecture as teacher of major architects and as drafter of the building regulations.
Selected works: buildings in Berlin: completion of *Arsenal*, 1699–1706. *Schwerin Palace*, c. 1702–1704. *Design of Tower of the Parochialkirche, Berlin*, 1713–1714 (carried out by Philipp Gerlach), destroyed.

Boumann the Elder, Jan (Johann)
1706 Amsterdam – 6.9.1776 Berlin. Architect, ship's architect, master carpenter and joiner. 1732 invited to Potsdam, where he worked for G. W. von Knobelsdorff; 1748 appointed Director of Works in Berlin; 1755 moved to Berlin. His buildings display Dutch stylistic influences.
Selected works: buildings in Berlin: *Berlin Cathedral*, 1747–1750 (with Knobelsdorff), demolished. *Hedwigskirche*, 1747–1773, site architect (following plans by Frederick II and Knobelsdorff). *Prince Henry's Palace* (now Humboldt University), 1748–1753 (following plans by Frederick II and Knobelsdorff). Buildings in Potsdam: *Dutch quarter*, 1737–1742. *City Hall*, 1753.

Brunsberg, Hinrich
c. 1350 probably in East Prussian state of Teutonic Knights – after 1428 presumably in Stettin. Architect. 1372 acquired civic rights in Danzig; 1400 first mentioned in *Liber querelarum* of the city of Stettin; 1428 last documentary mention in ecclesiastical records of Stettin. Had a workshop in Stettin for at least 30 years. Major architect of north German brick Gothic. One of the first architects in north Germany to develop an individual style.
Selected works: *Katharinenkirche*, Brandenburg, c. 1400. Works attributed to him: *Mariankapelle and choir of the St. Marien parish church, Stargard*, c. 1380–1400. *Marienkirche*, Königsberg/Neumark (Choina): choir 1389–1407, nave c. 1440–1459 (probably following Brunsberg's draft design). *City Hall*, Tangermünde, east wing and gable front, c. 1420 or 1430.

Chodowiecki, Daniel Nikolaus
16.10.1726 Danzig – 7.2.1801 Berlin. Painter, etcher and draftsman. Largely self-taught. 1743 apprentice merchant and painter of miniatures in Berlin, 1754 set up joint practice with his brother as enamel painter (learnt from the Augsburg painter Haid); studied at Bernhard Rode's private academy; 1764 member of the Berlin Academy of Arts; 1797 director of the Academy; decisive role in reviving the academy.
Most important German graphic artist of the 18th century. Central subject matter of his art is the family and every domestic life of the middle classes; numerous book illustrations

and pictures in calendars. His art often contains didactic and moral elements, revealing the influence of the Enlightenment.
Selected works: illustrations for: Basedow's *Pedagog. Elementarwerk*, J. K. Lavater's *Physiognomische Fragmente*, G. E. Lessing's play *Minna von Barnhelm*, Lawrence Sterne's *Empfindsame Reise durch Frankreich und Italien* (Sentimental Journey). Painting: *Cala's Farewell*, 1767, picture gallery, SMBPK Berlin.

Corinth, Lovis
21.7.1858 Tapiau, East Prussia – 1925 Zandvoort (Holland), painter and graphic artist. 1876 studied at Königsberg Academy of Art under Otto Günther; 1880 moved to Munich; 1887 moved to Berlin; 1891 moved to Munich; 1892 joined the newly established Munich Secession; 1893 co-founder of the Freie Vereinigung Münchner Künstler (Free Union of Munich Artists) and consequent expulsion from the Secession.
Selected works: *Self-portrait with Skeleton*, 1896, Städtische Galerie im Lenbachhaus, Munich. *Donna Gravida*, 1909, National Gallery, SMBPK Berlin. *Panorama of Lake Walchen, View from the promontory*, 1924, Wallraf-Richartz Museum, Cologne. *Ecce Homo*, 1925, Öffentliche Kunstsammlung, Basle.

Cornelius, Peter von
29.9.1783 Düsseldorf – 6.3.1867 Berlin. Painter. From 1798, studied at Düsseldorf Academy; 1811 trip to Rome; 1812 admitted to Lukasbund; 1821–1824 director of Düsseldorf Academy; from 1825, director of Munich Academy; 1840 King Frederick William IV appointed him Director-without-Portfolio in Berlin.
Leading representative of the Nazarenes; endeavored to revive German art by re-awakening interest in fresco painting.
Selected works: frescoes: *Story of Joseph*, Casa Zuccari of Consul General Bartholdy, Rome, since 1887 in National Gallery, SMBPK Berlin. *Mythological Scenes for Munich Glypthothek*, 1819, destroyed. *Trinity and the Last Judgment*, 1829, Ludwigskirche, Munich. Paintings: *Siegfried's Farewell*, 1816–1817, Wallraf-Richartz Museum, Cologne. *Holy Family*, Städelsches Kunstinstitut, Frankfurt am Main. Graphic work: *Illustrations for Goethe's "Faust"*, 1810–1816. *Nibelung illustrations*, from 1811–1812.

Degen, Dismar
before 1700 in Holland – 1751 presumably in Potsdam. Painter. Working c. 1730 in Pommersfelden; 1731 appointed to Potsdam by Frederick William I.
Painted landscape and historical pictures, especially battle scenes, including pictures of battles involving the Great Elector, hunting scenes, and portraits.
Selected works: *The Hunter's Gate*, c. 1735, Stern Hunting Lodge, SPSG Potsdam. *Construction of the Oranienburger Strasse in Berlin*, c. 1735, New Palace, SPSG Potsdam. *Monbijou House*, before 1740, Charlottenburg Palace, Berlin SPSG.

Dieussart, François
1600 Arquinghem (Hennegau) – 1661 London. Sculptor. 1622–1630 in Rome; 1622 enrolled in fraternity book of San Guiliano dei Fiamminghi; 1630 head of fraternity; from 1640 in England, working for Charles I, doing sculptural work for the palace of Whitehall; 1641 settled in Holland; did marble statues of the four Princes of Orange for the stadholder, Frederick Henry; 1647 member of St. Luke's guild in The Hague; 1647 presumably moved to Berlin after death of the stadholder Frederick Henry; 1647–1656 in the service of the Great Elector; later presumably resident in Brussels.
Selected works: *The Great Elector*, 1647, marble relief, Stichting Huis Doorn. *Electress Louise Henriette*, 1647, marble relief, Stichting Huis Doorn. *Dutch stadholders William I and William II of Orange*, 1646–1647, marble statues, formerly at Potsdam Palace, not preserved. *Philip William of the Palatinate-Neuburg, Mary of Orange*, both 1647, marble busts, Orangery Roundel), Sanssouci Park, SPSG Potsdam. *Prince William Henry of Brandenburg*, 1648, seated statue, sculpture collection, SPSG Potsdam. *Elector Frederick William of Brandenburg*, c. 1651–1652, marble statue, sculpture collection, SPSG Potsdam.

Ebenhech, Georg Franz
? – 21.2.1757. Sculptor, plaster worker, and ivory carver. Early 1740s had a sculpture workshop in Leipzig; moved to Berlin; 1751 honorary member of the Academy of Arts; collaborated with François Gaspard Adam on decorative and sculptural works for Sanssouci Park in Potsdam.
Selected works: Sanssouci Park, Potsdam: Abduction Roundel: *Rape of the Sabine woman, Paris and Helen, Pluto and Proserpine, Bacchus and Ariadne*, all c. 1750. Neptune grotto, Sanssouci Park, Potsdam: *Group of Naiads*, 1757. Sanssouci Palace, Potsdam, groups of figures on the architrave of the Marble Hall (Marmorsaal): *Painting, Sculpture, Architecture*. Berlin Opera House: *Figural ornamentation*. Katharinenkirche: *Twelve Apostles*.

Eosander von Göthe, Johann Friedrich Nilsson
(baptized) 23.8.1669 Stralsund – 22.5.1728 Dresden. Architect. 1685 worked in Riga; from 1692 in Berlin, court architect there from 1699; from 1707 site architect at the palace in succession to Schlüter; from 1709 principal director of works; 1713 major general in Swedish service, from 1722 in Saxon service.
Selected works: *Schönhausen Palace*, 1704, near Berlin. *Oranienburg Palace (extension)*, 1706–1709. *Monbijou Palace (center section)*, 1706–1708, Berlin (destroyed in war). *Charlottenburg Palace (dome and side wings)*, from 1704, Berlin. *Berlin Palace* (west wing and portal), 1707–1713 (war-damaged building blown up in 1950). *Uebigau Palace*, 1724–1726, near Dresden.

Erdmannsdorff, Friedrich Wilhelm von
18.5.1736 Dresden – 9.3.1800 Dessau. Architect. 1750–1754 studied at the Ritterakademie (school for young aristocrats) in Dresden; 1754–1757 studied at Wittenberg University; 1761–1763 in Italy; 1763 entered the service of the Dessau prince Leopold Frederick Francis (as friend, companion, and art adviser); joint journeys to Holland and England; 1765–1767 Italian tour with Leopold Frederick Francis; 1770–1771 another trip to Italy; 1775 trip to England with Leopold Frederick Francis; 1786 honorary member of the Royal Academy of Arts and Mechanical Sciences in Berlin; 1787–1789 (with interruptions) employed by Frederick William II of Prussia for architectural work in Berlin and Potsdam; 1789–1790 trip to Italy; 1791 trip to Weimar with Leopold Frederick Francis, and subsequent stays at the courts of Gotha, Kassel, and Karlsruhe; 1796 artistic director of the Chalkographic Society in Dessau and major architect of Early Classicist style in Germany.
Selected works: *Wörlitz Palace*, 1769–1773. Dessau: *Orangery*, 1793–1794, *Court theater*, 1798. Berlin Palace (Lustgarten wing): *Royal Chambers*, 1787–1789. Potsdam: *Marble Palace*, 1787–1788 (presumably as consultant).

Eyserbeck, Johann August
1762–1801. Landscape gardener. Son of Wörlitz court gardener Johann Friedrich Eyserbeck. 1777 studied under the Prince's Landscape, Pleasure and Orange Gardener Ernst Anton Oberheyde in Oranienbaum; 1782 apprentice gardener under the Landscape and Pleasure Gardener August Gottlob Ludwig in Winkler's Garden, Leipzig; 1782–1783 apprentice gardener in the Great Garden under the Court and Pleasure Gardener Johann Gottfried Hübler; 1786 or 1787 appointed to Potsdam; Court Gardener under Frederick William II.
Selected works: *New Garden (Neuer Garten)*, 1787–1797, Potsdam. Berlin: *Peacock Island (Pfaueninsel), park of Charlottenburg Palace*, (rebuilding).

Gärtner, Eduard
2.6.1801 Berlin – 22.2.1877 Berlin. Painter. 1811 first lessons in drawing from the court painter F. W. Müller in Kassel; 1813 return to Berlin; 1814–1820 worked at KPM (Royal Porcelain Factory); 1821 scene-painter at the studio of the court theater painter Carl W Gropius; 1825–1828 resident in Paris; 1828 settled in Berlin; 1829 member of the Berlin artists' society Berlinscher Künstler-Verein; 1833 full member of the Academy of Arts; 1837 and 1838 trips to Russia; from 1841 numerous study tours (Prague, March of Brandenburg, Bohemia, West Prussia), 1864–1870 trips to central Germany, north Germany and Austria; 1870 moved to Zechlin in the March of Brandenburg.
Most important German architectural painter of the 19th century, distinguished especially for his work chronicling the architecture of Berlin.
Selected works: *Stairwell in Berlin palace*, 1828, Berlin. *Charlottenburg Palace* and *Schlüter Courtyard of the Berlin City Palace*, both 1830, both SPSG Potsdam. *Unter den Linden with Monument of Frederick II*, 1853, National Gallery, SMBPK Berlin.

Gericke, Samuel Theodor
1665 Berlin (Spandau) – 12.7.1729 Berlin. Painter of historical scenes. From 1687 studied under G. Romandon at Elector's expense; 1694 visit to Rome with Elias Terwesten to make casts of antique works in the Papal collection for the newly established Academy; studied in Rome under Carlo Maratta; after his return 1696 court painter; from 1699 member and teaching professor of the Academy of Arts; 1705–1729 Director and Rector of the Academy.
Painted historical scenes and ceilings for the royal palaces.
Selected works: *Ceiling painting in Caputh Palace, corner cabinet*, 1687. *Altar* (design), 1715, the Nikolaikirche, Berlin. *Portraits of the Great Elector Frederick I and Frederick William I*, Magistrates' Court, Berlin City Hall.

Gerlach, Philipp
24.7.1679 Berlin (Spandau) – 17.9.1748 Berlin. Architect. While on military service, worked for the Building Administration; 1702 captain; 1707 succeeded royal director of works Martin Grünberg as head of city Building and Works department, Berlin; 1711 major of engineers; court architect to Frederick William I; 1720 architectural director of royal palaces. Planned the new town of Friedrichstadt in Berlin, and the reconstruction of Pariser Platz and Wilhelmstrasse.
Selected works: buildings in Potsdam: St. *Nikolai*, 1721–1724. *Garnisonkirche (Garrison Church)*, 1730–1735. Buildings in Berlin: *Supreme Court (Kammergericht)*, 1733–1735 (rebuilt 1965). *Marschall Palace*, 1735–1737. *Royal Gold and Silver Factory*, 1735–1737.

Gilly, David
7.1.1748 Schwedt – 5.5.1808 Berlin. Architect and writer on architecture. Father of the architect Friedrich Gilly. 1761 pupil at the Building Administration in the Neumark; 1770 master architect; from 1770 deputy to Chief Architect of Pomerania, C. Dornstein; 1776 appointed successor to Dornstein; from 1788 in Berlin; Privy Principal Head of Overall Planning and Control Dept and member of Principal Building Department; 1793 set up an architectural school (precursor of the Architectural Academy) in Berlin; 1799–1804 teacher at and director of the newly established Architectural Academy; 1802 member of the Academy of Arts; vice-director of the Principal Court Works Office; 1803–1806 vice-director of the Principal Works Department; various travels: 1801 Saxony and Bohemia, 1803 France; 1806 lost all his positions on dissolution of civil administration. His architecture is notable for its use of cubic forms with few classicizing features.
Written works on architecture: *Handbuch der Land-Baukunst* (Manual of National Architecture), Berlin 1797–1811. *Sammlung nützlicher Aufsätze und Nachrichten die Baukunst betreffend* (Notes on Architecture), Berlin 1799 ff. *Abriss der Cameral-Bauwissenschaft* (Outline of Building Finance), Berlin 1799. (With J. A. Eytelwein) *Praktische Anweisung zur Wasserbaukunst* (Practical Guide to Hydraulic Engineering), Berlin 1808–1818.
Selected works: *Paretz Palace and village*, 1796–1803. *Freienwalde Palace*, 1798–1799. *Vieweg House*, 1801–1804, Brunswick.

Gilly, Friedrich
16.2.1772 Altdamm near Stettinn – 7.8.1800 Karlsbad. Architect. Son of the architect David Gilly; studied under Langhans and Erdmannsdorf, and at the Academy in Berlin under G. Schadow and Chodowiecki; 1793 traveled to Paris; 1796 Principal Inspector of Court Works; 1797 study tours to England, France, southern Germany and Vienna; 1798 professor at the newly founded Architectural Academy his father had established; 1799 founded Privatgesellschaft junger Architekten (Private Society of Young Architects). Leading representative of the Berlin School of architecture, where his most important pupil was K. F. Schinkel; his numerous unrealized designs display influences of the architecture of the French Revolution.
Written works: *Einige Gedanken über die Notwendigkeit, die verschiedenen Theile der Baukunst in wissenschaftl. und prakt. Hinsicht möglichst zu vereinigen*, in *Sammlung nützlicher Aufsätze und Nachrichten die Baukunst betreffend*, published by his father's Royal Prussian Principal Works Dept, Vol 3/II, Berlin 1799.
Selected works: *Design for a National Monument*, 1797, Kupferstichkabinett, SMBPK Berlin. *Design for a National Theater in Berlin*, 1800, Academy of Arts, Berlin.

Glume the Younger, Friedrich Christian
25.3.1717 Berlin – 1752 Berlin. Sculptor. Pupil of his father Johann Georg Glume the Elder; worked at the court of Frederick II with J. A. Nahl under the direction of Knobelsdorff; participated in the sculptural decoration of numerous buildings in Berlin and Potsdam; principally sandstone sculptures in a late Baroque style.
Selected works: palace park, Rheinsberg: *Flora*, 1733. *Sphinxes on Steps*, c. 1741. Rheinsberg Palace: *Sculptural ornamentation*,

1737–1741. Berlin Opera House: *Sculptural decoration*, 1742–1743 (collaboration). Pleasure garden colonnade, Potsdam: *Sculptural decoration* (collaboration). Royal stables, Potsdam: *Horse Tamer*. French Church, Potsdam: *Façade decoration*, 1751–1753.

Gontard, Carl von (Carl Philipp Christian)
13.1.1731 Mannheim – 23.9.1791 Breslau. Architectect. 1741 came to the court of the Margrave Frederick and his wife Wilhelmina in Bayreuth, where he later became *maître de ballet*, but was persuaded by C. Galli-Bibiena to take up architecture; trained in architecture and drawing under the Bayreuth architect J. Saint Pierre and R. H. Richter from Berlin; 1749 employed as conductor at Court Works Office; 1750 sent by the Margrave to Paris for further training under J. F. Blondel; 1755 succeeded Saint Pierre as structural engineer in Bayreuth; from 1756 raised to rank of captain of engineers; 1764 moved to Potsdam to become Frederick II's architect-in-chief; from 1779 in Berlin as Royal Director of Works and member of the Immediate Construction Commission; 1788–1791 teacher at the Academy of Arts.
Most important architect of the late Fridercian era.
Selected works: buildings in Sanssouci Park, Potsdam: *New Palace Communs with Triumphal Arch*, by 1769. *Temples of Friendship and Antiquity*, 1768. Potsdam city: *Military Orphanage*, from 1771. Buildings in Berlin: *Royal, Hospital, and Mohrenstrasse Colonnades*, 1776 and 1786, *Royal Chambers in the Berlin Palace*, from 1785. *Domed towers of the Deutsche Kirche and Französische Kirche (German and French Churches) in Gendarmenmarkt* (after the collapse of the tower in the German cathedral in 1781, the work was carried out by G. C. Unger).

Gropius, Martin Carl Philipp
11.8.1824 Berlin – 13.12.1880 Berlin. Architect. 1843–1846 studied at the Trades Institute; 1849–1855 studied at the Architectural Academy in Berlin; associate of J. H. Strack; from 1856 independent architect; 1856–1865 also taught at the Academy; 1865 full-time at the Academy; 1866 became professor there; 1866–1880 partnership with Heino Schmieden; 1867 head of the educational side of the Arts & Crafts Museum founded jointly with him; from 1869 director of the Arts and Crafts School; member of the senate of the Academy of Arts and overall head of Prussian art schools.
Reformed art training and is considered principal representative of the post-Schinkel School. Also worked in arts and crafts, designing furniture, wallpaper, tiles and materials.
Selected works: buildings in Berlin: *Arts and Crafts Museum* (now Martin Gropius Building), 1875–1878 (with H. Schmieden). *University Surgical Clinic*, 1878–1883 (with H. Schmieden). *University Women's Clinic*, 1880–1882 (with H. Schmieden).

Grünberg, Martin
1655 near Insterburg, East Prussia – between 16 and 23.10. 1706 or 1707 in Berlin. Architect. 1674–1678 clerk at Drewitz Glassworks near Potsdam; clerk of works in Potsdam; 1682–1684 study tours to Italy and France; 1688 engineer; worked for J. A. Nering; 1695–1698 succeeded Nering as court architect; 1699 Director of Works in the Towns and in the Country; 1701 first architect member of the Academy of Arts in Berlin.
Representative of Dutch Baroque. Particularly distinguished for his work in Protestant church architecture.
Selected works: buildings in Berlin: *Sebastianskirche*, 1694. *Arsenal*, 1695–1698. *Garnisonkirche (Garrison Church)*, 1701–1703, destroyed. *Grunewald hunting lodge* (conversion), 1705. *Deutschen Kirche (German Church)* (carried out 1701–1708 by G. Simonetti, renovated 1881–1882 by H. von der Hude and J. Hernicke), Gendarmenmarkt.

Hackert, Jakob Philipp
15.9.1737 Prenzlau – 28.4.1807 San Piero di Careggi, Florence. Landscape painter and graphic artist. Son of the portrait painter Philipp Hackert; pupil of his father; from 1754 studied at the Academy of Arts in Berlin under its director Blaise Nicholas le Sueur; 1762–1765 in Stralsund and on the island of Rügen; 1765–1768 in Paris; from 1768 in Rome; from 1782 in Naples, 1786–1799 court painter under King Ferdinand IV there; 1799 fled to Florence following the Lazzaroni uprising. Hackert undertook many journeys, particularly to Italy. His landscape *vedute* are notable for their strict classicist compositions.
Selected works: *The Spree and Palace Bridge near Charlottenburg*, 1762, SPSG Potsdam. *Venus Pool in Berlin Tiergarten*, 1764, National Museum, Stockholm. *The Palazzina Borghese near Pratica di Mare*, 1780, National Gallery Nationalgalerie), SMBPK Berlin. *Gathering the Vintage near Sorrento*, 1784, Wallraf-Richartz Museum, Cologne. *Riverscape with Shepherd and Flock*, 1806, Nationalgalerie, SMBPK Berlin.

Hagemeister, Karl
12.3.1848 Werder/ Havel – 6.8.1933 Werder/Havel. Painter. From 1871 studied at the academy in Weimar under E. Preller Senior; 1873 struck up friendship with the painter Carl Schuch; study trips to Belgium, Holland and Italy; 1877 settled in Ferch; collaboration there with Carl Schuch; 1883 visit to Paris; 1907 on island of Rügen. Initially he painted still-lifes, hunting scenes, botanical studies and landscapes, but later preferred sea scenes (pictures of waves and billows). His later works are characterized by use of impasto.
Selected works: *Houses beside Lake Schwielow in Ferch*, 1878, National Gallery, SMBPK Berlin. *Marcher Landscape*, 1880, National Gallery, SMBPK Berlin. *Pool in the March with Duck Taking Off*, c. 1891, Bröhan Museum, Berlin. *Rocky Shore with Beech Tree*, 1913, Bröhan Museum, Berlin. *Waves in a Storm*, 1915, Bröhan Museum, Berlin.

Henry, Suzette, née Chodowiecka
26.7.1763 Berlin – 27.3.1819 Berlin. Painter. Daughter of Daniel Nikolaus Chodowiecki; pupil of her father and Anton Graff; from 1787 in Potsdam, from 1795 resident in Berlin; 1789 member of the Academy; from 1818 regularly represented at academy exhibitions; painted genre scenes, pictures of children and portraits.
Selected works: two series (eight paintings per series): *Good and Bad Upbringing*, 1800; *Happy and Unhappy Marriages*, 1802. Series (3 paintings) *The Pleasures of the People; the Middle Classes; and High Society*, 1804. Three paintings illustrating Wieland's "Oberon," 1812.

Hesse, Ludwig Ferdinand
23.1.1795 Belgard (Pomerania) – 8.5.1876 Berlin. Architect and painter. 1819 studied at the academies of art and architecture in Berlin; 1825 architectural exam; 1826–1827 study tours to Austria, south Germany and the Rhine; 1830 highways architect in Potsdam; 1832 inspector of court building works in Berlin; 1834–1835 and 1838–1839 trips to Italy and Sicily; trips to Russia and the Nordic countries; 1847 manager of Court Planning and Building Control Office; 1859 director of Court Planning and Building Control Office; 1865 Privy Director of Court Planning and Building Control Office; 1844–1863 worked in construction office in Potsdam, completing works by L. Persius; 1863 director of Palace Building Commission; 1843 member of the Academy of Arts; 1866 member of the senate of the Academy of Arts; 1871–1873 chairman of the Berliner gemeinnützige Baugesellschaft (Berlin charitable building association) founded by F. A. Stüler in 1847.
Representative of the Schinkel School, and principally active in Potsdam during reign of Frederick William IV.
Selected works: buildings in Potsdam: *Grape House*, 1849 (design by Frederick William IV). *Triumphal Arch*, 1850–1851 (design by F. A. Stüler, 1848). *Three Kings' Gate (Dreikönigstor)*, 1850–1851.

Heymüller, Johann Gottlieb
c. 1710–1715 Steyr – 1763 Potsdam. Sculptor. 1725–1735 presumably in Vienna; 1740–1746 in Bamberg; from 1746 in Potsdam. Carried out a large number of sculptural works in connection with the rebuilding and extensions of Potsdam city palace under Knobelsdorff's direction; took part in the building work in the town of Potsdam during the time of Frederick II; also did work at Sanssouci Park.
Selected works: Potsdam city palace: *Decorative Figures on West Wing*. Heads: statues of *Minerva* and *Hercules*; pediment reliefs: *Apollo with the Muses*, east wing; *Peace Offering*, west wing, 1750–1751; collaborated on *sculpture decoration of the stairwell* following its rebuilding by Knobelsdorrff. Carp pond, pleasure garden: *Triumph of Neptune* group (cast in lead by Heymüller and Benckert, design by J. A. Nahl, 1746); *Four Caryatids on the Obelisk in the Alter Markt. Attic Figures and Coat-of-Arms on City Hall*. Chinese House, Sanssouci Park: *Groups of Chinese Making Tea; Drinking Tea; Eating Pineappples. Bell-ringer; Fiddler; Horn-player; Clarinetist; Guitarist*, 1754–1757. Façade sculptures of art gallery in Sanssouci Park, Potsdam: *Philosophy. Historiography. Astronomy. Drawing. Study of Antiquity. Harmony. Natural Truth in Art*, all 1758–1760.

Hoffmann, Ludwig
30.7.1852 Darmstadt – 11.11.1932. Architect. Studied at the Academy of Art in Kassel; 1874 architectural studies at the Architectural Academy in Berlin and also under R. Lucae, F. Adler and J. H. Strack; 1879 Royal Government Architect; 1896 head of City Planning and Building Control Office. Built numerous school and administrative buildings in Berlin. Selected works in Berlin: *Marcher (Märkisches) Museum*, 1896–1908. *Frederick William University* (extension), now Humboldt University, 1913–1919. Leipzig: *Imperial Court*, 1887–1895.

Ihne, Ernst Eberhard von
23.5.1848 Elberfeld – 21.4.1917 Berlin. Architect. Briefly studied Modern Languages and Arts; prolonged visit to England; studied at the polytechnic in Karlsruhe; studied in Berlin at the Architectural Academy and from 1870–1872 in Paris at the Ecole des Beaux Arts; subsequently private architectural practice; 1878–1888 partnership with P. Stegmüller in Berlin; from 1888 court architect to Emperor William II; 1896 Privy Director of Planning and Control Office; 1899 member of the Academy of Building; 1906 ennobled; 1910 hon. member of the Ecole des Beaux Arts.
Built showpiece monumental buildings in neo-Baroque style for Emperor William II.
Selected works: buildings in Berlin: *New Royal Stables*, 1896–1902. *Emperor Frederick Museum* (now Bode Museum), 1897–1904. *Prussian State Library*, 1903–1914.

Kalide, Theodor
8.2.1801 Königshütte – 23.8.1863 Gleiwitz. Sculptor. Trained at the Royal Iron Foundry, Gleiwitz; 1819 model department, Iron Foundry, Berlin; pupil of J. G. Schadow at the Academy of Art; 1821 pupil of Christian Daniel Rauch; 1831 member of the Academy of the Arts; learnt the art of chasing from Louis François Coué; worked in Rauch's workshop principally on animal sculptures. His piece *Bacchante Riding a Panther* of 1846 aroused indignation because of its apparently liberal, naturalistic representation.
Selected works: *Equestrain Statue of Frederick William III*, post 1826–1828, Schinkel Pavilion, Charlottenburg Palace, SPSG Berlin. *Minister of State Count Reden*, 1850–1853, Königshütte.

Kaulbach, Wilhelm von
15.10.1805 Arolsen – 7.4.1874 Munich. Painter. 1822 studied at the Düsseldorf Academy under P. Cornelius; from 1826 in Munich, where in 1837 he became court painter of King Ludwig I of Bavaria; 1838–1839 visit to Rome; 1849 director of the Academy.
His work consists principally of historical scenes and portraits, but also illustrations; his most monumental paintings and murals are imbued with a classicizing pathos.
Selected works: *The Destruction of Jerusalem*, 1842–1847, Neue Pinakothek, Munich. *King Ludwig Surrounded by Scholars and Artists*, 1850, Neue Pinakothek, Munich. *Picture Cycle in stairwell of the New Museum (Neues Museum), Berlin*, 1847–1863 (destroyed in the war). *King Ludwig I as Grand Master of the Order of St. Hubert*, 1845, Neue Pinakothek, Munich.

Kiss, August
11.10.1802 Paprotzan/Upper Silesia – 24.3.1865 Berlin. Sculptor. Trained in his native ironworks and the iron foundry at Gleiwitz; further education in the foundry at Brieg-Liegnitz; from 1822 worked for Leopold Posch at the Royal Iron Foundry in Berlin, also attending Academy of Arts; 1825–1840 worked at workshop of Christian Daniel Rauch; 1830 teacher of chasing and modeling at the bronze foundry of the Crafts Institute; 1837 member of Academy; 1841 professor of the Academy.
Known best for his equine pieces. Worked almost solely in iron and bronze.
Selected works: *Amazon in Battle*, 1837–1842, Altes Museum, Berlin. *Equestrian Statue of Frederick the Great*, 1841, Breslau. *Statue for the Beuth Monument*, 1854–1861, Märkisches Museum, formerly Schinkelplatz, Berlin.

Knobelsdorff, Georg Wenzeslaus von
17.2.1699 Kuckädel Estate nr Crossen (Oder) – 16.9.1753 Berlin. Architect, painter, and landscape gardener. Pupil of the Prussian court painter Antoine Pesne; soon took up study of architecture instead; 1732 became a teacher and artistic adviser of the later King of Prussia, Frederick II; 1734 took part in Rhine campaign; 1736–1737 study tour to Italy; 1740 Director of Prussian palaces and gardens, trip to Paris.
Up to 1750 Frederick II's principal architect.
His buildings combine elements of Rococo with elements of English, Dutch and French Neo-classicism (Fridercian Rococo).
Selected works: *Rheinsberg Palace* (rebuilding and extension), 1737–1739. *Berlin Opera House*, 1741–1743. Rebuilding and

extension of Charlottenburg Palace in Berlin, 1740–1743, and of *Potsdam Palace*, 1744–1752. *Sanssouci Palace*, 1744–1748, Potsdam.

Knoblauch, Karl Heinrich Eduard
25.9.1801 Berlin – 29.5.1865 Berlin. Architect. Father of Edmund and Gustav Knoblauch. 1818 studied at the Berlin Academy of Art; 1824 co-founder of the Architektenverein (Association of Architects), chairman until 1862; 1828 passed out as architect; 1824–1830 various travels in Europe, including Italy (with F. A. Stüler); 1854–1861 editor of *Zeitschrift für praktische Baukunst* (Journal of Building Practice); 1845 member of the Academy of Arts; considerably involved in the reorganization of the architectural academy and development of new building regulations. First major private architect (not a civil servant) in Prussia. Active chiefly in building residences.
Selected works: buildings in Berlin: *Villa Busse*, 1837, Tiergarten (Zoo), destroyed. *Kroll Establishment*, 1842–1844, Tiergarten (Zoo), destroyed. *Arnim-Boitzenburg Palace*, pre-1857, Kreuzberg, destroyed. *Jewish Hospital Administration Building* (now Max Planck High School), 1858–1860, center. *Synagogue*, 1859–1866, center, Oranienburgerstrasse, rebuilt.

Kollwitz, Käthe (née Schmidt)
8.7.1867 Königsberg, East Prussia – 22.4.1945 Moritzburg Palace, nr Dresden. Graphic artist, sculptor, and painter. 1881 drawing lessons from E. Neide in Königsberg; 1885–1888 studied at the drawing academy of the Verein der Künstlerinnen (Woman Artists Society) in Berlin under K. Stauffer-Bern; 1888–1889 studied painting under L. Herterich in Munich; 1890 studies of elements of working-class life in Königsberg; 1904 spent several weeks in Paris working in the sculpture class of the Académie Julian, also visiting Rodin's workshop; 1907 Villa Romana Prize founded by Max Klinger, which goes with extensive study trip to Florence; 1919 first female member of the Academy of Arts, became a professor and was granted a studio at the Academy; 1914 younger of her two sons killed in World War I; 1927 travels to the Soviet Union (at invitation of its government); 1928 head of masters' workshop for graphic art at the Berlin Academy; 1933 Nazis force her to give up her studio at the Academy and quit the Prussian Academy; given a studio in the studio community in Klosterstrasse, but gave it up on the death of her husband in 1940; 1936 unofficial ban on exhibiting; 1943 moved in with the sculptor Margarete Böning in Nordhausen; 1944 Prince Ernest Henry of Saxony provided her with accommodation near Moritzburg Palace.
Selected works: graphic works: *The Revolt of the Weavers'* (cycle; three lithographs and three etchings, 1897. Wood carving series: *War* and *Proletariat*, 1922–1925. Lithographic series: *Death*, 1934–1935. Sculpture: *Parents*, 1924–1932, Roggevelde military cemetery near Dixmuiden (Flanders). *Mothers' Tower*, 1937–1938. *Pietà*, 1937–1938. *Lamentation*, 1938–1940.

Krebs, Konrad
1492 presumably in Büdingen – 31.8.–1.9.1540 Torgau. Architect. Trained as stonemason; from 1532 in Coburg as stonemason in employ of John Frederick the Magnanimous, Elector of Saxony; in Berlin from 22.4 to 1.6.1537 to hand over his design for a palace and to introduce his pupil Caspar Theiss as site architect of the palace.
Selected works: *Wittenberg Palace Church*, 1516. The *Moritzkirche* (collaboration), 1520, Coburg. *Hartenfels Palace (John Frederick Building)*, 1532–1536.

Krüger, Franz
3.9.1797 Badegast nr Köthen – 21.1.1857 Berlin. Painter and graphic artist. 1812–1814 studied at the Berlin Academy; 1825 member of the Berlin Academy of Arts, Prussian court painter and awarded professorial rank; from 1836 did works for St. Petersburg court; 1848–1849 in Dessau during revolutionary turmoil; Trips to St. Petersburg, 1846 trip to Paris; painted mostly parades, hunting scenes (nicknamed Horse Krüger) and portraits of Berlin society; his work is marked by precision of detail and sober depiction.
Selected works: *Opernplatz Parade*, 1824–1829, National Gallery, SMBPK Berlin. *A Prussian parade*, 1839, SPSG Potsdam. *Two Cuirassiers of the Emperor Nicholas I's Regiment*, 1839, SPSG Berlin.

Langerfeld, Rutger von
15 2.1635 Nijmegen – 15.3.1695 Berlin. Painter and architect. 1678 appointed court painter in Berlin by the Great Elector; 1689 court mathematician and court architect to Elector Frederick III (King Frederick I of Prussia); taught the Elector's sons, Princes Ludwig and Philip William, drawing and mathematics.
Selected works: ceiling paintings for the Berlin palace: *Perseus on Winged Steed* and *Rider in Antique Apparel*, c. 1683–1685, destroyed with the palace. Buildings: *Köpenick Palace* begun 1681 (completed by J. A. Nering). *Dorotheenstädtische Kirche*, 1678–1687, Berlin.

Langhans, Carl Gotthard
15.12.1732 Landeshut/Silesia – 1.10.1808 Grüneiche near Breslau. Architect. Father of the architect Carl Ferdinand Langhans. Dropped study of mathematics in favor of architecture; study trips to Italy (1768–1769), Holland, England and France; from 1775 head of Planning and Control Office in Breslau; 1786 invited to Berlin by Frederick William II; 1788 head of Principal Works Office there; member of the founding commission of the Architectural Academy. His design for the *Brandenburg Gate* (1788–1791) is considered the first high point of Neo-classical architecture in Germany.
Selected works: buildings in Berlin: *Colonnades in Mohrenstrasse*, 1785–1790. *Opera House* (rebuilding), 1787–1788. *Anatomy Theater, Veterinary College*, 1789–1790. *Theater, Charlottenburg Palace*, 1788.

Lehmbruck, Wilhelm
4.1.1881 Duisburg – 25.3.1919 Berlin. Sculptor, painter, and graphic artist. 1895–1899 studied at crafts school; 1901–1907 studied at Düsseldorf Academy, where he was a master pupil of K. Janssen; 1906 and 1912, study tours to Italy; 1910–1914 Paris; 1914 first major individual exhibition there; 1914–1917 Berlin, joined Free Secession and became its jury member; after outbreak of WWI became medical orderly; Jan–April 1916 in Strasbourg as "war painter in the field"; 1917–1918 Zürich, made contact with anti-war faction; 1919 Berlin; 1919 suicide. Among the leading representatives of German Expressionist sculpture.
Selected works: *Standing Youth*, 1913, Museum of Modern Art, New York. *Girl Meditating*, 1913–1914, Staatsgalerie, Stuttgart. *The Fallen Man* 1915–1916, Wilhelm Lehmbruck Museum, Duisburg.

Leistikow, Walter
25.10.1865 Bromberg/Bydgoszcz – 24.7.1908 Berlin. Landscape painter and graphic artist. Until 1887, studied under Hermann Eschke and Hans Gude; 1890–1893 teacher at the Berlin School of Art; 1892 co-founder of the Group of XI; 1899 leading role in the founding of the Berlin Secession, whose presidium he remained a member of until he died.
One of his favorite pictorial settings was the Marcher lake landscape around Berlin. His landscape paintings show stylistic influences of Art Nouveau and Impressionism. Also did craft designs for wallpaper, curtains, and glass windows.
Selected works: *Evening Mood on Lake Schlachten*, c. 1895, Berlin Museum. *Lake Grunewald*, 1898, National Gallery, SMBPK Berlin. *Evening Landscape in the March*, 1897, Ostdeutsche Galerie, Regensburg Museum.

Lenné, Peter Joseph
29.9.1789 Bonn – 23.1.1866 Potsdam. Landscape gardener and town planner. 1805–1808 trained in gardening in Brühl under his uncle Clemens Weyhe; 1811–1812 studied in Paris; study trips to Germany, Switzerland and Austria; commissioned to plan the palace park at Laxenburg near Vienna; plans for transforming the fortifications of Koblenz; 1816 invited to Potsdam; 1818 member of the Garden Directorate; 1822 co-founder of the Association for Promoting Horticulture in the State of Prussia; 1824 director of the royal gardens; 1824 established the National Tree Nursery and the Gardeners' College in Potsdam Deer Park, the first further education institutions for gardeners and landscape gardeners in Germany; 1830–1831 traveled to southern Germany and western Europe; 1837 trip to Brussels; 1844 trip to Paris; 1847 trip to Italy; 1854 General Director of Gardens; 1858 made honorary citizen of Potsdam; 1861 honorary doctor of University of Breslau; honorary member of the Prussian Academy of Arts. Considered a precursor of modern landscape design. Created a new type of park, the first German public park (in Magdeburg 1824). His park designs follow the style of English landscape gardens.
Selected works: Berlin: *Charlottenburg Palace park*, 1819. *Tiergarten* (zoo; transformation into a public park), 1833–1839. *Zoological Garden*, 1842. Potsdam: *Sanssouci Park*, 1816. *New Garden*, 1816. *Babelsberg Park*, 1833.

Lepsius, Reinhold
14.6.1857 Berlin – 16.3.1922 Berlin. Portraitist. Son of the Egyptologist Richard Lepsius, 1892 married the portraitist Sabine Graef; studied at the art school in Karslruhe; trained in Munich under Ludwig von Loefftz; influenced by Franz von Lenbach.
Selected works: *Carl Justi*, 1912, National Gallery, SMBPK Berlin. *Ernst Curtius* and *Field Marshal von Eichhorn*, Städelsches Kunstinstitut, Frankfurt am Main.

Lepsius, Sabine, née Graef
15.1.1864 Berlin – 1942 Berlin. Portrait painter, daughter of the painter Gustav Graef, wife of the portrait painter Reinhold Lepsius. Initial training from her father; 1884–1886 studied under Karl Gussow in Berlin; 1887–1889 studied in Paris under Lefèvre and Constant.
Selected works: *Poritrait of the Artist's Daughter*, Berlin, National Gallery, SMBPK Berlin.

Leygebe, Gottfried Christian
1630 Freystadt/ Silesia – 1683 Berlin. Sculptor, iron worker, and engraver. 1653 working in Nuremberg for the armorer Albrecht Liechtmann; employed solely on cutting iron; pupil of the sculptor and iron cutter Georg Pfründ; 1668 moved to Berlin and appointed Electoral master minter, medalist, and sculptor. Produced mainly medals and coins with portraits of the electoral family. Leygebe cut formes for Potsdam glassworks and arms and ornamental models for the artillery foundry.
Selected works: medals: *The Elector as a member of the English Order of the Garter*, 1663? *Return of the Elector from Prussia to Berlin*, 1669. *Electress Dorothea*, Birth of Princess Mary Amalia 1670. *The Heir Charles Emil* (1655–1674), *Return to Berlin from the Campaign in Alsace*, 1673. *The Heir Frederick William*, 1677, all Münzkabinett, SMBPK Berlin. *The Great Elector*, 1671, bronze relief, sculpture collection, SMBPK Potsdam. *The Great Elector as St. George*, 1680, sculpture collection, SMBPK Berlin.

Liebermann, Max
20.7.1847 Berlin – 8.2.1935 Berlin. Painter and graphic artist. Born to a distinguished Jewish manufacturing family. 1863–1864 taught by K. Steffeck; 1868–1872 studied at the art school in Weimar under P. Thumann, F. W. Pauwels and C. Verlat; 1871 went to Düsseldorf to study under the Hungarian painter Mihály Munkácsy; 1871 short visit to Holland; 1872 followed Munkácsy to Paris, where Jean-François Millet became his great model; from 1872 repeated visits to Holland; 1878 left Paris for Munich; 1882 member of the Cercle des XV (Circle of 15) in Paris; 1884 return to Berlin; 1889 member of the Société Nationale des Beaux Arts; 1892 co-founder of the XI group of artists; 1898 founder member of the Berlin Secession, 1899–1911 its first president; 1896 chevalier of the Legion d'Honneur; 1897 professorial status; 1898 member of the Academy of Arts; 1920 president, 1932 honorary president of the Prussian Academy of Arts; 1933 ban on painting and exhibiting; 1933 resigned from Academy.
His work encompassed landscapes, portraits and genre paintings, characterized by a combination of Realism and Impressionism.
Selected works: *Free Period in the Amsterdam Orphanage*, 1882, Städelsches Kunstinstitut, Frankfurt am Main. *Flax Barn in Laren*, 1887, National Gallery, SMBPK Berlin. *Portrait of Dr Max Linde*, 1897, Museum für Kunst und Kulturgeschichte, Lübeck.

Lisiewska, Anna Rosina
1713 or 10.6.1716 Berlin – 1783 Dresden. Painter. Daughter of Prussian court painter G. Lisiewski, sister of Anna Dorothea Therbusch and Christian Lisiewski, like them a pupil of her father. Mother of G. D. Matthieu. Imitated Pesne in Berlin; turned down an invitation to work in Dresden; 1756 went to Zerbst, following the death of her husband, the painter David Matthieu; later to Brunswick with her second husband, civil servant Ludwig de Gasc; appointed court painter in Brunswick; 1766–1767 visit to Holland. Painted mainly portraits, clearly manifesting influence of A Pesne initially and later D. Matthieu.
Selected works: *Lady Feeding a Parrot*, 1747, SPSG Potsdam. *Duchess Philippine Charlotte of Brunswick*, c. 1770, SPSG Potsdam.

Lisiewski, Christian Friedrich Reinhold
1725 Berlin – 11.6.1794 Ludwigslust. Painter. Son of Georg Lisiewski, and also his pupil; 1752–1772 court painter in Dessau; 1752 and 1755 worked in Leipzig and Dresden; 1772

return to Berlin, where he occasionally worked together with his sister Dorothea Therbusch; 1779 went to Ludwigslust, succeeding his deceased nephew G. D. Matthieu as court painter; 1783 honorary member of the Academy of Arts.
Chiefly painted portraits of the middle classes and the royal family.
Selected works: *Crown Prince Frederick Francis of Mecklenburg-Schwerin*, 1780, SPSG Potsdam. *Friedrich Balthasar Schönberg von Breukendorff (Colonizer of Netzebruch)*, SPSG Berlin.

Lohse, Adolph Hermann
30.8.1807 Berlin – 1867 Berlin. Architect. 1827 land surveyor's exam; 1828–1829 did his practical training in government service in Frankfurt an der Oder (hydraulic engineering) and under Langhans at the City Planning and Control Office in Berlin; studied at the Architectural Academy in Berlin; 1833 member of Association of Architects; 1840–1846 private architectural practice in Berlin; 1847 architect's exam; 1846–1849 national architect at the Ministry for Ecclesiastical Affairs); 1855–1856 travels (Paris, Belgium, England, Ireland, Scotland, Switzerland, Italy), partly with F. A. Stüler; 1856 inspector of works at the Ministerial Construction Commission; 1862 head of Court Planning and Control Office.
Selected works: *Palace of Prince Albrecht of Prussia*, 1850–1855, Dresden. *Villa Stockhausen*, Dresden.

Lynar, Rochus Guerini, Count of
25.12.1525 Maradi, near Florence – 22.12.1596 Spandau. Architect and fortifications engineer. Brought up at the Florentine court; friend of Cosimo I de' Medici, the Duke of Florence; equerry of the French Dauphin, later Henry II; 1550 Commissioner General for all royal fortifications; 1550s took active part in campaigns as an officer; 1554 in diplomatic service in Saxony, Hesse and Berlin; 1560 converted to Protestantism; 1561 constructed citadel of Metz, probably his first independent commission; from 1564 resident in Metz; 1567 Huguenot uprising in Metz led by Lynar; flees after failure of rebellion; 1568 colonel and military adviser in the Palatinate; 1569 principal architect for the fortifications of Dresden, colonel of artillery and domestic ordnance master in the service of the Elector of Saxony; at the same time, active as adviser in Hesse, Anhalt and the Palatinate; from 1577 in Dessau; from 1578 entered Brandenburg service in Berlin while retaining his earlier posts; general of artillery, ordnance master and architect to the Elector John George.
Major achievements also in economic affairs. Principally active as architect of fortifications and palaces.
Selected works: *Citadel*, 1561–1564 Metz. Buildings in Dresden: *Palace Bastion*, 1569, *Wagon House and wall of Arsenal*, 1570–1573, *Palace Mint Works*, 1570, *Sawmill*, 1570: all destroyed. *Transverse Building between the two courtyards at Berlin Palace* (site architect for construction and rebuilding of further parts), from 1579, destroyed. *Salt Works*, 1580, Beelitz, destroyed.

Memhardt, Johann
1607 Linz/Drau – 1678 Berlin. Architect. c. 1622 Protestant family emigrated to Holland, where he trained as a fortifications architect; c. 1638–1640 entered Brandenburg service; 1641 appointed engineer to the Elector; 1640–1650 mainly in Pillau, the later military port of Frederick William; from 1650 employed in Berlin; from 1656 inspector of all the Elector's buildings; from 1658 head of fortifications; 1669 mayor of Friedrichswerder; 1670–1671 passes the responsibility for fortifications to L. H. de Chieze because of overwork. His fortifications largely determined the urban structure of Berlin. No buildings of Memhardt's survive in Berlin.
Selected works: In the *Lustgarten*, Berlin: *Pleasure House and Ballroom*, 1650 and 1661. *Plan of Friedrichswerder*, 1762. Oranienburg: *Palace* (rebuilding), 1651–1655 (together with M. M. Smids).

Menzel, Adolph von
8.12.1815 Breslau – 9.2.1905 Berlin. Painter and graphic artist. Trained at the lithographic institute founded in 1818 by his father and moved to Berlin in 1830; 1832 took over the lithographic institute after death of his father; 1833 brief attendance at plaster classes at Academy of Arts; thereafter largely self-taught; 1834 member of Jüngeren Künstlerverein Berlin (Berlin Association of Younger Artists); travels in Germany, Austria and Bohemia; 1855 and 1867–1868 traveled to Paris, 1876 to Holland, 1881 and 1882 to northern Italy; 1853 member of the Royal Academy of Arts; 1870 Pour le mérite order; 1898 ennobled.
Considered the most important German painter between Realism and Impressionism.
Selected works: *The Balcony Room*, 1845, National Gallery, SMBPK Berlin. *Flute Concert*, 1850–1852, National Gallery, SMBPK Berlin. *Departure of King William I for the Army on July 31, 1870*, 1871, National Gallery, SMBPK Berlin. *Iron Rolling Mill*, 1875, National Gallery, SMBPK. *The Dinner Dance*, National Gallery, Berlin SMBPK.

Messel, Alfred
22.7.1853 Darmstadt – 24.3.1909 Berlin. Architect. 1873 architectural studies at the Academy of Art, Kassel; 1874 studied at the Architectural Academy in Berlin under J. H. Strack, R. Lucae, C. Boetticher and H. Ende; 1878–1888 employed in state service; 1882 architect's exam; 1883 travel scholarship to Italy; 1885–1893 assistant in building department of Charlottenburg Technical High School, Berlin; 1892 member of the Building and Savings Union, Berlin; 1893–1896 professor at the educational institute of the Arts and Crafts School; from 1896 private architectural practice; 1904 member of the Prussian Academy of Arts.
Important representative of the transition from historicist styles to Modernism.
Selected works: *Wertheim Warehouse*, 1893–1894, Berlin, destroyed in the war. *Landesmuseum, Darmstadt*, 1892–1905. *Bank*, 1899–1900, Behrenstrasse/Französische Strasse, Berlin. *Pergamon Museum* (plan), 1906–1909, Berlin (built by Ludwig Hoffmann).

Meyer, Johann Heinrich Gustav
14.1.1816 Frauendorf/Neumark – 27.5.1877 Berlin. Landscape gardener. Pupil and for many years colleague of P. J. Lenné at the Royal Court Gardens Directorate at Sanssouci and the Gardeners' Institute in Potsdam Deer Park; 1859 court gardener; 1870–1877 first city gardens director of Berlin.
Planned the first public parks, in which sports and play facilities were increasingly incorporated.
Selected works: Berlin: *Friedrichshain*, 1846–1848 (plan for extension 1868, construction 1874–1876). *Humboldthain*, 1869–1875 (design 1866), Wedding. *Small Tiergarten*, 1876, Moabit. *Gardens at the World Exhibitions of Paris (1867) and Vienna (1873).*

Mies van der Rohe, Ludwig
27.3.1886 Aachen – 17.8.1969 Chicago. Architect and designer. Trained as stonemason under his father; practical experience in various architectural and construction offices; from 1901 courses at evening and Sunday classes, the later Building Trades School; 1905–1907 worked for Bruno Paul in Berlin; 1908–1911 changes to Peter Behrens; from 1912 independent architect; 1918 member of the November Group and head of its architectural section; 1926–1932 vice-president of the Deutscher Werkbund; 1930–1933 directorate of Bauhaus; 1937 emigrated to the USA; architectural office in Chicago; 1938–1958 director of the architectural department of the Illinois Institute of Technology, Chicago; from 1945 on awarded numerous decorations and became a member of several academies.
Among the most important pioneers of modern architecture.
Selected works: *German Pavilion*, 1928–1929, Barcelona. *Haus Tugendhat*, 1928–1930, Brünn. *New National Gallery (Neue Nationalgalerie)*, 1962–1968 Berlin.

Nahl, Johann August the Elder
22.8.1710 Berlin – 22.10.1781 Kassel. Sculptor and interior designer. Trained under his father Johann Samuel Nahl, the Berlin court sculptor and colleague of Andreas Schlüter; visits to Paris and Rome; from 1735 in Strasbourg, where he worked on the plasterwork for the Palais Rohan as an assistant to Robert Le Lorraine; 1741 invited to Berlin by Frederick II; until 1746 worked as Director of Ornamentation of the interiors and the sculptural parts of the exteriors of Charlottenburg Palace in Berlin and Potsdam City Palace; visits to Strasbourg and Switzerland; 1755 took up employment with the Landgrave of Hesse in Kassel; 1777 director of the sculpture department of the Academy in Kassel.
Major decorator in the style of Prussian Rococo.
Selected works: Potsdam: *Library at Sanssouci Palace*, 1745–1747. Berlin: *Sculptural decoration of State Opera House* (direction). Kassel: *Interior decoration of Wilhelmstal House*. Karlsaue: *Horse Tamer*, 1767. Parish church of Hindelbank near Berne: *Tomb for Maria Magdalena Langhans*, 1751.

Nering, Johann Arnold
17.3.1659 (baptized) Wesel – 21.10.1695 Berlin. Architect. From 1676 trained in fortifications architecture; worked as engineer on construction of fortifications and great houses; 1677–1678 study tour of Italy; 1679–1680 worked for Dutch architect M. M. Smids in Berlin; from 1684 Principal Engineer; 1685 Colonel of Engineers; 1691 Principal Director of state building works in Brandenburg-Prussia.
After Schlüter, the most important Baroque architect in Berlin.
Selected works: *Palace chapel, Köpenick, Berlin*, 1682–1685. *Friedrichstadt* (plannin), 1688–1695. *Side Wing of Potsdam Palace*, begun 1683, destroyed. *Berlin Palace, Gallery Wing and various rooms, pleasure garden with orangery, and library*, 1679–1688, destroyed. *Oranienburg Palace* (rebuilding and extension), 1690–1694. *Charlottenburg Palace* (design), Berlin, commenced 1695. *Lange Brücke (Long Bridge)*, Berlin, 1692–1695, replaced by new structure 1894.

Persius, Friedrich Ludwig
15.2.1803 Potsdam – 12.7.1845 Potsdam. Architect. Pupil of K. F. Schinkel at the Architectural Academy, Berlin; worked for Schinkel until the latter's death; 1842 head of Prussian Planning and Control Office. Close confidant of Frederick William IV.
Along with Stüler, the most important pupil of Schinkel. His work is imbued with Schinkel's late Neo-classicism, also the influence of the Italian Renaissance and Early Christian buildings of Italy. Successfully blended architecture and the surrounding landscape.
Selected works: buildings in Potsdam: *Roman Baths*, 1829–1836, Sanssouci Park. *Heilandskirche (Church of the Redeemer)*, 1841–1844, Sacrow. *Pheasantry, 1842–1844, Sanssouci Park*. Steam-Engine House, Babelsburg, Potsdam, 1844–1845. *Friedenskirche (Church of Peace)*, 1844–1854, Sanssouci Park.

Pesne, Antoine
23.5.1683 Paris – 5.8.1757 Berlin. Painter of portraits and historical scenes. Pupil of his father Thomas Pesne and his uncle C. de la Fosse; trained at Academy in Paris; 1705–1710 in Italy; invited to Berlin; 1710 settled in Berlin; 1711 appointed Prussian court painter; travels to the courts of Dessau (1715), Dresden (1718, 1728–1729), London (1723) and Paris (1723 and 1724); 1720 admitted to Académie Royale, Paris; 1732 appointed Director of the Academy of Painting and Sculpture.
Court painter under Frederick I, Frederick William I and Frederick II (the Great), he was an important Rococo-period portraitist; numerous commissioned works on mythological or allegorical subjects for the palaces of Rheinsberg, Charlottenburg in Berlin, and Sanssouci in Potsdam.
Selected works: *Queen Sophia Dorothea*, c. 1745, SPSG Potsdam.

Poelzig, Hans
30.4.1869 Berlin – 14.6.1936 Berlin. Architect. 1889–1894 studied architecture at Technical High School in Berlin; 1899–1903 teacher, 1903–1916 director of the Academy of Arts and Crafts in Breslau; 1916–1920 head of city planning and control office in Dresden and lecturer at Technical High School; 1919 chairman of the Deutscher Werkbund; 1920 member of the November Group; moved to Berlin; head of a master studio at the Prussian Academy of Arts; 1923 professor at the Technical High School in Berlin; shortly after he had been appointed director of the United State Schools for free and applied art in Berlin, the Nazis sacked him in 1933.
Representative of an architectural style close to Expressionism.
Selected works: buildings in Berlin: *Grosses Schauspielhaus (theater)*, 1919. *Radio Building*, 1930.

Pückler-Muskan, Prince Hermann of
30.10.1785 Muskau – 4.2.1871 Branitz Palace, near Cottbus. Gardener and writer on gardens. From 1801, studied law in Leipzig; 1803 lieutenant of the Gardes du Corps in Dresden; 1804 resigned from the army; traveled to Switzerland, France and Italy; 1810 returned; 1811 became mediate prince of Muskau on the death of his father; 1813 a major in Russian service; adjutant to the Duke of Saxony-Weimar; lieutenant-colonel and military governor of Bruges; after the peace treaty, traveled around England; then lived alternately in Berlin, Dresden, and Muskau; 1815 had a park laid out in the English fashion in Muskau; various journeys: Algeria (1835), Greece (1836), Egypt (1837), Near East and Asia Minor (1839); 1840 returned to Muskau; 1845 sold the lordship of Muskau and retired to his paternal estates in Branitz, where he laid out another park.
Most popular travel writer of his time and important landscape designer. Influenced the design of the parks in Babelsberg, Ettersburg near Weimar, Altenstein near Liebenstein and Wilhelmsthal near Eisenach.

Written works: *Andeutungen über Landschaftsgärtnerei* (Hints on Landscape Gardening), 1834. *Tutti Frutti. Aus den Papieren des Verstorbenen*, 5 vols, 1834. *Jugendwanderungen* (Youthful Travels), 1835. *Briefe eines Verstorbenen. Ein fragmentarisches Tagebuch aus England, Wales, Irland and Frankreich, 1828–1829* (A Fragmentary Diary from England, Wales, Ireland and France, 1828–1829), four parts, 1830–1832.

Raschdorff, Julius
2.7.1823 Pless, Upper Silesia – 13.8.1914 Waldsieversdorf/Strausberg. Architect. Studied at the Architectural Academy in Berlin; 1854–1872 city architect in Cologne; from 1872 independent architect in Cologne; 1878–1911 taught at the Technical High School in Charlottenburg, Berlin; 1884–1886 member of the senate, and 1888–1889 head of the architectural department of the Technical High School; 1892 Royal Cathedral Architect.
Selected works: buildings in Berlin: *Main building of Technical High School, Charlottenburg* (now Technical University), 1878–1884 (with F. Hitzig and R. Lucae), partly demolished. *Chemistry lab of Technical High School, Charlottenburg*, 1882–1884. *English Church of St. Georg*, 1884–1885. *Cathedral*, 1892–1905 (reconstructed in different form from 1974).

Rauch, Christian Daniel
2.1.1777 Arolsen – 3.12.1857 Dresden. Sculptor. 1786–1791 studied under the court sculptor Friedrich Valentin in Helsen; 1795 employed in Christian Ruhl's workshop in Kassel, where he went to the local Academy; 1797 in Potsdam as valet of Frederick William II, then of Queen Louisa; made models part-time and attended evening life-classes at the Academy under J. Gottfried Schadow, also archeological lectures of Alois Hirt; 1804 quit royal service voluntarily, scholarship to Rome; in Rome, made friends with Berthel Thorwaldsen and Wilhelm von Humboldt, who gave him substantial assistance; 1811 returned to Berlin, commission for the tomb of Queen Louise (1811–1815, mausoleum in park of Charlottenburg Palace, Berlin); 1811–1818 alternately in Berlin, Rome and Carrara; 1819 joint studio with Friedrich Tieck, who had been his workshop manager in Carrara; from 1819, professor at the Academy of Arts in Berlin; member of numerous academies and artistic associations at home and abroad.
Most important German sculptor of Neo-classicism, with numerous pupils (including Ernst Rietschel, Friedrich Drake, August Kiss, Theodor Kalide, Reinhold Begas).
Selected works: *Bust of Goethe*, 1820, Museum der bildenden Künste, Leipzig. *Victoriae*, from 1832, Walhalla near Regensburg. *Equestrian Monument of Frederick the Great*, 1839–1851, Unter den Linden, Berlin.

Rode, Christian Bernhard
25.7.1725 Berlin – 24.6.1797 Berlin, painter and etcher. Pupil of Antoine Pesne; 1748–1750 pupil of Carle Van Loo in Paris; 1752–1754 in Italy; 1756 member of the Berlin Academy of Arts; 1783 director of the Academy.
His work is distinguished for its treatment of new materials, which he reproduced in large-scale paintings and etchings; a focal point of his painting is Prussian history (influenced by the poems of Rabener and Gellert, Gessner and K. W. Ramler); cycles for aristocratic houses and mansions, of which only that painted for the Count von Hahn at Neuhaus Estate (Holstein) remains in situ.
Selected works: *Morning, Noon, and Evening*, three ceiling paintings for the New Palace (Neues Palais) in Potsdam, 1767, SPSG. *Memorial for Princess Amalia of Prussia, 1780, SPSG Potsdam.* Allegory of the Foundation of the German League of Princes, 1786, Gemäldegalerie, SMBPK. *The Death of Frederick the Great*, c. 1787, SPSG Potsdam. *Allegory of the Outbreak of the Seven Years War*, 1785, Gemäldegalerie, SMBPK Berlin. *Frederick II and the Soldier's Wife*, 1791, Gemäldegalerie, SMBPK Berlin. *Frederick II and the Army Doctor*, c. 1795, Gemäldegalerie, SMBPK Berlin.

Romandon, Gedeon
1667 Venice – 1697 Berlin. Painter. From 1686 in Berlin; from 1687 court painter in Berlin to the Great Elector; from 1689 court painter to Elector Frederick III and curator of the Elector's pictures; 1696 professor at the newly established Academy of Arts; early 1690 at the court in London; 1695 visit to Italy on behalf of the Great Elector, to copy the most famous paintings.
Selected works: *The Great Elector*, 1687–1688, SPSG Potsdam; *Eleonora Louise Erdmuthe, Margravine of Brandenburg-Ansbach with Her Son Prince William Frederick*, c. 1688, Charlottenburg Palace, SPSG Berlin.

Schadow, Johann Gottfried
20.5.1764 Berlin – 27.1.1850. Sculptor and graphic artist. From 1776 drawing lessons from Giovanni Battista Selvino, an assistant in the workshop of court sculptor J. P. A. Tassaert, later from Madame Tassaert; from 1778 pupil of the court sculptor Tassaert and training at the Academy of Arts; from 1783 assistant in Tassaert's court sculpture workshop; 1785–1787 in Italy; briefly at the private academy of Alexander Trippel in Rome, friendship with Antonio Canova; 1787 return to Berlin; employed at the KPM (Royal Porcelain Factory); from 1788 successor to Tassaert as head of the court sculpture workshop; 1805 rector, from 1815 director of the Berlin Academy of Arts.
His principal works were done during the reign of Frederick William II (1786–1797). Schadow is considered the founder of the Berlin School of sculpture.
Selected works: *Tomb of the Count of the March*, 1790, formerly in Dorotheenstädt Kirche, Berlin, now in the National Gallery, SMBPK Berlin. *Quadriga on the Brandenburg Gate*, 1793, Berlin. *Group of Princesses*, 1795–1797, National Gallery, SMBPK Berlin. Busts: *Henriette Herz*, 1785 or post 1787, archives of the Prussian Academy of Arts, Berlin. *Frederick Nicholas*, 1798, Berlin Museum. *Frederick Gilly*, 1800–1801, archives of the Prussian Academy of Arts, Berlin. Monuments: *Field Marshal Gebhard Leberecht von Blücher*, 1819, Rostock. *Martin Luther Monument*, 1821, Wittenberg. *Statue of General von Zieten*, 1794, formerly in Wilhelmsplatz, Berlin (1857 replaced by a copy by A. Kiss).
Schadow's written works on technical aspects of sculpture: *Polyclet, oder von den Maassen nach dem Geschlechte und Alter, mit Angabe der wirklichen Naturgrösse nach dem rheinländischen Zollstocke and Abhandlung von dem Unterschied der Gesichtszüge und Kopfbildung der Völker des Erdbodens*, Berlin 1834. *National-Physionomieen oder Beobachtungen über den Unterschied der Gesichtszüge und die äussere Gestaltung des menschlichen Kopfes, in Umrissen bildlich dargestellt auf neun und zwanzig Tafeln, als Fortssetzung des Policlet*, Berlin 1835.

Schadow, Wilhelm (Friedrich W.) von
6.9.1788 Berlin – 19.3.1862 Düsseldorf. Painter. Son of the sculptor J. G. Schadow; from 1808 studied painting at the Berlin Academy of Art under F. G. Weitsch; 1810–1819 in Rome, where he joined the Nazarenes; 1814 converted to Catholicism; from 1819 professor and head of the master class for painting at the Academy of Arts in Berlin; 1826 succeeded Peter Cornelius as director of the Academy in Düsseldorf; 1829 co-founder of the Art Association for the Rhineland and Westphalia; 1830–1831 and 1839–1840 in Rome. Services to academic teaching by reorganization of the Academy.
Painted mainly religious and historical subjects; portraitist to the Prussian court.
Written works: *Meine Gedanken über eine folgerichtige Ausbildung des Malers* (Thoughts on Training Painters), 1828, reprinted in Racynski, *Geschichte der neueren deutsches Kunst* (History of the New German Art), 1836. *Über den Einfluss des Christenthums auf die bildende Kunst* (Christian Influence on Fine Art), Düsseldorf 1842. *Der moderne Vasari* (The Modern Vasari), novella, Berlin 1854.
Selected works: *Queen Louisa*, 1810, SPSG Potsdam. *Self-Portrait with Ridolfo Schadow and Bertel Thorwaldsen*, c. 1818, National Gallery, SMBPK Berlin. Frescoes in the Casa Bartholdy, Rome: *Joseph's Coat* and *Joseph in Prison*, 1816–1817, from 1887, National Gallery, SMBPK Berlin.

Schinkel, Karl Friedrich
13.3.1781 Neuruppin – 10.1841 Berlin. Architect and painter, also set-designer, graphic artist, craftsman, interior designer and writer on architecture. From 1798 pupil in the workshop of F. and D. Gilly, 1799–1800 student at the newly established Berlin Architectural Academy; 1800 first architectural commissions; 1803–1804 trips to France and Italy; 1810 admitted to the Prussian Supreme Buildings Commission; 1810 ordinary member of the Berlin Academy of Arts; from 1830, head of planning and control office of Technical Supreme Buildings Commission; 1838 Principal National Architectural Director.
Most important German architect of the first half of the 19th century; Schinkel's buildings largely determined the appearance of Berlin; main representative of Classicist architecture; also built in neo-Gothic style (Friedrichwerder Church 1824–1831, Kreuzberg Monument 1810–1818, Berlin); development of a new system of architecture introducing the latest structural engineering techniques (Architectural Academy, Berlin, 1831–1836).
Selected works: painting: *The Cathedral*, 1811, SPSG. *Cathedral Above a Town*, 1813, Bayerische Staatsgemäldesammlung, Munich. *Medieval Town by the Water*, 1813. *Greek Landscape*, 1815. *Greece in Her Prime*, 1825, all National Gallery, SMBPK Berlin. *Designs for the murals in the lobby of the Old Museum in Berlin*, 1831, carried out under the direction of P. Cornelius 1845, destroyed in the war.
Buildings in Berlin: *New Guard House*, 1816–1818. *Schauspielhaus* (theater), 1818–1821. *Schlossbrücke* (bridge), 1822–1824. *Tegel Palace, for W. von Humboldt*, 1820–1824. *Museum in the Lustgarten*, 1823–1830.
Buildings in Potsdam: *Pomona Temple*, 1800. *Charlottenhof Palace*, 1826–1829. *Gardeners' house*, 1829–1833. *Roman Baths*, 1829–1836. *Glienecke Palace*, 1824–1827. *Babelsberg Palace*, 1832–1835.

Schirmer, Johann Wilhelm
7.9.1807 Jülich – 11.9.1863 Karlsruhe. Landscape painter and etcher. From 1825 studied at the Düsseldorf Academy under H. C. Kolbe; from 1827 joint landscape studies and founding of a composition union with C. F. Lessing; 1830 teacher at the Düsseldorf Academy; professor there from 1839; 1854 head of the newly founded academy in Karlsruhe, until 1863 professor of landscape painting there; travels: Belgium (1830), Switzerland (1835, 1837, 1853), Normandy (1836), Italy (1839–1840), south of France (1851).
Painted both naturalistic landscapes (influenced by the Dutch painter J. van Ruisdael among others) and made-up ideal landscapes (influence of French artists Lorrain and Poussin). Most noted pupils: A Böcklin and Hans Thoma.
Selected works: *Geroldsau Valley near Baden-Baden*, 1855, Staatliche Kunsthalle, Karlsruhe. *Romantic Landscape (Altenahr Castle)*, 1828, Kunstmuseum, Düsseldorf.

Schlüter, Andreas
13.7.1659 Danzig – end of May 1714 St. Petersburg. Sculptor and architect. Trained in Danzig under the sculptor Sapovius; 1681–1693 worked in Wilanow near Warsaw and Zólkiew near Lvov as a sculptor; from 1694 in Berlin as court sculptor to Frederick III; 1695 traveled to France and Holland; 1696 trip to Italy; in the same year, participated as adviser in the founding of the Academy of Arts; 1699–1702 and 1704–1713 one of the four rectors of and 1704–1713 director of the Academy; 1698–1699 site architect at the Berlin arsenal; 1699–1706 site architect at the Berlin Palace; 1699 appointed palace architect, later principal architect; 1701–1701 member of the Academy of Sciences; 1707 with the imminent collapse of the Mint Tower, Schlüter was replaced as palace architect by Eosander von Göthe; from 1713 director of works to Peter I in St. Petersburg, where he also taught at the Academy of Art. Schlüter was important both as a sculptor and as an architect.
Selected works: sculptures: *Façade decoration and reliefs on Krasinski Palace*, 1689–1694, Warsaw. *Alabaster tombs of J. Sobieski and St. Danillowicz, 1688–1692, parish church, Zólkiew.* Architectural sculpture on Berlin Arsenal, *1696. Equestrian statue of the Great Elector*, 1696–1700, formerly on the Lange Brücke of the Berlin Palace, now in the *cours d'honneur* of Charlottenburg Palace. *Marble tomb male*, 1700, Nikolaikirche, Berlin. *Tomb of Queen Sophie Charlotte*, 1705. *Sarcophagus for Prince Frederick Ludwig of Orange*, c. 1708. *Tomb of King Frederick I*, 1713, all in crypt of Berlin Cathedral.
Buildings: *Arsenal*, 1698–1699, Berlin. *Berlin Palace*, 1698–1706, Baroque rebuild, destroyed in 1950). *Foundry*, 1698–1707, demolished 1872, Berlin. *Kamecke Palace*, 1711–1712, destroyed 1943, Berlin.

Strack, Johann Heinrich
6.7.1805 Bückeburg – 13.6.1880 Berlin. Architect. From 1824 studied at the Academy of Architecture and Art in Berlin; 1825 land surveyor exam; 1825–1832 worked for K. F. Schinkel; 1832–1837 private architectural practice; from 1838, joint publisher of *Architektonisches Album* (Architectural Albun); from 1839, lecturer (from 1841, professor) at the Academy of Arts; from 1842 court inspector of works; 1853–1854 traveled to Italy and Sicily as companion and drawing master of Prince Frederick William; 1854–1880 professor at the Architectural Academy; from 1859 head of court planning and control office and member of Technical Building Commission; 1862 excavations in Athens with E. Curtius and C. Boetticher; 1875 principal of Planning and Control Office; from 1876, Emperor's Architect to William I.
Representative of the Schinkel School who built in Berlin and Potsdam.
Selected works: buildings in Berlin: *Crown Prince's Palace* (extension), 1858–1860, modern building a reconstruction. *Victory column*, 1865–1873 (1938–1939 moved from Königsplatz to the Grosser Stern and heightened). *Plinth of Kreuzberg Monument*, 1875–1878.

Buildings in Potsdam: *Flatow Tower*, 1853–1856. *Justice Lobby* (reconstruction), 1871–1872, both in Babelsberg Park.

Stüler, Friedrich August
28.1.1800 Mühlhausen – 18.3.1865 Berlin. Architect. 1818–1819 student at the Architectural Academy in Berlin, university and Academy of Arts; 1820–1823 site architect in Naumburg and Schulpforta; 1824 founded Berlin Association of Architects jointly with K. H. E. Knoblauch; 1827–1829 worked at court planning and control office in Berlin under Schinkel; 1829 court inspector of works; 1834–1842 lecturer at the Architectural Academy; from 1842 member of the Supreme Building Commission; from 1850, ministerial adviser in Ministry of Trade, Crafts and Public Works; 1840–1845 (with Persius) successor to Schinkel as adviser to Frederick William IV in all building matters.
As an important representative of the Schinkel School, Stüler's work was mainly in the Berlin-Potsdam area, with occasional commissions in other parts of Prussia, also Russia, Stockholm, and Budapest.
Selected works: churches: *Nikolskoe*, 1834–1836 (with A Schadow). *Caputh*, 1852. *Matthäuskirche*, 1846, Berlin. *Glindow*, 1853. *Bornstedt*, 1854–1855. *Cathedral in the Lustgarten*, 1842–1858 (designs), Berlin (built 1893–1905 by J. Raschdorff).

Terwesten, Augustin
4.5.1649 Ouwerkerk – 21.1.1711 Berlin. Painter and etcher. Worked in his father's workshops as a modeler and engraver; learnt painting from Nicolaus Wieling and Willem Doudijns; 1672–1675 in Italy; 1675–1678 in France and England; from 1678 in The Hague as a freelance painter; co-founder of and teacher at the Drawing Academy; 1692 appointed court painter to the Elector of Brandenburg in Berlin; from 1696 member of the Academy of Arts; director of the Academy 1698, 1700–1701, 1704–1705, 1707–1708, 1710–1711.
Selected works: ceiling and wall decorations: Berlin Palace: *Red Room of the Elizabeth Apartments*, 1702. *Work Room of William II: Pandora Introduced into the Assembly of the Gods by Vulcan*, 1704. *Princess Mary Apartments: allegory of Frederick William I as Crown Prince*, all destroyed. Central block of Charlottenburg Palace, Berlin: *Amor Flees Psyche*, 1696. *Mercury Introduces Psyche to the Assembly of the Gods*, 1698. Painting: *Venus and Adonis*, c. 1700, Charlottenburg Palace, SPSG Berlin.

Theiss, Caspar
c. 1510(?) – c. 1550 Berlin, architect. Worked for Konrad Krebs on Hartenfels Palace in Torgau; 1537–1538 palace architect in Berlin; 1539–1544 recorded in documents in Berlin; head of the Elector's works department. Worked on numerous palace buildings; ran a company (chartered 1539) for exploiting the mineral wealth of the Middle March jointly with the Elector's adviser G. Brage, K. Buntschuh and master minters P. Mohlradt and A. Schreck; 1544 founded the Beelitz Saltworks Company; Theiss appointed Master of Mills.
Considered the first well-known Renaissance architect in the March of Brandenburg.
Selected works: *Berlin Palace: Palace Square wing, 1537–1540*. Erasmuskapelle, from 1540, destroyed 1950. *Grunewald Hunting Lodge*, 1542–1543. *Nikolaikirche, Spandau* (construction of the spire), 1540, destroyed.

Therbusch, Anna Dorothea, née Lisiewska
23.7.1721 Berlin – 9. 11.1782 Berlin. Painter. Daughter of the Prussian court portraitist G. Lisiewski (1674–1750), trained by her father, like her brother and sister (Anna Rosina, 1713–1783, Christian Friedrich Reinhold, 1725–1794); active as a painter from 1760; 1761 in Stuttgart at the court of Duke Charles Eugene of Württemberg to paint 18 *sopraporte* (overdoors) for the Mirror Room of the palace; 1763 in Mannheim as court painter of Elector Charles Theodore of the Palatinate; 1764 return to Berlin; from 1765 in Paris; 1767 member of the Académie Royale in Paris; 1768 member of the Viennese Academy; 1768 left Paris, returning to Berlin 1769–1770 via Brussels and Holland.
Besides historical and genre paintings, she did portraits of member of the Prussian royal family. Her work shows the influence of the French artists Pesne, Greuze, and Boucher.
Selected works: *Frederick William II as Prince of Prussia*, c. 1773, SPSG Potsdam. *Self-portrait*, 1782, Germanisches Nationalmuseum, Nuremberg. *Wilhelmine Encke*, 1776, SPSG Potsdam.

Tieck, Christian Friedrich
14.8.1776 Berlin – 12.5.1851, sculptor. 1789 studied under Sigismund Bettkober, at the same time going to drawing classes at the Academy, 1794 employed at the workshop of J. G. Schadow; 1797 scholarship to Rome, but because of the turmoil of war went to Paris; 1798 employed at workshop of Jacques-Louis David; 1801–1805 in Weimar to do decorative work on the new palace buildings; 1805 scholarship to Rome; 1808–1809 traveled to Coppet and Munich; 1812–1819 Carrara, where he did 25 colossal marble busts of well-known personalities for the Walhalla near Regensburg, on behalf of Ludwig, Crown Prince of Bavaria; 1819 returned to Berlin; 1830 director of the sculpture department of the National Gallery in Berlin; from 1839 vice-director of the Academy on various occasions. Received sponsorship from the Humboldt brothers and C. D. Rauch.
Representative of the idealized classicist style created by Rauch.
Selected works: *The Spirit of Grossbeeren*, 1821. *The Spirit of Culm*, 1821. On the Kreuzberg Monument, Berlin: *Bust of Crown Princess Elizabeth of Prussia*, 1825, SPSG Berlin.

Ury, Lesser
7.11.1862 Birnbaum, Posen – 18.10.1931 Berlin. Painter and graphic artist. 1879–1880 studied at the Academy in Düsseldorf under A. J. J. Müller; 1882 in Brussels to study at the Académie Royale des Beaux-Arts under J. F. Portaels, and in Paris to study under J. Lefebvre; 1884 settle in Volluvet, near Brussels; 1886 studied at the Academy of Fine Arts in Munich under J. K. Herterich; from 1887 resident in Berlin; traveled to Italy, London, and Paris.
Among the precursors of Impressionism in Germany. Of particular interest are his night pictures, in which sundry light effects contribute to the picture. Painted numerous urban landscapes of Paris, London, and Berlin.
Selected works: *Berlin Street Scene (Leipzig Platz)*, 1898. *Reclining nude*, both Berlinsche Galerie, Berlin. *Nollendorfplatz at Night*, 1925, National Gallery, SMBPK Berlin.

Vanloo, Charles Amédée Philippe
1719 Rivoli, near Turin – 15. 11. 1795, painter. (Called the Prussian Van Loo, to distinguish him from his uncle Charles-André (Carle) Van Loo.) Pupil of his father Jean-Baptiste Van Loo; studied at the Académie Royale in Paris; 1738–1742 in Italy (Rome, Naples, Florence); until 1745 in Aix at his father's house; 1745 return to Paris; 1747 member of the Academy; 1748 appointed to the court of Frederick II in Berlin: 1758–1763 Paris; from 1763 back in Berlin; 1769 return to Paris; 1770 professor of the Academy in Paris: 1790 recteur-adjoint.
Painted numerous decorative paintings and portraits for the buildings of Frederick II.
Selected works: ceiling paintings: *Apotheosis of the Great Elector*, 1751, formerly SPSG Potsdam. *Ganymede Introduced into Olympia by Hebe*, 1768, SPSG Potsdam.
Paintings: *Sacrifice of Iphigenia*, 1749, *School of Athens*, 1749, both SPSG Potsdam. *Princess Louise of Anhalt-Dessau as Diana*, 1765, formerly in Berlin Palace, now Huis Doorn. *Princess Louisa Amalia of Prussia*, 1765, SPSG Potsdam. *Princess Louise of Prussia*, 1766, SPSG Potsdam. *Embarcation for Cythera*, 1750, SPSG Berlin.

Weitsch, Friedrich Georg
8.8.1758 Brunswick – 30.5.1828 Berlin. Painter and etcher. Son and pupil of J. F. Weitsch; trained in Kassel by F. H. Tischbein, further training in Düsseldorf, Amsterdam, and Italy; 1787 court painter in Brunswick; 1794 member of the Berlin Academy of Arts; 1798 director of the Berlin Academy and Prussian court painter.
Painted numerous historical and landscape paintings, but especially portraits, in the style of F. A. Tischbein and Anton Graff; later influence of French portrait painting of the Empire.
Selected works: *Princesses Louise and Frederica Crowning the Bust of Frederick William II*, 1793, SPSG Berlin. *Johann Gottfried Schadow and Wife* (pair of portraits) 1795, National Gallery, SMBPK Berlin. *The School of Plato*, 1797, Stiftung Archiv, Berlin Academy of Arts. *Frederick William III and His Wife in Charlottenburg Park*, 1799, SPSG Berlin.

Werner, Anton von
9.5.1843 Frankfurt an der Oder – 4.1.1915 Berlin. Historical painter. From 1857, three-year training as house painter; from 1860 studied at the Berlin Academy; 1866 scholarship to Italy; 1862 moved to Karlsruhe, where he collaborated with the Academy teacher Adolf Schroedter; 1865 trips to Paris; 1867 at the World Exposition in Paris as representative of the southern German states; 1871 moved to Berlin; 1875–1915 director of the High School for Fine Arts. Head of a master studio independently of the High School; 1875–1877 and 1882–1911 member of the Prussian National Art Commission; 1887–1895, 1899–1901, 1906–1907 chairman of the Association of Berlin Artists; 1899–1900 and 1902–1906 chairman of the Co-operative of Members of the Royal Academy of Arts, fine arts section; 1908–1909 head of the National Gallery, Berlin; 1910 appointed privy counselor. Had a major effort on the Kaiser's art policies through his various offices; his historical paintings deal with scenes from Prussian history, which are presented with naturalistic precision but exaggerated so as to form state propaganda; painted portraits of members of the imperial family, the army, politicians, and churchmen.
Selected works: *The Emperor's Proclamation in Versailles*, National Gallery, SMBPK Berlin (four different versions). *The Coronation of Frederick I in Königsberg*, 1887, formerly in Berlin Arsenal, war loss. *The Crown Prince at the Court Ball in 1878*, 1895 National Gallery, SMBPK Berlin. *The Unveiling of the Richard Wagner Monument*, 1908, Berlinsche Galerie, Berlin.

Wichmann, Ludwig Wilhelm
10.10.1788 Potsdam – 28.6.1859 Berlin. Sculptor. Brother of Carl Friedrich Wichmann; 1800 employed in workshop of J. G. Schadow; 1809–1813 in Paris, employed in the workshop of François Bosio and Jacques-Louis David; return to Schadow's workshop; 1818 succeeded Emanuel Bardou as teacher of modeling at the Arts and Crafts School; 1819 member of the Academy of Arts and teacher of ornamentation; 1819–1821 trip to Italy with his brother Carl; established a joint workshop with his brother; 1832 became professor of the Berlin Academy Further trips to Rome: 1851–1852, 1854–1855, 1857–1858.
Major representative of the Neo-classicist school of sculpture in Berlin.
Selected works: busts: *Prince William*, 1808. *Henriette Sonntag*, 1829, Mittelrhein Museum, Koblenz. *Johann Friedrich Ancillon*, 1838, SMBPK Berlin. *Tobias Christoph Feilner*, National Gallery, Berlin SMBPK.
Sculptural figures: *Eight Statues of Battle Allegories* (to his own designs and designs by Rauch and Tieck), 1826, Kreuzberg Monument, Berlin. *Amor and Psyche*, 1826, SPSG Potsdam. *Nike Gives Fresh Heart to a Wounded Soldier*, 1853, Schlossbrücke (bridge), Berlin. *Statue of Johann Joachim Winckelmann*, 1840–1850, National Gallery, SMBPK Berlin.

Abbreviations:
SPSG = Stiftung Preussische Schlösser und Gärten Berlin-Brandenberg.
SMBPK = Staatliche Museen zu Berlin Preussischer Kulturbesitz.

Index of Places

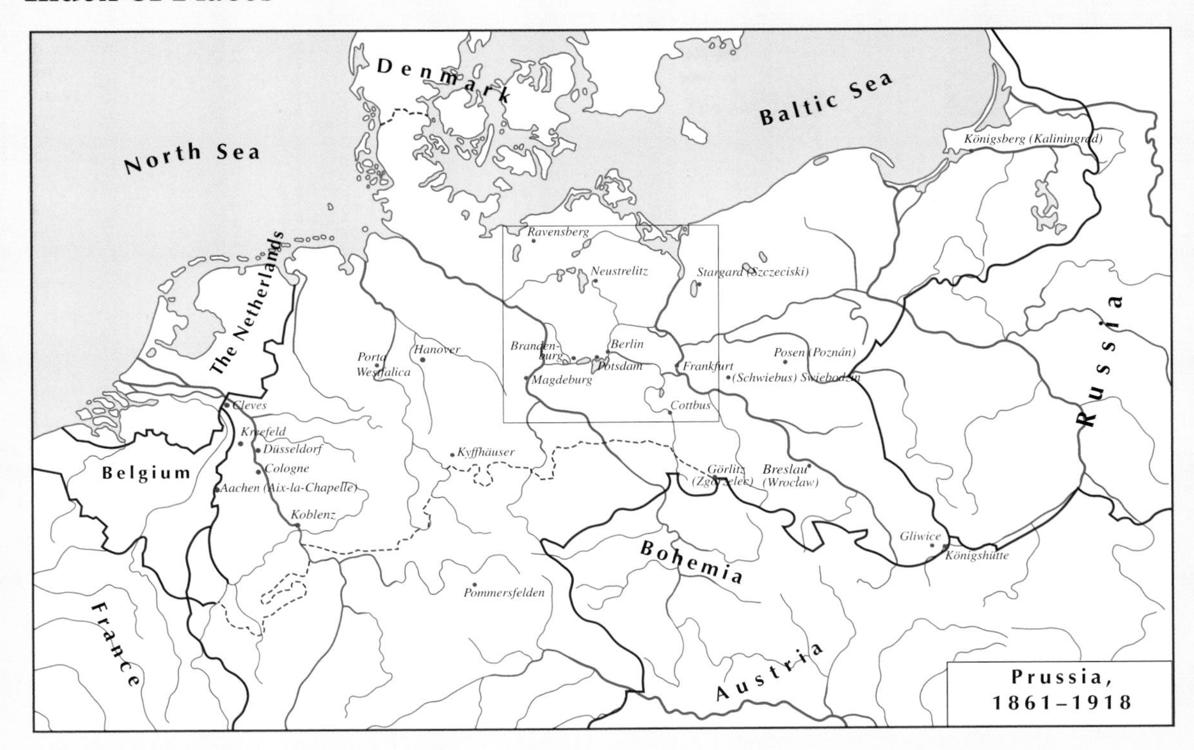

The present-day names of cities that are now part of Russia, Lithuania, or Poland appear in parentheses. Page numbers in italic in the lists of places and people indicate illustrations.

A

Aachen 393, 438
Alfeld an der Leine 447, *450*
Altlandsberg 42, 92
Altgolssen *494*
Angermünde *37*, 38, 40, *41*
Arneburg 32
Augsburg 63, 145, *146*, 151, 242

B

Baalbec 163
Bad Freienwalde 32
Bad Homberg von der Höhe *438*
Badingen 66
Bagow 67
Baumgartenbrück 346
Bayreuth 132, 164, *196*, 215, 222, 232f, 251
Beeskow 69
Belzig 34, *35*
Berlin 18, 46, 57, 66, *83*, 87, 107, 121, 122, 124, 132, 134, *136*, 138–142, 144, 147, 158f, 163, 170–179, 202, 225, 231, 243f, 252, 254, 258f, 261, *265*, 267, 296, 314, *351*, 369, 374, 393f, 446, 474, 476, 484, 494
AEG *13*, *439*, 441, 446, *447*, 447, *449*
Academy of Arts 10, 90, 122, 124, 126, 140f, 149, *177*, 232, 240, 276, 287, 295, 348, *355*, *356*, 361, *362*, 366, 378, 469
Architectural Academy 309, 313, 356, *381*, 420, 422f, 444
Arsenal (Zeughaus) 82, 92f, *95*, 124f, , *126*, 129, *456*, 459
Avenue of Victory (Siegesallee) *462*, 464
Blücher monument 356
Börsig Villa 430, 472
Brandenburg Gate *11*, 82, 276, 277, 349, 362, 369
Cathedral 81, 117, 383, *385*, *434*, 435
cemeteries 494–505, *494–505*
Central Markets, Alexanderplatz 420
Charlottenburg 78, 82, 147, 161, 173, 181, 420
Charlottenburg Palace, *see palaces*
churches
Böhemische 117
Buch Palace, *116*
Deutsche Kirche *223*
Dominican church (former) 81
Dorotheenstadt *348*
Dreifaltigkeitskirche 117, *498f*
Emperor William Gedächtniskirche *439*
Franciscan 42
Französische *223*
Friedrichwerdersche 309, *381*
Gedächtniskirche 437
Gnadenkirche 437
Hedwigskirche 176, *177f*, 220, 226
Marienkirche *40f*, 42f, 53, *56*, 57, *60*, 121, 127, *130*, *245*, *276*, 277
Matthäuskirche *331*
St. Michael *330*, 330
monastic 41, 62
Nikolaikirche *37*, 42f, *45*, 46f, 48, 57, *59*, *130*, 132
Parochialkirche *114*, 117
St. Peter and Paul 345
Sophienkirche 114
Thomaskirche *331*
Cölln 9, 62, 65, 76, 80, 82f, 124
commercial buildings in Friedrichstrasse *433*
courts
Central Law Court 427, *428*
City Court, Littenstrasse *13*
Criminal Court, Moabit 427
department stores 420, 443, *443–445*, 444
Dominican monastery 62
Faber Building *432*
FHP engine factory (AEG), Voltastrasse 445, *447*
Franciscan monastery 40
French Komödienhaus 223
Friedrichsfelde 78, 92, *93*
Friedrichshain 422, 445, 490, *492*
Friedrichstadt 83, 220
Friedrichswerder 82f
Gendarmenmarkt 83, 174, 220, *223*, 306, 454
Glienicke 86f, 186, 304, *319*, *340*, 345, 346
Bridge *304*, 328
casino 298, 303, 336
engine house 324
Grosse Neugierde *300*, 328
hunting-lodge 85
park 300
Grosser Hamburger Strasse 505
Grunewald 63f, *65*, 66
Hackesche Höfe 444
Hamburg Gate 218, 222
hospitals 331, *333*, *420*, 422, *442*
Hufeland Clinic, Buch *442*
Humboldt Harbour 422
Imperial Bank *422*
Joachimsthal Grammar School 430
KDW store 420, 444
Kaisergalerie shopping arcade *432*
Kaiser-Wilhelm-Strasse (now Karl Liebknecht Strasse) *419*, 420
Knorr Brake Works *449*
Köpenick 22, 32, 63, 88, *88f*, 90, 92, *93*, *102*, 105, 107, 136, 146
Körner Park 493
KPM (Royal Porcelain Manuactory) *255*, 255, 362, 380
Kreuzberg Monument 351
libraries
City (Unter den Linden) *437*
Royal *176*, *177*
Lindenhof Estate 493
Loewe armaments factory 445
Lustgarten *76*, *77f*, *309*
Museum Island (Museumsinsel) 436
museums *310f*, *313*, 384, *386*, 445
Bode Museum *435f*
Museum of Antiquity (Antikenmuseum) 351, 353
National Gallery (Nationalgalerie) 294, 430
Natural Science Museum (Naturkundemuseum) *430*
New Museum (Neues Museum) *315*, 392, 436
Old Museum (Altes Museum) 12, *308*, 309,
Old National Gallery (Alte Nationalgalerie) *431*
Pergamon 440, *441*
Rauch 356
Schinkel 356
Neuer Markt (New Market) *245*
New Guard House 452
New Mint *294*
Opera House 161, 162, 174, *176*, *177*
Oranienburg Gate 220, 222
Packhofanlage (goods depot) *420*, 422
palaces and great houses
Berlin (Stadtschloss) 6, 62, *63*, 64, 65, 67, *76–81*, 89, 91f, *93f*, 95–100, 121, 124, 126f, 129f, *131*, *140*, 141, 144, 146, 151–153, 191, 224, 229, 240, 272, *287–289*, *291*, 349, 351, *352*, 362, 364, 369, 392, 428, 456
Britz *241*
Louise Henrietta of Orange Chapel *78*
Charlottenburg *10*, 87, *100–106*, 129, 149, 163, *171*, 173, 179, 224, 227, *231*, 240, 284
Glienicke 298, 300
Grunewald hunting lodge 63f, *65*, 66
Lietzenburg, *see* Charlottenburg
Monbijou 171, *172*, 222
Niederschönhausen 107
Pless, Wilhelmstrasse 432
Pringsheim 429
Prince Henry (*now Humboldt University*) 174, *177*, 242, 428
Saldern 82
Peacock Island (Pfaueninsel) 290, *292f*, 323, 337f, 344–346
castle *292f*, 336, *337*
Pelikanhaus 444
police headquarters, Alexanderplatz 422
postal depot (Postfuhramt) 422, *423*
Prenzlauer Berg (housing estate) 490
Reichstag *418*, 427
Ritterhof 444
Rosenthal Gate 220, 222
Rotes Rathaus (Red City Hall) 49, 423, 426, 441
Royal Colonnades, Kleist park *222*
Royal Library (Königliche Bibliothek) *176*, *177*
Royal Technical University (*now Technical University*) 428, *429*, 490
Schiller Park 492
Schöneberg *416*, 420
Schönhausen (Niederschönhausen) 78, 92, 107
Spandau 32, 46, 67, 136
squares
Pariser Platz 82
Platz am Opernhause *176*, *177*
Viktoria-Luise-Platz 492
Wilhelmsplatz 235, 349
Wittenberg-Platz *416f*
stations
Anhalter *424*, 425–427
Hackescher Markt Station (formerly the Stock Exchange Station) 426
Hamburg 331, *334*
Stock Exchange 428, *429*
Synagogue, Oranienburg Strasse *332*, *423*
Tegel 92, 107, 299
Tempelhof 21, *490*
theaters
National *277*
Schauspielhaus 306, 384
Theater des Westens 443
Unter den Linden *64*, 80, 82, 83, 174f, *177*, 196, 220, 224, 428, 436
Villa Kamecke 82, 126, *129*

Villa Wiegand 446
Veterinary School *279*
Wehrmacht headquarters 422
Bernau *38*, 42, 46, 48, 50, 57, *59*, 70
Biesenthal 21
Blankenfelde 92
Boitzenburg 66
Bornim 86f, 92, 186
Bötzow (*later* Oranienburg) 21, 34, 87
Brandenburg (city) 8, 18, 21, 49, 57, 134, *495*
cathedral (St. Peter and Paul) *24f*, 25, 42
city hall, Old Town 61
Dominican church 41
Katharinenkirche *42*, 42, *46*, 48, *55*, 56, 69
Gotthardtkirche 25, 46, 47, *50*, 52, *61*
Breslau (Wrocław) 163, 363, 442, 444, *445*, 452, *454f*, 455
Briest 38
Brunswick *431*

C

Caputh *86*, 86f, 89, 100, 108, 141, 146f, 186
Chorin 8, 22, 26, 28, *29*, *31*, 31, 37, 40, 42, 53
Cleves (Kleve) 77, 85, 120, 122, 132, 136, 144
Cölln, *see* Berlin
Cologne *335*, 394, 424, *426*, 427, 438, 454f
Cottbus *444*

D

Danzig (Gdansk) 8, 10, 122, 138, 243
Darmstadt *351*
Demerthin 67
Dessau 66, 84, 242, 272, 495f
Deutsches Eck 462–463
Dolgelin 52
Dresden 153, *227*, 242, 244, 353, 416, 427, *431*
Düsseldorf 158, 374, 385, 386, 389, 393, *440*, 444

E

Eberswalde 37, 42, 52
Eisenhüttenstadt-Fürstenberg 47
Erfurt 56
Essen-Baldeney *430*

F

Fahrland 86
Frankfurt am Main 393, 424, *425*, 426, 429, 430, *431*, 454, 460
Frankfurt an der Oder 22, 42, 49, 57, 69, 70, *71*, 132
City Hall *49*, 50
civic church 47
Gertraudkirche *52f*, 54, 61
Marienkirche *6*, *36*, 37, 43, 45–47, 50, *52*, 53f, 57, 61, 69
Freyenstein 34, 66
Friedland 43, 50
Friedrichsthal 91, 100
Fürstenwalde 47, 57, *57*
Fürstenwerder 49

G

Gelnhausen 437f
Gernrode 18
Gleiwitz (Gliwice) 356
Glienicke, *see* Berlin
Glogau (Glogów) *277*
Golm 86
Goslar 437
Gotha 428, 497
Gransee 21, 66, *296*
Greifswald 43
Grimnitz (Uckermark/Ucker March) 63, 66, 147
Gross-Schönebeck 66

H

Hagen 445, 450, *451–453*
Halberstadt 55f, 56
Halle 90, 363
Hamburg 427, 497
Hanover 104, 141, 424, *425*, 426, 432
Harkort an der Wetter 452
Harlung (hill) 25
Havelberg 8, 18, 24, 26, 36, 37, 48, 53, *54f*
Hechingen *254*
Heidelberg 107
Heiligengrabe 26
Heltorf 387
Herrenhausen 107
Herrnhut 495
Herzberge 56
Himmelpfort 26
Hochkirch *369*
Hohenfinow 35
Hohenwalde 70, *71*
Homburg von der Höhe 437

J

Jerichow *21*, 22–25, *23*
Joachimstal 63, 66
Jüterbog 8, 38, 47, 50, 51, 56f

K

Karlsruhe 158, 436
Koblenz *462*
Königs Wusterhausen 67, 87, *108*, 109
Königsberg (East Prussia; Kaliningrad) 8, 18, 77, 101, 121, 124, 132, 134, 136, 144, 363, 456
Königsberg (Neumark) 48, 50
Kossenblatt *117*
Krefeld 459
Kronberg 436
Kulm *385*
Kunersdorf *497*
Küstrin (Kostrzyn) 63, 77, 88
Kyritz 48

L

Lauchhammer 356
Lehnin 8, 21, 26–31, 27, 37, 42
Leipzig 63, 152, 226, *351*, 427, 454
Leitzkau 22, 24
Lenzen 18, 32, 48, 132
Leuthen *398*
Lichterfelde 66
Liebenwalde 21, 34
Lieberose 69
Limburg 437
Lindow 26
Löwenburg 21
Luckau 47f
Luckenwalde 500
Ludwigsburg 158
Ludwigslust 242

M

Magdeburg 18, 22, 24, 43, 52, 233, 244, 363
Marienburg (East Prussia; Malbork) 8, *297*, *335*, 370f, *372*, 378
Marienfliess 26
Marienwalde (Neumark) 147
Mark 77
Meissen 22, 255
Meyenburg 34, 66
Mittenwalde 22, 47, 50, 57, *59*
Müncheberg 503

N

Nauen 164
Neubrandenburg 43, 48, 50
Neuruppin 164, 224, 272, 277, *278f*, 296
Niederhof *245*
Niederwald monument, Rüdesheim 13
Niemegk 51

O

Oderberg 21, 34
Oranienbaum 87
Oranienburg (*formerly* Bötzow) 21, 78, 87f, 100, 107, 122, 147
palace 90, *91*, 92, 107, 132f, 134, *135*, 141, 144, 149, 151, *164*, 168

P

Paradies monastery 26
Parduin 25
Paretz *284*
Pehlitzwerder (island) 22, 28
Peitz 67
Perleberg 8, 48, 51
Pillau 77
Pommersfelden 98
Porta Westfalica 463
Posen (Pozna) 438, *439*
Potsdam 18, 32, 87, 107f, *109–114*, 147, 159, 170, 179–220, 222, 231f, 254, 261, 290, *305*, 306, *357*, *400*
Babelsberg 50, 85, 304, *305*, 309, *328*, 336, 342f, *344f*, 345, 346, *361*
Barberini Palace 213
Bornstedt estate 343, *346*
Brandenburg Gate 110, 186, 217, *219*, 220
canal 217
churches
Bornstedt *346*, *497*
Französische Kirche 176, *221*
Garnisonkirche (Garrison Church) 112, *114*, *319*, *340*
Heiliggeistkirche (Church of the Holy Spirit) 114, *319*, *340*
Nikolaikirche 112, 116, *181*, *215*, *319*, *320*
Palace (Stadtschloss) 6, *85*, 118, 129, 134, 163, 167, *172*, *180*, 181, *183f*, 191, 204, 212, 216f, 224, 227, 272
pleasure garden 84, 85, 217, 226
Commissariat Department 321
Dutch quarter 110
Einstein tower 454
Grosse Stadtschule *113*
Hiller-Brandt house *213*, 215
Jägertor (Hunter's Gate) 217, 219
Jewish Cemetery, Pfingstberg *503*
Nauener Gate *218*, 219
Neustadt Gate *217*, 219
New Garden 277, *284*, *319*, *336f*, 341, 345–347
dairy 327
Gothic Library 277, *280*
Heiliger See 282
Marble Palace (Marmorpalais) *281*, 282, 284, *287*, *336*, 337, 366, 369, 392
Moorish Temple *281*
Orangery *10*, *282f*
pyramid (ice house) *282*
Pfingstberg 296, *297*, *319*, 345
Preacher's and school house 213
Sanssouci Park 186, *194–196*, *200*, 201, 204, *211*, *216*, *219*, *226*, 234, 346
Belvedere on Klausberg 204, *211*, *216*, 233
Charlottenhof 300, *302f*, 314, 316, 341, *342f*, 446
Commune 454
Communs *194*, 202, *204*, 220, 233, 266, 454
Chinese House 201, 224, 227, 229, *262*, *266*
church (Friedenskirche) 319, *320f*, *358*, 361
dairy 322
Dragon House *201*
engine house 325, *327*, 342
New Chambers (Neue Kammern) 194, 194–197, 216, 233f, *236f*, 251f, *257*
New Palace (Neues Palais) 86, 163, 167, 183, *194*, 202, *203–210*, *216*, 220, 233f, *235*, 240, *249*, *251f*, 257, *262*, *265*, 266, *267*, 272, 304, 342
pheasantry 316, 322, *325*
picture gallery 195, *199*, 227
Roman Baths *302*, 321, 341f
Sanssouci Palace *9*, 144, 163, *164*, 167, 181, *186–194*, 195, 199, 204, 212, 222, *224*, 225, 227, 229, *231*, 234, 238, 240, *246–248*, *266*, *272*, *275*, 318, 343
Schlossstrasse 1 *212*
squares
Alter Markt *179*, 213, *214*, 227
"Bassin" 110, 112, *113*
Neuer Markt 110
Steam Mill *324*
Stern Hunting Lodge 63, 110, *112*, 117
Temple of Friendship 203, *211*, 235
villas
Illaire 323, *325*
Jacobs 323
Persius 323, *324*
Schöningen *304*
Prenzlau 8, 40, 42, 43, 48f, 244
Pritzwalk 48
Putlitz 34

R

Rathenow *50*, 53f, 130
Ravensberg 77
Reichenow 70
Remagen 393
Rheinsberg *162*, 163, *164*, *167*, 167–170, 174, 179, *189*, 190, 194f, 201, 217f, 222f, 225, 227, 233, 238, *240*, 244, 272, 276
Ringenwalde 70
Rossow 53
Rostock 43, 356
Rüdersdorf 63
Rüdesheim 13

S

Sacrow 321, *322f*, 336, 344, *345*, *347*
St. Marienthal convent *351*
Schneeberg 60
Schönbrunn 95, 158
Schönebeck 63, 244
Schwedt 21, 88, 89
Schwerin 361
Schwiebus (Swiebodzin) 26
Seelow 52
Sonnenburg (Neumark) 77, 88
Spa 147
Stahnsdorf 500
Stendal *6*, 46, 48, *49*, *51*, 55, 56, *57*, 132
Stettin (Szczeczin) 42, 288
Stolpe 66
Stralsund 244, *245*
Strasbourg 297, 426
Strausberg 40, 41, 42

T

Tamsel 63
Tangermünde 32, 42, 46, 48, *49*, 50f, 62
Templin *48*, 49
Torgau 61, 63, 64, *368*
Trampe 66
Treuenbrietzen 42

U

Ulm 454

W

Weimar 450
Weissenfels 89
Werben 32, 50, 55
Wiesbaden 446
Wilsnack 48, 55
Wittenberg 60, 492
Wittstock 34, 48, 53, 57, 69
Wörlitz 234, 272, 277, 324, 337
Worpswede 478
Wriezen 503
Würzburg 98, 158
Wusterhausen 70

Z

Zehdenick 21, 26, 66
Ziesar 34
Zinna 8, *38*
Zossen 63
Zwettl 46, 47

Index of Persons

A

Achenbach, Andreas 400
Adam, François Gaspard 229, 231, *232f*
Adam, Lambert Sigisbert 225, 229, *230*, 231, *359*
Adam, Sigisbert-Michel 231
Adler, Friedrich *331*, 427
Adler & Sullivan 443
Afinger, Bernhard 353
Ahlborn, Wilhelm *386*
Albert the Bear 21, 24, 32, 34
Alberty, Jakob 349
Alexander, Prince William *348*, 349
Algarotti, Francesco 163, 213
Amalia of Solms, mother-in-law of the Great Elector 77, 84, 133, *213*
Arnim, Ferdinand von 314, *341*
Augusta of Saxony-Weimar 305
Augustus the Strong 87, 95, 97, 129, 142, 153, 248

B

Backert, Johann Hermann 124
Baluschek, Hans 485, *487*
Bantzer, Carl 478
Baraband, Jean the Elder 149
Barfuss, Field Marshal Johann Albrecht von *117*
Barlow, William Henry 425
Baron, Karl Christian Wilhelm von *215*, 244
Barth, Erwin 493
Bartsch, Johann Gottfried 138
Baudesson, Daniel 252
Baudouin Fils, Frères 266, 267
Bauer, Friedrich 492
Becherus, Friedrich 295
Becker, Carl *394*
Begas, Karl 356, 384, 385, 399, 400, 462 [not in biogs]
Begas, Reinhold 356, *461*, *473*, 483
Beger, Lorenz 122
Begeyn, Abraham Jansz *139*, 139
Behne, Adolf 447
Behrendt, Walter Curt 443, 454
Behrens, Peter *13*, 442, 445f, *447*, 449, 450, 452
Benckert, Johann Peter *183*, 225, 227, *228*, 232f, 235
Bendemann, Eduard 385f, *389*
Bérain, Jean 258
Berchem, Nicolaus 139
Berg, Max 452, *454*, *455*
Berger, Andreas *110*
Berger, Daniel 364, *370*
Berger, Heinrich 353
Berndt, Kurt 444
Bernhard, Karl 447, *449*
Bernhard, Philipp *279*
Berson, François *279*
Bettkober, Heinrich Sigismund 349
Bianchini, Francesco 204
Bièfve, Edouard de 393
Biermann, Carl Eduard *400*, 401
Biermann, Eduard *333*, *335*
Biller, Ludwig *151*
Biller II, Johann Ludwig *152*, 153
Biller, Johannes 153
Bismarck, Count Otto von 417, 456
Blankenstein, Hermann 420, 420, 422, 441
Bläser, Gustav 353, *354*
Blechen, Carl 10, 18, 374, *376–379*
Blesendorf, Constantin Friedrich *80*
Blesendorf, Samuel *84*, 139
Blondel, Jacques François 163
Blume, Christian Friedrich 261
Bodt, Jean de 93, 107f, *114*, 117, 129, 170, 179, 319
Boettiger, Carl August 292
Bogislav, Ernst 126
Böhme, K.W. 254
Böhme, Martin 151
Bohnstedt, Ludwig 428
Bollandt, Heinrich 132
Borrmann, J.B. 254
Boucher, François 240, 257
Boumann, Georg Friedrich *168*
Boumann, Jan (Johann) *110*, 112, *113*, 117, *176*, 220, *221*
Brasch, Bernhard Mattias *278f*
Bräunlich, Adolph 353
Brendel, Johann Gottlieb 288
Brenkenhoff, Friedrich Balthasar Schönberg von *243*
Breuer, Peter 462
Brodersen, Albert 492
Broebes, Jean Baptiste *85*, *92*
Brücke, Wilhelm 379, *380*
Brunsberg, Hinrich 34, 42, 47f, 50
Brunswick, Duke of 366
Brütt, Adolf 483, *484*
Büring, Johann Gottfried 195, *199*, 200–202, *218*, 218, *228*
Burnitz, Heinrich 428, 430

C

Calame brothers 227
Calandrelli, Alexander *431*
Calau, Benjamin 242
Campbell, Colen 163
Campen, Jacob van 84
Carove, Giovanni 89, 145
Carree, Michiel 139
Carstens, Asmus Jakob 366, 372, 373
Casteels, Alexander 139
Casteels, Joseph Franz 139
Catherine II (the Great) 244, 252, 282
Cauer, Ludwig 353, 462, *473*
Caulitz, Peter 139
Chambers, William 201, 272
Charlemagne 18, 122, 393
Charles, Prince of Prussia 297–299, *300*, 324, 340
Charles IV 45–47, 55, 62
Charles V 394
Charlotte, Queen 179
Charlotte of Prussia, Princess (later Alexandra Feodorovna) 350, *355*
Charpentier, René 129
Chiaramella, Francesco 67
Chièze, Philipp de 84, 86, 259
Chodowiecki, Daniel 243, *244*, 253, 363, 366, 369, 371
Clemens, Johan Frederik 369, 371
Cocceji, Samuel von 231
Cordes, Wilhelm 500
Corinth, Lovis 468, *469*, 477f, *482*
Cornelius, Peter 375, 385, 392, 394, 465
Coullodon, Jacques 152
Coullodon, Siméon 152
Coustou, Guillaume 231
Coxie, Anthonie de 105, 141f
Cranach the Elder, Lucas 57, 61, *65*, 132
Cranach the Younger, Lucas 132
Cunningham, Edward Francis 364, *369f*
Cybei, Giovanni Antonio *168f*
Czwiczek, Mathias 132, *133*

D

Dagly, Gerard *147*
Dähling, Heinrich Anton 376, 377
Damart, Bartholomé 130
Degen, Dismar 142f
Dessau, Leopold of 349
Diemar, Nathanael 243
Dieussart, Charles Philippe 92
Dieussart, François 120, *121*
Dillis, Johann Georg 378
Diterichs, Friedrich Wilhelm *116*, 181, 189
Dix, Otto 485
Dohna 91, 134
Dohna-Poinski 490
Donner, Georg Raphael 227
Dorothea of Holstein-Glücksburg (second wife of the Great Elector) *81*, 87f, *136*, 138, 144, 146, 179
Drake, Friedrich 353
Drentwett III, Abraham 153
Drentwett, Emanuel 153
Dubois, Charles Sylva 190, 240, 244
Dubuisson, Augustin 240
Dubut, Charles Claude 129
Duquesney, François-Alexandre 126, 425
Durand, Jean-Nicolas-Louis 296, 322
Dürer, Albrecht 57, 371, *373*, 470
Dusableau, G. *83*
Dyck, Sir Antony van 132, 136

E

Ebe & Bender, architectural partnership 429
Ebenhech, Georg Franz 194, 225f, *227*, 232, 235
Egells, machine maker 324
Eggers, Bartholomäus *119*, 121f, 124
Eggert, Herman 426f, 430
Elizabeth Christine, Queen (wife of Frederick II) 164, *239*
Elizabeth Henrietta Maria of Hesse-Kassel 146
Elizabeth, Queen (wife of Frederick William IV) 351, *352*, *354f*, *358*
Elizabeth, Tsarina of Russia 259
Elliger, Ottmar 136, 138
Endell, August 442
Engelbrecht, Johannes 153
Eosander, see Göthe, (Johann Friedrich) Eosander von
Erdmannsdorff, Friedrich Wilhelm von 272, 275f, 284, 288f, *290*, 296, 362, 364, 495
Erlach, Johann Bernhard Fischer von 95, 100, *176*, 217, 222
Eyserbeck, Johann August 281, 288, 327

F

Falbe, Joachim Martin *242*
Faltz, Raimund 122
Fechhelm, Carl Friedrich *176*, 244
Fechhelm, Carl Traugott *245*
Feilner, Tobias Christoph 309, 361
Feldmann, Christian Friedrich 167
Fischer, August 361
Fischer, Ferdinand August 361
Fischer, Theodor 454
Fischer von Erlach, see Erlach, Johann Bernhard
Flinck, Govert 132
Fontane, Theodor 164
Forster, Georg 338
Forster, Reinhold 338
Franke, Heinrich Christian Friedrich 242
Franz, Julius 349, 353, *356*
Frederica Louise of Hessen-Darmstadt (second wife of Frederick William II) 287, *288*
Frederica, Princess 349, 364
Frederick II, Emperor 22
Frederick I Hohenzollern, Margrave of Brandenburg (Frederick IV, Burgrave of Nuremberg) 9, 62, 80
Frederick I, King of Prussia (as Frederick III, Elector of Brandenburg) 64, 76, 80, 82f, 87f, 88f, 95f, 101, 107, *103*, 105, 116, 120–122, 124f, 129f, 138, 139f, 140, *141f*, 143, 147, 149, *151*, 170, 179, 202, 222f, 238, 240, *258*, 265, 459
Frederick II Irontooth, Margrave 9, 55, 62
Frederick III, Elector of Brandenburg (see Frederick I, King of Prussia)
Frederick II (the Great) 9f, 62, 85, 87, 95, 108, 110, 154, 158f, 161–163, *164*, *167*, 169, *170*, 171, *173*, 174, *175–177*, 179f, 181, 183, 186, *187*, *189*, *196*, 201, 204, *209f*, 213, *215*, 216f, 219f, *221*, *222*, 224f, 229, *231*, 235, 238, 240, 242f, 246, 248, 252f, *254f*, 257, *259f*, 265–268, 272, 275, 287, 294, 302, 317, 319, 325, 337, 343f, *353*, 362, 364, *368*, 369, *396*, 398, *431*, 435f, 461, 470
Frederick, prince heir of Brandenburg 146
Frederick Henry of Orange 84, 133
Frederick, Margrave 232
Frederick William 80, 110, *112*
Frederick William I (the "Soldier King") 10, 76, 78, *86*, 87, 108f, *113*, 114, *117*, 129, 131, 142f, *149*, *152*, 153, 158, 164, 167, 170, 186, 190, 203, 212, 216–217, 223, 238, 258f, 265, 348
Frederick William II 6, *260*, 261, 272, 275–277, 281f, 284, 287, *289f*, 292f, 296f, 337, *348*, 362–364, 368f, 382, 384
Frederick William III 272, *284*, 296f, 305, 338f, 342, *355*, 370, 381, 383f, 392
Frederick William IV 13, 158, 294, 300, 302, 314–317, 319, *320*, 330, 335, 341–343, 345, 351, *354–356*, *358*, 361, 375, 381, 398, *431*, 435
Frederick William of Brandenburg, Count 144, 383
Frederick William, Prince 350
Frederick William, Prince (firstborn son of the Elector Frederick III) *258*
Frentzel, G.J.F. *110*
Frentzen, Georg *426*, 427
Freydanck, Carl Daniel *340*, *347*
Frick, Friedrich 372
Friedrich, Caspar David 375f
Frisch, Johann Christoph 240, 290, 364, 366, 370
Fritsch 437, 439
Fromantiou, Hendrik de 138f
Fromery, Pierre 149
Füncke, Johann 162
Furttenbach, Joseph 495

G

Gaap II, Georg Lorenz 153
Gabriel, Jacques-Ange 282, 284
Gallait, Louis 393
Galland, Georg 484
Garnier, Charles 417, 435
Gärtner, Eduard *97*, 380, *381*, 383
Gasc, Anna Rosina de (née Lisiewska) 242
Gaul, August 462, *485*
Gayette, Pierre de 110, *113*, 114
Geiss, Moritz 361
Genelli, Hans Christian 275f
Gentz, Heinrich 290f, *294*, 295, 440
George William, Elector 132, 138
Gérard, François 382, *384*
Gericke, Samuel Theodor *138*, *141*
Gerlach, Philipp 114, 117
Gessner, Albert 490, *491*
Gibbons, Grinling *151*
Giese, Benjamin 232
Gilly, David 277, 295f, 331, 370
Gilly, Friedrich 288, 290, *294*, 296f, 309, 319, 324, 349, 370f, *372*, 379, 440
Ginzrot, August Christian 260, 261
Girardon, François 124
Girard, David *261*
Glume, Friedrich Christian 224–226
Glume, Johann Christian 169
Glume, Johann Georg 130
Godeau, Simeon 107, 109
Goethe, Johann Wolfgang von 244, 292, *351*, 386
Goldmann, Nicolaus 92
Golssenau, Vieth von *243*
Gontard, Carl (Philipp Christian) von 195, *201f*, 203, *204f*, *209*, *211f*, 213, 215, 220, 222f, 232, 272, 276, *281*, 282, *284f*, 287, 287, *289f*
Göthe, (Johann Friedrich) Eosander von 90–92, 100f, *103*, *104*, 105, 129, *199*
Gotzkowski, J.F.E. 254
Graeb, Carl *304*, 328, *400*, 401
Grael, Johann Friedrich 114, 167
Graff, Anton 231, 242, 243, 349
Grand Duke of Saxony-Weimar 351
Grässel, Hans 500
Great Elector Frederick William 9, 67, 76–78, 81–84, 92, 108, 118–121, 122, 124, 130, 132, 133, 134, 136, 138–140, 144, 148, 170, 179, 262, 265
Grenander, Alfred 445, *449*
Grieninger, J.G. 254
Grisebach, Hans 432, 434
Gropius & Schmieden, architectural partnership 422
Gropius, Walter 422, 447, *450*, 452, 455
Gros, Antoine Jean, Baron 384
Grünberger, Jonas, sculptor 69
Grünberger, Michael, sculptor 69
Grünberg, Martin 64, 90, 92f, 96, 100, 107, 112, 117
Grupello, Gabriel de 122, 124
Gubitz, Friedrich Wilhelm 371, 373
Guglielmi, Gregorio 242

H

Habermann, Hugo 469
Hackert, Jakob Philipp 244, *245*, 290
Hackert, Johann Gottlieb 244
Hagemeister, Karl 477, 478
Hagen, Hugo 349, *351*, 353
Hallerstein, Carl Haller von 294
Hamilton, Frans de 136, *138*
Hanff, Michael 77, 85
Harper, Johann 142, *143*, 240
Hase, Wilhelm 426, 432
Hasenclever, Johann Peter 389, *391*, *397*
Heine, Thomas Theodor *463*
Heinitschek, Matthias 261
Heinitz, Friedrich Baron Anton von 244, 276, 287, 362, 364, 371
Heintzy, Cornelius 124
Hempel, Gottfried 244

Hennicke, Julius *346*
Henrici, Karl 439
Henrietta Catherine of Nassau-Orange 84
Henry I, King 18
Henry, Prince *167–169*, 183, 189, *207*, 242, 272, 276
Henry of Orange 77
Henry, Suzette 366, *367*, 368
Herfert, Gottlieb 124
Hesse, Ludwig Ferdinand 314, *317f*, *354*, *359*
Heymüller, Johann Gottlieb 225, 227, *229*, 232f, 235
Hildebrandt, Theodor *388*
Hintze, Johann Heinrich *305*
Hirschfeld, Christian Cajus 495
Hirt, Aloys Ludwig 292, 382
Hirt, Michael Conrad 132
Hittorf, Jacques-Ingnaz 417
Hitzig, Friedrich 422, 426, 428, *429*, *456*
Hobrecht, James 416, 419, 490
Höder, Friedrich Wilhelm 240, 261
Hoesfeld, Karl Ludwig *297*
Hoffmann, Ludwig 427, 436, 441, *442*, 445, *492*
Hoffmann, Ludwig von 479
Holz, Ferdinand Wilhelm *334*
Honthorst, Gerard van 133
Honthorst, Willem van 133, 134, *134*, 136
Hopfgarten, Heinrich 361
Hopfgarten, Wilhelm 361
Hoppe, Otto *335*
Hoppenhaupt the Elder (Johann Michael) 203, *260*, 261
Hoppenhaupt the Younger (Johann Christian) 203f, *256*
Hoppenhaupt brothers 152, 227
Hoppenhaupt, Johann Christian 183, 194, 195, *195*, *206*, 248, 251
Hoppenhaupt, Johann Michael *170*, *173*, 183, *193*, 194, 203, 248, 251, *259*
Huaut, Amy 139
Huaut, Jean-Pierre 139
Huber, Thomas 200
Hübner, Rudolf Julius Benno *388*
Hulot, Guillaume 93, 129
Humboldt, Wilhelm von 231, 297, 351f
Hummel, Johann Erdmann 382, *383*
Hundrieser, Emil 463

I

Iffland, August Wilhelm 349
Ihne, Ernst von *436f*

J

Jacobi, Andreas 358
Jacobi, Johann 124f, 129
Jacobsthal, Eduard 426, *430*
Jakob VI, Philipp 153
Jamnitzer, Christoph 151
Jansen, Hermann *490*, 492, *493*
Joachim II, Elector 9, 61, 62f, 65f, 81, 121, *121*
John I, Margrave 22, 28
John George, Elector 65, 67
John Maurice of Nassau-Siegen 77, 82f, 85, 88, 133
John Sigismund 76
Jones, Inigo *213*, 282
Jordan, royal secretary 161
Jordan brothers 252

K

Kahle, Friedrich 361
Kahn, Louis 454
Kalckreuth, Leopold Count of 480
Kalide, Theodor 353, 361
Kambly, Johann Melchior 209, 251, *252f*, 254
Kändler, J.J. 254
Kaplunger, Rudolf 233
Kaulbach, Friedrich August von *459*, 485
Kaulbach, Wilhelm von 392, 393f, 465
Kemmeter, Johann Gottfried *164*, 167f
Kern, Leonhard 119, *120*
Kimpfel, Johann Christoph *287*
King, Charles 151
Kiss, August 351, 353, *357*, 361
Klenze, Leo von 294, 353, *355*, *431*
Klimsch, Fritz *478*, 482, *485*
Knaus, Ludwig *464*, 470
Knobelsdorff, Georg Wenzeslaus von *8f*, 10, 108, 152, 161f, *163f*, 164, 167f, *170*, 171, 174, *175*, *177*, *179f*, 181, *183f*, 186, *187*, 190, 194f, *199*, 200, 202, *209*, *211f*, *215*, 217–219, *221*, 222, 224, *225f*, 227, 232, 233, 238, *240*, 244, 248, 253
Knoblauch, Eduard 314, *332*
Koch, Wilhelm 361
Kolbe, Karl Wilhelm 384, *385*
Kollwitz, Käthe 468, 485, *487*
Krämer, Jean 447
Krebs brothers 361
Krebs, Konrad 63f
Kretschmar, Johann Carl Heinrich 368, 381
Krüger, Andreas 162, 240, *282*
Krüger, Andreas Ludwig *212*
Krüger, Franz 381, *382*, *384*
Krüger, Johannes 132

L

Labrouste, Henri 417
Lachmann, Ludwig 443
Lancret, Nicolas 238
Lange, A. F. M. 444
Langerfeld, Rutger von 88, 138
Langhans, Carl Gotthard 6, 10, *167*, *276f*, *280–282*, *284*, 285, *287f*, 290, 296, 306, 327, 362, 364
Langhans, Karl Friedrich *174*
Lauweriks, Jan Ludovicus Mathieu 450
Le Corbusier 447, 450, 452, 454
Ledoux, Claude Nicolas 276f, 281, 296
Ledoux, Jean-Nicolas *282*, 324
Legeay, Jean-Laurent *178*, 202, *204*
Lehmbruck, Wilhelm 485, 487
Leibl, Wilhelm 467, 469
Leistikow, Walter 474, *476*, 477f
Lemoyne, Jean Baptiste 231
Lenbach, Franz von 466, 468f, *476*, 477
Lenné, Peter Joseph 6, 10, *297f*, 300, 302, 305, 314–317, 328f, 331, 334, 337, 339–347, *351*, *356*, 419, 491, 496
Lepautre, Jean 89
Lepsius, Reinhold *468*, 477
Lepsius, Sabine 477, 484
Léquine, François 361
Lessing, Karl Friedrich 386f, *388*, 389, *390f*, 394
Le Sueur, Blaise Nicolas 240, 244
Leti, Gregorio 144–147
Levetzow, Konrad 292
Leygebe, Gottfried Christian 118, *119*, 139
Leygebe, Paul Carl *140*
Liberi, Pietro 134
Lichtenau, Countess 290
Lieberkühn (the Younger), Christian 253
Lieberkühn (the Elder), Johann Christian 153
Liebermann, Max 468, *469*, 474–478, *479f*, 482
Lier, Gysel van 132
Lievens, Jan 132f, *135*
Lisiewski, Christian Friedrich Reinhold 242, *243*
Lisiewski, Georg 242
Lorrain, Claude 167, 240
Lothar of Supplinburg 18
Louis XIV 9, 78, 85, 95, 97, 122, 124, 139, 147, 148, 158, 170, 246, 248
Louis XV 224, 229
Louise Henrietta of Orange (1st wife of the Great Elector) 77f, 84, 87f, 90, 119, 132, *133*, 134, *135*, 144, 147
Louise, Queen (wife of Frederick William III) 349, 355, 364, 373, 385
Lucae, Richard 419, 429f, 431
Ludwig I of Bavaria 392
Ludwig II of Bavaria 436
Ludwig of Prussia, Prince 350
Luther, Martin 61, 494
Lütke, Peter Ludwig 290, 377
Lynar, Count Rochus of 65–67, 134

M

Mächtig, Hermann 492, 500
Macke, August 485
Maddersteg, Michiel 139
Magnus, Eduard *399*, 400
Maison, Rudolf *435*
Makart, Hans 466
Manger, Heinrich Ludewig 159, 161, 201, *204*, 232, *283*
Männlich, Daniel 127, *130*, *144*
Mányoki, Adam 141f
Marck, Franz 485
Marot, Daniel 89, 258
Master Arnold *52*, 54
Matthieu, Georg David 242, 244
Maurice of Orange, Dutch stadholder 134
Meidner, Ludwig *488*
Meil, Johann Wilhelm *259*
Melchior de Polignac, Cardinal 224, 229, *231*, 359
Memhardt, Johann Gregor 62, *64*, *76*, 77f, 81f, 84f, *87*, 97, *107*, 121
Mendelsohn, Erich 454
Mendelsohn, Moses 231, *234*
Menzel, Adolph *193*, 392, 394, 395–398, 400, *401*, 466, *470–472*
Mercier, Philippe 139
Mercier, Pierre 149, 262
Merck, Johann Christof 142, 227
Merian, Matthäus the Younger 88, 138
Messel, Alfred *439*, 440–442, *443*, 444–446, *447*, 490
Meyer, Adolf 447, 450
Meyer, Friedrich Elias 233, 254, 255
Meyer, Gustav 491f
Meyer, Johann Friedrich *181*, *216*, 244
Meyerheim, Paul Friedrich 472, *467*
Michelet, Pierre 261
Micheli, Sigismondo 356
Michelis, Franz *319*
Mies van der Rohe, Ludwig 446f
Minne, Georg *451*
Möller, Karl Heinrich 353
Mönnich, Rudolf 427, *428*
Moshamer, Ludwig 455
Munch, Edvard 474f, *483*
Muthesius, Hermann 427, 439, 455
Mytens, Jan 136

N

Nagel, Johann Friedrich *113*
Nahl, Johann August 124, 152, 179, 183, *184*, *193*, 194, 224–226, 240, 248, *249*, 251, 259
Napoleon 10, 153
Napoleon III 436
Nash, John 298
Nason, Pieter 136
Nering, Johann Arnold 77, *78*, 82, 83, *84*, 85, 88–93, 95, 98, *100*, *102*, *107*, *114*, 116, 171, *225*
Neuhaus, Friedrich 334
Nicholas, Tsar 355, 381, *382*
Nosseni, Giovanni Maria 67
Nôtre, André Le 85, 107
Novi, Giovanni Baptista 144

O

Olbricht, Joseph Maria 442, 444, *446*
Orth, August 420, 425
Osthaus, Karl Ernst 450, 452
Otto I, King 18, 34
Otto II, Emperor 18
Otto III *393*
Otto III, Margrave 22, 28, 40
Otto IV, Margrave 31

P

Paglion, Thaddäus 69
Palladio, Andrea 10, 77, 163, 174, 202, 213, *214*, 282, 284f
Pally, Elli 261
Pecht, Friedrich 469, 471
Penny, Edward 369, *370*
Permoser, Balthasar 126f, 129, *131*
Persius, Ludwig *13*, 303, 305f, 314–316, 319, 321, 322–325, *327*, 329, 333, 342, *347*, 353
Pesne, Antoine *142*, *167*, 169, *173*, 173, 194, 204, 229, *238–240*, 242
Peter I of Russia *149*
Philip William of Brandenburg-Schwedt, Margrave *142*
Piehl, Rudolph 353
Pigalle, Jean Baptiste 225f, 229
Pitzler, Christoph 89
Poelaert, Joseph 427
Poelzig, Hans 442, 444f, 452, *455*
Polignac, see Melchior de Polignac
Post, Pieter 77, 88
Pückler-Muskau, Prince Hermann of 342f, *351*
Puhlmann, Johann Gottlieb *348*, *363*, 364
Pynacker, Adam 132

Q

Quellinus, Artus the Elder 121

R

Raczynski, Count Athanasius 393
Räntz brothers *211*, 231f, 234f
Räntz, Johann David *233*, *236f*
Räntz, Johann Lorenz Wilhelm 235, *236f*
Räntz, Lorenz Wilhelm *233*
Raphael 317, 384
Raschdorff, Julius 117, *429*, *434*, 435
Rathenau, Walther 445, 475
Rauch, Christian Daniel 10, 349, 351, *353*, *355*, 356, *358f*, 361
Ravesteyn, Jan Antonisz van 134
Reclam, Friedrich 242
Reclam II, Jean François 252
Reinhardt, Johann Christian 362
Rembrandt van Rijn 132, 134, *135*
Rethel, Alfred *393*, 394, *397*, 400
Reznicek, F. von 476
Ribestein, Michael *61*
Rode, Christian Bernhard 209f, 240, *241*, 244, 272, *279*, 364, 366, *367f*, 369, *370*
Romandon, Abraham *136*, 139
Romandon, Gedeon *136*, 139
Royen, Willem Frederik van *138*
Rubens, Peter Paul 134, 136
Ruischer, Johannes *64*, 134, 136, 138
Ryckwaert, Cornelius 77, 88

S

Sandrart, Joachim von 119, 136
Sarrazin, Jacques *227*
Schadow, Albert Dietrich 314
Schadow, Friedrich Gottlieb *110*
Schadow, Johann Gottfried 231, 275, 276, *288*, 296, *348–350*, 356, 358, 362, 363, *365*
Schadow, Ridolfo 382
Schadow, Wilhelm 369, 374, 377, 381f, *383*, 384–386, *388*
Scharnhorst, Gerhard von 351
Scheffler, Johann Karl 169, 233
Scheits, Andreas 141
Schenk (Scheutzlich), Hans 61, 63, 66
Schievelbein, Friedrich Anton 353
Schinkel, Karl Friedrich *10*, *13*, 164, *179*, *277*, 290, *295–313*, 314f, 319, 322–324, 328, 331, *338*, *351–353*, *357*, 361, *374f*, 376f, 385, *386*, 418, 422, 424, 454, 497, 501
Schirmer, Johann Wilhelm 389, *390*, 400
Schleuen, Johann David *90*
Schleuen, Johann Friedrich *194*, *199*
Schlüter, Andreas 10, 64, 78, 81, 92, 96, *97*, 98, *99f*, 101, 114, 118, 121, *122*, 122–127, 129, *130*, 131, 140, *141*, *151f*, 225, *235*, 427, 435, *436*
Schmalz, Otto *428*
Schmitz, Bruno *432*, 454, *460*, 463
Schnegg, Johann 233
Schoonjans, Anton 141
Schott, Walter *478*
Schroedter, Adolf 386, *389*
Schultheiss, Paul 61
Schulze, Friedrich 429, *430*
Schultze-Naumburg, Paul 437, *438*
Schulz, Wilhelm 480, *483*
Schwatlo, Carl 423
Schwechten, Franz *424*, 425, 427, 437, *438f*
Schwerin, Field Marshal Kurt von 231, *233*
Schwestermüller, David I *146*
Scott, Gilbert 425
Sehring, Bernhard 443f
Seidel, Heinrich *424*, *425*
Semper, Gottfried 416, 427, *431*, 422, 428, 442
Semper, Manfred *431*
Seydlitz, Friedrich Wilhelm von, General 231, *232*
Siemering, Rudolf 460, 463
Silber, Jonas 151
Sitte, Willi 491
Skarbina, Franz 477
Slevogt, Max 468, *481*, 482
Slotz, Michel-Ange 231
Smids, Michael Matthias 77, 83, 85

Sohn, Carl Ferdinand *388*, 398, *399*
Soller, August *330*
Sommer, Oskar 430
Sophie Charlotte (second wife of Frederick III/I) 82, 87, 95, *100*, 101, 107, 124, 127, 141, 171
Sophie Dorothea (wife of Frederick William I) 142, 152, 171, 252
Sophie Louise (3rd wife of Frederick III/I) 114, *140*, *258*
Spanheim, Ezechiel von 122
Spindler, Heinrich Wilhelm *196*, 250, 252, *253*
Spindler, Johann Friedrich *196*, 250, 253
Steiner, George 496
Steinhäuser, Karl *358*
Stier, Hubert 425f, 432
Storch, Johann 225
Strack, Johann Heinrich 294
Strack, Johann Heinrich *11*, *13*, 306, 314, 429, *431*, 472
Straub, Hans 151
Stridbeck, Johann 63, *82*
Stüler, Friedrich August 100, 294, *314f*, *317f*, *331*, 333, 335, 353, *354*, 422, 431
Suchodelez, Samuel von *110*

T
Tassaert, Jean Pierre 231, *233f*, 348f
Taut, Bruno 452, 455, 493
Terwesten, Augustin 90, 141, *141*
Terwesten, Matthäus 141
Tessin, Nicodemus 95f
Tessin, Nikolaus the Younger 105
Theiss, Caspar 9, 60, 63–66
Therbusch, Anna Dorothea 242, *243*
Thiede, August 428, *430*
Thiele, Johann Alexander 244
Thienpondt, Karl Friedrich 243
Thiersch, Friedrich von 427, 454
Thoemer, Paul *13*, 427, *428*
Thorvaldsen, Berthel 349, 356, *361*, 362, 382
Thulden, Theodor van 136
Tieck, Friedrich 349, 351, 352, 353, 356
Tieck, Ludwig *388*
Tischbein, Johann Heinrich Wilhelm 242
Troost, Paul Ludwig 437
Trübner, Wilhelm 469
Tuaillon, Louis 473, *475*

U
Unger, Georg Christian *177*, 195, 204, *211*, 215, 218, *219*, 220, 222, 232
Unger, Johann Friedrich 295
Ury, Lesser *474*, 475, 477

V
Vaillant, Jacques 89, 136f, 140
van de Velde, Henry 439, 442, 450, *451*, *453*, 454f
van der Lee, Pieter Fransen 148
van Lier, Gysel 133
van Loo, Charles Amédée Philippe *184*, 240, *241*
Veit, Philipp 393, 459
Vernet, Charles 383
Vigne, Charles 152
Viollet-le-Duc, Eugène-Emmanuel 417
Vollgold, Friedrich Alexander Theodor *361*
Vollmer, Johannes 426
Voltaire 161, 163, 171, *190*, 216f

W
Wach, Wilhelm 384
Waesemann, Friedrich 423
Wagner, Martin 420, 491, *493*
Wagner, Otto 432, 439, 442, 445
Walden, Herwarth 482
Wallbaum, Matthias 151
Wallot, Paul *418*, 427f, 430, 432
Walser, Friedrich 484
Wangenheim, A von 167
Warthmüller, Robert *465*, 470
Watteau, Antoine 190, 224, 238, 240, 249, *255*, 257
Weidemann, Friedrich Wilhelm 142, 240
Weitsch, Friedrich Georg 364, *365*, 370, *371*
Weitsch, Johann Friedrich 370
Wentzel, Johann Friedrich 96, 140
Werner, Anton von 401, 456, *457f*, 459, 476, 480
Weyhenmeyer, Georg Gottfried 125
Wichmann, Karl Friedrich 349, *350*
Wichmann, Ludwig Wilhelm 309, 349, *351*
Wiegand, Theodor 446
Wieling, Nicolaus *135*, 136, 141
William I, Kaiser 297, *351*, *401*, 459, 461f, 470, 502
William II, Kaiser 428, 435f, 440, *458*, 462–464, 473, 476, 482, 484
William III of Orange 90f, 95, 134, *141*
William Henry of Brandenburg, Prince (son of the Great Elector) 120
William, Prince (later Kaiser William I) 305
Wilhelmine of Bayreuth 164, 167, *211*, 232, 234
Willmann, Michael 134
Winkler, Nikolaus 57
Winterfeld, General von 231, *233*
Wislicenus, Hermann *459*
Wittig, Hermann 351
Wohler family of sculptors 233
Wohler, Johann Christoph 233, *235*
Wohler, Michael Christoph *235*
Wolff, Albert 353, *357f*, 361
Wolff, Emil 349
Wolff, Fritz 422
Wolff, Ridolfo 349
Wolff, Wilhelm 353
Wolgemut, Michael 57
Wolgast, Carl 353

Z
Zacharias, Friedrich *194*
Zille, Heinrich *487*

Further Reading

Books in English:
Avery, C., François Dieussart, Portrait Sculptor to the Courts of Northern Europe, in: Victoria & Albert Yearbook, Vol 4, London 1974
Baker, T., Frederick the Great and the Making of Prussia, London 1976
Carsten, F. L., The Origins of Prussia, Oxford 1968
Clelland, D. (ed), Berlin: An Architectural History, New York 1984
Corinth (exhibition catalog), Schuster, P–K, C. Vitali, and B. Butts, Munich/New York 1996
Crankshaw, E., Bismarck, London 1981
Feuchtwanger, E. J., Prussia: Myth and Reality, London 1970
Frey, L. and M. Frey, Frederick I.: The Man and His Times, Boulder and New York 1984
Haffner, Sebastiam, The Rise and Fall of Prussia, London 1980
Haftmann, Werner, German Art of the Twentieth Century, New York, 1972
Johnson, P. C., Mies van der Rohe, London 1978
Käthe Kollwitz (exhibition catalog), Elizabeth Prelinger, National Gallery of Art, Washington 1992
Klein, Mina D., and H. Arthur, Käthe Kollwitz: Life in Art, New York 1972
Koch, H. W., A History of Prussia, London 1978
Lindemann, G., History of German Art, New York 1971
Mitchell, O. C., A Concise History of Brandenburg-Prussia to 1786, London 1980
Parker, G., The Thirty Years War, London 1984
Pundt, H. G., Schinkel's Berlin, Cambridge (Mass) 1972
Schevill, F., The Great Elector, Chicago 1947
Watkins, D. and Tilman Mellinghoff, German Architecture and the Classical Ideal 1740–1840, London 1987
Wedgwood, C.V., The Thirty Years War, London 1938
Windsor, Alan, Peter Behrens, Architect and Designer, London 1981
Books in German:
750 Jahre Architektur in Berlin (exhibition catalog), IBA, Berlin 1987
Adler, Friedrich, Mittelalterliche Backsteinbauwerke des preussischen Staates, Berlin 1862 and 1898
Arndt, Monika, Die Ruhmeshalle im Berliner Zeughaus, Eine Selbstdarstellung Preussens nach der Reichsgründung, Berlin 1985
Badstübner-Gröger, Sybille, Bibliographie zur Kunstge-schichte von Berlin und Potsdam, Berlin 1968
Badstübner-Gröger, Sybille, Simson, Jutta von, Berlin und die Mark Brandenburg. Land zwischen Havel, Spree und Oder, Munich 1991
Baer, Ilse and Winfried, Schloss Charlottenburg, Berlin 1995
Bau- und Kunstdenkmale in Potsdam, Stadtkreis und Landkreis, Inst. für Denkmalpflege, Potsdam 1990
Baukunst in Brandenburg, Cologne 1992
Berckenhagen, Ekhardt, Die Malerei in Berlin vom 13 bis zum ausgehenden 18 Jahrhundert, Berlin 1964
Berlin um 1900 (exhibition catalog), Berlinische Galerie jointly with Akademie der Künste and Berliner Festspielen GmbH, Berlin 1984
Berlin und die Antike, Architektur, Kunstgewerbe, Malerei, Skulptur, Theater und Wissenschaft vom 16 Jahrhundert bis heute (exhibition catalog), Willmuth Arenhövel, Berlin 1979
Berliner Baukunst der Barockzeit, Die Zeich-nungen und Notizen aus dem Reisetagebuch des Architekten Christoph Pitzler (1657–1707), Lorenz, Hellmut, Berlin 1998
Berliner Kunstfrühling, Malerei, Graphik und Plastik der Moderne 1888–1918 aus dem Stadtmuseum Berlin (exhibition catalog), Dominik Bartmann, Berlin 1997
Bodenschatz, Harald Hans-Joachim Engstfeld and others, Berlin, Auf der Suche nach dem verlorenen Zentrum, Berlin 1995
Boeck, Wilhelm, Oranienburg, Geschichte eines preussischen Königsschlosses, Berlin 1938
Boockmann, Hartmut, Die Marienburg im 19 Jahr-hundert, Frankfurt am Main/Berlin/ Vienna 1982
Börsch-Supan, Eva; Berliner Baukunst nach Schinkel 1840–1870, Munich 1977
Börsch-Supan, Helmut, Berlin 1810. Bildende Kunst, Aufbruch unter dem Druck der Zeit, in: Kleist-Jahrbuch 1987
Börsch-Supan, Helmut, Die Deutsche Malerei von Anton Graff bis Hans von Marées 1760–1870, Munich 1988
Börsch-Supan, Helmut, Die Kunst in Brandenburg-Preussen, Ihre Geschichte von der Renaissance bis zum Biedermeier dargestellt am Kunstbesitz der Berliner Schlösser, Berlin 1980
Braun, Günther and Waltraud, Mäzenatentum in Berlin, Bürgersinn und kulturelle Kompetenz unter sich verändernden Bedingungen, Berlin/New York 1993
Brix, Michael, Monika Steinhauser (eds), "Geschichte allein ist zeitgemäss," in Historismus in Deutschland, Giessen 1978
Broebes, Jean-Baptiste, Vue de palais et maisons de plaisance de S M le Roy de Prusse, Augsburg 1733
Campbell, Joan, Der Deutsche Werkbund, Munich 1923
Cullen, Michael S., Kieling, Uwe, Der deutsche Reichstag, Berlin 1992
Das Brandenburger Tor 1791–1991, Aren-hövel, Willmuth and Rolf Bothe, Berlin 1991
Der Grosse Kurfürst, Sammler, Bauherr, Mäzen, Staatliche Schlösser und Gärten (exhibition catalog), Sanssouci, Potsdam 1988
Die Brandenburgisch-Preussische Kunstkammer. Eine Auswahl aus alten Beständen, Berlin 1981
Die mittelalterliche Plastik in der Mark Brandenburg, Lambacher, Lothar, Kammel, Frank Matthias, Berlin 1990
Doede, Werner, Die Berliner Secession, Berlin 1977
Dollinger, Hans, Preussen, Munich 1991
Drechsler, Maximiliane, Zwischen Kunst und Kommerz. Zur Geschichte des Ausstellungs-wesens zwischen 1775 und 1905, Munich 1996
Ebertshäuser, Heidi C. (ed), Kunsturteile des 19 Jahrhunderts, Munich 1983
Eggeling, Tilo, Studien zum friderizianischen Rokko, Berlin 1980
Ethos und Pathos. Die Berliner Bildhauerschule 1786–1914 (exhibition catalog), Staatliche Museen zu Berlin-Preussischer Kulturbesitz, Berlin 1990
Feist, Peter H. (ed), Geschichte der deutschen Kunst 1848–1890, Leipzig 1987
Friedrich Wilhelm II und die Künste. Preussens Weg zum Klassizismus (exhibition catalog), Stiftung Preussische Schlösser und Gärten Berlin-Brandenburg, Potsdam 1997
Friedrich Wilhelm IV. Künstler und König (exhibition catalog), Stiftung Preussische Schlösser und Gärten Berlin-Brandenburg, Potsdam 1995
Fritsche, Astrid, Der Pfingstberg in Potsdam, Potsdam 1995
Galland, Georg, Nationale Kunst, Leipzig 1910
Geist, Jonas and Klaus Kürvers, Das Berliner Mietshaus, Vols 1–3, Munich 1980, 1984, 1989
Giersberg, Hans Joachim, Adelheid Schendel, Potsdamer Veduten, Sanssouci, Potsdam 1984
Giersberg, Hans Joachim, Das Stadtschloss in Potsdam, Berlin 1998
Giersberg, Hans Joachim, Friedrich als Bauherr. Studien zur Architektur des 18 Jahrhunderts in Berlin und Potsdam, Berlin 1986
Gloger, Bruno, Friedrich Wilhelm, Kurfürst von Brandenburg, Berlin 1986
Gundlach, Wilhelm, Geschichte der Stadt Charlottenburg, Berlin 1905
Gurlitt, Cornelius, Die deutsche Kunst des 19 Jahrhunderts. Ihre Ziele und Taten, Berlin 1900
Günther, Harri, Peter Joseph Lenné, Gärten – Parke – Landschaften, Berlin 1985
Haffner, Sebastian, Preussen ohne Legende, Hamburg 1978
Hamann, Richard, Hermand, Jost, Deutsche Kunst und Kultur von der Gründerzeit bis zum Expressionismus, 4 vols Berlin 1959
Herrmann, Wolfgang, Deutsche Baukunst des 19 und 20 Jahrhunderts, Basle/Stuttgart 1977 (reprint of 1932/33 edition)
Herz, Rudolf, Berliner Barock, Bauten und Baumeister aus der ersten Hälfte des 18 Jahrhunderts, Berlin 1928
Hofmann, Werner, Das irdische Paradies. Motive und Ideen des 19 Jahrhunderts, Munich 1991
Hüter, Karl-Heinz, Architektur in Berlin 1900–1933, Dresden 1987
Junghanns, Kurt, Der Deutsche Werkbund. Sein erstes Jahrzehnt, Berlin 1982
Kathe, Heinz, Preussen zwischen Mars und Musen, Eine Kulturgeschichte von 1100 bis 1920, Munich/Berlin 1993
Kern, Josef, Impressionismus im Wilhelminischen Deutschland. Studien zur Kunst und Kunstgeschichte des Kaiserreichs, Würzburg 1989
Kieling, Uwe, Berlin, Baumeister und Bauten, Berlin/Leipzig 1987
Klingenburg, Karl-Heinz, Der Berliner Dom, Berlin 1987
Konter, Erich, Das Berliner Schloss im Zeitalter des Absolutismus, Architektursoziologie eines Herrschaftsortes, Berlin 1991
Kopisch, August, Geschichte der königlichen Schlösser und Gärten zu Potsdam, Berlin 1854
Kotsch, Detlef, Potsdam. Die Preussische Garnisonsstadt, Brunswick 1992
Kreisel, Heinrich and Georg Himmelheber, Die Kunstdes deutschen Möbels. Munich 1973
Kühn, Margarete, Preussische Schlösser in der Zeit vom Grossen Kurfürsten bis zu Friedrich Wilhelm IV, Berlin 1934
Kühn, Margarete, Schloss Charlottenburg, Berlin 1970 (Die Bauwerke und Kunstdenkmäler von Berlin Charlottenburg I)
Kunst in Berlin 1648–1987 (exhibition catalog), Berlin 1987
Die Kunst hat nie ein Mensch allein besessen (exhibition catalog), Akademie der Künste, Berlin 1996

Kunsttheorie und Kunstgeschichte in Deutschland (ed) Werner Busch and others:Vol 1 Kunstheorie; Vol 2, Architektur, Stuttgart 1985
Lammel, Gisold, Zwischen Legende und Wahrheit –Bilderfolgen zur brandenburgisch-preussischen Geschichte, Münster 1997
Mai, Ekkehard/ Waetzold, Stephan (ed), Kunstverwaltung, Bau und Denkmalpolitik im Kaiserreich, Berlin 1981
Malkowsky, Georg, Die Kunst im Dienste der Staatsidee, Berlin 1912
Materna, Ingo and Wolfgang Ribbe, Brandenburgische Geschichte, Berlin 1995
Mebes, Paul, Um 1800, Berlin 1907
Meier-Graefe, Julius, Entwicklungsgeschichte der modernen Kunst, 3 vols Stuttgart 1904
Mielke, Friedrich, Potsdamer Baukunst, Frankfurt am Main/Berlin 1992
Milde, Kurt, Neorenaissance in der deutschen Kunst des 19 Jahrhunderts, Dresden 1981
Mittenzwei, Ingrid and Erika Herzfeld, Brandenburg-Preussen 1648–1789. Das Zeitalter des Absolutismus in Text und Bild, Berlin 1987
Moeller van der Bruck, Arthur, Der preussische Stil, Berlin 1922
Müller, Hans, Die Königliche Akademie der Künste zu Berlin. 1696 bis 1896. Part I, Berlin 1896
Müller, Regina, Das Berliner Zeughaus. Die Baugeschichte, Berlin 1994
Muther, Richard, Geschichte der Malerei im XIX Jahrhundert, 3 vols, Munich 1893–1894
Nachtsheim, Stephan, Kunstphilosophie und empirische Kunstforschung 1870–1920, Berlin 1984
Nicolai, Friedrich, Beschreibung der königlichen Residenzstädte Berlin und Potsdam, Berlin 1769
Nitschke, Andreas, Kirchen in Potsdam, Berlin 1983
Olbrich, Harald (ed), Geschichte der deutschen Kunst 1890–1918, Leipzig 1988
Osborn, Max, Berlin, Leipzig 1909
Paret, Peter, Die Berliner Secession: Moderne Kunst und ihre Feinde im kaiserlichen Deutschland, Frankfurt am Main/Berlin/Vienna 1983
Paul, Barabara, Hugo von Tschudi und die moderne französische Kunst im Deutschen Kaiserreich, Mainz 1993
Pecht, Friedrich, Deutsche Künstler des 19 Jahrhunderts. Studien und Erinnerungen. Series 1, Nördlingen 1877
Peschken, Goerd, Das königliche Schloss in Berlin. Vol 1: Die Baugeschichte von 1688–1701, Munich 1992
Philipp, Klaus Jan, Um 1800. Architekturtheorie und Architekturkritik in Deutschland zwischen 1790 und 1810, Stuttgart/London, 1997
Posener, Julius, Berlin auf dem Wege zu einer neuen Architektur. Das Zeitalter Wilhelms II (Studien zur Kunst des 19 Jahrhunderts, Vol 40), Berlin 1979 (1995)
Potsdamer Schlösser und Gärten, Bau- und Gartenkunst vom 17 bis zum 20 Jahrhundert, Potsdam 1993
Preussen. Versuch einer Bilanz (exhibition catalog), Hamburg 1981
Preussische Königsschlösser in Berlin und Potsdam. Stiftung Schlösser und Gärten Potsdam-Sanssouci und Berlin, ed Hans-Joachim Giersberg and Jürgen Julier, Leipzig 1992
Pundt, Hermann, Schinkels Berlin, Frankfurt am Main/Berlin/Vienna 1981
Rasmussen, Jörg, Barockplastik in Norddeutschland (exhibition catalog), Hamburg/Mainz 1977
Reuther, Hans, Barock in Berlin, Meister und Werke der Berliner Baukunst 1640–1786, Berlin 1969
Schiedlavsky, Günter, Martin Grünberg, Ein märkischer Baumeister aus der Wende vom 17 zum 18 Jahrhundert, Burg 1942
Schmidt, Eva, Der preussische Eisenkunstguss, Technik, Geschichte, Werk, Künstler, Berlin 1981
Schneider, Wolfgang, Berlin, Eine Kulturgeschichte in Bildern und Dokumenten, Leipzig, Weimar 1983
Schönemann, Heinz, Karl Friedrich Schinkel. Charlottenhof, Stuttgart/London, 1997
Seidel, Paul, Die Kunst im Dienste der Staatsidee, Berlin 1907
Seiler, Michael, Pfaueninsel Berlin, Tübingen/ Berlin 1993
Sprengel, P. N., Handwerke und Künste, Berlin 1773
Streidt, Gert, Potsdam, Cologne 1996
Teeuwisse, Nicolaas, Vom Salon zur Secession. Berliner Kunstleben zwischen Tradition und Aufbruch zur Moderne 1871–1900, Berlin 1986
Theuerkauff, Christian, Die Bildwerke in Elfenbein des 16–19 Jahrhunderts, Berlin 1986 (Die Bildwerke der Skulpturengalerie Berlin, II)
Trier, Eduard and Willy Weyres (ed), Kunst des 19 Jahrhunderts im Rheinland, 3: Malerei, Düsseldorf 1979
Unter den Linden (exhibition catalog), Berlin 1997
Wiesinger, Liselotte, Das Berliner Schloss. Von der kurfürstlichen Residenz zum Königsschloss, Darmstadt 1989
Wimmer, Clemens Alexander, Sichtachsen des Barock in Berlin und Umgebung. Zeugnisse fürstlicher Weltanschauung, Kunst und Jägerlust, in: Berliner Hefte 2/1985
Wirth, Irmgard, Berliner Malerei im 19 Jahrhundert, Berlin 1990

Picture Credits

The editor and publisher made strenuous efforts right up to the date of going to press to discover all owners of copyright in illustrations and text. People and institutions that may possibly not have been contacted and wish to assert rights in illustrations or text used are asked to contact the publisher retrospectively.

Hans-Joachim Bartsch, Berlin: 249 bottom. **Artothek, Peissenberg:** 472. **Achim Bednorz, Cologne:** 20; 425 bottom; 426; 430 bottom right; 431 top; 438 right; 440; 446; 450; 451; 452 bottom courtesy Karl Ernst Osthaus Museum, Hagen. **Berlinische Galerie, Berlin:** 474; 488 bottom. **Bergman & Partner, Ingenieurgesellschaft MBH, Hanover:** 425 top. **Bismarck Museum, Friedrichsruh:** 457. **Bomann Museum, Celle:** 367 bottom right. **Brandenburgisches Landesamt für Denkmalpflege, Messbildarchiv, Waldstadt:** 63; 81; 117; 124; 125; 126 right; 127–129; 130 left and right; 180; 182; 183; 185; 260 top; 287–290; 291 bottom; 307; 315; 352 bottom; 353; 392. **Brandenburgisches Landeshauptarchiv, Potsdam:** 495 bottom. **Deutsches Archäologisches Institut, Berlin:** 80, photo: Peter Grunwald. **Deutsches Historisches Museum, Berlin:** 459 bottom; 464. **Cathedral, Berlin:** 385 left, photo: Klaus Frahm. **Klaus Frahm, Hamburg:** 2, 8–13; 41; 44; 56; 93; 94; 95; 101–103; 104 left and right; 105; 106; 109; 110 top; 111; 112 top and bottom; 113 top; 115; 116; 119 right; 123; 159–163; 165–167; 168; 169; 170 bottom left; 171–174; 178 bottom; 186; 187 bottom; 188–192; 193 bottom; 195 top; 196; 197; 198; 199 bottom; 200; 201; 202 top; 203; 205; 206 top; 207–211;212 top; 213; 214; 217–227; 230; 232; 234 center and right; 235; 236; 237; 246–248; 249 bottom; 250; 251; 252 bottom; 256; 257; 263–264; 266; 272; 273; 274; 275; 278 bottom; 279; 280; 281 bottom; 282; 283 top; 285; 286; 292; 293; 298; 299–303; 308; 309–311; 316–318; 320–323; 324 left and top right; 325–327; 329 top; 330–332; 333 bottom; 334; 336; 337; 338; 343–345; 347 bottom; 354; 355 top left; 357; 358; 360; 420 bottom; 421; 423; 430 top and bottom left; 433; 434; 435; 438 top; 441; 442; 445 bottom left; 447–449; 453; 485 top; 491; frontispiece; front cover; back cover; back cover flap. **Claudia Frehman, Archiv Heinpeter Schreiber, Cologne:** 444 bottom. **Germanisches Nationalmuseum, Nuremberg:** 242. **Hamburger Kunsthalle:** 241 top right; 396 top; 469 top; all photos: Elke Walford. **Hessisches Landesmuseum, Darmstadt:** 244. **Markus Hilbisch, Berlin:** 428; 445 top; 455. **Mewa Menzel GmbH:** 14; 72; 154; 268; 412; 515. **Hagen Immel, Potsdam:** 6; 7; 19–35; 37–40, 41 right; 42; 43; 45–50; 51 top; 52 left; 54; 55; 57–61; 67–71; 86 top; 296; 473 bottom; 484; 494; 495 top; 496; 505. **KPM-Archiv, Schloss Charlottenburg, Berlin:** 340; 347 top. **Kreismuseum, Heinsberg:** 399 bottom right. **Kulturamt der Stadt Goslar:** 459 top. **Kunstamt, Kreuzberg, Berlin:** 486, photo: Angelika Weidling. **Kunsthalle zu Kiel:** 476 bottom. **Kunstmuseum, Düsseldorf:** 390 top; 391 top; 393; 397 top; 399 top right; 478 bottom, photo: Werner Otto. **Kunstmuseum, St. Gallen:** 469 bottom. **Landesbildstelle, Berlin:** 414 top; 418; 419; 424; 429; 431 bottom; 432 bottom; 437; 443 bottom; 461; 492 bottom; 462 bottom. **Winfried Mausolf, Frankfurt an der Oder:** 36; 52 right; 53. **Museum der Bildenden Künste, Leipzig:** 482. **Museum Folkwang, Essen:** 374. 380 left, 470, photos: J Nober; **Marion Murza, Archiv Dr. Gerhard Murza:** 65; 88 top and bottom; 89; 91; 151. **Bernd Nicolai, Berlin:** 439 center. **Potsdam Museum:** 114 bottom left; 170 top; 179. **Plansammlung der Technischen Universität, Berlin:** 420 top. **Rheinisches Bildarchiv, Cologne:** 335 bottom. **Sächsische Landesbibliothek, Dresden:** 481. **Hans-Uwe Salge, Brandenburg:** 51. **Herbert Sander, Berlin:** 506; 507. **Staatsgalerie, Stuttgart:** 488 top. **Stadtverwaltung, Bad Kreuznach, Schloßparkmuseum und Römerhalle:** 473 top. **Städtische Galerie im Städel, Frankfurt am Main:** 389 bottom, photo: Ursula Edelmann. **Stiftung Archiv Akademie der Künste, Berlin:** 362; 371, photo: Christoph Schmidt; 458 top. 373 bottom, 377, photos: Roman März. **Stiftung Preussische Schlösser und Gärten Berlin-Brandenburg (SPSG), Plansammlung, Berlin:** 370 top. SPSG, **Plansammlung, Potsdam:** 87; 97 top; 107; 113 bottom; 164 top; 164 bottom, photo: Roland Handrick; 175; 176; 184 bottom; 187 top; 194; 199 top; 204; 206 bottom; 212 bottom; 278 top; 281 top; 283 bottom; 284; 291 top; 297 top; 304; 305; 313; 314; 328; 333 top; 335 top; 341; 346; 400 bottom; 458 bottom. **SPSG, Fotothek, Berlin:** 15 top right and bottom; 16; 17; 74 bottom right; 75 top center and right; 77; 96; 97 bottom; 98; 99 top and bottom; 100 top and bottom; 133; 135 top; 138 top left; 140; 141 bottom right; 142; 131; 176 bottom; 177 top; 184 top; 144; 150; 238; 243; 254; 268 bottom; 269 top right; 329 bottom; 350 right; 351 right; 380 right. 270 right; 365, 372, 381, photos: Jörg P. Anders.146 top left, 149, photos: Roland Handrick. 136, 138 bottom, 139, 141 top, 239, 245, 380 right, 385 right, 388 top, photos: Wolfgang Pfauder. **SPSG, Fotothek, Potsdam:** 73 bottom; 74 bottom left; 75 bottom; 108; 135 bottom; 137; 143 bottom left and bottom right; 122; 176 top; 155 top and bottom left; 181 top left; 231 left; 202 bottom; 215; 216; 258; 260 bottom; 261–267; 269 top left; 270 center left; 319; 338; 339; 342; 351 left; 352 top; 355 bottom left; 356; 365; 366; 369; 378; 412 bottom; 413 left; 414 right. 64, 86 bottom, 119 right, 121, 149 top, 181 bottom right, 152 top right, 153, 228/229, 231. 240, 241 top left, 249 top, 252 top, 253, photos: Roland Handrick. **Stiftung Staatliche Museen Berlin – Preussischer Kulturbesitz, Bildarchiv Preussischer Kulturbesitz:** 15 top left; 12, photo: Klaus Frahm; 270 center left; 271 bottom left, top right; 271 bottom right, photo: Lutz Braun (orig. private ownership); 413 top and bottom; 414 bottom left; 415, photo: Alfred Grohs; 348; 422; 436, photo: Klaus Frahm; 443 top; 444 top. **Alte Nationalgalerie:** 349 bottom; 376 top, photo: Karin März; 383 top; 391 bottom, photo: Walter Klein; 394; 399 left; 468; 475 bottom; 477, photo: Bernd Kuhnert; 478 top; 485 bottom. 375 top, 379, 383 bottom, 384, 386/7, 388 bottom, 395 bottom, 396 bottom, 471, photos: Jörg P. Anders. 349 top, 350 left, 382, 383, 398, 399 left, 401,466, 479 top, 480, photos: Klaus Göken. **Gemäldegalerie:** 241 bottom; 243 left; 368, photo: Jörg P. Anders. **Kunstbibliothek:** 14 bottom left; 193 top; 195; 270 top right. **Kunstgewerbemuseum:** 75 top left; 85; 145; 146 bottom right; 147, photo: Hans-Joachim Bartsch; 149 bottom; 151; 152 bottom; 255. **Kupferstichkabinett:** 84; 110 bottom; 114 top right; 155 right; 178 top; 259, 277 top; 306; 312; 370 bottom; 373 top; 375 bottom; 395 top; 73 top, 155 center, 269 center left, 294 bottom, 397 center and bottom, 483 top, 487 top, photos: Jörg P. Anders. **Skulpturensammlung:** 118, photo: Ducke; 119 left; 120, photos: Jörg P. Anders; 233, 234 left. **Staatsbibliothek, Haus 1:** 74 top; 76; 324 bottom. **Staatsbibliothek zu Berlin, Haus 2:** 62; 66; 82; 90. **Stiftung Stadtmuseum, Berlin:** 78; 83; 92; 143 top; 156; 157; 270 top left,; 271 top left; 276 left and right; 294 top; 297 bottom; 363; 367 top and bottom left; 400 top; 467 bottom; 487 bottom; 489 bottom; all photos: Hans-Joachim Bartsch. 416, 417, 439 top, photos: Max Missmann. **Verwaltung der Staatlichen Schlösser, Gärten und Seen Bayern, Munich** 134. **© VG Bild-Kunst, Bonn** 1998: 469 bottom; 474; 479 top and bottom; 480; 481; 486; 487 top; 488 bottom. **© VG Bild-Kunst and The Munch Museum/The Munch Ellingsen Group:** 483 top. **Wilhelm Lehmbruck Museum, Duisburg:** 489 top, photo: Bernd Kirtz. **Wallraf-Richartz Museum, Cologne:** 389 top; 390 bottom, photo: Walter Klein.

Acknowledgments

The publisher wishes to thank the Stiftung Preussische Schlösser und Gärten Berlin-Brandenburg for its generous support for this project. Special thanks are also due to Heidrun Klein of the Bildarchiv, Preussischer Kulturbesitz; to Petra Colm, Eleonore Degenhardt, Ingrid Knauth, Edith Themm, Margitta Tretter and Evelyn Zimmermann of the Stiftung Preussische Schlösser und Gärten, Berlin-Brandenburg; to Reiner Koppe of the Messbildarchiv, Brandenburgisches Landesamt für Denkmalpflege; to Thomas Wellmann of the Stiftung Stadtmuseum, Berlin; and to Andreas Heese from the Kupferstichkabinett of the Preussischer Kulturbesitz, Staatliche Museen zu Berlin. Our gratitude also to Herr Schulte-Wintrop of Stalling Medien for his profound patience, and to Uwe Kolsch, Thomas Ristow, and Sabine Vonderstein for their spontaneous willingness to assist.